Scott Mitchell

Sams **Teach Yourself** ASP.NET 3.5 Complete Starter Kit

SAMS 800 East 96th Street, Indianapolis, Indiana, 46240 USA

Sams Teach Yourself ASP.NET 3.5 in 24 Hours, Complete Starter Kit

ISBN-13: 978-0-672-32997-5
ISBN-10: 0-672-32997-2

Library of Congress Cataloging-in-Publication Data:

Mitchell, Scott.
Sams teach yourself ASP.NET 3.5 in 24 hours : complete starter kit / Scott Mitchell.
p. cm.
ISBN 0-672-32997-2
1. Active server pages. 2. Web sites—Design. 3. Microsoft .NET. I. Title.
TK5105.8885.A26M587 2008
005.2'76—dc22
2008014770

Printed in the United States of America

First Printing June 2008

Trademarks

All terms mentioned in this book that are known to be trademarks or service marks have been appropriately capitalized. Sams Publishing cannot attest to the accuracy of this information. Use of a term in this book should not be regarded as affecting the validity of any trademark or service mark.

Warning and Disclaimer

Every effort has been made to make this book as complete and accurate as possible, but no warranty or fitness is implied. The information provided is on an "as is" basis. The author and the publisher shall have neither liability nor responsibility to any person or entity with respect to any loss or damages arising from the information contained in this book or from the use of the CD or programs accompanying it.

Bulk Sales

Sams Publishing offers excellent discounts on this book when ordered in quantity for bulk purchases or special sales. For more information, please contact

U.S. Corporate and Government Sales
1-800-382-3419
corpsales@pearsontechgroup.com

For sales outside the U.S., please contact

International Sales
international@pearson.com

Editor-in-Chief
Karen Gettman

Executive Editor
Neil Rowe

Development Editor
Mark Renfrow

Managing Editor
Kristy Hart

Project Editor
Andrew Beaster

Copy Editor
Barbara Hacha

Indexer
Erika Millen

Proofreader
Kathy Ruiz

Technical Editor
Todd Meister

Publishing Coordinator
Cindy Teeters

Multimedia Developer
Dan Scherf

Book Designer
Gary Adair

Composition
Nonie Ratcliff

This Book Is Safari Enabled

The Safari® Enabled icon on the cover of your favorite technology book means the book is available through Safari Bookshelf. When you buy this book, you get free access to the online edition for 45 days.

Safari Bookshelf is an electronic reference library that lets you easily search thousands of technical books, find code samples, download chapters, and access technical information whenever and wherever you need it.

To gain 45-day Safari Enabled access to this book:

- Go to www.informit.com/onlineedition.
- Complete the brief registration form.
- Enter the coupon code 24DQ-UXWD-LCKF-B9DS-H2C9.

If you have difficulty registering on Safari Bookshelf or accessing the online edition, please email customer-service@safaribooksonline.com.

Contents at a Glance

Part IV: Site Navigation, User Management, Page Layout, AJAX, and Deployment

Table of Contents

About the Author

As editor and main contributor to 4GuysFromRolla.com, a popular ASP.NET resource website, **Scott Mitchell** has authored more than a thousand articles on Microsoft web technologies since 1998. In addition to his vast collection of online articles, Scott has written six previous books on ASP and ASP.NET: *Sams Teach Yourself Active Server Pages 3.0 in 21 Days* (Sams); *Designing Active Server Pages* (O'Reilly); *ASP.NET: Tips, Tutorials, and Code* (Sams); *ASP.NET Data Web Controls Kick Start* (Sams); *Teach Yourself ASP.NET in 24 Hours* (Sams); and *Teach Yourself ASP.NET 2.0 in 24 Hours* (Sams). Scott has also written a number of magazine articles and is a regular columnist for Microsoft's *MSDN Magazine*.

Scott's nonwriting accomplishments include speaking at numerous ASP.NET user groups and conferences across the country. Scott regularly teaches classes on ASP.NET and related web technologies at the University of California—San Diego University Extension. Scott also works as an independent software developer.

Scott can be reached at mitchell@4GuysFromRolla.com; his blog is available at www.ScottOnWriting.NET.

Dedication

This book is dedicated to my favorite person, Jisun.

Acknowledgments

Writing a book is an arduous and draining endeavor, a feat that would not be possible without the untiring patience and undying support of my wife and number one fan, Jisun. You make life unbearably fun and full of smiles.

Thanks also to Neil Rowe, Mark Renfrow, Andy Beaster, and the entire editorial team at Sams Publishing.

We Want to Hear from You!

As the reader of this book, *you* are our most important critic and commentator. We value your opinion, and we want to know what we're doing right, what we could do better, what areas you'd like to see us publish in, and any other words of wisdom you're willing to pass our way.

You can email or write me directly to let me know what you did or didn't like about this book—as well as what we can do to make our books stronger.

Please note that I cannot help you with technical problems related to the topic of this book, and that because of the high volume of mail I receive, I might not be able to reply to every message.

When you write, please be sure to include this book's title and author as well as your name and phone number or email address. I will carefully review your comments and share them with the author and editors who worked on the book.

Email: webdev@samspublishing.com

Mail: Neil Rowe
Executive Editor
Sams Publishing
800 East 96th Street
Indianapolis, IN 46240 USA

Reader Services

Visit our website and register this book at www.informit.com/title/9780672329845 for convenient access to any updates, downloads, or errata that might be available for this book.

Introduction

As the World Wide Web continues its meteoric growth, websites have matured from simple collections of static HTML pages to data-driven dynamic web applications. For example, websites such as eBay or Amazon.com are much more than a collection of HTML pages—they are complex applications that happen to be accessed through the Internet. Although many competing technologies exist for building data-driven websites, this book shows how to use the latest version of Microsoft's popular ASP.NET technology for creating web applications.

ASP.NET web applications are composed of individual ASP.NET web pages. As we will see in numerous examples throughout this book, these ASP.NET pages can display HTML, collect user input, and interact with databases. ASP.NET pages contain a mix of both HTML and source code. It is the source code of an ASP.NET page that allows for the more advanced features, such as accessing data from a database, or sending an email. The source code of an ASP.NET web page can be written in any one of a number of programming languages. For this book we will be using Microsoft's Visual Basic programming language. Don't worry if you've never programmed in Visual Basic, or even if you have never programmed at all. Starting with Hour 5, "Understanding Visual Basic's Variables and Operators," we spend three hours examining programming language concepts and the Visual Basic syntax.

To ease ASP.NET web page development, Microsoft provides a free development editor, Visual Web Developer, which is included in this book's accompanying CD. Visual Web Developer simplifies creating both the HTML and source code portions of ASP.NET pages. The HTML for an ASP.NET web page can be quickly created by using the Designer, which is a What You See Is What You Get (WYSIWYG) graphical editor. With the Designer, you can drag and drop various HTML elements onto an ASP.NET web page, moving them around with a few clicks of the mouse. Likewise, Visual Web Developer offers tools and shortcuts that help with creating an ASP.NET page's code.

Audience and Organization

This book is geared for developers new to ASP.NET, whether or not you've had past experience with HTML or programming languages. By the end of this book you'll be able to create and deploy your own dynamic, data-driven web applications using ASP.NET.

This book's 24 hours are divided into four parts. Part I introduces you to ASP.NET, HTML, Visual Web Developer, and Visual Basic. Hour 1, "Getting Started with ASP.NET 3.5," begins with an overview of ASP.NET and then walks you through installing the .NET Framework, Visual Web Developer, and other necessary components. Hour 3, "Using Visual Web Developer," showcases Visual Web Developer, which is the powerful development editor you'll be using throughout this book to create ASP.NET web pages. Hours 5, 6, and 7 examine the syntax and semantics of the Visual Basic programming language.

ASP.NET offers a variety of user interface elements for collecting user input, including text boxes, check boxes, drop-down lists, and radio buttons. In Part II you will see how to collect and process user input. Hour 10, "Using Text Boxes to Collect Input," examines using single-line, multi-line, and password text boxes, while Hour 11, "Collecting Input Using Drop-Down Lists, Radio Buttons, and Check Boxes," examines alternative user input controls.

Part III shows how easy it is to build data-driven websites with ASP.NET. Starting in Hour 13, "An Introduction to Databases," we begin our look at building websites that interact with databases. Typically, data-driven websites enable visitors to view, update, delete, and insert data into the database from an ASP.NET page. In Hour 15, "Displaying Data with the Data Web Controls," you will learn how to display database data in a web page. Hour 16, "Deleting, Inserting, and Editing Data," examines how to edit, insert, and delete data.

Part IV highlights tools provided by ASP.NET and Visual Web Developer that help with building professional, easy-to-use websites. In Hour 20, "Defining a Site Map and Providing Site Navigation," you'll see how to define a website's navigational structure and display menus, treeviews, and breadcrumbs. Hour 22, "Using Master Pages to Provide Sitewide Page Templates," examines master pages, which enable web designers to create a web page template that can be applied to all pages across the site.

Conventions Used in This Book

This book uses several design elements and conventions to help you prioritize and reference the information it contains:

By the Way boxes provide useful sidebar information that you can read immediately or circle back to without losing the flow of the topic at hand.

Did You Know? boxes highlight information that can make your Visual Basic programming more effective.

Did you Know?

Watch Out! boxes focus your attention on problems or side effects that can occur in specific situations.

New terms appear in a **semibold** typeface for emphasis.

In addition, this book uses various typefaces to help you distinguish code from regular English. Code is presented in a `monospace` font. Placeholders—words or characters that represent the real words or characters you would type in code—appear in *`italic monospace`*. When you are asked to type or enter text, that text appears in **`bold monospace`**. Menu options are separated by a comma. For example, when you should open the File menu and choose the New Project menu option, the text says "Select File, New Project."

Some code statements presented in this book are too long to appear on a single line. In these cases, a line-continuation character ➥ is used to indicate that the following line is a continuation of the current statement. Furthermore, some code listings include line numbers. These numbers are used to refer to specific lines of code in the text and are not part of the code syntax.

I hope you enjoy reading this book as much as I enjoyed writing it.

Happy Programming!

Scott Mitchell
mitchell@4guysfromrolla.com

PART I

Overview of ASP.NET 3.5

HOUR 1

Getting Started with ASP.NET 3.5

In this hour, we will cover

- What is ASP.NET?
- System requirements for using ASP.NET
- Software that must be installed prior to using ASP.NET
- Installing the .NET Framework, Visual Web Developer, and SQL Server 2005
- Taking a quick tour of Visual Web Developer
- Creating a simple ASP.NET web page and viewing it through a web browser

ASP.NET is an exciting web programming technology pioneered by Microsoft that allows developers to create **dynamic web pages**. Dynamic web pages are pages whose content is dynamically regenerated each time the web page is requested. For example, after you log on, the front page of Amazon.com shows books it recommends for you, based on your previous purchases. This is a dynamic web page because it is a single web page whose content is customized based on what customer is visiting. In this book we examine how to create dynamic ASP.NET websites quickly and easily.

Prior to ASP.NET, Microsoft's dynamic web programming technology was called Active Server Pages, or ASP. Although ASP was a popular choice for creating dynamic websites, it lacked important features found in other programming technologies. Microsoft remedied ASP's shortcomings with ASP.NET. ASP.NET version 1.0 was released in January 2002 and quickly became the web programming technology of choice for many. In November 2005, Microsoft released the much-anticipated version 2.0. Two years later, in November 2007, Microsoft released ASP.NET version 3.5.

Before we can start creating our first ASP.NET website, we need to install the .NET Framework, Visual Web Developer, and SQL Server 2005. The .NET Framework is a rich platform for creating Windows-based applications and is the underlying technology used to create ASP.NET websites.

Visual Web Developer is a sophisticated program for creating, editing, and testing ASP.NET websites and web pages. ASP.NET web pages are simple text files, so any text editor will suffice (such as Microsoft Notepad), but if you've created websites before, you know that using tools such as Microsoft FrontPage or Adobe Dreamweaver makes the development process much easier than using a generic text editor like Notepad. This is the case for ASP.NET, as well.

The third and final piece we'll need to install is SQL Server 2005. SQL Server is a database engine, which is a specialized application designed to efficiently store and query data. Many websites interact with databases; any e-commerce website, for example, displays product information and records purchase orders in a database. Starting with Hour 13, "An Introduction to Databases," we'll see how to create, query, and modify databases through both Visual Web Developer and ASP.NET pages.

This hour focuses on getting everything set up properly so that we can start creating ASP.NET web applications. Although it would be nice to be able to jump straight into creating ASP.NET pages, it is important that we first take the time to ensure that the pieces required for ASP.NET are correctly installed and configured. We create a very simple ASP.NET page at the end of this hour, but we won't explore it in any detail. We look at ASP.NET pages in more detail in the next hour and in Hour 4, "Designing, Creating, and Testing ASP.NET Pages."

What Is ASP.NET?

Have you ever wondered how dynamic websites like Amazon.com work behind the scenes? As a shopper at Amazon.com, you are shown a particular web page, but the web page's content is dynamic, based on your preferences and actions. For instance, if you have an account with Amazon.com, when you visit Amazon.com's home page your name is shown at the top and a list of personal recommendations is presented further down the page. When you type an author's name, a title, or a keyword into the search text box, a list of matching books appears. When you click a particular book's title, you are shown the book's details along with comments and ratings from other users. When you add the book to your shopping cart and check out, you are prompted for a credit card number, which is then billed.

Web pages in websites whose content is determined dynamically based on user input or other information are called **dynamic web pages**. Any website's search engine page is an example of a dynamic web page because the content of the search results page is based on the search criteria the user entered and the searchable documents on the web server. Another example is Amazon.com's personal recommendations. The books and products that Amazon.com suggests when you visit the home page are different from the books and products suggested for someone else. Specifically, the recommendations are determined by the products you have previously viewed and purchased.

The opposite of a dynamic web page is a **static web page**. Static web pages contain content that does not change based on who visits the page or other external factors. HTML pages, for example, are static web pages. Consider an HTML page on a website with the following markup:

```
<html>
<body>
  <b>Hello, World!</b>
</body>
</html>
```

Such a page is considered a static web page because regardless of who views the page or what external factors might exist, the output will always be the same: the text `Hello, World!` displayed in a bold font. The only time the content of a static web page changes is when someone edits and saves the page, overwriting the old version.

> **By the Way**
>
> Virtually all websites today contain a mix of static and dynamic web pages. Rarely will you find a website that has just static web pages, because such pages are so limited in their functionality.

By learning ASP.NET, you will learn how to create websites that contain dynamic web pages. It is important to understand the differences between how a website serves static web pages versus dynamic web pages.

> **By the Way**
>
> **Competing Web Programming Technologies**
>
> ASP.NET is only one of many technologies that can be employed to generate dynamic web pages. ASP.NET is the successor to Active Server Pages (ASP), which was Microsoft's earlier dynamic web-page creation technology. Other technologies include PHP, JSP, and ColdFusion.

By the Way

Personally, I find ASP.NET to be the easiest and most powerful technology of the bunch, which is why I'm writing a book about ASP.NET instead of one of the competing technologies. Moreover, the features and functionality of ASP.NET are head and shoulders above ASP. If you've created ASP pages in the past, you'll no doubt find that you can do the same things with ASP.NET but in a fraction of the time.

Did you Know?

If you have experience developing web applications with other web programming technologies, such as ASP, PHP, or JSP, you may already be well versed in the material covered in the next three sections. If this is the case, feel free to skip to the "Installing the ASP.NET Engine, Editor, and Database System" section.

Serving Static Web Pages

If you've developed websites before, you likely know that a website requires a **web server**.

A web server is a software application that continually waits for incoming **web requests**, which are requests for a particular URL (see Figure 1.1). The web server examines the requested URL, locates the appropriate file, and then sends this file back to the client that made the web request.

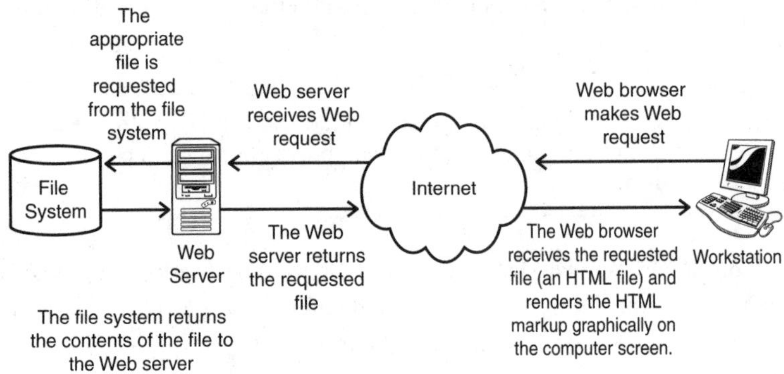

FIGURE 1.1 The web server handles incoming web requests.

For example, when you visit Amazon.com, your browser makes a web request to Amazon.com's web server for a particular URL, say `/books/index.html`. Amazon.com's web server determines what file corresponds to the requested URL. It then returns the contents of this file to your browser.

This model is adequate for serving static pages, whose contents do not change. However, such a simple model is insufficient for serving dynamic pages because the web server merely returns the contents of the requested URL to the browser that initiated the request. The contents of the requested URL are not modified in any way by the web server based on external inputs.

Serving Dynamic Web Pages

With static web pages, the contents of the web page are just HTML elements that describe how the page should be rendered in the user's web browser. Therefore, when a static web page is requested, the web server can send the web page's content, without modification, to the requesting browser.

This simple model does not work for dynamic web pages, where the content of the page may depend on various factors that can differ on a per-visitor basis. To accommodate dynamic content, dynamic web pages contain source code that is **executed** when the page is requested (see Figure 1.2). When the code is executed, it produces HTML markup as its result, which is then sent back to and displayed in the visitor's browser.

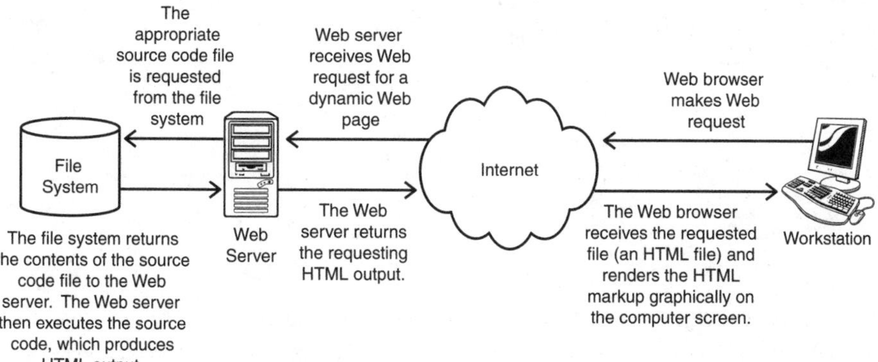

FIGURE 1.2 The content of a dynamic web page is created by executing the dynamic web page's source code.

This model allows for dynamic content because the content isn't actually created until the web page is requested. Imagine that we wanted to create a web page that displays the current date and time. To do this using a static web page, someone would need to edit the web page every second, continually updating the content so that it contained the current date and time. Clearly, this isn't feasible.

With a dynamic web page, however, the executed code can retrieve and display the current date and time. Suppose that one particular user visits this page on June 12, 2008, at 4:15:03 p.m. When the web request arrives, the dynamic web page's code is executed, which obtains the current date and time and returns it to the requesting web browser. The visitor's browser displays the date and time the web page was executed: June 12, 2008, 4:15:03 p.m. If another visitor requests this page 7 seconds later, the dynamic web page's code will again be executed, returning June 12, 2008, 4:15:10 p.m.

Figure 1.2 is, in actuality, a slightly oversimplified model. Commonly, the web server and the execution of the dynamic web page source code are decoupled. When a web request arrives, the web server determines whether the requested page is a static web page or dynamic web page. If the requested web page is static, its contents are sent directly back to the browser that initiated the request (as shown in Figure 1.1). If, however, the requested web page is dynamic—for example, an ASP.NET web page—the web server hands off the responsibility of executing the page to the **ASP.NET engine** (see Figure 1.3).

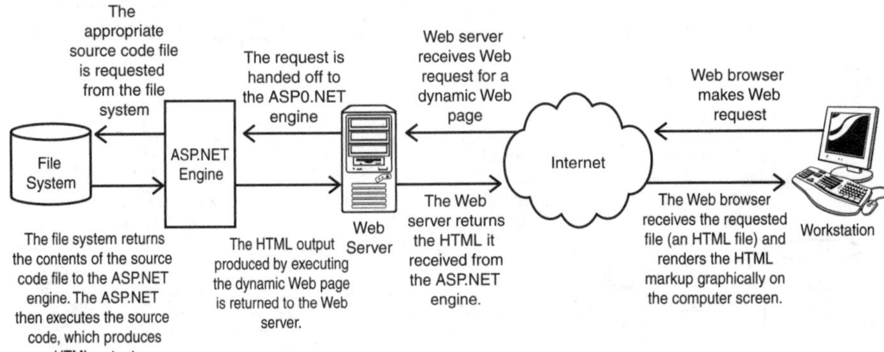

FIGURE 1.3 Execution of an ASP.NET web page is handled by the ASP.NET engine.

The web server can determine whether the requested page is a dynamic or static web page by the requested file's extension. If the extension is `.aspx`, the web server knows the requested page is an ASP.NET web page and therefore hands off the request to the ASP.NET engine.

By the Way

> The ASP.NET engine is a piece of software that knows how to execute ASP.NET web pages. Other web programming technologies, such as ASP, PHP, and JSP, have their own engines, which know how to execute ASP, PHP, and JSP pages.

When the ASP.NET engine executes an ASP.NET page, the engine generates the web page's resulting HTML output. This HTML output is then returned to the web server, which then returns it to the browser that initiated the web request.

Hosting ASP.NET Web Pages

To view an ASP.NET web page that resides on a web server, we need to request it through a browser. The browser sends the request to the web server, which then dispatches the request to the ASP.NET engine. The ASP.NET engine processes the requested page and returns the resulting HTML to the browser. When you're developing ASP.NET websites, the ASP.NET web pages you create are saved on your personal computer. For you to be able to test these pages, then, your computer must have a web server installed.

Fortunately, you do not need to concern yourself with installing a web server on your computer. Visual Web Developer, the editor we'll be using throughout this book to create our ASP.NET websites, includes a lightweight web server specifically designed for testing ASP.NET pages locally. As we will see in later hours, when testing an ASP.NET page, Visual Web Developer starts the **ASP.NET Development Web Server** and launches a browser that issues a request of the form: `http://localhost:`*`portNumber/ASP.NET_Page`*`.aspx`.

The `http://localhost` portion of the request tells the browser to send the request to your personal computer's web server, in contrast to some other web server on the Internet. The *`portNumber`* specifies a particular **port** through which the request is made. All web servers listen for incoming requests on a particular port. When the ASP.NET Development Web Server is started, it chooses an open port, which is reflected in the *`portNumber`* portion of the URL. Finally, the *`ASP.NET_Page`*`.aspx` portion is the filename of the ASP.NET page being tested.

Hosting ASP.NET pages locally through the ASP.NET Development Web Server has a number of advantages:

- **Testing can be done while offline**—Because the request from your browser is being directed to your own personal computer, you don't need to be connected to the Internet to test your ASP.NET pages.
- **It's fast**—Local requests are, naturally, much quicker than requests that must travel over the Internet.
- **Advanced debugging features are available**—By developing locally, you can use advanced debugging techniques, such as halting the execution of an ASP.NET page and stepping through its code line-by-line.
- **It's secure**—The ASP.NET Development Web Server allows only local connections. With this lightweight web server, you don't need to worry about hackers gaining access to your system through an open website.

The main disadvantage of hosting ASP.NET pages locally is that they can be viewed only from your computer. That is, a visitor on another computer cannot enter some URL into her browser's Address bar that will take her to the ASP.NET website you've created on your local computer. If you want to create an ASP.NET website that can be visited by anyone with an Internet connection, you should consider using a web-hosting company.

Web-hosting companies have a number of Internet-accessible computers on which individuals or companies can host their websites. These computers contain web servers that are accessible from any other computer on the Internet. The benefits of using a web-hosting company to host your site include

- **A publicly available website**—With a web-hosting company, any visitor who has an Internet connection can visit your website!
- **Use of a domain name**—You can register a domain name and have it point to your website so that visitors can reach your website through a name like www.mysite.com.
- **Ability to focus 100% on building your website**—Installing a web server, applying the latest security patches, properly configuring domain names, and so forth can be tricky tasks. By using a web-hosting company, you are paying for this service, which enables you to concentrate on building your website.

After you have settled on a web-hosting company and have set up your account, you are ready to move the ASP.NET pages from your computer to the web-hosting company. This process is referred to as **deployment**, and is covered in-depth in Hour 24, "Deploying Your Website." After a website has been successfully deployed, you, or anyone else on the Internet, can visit the site from their web browser.

Develop Locally, Deploy to a Web Host

Because there are different advantages for hosting a site locally versus hosting with a web-hosting company, often the best choice is to do both! I encourage you to develop, test, and debug your ASP.NET websites locally, through Visual Web Developer's built-in web server. After you have completed your site and are ready to go live, you can procure an account with a web-hosting company and deploy your site. This approach allows for the best of both worlds—an ideal development environment with the end result of a publicly accessible website!

The examples and lessons presented in Hour 1 through Hour 23 are meant to be created, tested, and debugged locally. Hour 24 contains step-by-step instructions for deploying your ASP.NET website to a web-hosting company.

Installing the ASP.NET Engine, Editor, and Database System

For a web server to be able to serve ASP.NET pages, it must have the ASP.NET engine installed. Recall that the ASP.NET engine is responsible for executing the ASP.NET web page and generating its resulting HTML. To install the ASP.NET engine, your computer must be running Windows XP, Windows Server 2003, Windows Vista, or Windows Server 2008. Even if your system does have the required operating system installed, you may need to take additional steps before you can start working with ASP.NET. For example, those using Windows XP need to have Service Pack 2 (SP2) installed. If you're uncertain whether your system meets the requirements, attempt the installation process. The installation program will inform you if there is some prerequisite for installation, such as Service Pack 2.

Three components need to be installed for us to work with the ASP.NET examples throughout this book. First, we must install the .NET Framework, which contains the core libraries required to execute an ASP.NET page. The ASP.NET engine is part of this .NET Framework. Following that, we need to install Visual Web Developer, which is the editor of choice for working with ASP.NET pages. Finally, we need to install SQL Server 2005, a database engine that is used extensively from Hour 14, "Accessing Data with the Data Source Web Controls," onward.

All three components can be installed through the single installation program included on this book's accompanying CD. To begin the installation process, insert the CD into your computer. This brings up the installation program starting with the screen shown in Figure 1.4. Click the Next button to progress through the subsequent two screens.

By the Way

> If your computer lacks the prerequisites, such as not having the latest service pack installed, the installation program informs you of the problem and gives you instructions on how to update your system. After you have updated your computer, rerun the installation program.

The book's CD is the installation CD for Microsoft's Visual Web Developer editor. Because Visual Web Developer is designed for developing ASP.NET websites, the installation process automatically installs the .NET Framework and other required ASP.NET tools. You can also install three optional packages, as shown in Figure 1.5.

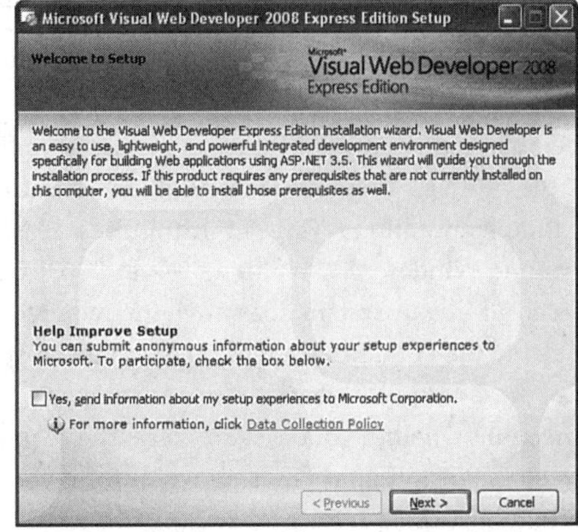

FIGURE 1.4 Start the installation process by inserting the CD into your computer's CD-ROM drive.

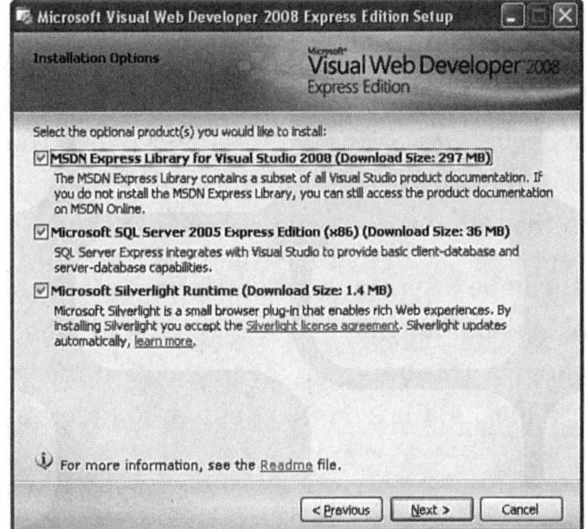

FIGURE 1.5 Make sure that you install SQL Server 2005 Express Edition.

The first optional package is MSDN Express Library for Visual Studio 2008. MSDN is Microsoft's collection of product documentation, whitepapers, code samples, and help files. Although all this information is accessible online at http://msdn2.microsoft.com, I encourage you to install MSDN locally on your computer. The local documentation can be searched and accessed quicker than its online counterpart and is still available even if your Internet connection is down.

The second optional package is Microsoft SQL Server 2005 Express Edition. This package is optional in the sense that Visual Web Developer will install successfully with or without SQL Server 2005; however, the latter half of this book's examples rely on SQL Server 2005 being installed. Therefore, make sure that this check box is selected.

The third package is for Microsoft's Silverlight runtime. Silverlight is a browser plug-in from Microsoft that is capable of displaying rich, interactive multimedia content. The Microsoft Silverlight runtime is required to view Silverlight applications in your browser. None of the examples in this book use Silverlight, so you may choose to not install it.

By the Way

The Microsoft SQL Server 2005 Express Edition and Microsoft Silverlight Runtime check boxes will not be displayed if you already have these components installed on your computer.

The next screen (see Figure 1.6) enables you to specify in what folder to install Visual Web Developer as well as what products will be installed and the disk space required. After double-checking that the correct packages are being installed, click the Install button to begin the installation process. The overall installation process will take several minutes. During the installation, you are kept abreast with what package is currently being installed as well as the overall installation progress (see Figure 1.7).

FIGURE 1.6
Specify the folder in which to install Visual Web Developer.

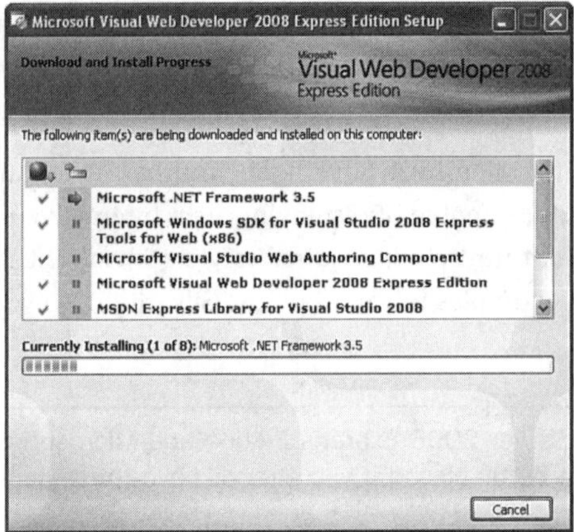

FIGURE 1.7
Monitor the installation's progress.

A Brief Tour of Visual Web Developer

When the installation process completes, take a moment to poke through Visual Web Developer. To launch Visual Web Developer, go to the Start menu, choose Programs, and click Microsoft Visual Web Developer 2008 Express Edition. Figure 1.8 shows Visual Web Developer when it loads.

When you open Visual Web Developer, the Start Page is initially shown. This Start Page includes a list of Recent Projects in the upper-left corner, a Getting Started section with some links for accomplishing common tasks in the bottom-left corner, and a list of recent articles on Microsoft's MSDN site in the right column.

On the left you'll find the Toolbox. When you view the Start Page, the Toolbox is empty, but when you work with an ASP.NET page, it contains the plethora of ASP.NET Web controls that can be added to the page. (We'll discuss what Web controls are and their purpose in the next hour.) Two other windows share the left region with the Toolbox: CSS Properties and Manage Styles. These windows are used to define style and appearance settings for the HTML and Web control elements within a web page.

To the right of the screen, you'll find the Solution Explorer. Again, on the Start Page this is empty, but when you load or create an ASP.NET website, the Solution Explorer will list the website's files. These files include database files, HTML pages, ASP.NET pages, image files, CSS files, configuration files, and so on. In addition to the Solution Explorer, the right portion of the screen is also home to the Database Explorer and Properties windows. The Database Explorer lists the databases associated with the project and provides functionality for creating, editing, and deleting the structure and contents of these databases. When you design an ASP.NET page, the Properties window displays information about the currently selected Web control or HTML element.

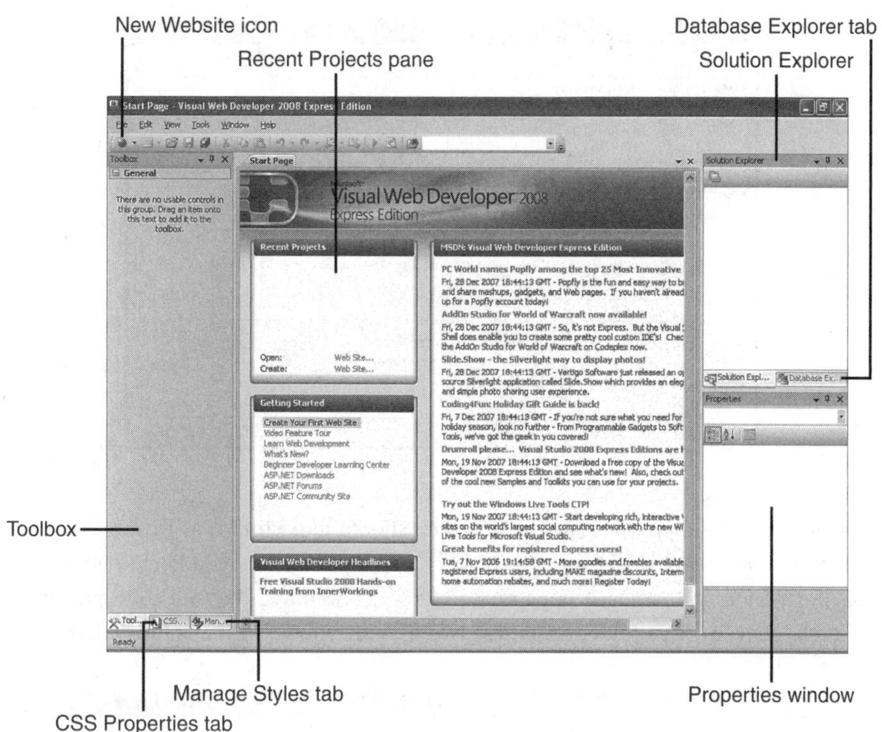

FIGURE 1.8
The Start Page shows when Visual Web Developer is loaded.

Creating a New ASP.NET Website

To create and design an ASP.NET page, we must first create an ASP.NET website. From Visual Web Developer, you can choose several ways to create a new ASP.NET website. You can go to the File menu and choose the New Web Site option; you can click the New Website icon in the Toolbar; or you can click the Create Web Site link in the Recent Projects pane of the Start Page.

All these approaches bring up the New Web Site dialog box, as shown in Figure 1.9. Let's take a moment to create a website. For now, don't worry about all the options available or what they mean because we'll discuss them in detail in Hour 3, "Using Visual Web Developer." Leave the Templates selection as ASP.NET Web Site, the Location drop-down list as File System, and the Language drop-down list as Visual Basic. The only thing you should change is the actual location of the website. Place the website in a folder named `MyFirstWebsite` on your desktop.

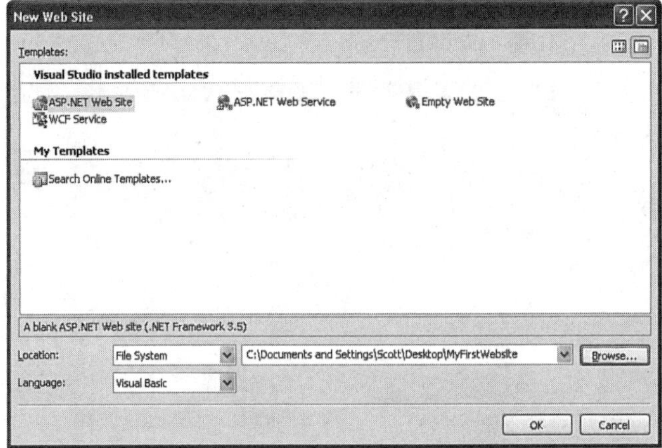

FIGURE 1.9
Create a new ASP.NET website in a folder on your desktop.

After you create the new website, your screen should look similar to Figure 1.10. When creating the new website, Visual Web Developer automatically created an `App_Data` folder, an ASP.NET page named `Default.aspx`, and a web configuration file (`web.config`). This folder and these two files are shown in the Solution Explorer.

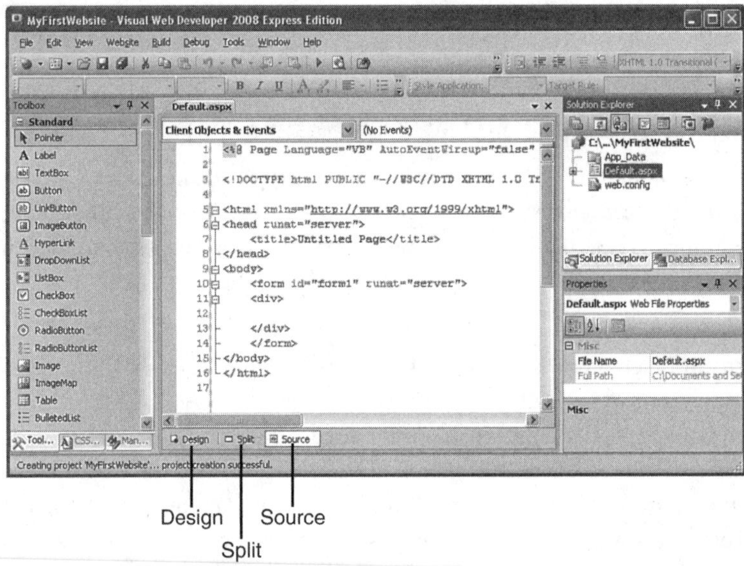

FIGURE 1.10
A new website has been created with an ASP.NET page, `Default.aspx`.

The `Default.aspx` page that was automatically created is opened and its contents are shown in the main window. Right now this ASP.NET page consists of just HTML. As we will see in future hours, ASP.NET pages can also contain Web controls and server-side source code. Typically, ASP.NET pages are broken into two files: one that contains the HTML markup and Web control syntax, and another that contains just the code. In fact, if you click the plus icon on `Default.aspx` in the Solution Explorer, you'll see that there's another file, `Default.aspx.vb`, that is nested. This is the source code file for `Default.aspx`.

By the Way

> Don't worry if you're feeling a bit overwhelmed. The point of this hour is to give a cursory overview of Visual Web Developer. Over the next three hours, we'll look at the portions of an ASP.NET page and the steps involved in creating and testing ASP.NET pages in much greater detail.

When you're working with the HTML elements and Web controls in an ASP.NET web page, you'll notice three views. The first is the Source view, which shows the page's underlying HTML markup and Web control syntax. This is the default view, and the one shown in Figure 1.10. The second view, called the Design view, provides a simpler alternative to specifying and viewing the page's content. In the Design view you can drag and drop HTML elements and Web controls from the Toolbox onto the design surface. You don't need to type in the specific HTML or Web control syntax. The third view, Split, divides the screen in half, showing the Source view in the top portion and the corresponding Design view in the bottom. You can toggle between the Source, Design, and Split views for an ASP.NET page by using the Design, Source, and Split buttons at the bottom of the main window.

Did you Know?

> You can reposition the Properties, Toolbox, Solution Explorer, Database Explorer, and other windows by clicking their title bars and dragging them elsewhere, or resize them by clicking their borders. If you accidentally close one of these windows by clicking the X in the title bar, you can redisplay it from the View menu.

Creating and Testing a Simple ASP.NET Web Page

To view or test an ASP.NET web page, a browser needs to make a request to the web server for that web page. Let's test `Default.aspx`. Before we do, though, let's add some content to the page, because right now the page's HTML will not display anything when viewed through a browser. From the Source view, place your cursor between the `<div>` and `</div>` tags in `Default.aspx` and add the following text:

```
<h1>Hello, World!</h1>
```

This displays the text **Hello, World!** in a large font. After entering this text, go to the Debug menu and choose the Start Without Debugging menu option. This starts the

ASP.NET Development Web Server and launches your computer's default browser, directing it to `http://localhost:portNumber/MyFirstWebsite/Default.aspx` (see Figure 1.11). The *portNumber* portion in the URL will depend on the port selected by the ASP.NET Development Web Server.

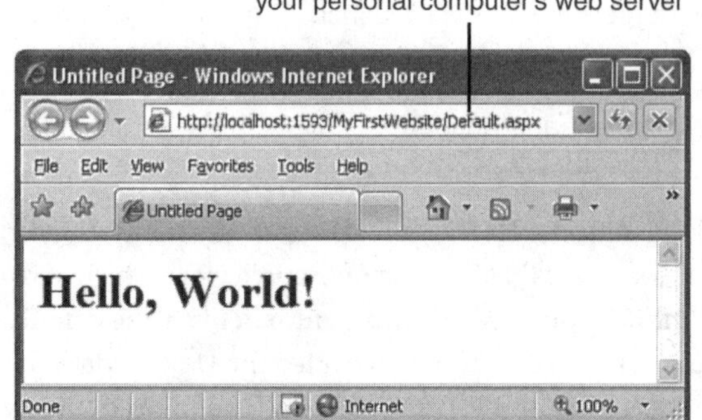

FIGURE 1.11
`Default.aspx`, when viewed through a browser.

This ASP.NET page isn't very interesting because its content is static. It does, however, illustrate that to view the contents of an ASP.NET page, you must start the ASP.NET Development Web Server and request the page through a browser.

You may be wondering what debugging is, and why I instructed you to start without it. We'll cover the differences between the Start Debugging and Start Without Debugging menu options in Hour 4.

Summary

Today virtually all websites contain dynamic web pages of one kind or another. Any website that allows a user to search its content, order products, or customize the site's content is dynamic in nature. A number of competing technologies exist for creating dynamic pages—one of the best is ASP.NET.

Throughout this book we'll be examining how to create interactive and interesting ASP.NET web pages. You will implement the examples using Visual Web Developer, a free editor from Microsoft designed specifically for working on ASP.NET websites. In the "Installing the ASP.NET Engine, Editor, and Database System" section, we looked at how to install Visual Web Developer, along with the .NET Framework and SQL Server 2005. In the "A Brief Tour of Visual Web Developer" section, we poked around Visual Web Developer and created our first ASP.NET web page, testing it through a browser. In Hour 3 we'll explore the Visual Web Developer environment in much greater detail.

We have just begun our foray into the world of ASP.NET. Over the next 23 hours we'll explore the ins and outs of this exciting technology!

Q&A

Q. ***What is the main difference between a static and a dynamic web page?***

A. A static web page has content that remains unchanged between web requests, whereas a dynamic web page's content is generated each time the page is requested. The dynamic content is typically generated from user input, database data, or some combination of the two.

For an example of a dynamic web page, consider the official website for the National Basketball Association (www.NBA.com), which lists team schedules, ongoing game scores, player statistics, and so on. This site's web pages display information stored in a database. Another example is a search engine site such as Google, which displays dynamic content based on both its catalog of indexed websites and the visitor's search terms.

Q. ***You mentioned that with Visual Web Developer we'll be using the ASP.NET Development Web Server. Are other web server systems available for serving ASP.NET pages?***

A. The ASP.NET Development Web Server is designed specifically for testing ASP.NET web pages locally. The computers at web-hosting companies use different web server software. Many web-hosting companies use Microsoft's Internet Information Server (IIS), which is a professional-grade web server designed to work with Microsoft's dynamic web technologies—ASP and ASP.NET.

If you are running Windows XP Professional, Windows Server 2003, Windows Vista, or Windows Server 2008, IIS may already be installed on your computer. If not, you can install it by going to Start, Settings, Control Panel, Add or Remove Programs, and clicking the Add/Remove Windows Components option.

I encourage you not to install IIS and to instead use the ASP.NET Development Web Server unless you are already familiar with IIS and know how to administer and secure it. The ASP.NET Development Web Server is more secure because it allows only incoming web requests from the local computer; IIS, on the other hand, is a full-blown web server and, unless properly patched and administered, can be an attack vector for malicious hackers.

Workshop

Quiz

1. What is the difference between a static web page and a dynamic web page?
2. What is the purpose of the ASP.NET engine?
3. True or False: ASP.NET web pages can be served from computers using the Windows ME operating system.
4. What software packages must be installed to serve ASP.NET web pages from a computer?
5. When should you consider using a web-hosting company to host your ASP.NET web pages?

Answers

1. The HTML markup for a static web page remains constant until a developer actually modifies the page's HTML. The HTML for a dynamic web page, on the other hand, is produced every time the web page is requested.
2. When the web server receives a request for an ASP.NET web page, it hands it off to the ASP.NET engine, which then executes the requested ASP.NET page and returns the rendered HTML to the web server. The ASP.NET engine allows for the HTML of an ASP.NET web page to be dynamically generated for each request.
3. False. ASP.NET pages can be served only from computers running Windows XP, Windows Server 2003, or Windows Vista.
4. For a computer to serve ASP.NET web pages, the .NET Framework and a web server that supports ASP.NET must be installed.
5. You should consider using a web-hosting company if you want your ASP.NET website to be accessible via the Internet. Typically, it's best to first develop the website locally and then deploy it to a web-hosting company when you are ready to go live.

Exercises

This hour does not have any exercises. We'll start with exercises in future hours, after we become more fluent with creating ASP.NET web pages.

HOUR 2

Understanding the ASP.NET Programming Model

In this hour, we will cover

- A quick primer on HTML semantics and syntax
- What content belongs in the HTML and source code portions of an ASP.NET web page
- Using Visual Web Developer to create new ASP.NET websites and web pages
- Adding Web controls to the HTML portion of an ASP.NET web page
- Specifying the functionality of an ASP.NET page through server-side source code
- Viewing an ASP.NET page through a web browser

Before we can start creating ASP.NET web pages, it is important that we have a solid understanding of the ASP.NET programming model. As we'll see in this hour, ASP.NET web pages are composed of two portions: a source code portion and an HTML portion. In this hour's first section, "Examining the HTML Portion of an ASP.NET Web Page," we'll look at what belongs in the HTML portion of an ASP.NET web page. The source code portion of an ASP.NET page is discussed in the second section, "Examining the Source Code Portion of an ASP.NET Web Page."

We will also see Visual Web Developer in action a number of times. This practice serves as a good introduction to Hour 3, "Using Visual Web Developer," which takes a more detailed look at the editor we'll be using throughout this book.

Examining the HTML Portion of an ASP.NET Web Page

As we discussed in the preceding hour, some fundamental differences exist between static web pages and dynamic web pages; the most profound one is that dynamic web pages contain a mix of HTML and server-side source code. Whenever a dynamic web page is requested, its code is executed, generating HTML. This dynamically generated HTML is then sent back to the requesting client.

In this section, we look at the HTML portion of a dynamic web page. In the section "Examining the Source Code Portion of an ASP.NET Web Page," we'll look at one of the more interesting parts of dynamic web pages—the source code.

Before we begin our examination of the HTML portion of an ASP.NET page, it is important to have an understanding of what HTML is, its syntactical rules, and how it is rendered in a web browser. This topic is tackled in the section, "A Brief HTML Primer." If you are already well versed in HTML syntax, feel free to skip ahead to the "Creating the HTML Portion of an ASP.NET Web Page Using Visual Web Developer" section.

A Brief HTML Primer

HTML, as you may already know, is a markup language that specifies how content should be displayed in a web browser. For example, to have a web browser display a message in bold, you could use the following HTML:

```
<b>This will be in bold.</b>
```

HTML is composed of **elements** that specify how the data should be rendered in a web browser. An element is composed of beginning and ending tags, such as

```
<elementName>... some content ...</elementName>
```

Here, `<elementName>` is referred to as the **start tag** and `</elementName>` is referred to as the **end tag** or **closing tag**. Many HTML elements apply various types of formatting to the content between their start and end tags; the formatting applied depends on the element name. As we saw earlier, text can be made bold by placing it between `<b>` and `</b>` tags. (The `<b>` element specifies that the content it contains be made bold.)

A plethora of HTML elements enable you to specify formatting in a web page. For more information on HTML and its myriad of elements, be sure to check out *Sams Teach Yourself HTML and CSS in 24 Hours* (ISBN: 978-0672328411), or go online to http://www.w3schools.com.

HTML elements that do not contain any content between their tags do not need to have an explicit closing tag. Instead, they can use a shorthand syntax that combines the starting and ending tag. That is, instead of explicitly specifying the starting and ending tags, like so:

```
<elementName></elementName>
```

The following shorthand syntax can be used:

```
<elementName />
```

Similarly, certain HTML elements disallow any inner content. Two common examples are the <br> and <hr> elements, which specify a line break and a horizontal line, respectively. These empty elements also use the shorthand syntax. For example, when adding a line break to the HTML of a web page, use the following syntax:

```
This will appear on one line...
<br />
And this will appear on a line beneath the text above...
```

Extraneous Whitespace

When a web browser renders HTML from a website, the whitespace in the markup—carriage returns, tabs, spaces, and so forth—do not affect the whitespace displayed in the browser. For example, consider the HTML shown in Listing 2.1, which contains several carriage returns, tabs, and extraneous spaces.

LISTING 2.1 A Snippet of HTML with Extraneous Whitespace

```
        <h1>Welcome to my Site!</h1>
<p>
<b>Welcome!</b>

You are                    now visiting my site!

<i>This is neat, I like
H
T
M
L
</i></p>
```

Watch Out!

The line numbers in Listing 2.1 are present simply to make it easier to refer to specific lines of markup in the listing. An HTML page would not contain these line numbers as part of its markup.

The HTML, when viewed through a browser, compresses the whitespace, as shown in Figure 2.1. Notice that any extra whitespace is reduced to a single space. For example, each carriage return between the `H`, `T`, `M`, and `L` letters in the markup is rendered as a single space between each of the letters in the browser. On line 5, the multiple spaces and tabs between **You are** and **now visiting my site!** are compressed into one space in Figure 2.1.

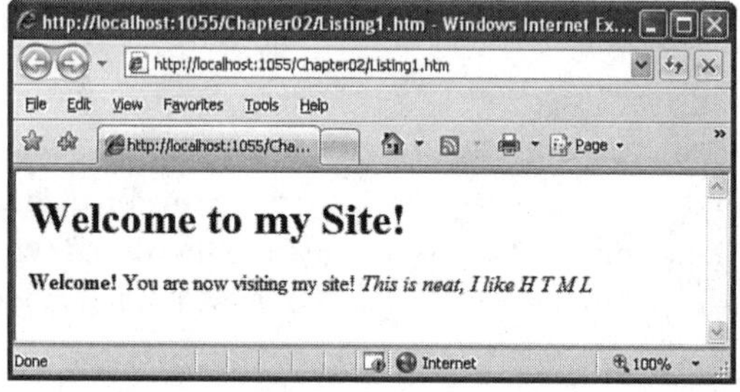

FIGURE 2.1 Extra white-space in the HTML is ignored by browsers.

Finally, note that some elements are rendered on a new line, whereas others follow after one another. For example, the content of the `<h1>` element appears on a separate line from the content of the `<p>` element. The `<b>` and `<i>` elements, however, have their content flow together on the same line.

HTML elements can be displayed in one of two ways: as **inline elements** or **block elements**. Inline elements do *not* introduce a carriage return after the closing tag, whereas block elements do. As you can tell from the rendered output in Figure 2.1, `<h1>` is a block element, and `<b>` and `<i>` are inline elements. (Although it might not be clear from the example, `<p>` is a block element.)

Did you Know?

You can find a complete list of inline and block HTML elements at www.htmlhelp.com/reference/html40/inline.html and www.htmlhelp.com/reference/html40/block.html, respectively.

With extraneous whitespace compressed by the browser, a natural question at this point is, "How do I position HTML elements?" That is, if no number of carriage returns or spaces affects the positioning of an HTML element, how do you create a web page where content appears to the right of other content or is indented?

HTML elements contain various style attributes that you can use to specify formatting and layout information, such as padding, margins, positioning, and how the content flows relative to other content on the page. These topics are a bit beyond the scope of this book, but we will examine some techniques to position elements throughout this book. Additionally, Visual Web Developer assists us in laying out elements.

Nested Tags

HTML tags can be **nested**, meaning that one set of HTML tags can appear within another. For example, if you wanted to have a web page display a message in both italic and bold, you would use both the `<i>` and `<b>` tags like so:

```
<i><b>This is both italic and bold</b>, whereas this is just italic</i>
```

In this example, the `<b>` tag is said to be inside the `<i>` tag. (Throughout this book I will also refer to nested tags as one tag being **contained within** the other, or **enclosed within**.)

The semantics of nested tags are fairly straightforward. In our example, the `<i>` tag indicates that everything within it should be formatted using italics. Next, the `<b>` tag indicates that everything within it should be bold. Therefore, the text **This is both italic and bold** will be formatted using both bold and italics, and **whereas this is just italic** will appear in italics.

There's no reason why the `<b>` tag must be inside the `<i>` tag and not the other way around. That is, you could also do

```
<b><i>This is both italic and bold</i>, whereas this is just bold</b>
```

The preceding two examples show how to use **properly nested tags**. Note that in our last example, the `<i>` tag that is contained within the `<b>` tag has both its starting and closing tag (`<i>` and `</i>`) before the closing `<b>` tag (`</b>`). An **improperly nested tag** is one whose start tag is contained within a tag, but its closing tag is not. The following HTML is an example of an improperly nested tag:

```
<i><b>This is both italic and bold</i>, but this is just bold</b>
```

Notice that the `<b>` tag's starting tag is contained within the `<i>` tag, but the closing `<b>` tag is not.

Creating the HTML Portion of an ASP.NET Web Page Using Visual Web Developer

The HTML portion of an ASP.NET web page is composed of both static HTML and **Web controls**. Web controls are programmatically accessible chunks of HTML, enabling developers to modify the HTML sent to the browser based on programmatic logic. Web controls also provide a means by which user input can be collected. They serve as the bridge between the HTML and source code portions of an ASP.NET page. We'll examine adding and working with Web controls in more detail later in this hour; starting with Hour 8, "ASP.NET Web Controls for Displaying Text," we'll spend significant time examining the array of Web controls at our disposal.

In the previous hour we saw that Visual Web Developer offers three views of an ASP.NET page's HTML portion. HTML content and web controls may be added to an ASP.NET web page through any of these views.

- **Source view**—You can either type in the HTML and web control syntax by hand or drag the desired HTML elements and Web controls from the Toolbox onto the Source view.
- **Design view**—This view presents a What You See Is What You Get (WYSIWYG) interface. You can add text to the page by typing, but HTML elements and Web controls can be added only by dragging them from the Toolbox and dropping them onto the design surface.
- **Split view**—This view shows both the Source and Design views.

In my experience, I've found most developers already familiar with HTML prefer typing in the HTML and web control syntax by hand, rather than using the drag-and-drop capabilities. Those coming from a background that did not include HTML exposure, however, usually find using the WYSIWYG designer to be a more intuitive and time-effective approach. Regardless of your past experiences, I encourage you to try both techniques and settle on the one that you are most productive with.

Whether you choose to manually type in or drag and drop the HTML elements and Web controls, I encourage you to use to Split view. In showing both the Source and Design views, the Split view illustrates the correspondence between the declarative syntax and how it is rendered in a browser.

To illustrate adding content to the HTML portion of an ASP.NET page, let's create a simple ASP.NET website with a single web page. To follow along, start Visual Web Developer and choose to create a new website by going to the File menu and choosing New Web Site. This displays the New Web Site dialog box, shown in Figure 2.2. Choose the ASP.NET Web Site template and set the Location drop-down list to File System and the Language drop-down list to Visual Basic.

By the Way

> The Location drop-down list indicates where the website will be saved. The examples in this book use the File System option, although other options are available. All the examples that we'll be examining in this book will use Visual Basic as the server-side programming language. Therefore, when creating new websites to follow along with examples from this book, leave the Language option as the default (Visual Basic).
>
> In Hour 3, we'll examine the New Web Site dialog box in greater detail.

After you click the New Web Site dialog box's OK button, Visual Web Developer creates the following folders and files in the directory you specified:

- **`App_Data`**—This folder, which is initially empty, will contain any data-related files. We'll begin our look at creating data-driven ASP.NET applications in Hour 13, "An Introduction to Databases."
- **`Default.aspx`**—This file contains the HTML portion of the `Default.aspx` ASP.NET page.
- **`Default.aspx.vb`**—This file contains the source code portion of the `Default.aspx` ASP.NET page.
- **`Web.config`**—This XML-formatted file contains configuration information for the website.

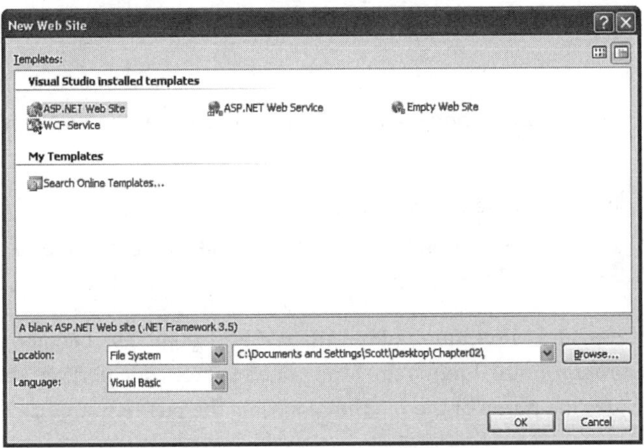

FIGURE 2.2
Choose to create a blank ASP.NET website.

Figure 2.3 shows Visual Web Developer after creating the new website. In the main window, Visual Web Developer has opened the file `Default.aspx`. By default, Visual Web Developer opens ASP.NET pages in the Source view. Figure 2.3 shows `Default.aspx`'s content displayed using the Split view. Use the Design, Split, and Source buttons in the bottom-left corner to toggle between these views.

Did you Know?

> To change the default view used by Visual Web Developer, go to the Tools menu and select Options. The General tab in the Options dialog box enables you to configure whether to start pages in Source view, Design view, or Split view.

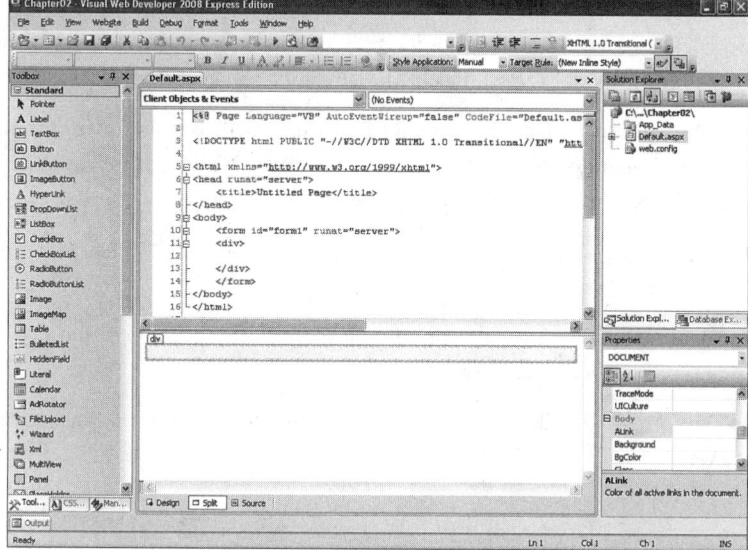

FIGURE 2.3
Congratulations! You have created your first ASP.NET website.

Notice that even though we have not yet added any content to our ASP.NET web page, some markup already exists.

At the top of the page is the **@Page directive**:

```
<%@ Page Language="VB" AutoEventWireup="false" CodeFile="Default.aspx.vb"
➥ Inherits="_Default" %>
```

This directive provides information about the ASP.NET page. The `Language` attribute indicates the programming language of the page's source code portion; the `CodeFile` attribute provides the name of the file that contains the page's source code.

When we look at an end-to-end example later in this hour, you'll find that not all content in an ASP.NET page is sent to the requesting browser. The `@Page` directive is one such fragment; its contents provide information to the ASP.NET engine on the web server, and therefore it is not rendered to the client.

After the `@Page` directive, you'll find the default HTML content Visual Web Developer adds when creating a new ASP.NET page. This includes an `<html>` element, which has nested within it `<head>` and `<body>` elements. Inside the `<body>` element is a `<form>` element, and inside the `<form>` element is a `<div>` element.

You may have noticed that the `<head>` and `<form>` tags in Figure 2.3 contain a `runat="server"` attribute. This is not a standard HTML attribute. In fact, the `<head>` and `<form>` elements in Figure 2.3 are not HTML elements at all! In an ASP.NET page, HTML tags that contain the `runat="server"` attribute are a special form of Web control. We discuss what, exactly, Web controls are and their place in an ASP.NET web page throughout this hour. Hour 9, "Web Form Basics," looks at the `<form>` element and its purpose in greater detail.

Editing the HTML Content Using the Designer

To edit the ASP.NET web page's HTML content, you can either use the Design view, which provides a WYSIWYG experience, or you can type the content through the Source view. Let's examine how to add content to our page using the designer. Specifically, let's add an HTML `<table>` that lists some popular Internet websites—Yahoo!, Google, MSN, and Ask.com—along with their logos.

By the Way

> The HTML `<table>` element creates a gridlike display consisting of a set of rows and columns. The `<table>` element is commonly used to lay out the contents of a web page, although other techniques are available. For more information on laying out HTML content, including a look at using `<table>`, check out www.w3schools.com/html/html_layout.asp.

Our first task to add is an HTML `<table>` to the page. Because we won't need the `<div>` element, go ahead and remove it. You can accomplish this by deleting the opening and closing `<div>` tags from the Source view or by right-clicking in the `<div>` region in the Design view and choosing the Delete menu option.

Did you Know?

> When using the Split view, keep in mind that if you make modifications in the Source view, the changes are not reflected in the Design view until you synchronize the two views. You can synchronize the views by clicking Click Here to Synchronize Views, which appears at the top of the Design view when the two views are out of sync, or by saving the ASP.NET page. To save the changes to your ASP.NET page, click the Save icon in the Toolbar, go to the File menu and choose Save, or press Ctrl+S.

Next, set the focus in the Design view so that the cursor is within the <form> element. Go to the Table menu and select Insert Table, which launches the Insert Table dialog box. From the Insert Table dialog box you can specify the number of rows and columns along with a variety of layout and formatting options.

Create a table with two columns and four rows. In the first column we will display the name of the website, and in the second column we will display the website logo. Set the table's width to 300 pixels, but do not specify a height. After making these changes the Insert Table dialog box on your screen should look similar to the one shown in Figure 2.4.

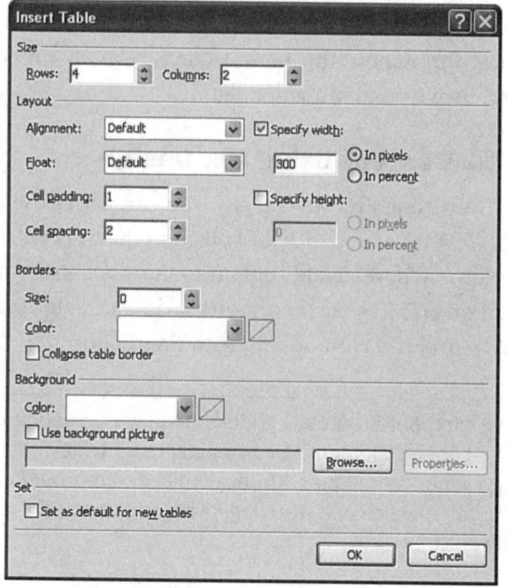

FIGURE 2.4
When inserting an HTML table, you can specify the number of rows and columns as well as the table's width and height.

Click the OK button to create the table. The Source view contains the <table>, <tr>, and <td> HTML elements used to construct the two-column, four-row table, whereas the Design view offers a WYSIWYG view of the table.

To add the websites' names to the table's left column, click inside the first column of each row in the Design view and type in the name. Entering the text into the Design view adds it to the corresponding section of the Source view, as well. Figure 2.5 shows the Source and Design views after the website names have been added to the table.

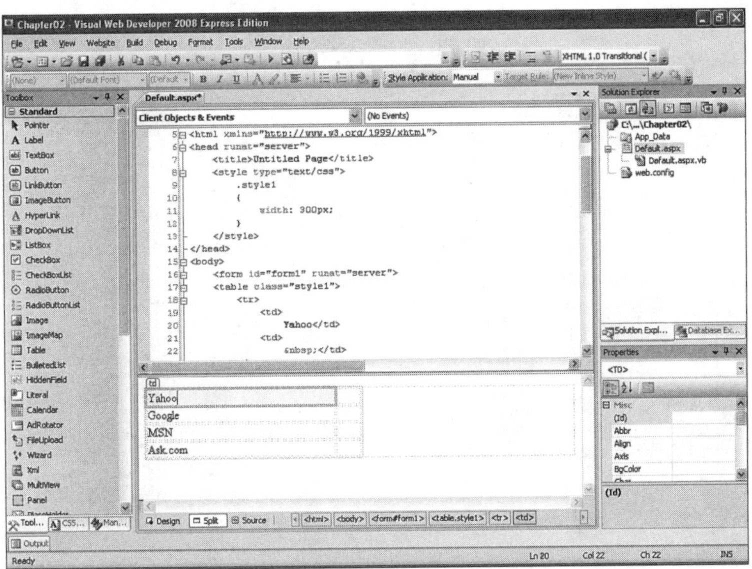

FIGURE 2.5
The first column contains the names of four websites.

Notice that the name of each website is displayed left-justified in a fairly plain-looking font. Let's spruce things up a bit by centering the name of each website and displaying it in a bold Arial font.

To accomplish this, start by selecting the text of a particular website. After it is selected, you can make the text bold by choosing the Font option from the Format menu. This launches the Font dialog box, from which you can update the font to display in a bold text. You can also turn the selected text bold by clicking the Bold icon in the Toolbar. To center the selected text, go to the Format menu and choose the Paragraph option. This displays the Paragraph dialog box, which includes an Alignment drop-down list. Select the Right option from the drop-down list. Finally, to make the font of the still-selected text Arial, click the list of fonts that is positioned beneath the Save icon in the Toolbar near the top-left corner.

Figure 2.6 shows Visual Web Developer after this formatting has been applied to all four website names.

By the Way

If you look closely at the HTML in the Source view, you will see that these formatting options are applied using **cascading style sheets**. Cascading style sheets, or CSS, is a technology for separating formatting and layout specifics from HTML elements. Visual Web Developer includes a number of tools for creating and managing styles.

For more information on CSS, refer to www.w3schools.com/css/.

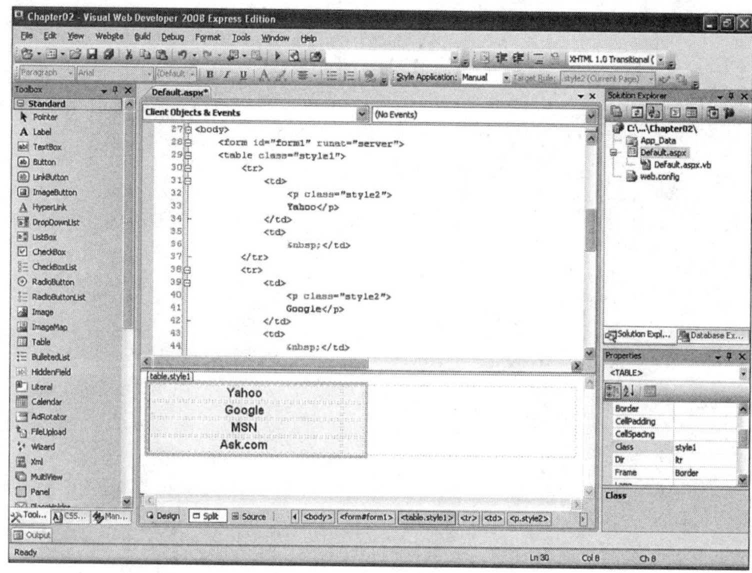

FIGURE 2.6
The website names have been centered, made bold, and changed to Arial font.

Now let's add the logos for each of the websites in the second column.

The Toolbox contains HTML elements and Web controls that can be dragged onto the WYSIWYG designer. By default, the Toolbox is shown on the left side of Visual Web Developer; if you do not see the Toolbox on your screen, you can display it by going to the View menu and selecting the Toolbox menu item.

There are nine tabs in the Toolbox:

- Standard
- Data
- Validation
- Navigation
- Login
- WebParts
- AJAX Extensions
- HTML
- General

Each tab contains a number of elements underneath it. By default, the Standard tab will be expanded, which includes items such as Label, TextBox, Button, LinkButton, and so on. The Toolbox with the Standard tab expanded is shown in Figure 2.7.

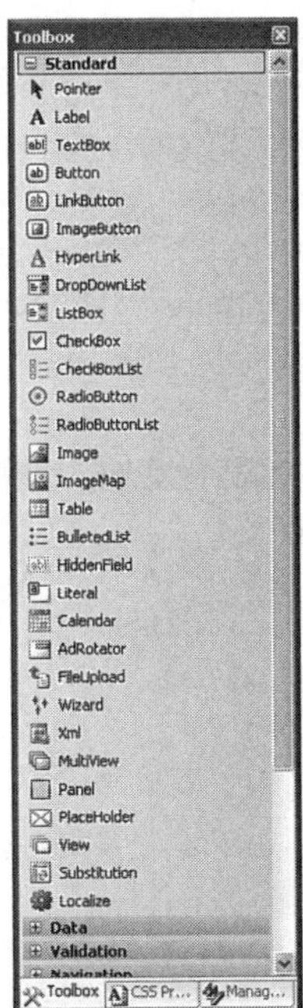

FIGURE 2.7 The Toolbox contains elements that can be dragged and dropped into the designer.

The Toolbox contains both Web controls and standard, static HTML elements. The HTML elements can be found in the Toolbox's HTML tab; all other tabs contain Web controls. At this point in our discussion, we've yet to explore the differences between Web controls and static HTML elements. When we finish examining the HTML portion and then turn to the source code portion of an ASP.NET page, the differences will become clearer. For now, just understand that unless you are adding items from the HTML tab onto the designer, you are adding Web controls to the page, and not HTML elements.

To add one of the items in the Toolbox to your ASP.NET web page, click the item you want to add and, while holding down the mouse button, move the mouse pointer over the location where you want the item to be placed and then release the mouse button.

As you can see from Figure 2.7, one of the items in the Standard tab is an Image Web control. We'll use this Web control to add the website logos in the second column of the `<table>`. Start by dragging and dropping four Image Web controls into the designer, one in each of the second columns of each of the four rows.

Figure 2.8 shows what you should see after the four Image Web controls have been added to the designer.

Note that each Image Web control currently displays a red square, green circle, and blue triangle. The reason is that we have yet to specify the URL of the image. The Image Web control has an `ImageUrl` property that specifies the URL of the image. Before we can assign the `ImageUrl` property, though, we first need to have the appropriate image files present for our website. Go to each search engine's home page, locate its logo, and save that logo to the same folder where you created your website. (To save an image in your browser, right-click the image and choose Save As.)

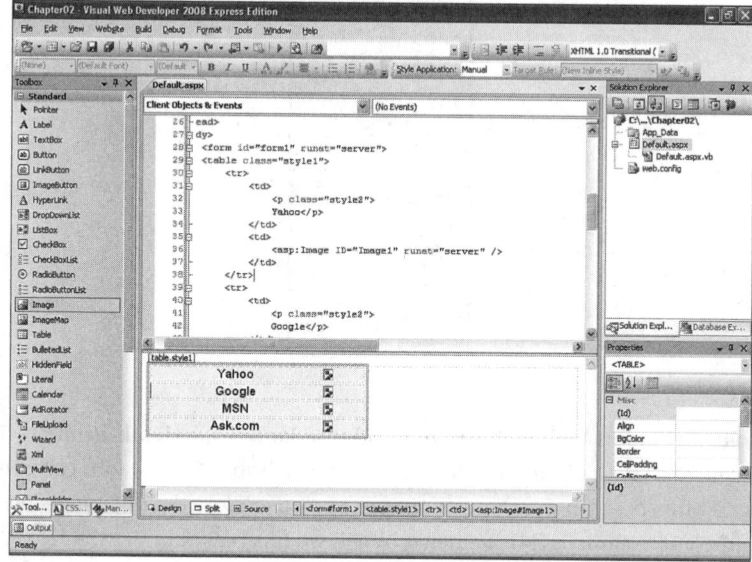

FIGURE 2.8
An Image Web control has been added to each row in the table.

After you have downloaded the four logos to your computer, you can edit the `ImageUrl` properties of the Image Web controls. The properties of a Web control can be viewed and altered through the Properties window, which resides, by default, in the lower-right corner. If you do not see the Properties window, go to the View menu and choose Properties Window.

To specify an Image Web control's `ImageUrl` property, click the Image Web control, which will load the control's properties in the Properties window. By default, the `ImageUrl` property's value is a blank string, meaning that no value for the `ImageUrl` property has been specified. You can either type in a value or click the ellipses to select a file.

Because we already have the image files in our website's root directory, click the ellipses. This displays the Select Image dialog box, shown in Figure 2.9. From here, you can choose which image to display in the Image Web control. For each of the four Image Web controls on your page, select the appropriate logo.

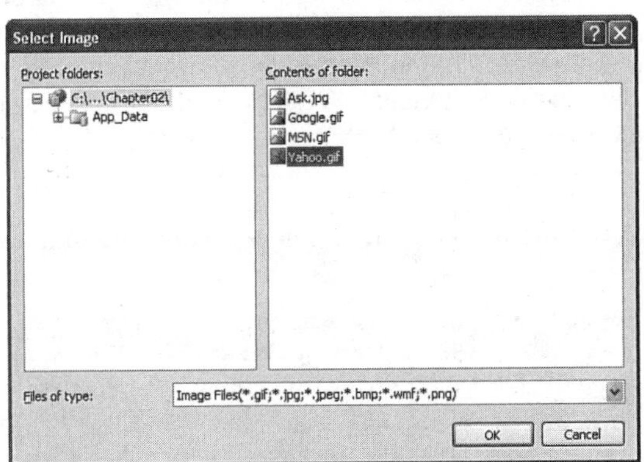

FIGURE 2.9 Choose the image to display in the Image Web control.

Did you Know?

> After you have added the four images, you may notice that the images are taller or wider than you like. To adjust an image's height or width, you can alter its `Height` and `Width` properties. To specify that an image should have a width, for example, of 100 pixels, set its `Width` property to a value of `100px`.

Atthis point we've created the HTML content, which includes both static HTML, such as `<table>`, along with Image Web controls. Note that we did not have to write a single line of HTML; rather, we chose various menu options, dragged and dropped Web controls from the Toolbox, and set properties via the Properties window.

To test your ASP.NET web page, go to the Debug menu and choose Start Without Debugging. Alternatively, you can press Ctrl+F5. This launches your default web browser and takes you to the open page. If you want Visual Web Developer to start on a specific page rather than the currently open page, right-click the desired start page in the Solution Explorer and choose the Set as Start Page option.

> Visual Web Developer provides you with two options to test your ASP.NET pages through a browser, both through the Debug menu: Start Debugging and Start Without Debugging. Both options automatically launch a browser, taking you to the specified start page, but the Start Debugging option also has the effect of running the debugger. The debugger is useful if you are troubleshooting the source code portion of an ASP.NET page. If you just want to view an ASP.NET page, though, and are not diagnosing any programmatic problems, you can start without debugging. We'll talk about working with the debugger in future hours.

By the Way

Personally, I choose Start Without Debugging if I don't need to use the services of the debugger. It's a snappier experience because Visual Web Developer doesn't need to load the debugger. However, there's nothing wrong if you always want to start with debugging. If you do attempt to use Start Debugging, your configuration file (`Web.config`) will need to be updated to indicate that the website is in debug mode. If this update is needed, Visual Web Developer informs you of this change and offers to make it on your behalf.

Figure 2.10 shows the ASP.NET web page when viewed through a web browser.

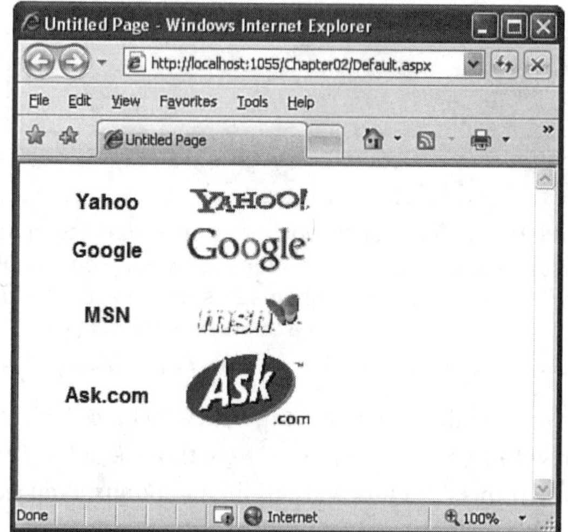

FIGURE 2.10 The ASP.NET web page when viewed through a browser.

Examining the HTML Content

Adding HTML and Web controls to an ASP.NET web page through the Design view saves a lot of typing. To appreciate the time the designer saves, take a moment to scan the bulk of markup present in the Source view. This lengthy markup is shown in Listing 2.2.

LISTING 2.2 The Markup Generated by the Designer

```
<%@ Page Language="VB" AutoEventWireup="false" CodeFile="Default.aspx.vb"
➥ Inherits="_Default" %>

<!DOCTYPE html PUBLIC "-//W3C//DTD XHTML 1.0 Transitional//EN"
➥   "http://www.w3.org/TR/xhtml1/DTD/xhtml1-transitional.dtd">

<html xmlns="http://www.w3.org/1999/xhtml">
<head runat="server">
    <title>Untitled Page</title>
```

LISTING 2.2 Continued

```
    <style type="text/css">
        .style1
        {
            width: 300px;
        }
        .style2
        {
            font-weight: bold;
            text-align: center;
            font-family: Arial;
        }
        .style3
        {
            font-weight: bold;
            text-align: center;
            font-family: Arial;
        }
    </style>
</head>
<body>
    <form id="form1" runat="server">
    <table class="style1">
        <tr>
            <td>
                <p class="style2">
                Yahoo</p>
            </td>
            <td>
                <asp:Image ID="Image1" runat="server" ImageUrl="~/Yahoo.gif" Width="100px" />
            </td>
        </tr>
        <tr>
            <td>
                <p class="style2">
                Google</p>
            </td>
            <td>
                <asp:Image ID="Image2" runat="server" ImageUrl="~/Google.gif" Width="100px" />
            </td>
        </tr>
        <tr>
            <td>
                <p class="style3">
                MSN</p>
            </td>
            <td>
                <asp:Image ID="Image3" runat="server" ImageUrl="~/MSN.gif" Width="100px" />
            </td>
        </tr>
        <tr>
            <td>
                <p class="style2">
                Ask.com</p>
```

LISTING 2.2 Continued

```
61:             </td>
62:             <td>
63:                 <asp:Image ID="Image4" runat="server"
➥ ImageUrl="~/Ask.jpg" Width="100px" />
64:             </td>
65:         </tr>
66:     </table>
67:     </form>
68: </body>
69: </html>
```

First, appreciate the quantity of HTML that the designer automatically generates. It added the various `<table>`-related elements along with the cascading style sheet information in the `<style>` element. Without a doubt, the designer knocked off several minutes of time it would have taken us to type this out by hand.

Next, study the syntax for the four Image Web controls (lines 36, 45, 54, and 63). The Google Image Web control (line 45) has the following markup:

```
<asp:Image ID="Image2" runat="server" ImageUrl="~/Google.gif" Width="100px" />
```

Web controls have an HTML-like syntax: They are represented by opening and closing tags; in the case where there is no inner content, as with the Image Web control, the shorthand syntax may be used. A Web control's opening tag can optionally contain attributes and, although not shown in this example, Web controls may contain content within their starting and closing tags.

Although a number of valid HTML elements exist, `asp:Image` is not one of them. In fact, none of the ASP.NET Web controls (all of whose tags have the notation `asp:`*`WebControlName`*) are valid HTML elements. This does not pose a problem, however, because the Web control syntax shown in our ASP.NET page in Visual Web Developer is not the markup that gets sent to the browser. Instead, the Web controls are rendered into valid HTML. When the browser requests this ASP.NET page, it is not sent an `<asp:Image>` element; instead, the Image Web control is rendered into an `<img>` element, which is a valid HTML element.

To see this conversion in action, return to viewing `Default.aspx` through a browser. Then, from your browser, view the HTML source received. (For Internet Explorer, go to the View menu and choose Source.) This opens Notepad and displays the contents of the HTML sent to your browser. Listing 2.3 shows the rendered HTML that was sent to my browser (Internet Explorer 7.0) when visiting `Default.aspx`.

LISTING 2.3 The HTML Received by the Browser When Visiting Default.aspx

```
<!DOCTYPE html PUBLIC "-//W3C//DTD XHTML 1.0 Transitional//EN"
➥ "http://www.w3.org/TR/xhtml1/DTD/xhtml1-transitional.dtd">

<html xmlns="http://www.w3.org/1999/xhtml">
<head><title>
   Untitled Page
</title>
    <style type="text/css">
        .style1
        {
            width: 300px;
        }
        .style2
        {
            font-weight: bold;
            text-align: center;
            font-family: Arial;
        }
        .style3
        {
            font-weight: bold;
            text-align: center;
            font-family: Arial;
        }
    </style>
</head>
<body>
    <form name="form1" method="post" action="Default.aspx" id="form1">
<div>
<input type="hidden" name="__VIEWSTATE" id="__VIEWSTATE"
➥ value="/wEPDwUJODM3MDQ0NzEzZGS0aDdy69DkIynhaY/njxxgxMDQEA==" />
</div>

    <table class="style1">
        <tr>
            <td>
                <p class="style2">
                Yahoo</p>
            </td>
            <td>
                <img id="Image1" src="Yahoo.gif"
➥ style="width:100px;border-width:0px;" />
            </td>
        </tr>
        <tr>
            <td>
                <p class="style2">
                Google</p>
            </td>
            <td>
                <img id="Image2" src="Google.gif"
➥ style="width:100px;border-width:0px;" />
            </td>
        </tr>
        <tr>
```

LISTING 2.3 Continued

```
52:             <td>
53:                 <p class="style3">
54:                 MSN</p>
55:             </td>
56:             <td>
57:                 <img id="Image3" src="MSN.gif"
➥ style="width:100px;border-width:0px;" />
58:             </td>
59:         </tr>
60:         <tr>
61:             <td>
62:                 <p class="style2">
63:                 Ask.com</p>
64:             </td>
65:             <td>
66:                 <img id="Image4" src="Ask.jpg"
➥ style="width:100px;border-width:0px;" />
67:             </td>
68:         </tr>
69:     </table>
70:     </form>
71: </body>
72: </html>
```

Although the markup in Listings 2.2 and 2.3 looks nearly identical, some subtle and important differences exist. Starting from the top, the `@Page` directive on line 1 in Listing 2.2 is not in the rendered HTML output shown in Listing 2.3. Next, notice how the `<form runat="server">` on line 28 in Listing 2.2 has been transformed into

```
<form name="form1" method="post" action="Default.aspx" id="form1">
```

There's also a hidden form field that's been added to Listing 2.3 (on line 29):

```
<input type="hidden" name="__VIEWSTATE" id="__VIEWSTATE"
➥ value="/wEPDwUJODM3MDQ0NzEzZGS0aDdy69DkIynhaY/njxxgxMDQEA==" />
```

We won't be discussing these transformations in this hour; this topic is left for Hour 9.

Last, note that the Image Web control syntax from Listing 2.2 has been replaced by standard `<img>` HTML elements in Listing 2.3, with the `ImageUrl` property transformed into the `src` attribute.

These changes highlight an important concept with ASP.NET pages: The markup present on the web server is not necessarily the markup that is sent to the requesting browser. When an ASP.NET page is requested, the ASP.NET engine renders the Web control syntax into its corresponding HTML. Also, as we'll see shortly, the rendering process involves the execution of any server-side code that we've written for the page. This server-side rendering process, which occurs when any ASP.NET page is requested, is what makes ASP.NET a dynamic web technology. The resulting HTML sent to the browser can be programmatically altered based on various criteria, such as database data, user input, and other external factors.

Examining the Source Code Portion of an ASP.NET Web Page

Now that we've examined the HTML portion of an ASP.NET web page, let's turn our attention to the source code portion. Although the HTML portion defines the layout of the ASP.NET page along with its static content, it's the source code portion where the content for the dynamic portions of the page is decided.

When adding a new ASP.NET page to your website, you can instruct Visual Studio to put the source code portion in one of two locations:

- **In a separate file**—The ASP.NET page is composed of two separate files, `*PageName*.aspx` and `*PageName*.aspx.vb`. The `*PageName*.aspx` file contains the HTML and Web control syntax, and the `*PageName*.aspx.vb` file contains the source code. This is how our current sample web page is structured, with `Default.aspx` and `Default.aspx.vb`.
- **In a `<script>` block in the same file**—The HTML and source code portions can reside in the same file. In this scenario, the source code portion is placed within a `<script runat="server">` element.

The examples in this book use the separate file technique, although either option is acceptable. Many developers prefer the separate file approach because it provides a cleaner separation between the HTML and source code portions. Furthermore, if you find yourself working in a large ASP.NET project, you'll more than likely be using the separate file approach. Hence, we'll stick with this technique for the examples in this book.

By the Way

ASP.NET web pages can have their source code portion written in any .NET programming language. The two most commonly used languages are Visual Basic and Visual C#. In this book, all our code examples use Visual Basic.

For more information on Visual Basic, consult Hours 5 through 7.

You can view the source code portion of an ASP.NET page that uses the separate file technique through any one of the following actions:

- Right-click the ASP.NET page in the Solution Explorer and choose View Code.
- Click the plus icon in the Solution Explorer for the ASP.NET page whose source code you want to edit. This lists its corresponding source code file, `PageName.aspx.vb`. Double-click the source code file to display its contents.
- In the Source or Design view of an ASP.NET page, right-click and choose View Code.

Take a moment to view the source code portion for `Default.aspx`. You should find the following content in `Default.aspx.vb`:

```
Partial Class _Default
    Inherits System.Web.UI.Page

End Class
```

These three lines are the bare minimum code that must exist in an ASP.NET page's source code portion. Specifically, this code defines a **class** called `_Default` that extends the `System.Web.UI.Page` class. Classes are a central construct of object-oriented programming, which is the programming paradigm used by ASP.NET. The next few sections provide an overview of object-oriented and event-driven programming; if you are already familiar with these concepts, feel free to skip ahead to the "Event Handlers in ASP.NET" section.

By the Way

> It is vitally important to remember that the ASP.NET page's source code portion is **server-side** code. As we discussed in Hour 1, "Getting Started with ASP.NET 3.5," when an ASP.NET page is requested, the ASP.NET engine executes the source code and returns the resulting HTML to the browser. Therefore, none of the ASP.NET page's source code is sent to the browser, just the resulting markup.

A Quick Object-Oriented Programming Primer

The source code portion of an ASP.NET web page uses a particular programming model known as **object-oriented programming**. Object-oriented programming is a paradigm that generalizes programming in terms of **objects**. A key construct of any object-oriented programming language is the **class**, which is used to abstractly define an object. Classes contain **properties**, which describe the state of the object; **methods**, which provide the actions that can be performed on the object; and

events, which are actions triggered by the object. Objects are instances of classes, representing a concrete instance of an abstraction.

Whew! This all likely sounds very confusing, but a real-world analogy should help. Think, for a moment, about a car. What things describe a car? What actions can a car perform? What events transpire during the operation of a car?

A car can have various properties, like its make, model, year, and color. A car also has a number of actions it can perform, such as drive, reverse, turn, and park. While you're driving a car, various events occur, such as stepping on the brakes and turning on the windshield wipers.

By the Way

In object-oriented terms, an object's actions are referred to as its **methods**.

This assimilation of properties, actions (hereafter referred to as methods), and events abstractly defines what a car can do. The reason this assimilation is an abstraction is that it does not define a specific car; rather, it describes features common to *all* cars. This collection of properties, methods, and events describing an abstract car is a class in object-oriented terms.

An object is a specific instance of a class. In our analogy, an object would be a specific instance of the car abstraction, such as a year 2000, forest green, Honda Accord. The methods of the car abstraction can then be applied to the object. For example, to drive this Honda to the store, I'd use the Drive method, applying the Turn method as needed. When I reached the store, I'd use the Park method. After making my purchases, I'd need to back out of the parking spot, so I'd use the Reverse method, and then the Drive and Turn methods to get back home. During the operation of the car object, various events might occur: When I'm driving to the store, the "Turning the steering wheel" event will more than likely transpire, as will the "Stepping on the brakes" event.

Examining Event-Driven Programming

Another important construct of the programming languages used to create ASP.NET web pages is the **event handler**. An event, as we just saw, is some action that occurs during the use of an object. An event handler is a piece of code that is executed when its corresponding event occurs. Programming languages that include support for handling events are called **event-driven**.

When an event occurs, it commonly is said that the event has **fired** or has been **raised**. Furthermore, an event handler, when run, is referred to as having been **executed**. Therefore, when an event fires (or is raised), its event handler executes.

For events to be useful, they need to be paired with an event handler. The event handler for the car's Starting event, for example, would run code that turns the crankshaft. When the "Stepping on the brakes" event fires, the executed code applies the brake pads to the brake drums.

You can think of ASP.NET web pages as event-driven programs. The source code portion of the ASP.NET web page is made up of event handlers. Furthermore, a number of potential events can fire during the rendering of an ASP.NET page.

Out-of-Order Execution

In ASP and PHP, two other dynamic web page technologies, the source code portion of a web page is executed serially, from top to bottom. If the source code section contains five lines of code, the first line of code is executed first, followed by the second, then the third, the fourth, and finally the fifth. This programming paradigm, in which one line of code is executed after another, is known as **sequential execution**. With sequential execution, the code is executed in order from the first line of code to the last. You know that code on line 5 will execute before code on line 10.

With event-driven programming, however, no such guarantees exist. The only serial portions of code in an event-driven program are those lines of code within a particular event handler. Often you can't make any assumptions about the order that the events will fire, and therefore you can't be certain of the order with which the corresponding event handlers will be called. Furthermore, in many cases you can't assume that a particular event will always fire.

Looking back at our car analogy, imagine that our car has the following events:

- Starting
- Stopping
- Applying brakes
- Starting windshield wipers

During a car's use—driving from home to the store, let's say—some events will definitely fire, such as the Starting and Stopping events. However others, such as "Starting windshield wipers," might not fire at all. Furthermore, although we can assume that the Starting event will be the first event to fire and Stopping the last, we can't say with any certainty whether or not the "Applying brakes" event will come before or after the "Starting windshield wipers" event.

When creating an ASP.NET page, you may optionally create event handlers for the plethora of events that may transpire during the ASP.NET page's life cycle. When an event fires, its corresponding event handler—if defined—executes. Returning to the car analogy, we may want to have event handlers for just the Starting and Stopping events. The code in the event handlers would be executed when the corresponding events fired. For example, imagine that our Starting event has an event handler that had the following two lines of code:

```
Begin Starting Event Handler
  Send signal to the starter to start turning the crankshaft
  Send signal to the fuel injector to send fuel to the engine
End Starting Event Handler
```

When the Starting event fires, the Starting event handler is executed. The first line of code in this event handler will execute first, followed by the second. Our complete source code for the car may consist of two event handlers, one for Starting and one for Stopping.

```
Begin Starting Event Handler
  Send signal to the starter to start turning the crankshaft
  Send signal to the fuel injector to send fuel to the engine
End Starting Event Handler

Begin Stopping Event Handler
  Send signal to the brake drums
  Decrease the fuel injector's output
End Stopping Event Handler
```

Even though the Starting event handler appears before the Stopping event handler in the source code, this does not imply that the Starting event handler will execute prior to the Stopping event handler. Because the event handlers are executed only when their corresponding event fires, the order of execution of these event handlers is directly dependent on the order that the events are fired and is unrelated to the location of the event handlers in the source code file.

By the Way

The code used to describe the Starting and Stopping events is not actual Visual Basic code, but is instead **pseudocode**. Pseudocode is not recognized by any particular programming language, but instead is a made-up, verbose, English-like language commonly used when describing programming concepts.

Event Handlers in ASP.NET

When writing the code for an ASP.NET page's code portion, you'll be creating event handlers that execute in response to specific ASP.NET-related events. One example of an ASP.NET event is the page's `Load` event, which fires every time an ASP.NET page is requested. If you have code that you want executed each time the page is requested, you can create an event handler for the `Load` event and place this code there.

There are a couple of ways to create the event handler for the `Load` event:

- If you are viewing the ASP.NET page's HTML portion through the Design view, you can double-click empty space within the Designer. Just be sure to double-click empty space, and not some existing Web control (like a Button or Image tag). If you double-click a Web control, you'll create an event handler for one of the events of that Web control.
- From the source code portion, you'll find two drop-down lists at the top. From the left drop-down list, select (Page Events). Then, from the right drop-down list, select Load (see Figure 2.11).
- Last, you can type in the necessary event handler syntax for creating the event handler and associating it with the page's Load event.

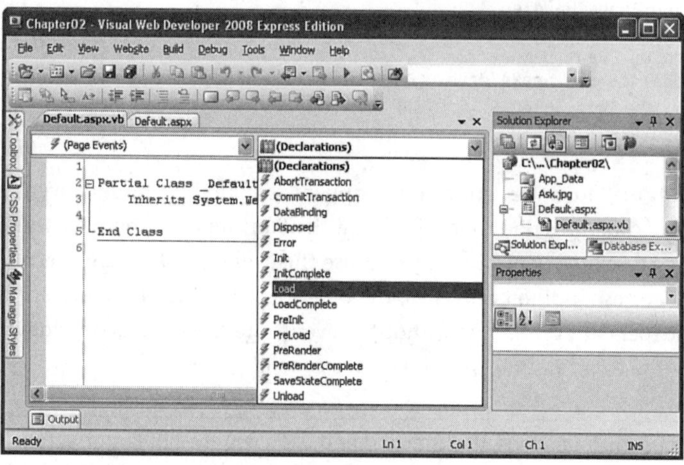

FIGURE 2.11 You can create the page's `Load` event handler from the drop-down lists.

Regardless of how you create the event handler, after you have done so, the syntax in your source code portion should resemble that in Listing 2.4.

LISTING 2.4 The `Page_Load` Event Handler Fires in Response to the Page's Load Event

```
1: Partial Class _Default
2:     Inherits System.Web.UI.Page
3:
4:     Protected Sub Page_Load(ByVal sender As Object, ByVal e As
➥ System.EventArgs) Handles Me.Load
5:
6:     End Sub
7: End Class
```

Whatever code you add between lines 4 and 6 will be executed whenever the ASP.NET page is visited through a browser.

Do *not* type the line numbers shown in Listing 2.4 into the source code portion. These line numbers appear in the code listings in this book simply to make it easier to refer to specific lines of code in the text.

As we will see in future hours, many events can fire during the rendering of an ASP.NET web page. In addition to page-level events (such as the `Load` event), Web controls have associated events as well. For example, one of the ASP.NET Web controls is the Button Web control. When the user visiting the web page clicks the Button Web control, the Button's `Click` event is fired; if an event handler is created for this event, the code within that event handler executes upon the Button being clicked. For now, though, we'll be working strictly with the page's `Load` event.

Programmatically Working with Web Controls

Earlier this hour, I mentioned that one difference between Web controls and static HTML content was that Web controls could be programmatically accessed, whereas static HTML content cannot. Web controls have a number of properties; for example, the Image Web control has an `ImageUrl` property that specifies the URL of the image to display. A Web control's properties can be read from and written to in the ASP.NET page's source code portion.

To illustrate this concept, let's enhance `Default.aspx` to contain some dynamic text at the top of the page. Specifically, let's add text to the page that says, **Welcome to my site, it is now *currentTime***, where *currentTime* is the current date and time on the web server. (The web server in this instance is your personal computer.)

To accomplish this, return to `Default.aspx` and add a Label Web control above the HTML `<table>`. A Label Web control is designed to display dynamic text in an ASP.NET page and is covered in detail in Hour 8, "ASP.NET Web Controls for

Displaying Text." To add the Label Web control, you can either drag the control from the Toolbox onto the Design or Source views or, if you'd rather, enter the following syntax in the Source view by hand:

```
<asp:Label ID="Label1" runat="server" Text="Label"></asp:Label>
```

After you've added the Label, change its `Text` and `ID` properties. Recall that this can be accomplished through the Properties window; if you are in the Source view, it may be quicker to edit the attributes value directly in the control's declarative markup rather than using the Properties window, although either approach will suffice.

Specifically, clear out the `Text` property and change the `ID` to `CurrentTime`. Figure 2.12 shows the Properties window after these changes have been made.

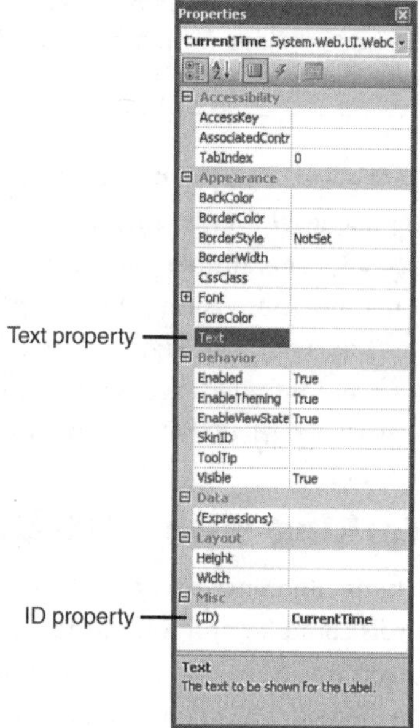

FIGURE 2.12
The Label's `ID` and `Text` properties have been altered.

After this change has been made, the syntax for the Label Web control in the Source view should now look like this:

```
<asp:Label ID="CurrentTime" runat="server"></asp:Label>
```

In the source code portion of this ASP.NET page, we're going to programmatically set the `Text` property of the `CurrentTime` Label Web control to the current date and time. To accomplish this, return to the source code portion and, in the `Page_Load` event handler added earlier, enter the following line of code (referring back to Listing 2.4, you would add this on line 5):

```
CurrentTime.Text = "Welcome to my site, it is now " & DateTime.Now
```

Notice that the Web control is referenced programmatically by its `ID` property value. To work with one of the `CurrentTime` Web control's properties in code, we use the syntax `CurrentTime.`*`PropertyName`*.

Did you Know?

When you start typing in the source code portion, Visual Web Developer displays a set of available keywords and Web controls. Moreover, after you type in `CurrentTime` and follow it with a period (`.`), the set of available properties and methods for this Web control are displayed. This listing of available keywords, Web controls, properties, and methods is known as **IntelliSense**, and it saves oodles of time!

When viewing an IntelliSense drop-down list, you can just type in the first few letters of the keyword, Web control, property, or method you want to select. When the keyword, Web control, property, or method you want to use is highlighted in the drop-down list, press the Tab key and Visual Web Developer will type in the rest for you.

If you do not see `CurrentTime` in the drop-down list or do not see a drop-down list after entering `CurrentTime` and typing a period, Visual Web Developer could not find a suitably named Web control in the ASP.NET page's HTML portion. Take a moment to ensure that the Label Web control's `ID` property is, indeed, `CurrentTime`.

Take a moment to view `Default.aspx` through a browser (see Figure 2.13). Now, at the top of your page, you'll find the message **Welcome to my site, it is now *currentTime***. If you refresh your browser, the *currentTime* displayed will be updated. This illustrates the dynamic nature of ASP.NET pages, because we now have a page whose content is not static, but rather based on the current date and time.

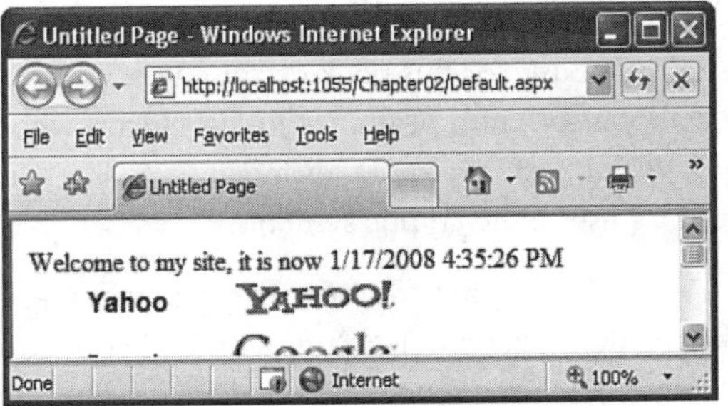

FIGURE 2.13 The ASP.NET page shows the current date and time.

As this example illustrated, a Web control's properties can be set either **declaratively** or **programmatically**. When a Web control property is specified through the Properties window or in the Web control syntax in the HTML portion, the property is said to be declaratively set. The `CurrentTime` Label's `ID` property was set declaratively, as were the Image Web controls' `ImageUrl` properties. When the property value is set through code, it is said to have been set programmatically. In this example we set the Label's `Text` property programmatically.

Summary

We covered quite a bit of material in this hour, starting with an examination of the HTML portion of an ASP.NET web page. Here, we saw how to add an HTML `<table>` and other static content through the Design view, as well as how to drag and drop Web controls onto the page. We also saw how to change the appearance of HTML content in the designer by using the options under the Format menu.

After studying the HTML portion of an ASP.NET web page, we moved on to the source code portion. Here, we went over a crash course in object-oriented and event-driven programming. We then saw how to provide code that would be executed each time an ASP.NET web page is visited.

The examples we examined in this hour and in the previous one have been pretty simple ones with limited real-world application. In Hour 4, "Designing, Creating, and Testing ASP.NET Web Pages," we'll create a more practical ASP.NET web page with more involved HTML and source code portions. First, though, we'll explore the Visual Web Developer editor in more detail.

Q&A

Q. ***Why are we building all our ASP.NET web pages using Visual Basic as the server-side programming language?***

A. I chose to use Visual Basic for this book because it is, in my opinion, an easier language to comprehend than Visual C# for developers who may be new to programming. Visual Basic syntax reads much more like everyday English, whereas Visual C# uses more cryptic symbols.

Furthermore, Visual Basic is not case sensitive, whereas C# is case sensitive, thereby making it more susceptible to typos and other frustrating errors. For this reason, languages that are not case sensitive are typically easier to pick up for those new to programming.

Q. ***When should I choose to use static HTML elements versus Web controls? That is, if I have to display static text, should I type in the text or use a Label Web control with its* `Text` *property set accordingly?***

A. For content that you know is going to be static, I recommend using HTML elements in contrast to Web controls. Of course, if the content is dynamic, such as the text displayed in the Label Web control in our last example in this hour, you'll want to use a Web control.

Some developers, however, prefer to use Web controls for all content, even static content. In fact, we did this in our first example, using an Image Web control rather than a static `<img>` HTML element. If you are unfamiliar with HTML syntax and markup, you may find it easier to use Web controls instead of having to research what HTML elements would be used (although many of the more common HTML elements are available through the Toolbox's HTML tab). There is a slight performance enhancement to using static HTML content instead of Web controls for static content, but don't let that minor impact sway your decision. Instead, use what you're most comfortable with. If you have an HTML background, you'll likely be more apt to use HTML elements for static markup; if you're new to HTML, Web controls may seem a more natural fit.

Workshop

Quiz

1. What does WYSIWYG stand for?

2. Is the following HTML properly nested?

```
<html><body>
<h1>My First Web Page</h1>
These are a few of my favorite <i>things:
<ol>
  <li>Jisun</li>
  <li>ASP.NET</li>
  <li>Basketball</li>
</ol></i>
</body></html>
```

3. What does the `@Page` directive do? Does it get rendered to the browser?

4. What is the name of the event handler you would use to have code execute each time the ASP.NET web page is loaded?

5. How can you add a Web control to an ASP.NET web page?

Answers

1. What You See Is What You Get.
2. Yes. There are no tags whose start tag appears after another tag's start tag (call that tag *t*), but whose end tag appears after *t*'s end tag.
3. The `@Page` directive supplies additional information to the ASP.NET engine, such as the server-side source code language used for the page and the location of the corresponding source code file. It is not rendered to the requesting browser.
4. The `Page_Load` event handler. Refer to Listing 2.4 to see an example of this event handler in the source code portion.
5. There are two ways. First, you can drag and drop the appropriate Web control from the Toolbox onto the designer. Second, you can enter the Web control syntax manually in the Source view.

Exercises

The purpose of these exercises is to help familiarize you with the Visual Web Developer editor.

1. The ASP.NET web page we created in the "Creating the HTML Portion of an ASP.NET Web Page Using Visual Web Developer" section contained an HTML `<table>` tag that was added by going to the Layout menu and selecting the Insert Table option. After an HTML `<table>` has been added to a web page, you can easily set the table's various display properties.

   For this exercise, open `Default.aspx` in the Design view and alter the `<table>` element's settings. If you click the HTML table so that it is highlighted, you will find that its properties are displayed in the Properties window. (You can also select the `<TABLE>` element from the drop-down list in the Properties window.) For this exercise, set the `Border` property to 3 and the `CellPadding` property to 5. Also, try setting the `BgColor` property. Notice that when you select this property from the Properties window, you can choose from an array of colors. You are invited to try setting the various HTML table properties to view their effects on the table in the designer.

2. For this exercise, add a message to the top of the `Default.aspx` web page that reads: **Here Are Some Popular Search Engines**. This text should be centered, appear above the message that displays the current time, and be displayed in a bold Arial font.

To accomplish this, start by positioning the cursor in the designer immediately before the Label Web control. Press Enter a few times to create some space. Then type in the text **Here Are Some Popular Search Engines**. After you have entered this text, select it with the mouse. Then choose the Arial font from the font drop-down list near the upper-left corner. Next, make the text bold by going to the Format menu and selecting Bold. Finally, center the text by going to the Format menu's Justify submenu and choosing the Center option.

As with exercise 1, you are encouraged to experiment with Visual Web Developer's formatting capabilities. See how the text looks with different fonts and formats. Note that you can add bulleted lists, numbered lists, and so on.

HOUR 3

Using Visual Web Developer

In this hour, we will cover

- Creating new websites and web pages
- Opening existing websites
- Customizing the editor through Visual Web Developer's Options menu
- Using techniques for laying out HTML content through the Design view
- Moving and resizing the assorted windows
- Accessing help through the installed documentation

In the preceding hour we looked at the ASP.NET programming model, noting how ASP.NET pages are composed of an HTML portion and a source code portion. Recall that the HTML portion of an ASP.NET web page consists of static HTML markup and Web control syntax; the code portion, separated out into its own file, is implemented as a class with various event handlers.

In the past two hours, you got a cursory look at Visual Web Developer, the development environment we'll be using throughout this book to build ASP.NET pages. In Hour 1, "Getting Started with ASP.NET 3.5," you installed Visual Web Developer and received a quick tour of its features. In the preceding hour we delved a bit deeper into Visual Web Developer's interface, looking at how to create a new ASP.NET website and how to use the Source and Design views and the source code editor.

Because we'll be using Visual Web Developer extensively throughout this book, it behooves us to take an hour to fully explore this tool. Visual Web Developer is a sophisticated and powerful programming editor, with a large number of features and capabilities. As with any profession, it's important to have a solid grasp of the tools at your disposal.

Creating a New Website

When you start Visual Web Developer, you will typically want to do one of two things: either create a new website or open an existing website. A website is a collection of resources: static and dynamic web pages, graphic files, style sheets, configuration files, and so on. In addition to the various files, a website may contain subdirectories, each of which may contain its own set of files and further subdirectories. A website is akin to a folder on your personal computer: It's a repository for files and subfolders.

To create a new website with Visual Web Developer, go to the File menu and select New Web Site or click the New Web Site icon in the Toolbar. Either of these actions brings up the New Web Site dialog box, shown in Figure 3.1.

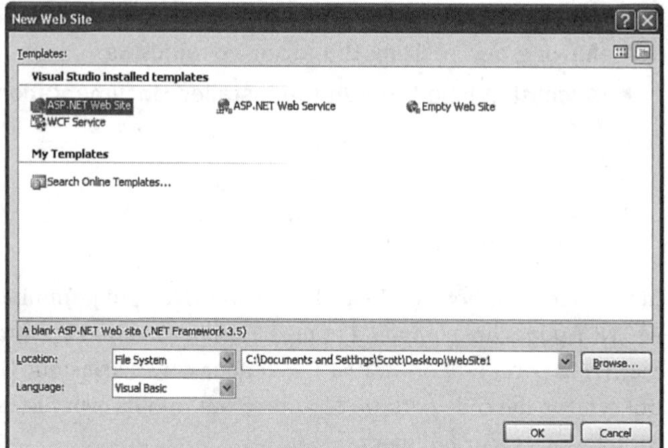

FIGURE 3.1 Create a new website from the New Web Site dialog box.

Choosing a Website Template

When creating a new website, you can choose among a number of available templates, such as the ASP.NET Web Site template, the ASP.NET Web Service template, the Empty Web Site template, and the WCF Service template. Regardless of what template is selected, a website will be created; the differences among the templates are what default files the template includes with the website. For example, in the preceding hour we saw that creating a new website using the ASP.NET Web Site template creates a website with an `App_Data` folder and three files: `Default.aspx`, `Default.aspx.vb`, and `web.config`. Creating a website using the Empty Web Site template creates the website but does not add any default folders or files.

Although you can choose from four different website templates, all the examples in this book are created using the ASP.NET Web Site template.

Specifying the Website's Location

Websites can be located either on your personal computer or on a remote computer. Typically, personal computers do not double as web servers; chances are the personal computer on which you're working right now does not host websites. Rather, you use your PC for your own ends—surfing the web, checking email, playing games, and so on. Publicly available websites are often hosted through web-hosting companies, which offer always-on computers with a persistent connection to the Internet. These computers' sole purpose is to host a website; they have web server software running on them, and they essentially sit around and wait for incoming requests. Upon receiving a request for a web page, they render the page and return the resulting markup to the requesting browser.

Often developers place a website on their own personal computer during the creation and testing phases. The site won't be accessible over the Internet, but that's okay because the site is not yet ready for the public. When a functional site is complete, it can be moved to a web-hosting company so that the site can be accessed by anyone with an Internet connection. Hour 24, "Deploying Your Website," looks at choosing a web-hosting company and moving your website's files from your local computer to the web-hosting company's.

When you create a new website on your local computer, you can host it in one of two ways:

- **Through the file system**—With this approach, you provide a directory on your hard drive that serves as the website's root directory. All of the site's associated files and folders will be placed in that specified directory.
- **Through IIS, Microsoft's web server**—If your personal computer has Internet Information Services (IIS) installed, you can host the website locally through IIS.

To host the site locally through the file system, select the File System option from the Location drop-down list. Next, click the Browse button to the right of the Location drop-down list. This brings up the Choose Location dialog box shown in Figure 3.2.

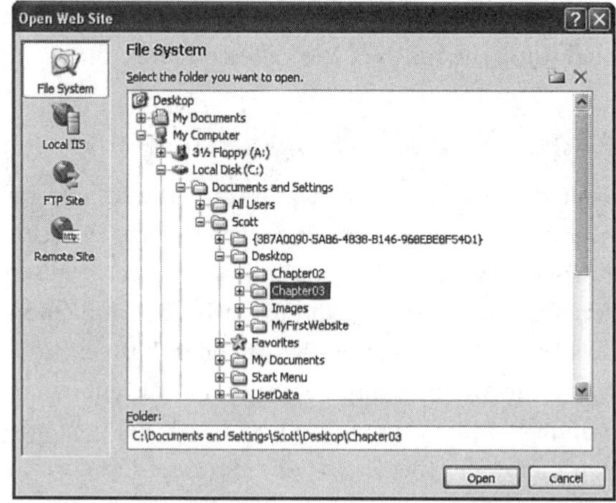

FIGURE 3.2 Choose the location where your website will reside.

The left column in the Choose Location dialog box lists the various locations the website can be saved to.

By the Way

> To host the website on a remote computer, select either the Remote Site or FTP Site for the location and then specify the associated configuration settings. When using an FTP site, you'll need to provide the FTP server, port, directory, and username/password, if anonymous access is not allowed. Similarly, if you choose to use the Remote Site setting, you'll need to specify the remote server's URL and, later, username and password information.

All the websites created throughout this book are located on the local file system.

Choosing the Source Code Programming Language

The setting chosen in the Language drop-down list specifies the programming language used by your ASP.NET web pages' code portions. Two options are available: Visual Basic and Visual C#. As discussed in the preceding hour, the Visual Basic language is used for the examples throughout this book.

By the Way

> If you have a programming background in Java or C/C++, you may be more familiar with Visual C# than Visual Basic. Visual Basic is typically preferred by those with a background in the BASIC language or those new to programming.
>
> If you are interested in learning more about Visual C#, check out Microsoft's Visual C# Developer Center (http://msdn.microsoft.com/vcsharp/).

To gain practice creating websites in Visual Web Developer, create a new website using the ASP.NET Web Site template. Locate the website on your computer's file system in a directory of your choice. Set the Language to Visual Basic.

As we saw in the preceding hour, this creates a website with an `App_Data` folder, a `Default.aspx` ASP.NET page (with a corresponding `Default.aspx.vb` file), and a configuration file, `web.config`. These files are listed in the Solution Explorer, which you can find in the upper-right corner. (If you do not see the Solution Explorer, go to the View menu and choose the Solution Explorer option.)

Opening Existing Websites

Now that we've created a website, let's see how to open this website at a later point in time. First, close the website by closing Visual Web Developer altogether, or by going to the File menu and choosing Close Project.

After closing your website, reopen it by going to the File menu and choosing the Open Web Site menu option. This lists the Open Web Site dialog box. This dialog box is nearly identical to the Choose Location dialog box shown in Figure 3.2.

Because you created your website locally through your personal computer's file system, open the site by selecting the File System icon in the left column and then navigating to the folder where you placed the website. Select the website's root folder and then click the Open button to open the website.

Opening the website will close the existing opened website (if any) and load the selected website's contents into the Solution Explorer. At this point you can work with the website as you normally would, creating and editing the web page HTML and source code portions.

Did you Know?

If you have recently worked with a particular website, there's a quicker way to open it with Visual Web Developer. The File menu contains a Recent Projects menu item that lists the most recently opened projects. Clicking a project name from the Recent Projects list opens that project.

Working with Web Pages and Other Content

A website is a repository of related files and subdirectories. Websites typically contain files of the following types:

- **Static web pages**—An HTML page is a static web page. Unlike an ASP.NET page, it contains only HTML content—no Web controls and no source code. As its name implies, the content of these types of files is static and cannot be altered based on user input, server-side data, or other criteria.
- **ASP.NET web pages**—ASP.NET pages are the dynamic web pages in your site. They are implemented as two files: `*PageName*.aspx`, which contains the HTML portion; and `*PageName*.aspx.vb`, which contains the source code portion.
- **Image files**—Most websites have various images, logos, and clip art. These image files typically are stored in the website, either in the root directory or in an `Images` subdirectory.
- **Configuration files**—ASP.NET websites contain a configuration file named `web.config` that provides server-side setting information.
- **Style sheet files**—Style sheets are files that instruct the browser how to format and display different types of content. For example, in your site you might want all content displayed in the Arial font and content within `<h1>` tags displayed in italics. You can specify this aesthetic information through cascading style sheet (CSS) rules defined in style sheet files. For more information, refer to www.w3schools.com/css/.
- **Script files**—In addition to server-side source code, a web page may contain **client-side script code**. This is code that is sent to and runs on the end user's web browser. Often this script is packaged in a separate script file on the web server, which the browser requests as needed.

This list enumerates the most commonly found file types on a web server, but it is hardly exhaustive. A rock band's website, for example, might include MP3 files available for download. Additionally, numerous ASP.NET-specific files can be added to your website to provide various types of functionality. We'll be learning about many of these different ASP.NET-specific file types throughout this book.

Adding Content to Your Website

After creating a new website or opening an existing one, you can add additional files and folders to the website through the Solution Explorer. From the Solution Explorer, right-click the website name; this brings up the context menu shown in Figure 3.3.

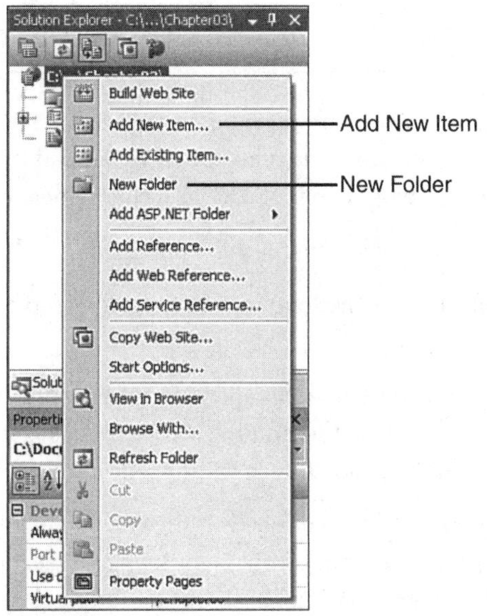

FIGURE 3.3 To add a new file or folder, right-click the website name in the Solution Explorer.

To add a new folder to your website, select the New Folder item from the context menu. To add a new file, choose Add New Item. Selecting Add New Item displays the Add New Item dialog box (see Figure 3.4). The Add New Item dialog box lists the variety of types of files that can be added. Notice that file types exist for each of the popular file types enumerated earlier, in addition to many others.

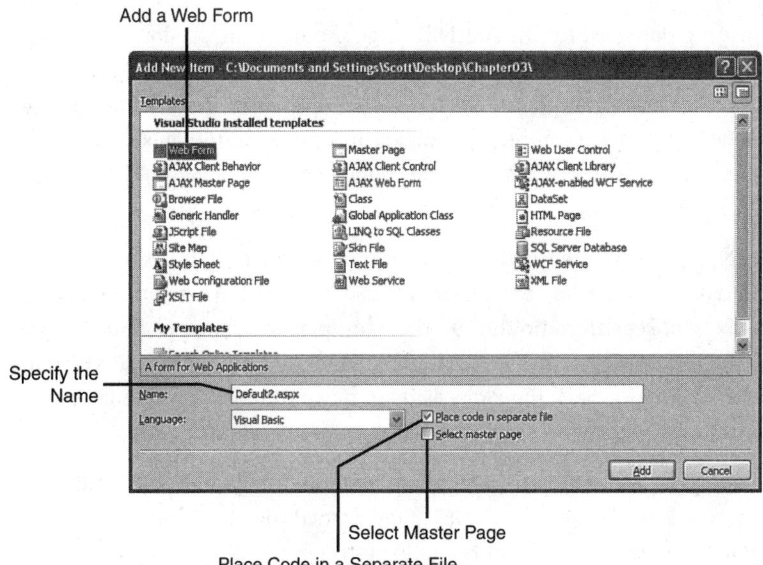

FIGURE 3.4 The Add New Item dialog box enables you to choose the type of file to add.

By the Way

> To add a new ASP.NET page to your website, add an item of type Web Form.

At the bottom of the Add New Item dialog box, you'll find a series of options. The options displayed depend on what file type you have decided to add. For Web Forms, which are the item type name for ASP.NET pages, there are four options:

- **Name**—This indicates what the file will be named.
- **Language**—This dictates the language of the page's server-side source code portion.
- **Place Code in Separate File**—This specifies whether the source code portion should be implemented as a second file (`*PageName*.aspx.vb`) or the page's declarative markup and source code will appear in the same file instead.
- **Select Master Page**—A master page is a sitewide template that can be applied to ASP.NET pages to maintain a consistent look and feel across the site. If you are using master pages, you can check this option to assign a master page to the newly created ASP.NET page.

By the Way

> Master pages are a very useful way to create a consistent page layout across all pages in your site. We'll discuss the benefits of master pages, along with how to use them in your ASP.NET website, in Hour 22, "Using Master Pages to Provide Sitewide Page Templates."

The Language drop-down list for the ASP.NET page's source code portion is set to the same language choice you specified when creating the website. However, a single ASP.NET website can have web pages that use different programming languages for their source code portions. I recommend against this approach and encourage you to stick with a single, unified programming language choice across all ASP.NET pages for a given website.

Although ASP.NET pages will work just as well if their source code portion is in the `.aspx` page in a server-side `<script>` block or if it is relegated to a separate file (*PageName*`.aspx.vb`), keep in mind that all the examples we will be working with in this book use the separate page model. Therefore, when adding a new ASP.NET page to your website, be sure to check the Place Code in a Separate File check box. Doing so will create both the *PageName*`.aspx` and *PageName*`.aspx.vb` files.

Let's practice adding a new ASP.NET page to our website. Imagine that in addition to `Default.aspx`, we need another ASP.NET page named `DisplayTime.aspx`. To add this page to your website, perform the following steps:

1. Go to the Solution Explorer and right-click the website name.
2. Choose Add New Item from the context menu.
3. From the Add New Item dialog box (see Figure 3.4), select to add an item of type Web Form.
4. Enter `DisplayTime.aspx` for the page's Name. Make sure that the Language setting is set to Visual Basic and that the Place Code in a Separate File check box is checked.
5. Click the Add button to create the new ASP.NET page.

You can follow these same steps to add other types of resources to your website. Of course, the options present in step 4 will differ depending on the type of item being added.

Adding Existing Content

Along with adding new content to your website, you can use Visual Web Developer to add existing content. You may already have an image file on your hard drive or an ASP.NET page from another project that you want to include in this project as well. If that's the case, you can add an existing item by right-clicking the website name in the Solution Explorer and choosing Add Existing Item.

Choosing this option displays the standard file browsing dialog box. From here, you can navigate to the folder on your hard drive that contains the content you want to add, select it, and click the Add button. This copies over the selected item to your website's directory, making it part of your website.

Moving, Renaming, and Deleting Content

Along with adding new folders and files, you can also move and delete files from the Solution Explorer. To move files among the folders in your website, drag the file from its existing location to a new folder.

To rename or delete a file or folder, start by right-clicking the item in the Solution Explorer. This brings up the context menu shown in Figure 3.5. As you can see from the figure, Rename and Delete menu items are available. Simply click the appropriate menu item to rename or remove the selected file or folder.

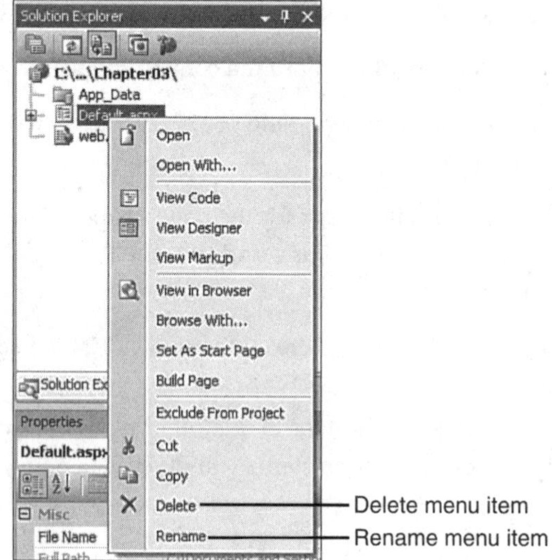

FIGURE 3.5 Select the appropriate menu item from the context menu.

Customizing the Visual Web Developer Experience

Like any robust programming editor, Visual Web Developer is highly customizable, enabling developers to configure the editor in a way that maximizes their productivity. Not only does Visual Web Developer give you fine-grained control over a variety of settings, but it also provides an easy way to export your unique settings to a single file. You can then re-create your environment at a new computer by importing your settings file. This makes it easy to move your settings from a desktop computer to a laptop; additionally, if you place your settings file on a website or keep it saved on a USB drive or web-based email account, you can easily re-create your development environment at *any* computer where you end up working!

In this section we'll examine how to customize Visual Web Developer. The bulk of the customizability is accomplished through the Options dialog box, which is available through the Tools menu. There are literally hundreds of settings, so we won't have the time to go through each and every one. Instead, we'll focus on the more germane ones. We'll also see how to alter the Visual Web Developer panes and their display settings, along with settings that aid with laying out HTML content in the Design view.

By default, the Visual Web Developer Options dialog box shows only the most pertinent options. To see all available options, check the Show All Settings check box.

By the Way

The screenshots throughout this book have been taken using the default Visual Web Developer settings. If you customize the environment to suit your preferences, some disparity may occur between your screen and the screenshots in this book.

The majority of the customizable settings in Visual Web Developer are accessible via the Options dialog box, which you can display by selecting the Options item from the Tools menu. Figure 3.6 shows the Options dialog box when first opened.

The Options dialog box is broken into various hierarchical categories, which are listed in the left column. Selecting an item from the list on the left displays its corresponding options on the right. As Figure 3.6 shows, the default category selected when opening the Options dialog box is the Environment category.

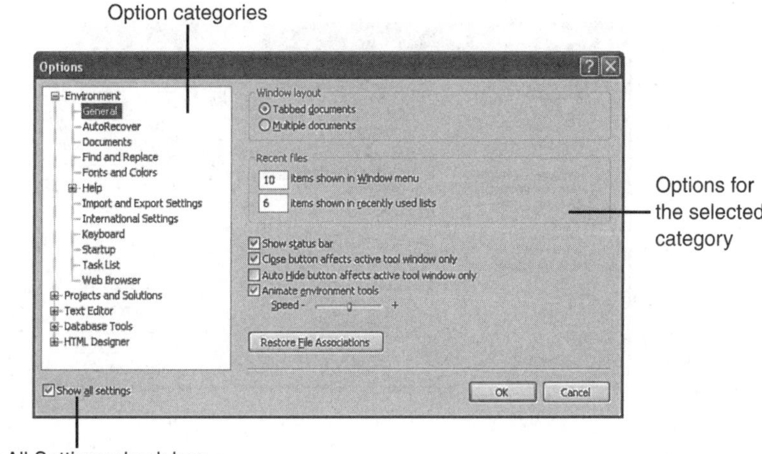

FIGURE 3.6 Customize your Visual Web Developer experience through the Options dialog box.

The Environment category has two settings worth exploring. The first is the AutoRecover setting. While you are working on a website, Visual Web Developer automatically saves copies of modified files every so often, based on a setting you provide (the default is every five minutes). These backup copies are kept around for a specified number of days (seven, by default). The AutoRecover feature protects against losing hours of work due to an unexpected shutdown. If your officemate LeRoy happens to walk past your desk and kick the power cord out of the wall, in the worst case you'll not have the last five minutes of changes saved (assuming you left the AutoRecover frequency as the default). If you have AutoRecover enabled (which it is, by default), backup copies of your modified files will be saved periodically to the `\My Documents\Visual Studio 2008\Backup Files\<projectname>` folder.

The final Environment setting we'll look at is the Fonts and Colors settings, which is shown in Figure 3.7. The Fonts and Colors settings dictate the fonts, sizes, and colors of the text used in Visual Web Developer. You can alter the fonts and colors for a variety of settings: the Visual Web Developer text editor, the printed output, various debugging windows, and so on. Furthermore, for each variety of setting, there are multiple display items whose font and color can be customized. For example, the default fonts and colors for the Text Editor setting's Plain Text is black, 10pt., Courier New; its setting for the Selected Text is white with a blue background, 10pt., Courier New.

Many developers tweak the Fonts and Colors settings to make it easier to see certain types of tokens in their source code. For example, in the version of Visual Web Developer I use at work, I have Numbers displayed as purple, bold, 10pt., Courier New text, and Strings displayed as turquoise, 10pt., Courier New text.

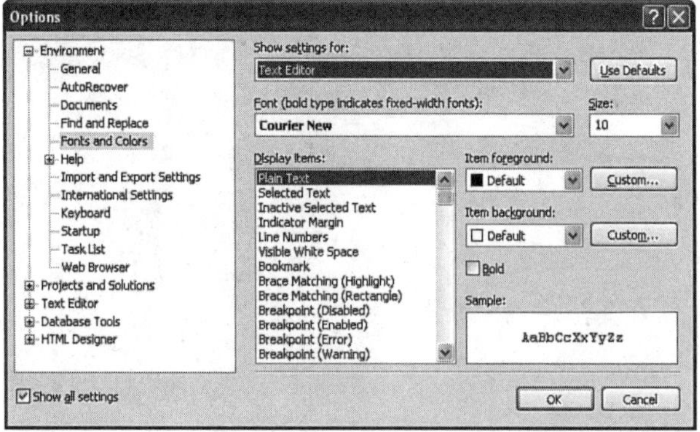

FIGURE 3.7 Specify the fonts, sizes, and colors of the text used in Visual Web Developer.

Another setting in the Options dialog box worth noting is the HTML Designer category. Expand this category and select the General item beneath it. On the right you should see an option titled Start Pages In with three options: Source View, Design View, and Split View. By default, when you're creating a new web page or opening an existing one, the page is opened in the Source view. If you prefer the Design view or Split view, you can change the default behavior here.

Did you Know?

When you have settled on the particular settings you find most conducive, take a moment to export your savings to a file. To accomplish this, go to the Tools menu and select the Import and Export Settings option. This will take you through a wizard where you can indicate what settings to export along with the filename and location to save the settings.

After you have exported your settings, you can re-create your personalized settings on another computer by importing this settings file. This capability is useful if you develop on both a desktop and laptop, depending on whether you're onsite or not, or if you are a contractor who moves jobs every few months but wants to maintain a consistent collection of settings.

Viewing, Moving, and Resizing Windows

The Visual Web Developer environment is made up of many windows that provide various tidbits of information. The window we've examined in most detail is the Solution Explorer, which lists the files and folders in the website. In the preceding hour, we saw two other windows: the Properties window, which listed the properties for the selected HTML element or Web control; and the Toolbox window, which listed the Web controls and HTML elements that could be dragged onto an ASP.NET page.

These are but three of the many windows available in Visual Web Developer. You can see a complete list of the available windows by going to the View menu.

Windows in Visual Web Developer each have a default position, size, and behavior. The position indicates where on the screen the window is placed and whether it is floating or docked. The Solution Explorer, for example, is in a docked position in the upper-right corner, by default; the Toolbox can be found in a docked position on the left. A docked window is one that's attached to a margin of the editor. When a docked window is shown, the content it displaces is moved elsewhere on the screen. A floating window is *not* attached to any margin; it floats above all other windows and content in the editor, covering it up rather than displacing it.

Each window also has a size. You can move your mouse to the margin of the window and click and drag to increase or decrease the window's width or height. Each docked window also has a behavior: It's either pinned or unpinned (the unpinned behavior is sometimes referred to as Auto-Hide behavior). A pinned window remains displayed regardless of whether your mouse is over the window. An unpinned window is displayed when you move your mouse over the window; it disappears when your mouse leaves the window's focus. You can toggle a docked window's pinned status by clicking the pin icon in each window's upper-right corner. Typically, I keep the Solution Explorer, Properties, and Toolbox windows pinned because they are commonly used; all other windows I'll make unpinned so they do not encroach on my screen's real estate.

In addition to being able to pin and unpin windows, you can also close a window. To remove a window from the screen, simply click the X icon in the upper-right corner of the window.

Did you Know?

> If you cannot find a window onscreen where you expect it, you may have moved it or accidentally closed it. You can display the needed window by going to the View menu and selecting the appropriate menu option.

If you do not like the position of a window, you can easily move it. Click on the top of the window and, holding down your mouse button, drag your mouse to the location where you want the window to appear.

A World of Help at Your Fingertips

ASP.NET is a rich, robust web development technology built on a platform known as the .NET Framework. This platform consists of hundreds of classes that provide the core functionality of the ASP.NET engine. Needless to say, it can take *years* to have a deep understanding of the framework and its capabilities.

Fortunately, the .NET Framework is well documented, and Visual Web Developer provides a variety of ways to access this help. When you installed Visual Web Developer you were prompted whether to install the MSDN Express Library for Visual Studio 2008. The MSDN Library is Microsoft's colossal collection of articles, whitepapers, technical documentation, knowledge base content, and frequently asked questions and answers. To view the library, go to the Help menu and choose Search, Contents, or Index. This launches the Microsoft Visual Studio 2008 Documentation program, from which you can browse through the help.

Did you Know?

> You can also search the MSDN Library online at http://msdn2.microsoft.com.

Another neat feature of Visual Web Developer is its **Dynamic Help**. As its name implies, Dynamic Help shows context-sensitive help based on where your cursor is in the source code or HTML portions of an ASP.NET page. For example, if you're in the Design view and you click a Button Web control in your page, Dynamic Help automatically displays help links with titles such as

- Button Class Technical Documentation
- Button Web Server Control Overview
- How to: Add Button Web Controls to a Web Forms Page
- How to: Add ImageButton Web Controls to a Web Forms Page

To display Dynamic Help, select the Dynamic Help option from the Help menu. This displays the Dynamic Help window (which you can resize, position, and pin just like any other window). The Dynamic Help window, if displayed, continually populates with context-sensitive help topics based on your actions in Visual Web Developer.

One of the most satisfying aspects of working with ASP.NET is that a large and friendly online community exists. There are many helpful forums that are great places to ask fellow ASP.NET developers questions when you get stuck. One very popular forum is Microsoft's MSDN Forums (http://forums.microsoft.com/msdn/). In fact, Visual Web Developer's Help menu includes a MSDN Forums menu option that, when clicked, loads the forum's search page. Another excellent forum is the ASP.NET Forums, online at http://forums.asp.net.

Did you Know?

Although a wealth of information is available through the MSDN Library and through Visual Web Developer's Community and Help menus, a vast array of information is also available online. A great place to start is Microsoft's official ASP.NET site, www.asp.net, which is home to the popular ASP.NET Forums as well as hundreds of excellent step-by-step tutorials and free "How To" videos.

When searching for ASP.NET resources, consider using Google's Microsoft-specific search, available at www.google.com/microsoft.html. This customized search page returns only results relating to Microsoft technologies and topics, which can help expedite your search for answers to your questions.

Summary

We spent this hour investigating Visual Web Developer in greater detail. It is important that you have a familiarity with this editor because you'll be using it throughout this book and beyond. Specifically, we looked at how to create and open websites in Visual Web Developer. Websites can be located either locally, on your personal computer, or remotely, with a web-hosting company. After you have created a website, you'll want to add various files and folders. This is easily accomplished through the Solution Explorer.

In this hour we also looked at customizing the environment through the Options dialog box and by repositioning and resizing windows. We concluded with a quick synopsis of Visual Web Developer's extensive built-in help system. The Dynamic Help capabilities are especially useful for developers new to ASP.NET.

In this hour and the previous two, we've covered a lot of ground. We've looked at the fundamentals of ASP.NET and the .NET Framework; installed the .NET Framework, Visual Web Developer, and SQL Server 2005 Express Edition; dissected the ASP.NET programming model; created our first ASP.NET web page, complete with HTML markup, Web controls, and server-side source code; and explored Visual Web Developer. We're now ready to build a nontrivial ASP.NET web page, which we'll tackle in the upcoming hour. This exercise will help hammer home many of the key points mentioned through these first three hours.

Q&A

Q. ***I want to use a web-hosting company to host my ASP.NET website. How do I determine whether a particular web-hosting company can host my ASP.NET application?***

A. The easiest way to ascertain whether a given web-hosting company can host your site is to simply ask. Be sure to tell the company that you are creating an ASP.NET 3.5 website using Visual Web Developer. For your ASP.NET site to be able to run on the company's servers, the web-hosting company must be running Microsoft's web server, IIS, along with the .NET Framework version 3.5. If these conditions are met, your site should run just fine.

We discuss choosing a web-hosting company and deploying an ASP.NET web application to the web-hosting company's computers in Hour 24.

Q. ***I have created a website on my local file system with the website located at folder X. I'd like to move the website to folder Y. Is this possible?***

A. Sure. To move the site, close Visual Web Developer and then move the website's folder from its current location to wherever else you'd like it to reside. After you have moved the files, reopen Visual Web Developer, go to the File menu, and choose the Open Web Site option. Browse to the *new* folder location and click Open. That's all there is to it!

Q. ***What are some online resources for ASP.NET information?***

A. Many free ASP.NET resources are available online. Your first destination should be Microsoft's official ASP.NET website, www.asp.net. This site has links to virtually every ASP.NET resource site on the Net, along with a very active online forum site (http://forums.asp.net/) that has received more than 2,000,000 posts from hundreds of thousands of users.

I run a popular online resource, 4GuysFromRolla.com, which has a messageboard, answers to frequently asked questions, and thousands of ASP.NET-related articles. Some other large and prominent ASP.NET sites include 15Seconds.com, ASPAlliance.com, and ASP101.com. There's also Microsoft's ASP.NET Developer Center, available at http://msdn.microsoft.com/asp.net/.

Workshop

Quiz

1. A website can be created or opened using two local and two remote techniques. What are these four techniques?
2. True or False: IIS stands for Internet Information Service and is Microsoft's web server software.
3. True or False: The ASP.NET Development Web Server and IIS are the same thing.
4. When you're adding a new Web Form (ASP.NET page) to your website, there's a check box titled Place Code in a Separate File. How will the created ASP.NET page differ based on whether this is checked?
5. How do you move and resize windows in Visual Web Developer?

Answers

1. The two local techniques are through the local file system or through a local version of IIS, Microsoft's web server software. (Keep in mind that for you to use the local IIS option, your personal computer must have IIS installed.) The two remote techniques are through a Remote Site or FTP Site. If you are using a web-hosting company, talk to the company to determine which approach to use and what values to use for the various settings.
2. True.
3. False. IIS is Microsoft's professional grade web server software. The ASP.NET Development Web Server is a lightweight web server that ships with Visual Web Developer to enable those who do not have IIS installed to be able to still develop, build, and test ASP.NET applications. IIS is designed to host real-world websites; the ASP.NET Development Web Server is designed solely for testing websites locally.
4. If you do *not* check the Place Code in a Separate File check box, only one file will be created for the ASP.NET page, *`PageName`*`.aspx`, and the page's source code will be placed within a server-side `<script>` block. Preferably, you'll check the Place Code in a Separate File check box, in which case *two* files will be created: *`PageName`*`.aspx` and *`PageName`*`.aspx.vb`. In this scenario, the HTML markup and Web control syntax reside in the former file, whereas the source code resides in the latter.

5. To move a window, click its title bar and drag the window to the desired location. To resize it, click the window's margins and drag the margin to the desired width and height.

Exercise

1. For more practice with Visual Web Developer, take a moment to create a new website. Along with the `Default.aspx` page, add a number of additional ASP.NET pages. In each page, add various content, much like we did in the preceding hour. Tinker around with the editor, not worrying about whether you're doing things right or wrong. Just experiment.

   After creating a couple of pages, visit each one in a browser by going to the Debug menu and choosing Start Without Debugging.

   If you're feeling adventurous, try adding some image files from your hard drive to the website. Next, have them displayed in your ASP.NET pages using Image Web controls, much like we did in the preceding hour. Again, focus more on the exploration than whether you are doing things the right way. Take your time and have fun; it's the best way to learn!

HOUR 4

Designing, Creating, and Testing ASP.NET Web Pages

In this hour, we will cover

- Creating the design requirements for a financial calculator
- Creating the user interface
- Adding the needed Web controls to the ASP.NET web page
- Writing the code for the ASP.NET web page's source code portion
- Testing the ASP.NET web page

In the past three hours we've spent quite a bit of time talking in very high-level terms about ASP.NET web pages, the ASP.NET programming model, and Visual Web Developer. We've looked at how to configure our computer to serve ASP.NET web pages, and we've looked at the role of the web server. We've examined the HTML and source code portions of an ASP.NET web page. And we've created some very simple ASP.NET web pages with Visual Web Developer.

In this hour we turn from these high-level discussions to actually designing, building, and testing a nontrivial, useful ASP.NET web page that illustrates the concepts discussed in the past three hours. Specifically, we'll be creating an ASP.NET web page that serves as a financial calculator.

Specifying the Design Requirements

In the process of creating any piece of software, whether a Windows desktop application or a dynamic web page, a number of development stages occur. First and foremost, the purpose of the software must be decided, along with what features and functionality the software should provide. After this, the software application must be created. Finally, it needs to be tested, and any bugs or errors that arise should be fixed.

These three steps—design, development, and testing—should always be performed when creating an ASP.NET web page, but too frequently, developers jump straight to the coding task without spending enough time in the planning stage.

This initial planning stage, sometimes called the **design requirements stage**, is vital for the following reasons:

- It lays down a road map for the software project. Having a road map helps in determining how much progress has been made, as well as how much work remains.
- The design requirements spell out precisely what features and functionality the software will provide.

To help get into the habit of designing before coding, let's spend a bit of time discussing what features will be present and what user interface elements will be employed in the financial calculator ASP.NET web page we will create this hour.

Without spending adequate time in the design requirements stage, you would be unable to accurately answer your boss when she asks, "How much longer will this take?" or "How much progress have you made?" Additionally, agreeing on a list of feature requirements—a task typically performed during the design requirements stage—avoids any confusion at the conclusion of the project when your boss or client wonders why a feature she thought was going to be present is not.

Formulating the Features for Our Financial Calculator

An important step in the design requirements process is to list the features you plan to provide in your application. So far, I have mentioned that we will create a financial calculator, but let's take the time to specifically define the features this calculator will provide.

Our financial calculator will be able to determine the monthly payments for a simple fixed-rate home **mortgage**. To determine the monthly payments required for a fixed-rate mortgage, we need three inputs:

- The amount of money being borrowed (the principal)
- The loan's annual interest rate
- The duration of the loan—typically 15 or 30 years (the loan's term)

The output of our financial calculator, along with these three inputs, gives us the features of our financial calculator. In a sentence: Our financial calculator will compute the monthly payment of a simple fixed-rate mortgage when provided the amount, duration, and interest rate of the mortgage.

Deciding on the User Interface

After describing the features that the application will have, the next stage in the design requirements phase is to create a **user interface**. The user interface, or **UI** for short, is the means by which the user interacts with the application. How will the user enter these inputs? How will the results be displayed?

With large applications, the user interface portion of the design requirements phase is usually very involved and can take quite some time; there may be dozens or hundreds of ASP.NET pages through which the user interacts with the website. For our financial calculator, however, the user interface is fairly straightforward and will exist on a single web page.

Essentially, our users need to be able to do two things: enter the three inputs discussed earlier and see the result of the calculation. These inputs can be entered via TextBox Web controls. The output of the financial calculator should show the mortgage's monthly cost.

Figure 4.1 shows the ASP.NET web page financial calculator when first visited by the user. Note the three text boxes for the three inputs. Additionally, there is a button labeled Compute Monthly Cost that the user is instructed to click after entering the required inputs.

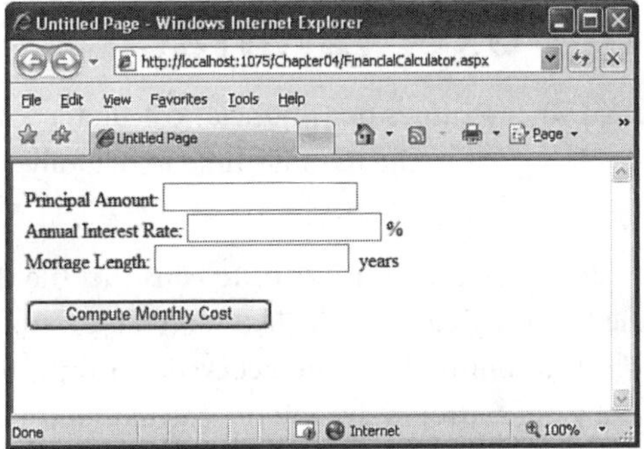

FIGURE 4.1
The user is asked to enter the three inputs.

Figure 4.2 shows the financial calculator after the user has entered the requested inputs and has clicked the Compute Monthly Cost button. Note that the output shows how much money the mortgage will cost per month.

To display the output of our calculation, we need to add a Label Web control to our ASP.NET page. We should place this Label Web control in the ASP.NET web page precisely where we want the final output to appear. As you can see from Figure 4.2, I have created the financial calculator so that the output appears below the input text boxes.

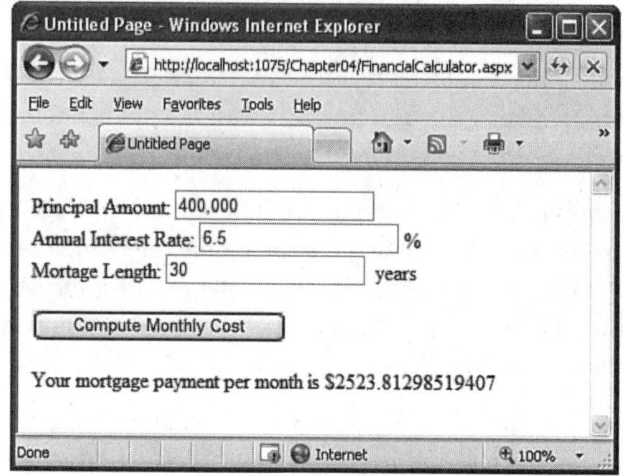

FIGURE 4.2
The monthly cost of the mortgage is shown.

Did you Know?

When creating a user interface for your web applications, you can use Visual Web Developer's WYSIWYG Design view to quickly create a mockup. Or, if you're more old-fashioned or if there's a power outage, you can use a trusty pencil and pad of paper as the canvas for your UI ideas.

Creating the User Interface

Now that we've decided what features our financial calculator will provide, as well as how the interface will appear to the user, it's time to actually start creating our ASP.NET web page.

The first task is to create the user interface (UI). To construct the UI shown in Figure 4.2, we add the following elements: a TextBox Web control for each of the three inputs; a Button Web control that, when clicked, performs the necessary computations; and a Label Web control to display the calculation.

After creating the user interface, we will turn our attention to writing the code to perform the financial computation.

Launch Visual Web Developer and create a new ASP.NET website on your computer's file system, just as we examined in the preceding hour. As we've seen, this creates a website with an ASP.NET page named `Default.aspx`. For practice, go ahead and delete this ASP.NET page and then add a new page named `FinancialCalculator.aspx`. When adding the `FinancialCalculator.aspx` ASP.NET page, remember to select the Web Form item type; also be sure to choose Visual Basic as the language and check the Place Code in a Separate File check box.

Adding the Three TextBox Web Controls

Let's start by adding the TextBox Web controls for our user's three inputs. Although we've yet to examine using the TextBox Web control in any of our previous examples, it's fairly straightforward. Just like with the Image and Label Web controls we added to our page in Hour 2, "Understanding the ASP.NET Programming Model," adding a TextBox Web control to a page is no different. Simply drag the TextBox from the Toolbox onto the page. After adding the TextBox to the page, you can configure its properties through the Properties window (or by typing them directly in the Source view, if you prefer).

Watch Out!

> One caveat is important to mention. When adding Web controls that collect user inputs—like TextBoxes, RadioButtons, DropDownLists, Buttons, and so on—you *must* place these Web controls within the page's **Web Form**. The Web Form is the name for that `<form runat="server">` markup we talked about in Hour 2. In short, you need to ensure that these controls appear between the opening and closing `<form>` tags.
>
> We'll be discussing *why* this is essential in detail in Hour 9, "Web Form Basics."

Before we drag a TextBox Web control onto the page, let's first create the title for the TextBox we're going to add. Because the first input is the amount of the mortgage, start by typing this title into the `FinancialCalculator.aspx` page's Design view: **`Principal Amount:`**.

Next, add a TextBox Web control after this title. To accomplish this, drag a TextBox control from the Standard tab in the Toolbox and drop it onto the page after the `Principal Amount:` title.

Take a moment to make sure your screen looks similar to Figure 4.3.

Currently, the TextBox Web control we just added has its `ID` property set to `TextBox1`. Because we will later need to programmatically refer to this `ID` to determine the value of the beginning mortgage principal entered by the user, let's choose an `ID` value that is representative of the data found within the TextBox. Specifically, change the `ID` property to `LoanAmount`.

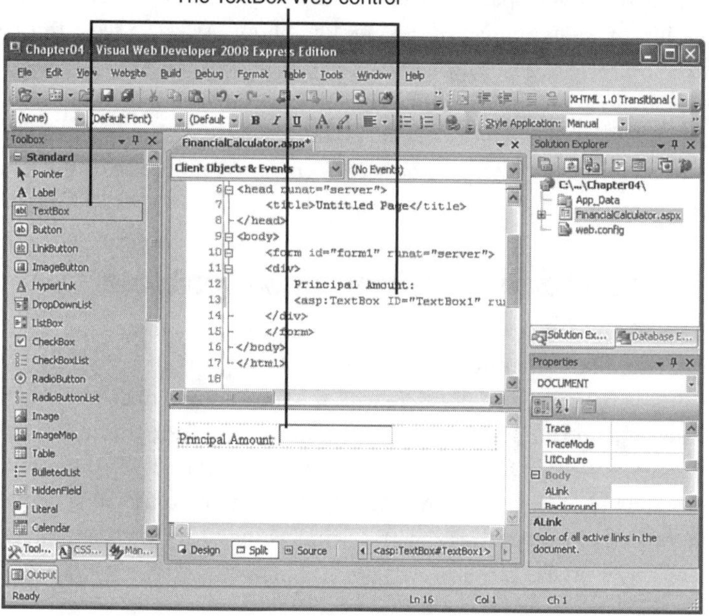

FIGURE 4.3 At this point you should have a title and a single TextBox.

Did you Know?

> To change a Web control's `ID` property, click the Web control, which will load the Web control's properties in the Properties pane in the lower-right corner. Scroll through the Properties pane until you see the `ID` property. This is the property value that you should change. Note that in the list of properties in the Properties pane, the `ID` property is denoted as (ID).

Now let's add the second TextBox, the mortgage interest rate. Add it just as we did in the previous TextBox Web control by first creating a title for the TextBox. Type in the title **`Annual Interest Rate:`**. Next, drag and drop a TextBox Web control after this title and change the TextBox's `ID` property to `Rate`.

Finally, add the third TextBox, the duration of the mortgage. Start by adding the title **`Mortgage Length:`**. Then drag and drop a TextBox Web control after the title. Set this TextBox's `ID` to `MortgageLength`.

Did you Know?

> You might want to type in some text after each TextBox Web control to indicate the units that should be entered into the TextBox. For example, after the Annual Interest Rate TextBox, you might want to add a percent sign so that the user knows to enter this value as a percentage. Similarly, you might want to enter the word **`years`** after the Mortgage Length TextBox. Figure 4.4 includes these optional additions.

Figure 4.4 shows the Design view after all three input TextBox Web controls have been added.

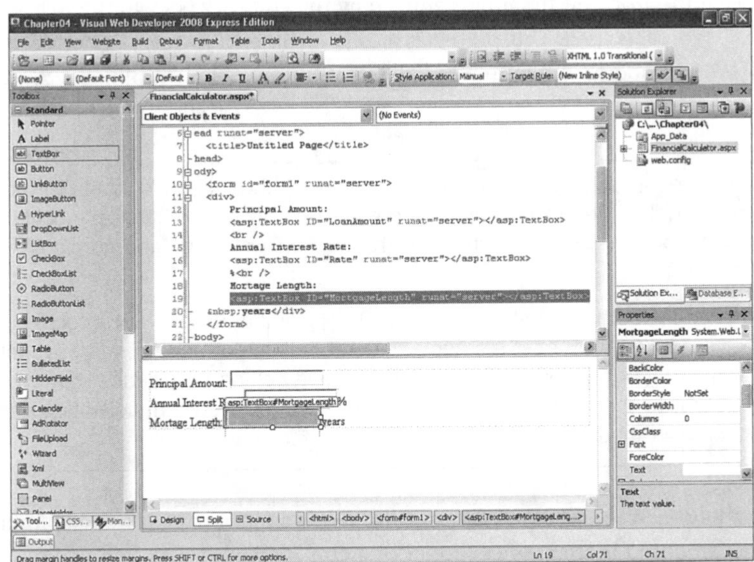

FIGURE 4.4 The Design view, after all three TextBox Web controls have been added.

Figure 4.4 shows the TextBox Web control titles in the standard font. Feel free to change the font or the aesthetics of the HTML portion however you see fit. Likewise, you can adjust the font, color, border, and other aesthetic settings of the TextBox Web controls through the Properties pane.

Adding the Compute Monthly Cost Button

After the user has entered inputs into the three TextBox Web controls, we need to take that information and perform the financial calculation. As we discussed in Hour 1, "Getting Started with ASP.NET 3.5," though, a temporal, physical, and logical disconnect exists between the client—the end user's web browser—and the server—the web server software that renders the ASP.NET pages.

When the user visits the `FinancialCalculator.aspx` ASP.NET web page via her browser, she is receiving HTML that contains the user interface we created from the Web controls and static HTML. After the user's browser receives our ASP.NET page's HTML, no communication occurs between the client and the server until the client explicitly makes a request back to the web server. Therefore, for the calculation to take place, the inputs entered by the user must be sent back to the ASP.NET web page (`FinancialCalculator.aspx`). After our ASP.NET web page receives these user-entered values, it can perform the financial computation and display the results.

For the client to transmit the inputs entered by the end user back to the web server, an HTML `<form>` is used. This process typically commences when a submit button is clicked. We can add such a button by adding a Button Web control to our ASP.NET web page.

By the Way

> The intricacies involved in having the browser send back a user's inputs to the appropriate web page are handled for us automatically by the browser's built-in functionality and the HTML produced by the ASP.NET web page and its Web controls.
>
> Although an in-depth understanding of this low-level plumbing is not a requisite, it is important to have at least a cursory understanding. For now, let me wave my hands and we'll not worry about what's happening behind the scenes; however, we will return to this topic, discussing the specifics involved with collecting and computing user input, in Hour 9.

To add a Button Web control, drag the Button Web control from the Toolbox onto the page, dropping it after the last input title and TextBox. When you add a Button Web control, the Button's caption reads "Button." To change this, click the Button, and then in the Properties window, change the `Text` property from Button to **`Compute Monthly Cost`**. Also, while in the Properties window, change the Button's `ID` property—listed in the Property window as (ID)—from the default `Button1` to `PerformCalcButton`.

Take a moment to make sure that your screen looks similar to Figure 4.5.

Creating a Label Web Control for the Output

The final piece we need to add to our user interface is a Label Web control to display the output of the financial calculation. Because the Label Web control will display the output (the amount of money the mortgage costs per month), the web page's final result will appear wherever you place the Web control. Therefore, if you want the output to appear at the bottom of your ASP.NET web page, drag and drop a Label Web control after the existing content in the designer. If you want the output to appear at the top of the web page, place it before the existing content in the designer.

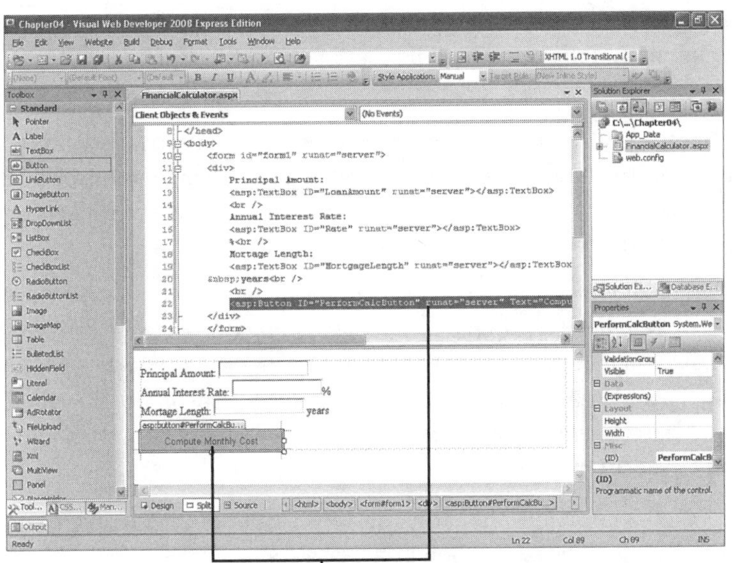

FIGURE 4.5
A Button Web control has been added.

After you have added the Label Web control, you will see that it displays the message "Label." The Label Web control displays the value of its `Text` property, which is configurable via the Properties window. Figure 4.6 shows Visual Web Developer after the Label Web control has been added.

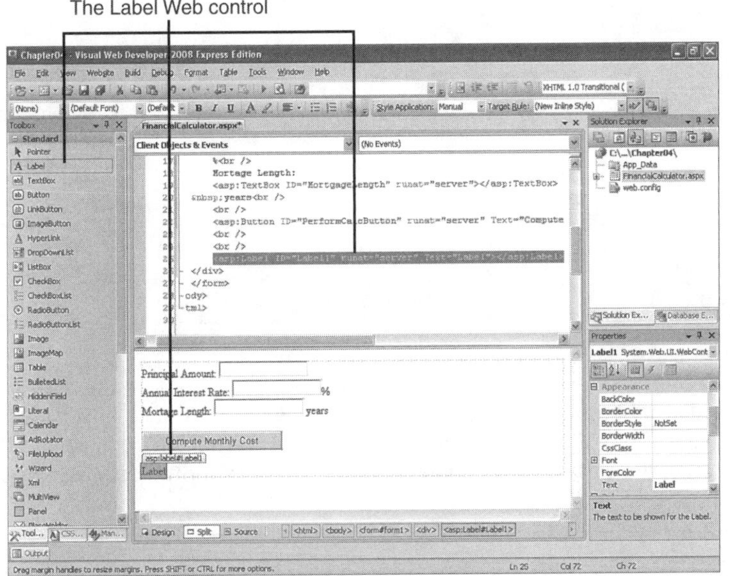

FIGURE 4.6
A Label Web control has been added to the ASP.NET web page.

Because we don't want this Label to display any content until the user has entered the three inputs and the calculation has been performed, clear out the Label's `Text` property.

To clear out the `Text` property value for the Label Web control, first click the Label so that its properties are loaded in the Properties pane. Then, in the Properties pane, locate the `Text` property and erase its value by clicking it and pressing Backspace until all the characters have been removed.

After you clear out the Label's `Text` property, the designer will show the Label Web control as its `ID` property, enclosed by brackets. Currently, the Label's `ID` property is `Label1`, meaning that in the designer you should see the Label Web control displayed as `[Label1]`. Go ahead and change the `ID` property of the Label from `Label1` to `Results`, which should change the Label's display in the designer from `[Label1]` to `[Results]`.

Figure 4.7 shows the designer after the Label Web control's `Text` property has been cleared out and its `ID` has been changed to `Results`.

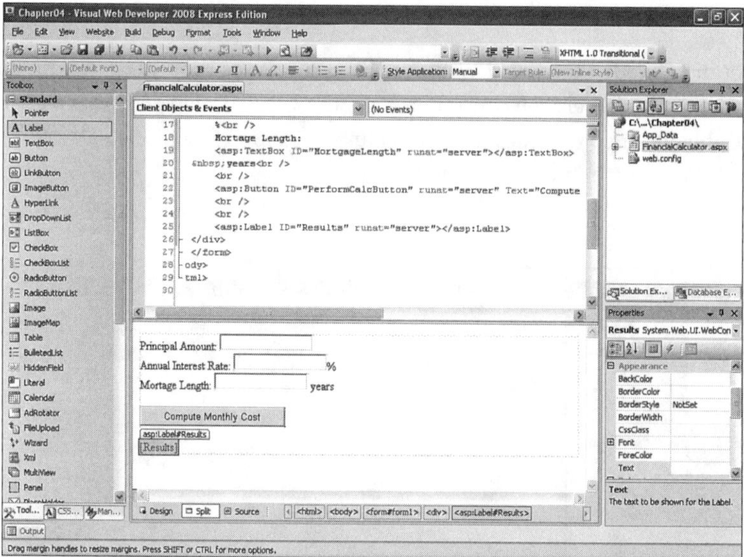

FIGURE 4.7
The Label Web control's ID has been changed to `Results`.

By the Way

At this point we have added the vital pieces of the user interface. If you want to add additional user interface elements at this time, perhaps a bold, centered title at the top of the web page or a brief set of instructions for the user, feel free to do so.

Writing the Source Code for the ASP.NET Web Page

Now that we have completed the HTML portion of our ASP.NET web page, all that remains is to write the code. The code reads the user's inputs, performs the calculations to arrive at the monthly cost for the mortgage, and then displays the results in the Label.

In Hour 2 we looked at the page's `Load` event and the corresponding `Page_Load` event handler. This event handler, which you can include in your ASP.NET web page's source code portion, is executed each time the web page is loaded. We will not be placing the source code to perform the monthly mortgage cost calculation in this event handler, though, because we do not want to run the calculation until the user has entered the principal, interest rate, and duration values and has clicked the Compute Monthly Cost button.

Button Web controls have a `Click` event that fires when the button is clicked. Therefore, what we want to do is create an event handler that is associated with the Compute Monthly Cost button's `Click` event. This way, whenever the Compute Monthly Cost button is clicked, the event handler that we provide will be executed.

Creating an event handler for a Button Web control's `Click` event is remarkably easy to accomplish with Visual Web Developer. The quickest way is to go to the Design view and double-click the Button Web control. This automatically creates the necessary event handler and whisks you to the page's source code portion, where you should see the following source code:

```
Partial Class FinancialCalculator
    Inherits System.Web.UI.Page

    Protected Sub PerformCalcButton_Click(ByVal sender As Object, ByVal e
➥As System.EventArgs) Handles PerformCalcButton.Click

    End Sub
End Class
```

Another way to create this same event handler is to go to the source code portion. At the top you'll find two drop-down lists. From the left drop-down list, select the Button Web control (`PerformCalcButton`) and then, from the right drop-down list, select the `Click` event. After you select the `Click` option, an event handler is automatically created for the Button's `Click` event with the same code as if you had double-clicked the Button in the Design view.

Note that the event handler is named `PerformCalcButton_Click`. More generically, Visual Web Developer names event handlers *`WebControlID_Event`*, where *`WebControlID`* is the name of the Web control and *`Event`* is the name of the event the event handler is wired to.

Any code that you write within the event handler will be executed whenever the `PerformCalcButton` button is clicked. Because we want to compute and display the monthly cost of the mortgage when this Button is clicked, we will put the code to perform this calculation in this event handler.

Reading the Values in the TextBox Web Controls

To calculate the monthly cost of the mortgage, we must first determine the values the user entered into the three TextBox Web controls. Before we look at the code to accomplish this, let's take a step back and reexamine Web controls, a topic we touched upon lightly in Hour 2.

Recall that when the ASP.NET engine is executing an ASP.NET web page, Web controls are handled quite differently from standard HTML elements. With static HTML content, the markup is passed directly from the ASP.NET engine to the web server without any translation; with Web controls, however, the Web control's syntax is rendered into a standard HTML element. Specifically, what's happening behind the scenes is that an object is created that represents the Web control. The object is created from the class that corresponds to the specific Web control. That is, a TextBox Web control in the HTML and Web control portion is represented as an object instantiated from the `TextBox` class in the source code portion. Similarly, the `Results` Label Web control is represented as an object instantiated from the `Label` class.

Recall that a class is an abstract blueprint, whereas an object is a concrete instance. When an object is created, it is said to have been **instantiated**. The act of creating an object is often referred to as **instantiation**.

Each Web control class has various properties that describe the state of the Web control. For example, the `TextBox` class has a `Columns` property that indicates how many columns wide the TextBox is. Both the `TextBox` and `Label` classes have `Text` properties that indicate that Web control's text content.

Did you Know?

A complete list of properties, methods, and events for the Web control classes, along with a description and sample code, can be found in the Visual Web Developer help. If you have enabled Dynamic Help, you can click the Web control that you want to learn more about, and the Dynamic Help window will be populated with technical documentation, articles, and other related information on that particular control.

Web control properties can be accessed in the ASP.NET page's source code section. Because the `Text` property of the TextBox Web control contains the content of the TextBox, we can reference this property in the Compute Monthly Cost button's `Click` event handler to determine the value the user entered into each TextBox.

For example, to determine the value entered into the `LoanAmount` TextBox, we could use the following line of code:

```
LoanAmount.Text
```

When the ASP.NET engine creates an object for the Web control, it names it using the Web control's `ID` property. Because we set the TextBox Web control's `ID` property to `LoanAmount`, the corresponding object in the source code portion is named `LoanAmount`. Consequently, to programmatically retrieve the `Text` property of the `LoanAmount` TextBox, we use the syntax `LoanAmount.Text`.

By the Way

Don't worry if the syntax for retrieving an object's property seems confusing. We discuss the syntax and semantics of the Visual Basic programming language in greater detail in Hours 5 through 7.

The Complete Source Code

Listing 4.1 contains the complete source code for our ASP.NET web page. Visual Web Developer has already written some of the code for us, namely the class declaration and the event handler definition. We need to enter the code between lines 4 and 35 into the `PerformCalcButton` Button's `Click` event handler.

Did you Know?

Keep in mind that you should *not* type in the line numbers shown in Listing 4.1. The line numbers are present in the code listing only to help reference specific lines of the listing when we're discussing the code.

Also, remember that IntelliSense can help expedite entering property names and alert you when there's a problem. For example, when referencing the `Text` property of the `LoanAmount` TextBox Web control, we use `LoanAmount.Text`. When you type the period (`.`) after typing in `LoanAmount`, you should see a drop-down list of available properties and methods for the TextBox Web control. You can then type in the first few letters of the property or method you want to use and press the Tab key to autocomplete the rest of the property or method name.

If you don't see a drop-down list after pressing the period key, something has gone awry. Did you mistype the `LoanAmount`? Did you not set the TextBox Web control's `ID` to `LoanAmount`?

LISTING 4.1 The Computation Is Performed in the `PerformCalcButton` Button's `Click` Event Handler

```
Partial Class FinancialCalculator
    Inherits System.Web.UI.Page

    Protected Sub PerformCalcButton_Click(ByVal sender As Object, ByVal e As
➥ System.EventArgs) Handles PerformCalcButton.Click
        'Specify constant values
        Const INTEREST_CALCS_PER_YEAR As Integer = 12
        Const PAYMENTS_PER_YEAR As Integer = 12

        'Create variables to hold the values entered by the user
        Dim P As Decimal = LoanAmount.Text
        Dim r As Decimal = Rate.Text / 100
        Dim t As Decimal = MortgageLength.Text

        Dim ratePerPeriod As Decimal
        ratePerPeriod = r / INTEREST_CALCS_PER_YEAR

        Dim payPeriods As Integer
        payPeriods = t * PAYMENTS_PER_YEAR

        Dim annualRate As Decimal
        annualRate = Math.Exp(INTEREST_CALCS_PER_YEAR *
➥ Math.Log(1 + ratePerPeriod)) - 1

        Dim intPerPayment As Decimal
        intPerPayment = (Math.Exp(Math.Log(annualRate + 1) / payPeriods)
➥ - 1) * payPeriods

        'Now, compute the total cost of the loan
        Dim intPerMonth As Decimal = intPerPayment / PAYMENTS_PER_YEAR

        Dim costPerMonth As Decimal
        costPerMonth = P * intPerMonth / (1 - Math.Pow(intPerMonth + 1,
➥ -payPeriods))


        'Display the results in the results Label Web control
        Results.Text = "Your mortgage payment per month is $" &
➥ costPerMonth
    End Sub
End Class
```

An in-depth discussion of the code in Listing 4.1 is provided toward the end of this hour in the "Examining the Source Code" section. For now, enter the code as is, even if there are parts of it you don't understand. One thing to pay attention to, though, is in lines 10 through 12. In these three lines we are reading the values of the three TextBox Web controls' `Text` properties and assigning them to variables `P`, `r`, and `t`.

By the Way

> If the source code in Listing 4.1 has you hopelessly lost and confused, don't worry. The point of this hour is to get you creating a useful ASP.NET web page. We will examine the source code for this page in more detail later in this hour. Additionally, we'll spend Hours 5 through 7 investigating the Visual Basic syntax in greater detail.
>
> The mathematical equations used to calculate the monthly interest cost can be found at www.faqs.org/faqs/sci-math-faq/compoundInterest/. A more in-depth discussion of these formulas can be found at http://people.hofstra.edu/Stefan_Waner/RealWorld/Summary10.html.

Testing the Financial Calculator

Now that we have completed the HTML and source code portions of our ASP.NET web page, it's time to test the financial calculator. To view the ASP.NET web page through your browser, go to the Debug menu and choose Start Without Debugging (or press Ctrl+F5 on your keyboard). This launches a web browser and loads `FinancialCalculator.aspx`.

By the Way

> The Start Without Debugging option visits the page without launching the debugger, whereas Start Debugging visits the page with debugging enabled.
>
> A **debugger** is a piece of software that can intercept running code, allowing a programmer to step through executing code one line at a time. Visual Web Developer's debugger is quite powerful and is a very helpful diagnostic tool when your page's programmatic output isn't what you expected. For now, just use Start Without Debugging; in the section "Using the Debugger," we'll examine the basics of debugging an ASP.NET page.

When first visiting the page, you should see three empty TextBoxes and the Compute Monthly Cost button, as shown in Figure 4.8.

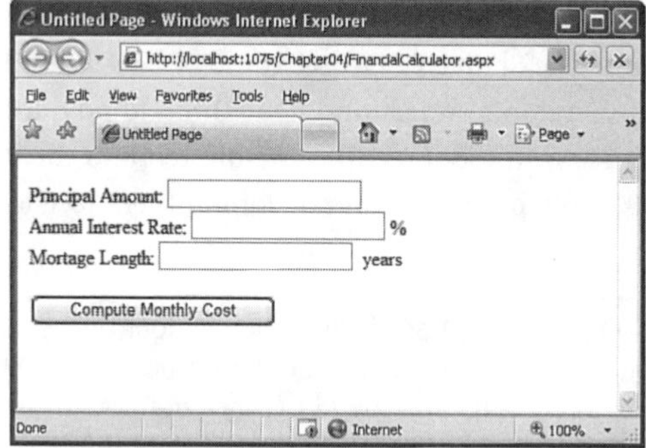

FIGURE 4.8 When the ASP.NET page is first visited, three TextBoxes await user input.

Enter some valid values into the TextBoxes and then click the Compute Monthly Cost button. When this button is clicked, the monthly cost is displayed beneath the TextBoxes and Button, as shown in Figure 4.9.

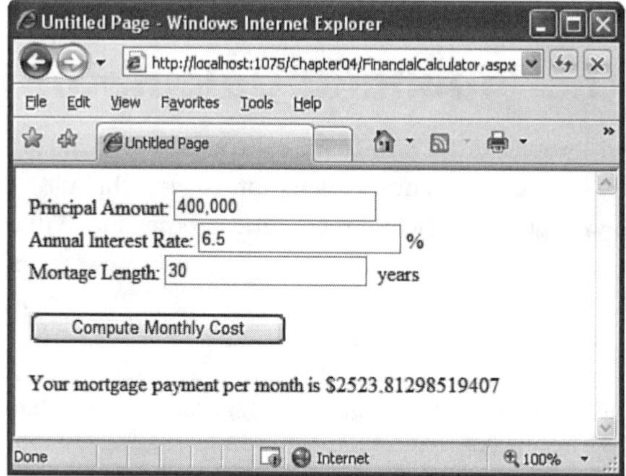

FIGURE 4.9 The output of the financial calculator is displayed when the Button is clicked.

Viewing the Rendered Source Code

When an ASP.NET page is requested by a browser, the ASP.NET engine on the web server renders the ASP.NET page and returns the resulting HTML to the browser. The Web controls are transformed into standard HTML elements, and the applicable event handlers in the source code portion are executed, potentially tweaking the resulting output further. (For example, in `FinancialCalculator.aspx` the `PerformCalcButton` Button control's `Click` event handler updates the `Results` Label Web control's `Text` property, which affects the resulting HTML for the page.)

You can see the page's rendered markup by viewing the page's source through the browser. All browsers allow you to view the markup they received; for Internet Explorer, go to the View menu and choose the Source option.

Viewing the resulting HTML markup can, at times, help with diagnosing a problem. Even if no problems exist, I encourage you to view the source often as you are learning ASP.NET. Doing so helps illustrate how Web controls get rendered into HTML.

Let's take a moment to examine the HTML output generated by `FinancialCalculator.aspx`, both when the page is first visited as well as after the user has entered values and clicked the Compute Monthly Cost button.

Listing 4.2 contains the HTML received when first visiting the ASP.NET page.

LISTING 4.2 **The HTML Markup Received by the Browser When First Visiting the Page**

```
<!DOCTYPE html PUBLIC "-//W3C//DTD XHTML 1.0 Transitional//EN"
➥ "http://www.w3.org/TR/xhtml1/DTD/xhtml1-transitional.dtd">

<html xmlns="http://www.w3.org/1999/xhtml">
<head><title>
    Untitled Page
</title></head>
<body>
    <form name="form1" method="post" action="FinancialCalculator.aspx"
➥ id="form1">
<div>
<input type="hidden" name="__VIEWSTATE" id="__VIEWSTATE"
➥ value="/wEPDwUKMTY1MDQyNjc5NWRk0P2vgXwmx2ZYXGDLcgiW4GDz5Cs=" />
</div>

    <div>
        Principal Amount:
        <input name="LoanAmount" type="text" id="LoanAmount" />
        <br />
        Annual Interest Rate:
        <input name="Rate" type="text" id="Rate" />
        %<br />
        Mortage Length:
        <input name="MortgageLength" type="text" id="MortgageLength" />
     years<br />
        <br />
        <input type="submit" name="PerformCalcButton"
➥value="Compute Monthly Cost" id="PerformCalcButton" />
        <br />
        <br />
        <span id="Results"></span>
    </div>

<div>
```

LISTING 4.2 Continued

```
31:
32:     <input type="hidden" name="__EVENTVALIDATION" id="__EVENTVALIDATION"
➥ value="/wEWBQL9hoydDwLio9b4CwK0hujeBAK4uu/
➥yAgK4kM+MBOI0DiB1FRIJYeJCNXwZKLYDTDmY" />
33: </div></form>
34: </body>
35: </html>
```

The HTML received by the browser looks pretty similar to the HTML content in the ASP.NET page's HTML portion, save for a few exceptions. First, the `@Page` directive that is found at the top of the ASP.NET page's HTML portion is not rendered. Second, the Web Form—`<form runat="server">`—is converted into a more detailed `<form>` tag (see line 8) and also includes some hidden form fields (see lines 10 and 32).

The TextBox, Button, and Label Web controls have also been transformed from their Web control syntax—`<asp:`*`WebControlName`*` runat="server" ... />`—to standard HTML elements. The TextBox Web controls have been converted into `<input type="text">` elements (lines 15, 18, and 21), the Label Web control into a `<span>` (line 27), and the Button Web control into `<input type="submit">` (line 24). Notice that the properties of the Web controls are translated into attributes in the controls' corresponding HTML elements. For example, the `ID` properties of the Web controls are rendered as `id` and `name` attributes in the resulting HTML elements.

After a user enters particular values into the three text boxes in his browser and clicks the Compute Monthly Cost button, the browser re-requests `FinancialCalculator.aspx` from the web server, but this time includes this user-entered information with the request. Submitting user-entered values back to the same web page is referred to as a **postback** and is the most common way user-entered information is relayed back to the web server for server-side processing.

On postback, the ASP.NET engine can determine that the postback was caused by the `PerformCalcButton` Button Web control being clicked and therefore raises the Button's `Click` event, which in turn causes the associated event handler to run. In addition, the `Text` properties of the three TextBox Web controls are updated to reflect the values entered by the user. The event handler for the Button's `Click` event then runs (refer back to Listing 4.1), computing the monthly cost for the mortgage based on the user's inputs. The event handler updates the `Results` Label Web control's `Text` property with this computed monthly cost. Finally, the page is rendered, generating the HTML that is sent back to the client.

The resulting markup from the postback has changed slightly from the first time the page was requested because now the TextBox Web controls' `Text` properties have values (based on the user's inputs), and the `Results` Label Web control's `Text` property is set to the monthly cost. Listing 4.3 shows the HTML received by the browser after the inputs have been entered and the Compute Monthly Cost button has been clicked.

LISTING 4.3 **The HTML Markup Received by the Browser After the User Has Clicked the Button**

```
<!DOCTYPE html PUBLIC "-//W3C//DTD XHTML 1.0 Transitional//EN"
➥ "http://www.w3.org/TR/xhtml1/DTD/xhtml1-transitional.dtd">

<html xmlns="http://www.w3.org/1999/xhtml">
<head><title>
    Untitled Page
</title></head>
<body>
    <form name="form1" method="post" action="FinancialCalculator.aspx"
➥ id="form1">
<div>
<input type="hidden" name="__VIEWSTATE" id="__VIEWSTATE"
➥ value="/wEPDwUKMTY1MDQyNjc5NQ9kFgICAw9kFgICCQ8PFgIeBFRleHQFNFlvdXIgbW9ydGd
➥hZ2UgcGF5bWVudCBwZXIgbW9udGggaXMgJDI1MjMuODEyOTg1MTk0MDdkZGTD5LjhyFZ2WhKJvA
➥tFb1JrZm8jlQ==" />
</div>

    <div>
        Principal Amount:
        <input name="LoanAmount" type="text" value="400,000"
➥ id="LoanAmount" />
        <br />
        Annual Interest Rate:
        <input name="Rate" type="text" value="6.5" id="Rate" />
        %<br />
        Mortage Length:
        <input name="MortgageLength" type="text" value="30"
➥ id="MortgageLength" />
     years<br />
        <br />
        <input type="submit" name="PerformCalcButton"
➥ value="Compute Monthly Cost" id="PerformCalcButton" />
        <br />
        <br />
        <span id="Results">Your mortgage payment per month
➥ is $2523.81298519407</span>
    </div>

<div>

    <input type="hidden" name="__EVENTVALIDATION" id="__EVENTVALIDATION"
➥ value="/wEWBQL9urXOCgLio9b4CwK0hujeBAK4uu/yAgK4kM+MBC6lrCSDFznHCrbrG7RzTdK
➥tGXV0" />
</div></form>
</body>
</html>
```

The HTML markup in Listing 4.3 has some very important differences from the HTML in Listing 4.2. The `Text` property of the three TextBox Web controls is now reflected in the corresponding `<input type="text">` HTML elements. Specifically, the value of the TextBox Web control's `Text` property has been emitted as a `value` attribute (lines 15, 18, and 21). Additionally, the Label Web control's `Text` property has been emitted as the inner content of the corresponding `<span>` tag (line 27).

The key points in this interaction are highlighted in Figure 4.10.

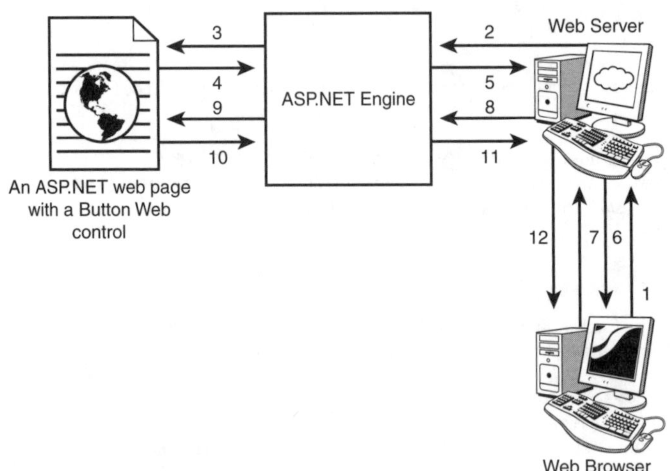

SEQUENCE OF STEPS:

1. The web browser requests the FinancialCalculator.aspx web page from the web server.
2. The web server hands off the request to the ASP.NET engine.
3. The ASP.NET engine executes the FinancialCalculator.aspx ASP.NET web page.
4. The ASP.NET web page's source code and web controls are rendered as HTML.
5. The ASP.NET Engine returns the resulting HTML to the web server.
6. The web server returns the resulting HTML to the web browser, which displays the web page.
7. The User clicks the button, which posts back the ASP.NET web page, re-requesting the FinancialCalculator.aspx web page from the web server.
8. The web server hands off the request to the ASP.NET engine.
9. The ASP.NET engine detects that the request is a postback, and the postback occurred because the button was clicked. Therefore, the Button's Click event is fired.
10. The ASP.NET web page is converted into HTML, just like in step 4.
11. Same as step 5.
12. Same as step 6.

FIGURE 4.10 Server-side code is executed only when the client makes a request to the server.

It's important to understand that the only way the code in an ASP.NET page's source code portion can run is when a request is made from the end user's browser to the web server. For pages on which the user is prompted to supply inputs, the server-side code does not execute until the user submits the form, which typically involves clicking a submit button (which is rendered by a Button Web control). This process is discussed in greater detail in Hour 9.

By the Way

> When you click the Compute Monthly Cost button, your browser is re-requesting the `FinancialCalculator.aspx` page from the web server, sending along your inputs. This entire interaction is likely happening in a split second on your computer, so you might not even realize this step is taking place. It just looks instantaneous: You click the button; the mortgage cost immediately appears on the page.
>
> The reason there is seemingly no delay in your testing is that in this case the client—your web browser—and the server—the ASP.NET Development Web Server—reside on the same machine, your personal computer. Your user experience when testing this ASP.NET page is so snappy because there is no network lag time. In a real-world setting, though, the client and server are typically separated physically, but connected via the Internet. This physical separation results in a short delay between clicking the button and seeing the result, with the actual delay time depending on a host of variables (whether the client has a low or high bandwidth connection to the Internet, the responsiveness of the web server, the route across which the request and response must travel over the Internet, and network congestion).

Testing Erroneous Input

When testing an ASP.NET page, it is important to not only test expected inputs, but also unexpected ones. For example, what will happen if the user enters a mortgage length of "Jisun"? Obviously, this is not a valid number of years.

Entering such an erroneous value will cause a runtime error, as shown in Figure 4.11.

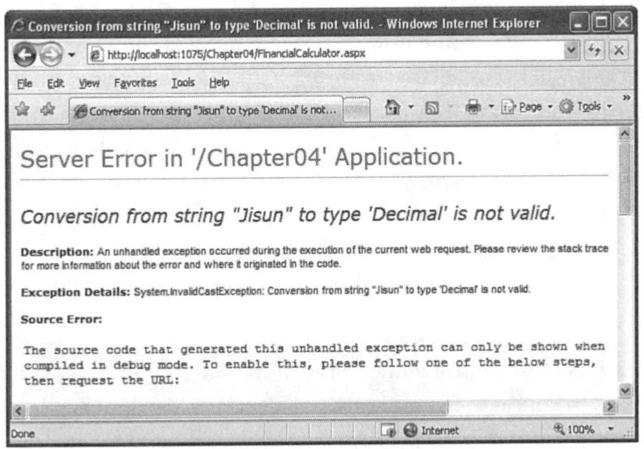

FIGURE 4.11
A runtime error will occur if the input is not in proper format.

Errors such as those shown in Figure 4.11 are an eyesore. Rather than displaying such error messages when the user enters erroneous input, it would be better to display a succinct message next to the text box(es) with erroneous input, explaining that the input is not in the right form.

The process of ensuring that user input is in the correct format is known as **input validation**. Fortunately, input validation is incredibly easy with ASP.NET. We'll examine ASP.NET's input validation features in Hour 12, "Validating User Input with Validation Controls."

Examining the Source Code

Although we've yet to take an in-depth look at the Visual Basic programming language, I believe it's worthwhile to take a moment to go over the source code for the ASP.NET page we just created, which can be found in Listing 4.1. We've already discussed the "filler" code inserted automatically by Visual Web Developer—the class definition and `Inherits` statement, as well as the event handler—so let's concentrate on the code within the event handler. This is the code that is executed when the user clicks the Compute Monthly Cost button. Its purpose is to read the user's inputs and calculate and display the monthly mortgage cost.

The first line of code in the event handler (line 5) is a comment. In Visual Basic, comments are denoted by an apostrophe (`'`); all other content on the line after an apostrophe is ignored. Comments serve a simple purpose: to make source code more readable for humans. Most of the code examples in this book include comments to make it easier for you to read and understand what's happening.

After the first comment are two constants. A constant is a value that cannot be changed programmatically. The two constants here—`INTEREST_CALCS_PER_YEAR` and `PAYMENTS_PER_YEAR`—define how often the interest is compounded and how many pay periods will occur each year throughout the life of the loan. By default these are both 12, indicating that the loan compounds every month and payments are made once per month. Next, on lines 10 through 12, the values from the three TextBox Web controls are read into variables. A variable is a construct that holds some value. The variables defined here are named `P`, `r`, and `t`, and are of type `Decimal`. The type of a variable indicates what sort of information it can hold. A `Decimal` is a predefined type in the .NET Framework that can hold large numbers with decimal places.

After these TextBox Web control values have been read in, the mathematical formulas needed to compute the monthly payment due are applied.

On lines 14 and 15 the variable `ratePerPeriod` is created and assigned the value of the interest rate each time it's compounded. Following that, the number of pay periods is recorded and stored in the `payPeriods` variable. Next, the annual interest rate is determined as well as how much interest per payment is due (and then how much interest is due per month). Finally, the cost per month is computed on line 30. The resulting output is then assigned to the `Text` property of the `Results` Label Web control.

The source code in Listing 4.1 is fairly readable, although the mathematical formulas might seem foreign. But I hope you'll agree that if you read through the lines of code, one at a time, it is clear what is happening. For example, on line 18, `payPeriods = t * PAYMENTS_PER_YEAR`, we are taking the value of `t` (the loan's term) and multiplying it by the number of payments made per year. This gives us the total number of payments made throughout the life of the loan. The point is that with Visual Basic's English-like syntax and semantics, even to someone with little to no programming background, it's possible to pick up the gist of the code by simply reading through it.

Don't worry if Listing 4.1 leaves you feeling lost and bewildered. Your code-reading acumen will greatly improve over the next three hours as we delve into the syntax of Visual Basic. By the time you finish working through Hour 7, "Working with Objects in Visual Basic," you'll have the Visual Basic background necessary for understanding all the examples throughout this book.

Using the Debugger

Over the course of creating ASP.NET pages, you'll undoubtedly run into problems where the page's source code portion isn't behaving as you'd expect. Perhaps a particular block of source code is not running when you expect it to, or the output you're seeing is different from what you expected. In such circumstances, your best friend is the **debugger**. A debugger is a special piece of software that can intercept a running program and provide the programmer a deep level of introspection into its inner workings. Unfortunately, we don't have the time or space to delve into the depths of debugging; instead, we'll just concentrate on some of the more common debugging tasks.

To use the debugger when testing an ASP.NET page, you need to go to the Debug menu and choose Start Debugging. If this is the first time you've attempted to debug this particular website, the Debugging Not Enabled dialog box appears, as shown in Figure 4.12. To debug an ASP.NET website, it must be configured to support debugging; by default, a new ASP.NET website project is *not* configured to support debugging. The Debugging Not Enabled dialog box warns you of this and offers to automatically alter the `web.config` configuration file to enable debugging support.

Did you Know?

> You can also start debugging by pressing F5 or the green play button icon in the toolbar.

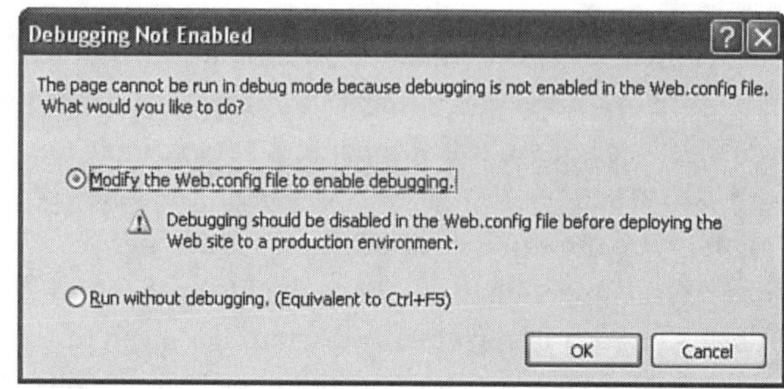

FIGURE 4.12 The Debugging Not Enabled dialog box warns you that the application is not configured for debugging.

Start debugging the application, selecting Modify the `Web.config` File to Enable Debugging radio button if necessary. Starting with debugging launches the debugger, fires up the browser, and visits the current page (`FinancialCalculator.aspx`), just as in Figure 4.8.

Watch Out!

> When launching the debugger, you may also get the Script Debugging Disabled warning. In addition to debugging server-side code, the debugger can also debug client-side code, which is code that is sent to and executed on the visitor's browser. To debug client-side script, however, Internet Explorer's script debugging features must be enabled. Because our page does not include any client-side script, it doesn't matter whether Internet Explorer's script debugging is disabled. Therefore, if you see this warning, feel free to dismiss it.

At this point you can't even tell that the debugger is running. The web page does not appear any different in the browser if the debugger is running. But with the debugger running, you can add one or more **breakpoints** to your ASP.NET page's source code portion. A breakpoint is a marker in the source code that, when reached, causes the program to halt, letting the debugger take over. When a breakpoint is reached, control automatically reverts to Visual Web Developer, allowing you to step through the execution of the code one line at a time.

Let's set a breakpoint. Leave the browser running and return to the `FinancialCalculator.aspx` page's source code portion in Visual Web Developer. Add a breakpoint to the line of code that reads `Dim P As Double = LoanAmount.Text` (line 10 in Listing 4.1). To accomplish this, place your cursor on this line of code and press F9; alternatively, you can click in the light gray left margin next to this line of code. In either case, a breakpoint will be set, which will display a red circle in the margin and highlight the line of code in red. Figure 4.13 shows the page's code portion in Visual Web Developer after this breakpoint has been set.

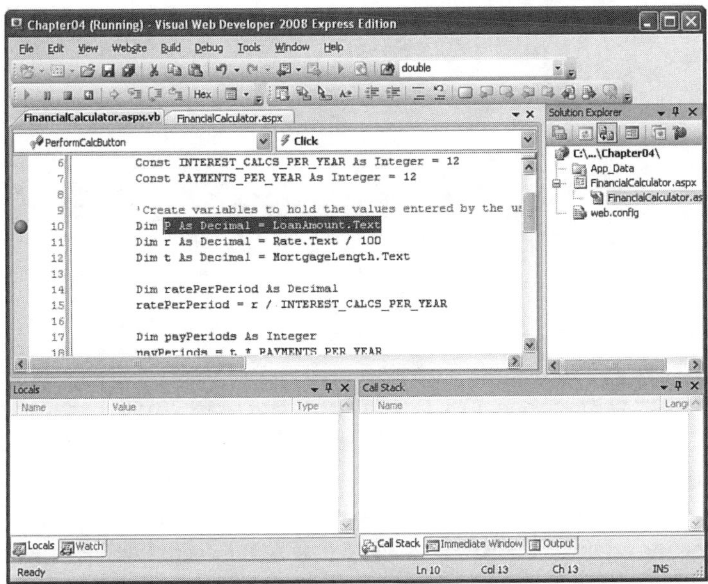

FIGURE 4.13
A breakpoint has been set.

Now return to the browser, enter some values into the text boxes, and click the Compute Monthly Cost button. Clicking the button causes a postback, which returns control to the ASP.NET page's source code portion, invoking the Button's `Click` event handler. As the event handler is executed, the `Dim P As Decimal = LoanAmount.Text` line of code is eventually reached. When this line is reached, the program halts and the debugger takes over. In Visual Web Developer, the current line of code being executed is highlighted yellow (see Figure 4.14); this current line of code is the line where we set the breakpoint moments ago.

From the debugger, we can inspect the values of various variables. For example, in the lower-left corner of Figure 4.14, you'll find the Locals window, which shows all the current variables and their values. Many of these variables have their default values. For example, the variables `annualRate`, `costPerMonth`, `intPerMonth`, and so on all have values of 0. The reason is that we've yet to reach the lines of code where these variables are assigned a value. As we step through the executing code, these values in the Locals window will be updated accordingly.

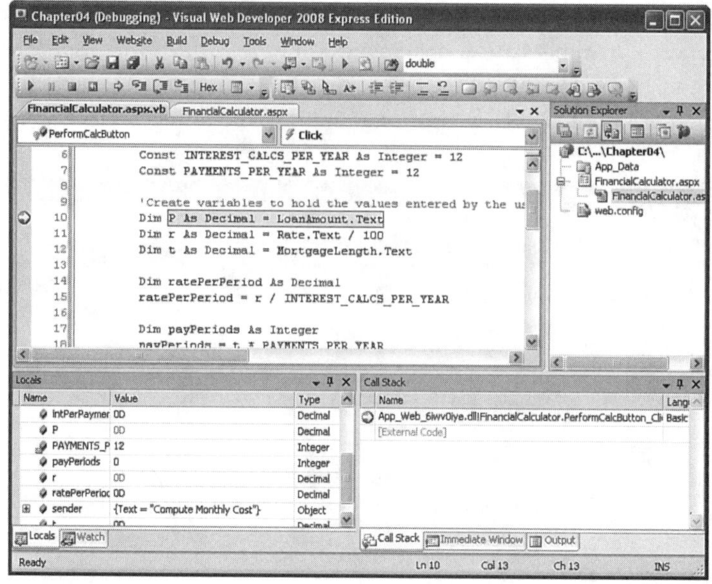

FIGURE 4.14 The breakpoint has been reached, halting program execution.

To move to the next line of code in the debugger, go to the Debug menu and choose Step Over, or press F10. Press F10 a couple of times and note how the yellow highlighted line moves further down the lines of code in the event handler, updating the values in the Locals window. If you want to run until the next breakpoint, press F5, or go to the Debug menu and choose Continue. Doing so in our example will return control to the browser because there are no other breakpoints.

> **Did you Know?** In addition to using the Locals window, you can determine the value of a variable by hovering your mouse pointer over the variable's name in the source code portion. Additional debugging windows can be of help. The Watch window allows you to specify particular variables or expressions whose values you want to monitor. A complete list of debugging-related windows can be found in the Debug menu's Windows submenu.

To stop debugging, go to the Debug menu and choose Stop Debugging. Alternatively, you can click the Stop icon in the Toolbar.

The preceding explanation is but a brief overview of Visual Web Developer's debugging capabilities. You can learn more about debugging at Microsoft's "Walkthrough: Debugging Web Pages in Visual Web Developer," available online at http://msdn2.microsoft.com/en-us/library/z9e7w6cs.

Summary

In this hour we saw how to create a useful ASP.NET web page. We started by outlining the page's features, including the output and needed user inputs. We then briefly discussed what the user interface should look like.

Next, we implemented the user interface by completing the HTML portion of the ASP.NET web page. With Visual Web Developer, this was a matter of typing in some text and dragging and dropping the needed TextBox, Button, and Label Web controls onto the page. Next, we turned our attention to the source code portion, creating and writing the code for the Compute Monthly Cost button's `Click` event handler. Following the design and development stages, we tested the ASP.NET web page by entering values into the three TextBoxes.

This hour concluded with discussion of the source code portion of the ASP.NET page and a look at Visual Web Developer's debugging capabilities.

Q&A

Q. ***How do I associate "event code" with a Web control that I've placed on a Web Form? Can I always just double-click the Web control in the Design view?***

A. In this hour we saw two ways to create an event handler for a Button Web control's `Click` event. The easiest approach is to double-click the Button Web control in the Design view. Double-clicking a Web control in the designer causes Visual Web Developer to create an event handler in the page's source code portion. For the Button Web control, a `Click` event handler is added.

However, most Web controls have several events, meaning we can, potentially, have numerous event handlers in our ASP.NET page's source code. Each Web control has a **default event**. When a Web control is double-clicked in the designer, an event handler is created for its default event. (As you may have guessed, the Button Web control's default event is its `Click` event.)

Adding an event handler for an event other than the default event requires that you go directly to the source code portion and pick the Web control and event from the two drop-down lists at the top.

Q. ***What would happen if I placed the financial calculation code in the*** `Page_Load` ***event handler instead of the*** `PerformCalcButton_Click` ***event handler?***

A. Recall that the source code in the `Page_Load` event handler executes every time the ASP.NET web page is requested. When the user visits the page for the first time, she has yet to enter the loan's principal, interest rate, or duration. Therefore, in attempting to compute the calculation, we will get an error because the code will attempt to perform numerical calculations on user-inputted values that have yet to be provided.

Because we want to perform the calculation only after the user has provided the required inputs, the source code for the calculation is placed in the Button's `Click` event handler.

Workshop

Quiz

1. Why is the design-requirements phase of software development an important one?
2. How can you add a TextBox Web control to an ASP.NET web page using Visual Web Developer?
3. Why did we add a Label Web control to our ASP.NET web page's HTML portion?
4. What will the ASP.NET page's output be if the user enters invalid characters into the TextBoxes? For example, what happens if the user enters "Way too much!" for the mortgage interest rate?
5. How do you add an event handler for a Button Web control's `Click` event with Visual Web Developer?
6. When using a TextBox Web control, what property is referenced to determine the value entered by the user?

Answers

1. The design-requirements phase outlines the specific features for the software project and the user interface. It is an important stage because, by enumerating the features, you can more easily determine the current progress of the project. Furthermore, there is no ambiguity as to what features will and will not be included in the final project.

2. There are two ways to add a TextBox Web control. You can drag a TextBox Web control from the Toolbox onto the page, or you can manually type in the TextBox's declarative syntax:

   ```
   <asp:TextBox runat="server" ID="ID"></asp:TextBox>
   ```

3. A Label Web control was added to the ASP.NET web page's HTML portion to indicate where the output of the financial calculator would appear.

4. If the user provides invalid input, a runtime error will occur. Refer to Figure 4.11 for the error message the user will receive.

5. To add an event handler for a Button Web control's `Click` event, double-click the Button in the designer. Alternatively, you can create the event handler by selecting the appropriate Web control and event from the two drop-down lists at the top of the source code portion.

6. The TextBox's `Text` property contains the value entered by the user. To reference this property in an ASP.NET web page's source code, use the following:

   ```
   TextBoxID.Text
   ```

Exercises

1. In this hour we saw how to use Visual Web Developer to create an ASP.NET web page with three TextBox Web controls, a Button Web control, and a Label Web control. Using this knowledge, create an ASP.NET web page that prompts the user for his name and age. After the user provides this information and clicks the submit button, have the page display a message for the user, depending on his age.

   This ASP.NET page will need two TextBox Web controls, a Button Web control, and a Label Web control. Set the TextBox Web controls' `ID` properties to `Name` and `Age`. The Button Web control should have its `Text` property set to "Click

Me." Set the Label Web control's ID property to Results and clear out its Text property. Then create an event handler for the Button Web control's Click event. Recall that this can be accomplished by double-clicking the Button in the designer.

Now, in the Click event handler, determine what message to display, based on the user's age. The code for this will look like this:

```
If Age.Text < 21 then
  Results.Text = Name.Text & ", you are a youngster!"
End If

If Age.Text >= 21 AND Age.Text < 40 then
  Results.Text = Name.Text & ", you are an adult."
End If

If Age.Text >= 40 then
  Results.Text = Name.Text & ", you are over the hill!"
End If
```

After you have entered the preceding source code into the Button Web control's Click event handler, save the ASP.NET web page and test it by visiting it through a browser.

2. For more practice with Visual Web Developer, take a moment to enhance the user interface of the FinancialCalculator.aspx web page we created in this hour. Some suggested enhancements include displaying the TextBox Web control titles in a more appealing font, adding some text at the top of the web page explaining the purpose of the financial calculator, and so on.

HOUR 5

Understanding Visual Basic's Variables and Operators

In this hour, we will cover

- What a programming language is
- What variables are and how to declare them
- How to assign values to variables
- What data types are and why they are important
- Visual Basic's operators and how to use them
- Typing rules

As discussed earlier, ASP.NET web pages are composed of two portions: an HTML portion, which contains HTML and Web controls; and a source code portion, which contains the ASP.NET web page's server-side code. You can write the source code for an ASP.NET page in one of two programming languages: Visual Basic or Visual C# (often referred to as just C#).

Most beginning developers find Visual Basic a much easier language to learn than C#, mainly because Visual Basic's syntax and structure are much closer to everyday English than C#'s. Therefore, all the source code portions of ASP.NET web pages discussed throughout this book use Visual Basic as the programming language.

If you are new to programming, you likely found the source code portions of the examples in Hours 2 and 4 to be a bit daunting. Don't worry; in this hour and the next two, we'll take an in-depth look at Visual Basic. By the end of these three hours, you'll be able not only to make sense of code similar to that in previous hours, but also to write it on your own.

The contents of this hour and the next two are geared toward readers who have had little to no programming experience. If you are already fluent with the Visual Basic programming language, feel free to skip ahead to Hour 8, "ASP.NET Web Controls for Displaying Text."

The Purpose of Programming Languages

When computers were first designed in the early twentieth century, they were created to carry out mathematical computations that, at the time, were performed by humans. Computers were preferred over humans because they could perform the calculations faster, could work around the clock, and were not susceptible to error. For example, a computer doesn't forget to carry the one when adding two numbers, an error every human has likely made at some point.

Computers then, as computers today, were built to accept a sequence of **instructions** and to carry out these instructions in the order in which they arrived. This made computers ideal for solving problems that could be broken down into a sequence of simple steps. For example, addition of large numbers can be broken down into simpler addition problems by first adding the numbers in the ones place, then the tens place, and so on, carrying over a digit into the preceding column if needed.

For a computer to solve a problem, though, it first needs to be told the precise sequence of steps to perform. Think of a computer as a very obedient young child, one who can understand only simple words and commands and will always do exactly as you instruct. For instance, if you want this child to go to sleep, you would have to tell him first to go to his bedroom, which might require that you first tell him to start walking toward the stairs. Then you would need to give instructions to step up the first step, then the second, and so on. After that, you might need to tell him to walk down the hall to his room. You would then need to tell him to open his door, to walk into his room, to lie down in bed, and finally, to fall asleep.

The verbal commands you give the child must be simple ones the child can understand. That is, if you said, "My beloved nipper, I fervently implore you to acquiesce to slumber," the child would wonder what in the world you were saying. Similarly, when you're providing instructions to a computer, the instructions must conform to a specific syntax and structure.

Specifically, computers understand commands only from particular **programming languages**. A programming language is a language with a well-defined syntax and semantics.

Multitudes of programming languages exist. When creating ASP.NET web pages, however, we are restricted to using .NET-compatible programming languages, such as Visual Basic and C#.

By the Way

> Many .NET-compatible programming languages exist, such as JScript.NET, COBOL.NET, Visual C++, and others. However, ASP.NET web pages are most typically created with either Visual Basic or C#. In fact, Visual Web Developer supports using only these two languages.

Concepts Common to All Programming Languages

Although many different programming languages exist, all share some common features, including the following:

- **A means to store data temporarily**—In Visual Basic, `variables` are used to store data. We'll be discussing variables in the next section, "Declaring and Using Variables."
- **A set of operators that can be applied to the data stored in variables**—One such operator is +, which sums the values of two variables. We'll look at the operators available in Visual Basic in the "Examining Visual Basic Operators" section.
- **A variety of control structures that can be used to alter the flow of instructions based on the value of variables**—The control structures in Visual Basic are covered in Hour 6, "Managing Program Flow with Visual Basic's Control Structures."
- **A way to modularize source code into reusable units**—In Visual Basic, code can be compartmentalized into subroutines and functions, as we'll see in the next hour.

In this hour we look at Visual Basic's syntax and semantics for storing and performing operations on data.

Declaring and Using Variables

A **variable** is a location in the computer's memory where you can temporarily store information, such as a number or a string.

By the Way

In a programming language, a **string** is a sequence of characters and is delimited by quotation marks. An example of a string is

```
"Hello, world!"
```

Variables have three components to them:

- A **value**, such as 5, or "Hello, world!"
- A **name**, which is used to refer to the value of the variable.
- A **type**, which indicates what types of values can be stored. For example, a variable of type `Integer` can store values like 5 and –858. A variable of type `String` can store values like "Hello, world!" and "Jisun is a toad."

Did you Know?

Because a variable's type dictates what data can be stored in the variable, a variable's type commonly is referred to as its **data type.**

Think of a variable as a box that can hold things only of a certain type. Each box has a name that you can use to reference the contents in a particular box. Figure 5.1 shows a box named `Age` that can accept integer values. We can place values like 29, 97, –3, 829, 294, and 1,334,128, into `Age`. In Figure 5.1, we've placed the value 29 into `Age`.

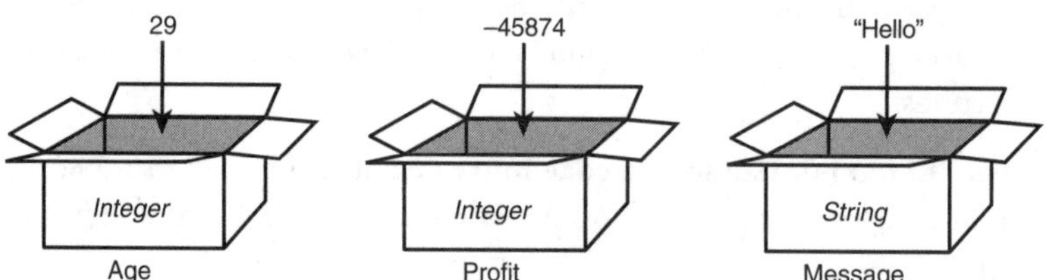

FIGURE 5.1 Think of a variable as a named box that can contain a certain type of value.

Assigning Values to Variables

The name and data type of a variable are **immutable**. That is, after the variable's name and type have been specified, they cannot change during the program's execution. The variable's value, on the other hand, is **mutable**, meaning that it can change over the course of the program's execution.

Variables alter their value through **assignment statements**. An assignment statement assigns a value to a variable using the = operator and has the following form:

```
variableName = value
```

This statement assigns *value* to the value of the variable *variableName*.

> The = operator is often referred to as the **assignment operator**. We will discuss this operation in more detail in the "Visual Basic's Assignment Operators" section.

Declaring a Variable

To use a variable, you must first **declare** the variable using the Visual Basic `Dim` statement. When declaring a variable, you must provide both the name and data type of the variable; you may optionally specify the value. For example, to create a variable named `Age` that accepts values of type `Integer`, you would use the following `Dim` statement:

```
Dim age as Integer
```

More generally, the `Dim` statement has the following form:

```
Dim variableName as type
```

We'll examine the `Dim` statement in much greater detail in the "Examining the `Dim` Statement" section. First, though, we need to look at the rules for naming variables, as well as the available variable types.

Rules for Naming Variables

Each programming language imposes its own set of rules for naming variables. Variable names in Visual Basic can start with an alphabetic character or an underscore character and be followed by zero to many underscores, alphabetic characters, or numeric characters.

> Variable names in Visual Basic may be anywhere from one character long to 16,383 characters long. They are not case sensitive, meaning that upper- or lowercase does not matter. Therefore, the variable name `Age` is equivalent to the variable names `AGE`, `age`, and `aGe`.

Some examples of *valid* variable names are

- `Age`
- `_xyz123abc`
- `message2`
- `txtPassword`

If a variable name begins with an underscore, it *must* be followed by at least one other character. That is, you cannot have a variable simply named _.

Some examples of *invalid* variable names are

- 3Age—Invalid because a variable name cannot start with a numeric character.
- _—Invalid because if a variable name begins with an underscore, it must be followed by at least one other character.
- 234—Invalid because a variable name cannot start with a numeric character.

When you're naming your variables, it is important to choose names that make sense given the information the variable will store. For example, if you are going to use a variable to store the product of two numbers, you might want to name that variable `Product`, or some other descriptive name, rather than using something ambiguous, like `x` or `variable3`.

Examining Variable Data Types

Recall that the data type of a variable dictates what type of value can be stored in the variable. For example, a variable of type `Integer` can store only values that are integers (negative and positive whole numbers).

If you have worked with ASP, ASP.NET's predecessor, you've likely had experience with VBScript, a watered-down version of Visual Basic 6.0, which was the version of Visual Basic that predated Microsoft's .NET platform. With VBScript, variables were **loosely typed**.

Loosely typed variables are variables that are declared without an explicit data type. Their type is inferred by their assigned value. In VBScript you could write code that looked like so:

```
1: Dim x
2: x = "Hello, World!"
3: x = 4
```

Note that the `Dim` statement on line 1 does not contain a type (that is, it does not read: `Dim x as String`). The type of `x` is dynamically inferred by the value assigned to it. Therefore, on line 2, when `x` is assigned the value "Hello, World!", which is a string, `x`'s type is considered to be of type `String`. On line 3, however, `x` is assigned the value 4, which is an integer. After line 3, `x`'s type now is considered to be of type `Integer`.

The opposite of loosely typed is **strongly typed**. In strongly typed programming languages, all variables must be declared to be of a certain type. After a variable has been declared to be a certain type, it can be assigned only values that correspond to that type.

By the Way

> With loosely typed languages, any value can be assigned to any variable, and the value being assigned determines the variable's type. With strongly typed languages, a variable's type is explicitly specified, and only values corresponding to the variable's type may be assigned to the variable.

Visual Basic is a strongly typed language. Therefore, all variables must be given an explicit data type, and the set of values that can be assigned to a given variable is limited by the variable's type.

Because each type has a predefined set of values that can be assigned, it is important to give your variable an appropriate data type. For example, in Hour 4, "Designing, Creating, and Testing ASP.NET Web Pages," we looked at an ASP.NET web page that calculated the monthly cost of a home loan. The variables used to hold the intermediary computations were of type `Decimal`, which is a numeric type that stores numbers with decimal places. Had we chosen to use variables of type `Integer`, the calculation would have come out incorrectly. Consider the interest rate involved in the calculation, which might be 0.065 (for a 6.5% interest rate). Such a number cannot be expressed as an integer. Rather, we would have to use 0 or 1 (or some other whole number), which would clearly produce an incorrect answer. For this reason, using the correct type is important.

Let's take a look at some of the most commonly used data types in Visual Basic.

Integer Types

Integers are whole numbers that can be either positive or negative. For example, 34, 76, –3,432, and 234,124 are all valid integers, whereas 12.4 and –3.14159 are not.

There are three types of integer data types, each differing in the range of numbers it can hold. The most common integer type is type `Integer`, which can accept values ranging from –2,147,483,648 to 2,147,483,647. To create a variable of type `Integer`, use the following syntax:

```
Dim variableName as Integer
```

If you need to store larger or smaller integer values, you can use the `Long` data type, which accepts integer values ranging from –9,223,372,036,854,775,808 to

9,223,372,036,854,775,807. To create a variable of type Long, use the following syntax:

```
Dim variableName as Long
```

If you need to store much smaller integer values, you can use the Short data type, which can store integers ranging from –32,768 to 32,767. To create a variable of type Short, use

```
Dim variableName as Short
```

Nonintegral Numeric Types

Integer variables cannot store numbers that have decimals. If you perform an operation that results in a number with decimal places and then assign this number to an Integer variable, the decimals will be truncated. If you need to work with variables that support decimal places, you must use one of Visual Basic's three **nonintegral numeric data types**.

The first nonintegral numeric data type is Single, which can accept values ranging from –3.4028235E+38 through –1.401298E–45 for negative values and from 1.401298E–45 through 3.4028235E+38 for positive values.

In scientific notation, the number following the E represents the number's **magnitude**. The magnitude specifies the number of decimal places in the number. For example, 6.45E+8 is equal to 6.45 * 10^8, or 645,000,000, and 6.45E–8 is equal to 6.45 * 10^–8, or 0.0000000645. Therefore, 3.4028235E+38 is a very, very big number!

To create a variable of type Single, use the following syntax:

```
Dim variableName as Single
```

A more precise nonintegral numeric data type that also allows for larger numbers is Double, which can accept values ranging from –1.79769313486231570E+308 through –4.94065645841246544E–324 for negative values and from 4.94065645841246544E–324 through 1.79769313486231570E+308 for positive values. To create a variable of type Double, use the following syntax:

```
Dim variableName as Double
```

The third and final nonintegral numeric data type is Decimal, which scales the decimal place by powers of 10. Decimals can have from 0 to 28 decimal places. With zero decimal places, the largest number a Decimal can have is

79,228,162,514,264,337,593,543,950,335 (the smallest being –79,228,162,514,264,337,593,543,950,335). The Decimal can have, at most, 28 decimal digits. Hence, the largest number with 28 decimal digits is 7.9228162514264337593543950335. To create a variable of type `Decimal`, use the following syntax:

```
Dim variableName as Decimal
```

Boolean Data Types

A Boolean variable is a variable that can be assigned only one of two values: `True` or `False`. To create a Boolean variable, use the `Boolean` variable type. The following syntax demonstrates how to create a variable of type `Boolean`:

```
Dim variableName as Boolean
```

String Types

A string is a sequence of characters. For example, "ASP.NET is fun!" is a string composed of 15 characters, the first being `A`, the second being `S`, and so on, with the 15th one being `!`. To create a variable that can store string values, use the type `String`. To create a variable of type `String`, use the following syntax:

```
Dim variableName as String
```

Date Types

To create a variable that stores dates, set the variable's data type to `DateTime` using the following syntax:

```
Dim variableName as DateTime
```

A `DateTime` variable can store dates between midnight on January 1, 0001, through 11:59:59 p.m. on December 31, 9999.

The `Object` Type

Visual Basic contains a catchall type, a data type that can be assigned any value. This base type is the `Object` type. The `Object` type is, by its nature, extremely flexible because you can assign a variable of any type to it. For example, as the following code shows, you can assign a string to a variable of type `Object`, and then an integer, and then a nonintegral number:

```
Dim catchall as Object
catchall = "Jisun"
catchall = 4
catchall = 3.14159
```

Despite its flexibility, you should rarely, if ever, create a variable of type `Object`. The benefit of using more specific types like `Integer`, `String`, and `Decimal` is that if you accidentally try to assign an inappropriate value to one of these variables, Visual Web Developer displays an error message.

Examining the `Dim` Statement

As we discussed earlier, you must declare a variable before you can use it. In declaring a variable in a strongly typed programming language, you must provide its name and data type. In Visual Basic, this is accomplished using the `Dim` statement.

In its simplest form, the `Dim` statement specifies the variable's name and type:

```
Dim variableName as type
```

To declare three variables of type `Integer`, you can use three separate `Dim` statements, such as:

```
Dim a as Integer
Dim b as Integer
Dim c as Integer
```

Or you can use one `Dim` statement, separating each variable name and type with a comma, such as

```
Dim a as Integer, b as Integer, c as Integer
```

You can also supply a comma-delimited list of variable names and just one type. In this instance, all the variable names appearing before the data type will share the same type. That is, you can declare three variables, `a`, `b`, and `c`, all to be of type `Integer` using the following syntax:

```
Dim a, b, c as Integer
```

Performing Assignment When Declaring a Variable

Using the syntax you've seen to this point, if you wanted to create a variable named a of type `Integer` and have it assigned the value 6, you'd write code like:

```
Dim a as Integer
a = 6
```

The preceding syntax is fine as is, but you can save yourself a line of code by combining the assignment and variable declaration. To do this, use the following syntax:

```
Dim a as Integer = 6
```

Or, more generally

```
Dim variableName as type = value
```

I find that merging a variable's declaration and assignment on the same line of code, if possible, results in more concise and readable code.

Examining Visual Basic's Operators

In mathematics there are numbers and operators. Numbers are values like 4, 17.5, and pi, whereas operators are actions performed on the numbers, like negate, add, subtract, multiply, and divide. Numbers, by themselves, aren't very interesting. But after you start applying operators to numbers, you can do all sorts of things, from balancing your checkbook to calculating the thrust needed to launch a satellite into orbit.

Visual Basic has variables and operators. Variables are like the numbers in mathematics. Visual Basic's operators—like those in mathematics—perform actions on variables. Many of the traditional mathematical operators are found in Visual Basic. For example, to add two numeric variables in Visual Basic, you use the + operator. To multiply two numeric variables, you use the * operator.

Different classes of operators exist, the most important being arithmetic operators, comparison operators, the concatenation operator, and assignment operators. We'll examine these four classes of operators in the following four sections.

Arithmetic Operators

The four most frequently used arithmetic operators in Visual Basic are +, -, *, and /, which perform addition, subtraction, multiplication, and division, respectively. These operators are referred to as **binary operators** because they operate on two variables.

For example, the following code adds the `Integer` variables `b` and `c` and assigns the sum to `a`:

```
Dim a, b, c as Integer
b = 15
c = 20
a = b + c
```

The - operator can be used both as a binary operator and as a **unary operator**. A unary operator is an operator that operates on just one variable. When the - operator is used as a unary operator, it performs the negation of a number. Consider the following code:

```
Dim a, b, c as Integer
b = 15
c = 20
a = -(b + c)
```

Here, a would be assigned the value –35. The - operator is used as a unary operator on the expression `b + c`, thereby negating the value returned by `b + c`.

By the Way

Note that parentheses can be used to determine the order of operations. If, in the preceding code snippet, instead of

```
a = -(b + c)
```

we had used

```
a = -b + c
```

a would have been assigned the value 5 because negation has precedence over addition. That is, when the expression `-b + c` is evaluated, b is negated first, and then its negated value is added to c. With `-(b + c)`, first b and c are summed, and then the resulting sum is negated.

The arithmetic precedence rules in Visual Basic mirror the standard precedence rules of mathematics. If you ever need to alter the order of operations, use parentheses to group those expressions that should be evaluated first.

The / operator always returns a nonintegral numeric value, even if the resulting quotient does not have a remainder. That is, the value returned by `4 / 2` is the nonintegral numeric value 2.0, not the integer value 2. Of course the / operator can also have a quotient with a decimal remainder; for example, the value returned by `3 / 4` is 0.75.

Exploring the Comparison Operators

Comparison operators are binary operators that compare the value of two variables. The six comparison operators are listed in Table 5.1. Comparison operators always return a Boolean value—`True` or `False`—depending on the operator and the value of the two variables being compared.

TABLE 5.1 Visual Basic's Comparison Operators

Operator	Description
<	Less than
<=	Less than or equal
>	Greater than
>=	Greater than or equal
=	Equal
<>	Not equal

The following statements evaluate to `True`:

```
4 < 8
3.14159 >= 2
"Bob" <> "Sue"
(10/2) = (20/4)
4 <= 4
```

The following statements evaluate to `False`:

```
7 > 100
"Bob" = "Frank"
(10/2) = 7.5
4 < 4
```

Comparison operators are commonly used in control structures. We explore control structures in detail in Hour 6.

Understanding the Concatenation Operator

The concatenation operator **concatenates** two string variables. Concatenating two strings produces a string that consists of the contents of the second string appended to the contents of the first. The string concatenation operator in Visual Basic is the ampersand, &.

Let's look at a quick code snippet to see how the concatenation operator works. Consider the following code:

```
Dim FirstWord as String = "ASP.NET"
Dim SecondWord as String = "is"
Dim ThirdWord as String = "neat"

Dim Sentence as String
Sentence = FirstWord & " " & SecondWord & " " & ThirdWord & "."
```

The variable Sentence will end up with the value "ASP.NET is neat." The first three string variables—FirstWord, SecondWord, and ThirdWord—are each declared and assigned the value. Next, the string variable Sentence is declared and is assigned the value of each of the three words concatenated together, with a space between each word and a period at the end.

To accomplish this, we use the & operator to join together six strings. First, the string FirstWord and " " are concatenated, resulting in the temporary string "ASP.NET ". I use the word *temporary* here because this string is immediately concatenated with SecondWord, resulting in "ASP.NET is", which is then concatenated with " ", resulting in "ASP.NET is ". Next, this is concatenated with ThirdWord, giving "ASP.NET is neat", and finally this is concatenated with ".", resulting in "ASP.NET is neat.", which is then assigned to the variable Sentence.

By the Way

Inserting the Value of a Variable into a String

In many situations, we may want to insert the value of a string variable into another string. For example, imagine that we have a variable called UserFirstName that contains the user's first name, and we want to display a message on the web page that reads "Hello, *FirstName*", where *FirstName* is the value of the variable UserFirstName. That is, if the value of UserFirstName is "Scott", we want the message "Hello, Scott" to appear.

To accomplish this, we would use code like

```
Dim Output as String
Output = "Hello, " & UserFirstName
```

It is important to realize that after these two lines of code execute, the variable Output will contain the value "Hello, *FirstName*", where *FirstName* is the value of UserFirstName. Note that we did *not* use

```
Dim output as String
output = "Hello, UserFirstName"
```

Had we used this syntax, the value of Output would be precisely as we indicated: "Hello, UserFirstName". To insert the value of UserFirstName into the string Output, we need to concatenate the string "Hello, " with the value of UserFirstName. This is done using the concatenation operator, not by simply typing the variable name into the string.

Visual Basic's Assignment Operators

The most common assignment operator is the = operator, which takes the form

```
variableName = value
```

For example, to assign the value 5 to an integer variable, we can use the following code:

```
Dim Age as Integer
Age = 5
```

The value assigned to a variable can be things more complex than simple values like 5. The value can be an expression involving other operators. For example, we might want to add two numbers and store their sum in a variable. To accomplish this, we could use code like

```
'Create three integer variables
Dim sum, number1, number2 as Integer
number1 = 15
number2 = 20

'Assign the sum of number1 and number2 to sum
sum = number1 + number2
```

Shorthand Versions for Common Assignments

In many situations we need to routinely update a variable's value in some fashion. One of the most common applications of this is in a loop, where we increment (or decrement) the value of a variable by a certain amount in each iteration. We'll see some concrete examples of loops in the next hour.

We could use the following code to increment a variable by 1:

```
Dim SomeIntegerVariable as Integer = 0

...
SomeIntegerVariable = SomeIntegerVariable + 1
...
```

Initially, `SomeIntegerVariable` is declared with an initial value of 0. Sometime later we want to increment the `SomeIntegerVariable` by 1. This involves adding 1 to the current value of `SomeIntegerVariable` and then storing the new value back into `SomeIntegerVariable`. If `SomeIntegerVariable` equals 0, then

```
SomeIntegerVariable = SomeIntegerVariable + 1
```

will take the value of `SomeIntegerVariable` (0), add 1 to it (yielding 1), and store 1 into `SomeIntegerVariable`. The next time the line

```
SomeIntegerVariable = SomeIntegerVariable + 1
```

is encountered, `SomeIntegerVariable` will equal 1. This line of code will first evaluate `SomeIntegerVariable + 1`, which is the value of `SomeIntegerVariable` (1) plus 1. It will then assign this value (2) back into `SomeIntegerVariable`. As you can see, this line of code increments the value of SomeIntegerVariable by 1 regardless of the current value of SomeIntegerVariable.

Because incrementing the value of a variable is a common operation, Visual Basic provides an alternative assignment operator to reduce the amount of code we need to write. This shorthand operator, +=, has the form

```
variableName += value
```

and has the effect of adding *value* to the current value of *variableName* and then storing the resulting value of this addition back into *variableName*. The following two lines have the same meaning and produce the same results—they increment SomeIntegerVariable by 1:

```
SomeIntegerVariable = SomeIntegerVariable + 1
```

and

```
SomeIntegerVariable += 1
```

In addition to +=, a number of other shorthand assignment operators exist, as shown in Table 5.2. Along with the shorthand arithmetic operators, you'll notice the shorthand concatenation operator, &=. This and the += operator are the two shorthand assignment operators we'll use most often.

TABLE 5.2 The Shorthand Assignment Operators

Operator	Description
+=	*variable += value* adds *value* to the value of *variable* and then stores this resulting value back into *variable*.
-=	*variable -= value* subtracts *value* from the value of *variable* and then stores this resulting value back into *variable*.
*=	*variable *= value* multiplies *value* to the value of *variable* and then stores this resulting value back into *variable*.
/=	*variable /= value* divides *value* into the value of *variable* and then stores this resulting value back into *variable*. Recall that the / operator returns a nonintegral value.
&=	*variable &= value* concatenates *value* to the value of *variable* and then stores this resulting value back into *variable*.

Learning Visual Basic's Type Rules

Recall that Visual Basic is a strongly typed language. This implies that all variables declared in a Visual Basic program must be given an explicit data type.

Furthermore, the set of values that can be assigned to a variable is limited by the variable's type. That is, a variable that is of type `Integer` can be assigned only positive or negative whole number values that range between, approximately, positive two billion and negative two billion.

What happens, though, when you try to assign a nonintegral number to an integer variable, or when you try to assign an integer to a nonintegral numeric variable? What about when you try to assign a string variable to a nonintegral numeric variable, or an integer variable to a string variable?

Because Visual Basic is strongly typed, a value of one type cannot be assigned to a variable of a different type, which means you should not be able to assign an integer value to a nonintegral numeric variable. However, the following code will work:

```
Dim NonintegralVariable as Single
NonintegralVariable = 5
```

Why does the preceding code snippet not produce an error? After all, doesn't it violate the typing rules of Visual Basic by assigning an integer value to a nonintegral numeric variable?

Such an assignment is legal because, behind the scenes, Visual Basic **casts** the integer value (5) into a nonintegral value (5.0) and then assigns it to the nonintegral numeric variable.

Understanding Casting

Casting is the process of changing the type of a variable or value from one type to another. There are two types of casting: implicit casting and explicit casting.

Implicit casting is casting that occurs without any needed intervention or instructions by the programmer. In the previous code snippet, implicit casting is utilized because the integer variable 5 is cast to a nonintegral representation of 5.0 without any extra code provided by us, the programmers.

The documentation accompanying the .NET Framework SDK refers to implicit casting as **coercion**.

Explicit casting, on the other hand, requires that we, the programmers, explicitly indicate that a cast from one type to another should occur. To explicitly cast a variable from one type to another, use Visual Basic's built-in `CType` function, which has the following syntax:

```
CType(variableName, typeToCastTo)
```

The `CType` function casts the variable *`variableName`* from its current type to the type specified by *`typeToCastTo`*. The following code snippet explicitly casts a value of type `Integer` to type `Single`:

```
Dim NonintegralVariable as Single
NonintegralVariable = CType(5, Single)
```

Did you Know?

> In addition to Visual Basic's `CType` function, a `Convert` class in the .NET Framework contains functions of the form `To`*`DataType`*. In lieu of `CType`, we could use the `Convert` class's `ToSingle` function to explicitly cast a value of type `Integer` to type `Single`:
>
> ```
> NonintegralVariable = Convert.ToSingle(5)
> ```

Widening and Narrowing Casts

Visual Basic can be run in one of two modes: strict and nonstrict. In the strict mode, implicit casting is allowed only for **widening casts**. In a widening cast, the set of legal values for the initial data type is a subset of the set of legal values for the target data type. For example, a cast from an integer type to a nonintegral type is a widening cast because every possible integer value can be expressed as a nonintegral value.

Another example of a widening cast is casting a variable of type `Integer` to a variable of type `Long`. This is a widening cast because any legal value for an `Integer` is included in the set of legal values for a `Long`.

The opposite of a widening cast is a **narrowing cast**. Consider casting a nonintegral numeric type to an integer type. Variables of nonintegral types can hold values that can be accurately cast to integral types. The nonintegral value 5.0, for example, can be accurately cast to the integral value 5. But what about nonintegral values like 3.14? There is no integer value that can represent 3.14 precisely. When we're casting 3.14 to an integer, the resulting integer value is 3; the remainder is dropped.

> In a narrowing cast there is the potential for lost information. When we're casting 3.14 to an integer, the 0.14 portion of the number is lost in the narrowing cast.

Rules for Implicit Casting

Considering that narrowing casts can result in a loss of data, should Visual Basic allow for implicit narrow casts, or would it be prudent for the language to require that an explicit cast be used if a narrowing cast is required?

Truly strongly typed programming languages would require that all narrowing casts be explicit. In this case, if you tried to use code that would invoke an implicit narrowing cast, an error would result. That is, in a truly strongly typed programming language, the following code would produce an error:

```
Dim Quotient as Integer
Quotient = 8 / 4
```

The reason this would result in an error is that the / operator returns a nonintegral number (2.0), which must be cast to an integer to assign it to `Quotient`. However, this cast is a narrowing cast. In a truly strongly typed language, you would have to provide an implicit cast, like so:

```
Dim Quotient as Integer
Quotient = CType(8 / 4, Integer)
```

or

```
Dim Quotient as Integer
Quotient = Convert.ToInteger(8 / 4)
```

Older versions of Visual Basic allowed for implicit narrowing casts, however. Consequently, if Visual Basic implemented the rules inherent to truly strong typed programming languages, old Visual Basic code could not be reused as is in programs created with today's version of Visual Basic; rather, the programmer would have to alter the code to include explicit casting.

The designers of Visual Basic decided to take a middle-of-the-road approach. By default, implicit narrowing casts are permitted, meaning that the code

```
Dim x as Integer
x = 8 / 4
```

will run without error, assigning the integer value 2 to the variable `x`.

Watch Out!

> Keep in mind that casting a nonintegral number to an integer drops the remainder portion of the nonintegral number. That is, after the following code is executed, the value of `Quotient` will be 0:
>
> ```
> Dim Quotient as Integer
> Quotient = 3 / 4
> ```

To disallow implicit narrow casting in an ASP.NET page's source code portion, open the page's source code file and add `Option Strict On` at the top. With this option turned on, Visual Basic reports any implicit narrowing casts as errors in Visual Web Developer.

Listing 5.1 shows the contents of an ASP.NET page's source code file with `Option Strict On` (line 1). Because of this setting, Visual Web Developer reports that the implicit narrowing cast in the `Page_Load` event handler is an error (see Figure 5.2).

LISTING 5.1 Implicit Narrowing Casts Are Disallowed Because of the `Option Strict On` Setting

```
 1: Option Strict On
 2:
 3: Partial Class _Default
 4:     Inherits System.Web.UI.Page
 5:
 6:     Protected Sub Page_Load(ByVal sender As Object, ByVal e As
    ➥ System.EventArgs) Handles Me.Load
 7:         Dim Quotient As Integer
 8:         Quotient = 8 / 4    'An implicit narrowing cast!
 9:     End Sub
10: End Class
```

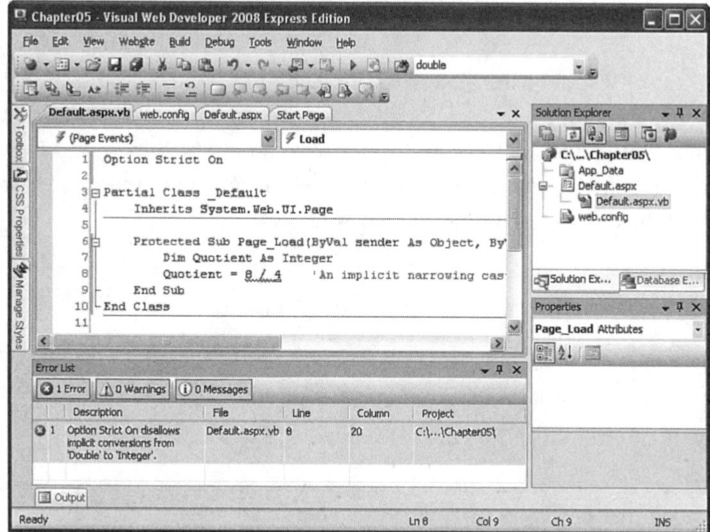

FIGURE 5.2 A compile-time error occurs if `Option Strict On` is set and an implicit narrowing cast is found.

By the Way

For this book, I will *not* be adding `Option Strict On` in the ASP.NET code files. In some code examples there may be implicit narrowing casts. If you choose to add `Option Strict On`, you will have to add the appropriate explicit cast syntax for these examples.

Summary

In this hour we examined the syntax and semantics for variables and operators in Visual Basic. Variables are defined by three properties: their name, their data type, and their value. The name and data type of a variable are specified when the variable is declared and are immutable. Variables are declared in Visual Basic via the `Dim` statement in the following fashion:

```
Dim variableName as type
```

The type of a variable dictates what values the variable can contain. Each type has a set of legal values. For example, a variable of type `Integer` can store negative or positive whole numbers that range from –2,147,483,648 to 2,147,483,647.

A variable is assigned a value via an assignment statement, which is = in Visual Basic. Along with the assignment operator, there are a number of other operators in Visual Basic, including arithmetic operators, like +, -, *, and /; comparison operators, like <, <=, >, >=, =, and <>; and the string concatenation operator, &.

When you're assigning a value to a variable, it is vital that the type of the value matches the type of the variable. If the types do not match, Visual Basic may be able to implicitly cast the value's type into the needed type.

Casts can be implicit or explicit, narrowing or widening. An explicit cast can be declared by using Visual Basic's built-in `CType` function or by using the `Convert` class's methods. Visual Basic, by default, allows for implicit, narrowing casts. However, when you specify `Option Strict On` in ASP.NET web page's source code file, implicit narrowing casts are not allowed.

In the next hour we will look at control structures in Visual Basic. Control structures allow for changes in the program's instruction execution. Commonly, this is translated into having specified portions of code executed repeatedly until some condition is met, or encapsulating a series of related instructions in a subroutine or function, which can then be invoked in a single line of code.

Q&A

Q. *Are the shorthand assignment operators used often in practice?*

A. Visual Basic contains a number of shorthand assignment operators, such as +=, -=, *=, and so on. These operators first perform a mathematical computation (such as addition in the case of +=) and then an assignment. They are used in the following form:

```
variable += expression
```

They have the effect of applying the operation to the value of *`expression`* and the current value of *`variable`*, and then storing the result back in *`variable`*.

In earlier versions of Visual Basic, the shorthand assignment operators did not exist. Therefore, if a developer wanted to increment a variable by one, she'd have to use the more verbose code:

```
variable = variable + 1
```

in contrast to the more succinct option that is available in Visual Basic today:

```
variable += 1
```

Shorthand assignment operators are used quite often in practice because of this succinctness. In fact, in a number of examples throughout this book, we'll see these shorthand assignment operators in use.

Q. ***Are there any advantages to using `Option Explicit On`?***

A. Recall that specifying `Option Strict On` in the ASP.NET page's code file configures Visual Basic so that implicit narrowing casts are not allowed. Setting it to `Option Strict Off` (or simply omitting the statement) allows implicit narrowing casts.

Personally, I prefer to omit the `Option Strict On` statement because it leaves the code less cluttered. However, implicit casting is more error prone because a variable may be automatically cast from one type to another without your knowledge. As we discussed earlier in this hour, the / operator returns a non-integral result. The following code, however, will not produce an error message unless you've added `Option Strict On`:

```
Dim Quotient as Integer
Quotient = 10 / 3
```

Here, the value of `10 / 3` will be 3.33333.... However, because the result is assigned to `Integer` the value 3.33333... is implicitly cast to an `Integer` value (3), truncating the decimal portion.

To see why implicit casting can lead to potential errors, imagine that at some point later in your code, you display a particular message if `Quotient` is greater than 3. This conditional code will never execute because `Quotient` is equal to 3, not greater than 3.

Workshop

Quiz

1. What is the one mutable property of a variable, and how is it changed throughout the execution of the program?

2. If you wanted a variable to store whole numbers with values from 0 up to a value no greater than 10,000, what data type should you use?

3. Does the following code contain an implicit narrowing cast?

```
Dim a, b as Integer
b = 10
a = b / 2
```

4. Does the following statement evaluate to `True` or `False`?

```
(4 / 3) = 1
```

5. Does the following statement evaluate to `True` or `False`?

```
CType(4 / 3, Integer) = 1
```

Answers

1. The value of a variable is the only mutable property; the name and data type are immutable. The value of a variable is changed via the assignment statement, which assigns a new value to a variable.

2. You could use the `Short`, `Integer`, or `Long` data types. In the examples throughout this book, when storing integer data we will use the `Integer` data type.

3. Yes. The / operator always produces a nonintegral result, so `b / 2` will return the value 5.0. Because this value must be cast to an integer to be assigned to `a`, a narrowing cast must be performed. The cast is implicit because there is no call to `CType` to explicitly cast the nonintegral type to an integer type.

4. It evaluates to `False`. The division `4 / 3` will produce the value 1.333333..., which is not equal to 1.

5. It evaluates to `True`. The division `4 / 3` will produce the value 1.333333..., but when this is cast to type `Integer`, the remainder will be truncated, resulting in the value 1. Because 1 = 1, this will return `True`.

Exercises

There are no exercises for this hour mainly because all that we know how to do in Visual Basic at this point is declare variables and assign values to these variables.

In the next hour we will look at Visual Basic control structures, which allows for code to be executed repeatedly or conditionally. After we have covered this material, you'll be ready for some Visual Basic exercises.

HOUR 6

Managing Program Flow with Visual Basic's Control Structures

In this hour, we will cover

- Using conditional statements
- Identifying the types of looping constructs Visual Basic supports
- Using `For` loops
- Using `Do` loops
- Understanding the differences between subroutines and functions
- Using subroutines and functions

In the preceding hour we looked at variables and operators in Visual Basic, two important concepts in any programming language. In this hour we examine an equally important aspect of all programming languages: **control structures**.

Control structures are constructs that alter the control flow during a program's execution. Without control structures, programs are executed by running the first line of code, then the second, and so on, where each line of code is executed precisely once in the order in which it appears.

Control structures, however, alter the order of instruction execution and can allow for a group of instructions to execute more than once. In this hour we examine conditionals, loops, subroutines, and functions.

Understanding Control Structures

A computer is good at doing one thing and one thing only—executing a series of instructions. From the computer's point of view, it is handed a sequence of instructions to execute, and it does so accurately and quickly.

The instructions executed by the computer are spelled out using a programming language, such as Visual Basic. For example, if you want the computer to create an integer variable, assign the value 4 to it, and then multiply the variable's value by 2, you could use the following code:

```
'Create a variable of type Integer and assign it the value 4
Dim SomeVariable as Integer = 4

'Multiply the value of SomeVariable by 2
someVariable *= 2
```

When this program is executed, the first line of code is executed (the `Dim` statement), which declares a variable of type `Integer` and assigns it the value 4. Next, the code `SomeVariable *= 2` is executed, which multiplies the value of `SomeVariable` by 2 and then assigns the result (8) to `SomeVariable`.

By the Way

> The lines of code in this snippet are executed exactly once, with the first line of code executing before the second. This style of code execution is known as **sequential flow.**

But what if we want to execute the `SomeVariable *= 2` line of code only if `SomeVariable` is less than 5? Or perhaps we want to continue to double the `SomeVariable`'s value until it is greater than 100. To perform conditional or repetitive logic, we need to use control structures.

There are three primary types of control structures:

- The conditional control structure, which executes a set of instructions only if some condition is met
- Looping control structures, which repeatedly execute a set of instructions until some condition is met
- Modularizing control structures, which group sets of instructions into modules that can be invoked at various places in the program

In this hour we examine the syntax and semantics of all three types of control structures.

Exploring the Conditional Control Structure

The conditional control structure is used to conditionally execute a set of instructions. The syntax for the conditional control structure, in its simplest form, is given as

```
If condition Then
   Instruction1
   Instruction2
   ...
   InstructionN
End If
```

Here, *`condition`* is a Boolean expression, one that evaluates to either `True` or `False`. If *`condition`* evaluates to `True`, instructions *`Instruction1`* through *`InstructionN`* are executed. If *`condition`* evaluates to `False`, these instructions are skipped and therefore are not executed.

By the Way

Conditional statements are commonly referred to as `If` statements.

To practice using conditional statements, let's create an ASP.NET page that displays either "Good morning," "Good afternoon," or "Good evening," depending on the hour of the day.

Did you Know?

The current hour can be determined via `DateTime.Now.Hour`. This returns an integer value between 0 and 23, where 0 is midnight, 9 is 9:00 in the morning, 13 is 1:00 in the afternoon, and so on.

To start, create a new ASP.NET website on your computer's file system. Next, add a new ASP.NET page named `TimeAppropriateMessage.aspx`. From the Toolbox, drag and drop a Label Web control onto the page. Next, change the Label's `ID` property to `Message` and clear out its `Text` property. We will use this Label to display the "Good morning," "Good afternoon," or "Good evening" message.

At this point your screen should look similar to Figure 6.1.

We now need to add code that displays a message based on the current hour. This code needs to execute when the page first loads, so create an event handler for the page's `Load` event. As previously discussed, you can accomplish this in one of two ways: either double-click the page in the Design view, or go to the ASP.NET page's source code portion and select (Page Events) from the left drop-down list and Load from the right one.

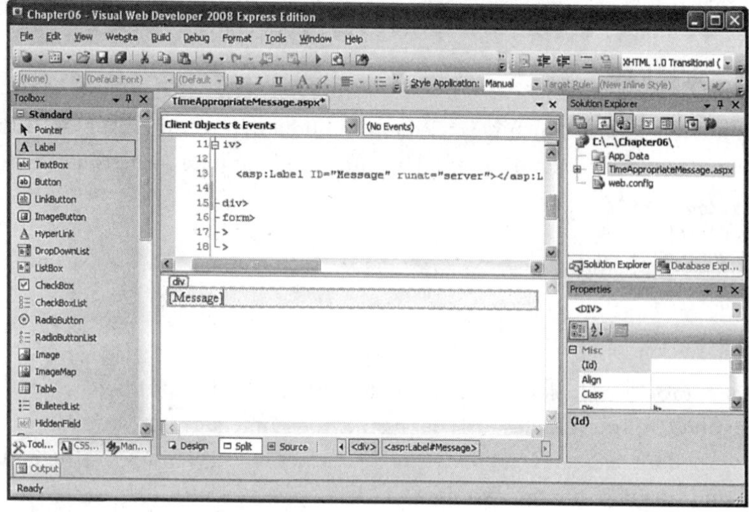

FIGURE 6.1
A Label control has been added.

After you have created the Page_Load event handler, enter the code shown in Listing 6.1.

LISTING 6.1 A Different Message Is Displayed Based on the Current Hour

```
Partial Class TimeAppropriateMessage
    Inherits System.Web.UI.Page

    Protected Sub Page_Load(ByVal sender As Object, ByVal e As
    ➥ System.EventArgs) Handles Me.Load
        If DateTime.Now.Hour >= 6 And DateTime.Now.Hour < 12 Then
            Message.Text = "Good morning."
        End If

        If DateTime.Now.Hour >= 12 And DateTime.Now.Hour <= 17 Then
            Message.Text = "Good afternoon."
        End If

        If DateTime.Now.Hour > 17 Or DateTime.Now.Hour < 6 Then
            Message.Text = "Good evening."
        End If
    End Sub
End Class
```

After entering the code in Listing 6.1, view the page through a browser by going to the Debug menu and choosing Start Without Debugging. You should see the message "Good morning" if the current hour is after 6 a.m. but before noon, "Good afternoon" if it's noon or later but before 5 p.m., and "Good evening" if it's after 5 p.m. and before 6 a.m.

By the Way

> Because the code in Listing 6.1 is executed on the web server, the message displayed is based on the current time of the machine where the web server is running. If your ASP.NET web page is being hosted by a web-hosting company that is in another time zone, the output you see may not be reflective of the current time in your time zone.

The code in Listing 6.1 works by using three `If` statements. The first one (lines 5–7) checks to see whether the current hour is greater than or equal to 6 and less than 12.

Note that the condition on line 5 contains two conditional statements: `DateTime.Now.Hour >= 6` and `DateTime.Now.Hour < 12`. These two conditions are joined by the keyword `And`. Visual Basic contains two keywords for joining conditional statements: `And` and `Or`. The semantics of `And` and `Or` are just like their English counterparts. That is, the expression *`condition1`* `And` *`condition2`* will return `True` if and only if both *`condition1`* and *`condition2`* are true, whereas the expression *`condition1`* `Or` *`condition2`* will return `True` if either *`condition1`* or *`condition2`* is true (or if both *`condition1`* and *`condition2`* are true).

Did you Know?

> Parentheses can be used to specify the order of operations and help make compound conditionals more readable. For example, if we wanted to run a sequence of instructions if the hour was between 9 and 12, or if the hour was 17, we could use a statement like this:

```
If (DateTime.Now.Hour >= 9 And DateTime.Now.Hour <= 12) Or
➥ (DateTime.Now.Hour = 17) then
   ' ... Instructions ...
End If
```

So, if the current hour is both greater than or equal to 6 and the current hour is less than 12, then the condition on line 2 is true, and line 3 will be executed, which causes the message "Good morning" to be displayed.

Another conditional statement is found on line 9. This one checks to see whether the current hour is between noon and 5 p.m. (Because the hour is returned as a value between 0 and 23, 5 p.m. is returned as 17.) If the hour is both greater than or equal to 12 and less than or equal to 17, line 7 is executed and the message "Good afternoon" is displayed.

A third condition on line 13 checks to see whether the hour is greater than 17 or whether the hour is less than 6. If either of these conditions is true, the code on line 11 is executed, which displays the message "Good evening."

All three conditional statements in Listing 6.1 are executed, but precisely one of the conditions will return `True`, meaning that only one message is displayed.

Executing Instructions If the Conditional Is False

The `If` statement executes a set of instructions if the supplied conditional is true, but what if we want to execute some instructions if the condition is false? For example, suppose that some string variable named `password` contains the password for the user visiting our website. If the `password` variable is equal to the string "shazaam", we want to display some sensitive information; if, however, the password is not "shazaam", the user has entered an incorrect password, and we need to display a warning message.

We can accomplish this using the following code:

```
If password = "shazaam" then
  'Display sensitive information
End If

If password <> "shazaam" then
  'Display message informing the user they've entered an
  'incorrect password
End If
```

However, there is an easier way to accomplish this using the `Else` clause. The source code that appears within the `Else` portion is executed when the condition evaluates to `False`. The general form of an `If` statement with an `Else` clause is

```
If condition Then
   Instruction1
   Instruction2
   ...
   InstructionN
Else
   ElseInstruction1
   ElseInstruction2
   ...
   ElseInstructionN
End If
```

If *`condition`* is true, *`Instruction1`* through *`InstructionN`* are executed, and *`ElseInstruction1`* through *`ElseInstructionN`* are skipped. If, however, *`condition`* is false, *`ElseInstruction1`* through *`ElseInstructionN`* are executed, and *`Instruction1`* through *`InstructionN`* are skipped.

Using the Else statement, we can reduce the password-checking code from two conditionals down to one, as the following code illustrates:

```
If password = "shazaam" then
  'Display sensitive information
Else
  'Display message informing the user they've entered an
  'incorrect password
End If
```

An If statement cannot have more than one Else clause.

Performing Another If Statement When the Condition Is False

In addition to the Else statement, If statements can have zero to many ElseIf statements. An ElseIf clause follows an If statement, much like the Else, and has a condition statement like the If statement. The instructions directly following the ElseIf are executed only if the If statement's condition, as well as all of the preceding ElseIf conditions, are false and the condition of the ElseIf in question is true.

This description may sound a bit confusing. An example should help clear things up. First, note that the general form of an If statement with ElseIf clauses is as follows:

```
If condition Then
   Instruction1
   Instruction2
   ...
   InstructionN
ElseIf elseIf1Condition
   ElseIf1Instruction1
   ElseIf1Instruction2
   ...
   ElseIf1InstructionN
ElseIf elseIf2Condition
   ElseIf2Instruction1
   ElseIf2Instruction2
   ...
   ElseIf2InstructionN
...
ElseIf elseIfNCondition
   ElseIfNInstruction1
   ElseIfNInstruction2
   ...
   ElseIfNInstructionN
```

```
Else
   ElseInstruction1
   ElseInstruction2
   ...
   ElseInstructionN
End If
```

If `condition` is true, instructions `Instruction1` through `InstructionN` are executed and the other instructions are skipped. If, however, `condition` is false, the first `ElseIf` condition, `elseIf1Condition`, is evaluated. If `elseIf1Condition` is true, instructions `ElseIf1Instruction1` through `ElseIf1InstructionN` are executed and all other instructions are skipped. If, however, `elseIf1Condition` is false, the second `ElseIf` condition, `elseIf2Condition`, is evaluated. If it is true, then instructions `ElseIf2Instruction1` through `ElseIf2InstructionN` are executed. If, however, `elseIf2Condition` is false, the third `ElseIf` condition is evaluated, and so on. If the `If` statement's initial condition is false and if all the `ElseIf` conditions are false, the `Else`'s instructions (`ElseInstruction1` through `ElseInstructionN`) are executed.

Take a moment to look back at Listing 6.1; notice that we used three conditions: one to check whether the time was between 6 a.m. and noon, one to check whether the time was between noon and 5 p.m., and one to check whether the time was after 5 p.m. or before 6 a.m.

We can accomplish this with a single `If` statement using either two `ElseIf`s or one `ElseIf` and an `Else`. The code for using two `ElseIf`s is as follows:

```
If DateTime.Now.Hour >= 6 And DateTime.Now.Hour < 12 then
  Message.Text = "Good morning."
ElseIf DateTime.Now.Hour >= 12 And DateTime.Now.Hour <= 17 then
  Message.Text = "Good afternoon."
ElseIf DateTime.Now.Hour > 17 Or DateTime.Now.Hour < 6 then
  Message.Text = "Good evening."
End If
```

The code for using an `ElseIf` and an `Else` looks like this:

```
If DateTime.Now.Hour >= 6 And DateTime.Now.Hour < 12 then
  Message.Text = "Good morning."
ElseIf DateTime.Now.Hour >= 12 And DateTime.Now.Hour <= 17 then
  Message.Text = "Good afternoon."
Else
  Message.Text = "Good evening."
End If
```

Working with Visual Basic's Looping Control Structures

The next three sections cover two of Visual Basic's looping constructs: `For ... Next` loops and `Do ... Loop` loops. Looping control structures allow for a set of instructions to be executed a repeated number of times. The number of times the code is repeated can be a fixed number of times, such as with `For ... Next` loops, or repeated until some condition is met, such as with `Do ... Loop` loops.

These two looping constructs are fundamentally equivalent, although they have differing syntax. They both accomplish the same task—repeating a set of instructions a certain number of times.

Using `For ... Next` Loops

If you need to execute a certain set of instructions a specific number of times, consider using the `For ... Next` looping control structure. The `For ... Next` loop has the following syntax:

```
For integerVariable = start to stop
  Instruction1
  Instruction2
  ...
  InstructionN
Next
```

Did you Know?

`For ... Next` loops are often referred to as `For` loops.

The semantics of the `For` loop are as follows: The variable *`integerVariable`*, which should be an integer variable type (`Short`, `Integer`, or `Long`), is referred to as the **looping variable**. It is initially assigned the value *`start`*.

By the Way

The looping variable does not necessarily need to be an integer; it can be any numeric type. However, in practice the overwhelming majority of `For ... Next` loops use an integer looping variable.

After the looping variable is assigned the *`start`* value, instructions *`Instruction1`* through *`InstructionN`* are executed. After these instructions are executed, the value of the looping variable is incremented by one. If, at this point, the value of the looping variable is less than or equal to *`stop`*, the process is repeated—instructions *`Instruction1`* through *`InstructionN`* are executed again and the value of the looping variable is incremented. The loop continues to execute, with the value of the looping variable incremented at each iteration, until the looping variable is greater than *stop*.

By the Way

Instructions *Instruction1* through *InstructionN* are commonly referred to as the **body** of the loop.

So, to display the message "Hello, World!" in the user's browser three times, put the following For ... Next loop in the ASP.NET web page's Page_Load event handler:

```
Dim i as Integer
For i = 1 to 3
  LabelWebControl.Text &= "Hello, World!"
Next
```

The code starts by creating an integer variable named i. When the For loop executes, i is initially assigned the value 1. Then the body of the loop is executed, which concatenates the string "Hello, World!" to the current value of some Label Web control's Text property. (Recall that &= is an operator that takes the value of the variable on the left side and concatenates to it the value on the right side, saving the resulting concatenation back to the variable on the left side.)

After the body finishes executing, the value of i is incremented by one. A check is then made to see whether i's current value is less than or equal to 3. At this point, i equals 2, so the loop body is executed again, which again concatenates "Hello, World!" to the Label's Text property. As before, i is incremented and compared to 3. i is still less than or equal to 3, so the loop body executes again. After concatenating "Hello, World!" to the Label's Text property, i is (again) incremented and now equals 4. At this point, i is not less than or equal to 3, so the For loop body does not execute. Instead, the line of code immediately following the Next executes.

By the Way

Incrementing (or Decrementing) the Looping Variable by Values Other Than One

The standard For loop syntax increments the looping variable by one after each iteration of the loop body. If you need to increment (or decrement) the looping variable by a different value, add the Step keyword to the For statement like so:

```
For integerVariable = start to stop Step stepAmount
  Instruction1
  Instruction2
  ...
  InstructionN
Next
```

By the Way

For example, the following `For ... Next` loop displays the even numbers between 0 and 10 in a Label Web control:

```
Dim evens as Integer
For evens = 0 to 10 Step 2
  LabelWebControl.Text &= evens & " is an even number.<br />"
Next
```

To have the looping variable decremented at each iteration, set the step amount to a negative value.

Do ... Loop Loops

The `Do ... Loop` loop, often referred to as a `Do` loop, executes the loop body while a condition holds true. The syntax for such a loop is as follows:

```
Do While condition
  Instruction1
  Instruction2
  ...
  InstructionN
Loop
```

As with conditional statements, *`condition`* is an expression that evaluates to a Boolean value. When the `Do` loop is encountered, the condition is checked. If it evaluates to `True`, the loop body—instructions *`Instruction1`* through *`InstructionN`*—is executed. After the loop body has executed, the condition is checked again. If it is still `True`, the loop body is executed again. This process repeats until the condition evaluates to `False` after the execution of the loop body.

Did you Know?

A `Do` loop can also be constructed so that its loop body is executed repeatedly *until* a condition is met. The syntax for this form of the `Do` loop is

```
Do Until condition
  Instruction1
  Instruction2
  ...
  InstructionN
Loop
```

The following `Do` loop displays the even numbers between 0 and 10 in a Label Web control:

```
Dim number as Integer = 0
Do While number <= 10
  LabelWebControl.Text &= number & " is an even number.<br />"

  number += 2
Loop
```

Here, the `Integer` variable `number` is created and assigned the value 0. The `Do` loop then iterates while the value of `number` is less than or equal to 10. Because 0 (number's initial value) is less than or equal to 10, the loop body executes and the message "0 is an even number" is appended to a Label Web control's `Text` property. The value of `number` is incremented by 2 and the `Do` loop's condition is checked. Because the value of `number` is 2, which is less than or equal to 10, the loop body is executed again. This continues until the end of the sixth iteration, after which `number` has the value 12.

`Do` loops bodies usually have a line of code that updates the variable used in the condition. If you forget this line of code, your loop will become an **infinite loop**, one that never ends. For example, imagine what would happen if we removed the `number += 2` line of code from the previous `Do` loop example. Clearly, the value of number would remain 0 after each iteration, meaning that the body would continuously execute, never ending.

Exploring the Modularizing Control Structures: Subroutines and Functions

In addition to loops and conditionals, Visual Basic allows for **modularizing control structures**. A modularizing control structure may contain many lines of source code, can accept zero to many input parameters, and can optionally return a value. Furthermore, these modules can then be called from any location in the Visual Basic code.

There are two flavors of modularization control structures: **subroutines** and **functions**. Subroutines are modularization control structures that do not return any value, whereas functions always return a value. Subroutines and functions are handy for encapsulating programming logic.

Let's use a subroutine to encapsulate the logic behind displaying a repeated text message. Start by creating a new ASP.NET web page named `SubroutineLesson1.aspx`. Add a Label to the page's HTML portion, clearing out its `Text` property and settings its `ID` to `Output`. Next, create an event handler for the page's `Load` event. Imagine that we want this ASP.NET page to display the string "Welcome to my Website" precisely four times. To accomplish this, we can use a simple `For` loop that concatenates the string "Welcome to my Website" to the `Output` Label's `Text` property in the loop body.

Listing 6.2 contains the source code that you should enter into the page's source code portion.

LISTING 6.2 The `Page_Load` Event Handler Displays a Message Four Times

```
 1: Partial Class SubroutineLesson1
 2:     Inherits System.Web.UI.Page
 3:
 4:     Protected Sub Page_Load(ByVal sender As Object, ByVal e As
    ➥ System.EventArgs) Handles Me.Load
 5:         Output.Text = String.Empty
 6:
 7:         Dim i As Integer
 8:         For i = 1 To 4
 9:             Output.Text &= "Welcome to my Website<br />"
10:         Next
11:     End Sub
12: End Class
```

Notice that on line 5 we clear out the Label Web control's `Text` property programmatically. We accomplish this by setting the `Text` property to an empty string. An empty string can be denoted in one of two ways: using `String.Empty`, as on line 5, or using a string literal with no contents (`""`). The code's output would be identical if we replaced line 5 with `output.Text = ""`.

After you have entered this code, view the page through a browser. Notice that this web page displays the message "Welcome to my Website" four times, as shown in Figure 6.2.

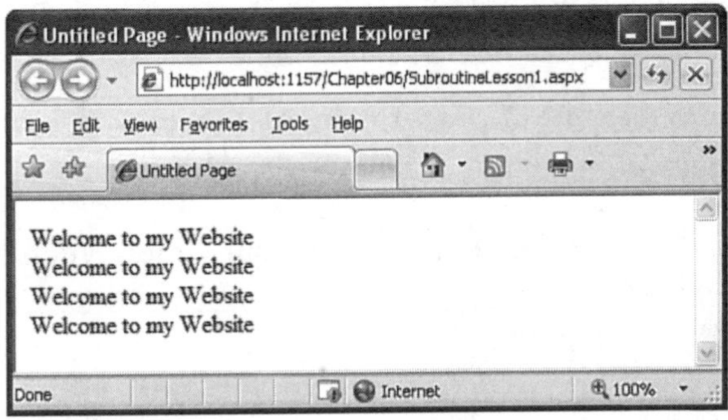

FIGURE 6.2
The "Welcome to my Website" message is displayed four times.

Now, imagine that we also wanted a Button Web control on the web page that, when clicked, would display the message "Welcome to my Website" four times as well.

To accomplish this, we first need to add a Button Web control to the page. Return to the HTML portion of the ASP.NET page and drag and drop a Button from the Toolbox onto the page. Set the Button's `ID` to `DisplayMessage` and its `Text` property to **Display Message**. At this point your screen should look similar to Figure 6.3.

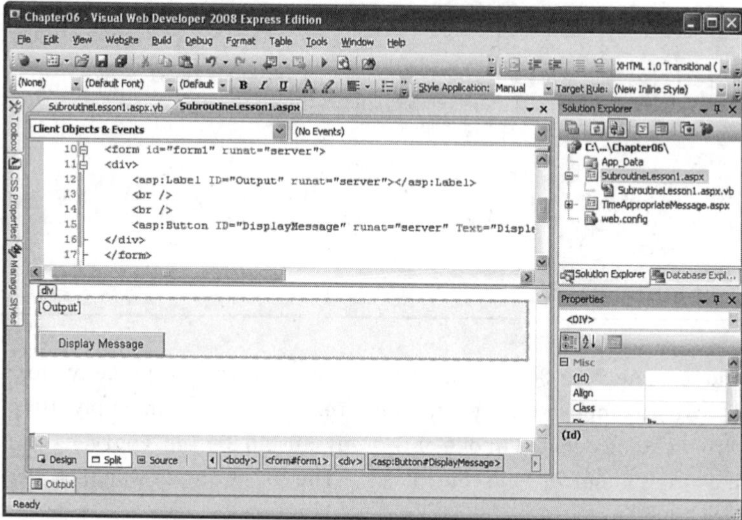

FIGURE 6.3
A Button Web control has been added.

Recall from our discussions in Hour 4, "Designing, Creating, and Testing ASP.NET Web Pages," that when the Button is clicked, the Button's `Click` event handler is executed. Therefore, add an event handler for the Button's `Click` event. To have the message "Welcome to my Website" displayed four times when the Button is clicked, copy the code in the `Page_Load` event handler to the Button's `Click` event handler.

Listing 6.3 contains the ASP.NET page's source code portion with the added `Click` event handler (lines 11 through 16), which you should enter.

LISTING 6.3 The Message Is Displayed Four Times When the Button Web Control Is Clicked

```
 1: Partial Class SubroutineLesson1
 2:     Inherits System.Web.UI.Page
 3:
 4:     Protected Sub Page_Load(ByVal sender As Object, ByVal e As
        ➥ System.EventArgs) Handles Me.Load
 5:         Output.Text = String.Empty
 6:
 7:         Dim i As Integer
 8:         For i = 1 To 4
 9:             Output.Text &= "Welcome to my Website<br />"
10:         Next
```

LISTING 6.3 Continued

```
    End Sub

    Protected Sub DisplayMessage_Click(ByVal sender As Object, ByVal e
    ➥ As System.EventArgs) Handles DisplayMessage.Click
        Dim i As Integer
        For i = 1 To 4
            Output.Text &= "Welcome to my Website<br />"
        Next
    End Sub
End Class
```

With this addition to the ASP.NET web page, when you first visit the web page, the message "Welcome to my Website" is displayed four times (from the Page_Load event handler). Additionally, the "Display Message" Button is displayed. Figure 6.4 shows SubroutineLesson1.aspx after the code from both Listings 6.2 and 6.3 has been added to the source code portion.

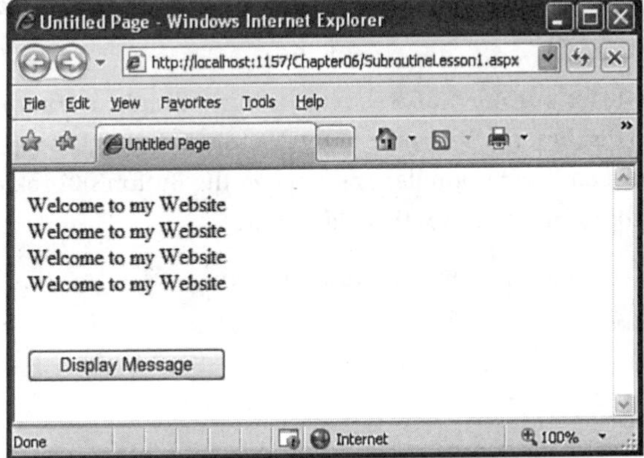

FIGURE 6.4
A Button Web control is displayed after the message.

When the button is clicked, the ASP.NET page is posted back, which causes the Button's Click event handler to execute. In addition to the Button's Click event handler being executed, the Page_Load event handler is executed as well because the page is being loaded again. This causes the message "Welcome to my Website" to be displayed eight times, as shown in Figure 6.5.

By the Way

In Hour 4, we briefly discussed the series of actions that happen when a Button Web control is clicked. If you are still a bit confused, don't worry; we'll be covering this topic more in Hour 9, "Web Form Basics."

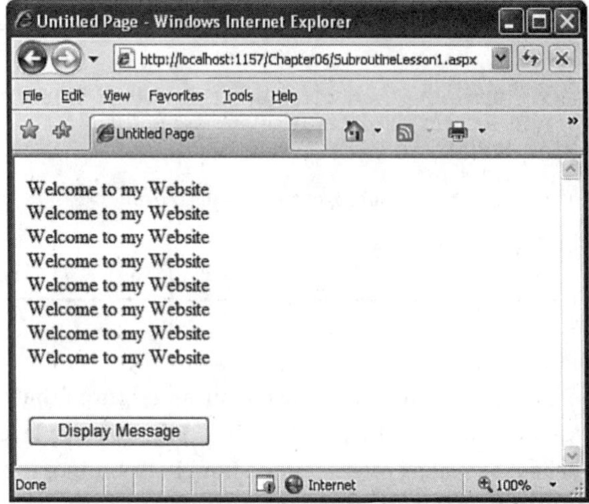

FIGURE 6.5 The "Welcome to my Website" message is displayed eight times after the button is clicked.

Reducing Code Redundancy Using Subroutines and Functions

Although the code for our ASP.NET web page is fairly simple, it contains redundancies. The code to display the "Welcome to my Website" message is repeated twice: once in the `Page_Load` event handler and once in the Button's `Click` event handler. We can use a subroutine to reduce this redundancy.

Subroutines are created using the following syntax:

```
Sub SubroutineName()
  Instruction1
  Instruction2
  ...
  InstructionN
End Sub
```

The code that appears between the `Sub` and `End Sub` lines is referred to as the **body** of the subroutine and is executed whenever the subroutine is **called**. A subroutine is called using the following syntax:

```
SubroutineName()
```

For our ASP.NET web page, let's create a subroutine named `ShowWelcomeMessage` that has as its body the code to display the "Welcome to my Website" message four times. We can then replace the code that displays the message four times in the `Page_Load` and Button `Click` event handlers with a call to the `ShowWelcomeMessage` subroutine.

Replace the source code contents entered from Listings 6.2 and 6.3 with the source code provided in Listing 6.4.

LISTING 6.4 **The Code to Display the "Welcome to my Website" Message Is Moved to a Subroutine**

```
 1: Partial Class SubroutineLesson1
 2:     Inherits System.Web.UI.Page
 3:
 4:     Protected Sub Page_Load(ByVal sender As Object, ByVal e As
    ➥ System.EventArgs) Handles Me.Load
 5:         Output.Text = String.Empty
 6:
 7:         ShowWelcomeMessage()
 8:     End Sub
 9:
10:     Protected Sub DisplayMessage_Click(ByVal sender As Object, ByVal
    ➥ e As System.EventArgs) Handles DisplayMessage.Click
11:         ShowWelcomeMessage()
12:     End Sub
13:
14:     Private Sub ShowWelcomeMessage()
15:         Dim i As Integer
16:         For i = 1 To 4
17:             Output.Text &= "Welcome to my Website<br />"
18:         Next
19:     End Sub
20: End Class
```

Listing 6.4 has encapsulated the code to display the "Welcome to my Website" message four times in a subroutine (lines 14–19). The body of the subroutine can be invoked from anywhere else in the ASP.NET page's source code portion by calling the subroutine (see lines 7 and 11).

View the page through a browser by going to the Debug menu and choosing Start Without Debugging. Upon first loading the page, you should see the same output shown in Figure 6.4: the message "Welcome to my Website" displayed four times, followed by the "Display Message" Button. By clicking the Button, you should see the output shown in Figure 6.5.

Strive to reduce code redundancy by modularizing repeated code into a subroutine or function. Redundant code has a number of disadvantages, such as making the code harder to read (because of its increased length), harder to update (because changes to the redundant code require updating the code in multiple places), and more prone to typos (because you have to reenter the code multiple times, the chances of making a mistake increase).

Passing in Parameters to a Subroutine or Function

In Listing 6.4 we used a subroutine to display a message four times. But what if we wanted to generalize the `ShowWelcomeMessage` subroutine so that instead of always displaying the message "Welcome to my Website", any message could be displayed four times?

Subroutines can be generalized in this manner through the use of `parameters`. A parameter is a value that is passed into the subroutine when the subroutine is called. A subroutine must explicitly spell out what parameters are allowed in its definition, as the following syntax illustrates:

```
Sub SubroutineName(Param1 as Type, Param2 as Type, ... ParamN as Type)
  Instruction1
  Instruction2
  ...
  InstructionN
End Sub
```

`Param1` through *`ParamN`* are referred to as the subroutine's `parameters`. A subroutine may have zero to many parameters. Because Visual Basic is a strongly typed language, each parameter must have a type. The instructions in the subroutine's body can access these parameters just like they would any other variable.

Let's take a moment to rewrite the `ShowWelcomeMessage` subroutine from Listing 6.4 so that any message can be displayed four times. To accomplish this, the `ShowWelcomeMessage` subroutine needs to accept a string parameter that indicates the message to display:

```
Sub ShowWelcomeMessage(ByVal message as String)
  Dim i as Integer
  For i = 1 to 4
    Output.Text &= message
  Next
End Sub
```

With this change, the `ShowWelcomeMessage` subroutine accepts a parameter named `message` of type `String`. In the subroutine's body, instead of using `Output.Text &= "Welcome to my Website<br />"`, which would display the message "Welcome to my Website", we use `Output.Text &= message`, which concatenates the value of the `message` variable to the `Output` Label's `Text` property.

Use the following code to call this updated version of the `ShowWelcomeMessage` subroutine:

```
ShowWelcomeMessage(messageToDisplay)
```

To display the message “Welcome to my Website”, call the subroutine like this:

```
ShowWelcomeMessage("Welcome to my Website<br>")
```

By the Way

Each subroutine parameter has a keyword that specifies low-level details on how the parameter is sent from the caller to the subroutine. There are two possible values: `ByVal` and `ByRef`. A thorough discussion of these two keywords and the effects they have is beyond the scope of this book. For all examples in this book, we'll be using `ByVal`, which is the default. In fact, when typing in the subroutine parameters, you can omit the `ByVal` keyword; Visual Web Developer will add it automatically.

Let's use this updated version of the `ShowWelcomeMessage` subroutine to create a page whose output is exactly identical to that of Listing 6.4. Start by creating a new ASP.NET web page named `SubroutineLesson2.aspx`. As with `SubroutineLesson1.aspx`, add Label and Button Web controls to the page with the same `ID` and `Text` values used previously. Also, be sure to create the event handlers for the page's `Load` event and the Button's `Click` event. After you have done this, enter the source code in Listing 6.5.

LISTING 6.5 The `ShowWelcomeMessage` **Subroutine Accepts a Parameter**

```
Partial Class SubroutineLesson2
    Inherits System.Web.UI.Page

    Protected Sub Page_Load(ByVal sender As Object, ByVal e As
    ➥ System.EventArgs) Handles Me.Load
        Output.Text = String.Empty

        ShowWelcomeMessage("Welcome to my Website<br>")
    End Sub

    Protected Sub DisplayMessage_Click(ByVal sender As Object, ByVal
    ➥ e As System.EventArgs) Handles DisplayMessage.Click
        ShowWelcomeMessage("Welcome to my Website<br>")
    End Sub

    Sub ShowWelcomeMessage(ByVal message As String)
        Dim i As Integer
        For i = 1 To 4
            Output.Text &= message
        Next
    End Sub
End Class
```

When viewing this page through a browser, you should initially see the same output shown in Figure 6.4; clicking the Button should display the output shown in Figure 6.5.

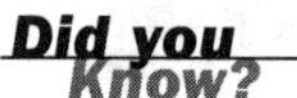

A subroutine may have more than one parameter. To create a subroutine with multiple parameters, list the parameters and their types using a comma to separate each parameter.

Returning Values with Functions

Visual Basic's two modularizing control structures—subroutines and functions—have quite a bit in common. Both can have zero to many parameters. Both are used to reduce code redundancy and encapsulate logic. The key difference between subroutines and functions is that a function returns a value, whereas a subroutine does not. In Listing 6.5 we made `ShowWelcomeMessage` a subroutine instead of a function because no value is returned. However, there are times when some modularized bit of logic needs to return a value, and in those cases we would use a function.

In Hour 4 we created a financial calculator web page that accepted some inputs—the mortgage amount, the interest rate, and so on—and determined the monthly cost. This was accomplished in a little less than 20 lines of code and was coded directly within the Button control's `Click` event handler. A more modular approach would be to place this logic in a function and then have the `Click` event handler call the function.

A function's syntax differs from a subroutine's syntax in a few ways. First, instead of using the `Sub ... End Sub` keywords, use `Function` and `End Function`. Second, because a function returns a value, we must specify the type of the value returned by the function. Finally, in the function body, we need to actually return some value. This is accomplished via the `Return` keyword.

The general syntax of a function is as follows:

```
Function FunctionName(Param1 as Type, ..., ParamN as Type) as ReturnType
  Instruction1
  Instruction2
  ...
  InstructionN
End Function
```

The *`ReturnType`* specifies the type of the value returned by the function. As with subroutines, functions can have zero to many input parameters. Functions are called in an identical fashion to subroutines, but because functions return a value, you may see a function call in an expression, like so:

```
Dim costPerMonth as Decimal
costPerMonth = ComputeCostPerMonth(P, r, t)
```

Here `ComputeCostPerMonth` is a function that accepts three inputs and returns a `Decimal` value. Typically, you assign the result of a function to a variable, although you can call a function and disregard its result, as in

```
ComputeCostPerMonth(P, r, t)   'disregards the return value
```

Let's create a function to compute the monthly cost of a mortgage. If you created the `FinancialCalculator.aspx` web page from Hour 4, you can cut and paste the source code from the `PerformCalcButton_Click` event handler into the new function, `ComputeCostPerMonth`. The code for the new function is given in Listing 6.6.

LISTING 6.6 The `ComputeCostPerMonth` Function Computes the Monthly Cost of a Mortgage

```
Function ComputeMonthlyCost(P as Decimal, r as Decimal, t as
➥ Decimal) as Decimal
  'Specify constant values
  Const INTEREST_CALCS_PER_YEAR as Integer = 12
  Const PAYMENTS_PER_YEAR as Integer = 12

  Dim ratePerPeriod as Decimal
  ratePerPeriod = r / INTEREST_CALCS_PER_YEAR

  Dim payPeriods as Integer
  payPeriods = t * PAYMENTS_PER_YEAR

  Dim annualRate as Decimal
  annualRate = Math.Exp(INTEREST_CALCS_PER_YEAR *
  ➥ Math.Log(1 + ratePerPeriod)) - 1

  Dim intPerPayment as Decimal
  intPerPayment = (Math.Exp(Math.Log(annualRate + 1) / payPeriods)
  ➥ - 1) * payPeriods

  'Now, compute the total cost of the loan
  Dim intPerMonth as Decimal = intPerPayment / PAYMENTS_PER_YEAR

  Dim costPerMonth as Decimal
  costPerMonth = P * intPerMonth / (1 - Math.Pow(intPerMonth+1,
  ➥ -payPeriods))

  Return costPerMonth
End Function
```

The `ComputeMonthlyCost` function accepts three parameters, all of type `Decimal`, and returns a value of type `Decimal`. Recall from Hour 4 that to compute the monthly cost of a mortgage, we need three bits of information: the mortgage principal (`P`), the interest rate (`r`), and the duration of the mortgage (`t`). The `ComputeMonthlyCost` function receives these three values as input parameters and uses them to compute the monthly mortgage cost. It then returns this final calculation using the `Return` statement (line 24).

By the Way

> The code in Listing 6.6 from lines 2 through 22 was taken directly from the `PerformCalcButton_Click` event handler in the `FinancialCalculator.aspx` page created in Hour 4.

Now that we have the `ComputeMonthlyCost` function written, we can call it from the `PerformCalcButton_Click` event handler, which is the event handler that fires whenever the page's Button Web control is clicked. The event handler's code replaces the computation with a call to `ComputeMonthlyCost`, as shown in Listing 6.7.

LISTING 6.7 The `PerformCalcButton_Click` Event Handler Calls the `ComputeMonthlyCost` Function

```
1: Protected Sub PerformCalcButton_Click(ByVal sender As Object, ByVal e
   ➥ As System.EventArgs) Handles PerformCalcButton.Click
2:    'Create variables to hold the values entered by the user
3:    Dim P as Decimal = loanAmount.Text
4:    Dim r as Decimal = rate.Text / 100
5:    Dim t as Decimal = mortgageLength.Text
6:
7:    Results.Text = "Your mortgage payment per month is $" &
      ➥ ComputeMonthlyCost(P, r, t)
8: End Sub
```

On lines 3–5, the values entered by the user into the loan amount, interest rate, and mortgage length TextBox Web controls are read and stored into local variables `P`, `r`, and `t`. Then, on line 7, the `Text` property of the `Results` Label is assigned the string "Your mortgage payment per month is $", concatenated with the `Decimal` value returned by `ComputeMonthlyCost`.

Watch Out!

> If you have set `Option Strict On`, the code in Listing 6.7 will generate an error because lines 3, 4, and 5 use implicit casting to cast a value of type `String` (`loanAmount.Text`, `rate.Text`, and `mortgageAmount.Text`) into a `Decimal`. To remedy this, use the `Convert.ToDecimal` method like so:

```
Dim P as Decimal = Convert.ToDecimal(loanAmount.Text)
```

Where Do Event Handlers Fit In?

Virtually all the ASP.NET examples throughout this book use **event handlers**, which are a way to modularize code that is executed in response to a particular event. Event handlers, as you may have noticed, are implemented as subroutines because they never return a value.

Consider the `Page_Load` event handler, which has the following definition:

```
Protected Sub Page_Load(ByVal sender As Object, ByVal e As System.EventArgs)
➥ Handles Me.Load
  ...
End Sub
```

As you can see, the Sub and End Sub statements indicate that the event handler is implemented as a subroutine. In addition, the `Page_Load` event handler accepts two parameters: the first of type `Object` and the second of type `EventArgs`. The details of these parameters are unimportant for now; in later hours we'll examine their meaning in more depth.

Finally, note that an event handler's subroutine definition ends with `Handles` *`ObjectName.EventName`*. *`ObjectName.EventName`* is the event that is associated with this event handler. That is, when the specified event fires, the event handler executes. It's the `Handles` keyword that wires up the specified event to this event handler.

The important information to grasp here is that an event handler is a subroutine. An event handler provides a modularized chunk of code that is executed whenever its corresponding event fires, and that corresponding event is spelled out in the `Handles` clause.

> While Visual Web Developer automatically gives each event handler a name of the form *`ObjectName_EventName`*, this name does not have any impact on the event handler's functionality. Rather, it's the `Handles` keyword that ties an event handler to an event. For example, you could rename the `Page_Load` event handler to `RunWheneverThePageIsLoaded`; as long as you kept the `Handles Me.Load` keyword in the subroutine definition, the event handler would execute on each and every page load.

Summary

In this hour we looked at Visual Basic's control structures. Control structures alter the program flow from a sequential, one-line-after-the-other model, to one where lines of code can be conditionally executed or executed repeatedly until some specified condition is met.

Visual Basic supports conditional control structures through the `If` statement. The `If` statement evaluates a condition and, if it is true, executes the instructions following the `Then`. In addition to the `If ... Then` portion, `If` statements may include `ElseIf` and `Else` clauses.

Visual Basic has a number of looping constructs, the two most common ones being the `For` loop and the `Do` loop. The `For` loop starts by assigning an initial value to its looping variable and then executes the loop body. At the end of the body, the looping variable is incremented. The `For` loop continues executing its body until the looping variable has surpassed the specified bounds. The `Do` loop is more general. Rather than having a looping variable, it executes the loop body until a specified condition is met.

We also looked at modularization control structures: the subroutine and function. Both the subroutine and function allow for programming logic to be encapsulated, both can accept zero to many parameters, and both are called using the same syntax. The difference between the two is that a function returns a value, whereas a subroutine does not.

The next hour, "Working with Objects in Visual Basic," will be our last hour focusing specifically on Visual Basic's syntax and semantics. After that, we'll turn our attention back to ASP.NET's Web controls.

Q&A

Q. ***What is the difference between a subroutine and a function?***

A. Subroutines and functions both are modularization control structures that can accept zero or more input parameters. However, a function returns a value, whereas a subroutine does not.

Q. ***I see that the* `Sub` *keyword in an event handler is prefaced with the keyword* `Protected`*. I've also seen code examples that added the keywords* `Private` *or* `Public` *in the subroutine and function definitions. Are they necessary? When I'm creating a subroutine or function, what should I be using?***

A. In its simplest form, a subroutine merely spells out the subroutine's name and input parameters, whereas a function must include its name, input parameters, and return value. However, in addition to these bare minimum pieces of information, a number of additional keywords may be included.

One such set of keywords is the **access modifier** keywords. These are the keywords that precede `Sub` or `Function`, and include these options: `Private`,

Protected, Public, Friend, or Protected Friend. These access modifiers define how other classes and derived classes can use the subroutines and functions. The details aren't important for the code examples we'll be examining throughout this book, so you may use any access modifier, or leave it out altogether (in which case the default access modifier, Private, is used). However, event handlers, *must* be marked Protected. To ensure the appropriate access modifier for event handlers, let Visual Web Developer create them for you and don't change their access modifiers.

Q. ***When calling a function, must its return value be assigned to a variable?***

A. Recall that functions always return a value. Typically, the return value of a function is either used in an expression or stored in a variable. However, it is not required that the return value of a function be used at all. Imagine that we had a function called SaveCustomerInformation(*name*, *age*) that took as input parameters the name and age of the customer and saved this information in a database. The return value of this function might be a DateTime variable that indicated the last time the customer's information was updated. In certain situations, we might not care about when the customer's information was last updated; all we want to do is update the customer's information. In such a case, we could call the function and disregard its return value. This is accomplished by calling the function just like we would a subroutine:

```
SaveCustomerInformation("Scott", 29)
```

Workshop

Quiz

1. True or False: Conditional control structures alter the control flow of a program.

2. If we wanted to print out a message five times if the current hour was past 12, what control structures would we need to use?

3. Is the following For ... Next loop an example of an infinite loop?

```
Dim i as Integer
For i = 10 to 20 Step -1
  ' Instructions
Next
```

4. True or False: Functions and subroutines must always have at least one input parameter.

Answers

1. True. Computer programs execute sequentially by default; however, control structures allow for more flexible control flow scenarios.
2. We'd need to use two controls structures: a conditional control structure to evaluate if the hour is past 12 and a looping control structure to output the message five times. The code for this might look like so:

```
Dim i as Integer
If DateTime.Now.Hour >= 12 then
  For i = 1 to 5
    LabelWebControl.Text &= "This is my message to you.<br>"
  Next
End If
```

3. Yes. It is an infinite loop because, at each loop iteration, the looping variable is decreased by 1 (due to the `Step -1`). Therefore, the looping variable, which starts at 10, will never reach the loop termination value, 20. This means that this loop will run forever.
4. False. Subroutines and functions can have zero or more input parameters. It is not required that they have more than zero.

Exercises

1. A common mathematical function is the *factorial function*. The factorial function takes an integer input *n* that is greater than or equal to 1 and computes `n * (n-1) * ... * 2 * 1`. In mathematical texts, factorial is denoted with an exclamation point, as in `n!`.

   For this exercise, write a function called `Factorial` that takes a single `Integer` input and returns an `Integer` corresponding to the factorial of the inputted parameter. To help get you started, your function will look like this:

```
Function Factorial(n as Integer) as Integer
  ' Write code here to compute n!
  ' Return the value n!
End Function
```

   Note that:

```
1! = 1
2! = 2 * 1 = 2
3! = 3 * 2 * 1 = 6
4! = 4 * 3 * 2 * 1 = 24
5! = 5 * 4 * 3 * 2 * 1 = 120
```

After you have written this `Factorial` function, add a `Page_Load` event handler that calls the function, displaying on the ASP.NET web page the values of 1! through 5!.

Hint: The `Factorial` function will need to contain a looping construct from 1 to *n*, where, at each iteration, a variable is multiplied by the value of the looping variable.

HOUR 7

Working with Objects in Visual Basic

In this hour, we will cover

- The difference between objects and classes
- Creating an object
- Setting an object's properties
- Calling an object's methods
- Handling an object's events
- Examples of creating objects from classes in the .NET Framework

In Hour 5, "Understanding Visual Basic's Variables and Operators," we looked at using variables and operators in Visual Basic. In Hour 6, "Managing Program Flow with Visual Basic's Control Structures," we looked at control structures, such as `If` statements, looping constructs, and subroutines and functions. We need to discuss one more important topic regarding Visual Basic before returning to ASP.NET. Specifically, we need to examine how to use objects in Visual Basic.

The key component of an object-oriented programming language like Visual Basic is the **object**, which is an instance of a **class**. In this hour we reexamine the relationship between an object and a class and discuss the role of classes and objects in Visual Basic, the .NET Framework, and ASP.NET web pages.

Whether you realize it or not, you've already used an assortment of objects in the source code you've written in previous hours. Each ASP.NET Web control, for example, exists as an object in the source code portion. When setting the `Text` property of a Label control or handling the `Click` event of a Button Web control, you are working with objects.

Reexamining the Role of Classes and Objects

In Hour 2, "Understanding the ASP.NET Programming Model," we discussed the ideas behind object-oriented programming. To refresh your memory, object-oriented programming is a programming paradigm in which the object is a key construct of the programming language. Objects contain methods, properties, and events. Properties define the state of the object, methods perform actions, and events commonly represent state changes or indicate that some action has transpired.

By the Way

> Recall that in Hour 2 we described object-oriented programming using a car as an analogy. The properties of the car were such things as make, model, and color; its events were stepping on the brakes and turning on the windshield wipers; and its methods were drive, reverse, turn, and so on.
>
> The list of properties, methods, and events that describe a car is referred to as a **class**, whereas an actual, concrete instance of a car, such as a 2005 silver Porsche Boxster, is referred to as an **object**.

Classes are the abstractions from which objects are created. To understand the relationship between a class and an object, think of a calculator. A calculator may have properties like current battery power, current value on the screen, last operation entered, and others. It might have methods like add, subtract, and so on. Its events might include clearing the last computation and turning off. If you were to sit down and list all the properties, methods, and events that a calculator has, this list would be equivalent to a class. This list is an abstract idea of what a calculator is and what it does. It clearly is not a concrete representation of a calculator; you cannot use the list to compute the product of 19.34 and 78.

An object, on the other hand, is a concrete representation of the class. The actual calculator that supports the properties, methods, and events outlined by the class is an object and is said to be an **instance** of the class it represents.

By the Way

> To summarize, a class is an abstract definition, a simple list of properties, methods, and events that are supported. An object, however, is an instance of the class, a concrete "thing" whose properties we can set, whose methods we can call, and whose events can fire.

The Role of Objects in an ASP.NET Web Application

Recall from our earlier discussions that the .NET Framework contains a plethora of classes that allow for a variety of functionality. For example, each and every Web control that can be used in an ASP.NET page is represented by a class in the .NET Framework.

Classes in the .NET Framework allow for an email to be sent from a web page, for data to be retrieved from a database, for an image to be created, and so on. The code in your ASP.NET pages can utilize the variety of functionality present in the .NET Framework.

To use one of the classes in the .NET Framework, we first must create an object from the particular class whose functionality we are interested in. After we have an object, we may need to set some of the object's properties and call some of its methods. Additionally, we may need to create event handlers for some of its events.

The Four Common Tasks Performed with Objects

When using objects, we'll perform four tasks again and again:

- **Instantiation**—Before we can work with an object, we need to create an instance of the object from the desired class. This is a required step that must be performed before working with an object.
- **Setting property values**—In most scenarios we will need to set one or more properties of the object we're working with. Remember that properties are values that describe the state of the object. For example, a class that represents an email message might have properties like `Body`, `Subject`, `To`, `From`, `Cc`, and forth.
- **Calling methods**—When using objects, we will always call one or more of the object's methods. A class that sends email messages, for example, might have a method called `Send` that sends a specified email message. To send an email using this class, we would first create an instance of the class; then set its `Body`, `Subject`, `To`, `From`, and other pertinent properties; and then call its `Send` method.
- **Creating event handlers**—In some cases we will need to run a set of instructions only when a particular event for a particular object fires. This can be accomplished by creating an event handler that's wired up to the object's pertinent event. We've created event handlers for a Button Web control's `Click` event and for the page's `Load` event in previous hours.

The remainder of this hour examines the Visual Basic syntax required to accomplish these four tasks.

Creating an Object

In addition to properties, methods, and events, classes contain **constructors**. A constructor is a special method that is used to create an instance of the class.

In a later section, "Calling an Object's Methods," we'll discuss what, exactly, methods are. For now, you can think of a method as a function or subroutine. Like functions and subroutines, methods are a means of encapsulating a number of program instructions; they can have zero or more parameters and may return a value.

Constructors always have the same name as the class. For example, one of the classes used to programmatically work with database data is the `SqlCommand` class. The constructor for this class is a method named `SqlCommand`.

To create an instance of an object, use the following syntax:

```
Variable = New Constructor()
```

The constructor *`Constructor`* creates and returns an object from the class named *`Constructor`*. Because Visual Basic is a strongly typed language, the type of *`Variable`* must be the same type as the class whose constructor is being called. For example, to create an instance of the `SqlCommand` class, we would first create a variable whose type was of `SqlCommand` as follows:

```
Dim MyCommand as SqlCommand
```

Then we would assign to this variable the object returned by the constructor:

```
MyCommand = New SqlCommand()
```

The first line of code creates a variable named `MyCommand` of type `SqlCommand`. The second line of code calls the constructor, creating a new `SqlCommand` object; this new object is then assigned to `MyCommand`.

Before working with an object, we must first create an instance of the object. This process is commonly called **instantiation**. We can instantiate an object like this:

```
Dim Variable as type
Variable = New Constructor()
```

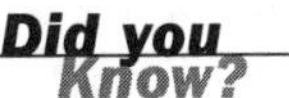

Or by combining the two statements on one line, like this:

```
Dim Variable as type = New Constructor()
```

For example, the following code declares a variable named `MyCommand` and assigns to it a new `SqlCommand` object:

```
Dim MyCommand as SqlCommand = New SqlCommand()
```

Constructors with Parameters

Constructors, like functions and subroutines, can have zero or more parameters. Additionally, classes may have more than one constructor. When constructors accept one or more parameters, the parameter values are typically used to specify initial values for the classes' various properties. For example, the `SqlCommand` class has a constructor that accepts zero parameters, as well as one that accepts a string parameter. The constructor that accepts zero parameters does not assign any initial value to any of its properties. The constructor that accepts a string parameter, however, assigns the passed-in parameter value to the object's `CommandText` property.

By the Way

In general, any class method (such as the constructor) can have multiple versions; each accepts a different number of input parameters. A single method that has multiple versions that accept different numbers of parameters are referred to as **overloaded**.

Constructors that accept more than one parameter are used for reducing the amount of code that needs to be written. For example, to create a `SqlCommand` object and set its `CommandText` property, we need to use the following two lines of code:

```
Dim MyCommand as SqlCommand = New SqlCommand()
MyCommand.CommandText = "some value"
```

However, by using the `SqlCommand` constructor that accepts a string parameter, we can condense these two lines into one:

```
Dim MyCommand as SqlCommand = New SqlCommand("some value")
```

By the Way

Most classes have more than one constructor—one that accepts zero parameters and a number of others that accept one, two, three, four, or even more parameters. The constructor that accepts zero parameters is referred to as the **default constructor**.

Setting an Object's Properties

After creating an object, we may need to set some of its properties. To reference an object's properties, use the following syntax:

```
ObjectVariable.PropertyName
```

Here, *ObjectVariable* is the name of the object variable. That is, in the code

```
Dim myCommand as SqlCommand
myCommand = New SqlCommand()
```

the *ObjectVariable* is `myCommand`. The *PropertyName* is the name of the property that you want to access. Properties are used just like variables; they can be assigned values, they have types, and they can be used in expressions.

Typically, you assign a value to a property just once and then call one of the object's methods, which uses the value of the property in some manner.

For example, to send an email message from an ASP.NET page, we use the `MailMessage` class. When an instance of this class is created, a number of properties need to be set, such as `From`, `To`, `Subject`, and others. The following code snippet demonstrates how to create an instance of this class and set its properties:

```
'Create an instance of the MailMessage class
Dim MyMailMessage As MailMessage = New MailMessage()

'Set the From, To, Subject, and Body properties
MyMailMessage.From = "someone@example.com"
MyMailMessage.To = "someoneElse@example.com"
MyMailMessage.Subject = "Email Subject"
MyMailMessage.Body = "Hello!"
```

Not all properties can necessarily be written to and read from. Some classes mark certain properties as **read only** or **write only**. The vast majority of properties, however, are both readable and writeable. When examining a new class and its properties, I'll point out whether any properties are read only or write only.

Calling an Object's Methods

An object's methods are called just like other subroutines and functions, except that the name of the object whose method you want to call must precede the method name. That is, the syntax for calling an object's method is as follows:

```
ObjectVariable.MethodName(param1, param2, ..., paramN)
```

Methods in classes are semantically equivalent to subroutines and functions. Methods in classes can accept zero to many input parameters and can optionally provide a return value.

As we discussed earlier, the `SqlCommand` class is used for programmatically working with database data. In using the `SqlCommand` class, we must specify the database to retrieve the data from, as well as what data to retrieve. These two bits of information are specified via the `Connection` and `CommandText` properties. The `SqlCommand` class's `ExecuteReader` method, when executed, returns the data specified by the `CommandText` property from the database specified by the `Connection` property.

Before calling the `ExecuteReader` method, we first must create an instance of the `SqlCommand` class and set its `Connection` and `CommandText` properties. The following code snippet demonstrates the syntax for calling a method:

```
'Create an instance of the SqlCommand class
Dim MyCommand as SqlCommand = New SqlCommand()

'Set the Connection and CommandText properties
MyCommand.Connection = ...
MyCommand.CommandText = "..."

'Call the ExecuteReader() method
Dim MyReader as SqlDataReader
MyReader = myCommand.ExecuteReader()
```

As you can see in this code snippet, the `ExecuteReader` method returns an object of type `SqlDataReader`. This `SqlDataReader` object contains the data specified by the `CommandText` property.

Methods that return a value are similar to functions; some methods do not return a value, making them similar to subroutines. Also, methods—both ones that do and ones that do not return a value—can have zero to many input parameters.

Creating Event Handlers for an Object's Events

In addition to methods and properties, objects may also have events. Events typically represent a state change or indicate that some action has transpired. For example, the ASP.NET Button Web control has a `Click` event that indicates that the user has performed some action, namely that she's clicked the button in her browser. A good example of an event representing a state change is the TextBox Web control's `TextChanged` event, which is fired on postback if the TextBox's text content has been changed.

In many scenarios, we will need some code that we've written to run in response to a particular event firing. To accomplish this, we must create an **event handler**. An event handler is a subroutine with a particular set of input parameters that is wired to a particular event. This wiring process, which we'll examine shortly, causes the event handler to be executed whenever the event is raised.

All event handlers in a .NET program must be created as a subroutine and must accept precisely two input parameters: the first one must be of type `Object` and the second must be of a type derived from `EventArgs`. For example, the event handler for a Button Web control's `Click` event (which Visual Web Developer can create for us automatically) has the following signature:

```
Protected Sub Button1_Click(ByVal sender As Object, ByVal e As
➥ System.EventArgs) Handles Button1.Click
  ...
End Sub
```

This statement defines a subroutine named `Button1_Click` that serves as an event handler for `Button1`'s `Click` event.

As you can see, the first parameter passed into the event handler named `sender` is of type `Object`. When an event is raised, the object that raised the event is passed in as `sender`. The second parameter is of type `EventArgs`. This second parameter can contain additional event-related information. In this event handler, as well as the `Page_Load` event handler, no additional information is passed in. However, in future hours we will see examples of event handlers that are sent additional information through this second input parameter.

Along with these two input parameters, the event handler's definition includes the `Handles` keyword. This keyword is responsible for wiring the event handler to a particular event. In the case of the `Button1_Click` event handler, the subroutine is wired to `Button1`'s `Click` event. `Button1` is an object representing the Button Web control defined in the page's HTML portion with `ID Button1`.

By the Way

> You can create an event handler in Visual Basic by typing in the appropriate syntax by hand. However, Visual Web Developer can autogenerate event handler syntax for you. As we saw in previous hours, double-clicking a Web control in the Design view creates an event handler for the Web control's default event. Alternatively, you can go to the source code portion and select the appropriate object and event from the drop-down lists at the top.

Summary

In this hour we reexamined the concepts behind objects and classes. To use an object, we first must create it. This is accomplished using the Visual Basic `New` keyword along with a constructor. As we saw, a constructor is a method that has the same name as the class and returns an instance of the class. For example, to create an instance of the `SqlCommand` class, we could use

```
Dim MyCommand as SqlCommand
MyCommand = New SqlCommand()
```

After an object has been created, we can set its properties, call its methods, and create event handlers. An object's properties are accessible by listing the object's name, followed by a period (`.`), followed by the property name. For example, to access the `CommandText` property of the `MyCommand` object, we would use the following syntax:

```
MyCommand.CommandText
```

Properties have the same semantics as ordinary variables; they have a type and can be used in expressions or assigned values.

An object's methods are called by listing the object's name, followed by a period, followed by the method's name. Methods are like subroutines and functions in that they may accept zero or more input parameters and can optionally return a value.

Objects can also have a number of events that fire at different times during the object's lifetime; when an event fires, we may want to execute some code. Event handlers are special subroutines that are wired up to a particular event and execute when that specified event fires. Event handlers must accept two input parameters and use the `Handles` keyword to indicate the particular event that they execute in response to. Although an event handler's syntax can be entered manually, Visual Web Developer will easily create the appropriate event handler syntax: just specify the object and event from the drop-down lists at the top of the source code portion of an ASP.NET page.

This hour concludes our in-depth examination of Visual Basic. In the next hour we will look at the two ASP.NET Web controls that are used for displaying text: the Label and Literal Web controls. Following that, we spend the next several hours examining how to collect and process user input.

Q&A

Q. *This hour showed us how to use classes in the .NET Framework, but is it possible to create our own classes?*

A. With object-oriented programming languages like Visual Basic, you can create your own classes. However, doing so is beyond the scope of this book. Although we'll be using a number of the .NET Framework classes throughout the course of this book, won't ever need to create our own classes.

Q. *Will we be examining how to send email messages from an ASP.NET page in this book?*

A. No, I'm afraid we won't have the time to dissect sending an email message from an ASP.NET page. However, a plethora of online articles show how to accomplish this common task.

The two classes used in ASP.NET 3.5 for sending email messages are the `MailMessage` and `SmtpClient` classes. For more information on using these classes, check out my article "Sending Email in ASP.NET," available online at http://aspnet.4guysfromrolla.com/articles/072606-1.aspx.

Workshop

Quiz

1. What are the four actions commonly performed on objects?
2. True or False: The .NET Framework contains classes that we will use in our ASP.NET pages.
3. In the past two hours, we examined a number of fundamental programming concepts. In this hour, we looked at objects, which have properties, methods, and events. What programming concept is analogous to an object's properties?
4. What programming concept is analogous to an object's methods?
5. In Visual Basic, what keyword in the subroutine definition indicates that the subroutine should be called when a specified event fires?

Answers

1. Before objects can be used, they must first be instantiated. After an object instance exists, its properties can be set and its methods called. Event handlers may need to be created to have code executed in response to the firing of an object's event.
2. True. In fact, all ASP.NET Web controls are implemented as classes in the .NET Framework.
3. Properties are analogous to variables.
4. Methods are analogous to subroutines and functions.
5. The `Handles` keyword.

Exercises

There are no exercises for this hour.

HOUR 8

ASP.NET Web Controls for Displaying Text

In this hour, we will cover

- Displaying text using the Literal and Label Web controls
- Using the Literal Web control
- Using the Label Web control
- Understanding the differences between the Literal and Label Web controls
- Altering the appearance of the Label Web control

We'll be examining a variety of Web controls throughout this book. Web controls, like regular HTML markup, are placed in the ASP.NET page's HTML portion. But unlike HTML elements, Web controls can be accessed programmatically from the page's code. In this manner, Web controls serve as an intermediary between the source code and HTML portions of an ASP.NET page.

ASP.NET's various Web controls can be divided into a number of categories, such as Web controls that are used to display text, Web controls that are used to collect user input, Web controls that are used to display data from a database, and so on. In this hour we examine the two ASP.NET Web controls used for displaying text.

Examining the Web Controls Designed for Displaying Text

Recall from our discussions in Hour 4, "Designing, Creating, and Testing ASP.NET Web Pages," that when an ASP.NET web page is visited through a browser, the ASP.NET engine executes the page, producing HTML that is then sent back to the web server. The HTML produced by an ASP.NET web page can come from

- The static HTML in the HTML portion
- The HTML that is rendered by the page's Web controls

The static HTML in the HTML portion is passed on to the browser exactly as it's typed in. However, the HTML produced by a Web control depends on the values of its properties.

Two ASP.NET Web controls are designed for displaying text: the Literal Web control and the Label Web control. The differences between the Literal and Label Web controls lie in the HTML produced by each control. The Literal Web control's rendered markup is the value of its `Text` property. The Label Web control, on the other hand, has a number of formatting properties, such as `BackColor`, `ForeColor`, `Font`, and so on, that specify how the Label's `Text` property should be displayed.

Using the Literal Web Control

The Literal Web control is one of the simplest Web controls. The HTML rendered by the Literal Web control is precisely the value of its `Text` property.

To illustrate the Literal's behavior, let's create an ASP.NET page that has a Literal control. Start by creating a new ASP.NET web page named `LiteralControl.aspx`. Next, drag the Literal control from the Toolbox onto the page. Figure 8.1 shows the Design view after the Literal control has been added.

Make sure that the Literal Web control you just added is selected, and then examine the Properties window in the lower-right corner. Note that the Literal Web control has only six properties. These six properties, as displayed in the Properties window, are

- Text
- EnableViewState
- Mode
- Visible
- (Expressions)
- (ID)

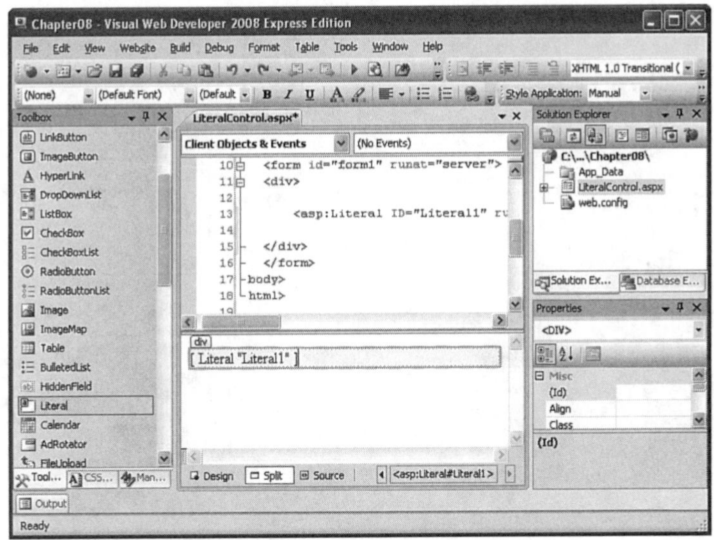

FIGURE 8.1
A Literal Web control has been added to the designer.

The only two properties that we will work with in this hour are the `ID` and `Text` properties. The `ID` property uniquely names the Web control so that its properties can be referenced in the source code portion of the ASP.NET web page. The `Text` property is the value that is displayed in the ASP.NET web page when the Literal Web control is rendered.

When the Literal Web control's `Text` property is not set, the Literal Web control is shown in the designer as

```
[Literal "ID"]
```

where *`ID`* is the value of the Literal Web control's `ID` property. In Figure 8.1 the Literal control is displayed as `[Literal "Literal1"]` because the `Text` property is not set and the `ID` property value is `Literal1`.

If the `Text` property is set to some value, though, the designer displays this value. For example, take a moment to change the Literal Web control's `Text` property to **Hello, World!** Figure 8.2 shows the designer after this change has been made. Note that the Literal Web control is displayed in the designer as the text "Hello, World!"

Now that we've added this Literal Web control and set its `Text` property, let's view this ASP.NET page through a browser. Go to the Debug menu and choose Start Without Debugging. Figure 8.3 shows the `LiteralControl.aspx` web page when viewed through a browser. Note that the output is simply the value "Hello, World!"

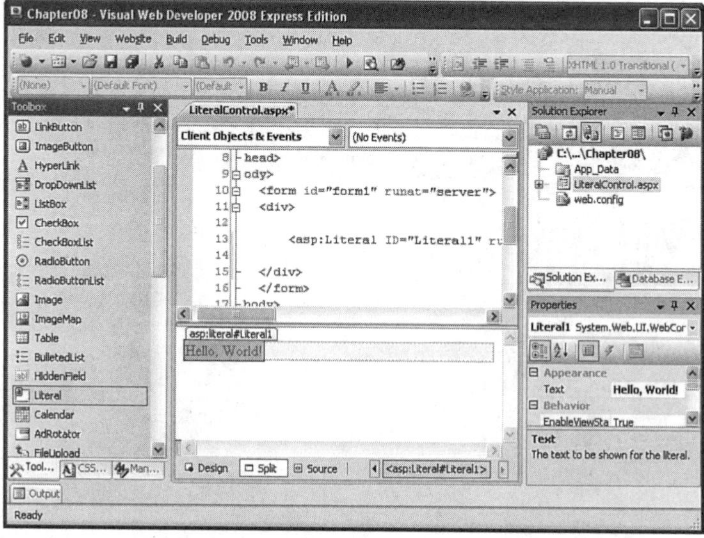

FIGURE 8.2 The Literal Web control is displayed as "Hello, World!" in the designer.

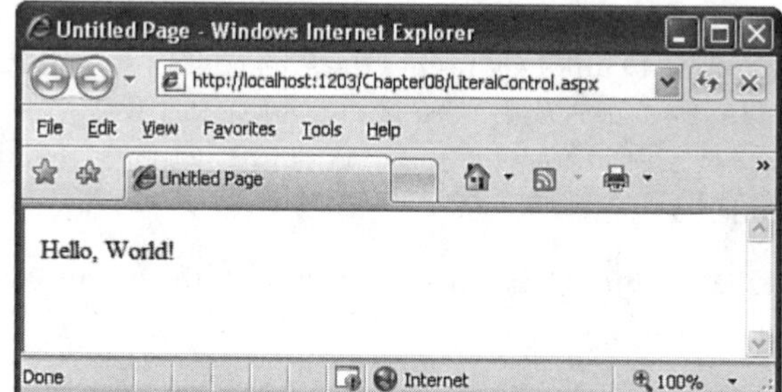

FIGURE 8.3 LiteralControl.aspx, when viewed through a web browser.

Setting the Literal Control's `Text` Property Programmatically

As we just saw, the `Text` property of the Literal Web control can be set through the Properties window. If you know what the `Text` property's value should be, nothing is wrong with using this approach. However, if you want the value of the `Text` property to be dynamic, you will have to set the property value through the source code portion of the ASP.NET page.

For example, imagine that you wanted to use a Literal control to display the current date and time. Programmatically, the current date and time can be retrieved by the `DateTime.Now` property.

To set the Literal control's `Text` property programmatically, use the following syntax in the source code portion:

```
LiteralControlID.Text = value
```

Here, *`LiteralControlID`* is the value of the Literal Web control's `ID` property, and *`value`* is the string value to assign to the Literal Web control's `Text` property.

Let's create an ASP.NET web page that uses a Literal Web control to display the current date and time. Start by creating a new ASP.NET web page named `LiteralTime.aspx` and then drag and drop a Literal Web control onto the designer. There's no need to set the `Text` property through the Properties window because we will be setting this property programmatically. We should, however, rename the Literal Web control's `ID` property from the ambiguous `Label1` to something more descriptive, such as `CurrentTime`.

After you have added the Label Web control and changed its `ID` property to `CurrentTime`, take a moment to compare what your screen looks like with Figure 8.4.

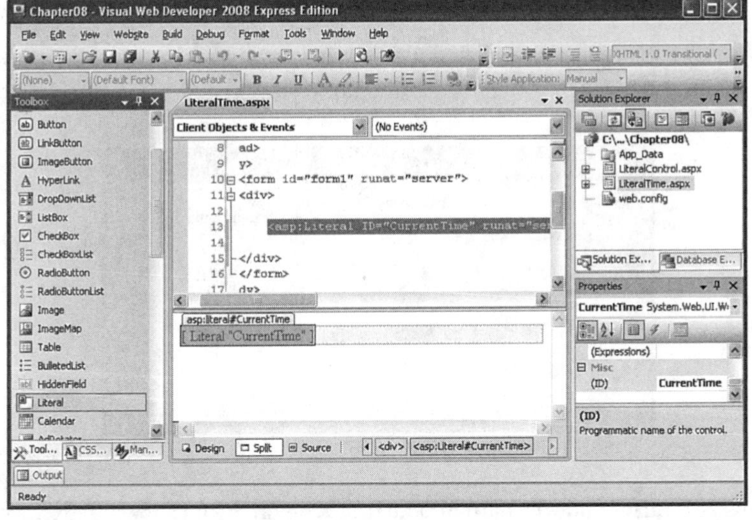

FIGURE 8.4 The designer after the Literal Web control has been added and its `ID` property set.

After you've added the Literal Web control and set its `ID` property to `CurrentTime`, you're ready to add the needed source code. For this ASP.NET web page, we want the Literal Web control's `Text` property set to the current date and time whenever the page is visited. Therefore, create an event handler for the page's `Load` event.

Enter the following code into the Page_Load event handler:

```
CurrentTime.Text = DateTime.Now
```

At this point your ASP.NET page's source code portion should be identical to the code in Listing 8.1.

LISTING 8.1 The Current Date and Time Is Displayed in the `CurrentTime` Literal Control

```
1: Partial Class LiteralTime
2:     Inherits System.Web.UI.Page
3:
4:     Protected Sub Page_Load(ByVal sender As Object, ByVal e
➥ As System.EventArgs) Handles Me.Load
5:         CurrentTime.Text = DateTime.Now
6:     End Sub
7: End Class
```

Whenever a browser requests the `LiteralTime.aspx` web page, the ASP.NET engine executes the page. The `Page_Load` event handler is fired, and the source code within that event handler is executed. The code on line 5 sets the `CurrentTime` Literal control's `Text` property to the current date and time.

Save the ASP.NET web page and view it through a web browser. Figure 8.5 shows `LiteralTime.aspx` when viewed through a browser.

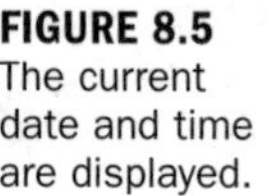

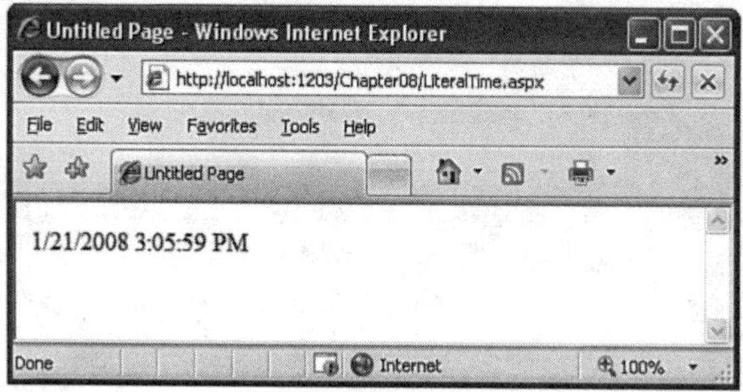

FIGURE 8.5 The current date and time are displayed.

To convince yourself that the current date and time are being shown, refresh your web browser every few seconds, noting that the time displayed is updated accordingly. When refreshing your web browser, the entire page execution process is repeated—the `Page_Load` event handler sets the Literal's `Text` property to the current date and time and the Literal control is rendered, sending down the value of its `Text` property to the requested browser.

By the Way

What do you think the output of the `LiteralTime.aspx` web page would be if we changed the code in the `Page_Load` event handler from

```
CurrentTime.Text = DateTime.Now
```

to

```
CurrentTime.Text = "The current time is: " & DateTime.Now
```

I encourage you to try this code change to see how the output differs.

The Literal Web control does not contain any properties to specify the format of its output. That is, no properties specify that the text should be displayed in a larger font, or that it should be underlined. If you need to format the Literal control's output, you have to insert the appropriate HTML in the control's `Text` property. For example, to display the current time in a bold font, you need to explicitly include the HTML bold element (`<b>`):

```
CurrentTime.Text = "<b>" & DateTime.Now & "</b>"
```

Clearly, the Literal Web control is not well suited for displaying formatted text. The Label Web control, which we'll examine in the next section, has a host of properties that make formatting the output a breeze.

The Literal Web control is most useful in scenarios in which you need precise control over the rendered output. The Label control's emitted markup depends on both its `Text` property and its formatting properties. The Literal control, on the other hand, offers finer control over the output because it emits just the value of its `Text` property—nothing more, nothing less.

Using the Label Web Control

The Label Web control differs from the Literal Web control in that it contains a number of formatting properties that, when set, specify how the `Text` property should be displayed in the user's web browser. For example, we can display the Label text in a bold font by setting the control's `Font` property's `Bold` subproperty to `True`; to have the text displayed in a red font, set its `ForeColor` property to `Red`.

Let's create a new ASP.NET web page to demonstrate using the Label Web control. Start by creating an ASP.NET page named `LabelControl.aspx`; next, drag a Label Web control onto the page. Select the Label and note its list of properties in the Properties window. There are far more properties listed here than with the Literal Web control.

First, set the Label Web control's `Text` property to **Hello, World!** After you have done this, your screen should look like Figure 8.6.

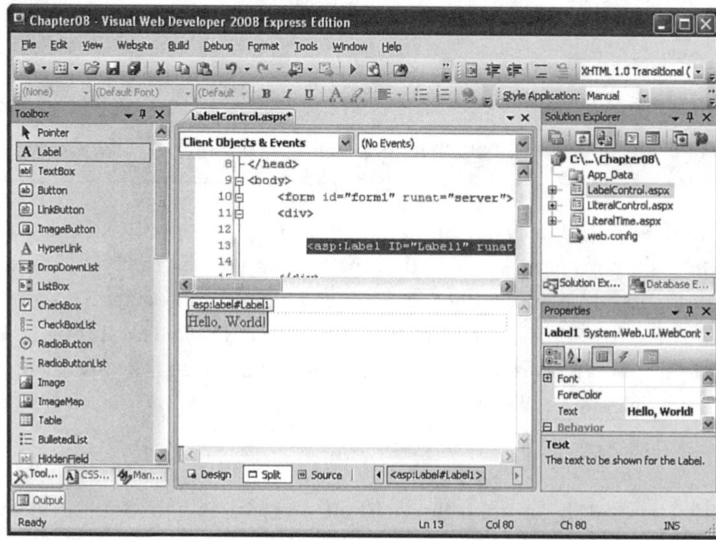

FIGURE 8.6 A Label Web control has been added and its `Text` property has been set.

Let's configure the Label so that it displays its content in a bold font. To accomplish this, select the Label Web control to load its properties in the Properties window. One of the properties listed is `Font`. To the left of this property name, you'll find a plus, which indicates that this property has subproperties. Click the plus sign to expand these subproperties.

The subproperties of the `Font` property are listed in Table 8.1. One of these subproperties is `Bold`, which defaults to a value of `False`. Change this value to `True`. This has the effect of making the Label Web control's text in the designer appear bold, as you can see in Figure 8.7.

TABLE 8.1 The Subproperties of the Label Web Control's `Font` Property

Subproperty Name	Description
`Bold`	A Boolean value indicating whether the `Text` property will be displayed in a bold font.
`Italic`	A Boolean value indicating whether the `Text` property will be displayed in an italic font.
`Name`	The preferred font to use when displaying the text. Common font choices include Arial, Helvetica, and Verdana.

TABLE 8.1 Continued

Subproperty Name	Description
`Names`	A sequence of font names. If the browser visiting the page does not support one of the fonts, it will try using the next listed one.
`Overline`	A Boolean value indicating whether the `Text` property will be displayed with an overline.
`Size`	The size that the `Text` property will be displayed in. You can choose settings such as `Smaller`, `Medium`, `Larger`, and so on. You can also enter a point value, like 14pt.
`Strikeout`	A Boolean value indicating whether the `Text` property will be displayed with a strikeout.
`Underline`	A Boolean value indicating whether the `Text` property will be displayed underlined.

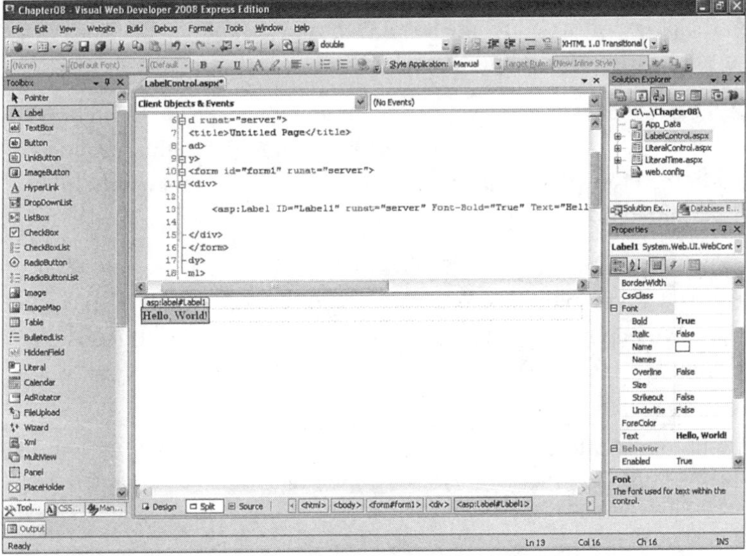

FIGURE 8.7 The Label Web control's `Bold` subproperty has been set to `True`.

Go ahead and view the ASP.NET page through a web browser. When viewing the `LabelControl.aspx` page through a browser, you should see the message "Hello, World!" in a bold font, just like what is shown in the designer.

Examining the Formatting Properties of the Label Web Control

The Label Web control contains a number of formatting properties. We've already seen how to make the text of the Label Web control bold. Numerous other Label Web control formatting properties are worth examining. These formatting properties can be divided into the following classes: color properties, border properties, font properties, and miscellaneous properties. We'll examine each of these classes of properties in the next four sections.

Looking at the Color Properties

The Label Web control contains two properties for specifying the color of the outputted text: `ForeColor` and `BackColor`. If you couldn't guess, `ForeColor` specifies the text's foreground color, whereas `BackColor` specifies its background color.

Let's create a new ASP.NET web page to try out these two color properties. Create an ASP.NET web page named `ColorLabel.aspx` and drag and drop a Label Web control onto the page. After adding the Label Web control, change the `Text` property to **This is a test of the color properties.**

Now, set the `BackColor` to a dark blue color and the `ForeColor` to white. To accomplish this, make sure that the Label Web control is selected so that its properties are displayed in the Properties window. Then find the `BackColor` property in the Properties window.

Selecting the `BackColor` property displays the More Colors dialog box shown in Figure 8.8. The More Colors dialog box allows you to pick a color from the palette on the left. If you do not see a color you like in the palette, click the Custom button, which presents an interface where you can specify the precise color settings.

If you want to replicate a color shown somewhere on your screen, click the Select button. This turns your mouse cursor into an eyedropper icon. Click the eyedropper on the color you want to replicate, and the More Colors dialog box selects that precise color.

Choose a dark blue color from the palette and click OK to assign the color selection to the `BackColor` property.

The Label Web control's `ForeColor` property indicates the foreground color of the text displayed. When the `ForeColor` property is selected, the same More Colors dialog box appears. Set the `ForeColor` to white.

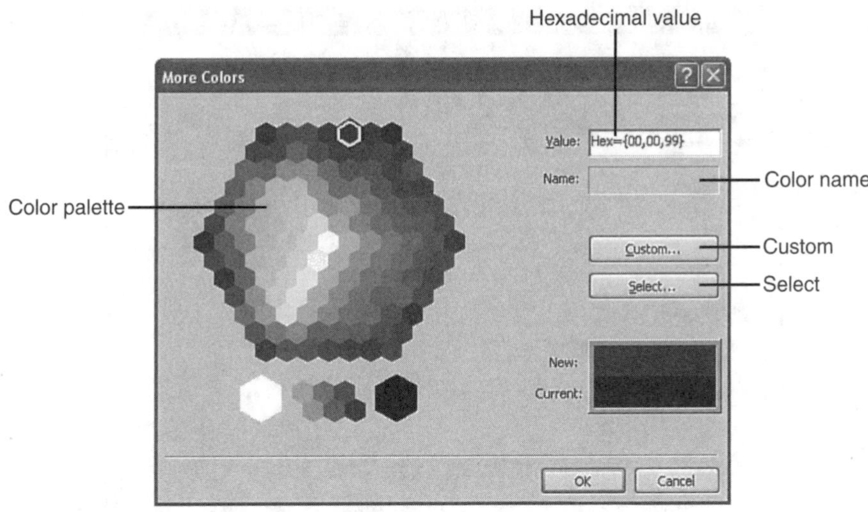

FIGURE 8.8 Pick a color from the More Colors dialog box.

By the Way

How Colors Are Expressed in HTML

Colors in a web page are typically expressed in one of two ways: as a named color; or as a hexadecimal string specifying the amount of red, green, and blue that, mixed together, makes up the color.

There are only 16 "official" named colors (although most browsers support many unofficial named colors, as well). Some of the official named colors include black, white, red, green, blue, orange, and yellow.

Colors can also be expressed based on its quantities of red, green, and blue, with values ranging from 0 to 255. This information is typically denoted as a six-character hexadecimal string. Hexadecimal is an alternative numbering system that has 16 digits—0, 1, 2, ..., 8, 9, A, B, ..., E, F— instead of 10. The numbers 0 through 255 can be represented in hexadecimal as 00 through FF. A color, then, can be denoted using hexadecimal as *RRGGBB*, where *RR* is the amount of red, *GG* the amount of green, and *BB* the amount of blue.

As Figure 8.8 shows, the More Colors dialog box displays the hexadecimal value for the selected color as `Hex={RR, GG, BB}`. It also includes a Name label that shows the color's associated defined name, if one exists.

For more information on the hexadecimal system and how colors can be denoted using hexadecimal, see www.mathsisfun.com/hexadecimal-decimal-colors.html.

At this point we've set three of the Label Web control's properties. We set the `Text` property to "This is a test of the color properties," the `BackColor` to a dark blue color, and the `ForeColor` to white. The designer should show the text "This is a test of the color properties" in a white foreground color with a dark blue background color, as shown in Figure 8.9.

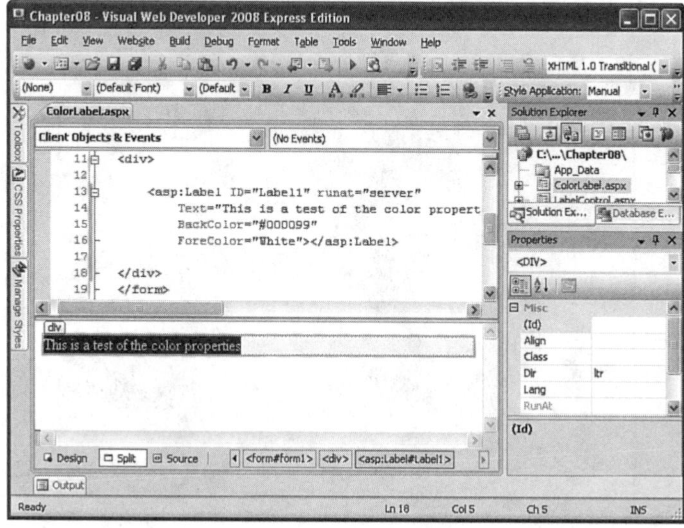

FIGURE 8.9
A Label with a white foreground and dark blue background is shown in the designer.

Figure 8.10 shows this page when viewed through a browser. As you would expect, the display in the browser matches the display in Visual Web Developer's designer.

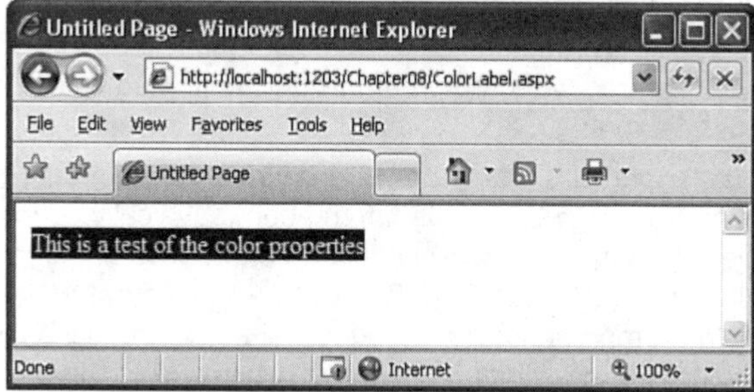

FIGURE 8.10
A Label with a white foreground and dark blue background is shown in the browser.

Examining the Border Properties

It is possible to put a border around the text displayed by a Label Web control.

To practice adding a border, create a new ASP.NET page titled `BorderLabel.aspx`. Drag and drop a Label Web control onto the page and set its `Text` property to **Testing the border properties.** Next, click the Label's `BorderStyle` property. This should open a drop-down list that contains various options for the style of border to be placed around the Label Web control. These options are enumerated in Table 8.2.

TABLE 8.2 **The** `BorderStyle` **Property Can Be Set to Any One of the Following Values**

Border Style	Description
`NotSet`	The default option. The border around the Label Web control depends on external style sheet rules.
`None`	No border is displayed.
`Dotted`	A dotted border is displayed.
`Dashed`	A dashed border is displayed.
`Solid`	A solid border is displayed.
`Double`	A double border is displayed.
`Groove`	A grooved border is displayed.
`Ridge`	A ridged border is displayed.
`Inset`	An inset border is displayed.
`Outset`	An outset border is displayed.

Select the `Solid` option for the `BorderStyle` property. In the designer, you see a solid border appear around the edges of the Label Web control. At this point your screen should look similar to Figure 8.11.

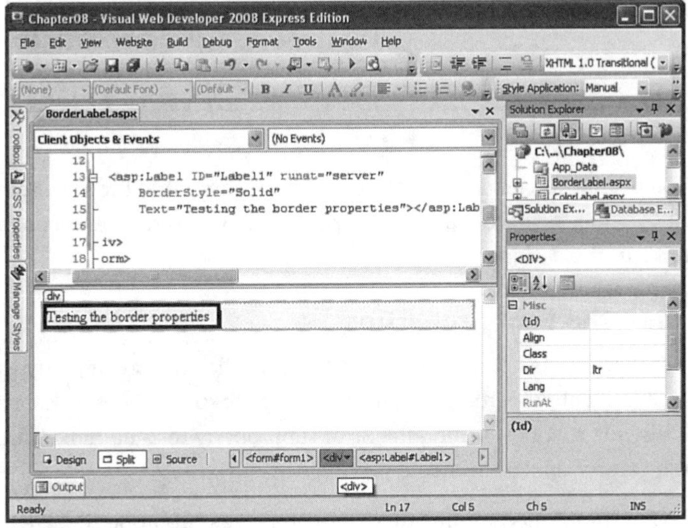

FIGURE 8.11 The Label Web control has a solid border.

Note that the border displayed in Figure 8.11 is black. We can change the border's color via the `BorderColor` property. The interface for selecting the `BorderColor` property is identical to that used for selecting the `BackColor` and `ForeColor` properties. Set the `BorderColor` to red.

In addition to the `BorderStyle` and `BorderColor` properties, there's a `BorderWidth` property as well. Go ahead and enter a value of 2 as the `BorderWidth` property, which creates a border 2 pixels wide.

Figure 8.12 shows the Design view after the `BorderColor` and `BorderWidth` properties have been set. Your screen should look similar.

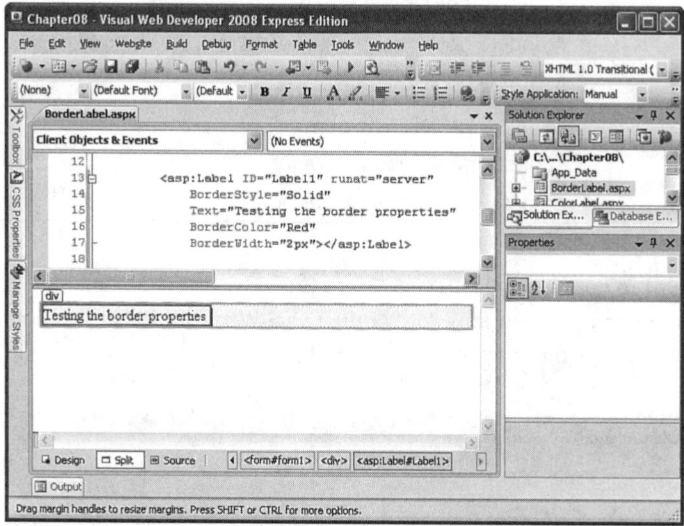

FIGURE 8.12 The designer contains a Label Web control with a solid red border 2 pixels thick.

Take a moment now to view this ASP.NET web page through a browser. You should see the text "Testing the border properties" displayed with a red, solid border 2 pixels thick, just like in the designer.

Delving into the Font Properties

As we saw earlier in this hour, the Label Web control has a `Font` property that contains a number of subproperties, such as `Bold`, `Italic`, `Underline`, `Name`, and others. We already saw how setting the `Bold` subproperty to `True` makes the text of a Label Web control appear in a bold font.

To further our examination of the other `Font` property's subproperties, create a new ASP.NET page named `LabelFont.aspx`, and drag a Label Web control onto the designer. Set this Web control's `Text` property to **Working with the Font properties.** Next, expand the Label's `Font` property by clicking the plus sign to the left of the

`Font` property name. This will list its subproperties. (You can find a complete list of the `Font` property's subproperties in Table 8.1.)

Let's set some of the `Font` property's subproperties. Start by setting the `Italic` subproperty to `True`, which will make the Label's text appear in an italic font in the designer. Next, under the `Name` property, choose the font name Arial. Finally, set the `Size` subproperty to `22pt`. This will cause the Label Web control's text in the designer to enlarge to a 22-point size.

Figure 8.13 shows Visual Web Developer at this point. If you're following along, your screen should look similar.

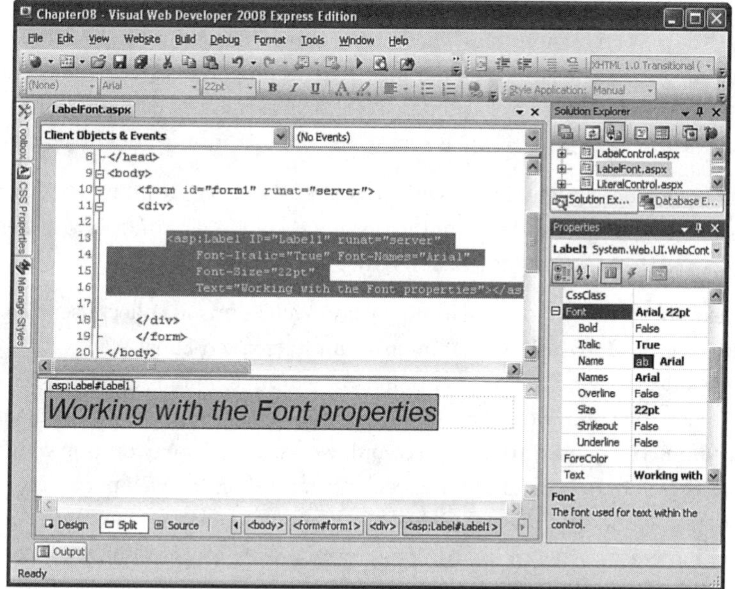

FIGURE 8.13
A Label Web control with some `Font` property subproperties set.

The Miscellaneous Properties

The remaining Label Web control properties can be classified as miscellaneous properties. For example, there is a `ToolTip` property. If you specify a value for the `ToolTip` property, it is displayed in a light yellow box whenever a visitor hovers his mouse pointer over the label's text. Figure 8.14 shows an ASP.NET web page that has its `ToolTip` property set to "This is a tooltip."

Two other miscellaneous Label Web control properties are `Height` and `Width`. These two properties can be set to specific values through the Properties window.

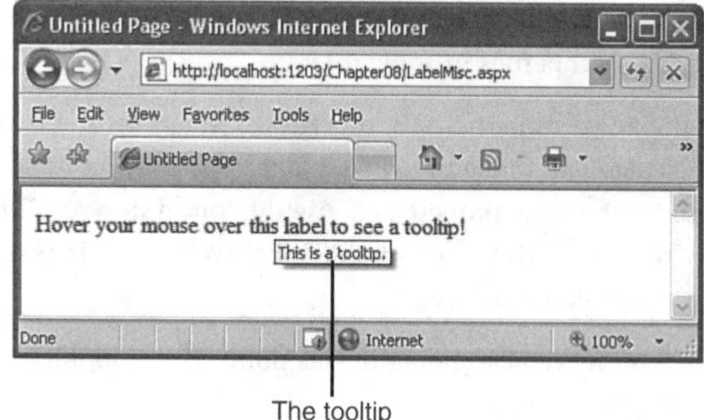

FIGURE 8.14 A tooltip is displayed when the mouse pointer hovers over the Label Web control.

The `Visible` property determines whether the Label Web control is rendered when the ASP.NET page is executed. If the `Visible` property is set to `True` (the default), the Label Web control's rendered HTML is sent to the browser. If, however, `Visible` is set to `False`, no HTML is sent to the browser for the Label Web control.

You may be wondering why in the world anyone would ever want to use this property. If a page developer doesn't want to display a Label Web control, why create it and set its `Visible` property to `False`? Why even create it in the first place?

In the next few hours, when we examine using Web Forms to collect user input, we'll see scenarios in which we just might want to create a Label Web control and hide it initially, showing it at a later point. For example, imagine that we had an ASP.NET page that prompted the user for her username and password. If the user provides an incorrect username or password, we want to display an appropriate message. Therefore, we can place a Label Web control on the web page that has such a message and initially set its `Visible` property to `False`. Then, if the user enters an incorrect password, we can programmatically set the Label Web control's `Visible` property to `True`, thereby displaying the message in response to an invalid password.

By the Way

> The remaining Label Web control properties—`AccessKey`, `AssociatedControlID`, `CssClass`, `Enabled`, `EnableTheming`, `EnableViewState`, (Expressions), `SkinID`, and `TabIndex`—are beyond the scope of this book. We will not use these Label Web control properties in any of the examples in this book.

Summary

In this hour we looked at the two ASP.NET Web controls designed for displaying text output: the Literal Web control and the Label Web control.

When the Literal Web control is rendered, its `Text` property is returned as its HTML. No formatting is applied, and no extraneous HTML tags are added.

The Label Web control is useful for displaying formatted text. For example, use the Label control if you want to display some text in a bold font or with a yellow background color. The Label Web control has a number of formatting properties, such as `BackColor`, `ForeColor`, `Font`, `BorderColor`, `BorderStyle`, and so forth.

Now that we've examined how to use the Literal and Label Web controls, we're ready to turn our attention to the Web controls that are designed to collect user input, such as the TextBox, DropDownList, RadioButton, and others. Before we do, though, we need to examine how an ASP.NET web page collects data from a web visitor and returns that data to the web server. We'll tackle this subject in the next hour, "Web Form Basics."

Q&A

Q. ***Is there any difference in the HTML sent to the browser for a Literal and a Label Web control?***

A. Recall from our discussions in this hour that when the ASP.NET engine executes an ASP.NET page, the Web controls are rendered into HTML. The precise HTML generated depends on the Web control and the values of its properties.

ASP.NET offers two Web controls for displaying text: the Literal and Label. If you create an ASP.NET page with Literal and Label Web controls and set the `Text` property of both to the same value—**This is a test**—when you visit the page through a browser it may appear as if both Web controls produce the same HTML output. However, the Label Web control produces slightly different HTML than the Literal Web control.

In such a web page, the HTML produced by the Literal control is

```
This is a test
```

Note that the HTML produced by a Literal control is literally the value of its `Text` property.

The Label Web control, however, actually uses a `<span>` HTML element to display its `Text` property. The HTML generated by the Label Web control in this example is

```
<span>This is a test</span>
```

The Label Web control wraps its `Text` property in a `<span>` HTML element so that it can add formatting. For example, if the Label Web control's `Font` property's `Bold` subproperty is set to `True`, the following HTML is rendered:

```
<span style="font-weight:bold;">This is a test</span>
```

Q. *In this hour we saw how to set the Label's formatting properties through the Properties window. Can they also be set programmatically, in the ASP.NET page's source code portion?*

A. All of the Label's properties may be set declaratively—through the Properties window—or programmatically. For example, in Hour 6, "Managing Program Flow with Visual Basic's Control Structures," we created an ASP.NET page that displayed a different message depending on the hour of the day. The page's code portion used conditional statements and programmatically set the Label control's `Text` property based on the value returned by `DateTime.Now.Hour`. I invite you to go back and augment this page so that the formatting is also adjusted based on the time of day.

In particular, if the message "Good morning" is displayed, have it rendered in a bold font. For "Good afternoon" set the `ForeColor` property to red. And for "Good evening" have the message underlined and italicized.

I'll get you started with the "Good morning" message. The following code sets the Label's `Text` property to "Good morning" and its `Font` properties `Bold` subproperty to `True` if the current hour is between 6:00 a.m. and noon:

```
If DateTime.Now.Hour >= 6 And DateTime.Now.Hour < 12 Then
    Message.Text = "Good morning."
    Message.Font.Bold = True
End If
```

Workshop

Quiz

1. What must you do to display formatted text with the Literal Web control?
2. What must you do to display formatted text with the Label Web control?
3. True or False: The Literal Web control contains only a single property, `Text`.
4. True or False: The Label Web control contains only a single property, `Text`.
5. Recall that when the ASP.NET engine executes an ASP.NET web page, it renders the Web controls into their corresponding HTML. What factor or factors determine the HTML generated by a particular Web control?
6. What purpose do the Literal and Label Web controls serve?
7. Why is it said that Web controls are an intermediary between an ASP.NET web page's HTML and source code portions?

Answers

1. The Literal Web control does not have any formatting properties. Instead, its rendered HTML is precisely the value of its `Text` property. Therefore, if you want to decorate the Literal Web control's output with any kind of formatting, you must enter the appropriate HTML elements or CSS styling directly in the `Text` property.
2. The Label Web control contains a number of formatting properties that can be used to specify the resulting text's formatting. Therefore, you can display formatted text by configuring the appropriate properties.
3. False. The Literal Web control also contains an `ID` property, among others.
4. False. In addition to its `Text` property, the Label Web control contains a plethora of formatting properties, an `ID` property, and several other less germane properties.
5. The HTML generated by a Web control depends on the Web control's properties' values.
6. The Literal and Label Web controls are the two Web controls designed to display text.

7. Web controls are said to be an intermediary between the HTML portion and source code portions of an ASP.NET web page because they are placed in the HTML portion and generate HTML, but can be programmatically accessed in the source code portion.

Exercises

1. Create an ASP.NET web page that uses a Literal Web control to display the web page's URL. Rather than hard-coding the URL into the Literal's `Text` property, set the `Text` property programmatically in the `Page_Load` event handler. Note that you can obtain the current page's URL via `Request.Url.ToString()`.

   Your ASP.NET page should contain a Literal Web control with its `ID` property set to some value (for example, `UrlDisplay`). Then, in the page's `Page_Load` event handler, add the following code:

   ```
   UrlDisplay.Text = Request.Url.ToString()
   ```

2. Create an ASP.NET page and add a Label Web control. Set its `Text` property to **What pretty text!** and then set a number of its formatting properties. Feel free to specify whatever formatting property values you'd like, but be sure to set at least five formatting properties. Try out formatting properties that were not closely examined in this hour.

3. For this exercise, create an ASP.NET web page that uses a Label Web control to display the IP address of the visitor visiting the web page. (An IP address is a series of numbers that identifies a computer on the Internet. If you are serving the ASP.NET pages from your own computer, your IP address will be 127.0.0.1.)

   The visiting user's IP address can be obtained via `Request.UserHostAddress`. Therefore, to complete this exercise, you will need to create a Label Web control and set its `ID` property. Then you need to create a `Page_Load` event handler in the ASP.NET page's source code portion that contains the following code:

   ```
   LabelID.Text = Request.UserHostAddress
   ```

PART II

Collecting and Processing User Input

HOUR 9

Web Form Basics

In this hour, we will cover

- How user input is gathered through HTML
- What a Web Form is
- Using a Web Form in an ASP.NET web page
- Identifying properties of Web Forms
- Collecting user input in an ASP.NET web page
- Examining how the Web Form persists the state of its Web controls

To create a useful web application, we must be able to somehow collect user input and return to the user a web page customized to the input entered. For example, search engines like Google accept a user's search term and then display a page with the results based on the search query. Sites like Amazon.com read a shopper's credit card numbers so that they can correctly bill shoppers for their purchases.

HTML was designed with these needs in mind, as evidenced by the various HTML elements designed to aid in collecting user input. The HTML `<input>` element, for example, can be used to display a text box, check box, radio button, or drop-down list. After the user enters information into these `<input>` elements, the HTML `<form>` element specifies the web page that the input should be sent to.

With ASP.NET we do not need to enter such HTML elements directly. Rather, we use the appropriate Web controls, which, when rendered, produce the necessary HTML elements. If we need a text box on our ASP.NET page, instead of adding an `<input>` HTML element, we add a TextBox Web control. Similarly, instead of using the HTML `<form>` element, our ASP.NET web pages use Web Forms. We'll discuss Web Forms and their semantics in this hour.

Gathering User Input in an HTML Web Page

Imagine that we wanted to create a web page that calculated a user's Body Mass Index, or BMI.

By the Way

> The Body Mass Index is a ratio of a person's height to weight. BMI is commonly used as a quick determination of whether one is underweight, at a healthy weight, overweight, or obese. For more information about BMI, see www.cdc.gov/nccdphp/dnpa/bmi/.

To determine someone's BMI, we need to know his height and weight. For the time being, imagine that we want to create this web page without using HTML instead of ASP.NET's Web controls to generate the text boxes needed for collecting the user's height and weight.

When HTML was designed, two elements were created to facilitate collecting user input. These two HTML elements are the `<form>` element and the `<input>` element. Although a thorough understanding of these elements is not needed for collecting user input in an ASP.NET web page, having a strong grasp on the concepts of how user input is collected from a web page is important. Therefore, let's briefly examine the `<input>` and `<form>` elements and see how they work in conjunction to allow a web page to collect user input.

Examining the <input> HTML Element

The `<input>` element can be used to create a text box, a radio button, a check box, or a button. The `<input>` element's type attribute specifies what type of user input control is displayed in the user's web browser. For example, if you wanted to create an HTML web page that contained a text box, you could use the following HTML:

```
<input type="text">
```

To display a check box, you would use

```
<input type="checkbox">
```

> We will not delve into the HTML specifics for collecting user input in this book. For more information on this topic, check out www.w3schools.com/html/html_forms.asp.

Because our web page needs two text boxes—one for the person's height in inches and one for the person's weight in pounds—we use two `<input>` elements, both with `type="text"`.

Listing 9.1 contains the preliminary HTML web page for our BMI calculator. Keep in mind that this page is far from complete!

LISTING 9.1 Our First Draft of the BMI Calculator

```
1: <html>
2: <body>
3:   <h1>BMI Calculator</h1>
4:   <p>Your Height (in inches): <input type="text" name="height" /></p>
5:
6:   <p>Your Weight (in pounds): <input type="text" name="weight" /></p>
7: </body>
8: </html>
```

Listing 9.1 displays two text boxes, one for the user's height and one for weight. The `<input>` elements on lines 4 and 6 each contain a `name` attribute. The `name` attribute is needed to uniquely identify each `<input>` element. As we will see in the next section, "Passing the Input Back to the Web Server Using the `<form>` Element," the `<input>` element's `name` attribute is used when sending the contents of the various `<input>` elements back to the web server.

Figure 9.1 shows the code in Listing 9.1 when viewed through a browser.

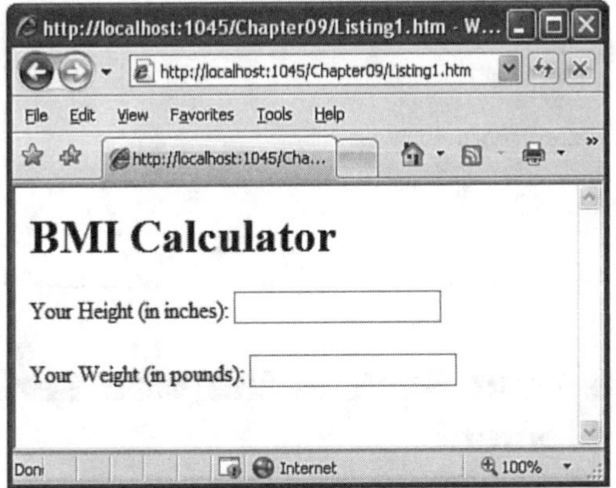

FIGURE 9.1 The user is presented with two text boxes.

In addition to the two text boxes, we need some way for the user to indicate to the web browser that she has completed entering her data. To accomplish this, a **submit button** is used. A submit button is a button that, when clicked by the user, indicates to the web browser that the user has finished entering her input. The HTML for a submit button is as follows:

```
<input type="submit" value="Text to Appear on Submit Button">
```

Listing 9.2 contains the HTML from Listing 9.1, but augmented with the submit button (line 8). Figure 9.2 shows the HTML from Listing 9.2 when viewed through a browser.

LISTING 9.2 Our Second Draft of the BMI Calculator

```
 1: <html>
 2: <body>
 3:    <h1>BMI Calculator</h1>
 4:    <p>Your Height (in inches): <input type="text" name="height" /></p>
 5:
 6:    <p>Your Weight (in pounds): <input type="text" name="weight" /></p>
 7:
 8:    <p><input type="submit" value="Calculate BMI" /></p>
 9: </body>
10: </html>
```

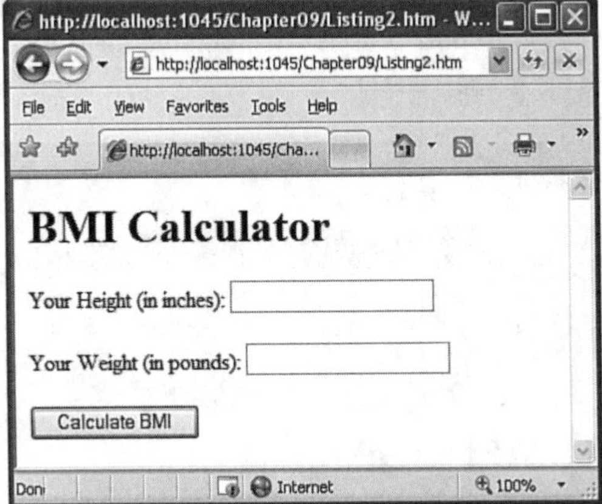

FIGURE 9.2
A submit button has been added.

Passing the Input Back to the Web Server Using the `<form>` Element

Recall from our discussions in Hour 1, "Getting Started with ASP.NET 3.5," that when a user requests a web page from a web server, the web server sends the web page's HTML to the user's browser, which is then rendered in the browser. For the browser to receive this HTML, the web browser and web server must communicate with one another, but after the web browser has received the HTML from the server, this communication ends.

The key point to take away from this discussion is that a physical, logical, and temporal disconnect exists between the web server and the web browser. The web server has no idea whether the user is still viewing the page or entering information into the page's text boxes, check boxes, or other inputs.

Because of this disconnect between the web browser and the web server, the web browser needs some way to let the web server know the values the user entered into any input fields. This is accomplished via the HTML `<form>` element.

The `<form>` element contains within it the `<input>` elements used to collect the user input, as well as the submit button. When the `<form>` element's submit button is clicked, the form is said to have been **submitted**. When a form is submitted, a specified web page is requested by the browser, and the data entered into the various `<input>` elements within the `<form>` are sent to this web page.

This description of the `<form>` element leaves two questions unanswered:

- When the `<form>` is submitted, how does it know what web page to send the contents of its `<input>` elements to?
- How, exactly, are the contents of the `<input>` elements sent to this web page?

We can answer these two questions by examining the `action` and `method` attributes of the `<form>` element. The `action` attribute specifies the URL that the browser is directed to after the `<form>`'s submit button is clicked. Therefore, it is the value of the `action` attribute that indicates the web page that is visited after the `<form>` is submitted.

The contents of the `<input>` elements are compacted into a single string and are sent in a specific format. Precisely, the format used is as follows:

```
InputName1=InputValue1&InputName2=InputValue2&...&InputNameN=InputValueN
```

Here, *`InputName1`* is the value of the first `<input>` element's name attribute, and *`InputValue1`* is the value the user entered into this `<input>` element. *`InputName2`* is the value of the second `<input>` element's `name` attribute, and *`InputValue2`* is its value, and so on. Note that each `<input>` elements name and value are separated by an equal sign (=), and each pair of names and values is separated by an ampersand (&).

The `method` attribute determines how this string of `<input>` element names and values is sent to the web server. The method attribute can have one of two values: `GET` or `POST`. If method is set to `GET`, the contents of the `<input>` elements are sent through the **querystring**. The querystring is an optional string that can be tacked on to the end of a web page's URL. Specifically, if a website URL has a question mark in it (?), everything after the question mark is considered the querystring.

You have probably seen web pages whose URL looks like

```
http://www.example.com/somePage.htm?Name=Scott&Age=21
```

Here, the contents after the question mark are considered the querystring.

If method is set to `POST`, the `<input>` elements' contents are sent through the HTTP headers, meaning there is no querystring tacked onto the end of the URL.

By the Way

> Whenever a web browser requests a web page, it sends HTTP headers in addition to the requested URL. These are simple strings of text. One such HTTP header is the User-Agent header, which sends information on the type of browser making the web request.
>
> When the method attribute is set to `POST`, the HTTP Post header is used to send along the contents of the `<input>` elements. When this information is placed within the HTTP Post header, the querystring is left uncluttered.

Let's augment Listing 9.2 to include a `<form>` element that contains `action` and `method` attributes. Listing 9.3 is this augmented HTML page.

LISTING 9.3 A `<form>` Element Has Been Added

```
 1: <html>
 2: <body>
 3:
 4:   <form method="GET" action="SomePage.htm">
 5:     <h1>BMI Calculator</h1>
 6:     <p>Your Height (in inches): <input type="text" name="height" /></p>
 7:
 8:     <p>Your Weight (in pounds): <input type="text" name="weight" /></p>
 9:
10:     <p><input type="submit" value="Calculate BMI" /></p>
11:   </form>
12:
13: </body>
14: </html>
```

The `<form>` element—spanning from line 4 to line 11—encloses the two `<input>` elements that generate the two text boxes and the submit button `<input>` element. The `<form>`'s `action` attribute is set to `SomePage.htm`, and the `method` attribute is set to `GET`.

When the user visits the HTML page shown in Listing 9.3, he will be presented with two text boxes and a submit button, as was shown in Figure 9.2. After the user enters his height and weight and clicks the submit button, the web browser requests the web page, as follows:

```
SomePage.htm?height=heightEnteredByUser&weight=weightEnteredByUser
```

Figure 9.3 shows the web browser's Address bar after the user has visited the HTML page generated by Listing 9.3 and has entered the value 72 for height and 168 for weight.

The user's inputs are encoded in the querystring
http://localhost:1045/Chapter09/SomePage.htm?height=72&weight=168

FIGURE 9.3
The querystring contains the values entered into the height and weight text boxes.

By the Way

> `SomePage.htm` would likely read the values in the querystring, perform some calculation on these values, and then display the results to the user. Starting in the "Dissecting ASP.NET Web Forms" section, we'll see how to programmatically process user input in an ASP.NET page.

Comparing Postback Forms and Redirect Forms

If the `<form>`'s `method` attribute on line 4 in Listing 9.3 is changed to `POST`, when the user submits the form, she is still directed to `SomePage.htm`, but no information will be passed through the querystring. Rather, the names and values of the `<input>` elements— `height=`*`heightEnteredByUser`*`&weight=`*`weightEnteredByUser`*—will be hidden from sight, passed through the HTTP headers instead.

As we saw, the `<form>`'s `action` attribute specifies the web page that the browser requests after the `<form>` is submitted. In Listing 9.3, this web page was `SomePage.htm`. Such forms are typically called **redirect forms** because, when submitted, they redirect the user to a different page.

Imagine, though, what would happen if the `action` property were set to the same URL as the page that contains the `<form>` element. Suppose we create an ASP.NET web page called `PostbackFormExample.htm` that has the following HTML:

```
<html>
<body>
  <form method="POST" action="PostbackFormExample.htm">
    <p>What is your age? <input type="text" name="age" /></p>
    <p><input type="submit" value="Click to Continue" /></p>
  </form>
</body></html>
```

When the user first visits `PostbackFormExample.htm`, she will be shown a text box labeled "What is your age?" Underneath this text box, she will see a submit button titled Click to Continue. After entering her age into the text box and submitting the `<form>`, what will happen? Because the method attribute is set to `POST`, the `<input>` text box's data will be sent via the HTTP Post header. Because the `action` attribute is set to `PostbackFormExample.htm`, the user will be sent *back* to `PostbackFormExample.htm` (but this time with information passed in through the HTTP Post header).

Such `<form>`s are called **postback forms** because they use the `POST` method and because when the `<form>` is submitted, the user is sent back to the same page. With a postback form, the `<form>`'s `<input>` elements' data is posted back to the same web page.

Figure 9.4 shows a pictorial representation of both a redirect form and a postback form. Note how the postback form sends the contents of its `<input>` elements back to itself, whereas a redirect form forwards the contents to a different web page.

FIGURE 9.4
Postback forms differ from redirect forms.

Postback Web Form Example

A postback form is one whose ACTION property is set to the URL of the page the form appears on (i.e., Page1.htm). When the form is submitted, the user's browser requests the same page (Page1.htm), passing the form field inputs through either the querystring or HTTP Post headers.

Redirect Form Example

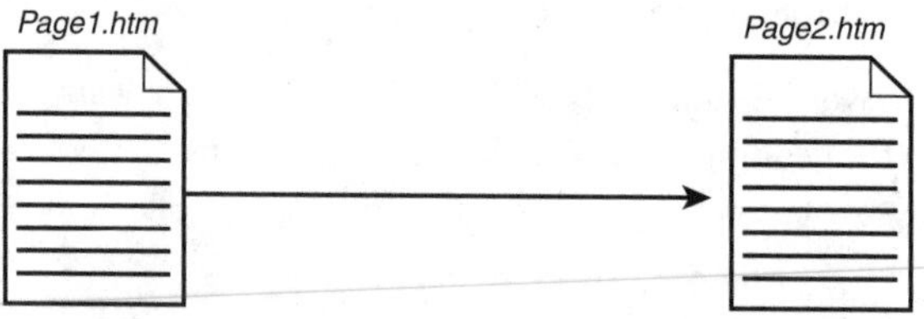

With a redirect form, Page1.htm has a form whose ACTION property is set to Page2.htm. When the form is submitted, the user requests the Page2.htm web page, passing along the form field data in either the querystring or HTTP Post headers.

Dissecting ASP.NET Web Forms

Collecting user input in an ASP.NET page is much simpler than the techniques discussed in the preceding section. To collect user input, the ASP.NET page must contain a **Web Form**. A Web Form is a Web control that has the following syntax:

```
<form runat="server">
  ...
</form>
```

When you create a new ASP.NET page in Visual Web Developer, a Web Form is automatically added. To demonstrate that this is the case, let's create a new ASP.NET page, one that we'll build on throughout the remainder of this hour. Name this new ASP.NET page `BMICalculator.aspx`.

After the new file is created, go to the Source view if you are not already there, and inspect the HTML that was automatically injected into this page. As Figure 9.5 shows, the HTML portion already contains a Web Form (the `<form runat="server">` on line 10).

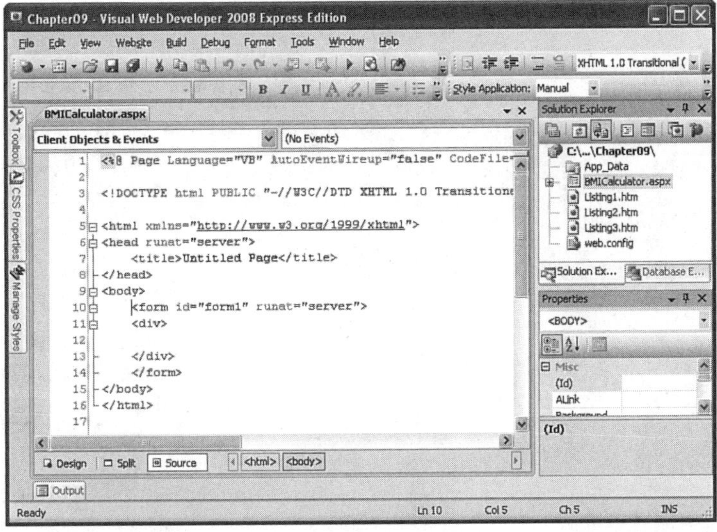

FIGURE 9.5
A Web Form is automatically included in new ASP.NET pages created by Visual Web Developer.

Adding Web Controls to Collect User Input

In an HTML web page, user input is collected using a number of `<input>` elements, which can provide a variety of input media, such as text boxes, check boxes, radio buttons, and so on. Additionally, a `<form>` must encase these `<input>` elements and have its `method` and `action` properties specified.

With an ASP.NET page, collecting user input is much simpler. As we've seen already, we need a Web Form, which Visual Web Developer has already added for us. In addition, we need the Web controls into which the user will enter his input.

For example, if we want to provide the user with a text box to enter his input, we would use a TextBox Web control. If we want to have the user enter his input via a radio button, we would use a RadioButton Web control. These various Web controls must be placed within the Web Form.

Earlier in this hour we looked at creating an HTML page to collect user input for a BMI calculator. The BMI calculator needs to collect two bits of information from the user: height and weight. These two pieces of information can be provided via two text boxes. Therefore, let's add two TextBox Web controls to our `BMICalculator.aspx` ASP.NET page.

Before you add the first TextBox Web control, though, type in the title to precede the TextBox Web control: **`Your height (in inches):`**.

After you've typed in this text, drag and drop a TextBox Web control from the Toolbox onto the designer. Figure 9.6 shows the Visual Web Developer after adding this first TextBox Web control.

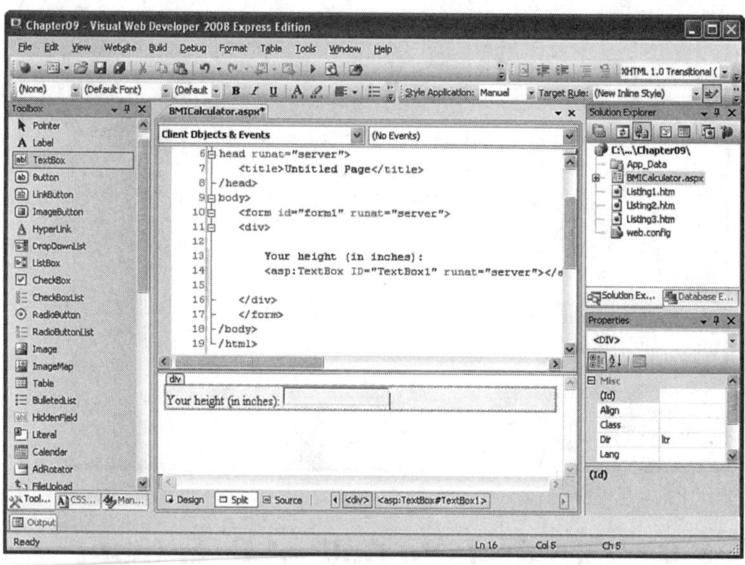

FIGURE 9.6
The first TextBox Web control has been added.

Now add the title for the second TextBox Web control. Specifically, enter the text: **`Your weight (in pounds):`**. After entering this text, drag a TextBox Web control onto the page. Take a moment to ensure that your screen looks similar to Figure 9.7.

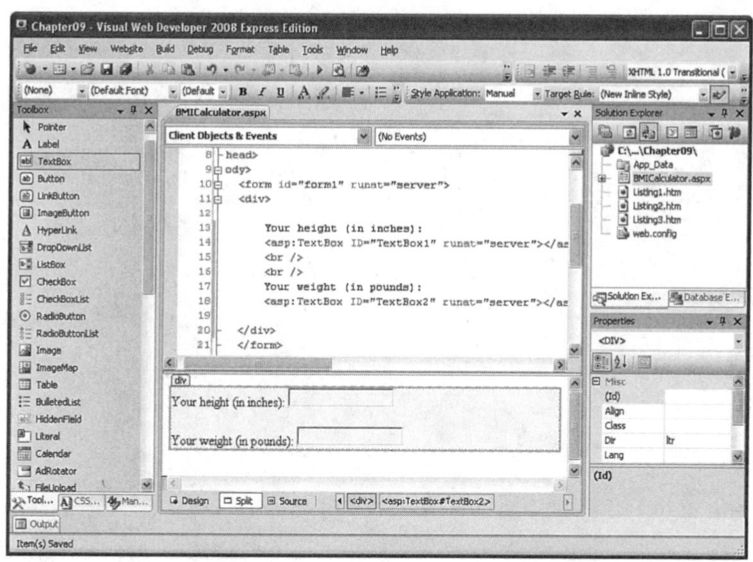

FIGURE 9.7
The second TextBox Web control has been added.

At this point we have added two TextBox Web controls to the ASP.NET page. We are still missing one Web control, though. Recall from our earlier discussion that the browser needs to know when the user has completed entering his input. This was accomplished in the HTML web page in Listing 9.2 by adding a submit button.

We need to add a submit button to our ASP.NET page as well. To accomplish this, drag and drop the Button Web control from the Toolbox onto the page, placing it beneath the two TextBox Web controls.

Figure 9.8 shows the designer after the Button Web control has been added.

The next step is to set the properties of these various Web controls. The Button Web control, for example, is currently displaying the text "Button," which we can change to a more descriptive message by changing the Button Web control's `Text` property. Also, the `ID` properties of the three Web controls are still set to their default values, which are not very descriptive.

Take a moment to change the properties of these Web controls. Change the Button control's `ID` property to `CalculateBMI` and set its `Text` property to **Calculate BMI**. After you change the `Text` property, the text appearing on the Button in the designer should change as well.

Next, change the `ID` properties of the two TextBoxes to `Height` and `Weight`.

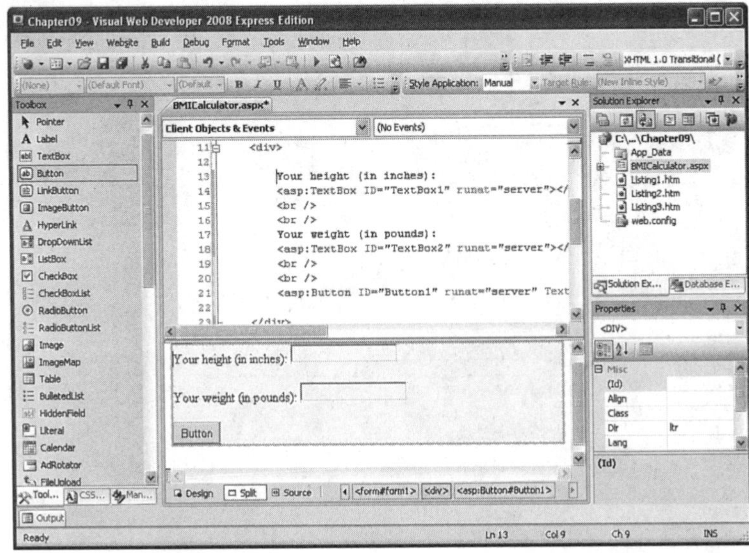

FIGURE 9.8 The final input Web control—the Button Web control—has been added.

Testing the `BMICalculator.aspx` ASP.NET Page

Let's examine the `BMICalculator.aspx`'s user interface through a browser. Go to the Debug menu and choose Start Without Debugging. This launches a web browser and directs it to `BMICalculator.aspx`. The output you see should be identical to that shown in the designer in Figure 9.8.

After you have visited the ASP.NET web page through your browser of choice, take a moment to view the HTML that was sent to your browser. Listing 9.4 shows the source code received when visiting `BMICalculator.aspx` through a browser.

LISTING 9.4 The Browser Receives `<form>` and `<input>` Elements

```
<!DOCTYPE html PUBLIC "-//W3C//DTD XHTML 1.0 Transitional//EN"
➥ "http://www.w3.org/TR/xhtml1/DTD/xhtml1-transitional.dtd">

<html xmlns="http://www.w3.org/1999/xhtml" >
<head><title>
    Untitled Page
</title></head>
<body>
    <form name="form1" method="post" action="BMICalculator.aspx"
➥id="form1">
<div>
<input type="hidden" name="__VIEWSTATE" id="__VIEWSTATE"
➥ value=" /wEPDwULLTExNTc2NTI3OTlkZJ14lafYUKkP1ite6Wd2kKJ1mR/d" />
</div>

```

LISTING 9.4 Continued

```
13:     <div>
14:         Your height (in inches):
15:         <input name="Height" type="text" id="Height" /><br />
16:         <br />
17:         Weight (in pounds):
18:         <input name="Weight" type="text" id="Weight" /><br />
19:         <br />
20:         <input type="submit" name="CalculateBMI" value="Calculate BMI"
➥ id="CalculateBMI" />
21:     </div>
22:
23: <div>
24:
25:     <input type="hidden" name="__EVENTVALIDATION" id="__EVENTVALIDATION"
➥ value=" /wEWBALG+8PhBgLzj/DXAQLUj/
➥DXAQL5loSvCu1r+ovlIsichSbzWaNft98Nba69" />
26: </div></form>
27: </body>
28: </html>
```

The first thing to notice from Listing 9.4 is that the Web Form and Web controls produce roughly the same HTML that we crafted by hand in Listing 9.3. This is a powerful concept because it makes our job as ASP.NET developers easier. We do not to have to worry about HTML specifics. Rather, we can focus on building our page's user interface by adding the necessary Web controls to our page.

By the Way

ASP.NET's Web control model relieves developers from having to know HTML details. Rather, ASP.NET developers can focus on creating the user interface as they see fit (by dragging and dropping controls onto the designer), and working on the source code portion of their ASP.NET web pages.

Before we move on, I want to point out three important concepts illustrated in Listing 9.4. First, notice that the Button Web control is rendered as a submit button (line 20). That means that when this button is clicked, the `<form>` will be submitted.

Next, note that the Web Form in our ASP.NET web page is rendered as a postback `<form>` element (line 8). (Recall that a postback form is one that has its `method` attribute set to `POST` and its `action` set to its own URL.) This means that when the user clicks the Button Web control, the `<form>` will submit, causing the page to be reloaded.

By the Way

As Listing 9.4 shows, ASP.NET Web Forms are rendered as postback forms. The terms **postback** and **posted back** are used to describe the process of a Web Form being submitted. For example, you might say, "Clicking the Button Web control causes a postback," or "There was an error when the page posted back."

Finally, pay attention to the `<input>` elements on lines 10 and 25. They are hidden `<input>` elements (note that their `type` attributes are set to `hidden`), meaning that they are not displayed in the browser. These hidden `<input>` elements are produced when the Web Form is rendered and provide information used by the ASP.NET engine when the Web Form is submitted. A thorough discussion of these hidden `<input>` elements accomplish is an advanced topic that we will not discuss in this book.

Web Forms Remember the Values the Users Enter

While you have `BMICalculator.aspx` loaded into your browser, take a moment to fill some values into the two text boxes and then click the Calculate BMI button. What happens? At first glance, it may appear that nothing happened. The same web page is shown, and the text boxes contain the values you entered.

However, something has happened. Specifically, when you clicked the submit button, the `<form>` was submitted. Because this `<form>` is a postback form, the same web page was reloaded, which is why you still see the same web page in your browser. In fact, the HTML markup sent to your web browser has changed, but ever so slightly. If you view the HTML received by your browser after entering some data into the text boxes and submitting the form, you'll see that the TextBox Web controls' rendered `<input>` elements now contain a `value` attribute containing the input you entered into the text box.

To better understand what has just happened, take a look at Figure 9.9. This figure shows `BMICalculator.aspx` after the values 72 and 168 have been entered into the height and weight text boxes and the submit button has been clicked.

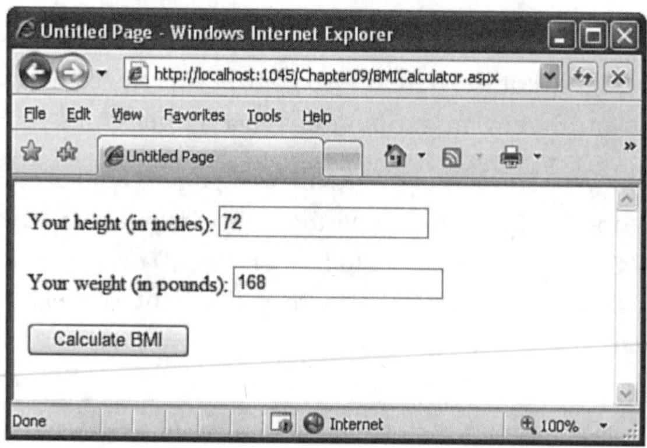

FIGURE 9.9 The text boxes have had values entered into them, and the form has been submitted.

The HTML sent to the browser in Figure 9.9 is shown in Listing 9.5. Note that the HTML in Listings 9.4 and 9.5 is nearly identical, the only exception being that the `<input>` elements on lines 15 and 18 of Listing 9.5 differ from lines 15 and 18 of Listing 9.4. Specifically, the `<input>` elements in Listing 9.5 have a value attribute set to the value entered into each respective text box (see Figure 9.9).

LISTING 9.5 The HTML Received by the Browser After the Form Has Been Submitted

```
 1: <!DOCTYPE html PUBLIC "-//W3C//DTD XHTML 1.0 Transitional//EN"
➥ "http://www.w3.org/TR/xhtml1/DTD/xhtml1-transitional.dtd">
 2:
 3: <html xmlns="http://www.w3.org/1999/xhtml" >
 4: <head><title>
 5:     Untitled Page
 6: </title></head>
 7: <body>
 8:     <form name="form1" method="post" action="BMICalculator.aspx"
➥id="form1">
 9: <div>
10: <input type="hidden" name="__VIEWSTATE" id="__VIEWSTATE"
➥ value=" /wEPDwULLTExNTc2NTI3OTlkZJ14lafYUKkP1ite6Wd2kKJ1mR/d" />
11: </div>
12:
13:     <div>
14:         Your height (in inches):
15:         <input name="Height" type="text" value="72" id="Height" /><br />
16:         <br />
17:         Weight (in pounds):
18:         <input name="Weight" type="text" value="168" id="Weight" /><br />
19:         <br />
20:         <input type="submit" name="CalculateBMI" value="Calculate BMI"
➥ id="CalculateBMI" />
21:     </div>
22:
23: <div>
24:
25:     <input type="hidden" name="__EVENTVALIDATION" id="__EVENTVALIDATION"
➥ value=" /wEWBALG+8PhBgLzj/DXAQLUj/
➥DXAQL5loSvCu1r+ovlIsichSbzWaNft98Nba69" />
26: </div></form>
27: </body>
28: </html>
```

To understand why the TextBox Web controls rendered different HTML markup after the form was submitted (Listing 9.5) than before (Listing 9.4), let's step through the sequence of steps that transpires in the ASP.NET engine on postback.

The TextBox Web control has a `Text` property. If this property is set to some value, the HTML rendered by the TextBox Web control is different than if this property is not set at all. If the `Text` property is not set, the HTML rendered by the TextBox Web control is simply

```
<input name="ID" type="text" id="ID" />
```

where *`ID`* is the value of the TextBox control's `ID` property.

For example, on line 15 in Listing 9.4 you can see that the first TextBox Web control, whose `ID` property is set to `Height`, produces the following rendered markup:

```
<input name="Height" type="text" id="Height" />
```

If, however, the `Text` property is set to some value, the `value` attribute is included in the TextBox control's rendered markup like so:

```
<input name="ID" type="text" value="Text" id="ID" />
```

where *`Text`* is the value of the TextBox control's `Text` property.

When the `BMICalculator.aspx` page was first visited, the `Text` property of the TextBox Web controls was not set, as evidenced by the HTML markup produced (see lines 15 and 18 in Listing 9.4). When the user enters some values into these two text boxes, such as 72 in the height text box and 168 in the weight text box, and then submits the form, the `Text` properties of the TextBox Web controls are set to the values entered by the user. Then, when the TextBox Web controls are rendered, they include a `value` attribute whose value corresponds to the input entered by the user (see lines 15 and 18 in Listing 9.5).

Writing the Code for `BMICalculator.aspx`

Note that when we enter values into the text boxes and submit the form, the web page is reloaded (because we're using a postback form) and the values entered into the text boxes are persisted across the postback. Although this is fine and good, we still need to provide code to actually perform the Body Mass Index calculation. The BMI calculation is quite simple and is shown in Figure 9.10.

The code required for this calculation is fairly straightforward and is shown in Listing 9.6.

LISTING 9.6 The Code for the BMI Calculation

```
'Find out the person's height and weight
Dim UsersHeight as Integer = Height.Text
Dim UsersWeight as Integer = Weight.Text

'Calculate the person's BMI
Dim BMI as Decimal
BMI = (UsersWeight / (UsersHeight * UsersHeight)) * 703
```

LISTING 9.6 Continued

```
 8:
 9: 'Output the BMI value
10: LabelWebID.Text = "Your BMI is " & BMI
```

English Formula:

$$BMI = \left(\frac{WeightInPounds}{HeightInInches^2} \right) \cdot 703$$

Metric Formula:

$$BMI = \frac{WeightInKilograms}{HeightInMeters^2}$$

FIGURE 9.10 The BMI is a ratio of weight to height.

On line 2 an `Integer` variable named `UsersHeight` is declared and assigned the value of the `Height` TextBox control's `Text` property. Following that, an `Integer` variable named `UsersWeight` is declared and assigned the value of the `Weight` TextBox control's `Text` property. Next, on line 6, a `Decimal` variable named `BMI` is created; it is then assigned the person's BMI as defined by the formula in Figure 9.10 (see line 7).

By the Way

> The code in Listing 9.6 outputs the BMI to a Label Web control, but we have not yet added a Label to our ASP.NET page. Take a moment to do so. Set the Label control's `ID` to an appropriate value and then have the BMI calculation assigned to its `Text` property. Refer to the preceding hour for more information on the Label Web control.

Clearly, this code must appear in our ASP.NET web page's source code portion, but where? We want this code to run whenever the user submits the form. The form is submitted when the Button is clicked. Therefore, this code should execute when the Button Web control's `Click` event fires.

To add a `Click` event handler for the button, double-click the Button Web control in the Design view. This takes you to the page's source code portion with the appropriate event handler created. Now add the code from Listing 9.6 inside the `Click` event handler.

After you have added this code, view the ASP.NET page through a browser. When you first visit the page, you should see two empty text boxes and a button labeled Calculate BMI; Figure 9.11 shows the browser when the page is first visited.

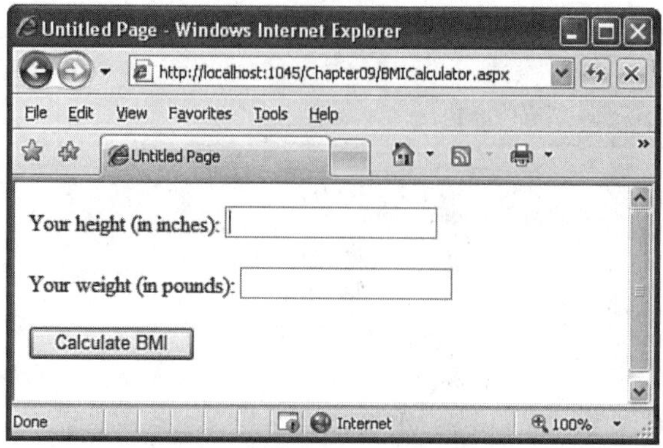

FIGURE 9.11 The final `BMICalculator.aspx` ASP.NET web page when it is first visited.

Now enter some appropriate values into the two text boxes and click the Calculate BMI button. If you enter my height and weight—70 and 164—you should see the output shown in Figure 9.12.

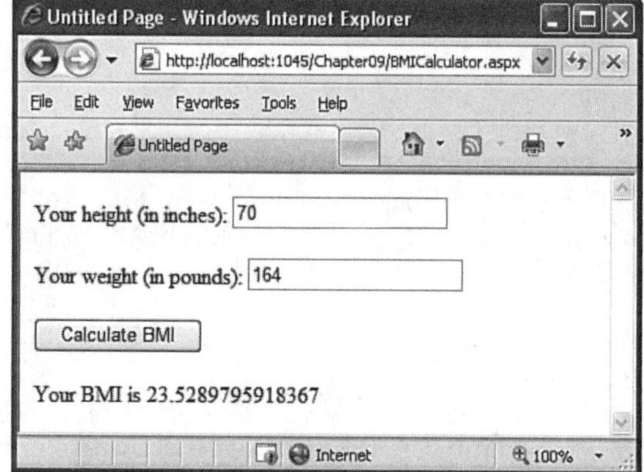

FIGURE 9.12 The user's BMI is displayed.

Did you Know?

To determine what the various BMI ratings mean, visit http://nhlbisupport.com/bmi/bmicalc.htm. Briefly, a healthy BMI range is between 18.5 and 24.9. Persons with a BMI of 25.0 to 29.9 are considered overweight, whereas a BMI over 30 indicates obesity. (BMI conclusions can be inaccurate for athletes and the elderly.)

If you omit entering values for your height or weight or enter noninteger values into these text boxes, you will get an error when submitting the page. Similarly, if you enter a negative value for your weight, the computed BMI will be a negative number itself.

In Hour 12, "Validating User Input with Validation Controls," we'll examine how to use a special kind of Web control that ensures a user's input is in an acceptable form and within acceptable boundaries.

Summary

In this hour we examined how user input can be collected in an ASP.NET web page. We started by examining the HTML elements needed to collect user input, which include a number of `<input>` elements for each text box, check box, radio button, or drop-down list; and a `<form>` element, inside which the `<input>` elements must be enclosed. Additionally, a submit button is needed.

With ASP.NET web pages, we do not need to worry about creating these HTML elements by hand. Rather, we can use appropriate Web controls, such as the TextBox Web control for displaying a text box, a CheckBox Web control for displaying a check box, and so on. To collect a user's input, these Web controls must be placed inside a Web Form. A Web Form, as we saw, is a Web control of the following form:

```
<form runat="server">
  ...
</form>
```

Visual Web Developer automatically generates the declarative markup for a Web Form when creating a new ASP.NET page.

In addition to Web controls to collect the user's input, a Button Web control should be added in the Web Form. The Button Web control is rendered as a submit button. When clicked, the form is submitted via a postback. If you have source code that you want to execute whenever the Web Form is submitted, you can place it in the Button Web control's `Click` event handler. To add a `Click` event handler, double-click the Button Web control from the Design view.

Now that we have seen how an ASP.NET page can collect user input and perform calculations on this input, we're ready to examine the Web controls for collecting user input in much finer detail. In the next hour we'll focus on examining the TextBox Web control. Following that hour, we'll look at collecting a user's input using the DropDownList, RadioButton, and CheckBox Web controls.

Q&A

Q. ***Sometimes when I refresh my browser on a web page with a form, I receive the message*** `"This page cannot be refreshed without resending the form information"` ***or*** `"The page contains POSTDATA. Do you want to refresh?"` ***What does this mean?***

A. Recall that there are two ways a form can submit its values: through the querystring or through the HTTP Post headers. When a postback form is used, the form uses the HTTP Post headers and submits the form to the same URL. (Refer to Figure 9.4 for a graphical depiction of how postback forms work.)

When you ask your browser to refresh the page after you have submitted a postback form, the browser doesn't know whether you want to refresh without resubmitting the user's inputs or if you want to refresh by resending the HTTP Post headers. Therefore, it asks if you want to resend the form information.

You may also notice this behavior when clicking the Back button to return to a page that has been requested via a postback.

Q. ***Why do ASP.NET Web Forms use postback? Why not direct the user to another page or pass the information along in the querystring?***

A. ASP.NET Web Forms use postback forms over alternative methods for a number of reasons. The most important is that postback forms allow the ASP.NET Web controls to maintain their state across postbacks. Recall that when a user enters a value into a TextBox Web control and submits the form, the ASP.NET page is posted back and the TextBox Web control's `Text` property is updated to the value the user entered. For the TextBox Web control's `Text` property to be updated with the value the user entered, the Web Form must submit back to the same page that contains the TextBox Web control. (A lengthy discussion on why this is the case is beyond the scope of this book.)

Additionally, the HTTP Post headers are used rather than the querystring because often a large amount of data is being passed back in the Post headers. Some older browsers have a limit on the amount of information that can be passed through the querystring. Furthermore, it would be unsightly to have such a mangled querystring.

Workshop

Quiz

1. What are the germane differences between a form with its `method` attribute set to `GET` versus a form with its `method` attribute set to `POST`?

2. Imagine that you saw the following querystring:

   ```
   SomePage.aspx?SSN=123-45-6789&age=29&gender=M
   ```

   What does this tell you about the form that the user filled out?

3. What are the differences between postback forms and redirect forms?

4. What types of forms do ASP.NET Web Forms use?

Answers

1. A form with its `method` attribute set to `GET` passes its form values through the querystring. A form with its `method` attribute set to `POST` passes its form values through the HTTP Post headers. When passing information through the querystring, it appears in the browser's Address bar (see Figure 9.3). With the HTTP Post headers, however, the information is hidden from sight. Realize that ASP.NET Web Forms use the HTTP Post header to pass form value information.

2. Because the information is passed in the querystring, it is obvious that the form's `action` property was set to `GET`. Also, based on the values in the querystring, it can be determined that three form fields were on the page with the names `SSN`, `age`, and `gender`, and that the user entered the values `123-45-6789`, `29`, and `M` for the three form fields.

3. Postback forms are forms whose `method` attribute is set to `POST` *and* whose `action` attribute is set to the same URL that the form exists on. That is, if the web page `Page1.aspx` has a postback form, its form's `method` attribute will be set to `POST` and its `action` property to `Page1.aspx`.

   Redirect forms are ones whose `action` attribute is set to a URL other than the URL the form exists on. That is, if the web page `Page1.aspx` has a redirect form, its form's `action` attribute is set to some other web page's URL, such as `Page2.aspx`. Redirect forms can have a `method` attribute of either `POST` or `GET`.

   (Refer to Figure 9.4 for a graphical representation of the differences between postback forms and redirect forms.)

4. ASP.NET Web Forms use postback forms.

Exercises

There are no exercises for this hour. Web Forms, by themselves, are quite useless. To make Web Forms useful, we need to add Web controls designed for collecting a user's input. In the next hour, "Using Text Boxes to Collect Input," we'll see how to use the TextBox Web control to collect user input. At the end of this next hour, we'll work on a number of exercises that examine the use of Web Forms.

HOUR 10

Using Text Boxes to Collect Input

In this hour, we will cover

- Creating multiline text boxes
- Creating password text boxes
- Specifying the number of columns in a text box
- Indicating the maximum number of characters that can be entered into a text box
- Changing the look and feel of the text box by changing the font size, font name, and color of the text box

In Hour 9, "Web Form Basics," we examined how to collect user input through an ASP.NET page. In doing so we created a BMI Calculator that that prompts visitors for two pieces of information: their height and weight. Two TextBox Web controls were used to collect this information.

The TextBox Web control contains a number of properties that specify its appearance. For example, the `TextMode` property specifies whether the text box consists of a single line (the default) or multiple lines. The `Columns` and `Width` properties specifies how wide the text box should be. The various formatting properties—`Font`, `ForeColor`, `BackColor`, `BorderStyle`, and so on—can be used to enhance the TextBox's appearance.

Learning About the TextBox Web Control Basics

As you already know, when an ASP.NET page is visited, its Web controls are rendered into HTML. The Label Web control, for example, is rendered as a `<span>` tag whose content is the Label's `Text` property. The TextBox Web control, as we saw in the preceding hour, is rendered into an `<input>` tag whose `type` attribute is set to `text`.

Text boxes are an ideal user interface element for collecting general user input, such as a person's name, mailing address, or credit card number.

Did you Know?

> For certain types of user input, a text box might not be the best choice. In the next hour we examine other Web controls designed for collecting user input and learn why they are better suited than the TextBox Web control for some situations.

In this hour we examine the various types of text boxes—such as password text boxes and multiline text boxes—as well as how to alter their appearance. Before we begin this exploration, though, let's practice adding a TextBox Web control to an ASP.NET page and displaying the value the user entered.

To do this, start by creating a new ASP.NET page named `TextBoxPractice.aspx`. We will add two TextBox Web controls to this page to collect the user's name and age.

Start by entering the following text to the page: **`Your name:`**. Next, drag a TextBox Web control from the Toolbox onto the page. Then enter the text **`Your age:`** and another TextBox Web control. Finally, as with all Web Forms, we need a Button Web control. Add this below the two TextBox controls.

Figure 10.1 shows Visual Web Developer after these three Web controls have been added. Take a moment to make sure that your screen looks similar.

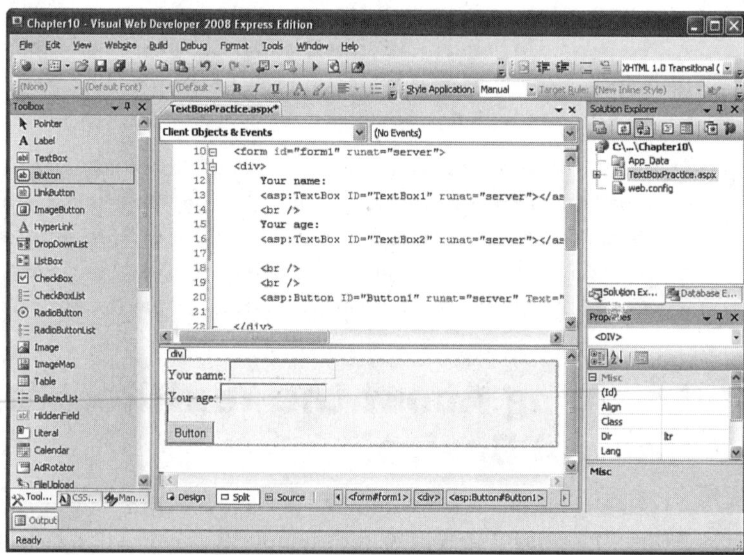

FIGURE 10.1 Two TextBox Web controls and a Button Web control have been added to the page.

Now that we've added our three Web controls to the page, let's set their properties. Start with the first TextBox Web control. Because this Web control is used to collect the user's name, set its `ID` property to `Name`. Set the second TextBox Web control's `ID` property to `Age`.

Finally, set the Button Web control's `ID` property to `SubmitButton` and its `Text` property to "Click Me."

Take a moment to test this ASP.NET page through a browser by going to the Debug menu and choosing Start Without Debugging. Figure 10.2 shows the web page when visited through a browser.

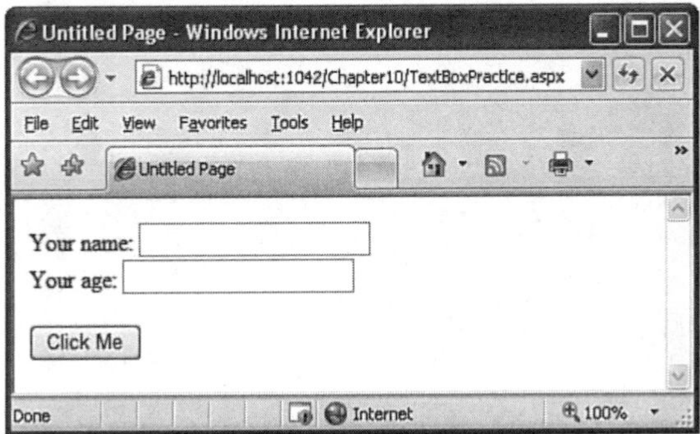

FIGURE 10.2 The ASP.NET page, when visited through a browser, displays two text boxes and a button.

Performing an Action When the User Submits the Form

Currently, the `TextBoxPractice.aspx` ASP.NET page performs no action when the form is submitted. Typically, though, when the user submits information, you will do something with it. You might perform a calculation on the data entered and present some computed value to the user. As we will see in later hours, you may display data from a database based on the input provided by the user.

The best place for processing the user's input is in an event handler for the Button Web control's `Click` event. As we saw in the preceding hour, adding an event handler for the Button's Click event is easy. Double-click the Button Web control in the Design view, or go to the source code portion and select the Button Web control and the `Click` event from the left and right drop-down lists at the top. After the `Click` event handler has been created, all that remains is to write the code to process the user's input. For this ASP.NET page, let's simply display the user's input using a Label.

Start by adding a Label Web control to the `TextBoxPractice.aspx` ASP.NET page. You can add this anywhere in the HTML portion; if you want to follow along with my example, add it beneath the Button Web control. Set the Label control's `ID` property to `Results` and clear out its `Text` property. Figure 10.3 shows Visual Web Developer after this Label has been added and its properties set.

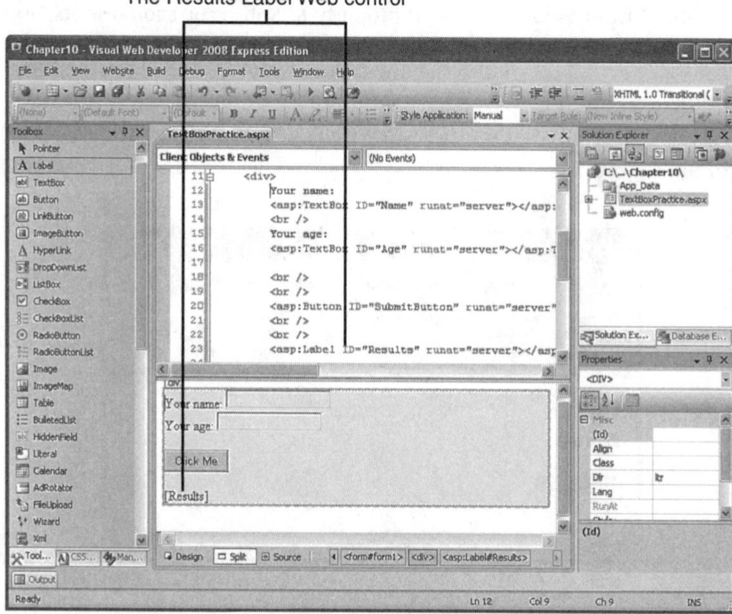

FIGURE 10.3 A Label Web control has been added to `TextBoxPractice.aspx`.

By the Way

> Feel free to set any of the Label's aesthetic properties, such as `Font`, `BackColor`, `ForeColor`, or others.

With the Label Web control in place, we're ready to add the code for the Button's `Click` event handler. Listing 10.1 shows what the ASP.NET page's source code portion should look like after you have added the necessary code to the `Click` event handler. Note that you will need to manually type in only lines 5 and 6; all the other lines of code should already be there, courtesy of Visual Web Developer.

LISTING 10.1 The `Click` Event Handler Displays the User's Name and Age in the `Results` Label Web Control

```
1: Partial Class TextBoxPractice
2:     Inherits System.Web.UI.Page
3:
4:     Protected Sub SubmitButton_Click(ByVal sender As Object, ByVal e As
➥ System.EventArgs) Handles SubmitButton.Click
5:         Results.Text = "Hello, " & Name.Text
```

LISTING 10.1 Continued

```
        Results.Text &= ". You are " & Age.Text & " years old."
    End Sub
End Class
```

The code in the event handler sets the `Results` Label's `Text` property so that it displays the user's entered name and age.

Figure 10.4 shows `TextBoxPractice.aspx` when visited through a browser. The screenshot was taken after a user entered his name and age and submitted the form by clicking the Click Me button.

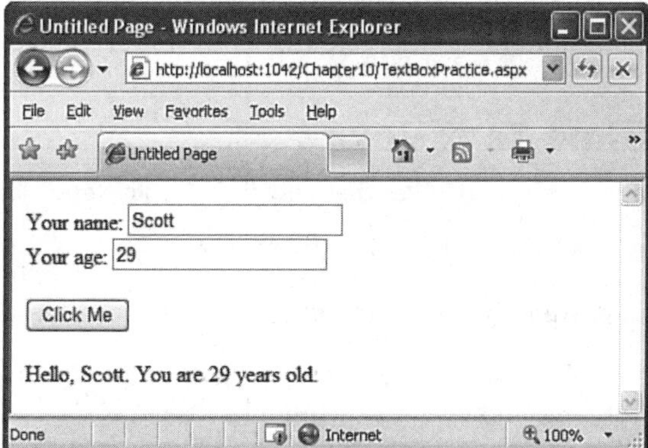

FIGURE 10.4 The user's supplied name and age are displayed.

`TextBoxPractice.aspx` demonstrates the basics of using TextBox Web controls in an ASP.NET web page. For the remainder of this hour, we will focus on the various properties of the TextBox Web control and see how these properties alter the appearance and behavior of the resulting text box in the user's browser.

Creating Multiline and Password Text Boxes

Take a moment to examine the text boxes in Figure 10.4. Note that these text boxes allow for a single line of text. As you likely know from your Internet surfing experience, text boxes come in other forms. The two variants of the text box are multiline and password.

A multiline text box contains more than one row of text. This type of text box is commonly used when a large amount of text may be needed. Consider a news site that allows visitors to leave comments about the various stories and opinion articles published online. Typically, multiline text boxes are used because a user may enter a lengthy comment. (See Figure 10.5 for an example of a multiline text box.)

Password text boxes mask the user's input with asterisks (*). Password text boxes are useful for collecting sensitive input from the user, such as her password or personal identification number (PIN). The masked input prevents an onlooker from being able to glance over the web user's shoulder to determine the password or other sensitive information. (See Figure 10.6 to see an example of a password text box.)

The TextBox Web control contains a `TextMode` property that specifies how the resulting text box is displayed: as a single line text box, as a multiline text box, or as a password text box. As we have seen, the TextBox Web control displays a single line text box by default. In the next two sections, we examine how to have the TextBox Web control render as a multiline text box and a password text box.

Using Multiline Text Boxes

Creating a multiline text box involves the following simple steps:

1. Add a TextBox Web control to the ASP.NET page.
2. Set the TextBox Web control's `TextMode` property to `MultiLine`.
3. Set the TextBox Web control's `Columns` and `Rows` properties to specify the number of columns and rows for the multiline TextBox.

Let's practice using a multiline text box. Create a new ASP.NET page named `MultiLineTextBox.aspx`. Next, type the following text into the page: **`Share your thoughts:`**.

The first step in creating a multiline text box is to add the TextBox Web control to the web page. So, drag and drop a TextBox Web control from the Toolbox onto the page beneath the "Share your thoughts:" text. Set the TextBox control's `ID` property to `UsersThoughts`.

Next, set the TextBox control's `TextMode` property to `MultiLine`. To accomplish this, select the TextBox Web control so that its properties are loaded in the Properties window. Then scroll down through the list of properties until you reach the `TextMode` property.

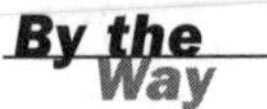

By default, the `TextMode` property is set to the value `SingleLine`, which creates a standard, single-line text box like the ones shown in Figure 10.4.

Clicking the TextMode property drops down a list of three options: SingleLine, MultiLine, and Password. Select the MultiLine option. At this point, we can adjust the number of columns and rows in the multiline text box by setting the TextBox control's Columns and Rows properties. Go ahead and set these two properties to values of 25 and 5, respectively.

Figure 10.5 shows Visual Web Developer after these steps have been completed.

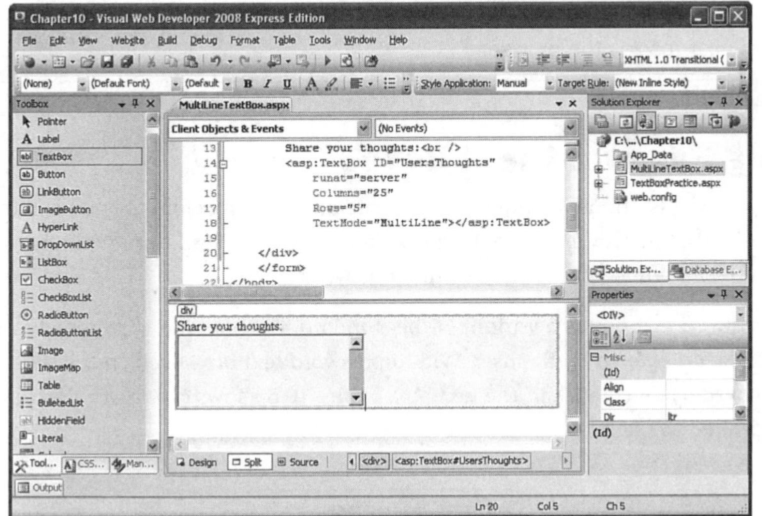

FIGURE 10.5 A multiline TextBox Web control with 25 columns and 5 rows has been added to the page.

By the Way

> For practice, you are encouraged to complete the MultiLineTextBox.aspx web page by adding a Button Web control and providing code in the Button's Click event handler that displays the text the user entered in a Label.

In addition to using the Columns and Rows properties to specify the size of the multiline TextBox , you can also resize the TextBox Web control directly by clicking the TextBox in the designer and selecting one of the resize icons on the bottom, right, or bottom-right corner. Resizing a TextBox in this way adjusts the TextBox Web control's Height and Width properties rather than its Columns and Rows properties.

The difference between these two methods is that if you set the Height and Width properties, the text box displayed in the user's browser will have the exact size specified by these properties, regardless of the font used within the text box. In other words, the text box will be the same dimensions regardless of whether its text is displayed in a large- or small-sized font. However, if you specify the size through the Columns and Rows properties, the rendered text box's dimensions will depend on the size of the font being used for the text box. There will always be the specified number of columns and rows, so if a large font size is used, the text box will be larger than if a smaller font size is used.

Did you Know?

In addition to specifying absolute sizes for the TextBox control's `Width` and `Height` properties, you can also specify relative sizes in terms of percentages. For example, if you want the rendered text box to be as wide as the browser window, set its `Width` property to 100%. What's more, when specifying a percentage for the TextBox's `Height` or `Width` properties, its dimensions will dynamically change as the user resizes the browser.

Using Password Text Boxes

Many web applications require users to create an account before they can enjoy the services of the site. For example, to check your email at GMail.com, you must first sign in by providing your username and password.

The password text box is a variant of the standard text box and is designed to hide the text being entered by the user. With a password text box, each character entered is displayed as an asterisk in the text box. Figure 10.6 shows a password text box that has had the text "My password" typed into it.

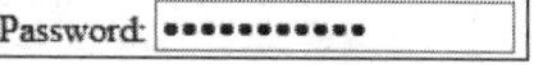

FIGURE 10.6 A password text box masks the text entered by the user.

To create a password text box in an ASP.NET web page, we need to add a TextBox Web control and set its `TextMode` property to `Password`. Create an ASP.NET page named `PasswordTextBox.aspx`, type the text **`Username:`** into the page, and then add a TextBox Web control. Set this TextBox's `ID` to `Username`. On the next line, type in the text **`Password:`** and then add another TextBox Web control. Set this second TextBox control's `ID` property to `UsersPassword` and its `TextMode` property to `Password`.

Add a Button Web control beneath these two TextBoxes and set its `ID` and `Text` properties to `LoginButton` and "Login," respectively.

After you perform these steps, your screen should look similar to Figure 10.7.

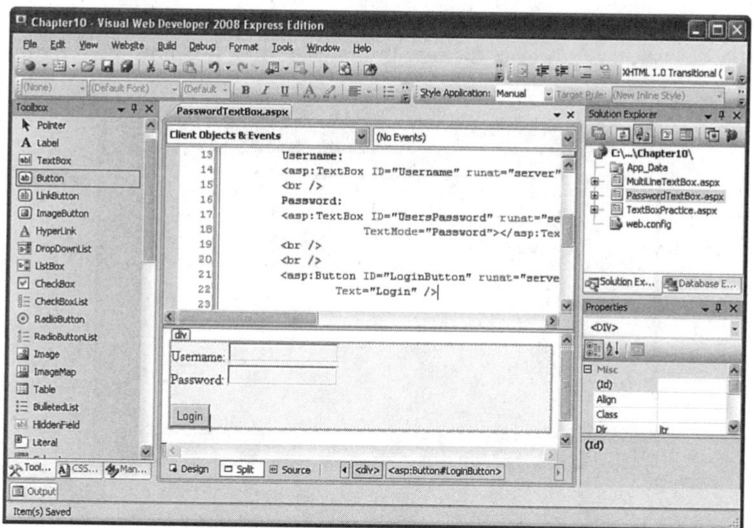

FIGURE 10.7
The ASP.NET web page has two TextBox Web controls and a Button Web control.

Password Text Box Values Are Not Continued Across Postbacks

The password text box has some potentially unexpected behavior when viewed through a browser. Visit the page and enter some text into the two text boxes. Note that the username text box behaves like a normal text box, but the password text box has its input masked by asterisks. Figure 10.8 shows the `PasswordTextBox.aspx` ASP.NET web page when viewed through a browser after values have been entered into the two text boxes.

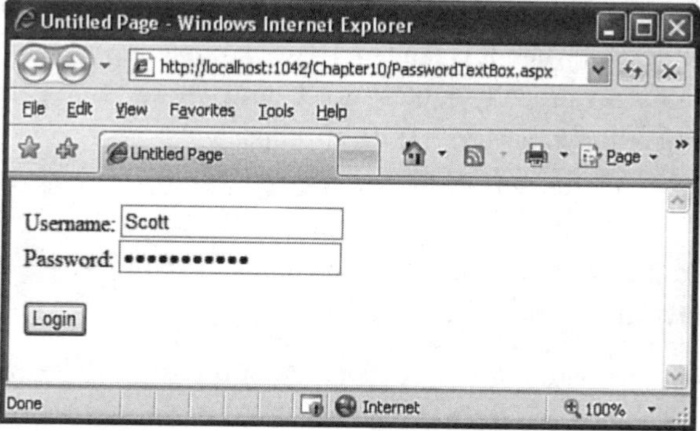

FIGURE 10.8
The text in the password text box is masked by asterisks.

After you have entered information into the two text boxes, submit the form by clicking the Login button. Clicking the button causes the form to postback. Notice that the text entered into the password text box has disappeared on postback, as Figure 10.9 illustrates. However, the text in the username text box still remains.

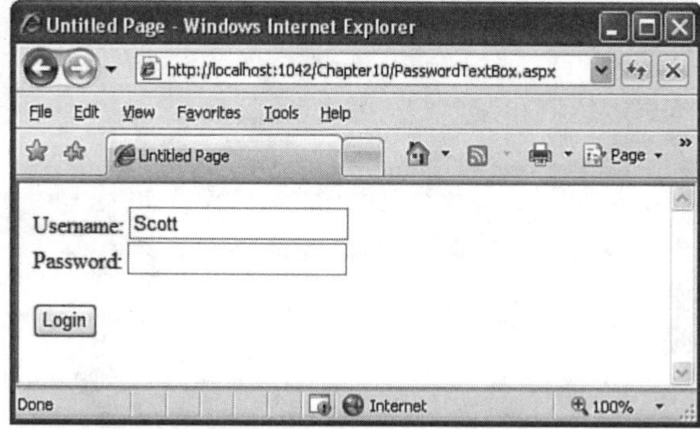

FIGURE 10.9
When the Web Form is posted back, the text in the password text box is not redisplayed.

Why did the text in the username text box remain, but the text in the password text box disappear? Recall that when the submit button is clicked, the Web Form is submitted and the data the user entered into the text boxes is sent back to `PasswordTextBox.aspx`.

When the request for `PasswordTextBox.aspx` arrives at the web server, the ASP.NET engine is invoked to produce the proper HTML output for the page. The ASP.NET engine determines that the page has been posted back and sets the `Text` properties of the two TextBox Web controls to the values entered by the user.

With TextBox Web controls whose `TextMode` property is set to `SingleLine` or `MultiLine`, the value of the `Text` property is expressed in the HTML generated by the TextBox Web control when it is rendered. For example, a single line TextBox Web control whose `Text` property equals "Scott" and whose `ID` property equals `TextBox1` will render the following HTML markup:

```
<input name="TextBox1" type="text" value="Scott" id="TextBox1" />
```

However, when a password text box is rendered, the `Text` property is not expressed in the resulting HTML for security reasons.

To understand why rendering the `Text` property for a password TextBox poses a security threat, imagine for a moment that the ASP.NET engine did include the `Text` property in the rendered markup. If we had a TextBox Web control with its `ID` property set to `TextBox2`, its `TextMode` property set to `Password`, and its `Text` property set to `password123`, the following HTML would be rendered:

```
<input name="TextBox2" type="text" value="password123" id="TextBox2" />
```

Now imagine that a user visits a web page where he is prompted for his username and password, and imagine that after he enters his correct username and password, the ASP.NET page displays some information specific to his user account in a Label Web control on the same web page.

If the user gets up from his computer to get a quick drink of water, an unscrupulous co-worker could go to the user's browser and view the received HTML, which would include the markup:

```
<input name="TextBox2" type="text" value="password123" id="TextBox2" />
```

(This assumes `password123` was the person's password.)

The co-worker now knows the user's password. To help prevent this, the `Text` property is not rendered for password TextBoxes.

By the Way

> Once a month or so, a person will ask the following question on one of the ASP.NET newsgroups or messageboards: "Why is it that when I set a password TextBox Web control's `Text` property, it does not appear when I visit the ASP.NET page through a browser?" Now you can answer this type of question!

Examining the TextBox Web Control's Properties

So far in this hour, we have looked at one property in particular—the `TextMode` property—which is used to specify whether the TextBox Web control should be rendered as a standard text box, a multiline text box, or a password text box. In addition to this property, there are a number of other TextBox Web control properties. The remainder of this hour examines the most germane ones.

Specifying the Length of a Text Box

Sometimes you may need to use the TextBox Web control to collect information from users, such as their age or the two-letter abbreviation of the state they live in. In such cases, the users' input will be only a few characters long. However, as you can see with the `Age` text box in Figure 10.4, the text box displayed in the web browser is much larger than it needs to be for such cases.

You can specify how many columns wide the text box should be by setting the TextBox Web control's `Columns` property. Open the `TextBoxPractice.aspx` page, which we created in the first example in this hour (see Figure 10.4). Adjust the `Age`

TextBox Web control's `Columns` property so that the text box into which the user enters his age is more appropriately sized. Specifically, set this TextBox's `Columns` property to a value of 3.

After you set the `Columns` property to 3, the text box displayed in the designer will shrink from its default width to a width of three columns. Refer to Figure 10.10 for a screenshot of Visual Web Developer after this property has been set.

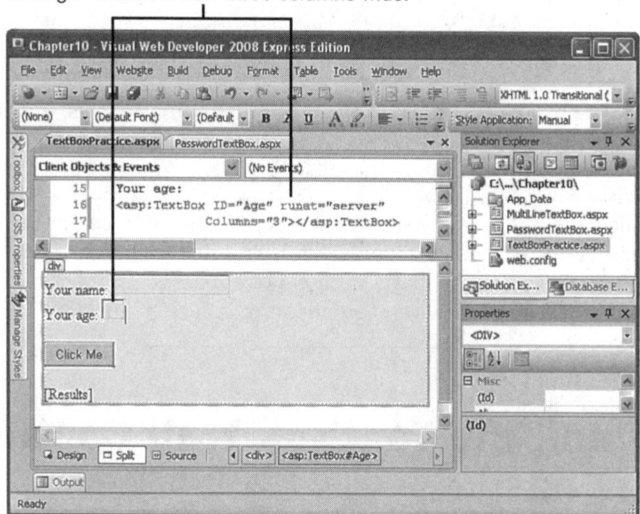

FIGURE 10.10 The age text box is three columns wide.

You can also resize the TextBox through the designer by clicking the TextBox and selecting one of the resize icons on the bottom, right, or bottom-right corner. Doing so sets the TextBox's `Height` and `Width` properties. As discussed at the end of the "Using Multiline Text Boxes" section, the `Height` and `Width` properties specify the absolute size of the resulting text box, whereas the `Columns` property dictates the number of columns to display, making the size of the rendered text box relative to the text box's font size.

Did you Know?

> Be sure to have your TextBox Web controls properly sized for the input you are expecting users to enter. Properly sized text boxes help ensure that users enter the data in the correct format. For example, if you want users to enter a short description about themselves, they will be more apt to enter a shorter description if you provide them with a single-line text box than if you provide them with a multiline text box.

Limiting the Number of Characters a User Can Enter into a Text Box

Adjusting the size of the text box by setting the TextBox Web control's `Columns` property does not regulate how much text the user can enter. Even if you create a TextBox Web control that's just three columns wide, the user can still enter hundreds of characters of text.

Sometimes you may want to limit the amount of text a user may enter into a particular text box. For example, sites like eBay allow only 80 characters to be entered when providing feedback about another buyer or seller.

Websites typically limit the number of characters that can be entered into a text box for two reasons. First, it is usually easier to format data for display at a later time by limiting the number of characters that can be supplied by the user. For example, the feedback a user enters at eBay about a buyer or a seller can be viewed by other eBay users in a feedback summary page. This summary page is clean and concise because no one user can enter more than 80 characters of feedback at a time.

Second, sites like eBay use databases to store the information their users enter. When you're setting up a database, you must specify the maximum number of characters for text fields in advance. Therefore, this feedback limit is in place because of the limit imposed by those who designed eBay's database tables. (We'll be examining how to create and use databases later in this book, starting with Hour 13, "An Introduction to Databases.")

To set a limit to the number of characters that can be entered into a TextBox Web control, set its `MaxLength` property accordingly. In our `TextBoxPractice.aspx` example, we may want to limit the `Age` text box to a maximum of three characters (because it would be impossible for a visitor to have an age greater than 999).

To do so, set the `Age` TextBox Web control and set its `MaxLength` property to 3. After you have made this change, view `TextBoxPractice.aspx` through a browser. Try to type more than three characters into the `Age` text box—you can't!

Watch Out!

Although you might think that a `MaxLength` value of 0 would not permit users to enter information into the text box at all, it means quite the opposite. A `MaxLength` value of 0 means that no restrictions exist on the amount of information users can enter into the text box.

Advanced users can circumvent the text box restrictions imposed by the `MaxLength` property. Therefore, the `MaxLength` property does not guarantee that a user's supplied input will be less than the `MaxLength` setting. The Q&A section in Hour 12, "Validating User Input with Validation Controls," discusses how to ensure that a user has entered no more than a specified number of characters into a particular text box.

Furthermore, the `MaxLength` property works only with single line and password text boxes. If you set your TextBox Web control's `TextMode` property to `MultiLine`, the `MaxLength` property is ignored. There is a workaround for limiting the number of characters that can be entered into a `MultiLine` text box, but it involves the use of the ASP.NET validation controls. This topic is also addressed in the Q&A section in Hour 12.

Aesthetic Properties—Changing the Text Box's Font and Color

The Label Web control has a number of aesthetic properties, such as `BackColor`, `ForeColor`, `Font`, and so on. In Hour 8, "ASP.NET Web Controls for Displaying Text," we examined these various properties, looked at how to specify them, and observed the visual effect they had on the text displayed by the Label Web control.

The TextBox Web control has the exact same set of formatting properties as the Label Web control, which is summarized in Table 10.1.

TABLE 10.1 The Aesthetic Properties of the TextBox Web Control

Property	Description
`BackColor`	Specifies the background color of the text box.
`BorderColor`	Specifies the color of the text box's border.
`BorderStyle`	Specifies the style of the text box's border.
`BorderWidth`	Specifies the width of the text box's border.
`Font`	Specifies the font properties for the text entered by the user into the text box. Recall that the `Font` property has a number of subproperties, including `Name`, `Size`, `Bold`, and others.
`ForeColor`	Specifies the color of the text entered into the text box by the user.

Let's create a new ASP.NET page called `PrettyTextBox.aspx`, in which we'll create a number of TextBox Web controls to observe the effects of various formatting properties. After you create the ASP.NET page, add two TextBox controls.

For the first TextBox, set its `BackColor` property to yellow. Next, add a border by setting its `BorderColor`, `BorderStyle`, and `BorderWidth` properties to black, dotted, and "5px," respectively. These settings result in a TextBox with a yellow background and a black, dotted border 5 pixels wide (see Figure 10.11).

For the second TextBox Web control, set the `Font` property's `Bold` subproperty to `True`, the `Name` subproperty to Comic Sans MS, and the `Size` subproperty to `Large`. Set the `ForeColor` property to red. The text typed into this text box will be large, red, and displayed with the Comic Sans MS font.

Figure 10.11 shows Visual Web Developer after these properties have been set. (Some of the color differences may not be noticeable in the figure.)

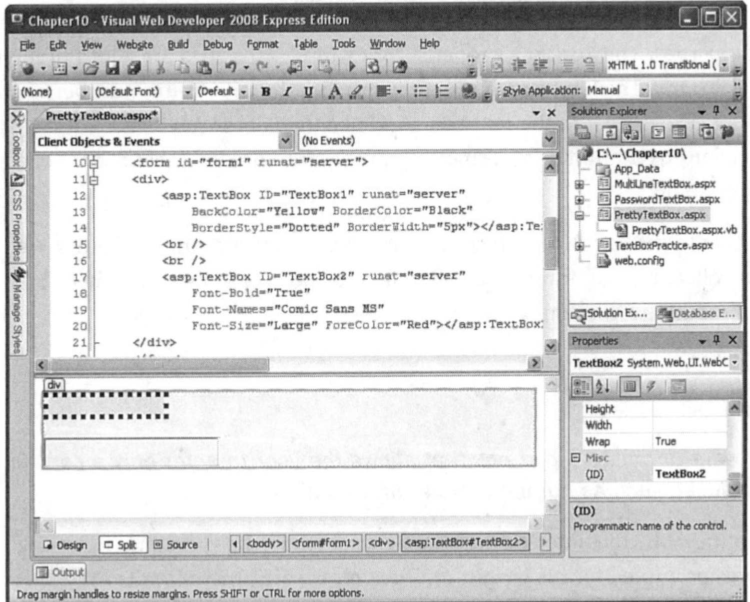

FIGURE 10.11 Both TextBox Web controls have had a number of their aesthetic properties set.

Take a moment to view the `PrettyTextBox.aspx` ASP.NET page through a browser (see Figure 10.12). When viewing the page, type some text into the second text box and note that it is red, large, and in the Comic Sans MS font.

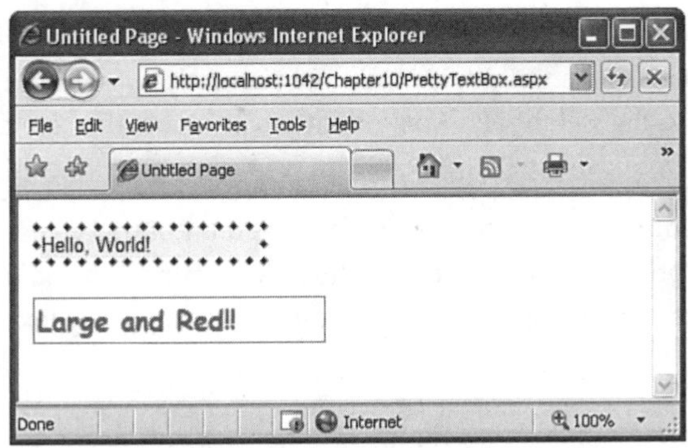

FIGURE 10.12 The `PrettyTextBox.aspx` ASP.NET page, when viewed through a browser.

Summary

In this hour we looked at one of the most commonly used Web controls for collecting user input: the TextBox. The TextBox Web control can be used to create three types of text boxes: a single line text box, a multiline text box, or a password text box. Use the TextBox control's `TextMode` property to specify what kind of text box to render.

In addition to the `TextMode` property, the TextBox Web control contains a number of other properties. The `Columns` property, for example, specifies the width of the text box in columns. The `MaxLength` property specifies the maximum number of characters a user can enter into the text box. And like the Label Web control, the TextBox control contains a number of formatting properties, such as `BackColor`, `ForeColor`, `Font`, and so on.

In addition to the TextBox Web control, ASP.NET offers a number of other Web controls for collecting user input. We will look at using drop-down lists, check boxes, and radio buttons in the next hour.

Q&A

Q. ***I want to create a text box that allows the user to enter only a certain type of input, such as numbers. How can I do this?***

A. In the BMI calculator example we examined in the preceding hour, the user was prompted for his weight and height. Clearly, these inputs must be numeric ones. As we saw, if the user enters some input like **`Sam`** as his weight, it breaks the BMI calculator.

Therefore, you might think that an ideal solution would be to create a text box into which the user can enter only numbers. Such masked text boxes, as they are called, are rarely, if ever, used on web pages for a number of reasons.

First, although a masked text box would prevent the user from entering something like **`Sam`** as his weight, it would not prevent the user from entering nothing into the weight text box, or entering weights that are clearly out of sensible bounds, like 0 or 999,999.

Second, creating masked text boxes requires a bit of tricky client-side JavaScript programming. Users who have JavaScript disabled in their browser would therefore be able to enter any values into a masked text box.

Finally, and perhaps most important, users are not accustomed to masked text boxes on web pages. Therefore, the inclusion of masked text boxes would likely irritate users and lead them to conclude that your website was fundamentally different from the many websites they're used to.

As we will see in Hour 12, it is quite easy to ensure that a user's text box input conforms to a certain format.

(There are, however, masked input ASP.NET controls you can purchase. The nice thing about these third-party controls is that they take care of the tricky client-side JavaScript needed. You just drag and drop them onto your ASP.NET page, much like you would a regular TextBox. I've used and have been pleased with the masked input controls available at www.peterblum.com.)

Q. ***Why does the* `MaxLength` *property not work with a* `MultiLine` *TextBox Web control?***

A. The `SingleLine` and `Password` TextBox Web controls render as an `<input>` HTML element; if the TextBox control's `MaxLength` property is specified, its value is rendered in the `<input>` element's `maxlength` attribute. If the browser sees an `<input>` element with a `maxlength` attribute, it limits the number of characters the user can enter.

`MultiLine` TextBoxes, however, are rendered as the `<textarea>` HTML element. The HTML specification does not permit `maxlength` attributes for `<textarea>` elements.

Despite this limitation, it is still possible to restrict the number of characters entered into a `MultiLine` TextBox. In the Q&A section in Hour 12, we'll examine one such workaround.

Q. ***I have a Web Form with TextBox and Button controls. If I press Enter after typing my input into a text box, the Web Form posts back. But I've noticed that in some situations the Button's* `Click` *event handler doesn't execute. Any ideas what's going on here?***

A. If a visitor hits the Enter key while focused in a single line or password text box, the browser submits the form. When the form is submitted, the submit button's `Click` event should fire and the event handler (if present) should execute. But there are two common cases when this expected behavior doesn't unfold.

The first scenario is when the Web Form contains only one TextBox. The second scenario occurs when there are multiple Button Web controls on the page. For a more thorough explanation of these scenarios, as well as workarounds, check out "Two Common Pitfalls When Submitting a Web Form Using the Enter Key," available online at http://aspnet.4guysfromrolla.com/articles/010908-1.aspx.

Workshop

Quiz

1. What are the possible values of the TextBox Web control's `TextMode` property?
2. If you wanted to create a multiline text box with 40 columns and 5 rows, what TextBox Web control properties would you need to set?
3. True or False: T he `MaxLength` property works equally as well for single line, password, and multiline text boxes.
4. What TextBox Web control property contains the text that was entered by the user?
5. What Web control that we've examined in previous hours has the same formatting properties as the TextBox Web control?
6. If you set the `Text` property of a TextBox Web control whose `TextMode` is set to `Password`, no text will appear in the text box when viewed through a web browser. Why is this the case?

Answers

1. The TextBox Web control supports three possible values for its `TextMode` property: `MultiLine`, `Password`, and `SingleLine`. The default value is `SingleLine`.
2. To create such a text box, you would need to set the TextBox Web control's `TextMode` property to `MultiLine`, its `Columns` property to 40, and its `Rows` property to 5.
3. False. The `MaxLength` property has no effect with the multiline TextBox.
4. The `Text` property.

5. The Label Web control.

6. Password text boxes cannot have their `Text` property programmatically set, nor do they persist this value across postbacks. The reason is that doing so would serve as a security risk because a nefarious user could simply examine the HTML received by the browser to determine the user's password.

Exercises

1. For this exercise we'll create an ASP.NET web page that prompts the user for two integers and then computes and displays the integers' greatest common divisor. (The greatest common divisor of two integers `a` and `b`, commonly denoted `gcd(a,b)`, is the largest number that divides both `a` and `b` without a remainder. For example, `gcd(49, 21)` is 7.)

   Because the user needs to provide two integers, you'll need two TextBox Web controls. Set the `ID` property of the first Web control to `a`, and the second to `b`. You'll also need to add a Button Web control, as well as a Label Web control. Set the `ID` property of the Label Web control to `Results` and clear out its `Text` property.

   As with the BMI calculator example from the preceding hour, you'll need to create an event handler for the Button Web control's `Click` event. This event handler needs to compute the greatest common divisor of the values entered into the `a` and `b` TextBox Web controls and display it in the `Results` Label.

   The greatest common divisor of two integers can be quickly computed using the Euclidean Algorithm. If you are not familiar with the details of this algorithm, don't worry, the following pseudo code should get you started:

```
'Assign the maximum of a and b to x and the minimum to y
If a.Text < b.Text then
  x = b.Text
  y = a.Text
Else
  x = a.Text
  y = b.Text
End If

'Compute the remainder of x / y
z = x mod y
While z <> 0
  x = y
  y = z

  z = x mod y
End While

gcd = y
```

`Mod` is an operator in Visual Basic. *x* `Mod` *y* returns the remainder of `x / y`. For example, `13 Mod 5` returns 3, because 5 divides 13 two times, with 3 left over.

For more information on the Euclidean Algorithm, check out http://en.wikipedia.org/wiki/Euclidean_algorithm.

2. Given two integers `a` and `b`, their least common multiple, commonly denoted `lcm(a,b)`, is the smallest integer that is a multiple of both `a` and `b`. For example, the least common multiple of 6 and 4 is 12 because 12 is both a multiple of 6 (6 times 2) and 4 (4 times 3) and is the smallest such multiple. For this exercise, create an ASP.NET web page that accepts two integer inputs from the user and computes the least common multiple.

Fortunately, computing the least common multiple of two numbers is quite simple after you compute the greatest common divisor of the two numbers. Specifically,

```
lcm(a,b) = (a * b) / gcd(a,b)
```

Therefore, for this exercise you should create a function named `GCD` that takes in two integer inputs and returns an integer value. You can cut and paste the greatest common divisor code that you entered in for exercise 1.

As with the previous exercise, be sure to include two TextBox Web controls, a Button Web control, and a Label Web control. The Button Web control's `Click` event handler should compute the least common multiple of the two integers entered by the user using the `GCD` function and display it in `Results`.

HOUR 11

Collecting Input Using Drop-Down Lists, Radio Buttons, and Check Boxes

In this hour, we will cover

- Ideal times for using Web controls other than the TextBox Web control
- Adding DropDownList Web controls to an ASP.NET web page
- Programmatically accessing a selected value and text from a DropDownList Web control
- Using the RadioButton Web control
- Grouping related RadioButton Web controls
- Using the CheckBox Web control
- Programmatically determining whether a particular CheckBox Web control is checked

In the preceding hour we saw how to collect user information through the TextBox Web control. The text box, however, is not always the best tool for collecting a user input. For example, imagine that you wanted to create a web page where the user answered a bunch of yes/no questions. Would it make sense to require the user to type in the words "Yes" or "No" for each question?

Fortunately, alternative Web controls exist for collecting user input, such as the DropDownList Web control, the RadioButton Web control, and the CheckBox Web control. We examine these three Web controls in this hour.

Examining the Different Types of User Input Classifications

So far we have explored only one Web control for collecting user input, the TextBox Web control. As we have seen in the examples thus far in the book, the TextBox Web control presents users with a text box into which they can type their input.

Text boxes, however, are not the only means by which user input can be collected. As we will see in this hour, other input collection Web controls include the DropDownList, the CheckBox, and the RadioButton. The DropDownList Web control presents users with a list of options, from which they may choose one. The CheckBox Web control displays a box that can be ticked or cleared to indicate a yes or no type answer. And the RadioButton Web control presents users with a single, selectable option. Typically, a series of RadioButton controls are used, with each radio button representing a single option from which the visitor can select only one of the available choices.

Given that a number of Web controls are designed to collect user input, you may be wondering when you should use a TextBox versus a DropDownList, CheckBox, or RadioButton. The type of Web control you use depends on the kind of input that is being collected.

Input collected from users can be classified into various types. The following classifications group input in terms of their restrictiveness, from the most restrictive form of input, to the least:

1. Boolean input
2. Input selected from an allowable list of choices
3. General text input

The first classification, Boolean input, is input that can be inputted in only one of two ways. For example, an online survey may ask you for your gender, which can be only one of two values, Male or Female. A sign-up web page may ask if you want to receive their weekly email newsletter, which can be answered in one of two ways: yes or no.

A slightly more general input classification is input selected from a list of acceptable choices. If you live in the United States and are filling out your address on an online form, you are asked to specify the state you live in from a list of the 50 states.

General text input is the most flexible of the three categories. Input that falls into this category includes filling in your name and address on an online form or entering your comments on an online messageboard site.

Using an Appropriate Web Control

When collecting user input, you must decide what Web control to use. For example, when prompting users for their gender, you could use a TextBox Web control, having them type in whether they are Male or Female. However, this approach lends itself to user error. A visitor may misspell Female or type in Woman instead. A less error-prone approach would be to use a DropDownList Web control with two options: Male and Female.

Other Boolean inputs work best with check boxes. For example, many websites require you to create an account to access certain portions of the site. When registering for a user account, you typically find a check box labeled something like I Agree to the Terms or Keep Me Abreast of New Products from Your Company.

In this same account-creation page, users may be prompted to specify how they learned about the website. Rather than requiring users to type in an explanation, many websites will provide a drop-down list that contains a number of potential choices, such as Read About It in Print, Heard About It from a Friend, and so on. A drop-down list or a series of radio buttons work well here.

Did you Know?

> When you're prompting the user to select one choice from a series of acceptable answers, either a drop-down list or a series of radio buttons will suffice. If users can choose from many available options, however, a list of radio buttons can become cumbersome and take up valuable screen real estate. A good general rule is to stick with the drop-down list when presenting more than five options. For five or fewer options, either a series of radio buttons or a drop-down list will get the job done.

Input that falls into the general text input category, such as a person's name or mailing address, must be entered via text boxes.

The point of this discussion is to highlight that different classes of user input exist, and the best Web control for one class of input may not be the best for another. Keep this in mind as you work through this hour.

Table 11.1 summarizes the classifications of user input and what types of Web controls typically work best.

TABLE 11.1 Choose an Appropriate Web Control Based on the Data Being Collected

Class of User Input	Description	Web Control(s) to Use
Boolean	The user can select only one of two potential values.	DropDownList, CheckBox, or two RadioButtons
One selection from a list of acceptable answers	The user must select one option from a finite list of acceptable options.	DropDownList or a series of RadioButtons
General text	The user can provide text input in any form.	TextBox

Examining the DropDownList Web Control

For certain forms of input, users must select precisely one option from a list of suitable choices. For example, a software company might want to create a support site where users can find answers to common questions about the company's various software products. When a user is searching for an answer to his question, it would be helpful if, along with searching for certain keywords, he could select what particular software product he was having trouble with.

In such a scenario, a suitable Web control for collecting this bit of input would be a DropDownList Web control. The DropDownList Web control creates a drop-down list of one to many options from which the user can choose.

Figure 11.1 shows an example of a drop-down list in an HTML web page.

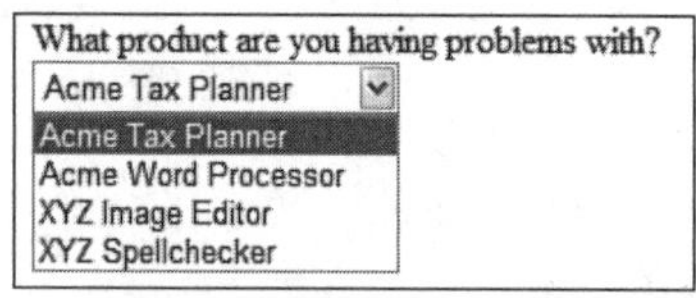

FIGURE 11.1 With a drop-down list, the user can select one option from a list of options.

Adding Options to the DropDownList Web Control

When using the DropDownList Web control, you must specify the drop-down list's **list items**. The list items are the allowable choices that the user can select from. Each individual option in the list of choices is a list item.

There are two ways to specify a DropDownList Web control's list items. This first method, which we'll examine in this hour, is to enter the list items by typing them in, one after another. This approach works well if you know in advance what list items the user should be presented with. For example, if you are using a DropDownList Web control to present the user with a list of the 50 states in the United States, this method is sufficient.

Imagine, however, that you wanted to populate the choices shown in the DropDownList Web control based on some external input. An online banking website, for example, might allow customers to have more than one account, such as a savings account, a checking account, a money market account, and so on. Some customers may have only a checking account, whereas others may have checking and savings accounts.

When the user first logs on to the website, you might want to have the user select which of her accounts (assuming she has multiple accounts) she wants to start working with. These options could be presented in a DropDownList Web control. However, the accounts shown depend on what accounts the customer has opened with the bank. Therefore, the list items shown in the DropDownList Web control depend on external input—namely, the currently logged on user's open accounts.

To handle situations like this, you can store the list items in a database. Then, when using the DropDownList Web control, you can indicate that the list items to be displayed in the drop-down list should come from the database. We'll examine this mode of specifying list items in Hour 17, "Working with Data-Bound DropDownLists, RadioButtons, and CheckBoxes."

Adding a DropDownList Web Control to an ASP.NET Web Page

To demonstrate using a DropDownList Web control and adding list items to it, create a new ASP.NET page named `DropDownList.aspx`. Type in the text **`What is your favorite ice cream flavor?`** and then drag a DropDownList Web control from the Toolbox onto the page. Set the DropDownList control's `ID` property to `Flavors`.

Watch Out!

> Be certain that you add a DropDownList Web control to the ASP.NET web page, not a ListBox Web control. The DropDownList Web control allows the user to select precisely one item from a list of acceptable ones. The ListBox Web control, on the other hand, allows the user to select zero or more list items. (We will not cover the ListBox Web control in this book.)

Next, add a Button Web control beneath the DropDownList. At this point your screen should look similar to Figure 11.2.

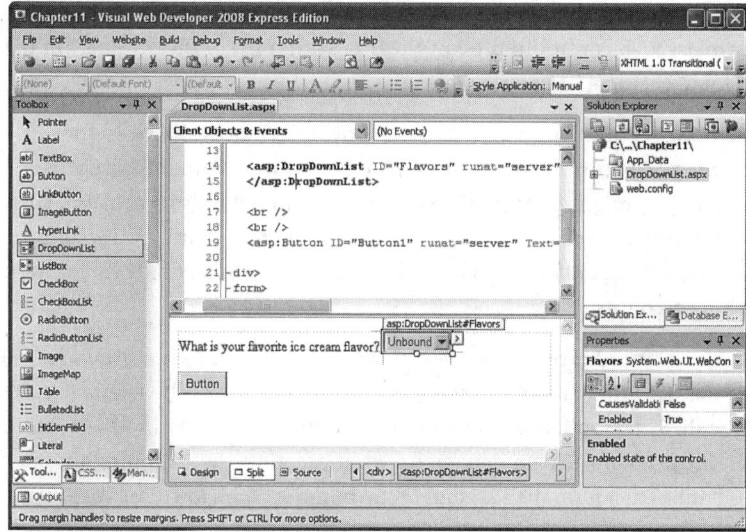

FIGURE 11.2
A DropDownList Web control and Button Web control have been added to the designer.

At this point we've yet to add any list items to the DropDownList Web control. If you view the ASP.NET web page through a browser at this point, you'll be presented with an empty drop-down list, as shown in Figure 11.3.

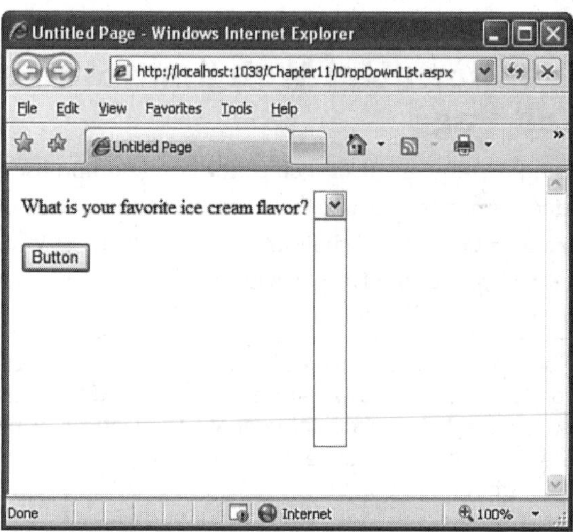

FIGURE 11.3
The drop-down list is empty; it contains no items for the user to choose from.

The DropDownList control's list items are contained in the control's `Items` property. To add list items to the DropDownList Web control, we need to edit this property. Select the DropDownList so that its properties are loaded in the Properties window, and then scroll down to the `Items` property. You should see that the property value currently reads (Collection). As Figure 11.4 shows, if you click this property value, a button with a pair of ellipses will appear to the right of (Collection).

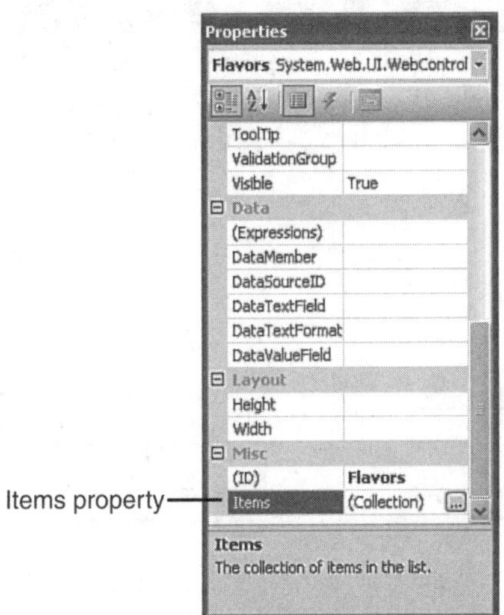

FIGURE 11.4
Clicking the `Items` property reveals a button with a pair of ellipses.

Go ahead and click this button; when you do so, the ListItem Collection Editor dialog box will appear. This dialog box, shown in Figure 11.5, allows you to add and remove list items from the DropDownList Web control.

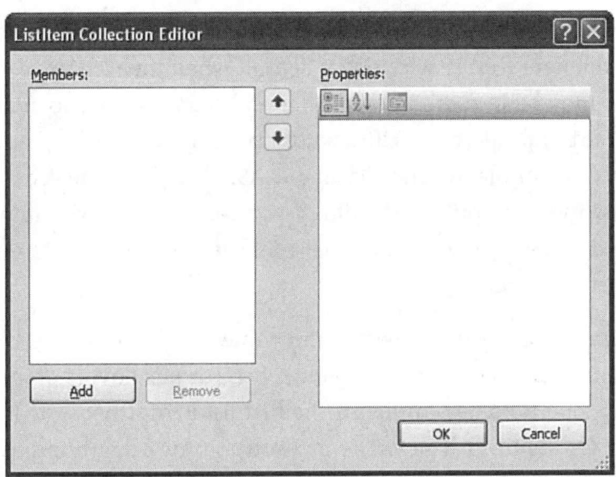

FIGURE 11.5
The ListItem Collection Editor dialog box allows you to manage the options for a DropDownList Web control.

Let's add the ice cream flavors Vanilla, Chocolate, and Strawberry to the DropDownList. To add a new list item, click the Add button.

After you click the Add button, a new list item is added; its properties are displayed on the right. As Figure 11.6 shows, list items have four properties: `Enabled`, `Selected`, `Text`, and `Value`.

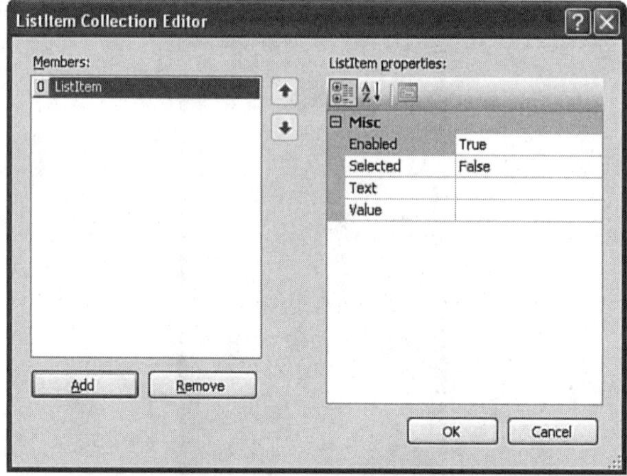

FIGURE 11.6 After you have added a new list item, you can specify its properties.

The first property, `Enabled`, expects a Boolean value (either `True` or `False`). `Enabled` indicates whether the particular list item is present in the rendered drop-down list. For example, if you have a DropDownList Web control with three list items—Vanilla, Chocolate, and Strawberry—and set Chocolate's `Enabled` property to `False`, the drop-down list shown in the user's browser would have only two items—Vanilla and Strawberry.

The second property, `Selected`, also expects a Boolean value and indicates whether the list item is the item that is selected by default when the web page loads. Because many list items may be in a drop-down list, and because only one item is shown at a time, the `Selected` property specifies what list item is selected when the web page is first loaded. For example, when visiting our ASP.NET page, the drop-down list will, by default, show the first option—Vanilla. If you want the Strawberry option to be the item selected by default, you can either make it the first list item or set its `Selected` property to `True`.

The `Text` and `Value` properties expect string values. The `Text` property is the text that is displayed to the user in the drop-down list. For our flavors of ice cream, we'd want the `Text` property to be Vanilla for the first list item, Chocolate for the second, and Strawberry for the third. The `Value` property, on the other hand, is not seen by the user. It serves as a means to pass along additional information with each list item.

> **By the Way**
>
> The `Value` property is typically used when displaying list items from a database. In this hour we won't examine the `Value` property further; instead, we will be setting only the `Text` property.

Now that you understand the roles of the four list item properties, go ahead and set the `Text` property for the list item just added to Vanilla. Add another list item and set its `Text` property to Chocolate. Finally, add a third list item and set its `Text` property to Strawberry.

> **By the Way**
>
> If you don't specify a `Value` property for a list item, the ListItem Collection Editor automatically sets the `Value` to the same value as the `Text` property.

After you have added the Vanilla, Chocolate, and Strawberry list items, the ListItem Collection Editor should look similar to the one shown in Figure 11.7.

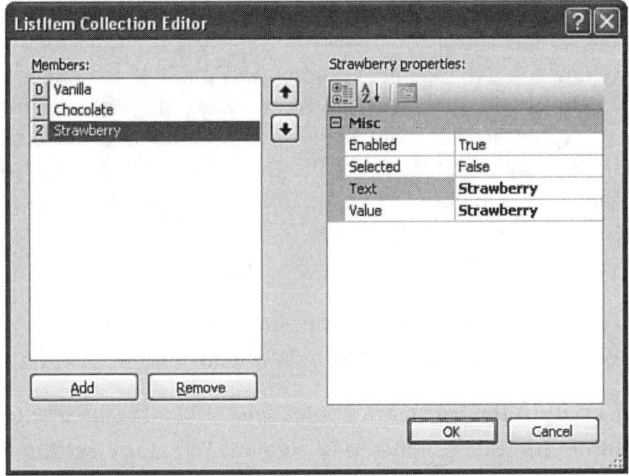

FIGURE 11.7 Three list items have been added.

> **Did you Know?**
>
> You can rearrange the order of the list items through the ListItem Collection Editor. To do so, click the list item in the left text box whose position you want to alter. Then click the up and down arrows in the middle of the ListItem Collection Editor dialog box to move that particular list item up or down with respect to the other list items.

Finally, click OK on the ListItem Collection Editor dialog box. Note that the DropDownList Web control in the designer has changed so that it shows the word Vanilla as its selected list item.

Let's check out our progress by visiting `DropDownList.aspx` through a browser (see Figure 11.8). Note that all three ice cream flavors, which weren't present before we added the three list items via the ListItem Collection Editor, are now listed. (Refer to Figure 11.3 to see the output prior to adding list items.)

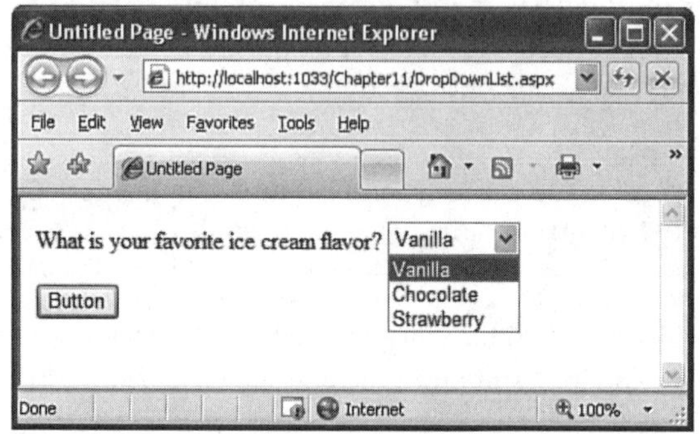

FIGURE 11.8 The web page presents the user with the three ice cream flavor options.

By the Way

When you're visiting the `DropDownList.aspx` web page, if you choose a list item from the drop-down list (for instance, the Strawberry list item) and then submit the form by clicking the button, the page will be posted back and the Strawberry item will remain selected. This indicates that the DropDownList Web control maintains the selected item across postbacks, just like the TextBox Web control maintains its `Text` property value across postbacks.

To have the ASP.NET page take some action when the form is submitted, we need to create a `Click` event handler for the Button Web control.

For now, let's just output the ice cream choice selected by the user in a Label Web control. To facilitate this, add a Label to `DropDownList.aspx`, setting its `ID` property to `Results` and clearing out its `Text` property. Also, set the Button Web control's `ID` property to `SubmitButton` and its `Text` property to "Click Me."

Next, double-click the Button Web control. This will, as you know, add an event handler for the Button's `Click` event. Add the following line of code to the event handler:

```
Results.Text = "You like " & Flavors.SelectedItem.Text
```

As this source code illustrates, the DropDownList Web control's selected list item can be accessed using

```
DropDownListID.SelectedItem
```

Recall that each list item has the properties `Enabled`, `Selected`, `Text`, and `Value`. So, to retrieve the `Text` property, we use

```
DropDownListID.SelectedItem.Text
```

If we wanted to work with the `Value` property, we could use

```
DropDownListID.SelectedItem.Value
```

By the Way

> In addition to the `Enabled`, `Selected`, `Text`, and `Value` properties of the DropDownList Web control's `SelectedItem` property, you may have noticed a fifth property: `Attributes`. You can use this property to set HTML attributes in the markup rendered by the DropDownList Web control. This property is rarely needed in practice, so we won't discuss it further.

After you have added the code to the Button Web control's `Click` event handler, view the page through a browser. When the page loads, select a particular flavor and click the Click Me button. This will cause the form to postback, at which point you should see the message "You like *flavor*" (where *flavor* is the ice cream flavor you selected from the drop-down list).

Figure 11.9 shows `DropDownList.aspx` after the Strawberry flavor has been selected and the Click Me button has been clicked.

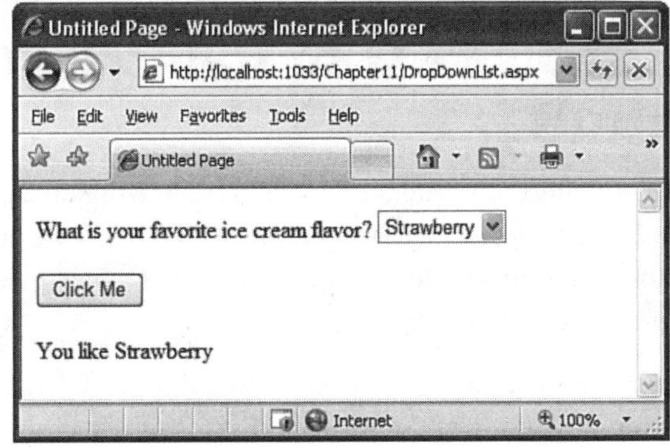

FIGURE 11.9 The text of the selected ice cream flavor is display in the Label Web control.

The DropDownList Web Control's Formatting Properties

The DropDownList Web control has a handful of formatting properties. These formatting properties function the same way as those found in the Label and TextBox Web controls. Table 11.2 lists these formatting properties.

TABLE 11.2 The Formatting Properties of the DropDownList Web Control

Property	Description
`BackColor`	Specifies the background color of the drop-down list.
`Font`	Specifies the font properties for the text entered by the user into the drop-down list. Recall that the `Font` property has a number of subproperties, such as `Name`, `Size`, `Bold`, and so on.
`ForeColor`	Specifies the color of the text in the drop-down list.

You may have noticed that Table 11.2 is missing some of the formatting properties examined in earlier hours, namely the border-related properties. Although these are, technically, properties of the DropDownList Web control, you won't find them in the Properties window in Visual Web Developer.

These border-related formatting properties are omitted from the Properties window because most browsers do not render border-related CSS settings for drop-down lists.

Selecting One Option from a List of Suitable Choices with RadioButton Web Controls

Radio buttons offer an alternative means for choosing one option from a list of allowable choices. You have probably seen and used radio buttons on web pages before. Radio buttons are small circles that, when selected, have a black circle displayed within them. See Figure 11.10.

Radio buttons can be grouped into a series of related radio buttons. In a related group of radio buttons, only one of the radio buttons from the group can be selected at a time. For example, if there are three related radio buttons and the first one is selected, neither the second nor the third one can be selected; if the second is selected, neither the first nor the third one can be selected; and so on. Another way to put it is that related radio buttons are **mutually exclusive**.

To create a radio button in an ASP.NET page, use the RadioButton Web control. The RadioButton Web control, when rendered, produces the HTML for creating a single radio button. Therefore, if the user is to select one option from a list of three, for instance, we must add three RadioButton Web controls to the page.

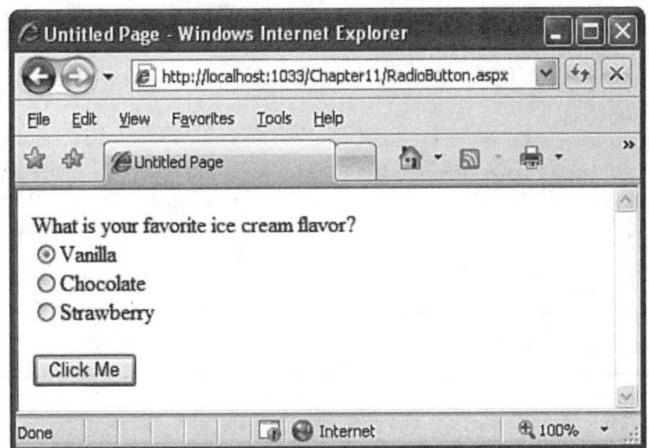

FIGURE 11.10
Radio buttons allow the user to select one option from a list of options.

Create a new ASP.NET page named `RadioButton.aspx`. This page will function like the `DropDownList.aspx` page, prompting the users to select their favorite ice cream flavor.

After you creating the new ASP.NET page, type in the text `What is your favorite ice cream flavor?`. Beneath this text, add the first RadioButton Web control to the page. The designer displays the RadioButton control as a radio button followed by the value of the RadioButton control's `ID` property (in brackets).

You may have noticed that the Toolbox contains both a RadioButton Web control and a RadioButtonList Web control. The RadioButtonList Web control is used when the options for the radio buttons are stored in a database. We will look at using the RadioButtonList Web control in Hour 17.

Figure 11.11 shows the designer after the first RadioButton Web control has been added.

Now change the `ID` property of the RadioButton Web control you just added from `RadioButton1` to `Vanilla`. Add two more RadioButton Web controls, each one beneath the other, and set their `ID` properties to `Chocolate` and `Strawberry`. Finally, add a Button Web control beneath all three RadioButton Web controls. Set the Button's `ID` property to `SubmitButton` and its `Text` property to "Click Me".

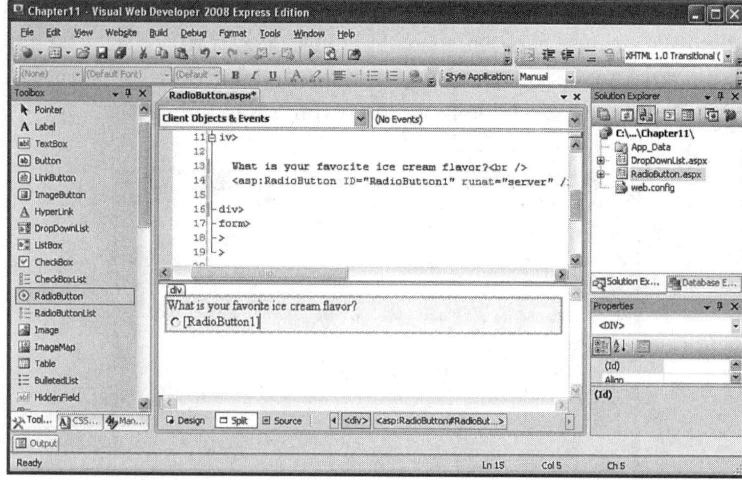

FIGURE 11.11 A RadioButton Web control has been added to `RadioButton.aspx`.

Figure 11.12 shows Visual Web Developer after the additional RadioButton controls and the Button have been added.

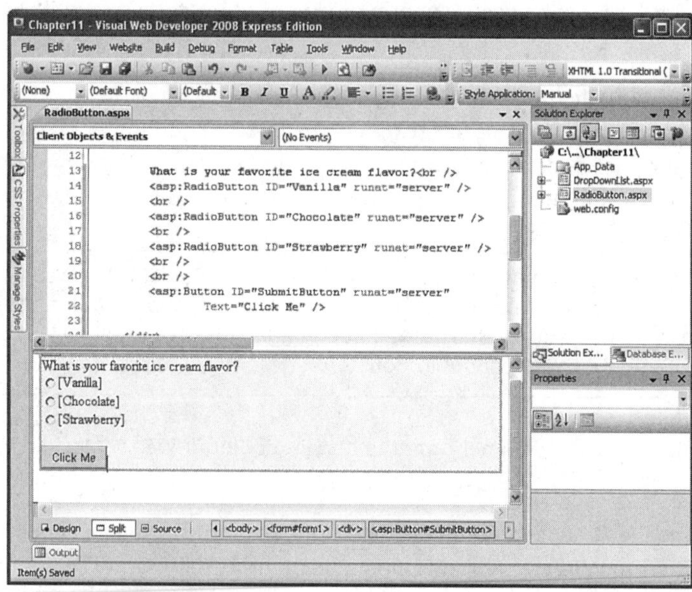

FIGURE 11.12 The `RadioButton.aspx` page now contains three RadioButton Web controls and a Button Web control.

Take a moment to view the `RadioButton.aspx` ASP.NET web page through a browser. As you do this, take note of two things. First, there are only three radio buttons and no text explaining what each radio button represents. Second, you can select more than one radio button. (To see this, click the first radio button and then click the second—both radio buttons will be selected.) Figure 11.13 shows the `RadioButton.aspx` web page when viewed through a browser, highlighting these two issues.

Using the `Text` and `GroupName` Properties

As Figure 11.13 shows, there is no text next to the radio buttons. We need to add some text explaining what choice the resulting radio button represents. To accomplish this, set the RadioButton Web control's `Text` property to the appropriate text. For the `RadioButton.aspx` web page, set the first RadioButton Web control's `Text` property to "Vanilla," the second's to "Chocolate," and the third's to "Strawberry." After you do this, your screen should look similar to Figure 11.14.

Now we need to group the three RadioButton Web controls so that the user can select only one option from the three. The RadioButton Web control contains a string property named `GroupName`. Those RadioButton Web controls on a web page that have the same value for their `GroupName` properties are considered to belong to the same group. Therefore, to group the three RadioButton Web controls (so that the user can select only one flavor of the three), set the `GroupName` property for the three RadioButton Web controls to the value `Flavors`.

What value you use for the `GroupName` property isn't important; what matters is that all related RadioButton Web controls have the same `GroupName` value. We could have set the `GroupName` property of all three RadioButton Web controls to "ScottMitchell," and the result—the user now being able to select only one of the three radio buttons—would be the same.

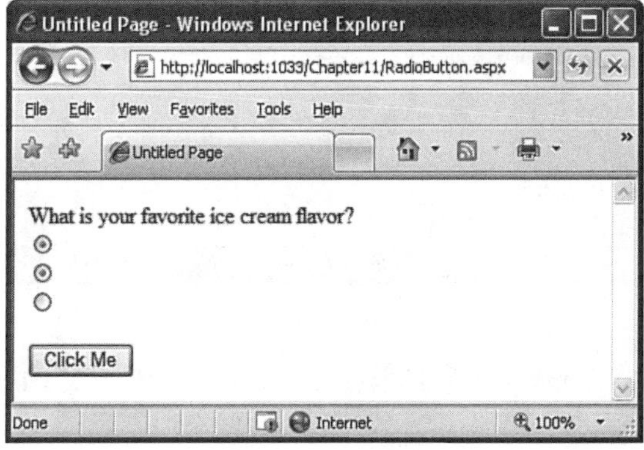

FIGURE 11.13
There is no text explaining what each radio button represents, and multiple radio buttons can be selected.

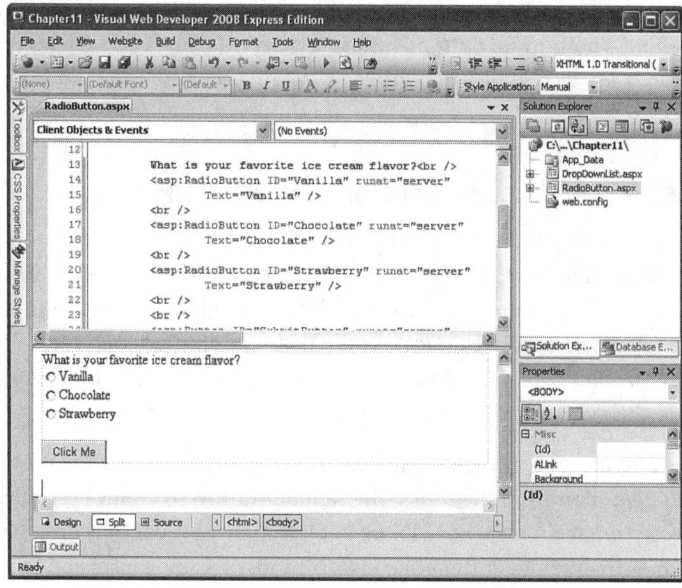

FIGURE 11.14 Text has been added next to each RadioButton Web control.

View the `RadioButton.aspx` web page through a browser. Now that we've specified the `Text` and `GroupName` properties for each of the three RadioButton Web controls, each radio button includes descriptive text and the three radio buttons are mutually exclusive. Figure 11.15 shows the page when visited through a browser.

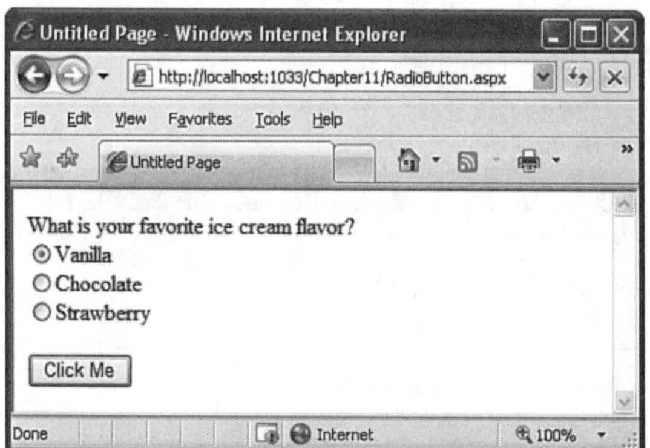

FIGURE 11.15 The radio buttons have text explaining what they represent and are mutually exclusive.

Determining What RadioButton Web Control Was Selected

Adding the RadioButton Web controls to the ASP.NET page, setting their `Text` properties, and making them mutually exclusive is only half of the battle in collecting and processing user input via radio buttons. The other half is determining what option the user selected. Each RadioButton Web control has a `Checked` property, which returns `True` if the RadioButton control is selected, `False` otherwise.

Therefore, to determine if the `Vanilla` RadioButton control was selected, we can use an `If` statement like this:

```
If Vanilla.Checked then
  'The vanilla radio button was selected.
End If
```

Let's have this page display the flavor the user chose using a Label Web control, much like we did with the DropDownList Web control example earlier in this hour. Add a Label to the page, clear out its `Text` property, and set its `ID` property to `Results`.

Next, create an event handler for the Button control's `Click` event and add the code shown in Listing 11.1 to it.

LISTING 11.1 **The Code for the Button's `Click` Event Handler**

```
1:  If Vanilla.Checked then
2:    Results.Text = "You like Vanilla"
3:  ElseIf Chocolate.Checked Then
4:    Results.Text = "You like Chocolate"
5:  ElseIf Strawberry.Checked Then
6:    Results.Text = "You like Strawberry"
7:  End If
```

The code in Listing 11.1 starts by checking to see if the first RadioButton Web control, `Vanilla`, was selected (line 1). If it was (that is, if `Vanilla.Checked` is `True`), then the `Results` Label Web control has its `Text` property set to "You like Vanilla" on line 2. Similarly, if `Chocolate` was the selected RadioButton, then the `Results` Label's `Text` property is set to "You like Chocolate" (lines 3 and 4). Finally, if the `Strawberry` RadioButton control is checked, "You like Strawberry" is displayed (lines 5 and 6).

Did you Know?

> Realize that all three conditionals—`Vanilla.Checked`, `Chocolate.Checked`, and `Strawberry.Checked`—may be `False`. This case occurs if the user does not select a radio button before clicking the Click Me button. If you want to ensure that at least one option in a radio button will be selected, set one of the RadioButton control's `Checked` properties to `True`. Doing so will cause the browser to select that radio button when the page loads, thereby ensuring that one of the radio buttons in the group will be selected.

A Look at the Formatting Properties

Just like the DropDownList, TextBox, and Label Web controls, the RadioButton Web control offers the same set of formatting properties. As you may have already guessed, *all* Web controls contain these properties. (For this reason I won't mention the formatting properties when discussing future Web controls.)

> Recall that the DropDownList Web control lacks the border-related formatting properties. The RadioButton, on the other hand, does have these border-related properties (`BorderColor`, `BorderStyle`, and `BorderWidth`).

Using the CheckBox Web Control

In the "Examining the Different Types of User Input Classifications" section at the beginning of this hour, we examined three classes of user input. The most restrictive class of user input was the Boolean input class, as it is input that can be answered in only one of two ways. The check box is an ideal candidate for collecting user input that falls into this category. The check box, as you've no doubt seen in use before, is a square box that can be checked or unchecked.

Check boxes can also be used for presenting a list of options from which the user can select multiple choices. In our previous two examples—`DropDownList.aspx` and `RadioButton.aspx`—users can select only one flavor of ice cream as their favorite. If we use three check boxes, however, users can select zero, one, two, or three flavors.

The CheckBox Web control adds a check box to an ASP.NET page. Like the RadioButton Web control, a single CheckBox Web control displays a single check box, so to create a page with three check boxes, for example, we must add three CheckBox Web controls.

Let's create an ASP.NET page to demonstrate using the CheckBox Web control. Create a new page named `CheckBox.aspx`. This web page will be similar to the previous two examples in that we will be prompting users for their favorite ice cream flavors. With check boxes, however, users will be able to choose more than one flavor if they so desire.

After you have created the new ASP.NET page, type in the text **`What are your favorite ice cream flavors?`**. Next, drag three CheckBox Web controls from the Toolbox onto the page, one after another. Place a Button Web control beneath the CheckBox controls and a Label Web control underneath the Button.

By the Way

> In addition to the CheckBox Web control, the Toolbox includes a CheckBoxList Web control. The CheckBoxList Web control generates a list of check boxes from data found in a database. We'll examine using the CheckBoxList in Hour 17.

Set the properties for the Web controls we just added. First, clear the Label Web control's `Text` property and set its `ID` to `Results`. Next, set the Button control's `Text` property to "Click Me" and its `ID` property to `SubmitButton`. For the three CheckBox Web controls, set their `Text` and `ID` properties just like we did for the three RadioButton Web controls in the previous example: set the first CheckBox Web control's `Text` property to `Vanilla` and its `ID` to `Vanilla`; set the second CheckBox Web control's `Text` property to `Chocolate`; and so on.

After you have set these Web controls' properties, your screen should look similar to Figure 11.16.

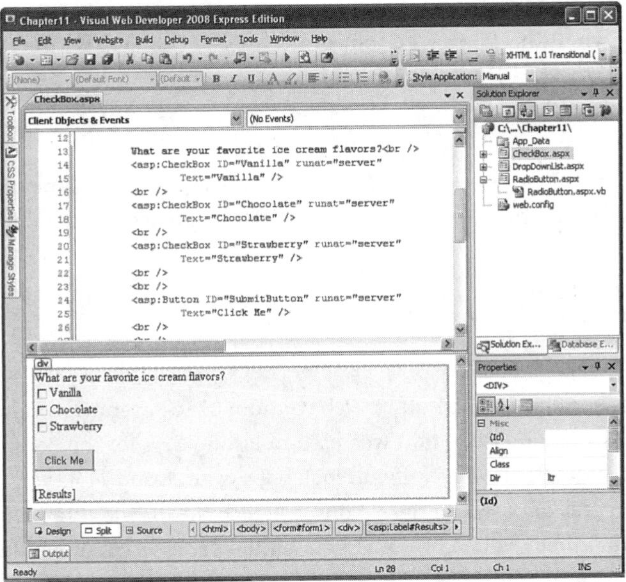

FIGURE 11.16
The ASP.NET page has three CheckBox Web controls.

Take a moment to view `CheckBox.aspx` through a browser. In Figure 11.17 you can see that the page lists three check boxes and that more than one of the three check boxes can be checked.

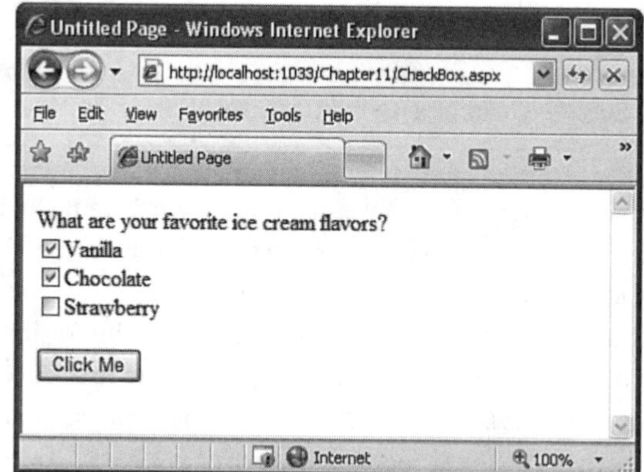

FIGURE 11.17 The user can select zero to three ice cream flavors.

Determining What Check Boxes Have Been Checked

To determine what CheckBox Web controls have been checked, we use the same syntax as with the RadioButton Web controls, namely:

```
CheckBoxID.Checked
```

The `Checked` property returns `True` if the check box is checked, `False` otherwise. Consequently, to determine if the `Vanilla` check box is checked, the following code will suffice:

```
If Vanilla.Checked then
  'The vanilla CheckBox is checked
End If
```

Add an event handler for the Button Web control's `Click` event. You may be tempted to use the same code that was used in Listing 11.1 for the RadioButton Web controls example. However, if you look back over Listing 11.1, you will see that `ElseIf` statements are used on lines 3 and 5, which means the conditional statements following them will be evaluated only if the previous conditional statement was `False`. To put it another way, line 3 in Listing 11.1 will be evaluated only if the condition on line 1—`Vanilla.Checked`—is `False`.

Therefore, the code in Listing 11.1 displays only the name of the first selected ice cream flavor. This is not a problem for the RadioButton Web control example because the user can select only one of the three radio buttons. However, with check boxes we need to allow for multiple ice cream flavors to be listed in the Label Web control because multiple ice cream flavors may be selected. Therefore we need to use three separate `If` statements.

Listing 11.2 contains the source code to add to the `Click` event handler.

LISTING 11.2 The User's Ice Cream Preferences Are Displayed

```
 1:   'Clear out the value of the results Text property
 2:   Results.Text = ""
 3:
 4:   If Vanilla.Checked then
 5:     Results.Text &= "You like Vanilla."
 6:   End If
 7:
 8:   If Chocolate.Checked then
 9:     Results.Text &= "You like Chocolate."
10:   End If
11:
12:   If Strawberry.Checked then
13:     Results.Text &= "You like Strawberry."
14:   End If
```

The code in Listing 11.2 starts by clearing out the `Results` Label Web control's `Text` property (line 2). Next, on lines 4, 8, and 12, the `Checked` property is examined for the three CheckBox Web controls. If the check box is checked, an appropriate message is concatenated with the current value of the `Results` Label control's `Text` property.

For example, on line 8, the `Chocolate.Checked` property is examined. If this property returns `True`, that means the `Chocolate` check box was selected, and line 9 is executed. On line 9, the `Results` Label Web control's `Text` property has its current value concatenated with the string "You like Chocolate."

By the Way

Recall from Hour 5, "Understanding Visual Basic's Variables and Operators," that the &= operator takes the value of the variable on its left side, concatenates it with the expression on the right side, and then assigns the resulting concatenated value to the left-side variable. That is, the following two statements are equivalent:

```
Variable = Variable & "Some string"
```

and

```
Variable &= "Some string"
```

Figure 11.18 shows the `CheckBox.aspx` web page when viewed through a browser. Here the visitor has selected multiple check box choices and submitted the form. Note that all of the user's checked choices are listed in the Label Web control at the bottom of the web page.

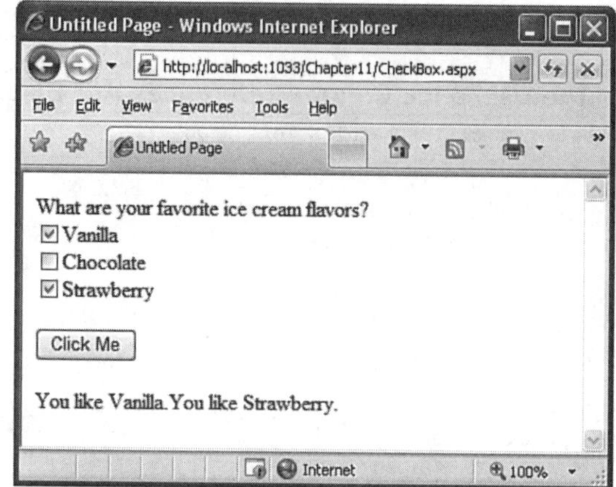

FIGURE 11.18 Users can select multiple ice cream flavors as their favorites.

Summary

In this hour we examined three Web controls commonly used to collect user input: the DropDownList, RadioButton, and CheckBox Web controls. These Web controls are typically used when the user's input is restricted to either a subset of available options or just one of two options.

When adding a DropDownList Web control to an ASP.NET page, we need to explicitly specify those list items that should appear in the drop-down list. Fortunately, this is a simple task through Visual Web Developer's ListItem Collection Editor dialog box (refer to Figure 11.5). In the ASP.NET source code portion, the list item that was selected can be determined via the DropDownList Web control's `SelectedItem` property.

Like drop-down lists, radio buttons allow the user to select one option from a series of allowable choices. Specifically, a radio button is needed for each option, and these radio buttons must be made mutually exclusive with one another so that the user can select only one radio button from the group of related radio buttons. The RadioButton Web control creates a single radio button. To group multiple RadioButton Web controls (so that the user can select only one radio button from the group), give each grouped RadioButton control the same value for its `GroupName` property. Use the RadioButton Web control's `Checked` property to determine whether the user selected a particular RadioButton control.

With radio buttons and drop-down lists, the user can choose only one option from a list of options. A list of check boxes, however, permits the user to choose multiple options. Use the CheckBox Web control to render a check box in the browser. Like the RadioButton, the CheckBox Web control has a `Checked` property that indicates whether the check box was selected.

Now that we've examined the most common Web controls used for collecting input, we're ready to learn how to ensure that the entered input is valid. For example, if users are prompted to enter their age, the value entered should be numeric and within an acceptable range (for instance, between 0 and 110). In the next hour we'll examine ASP.NET's validation Web controls, which are Web controls designed to validate input data.

Q&A

Q. ***If I use a DropDownList or series of RadioButton Web controls to let the user choose one option from, for example, 50 legal choices, does this mean I have to enter in all 50 choices by hand?***

A. With what you know now, the answer is yes. In Hour 17, we will examine how to populate the DropDownList Web control with data from a database. Furthermore, we will see how to create a series of radio buttons or check boxes from database data using the RadioButtonList and CheckBoxList Web controls.

Q. ***I have created a DropDownList with 10 list items on an ASP.NET page. Now I want to provide this same DropDownList Web control on a different ASP.NET page. Obviously, I can accomplish this by creating a new DropDownList control on the second page and reentering the 10 options by hand. Is there an easier or quicker way?***

A. If you want to copy a DropDownList Web control and its list items from one ASP.NET page to another, start by opening both pages in Visual Web Developer. From the designer, select the DropDownList from the source page and copy it to the Clipboard by pressing Ctrl+C or by going to the Edit menu and choosing Copy. Then go to the target page and paste the control in the appropriate location on the page.

Q. ***When I'm displaying a series of radio buttons, none of the radio buttons are selected by default. This means that a user can submit the Web Form without having picked one of the options. How do I require the user to select one of the radio buttons?***

A. When a user first visits a page, none of the radio buttons are selected. This means a user can simply not choose one of the options in the group by virtue of not clicking on any radio button in the group.

Usually, you want the user to select one of the options. To accomplish this, have one of the radio buttons in the group selected by default. In Visual Web Developer, click the RadioButton Web control that you want selected by default. This will load its properties in the Properties window. From there, set the RadioButton control's `Checked` property to `True`.

Keep in mind that only one of the radio buttons in the group can be selected by default. If you set the `Checked` property to `True` for multiple RadioButton Web controls in the group, the user's browser will select only one of the radio buttons.

Workshop

Quiz

1. Imagine that you were creating an online multiple-choice quiz that presented visitors with a question and five possible answers. Assuming that each question can have only one answer selected, what user input Web control would be best suited for this web page?
2. Imagine that you need a user to specify what time zone they live in. What user input Web controls could be used for this task, and what ones could not be used? What user input Web control would be the best option?
3. True or False: The DropDownList Web control can be used to select multiple items from a list of available options.
4. Imagine a web page where users could specify how many countries they've visited from a list of 100 countries. Why would using a series of CheckBox Web controls make sense here?
5. For the example in Question 4, precisely how many CheckBox Web controls would be on this ASP.NET page?
6. What CheckBox Web control property specifies whether a check box was checked?
7. What is the major difference between a series of RadioButton Web controls and a series of CheckBox Web controls?
8. If you wanted to add five RadioButton Web controls to an ASP.NET web page so that users could select only one of the five resulting radio buttons, what property of each of the RadioButtons would you need to set?

Answers

1. Because users can select precisely one option from a list of options, either a DropDownList Web control or a series of RadioButton Web controls would suffice. The best choice would likely be a series of RadioButton controls because virtually all existing online quizzes use radio buttons for the quiz user interface.
2. This information could be provided via a text box, a series of radio buttons, or a drop-down list. A series of check boxes would not be suitable because a single user cannot live in multiple time zones. The best user input Web control for the job, though, would likely be a series of RadioButtons or a DropDownList.
3. False. The DropDownList Web control allows users to select only *one* item from a list of items.
4. A series of CheckBox Web controls would allow users to select more than one option. Had we opted to use, for instance, RadioButton Web controls, the users would be able to select only *one* country from the list of 100.
5. A CheckBox Web control would be needed for each option. Because there are 100 countries from which the users can select, there would need to be 100 CheckBox Web controls on the page.
6. The `Checked` property.
7. The RadioButton Web control is designed to allow users to choose precisely one option from a list of available options. The CheckBox Web control, on the other hand, is designed so that users can choose zero or more options. Therefore, a series of RadioButton Web controls would restrict users to selecting just one option from the array of options, whereas a series of CheckBox Web controls would allow users the flexibility to choose several of the available options.
8. RadioButton Web controls are grouped via the `GroupName` property. To group the five radio buttons, set their `GroupName` properties to the same value.

Exercises

1. The book you have in your hands is my seventh book on ASP and ASP.NET. As a shameless plug for my other books, please create an ASP.NET page that allows the user to indicate what other books of mine she has read. That is, create six CheckBox Web controls, each with its `Text` property set to the title of

one of my six other books. In case for some odd reason you are not familiar with my body of work, the six titles are (1) *Sams Teach Yourself Active Server Pages 3.0 in 21 Days;* (2) *Designing Active Server Pages;* (3) *ASP.NET: Tips, Tutorials, and Code;* (4) *ASP.NET Data Web Controls;* (5) *Sams Teach Yourself ASP.NET in 24 Hours;* and (6) *Sams Teach Yourself ASP.NET 2.0 in 24 Hours.*

In addition to creating the six CheckBox Web controls, create a Button Web control and a Label Web control. In the Button Web control's `Click` event handler, count the number of books that the reader has read and emit an appropriate message. If I may so humbly suggest, if the user has read, for instance, five or more of my books, you might display the message "You are indeed a wonderful person," whereas if the user has yet to read any of my other books, you could emit a message like "It is absolutely imperative that you go to your nearest bookstore without delay and pick up one (or more) of Scott's books!"

2. For this exercise, create a short online quiz. Make sure the quiz has at least three questions and that each question has at least three possible answers. Each question should have exactly one correct answer.

   After the questions, there should be a Button Web control that, when clicked, will display the user's score. If you are interested in a more difficult challenge, in addition to displaying the user's score, list the correct answer to each question that was incorrectly answered.

HOUR 12

Validating User Input with Validation Controls

In this hour, we will cover

- The various classes of input validation
- How to use the RequiredFieldValidator to ensure that the user has provided input
- How to use the CompareValidator
- How to ensure that the user's input falls between a range of values by using the RangeValidator
- How to use the RegularExpressionValidator

As we have examined in previous hours, collecting user input through an ASP.NET page is a relatively easy task. Unfortunately, when we're collecting a user's input, there is no guarantee that it has been provided in an acceptable format. Consider a page that prompts the user for his weight, much like we did with the BMI calculator a few hours ago. What should happen if the user enters a value like "Far too much"?

Ensuring that user input is in a proper format is a technique known as **input validation** and is the topic for this hour. ASP.NET makes input validation a breeze thanks to its **validation controls**. We examine how to use four validation controls in this hour: the RequiredFieldValidator, the CompareValidator, the RangeValidator, and the RegularExpressionValidator.

Examining the Need for User Input Validation

In the past two hours, we've looked at using TextBoxes, DropDownLists, RadioButtons, and CheckBoxes to collect user input. Often, we need the user's input to be in a certain format or to conform to some set of guidelines. **Input validation** is the process of ensuring that the data entered by a user is in the proper format and/or meets certain constraints.

For example, imagine that you wanted to collect the following information from a user:

- Name
- Age
- ZIP code

To collect this input, you would probably use three TextBox Web controls, one for each of the three inputs. When presented with a text box, users can enter any value they choose, or they may enter no input at all. For example, when prompted to enter his age, the user could leave the text box empty. Or he may choose to enter **29**. Or, instead of entering **29**, he may use an alternative representation for **29**, like **`twenty-nine`**. Or the user might enter something nonsensical, like **`I am a Jisun`**.

More likely than not, we want the user to enter his age as a number because a number is less ambiguous than a string. (That is, **29** is unambiguous, because it's the only numerical way to specify the value; with text, however, 29 can be written as **`twenty-nine`**, **`twenty nine`**, **`Twentynine`**, **`Twenty Nine`**, and so forth.) Furthermore, a number can be used in mathematical calculations, whereas a string like **`twenty-nine`** cannot.

Even if we ensure that users enter their age as a number, users can still enter bad input. Values like –540.149, 750, and 0.576 are valid numbers, but not valid ages.

Types of Input Validation

The validation requirements we just discussed for collecting a user's age highlights that different classes of input validation exist. For instance, ensuring that users enter a value for their age and ensuring that the age is entered as a number are both considered forms of input validation, but they differ in that the former simply checks to see whether a value is entered, and the latter ensures that the entered data is in a predefined format.

Input validation can be broken into five distinct classes. Let's examine these five classes.

Required Field Input Validation

The first type of input validation is required field validation. Required field validation is used to ensure that a value has been entered for a particular form field. For example, when filling out shipping information at an e-commerce website, required fields would include the street address, city, state, and ZIP code; optional fields might include special shipping instructions.

Data Type Validation

For numeric inputs, it is often important that the input be entered as a number, not a string. That is, when users are prompted for the year they were born, it is important that they enter the year as four digits, such as **`1978`**, rather than as a string, such as **`Nineteen seventy eight`**.

Humans think in terms of language, whereas computer programs work in terms of data. Data type validation helps ensure that the text entered by the user can be converted into the data format needed by the code.

Range Input Validation

For certain numeric inputs, it is important that the value falls within a certain range of numbers. For example, if a user is prompted for her age, we might want to ensure that the value entered is between 0 and 150.

Comparison Validation

Another typical class of input validation for numeric inputs is a comparison validation. Consider a web page that asks visitors to enter their annual income. For the input to be valid, the income amount needs to be a numeric value greater than or equal to 0.

Alternatively, we may need to compare the value of one user input with the value of another. Imagine that in addition to their income, users were asked to provide their income tax burden. Because a person's income tax cannot exceed her total income, we would want to ensure that the value entered for the income tax entered was less than the value entered for her income.

Pattern Validation

Certain types of string input must conform to a particular format. For example, mailing addresses in the United States include a ZIP code, which is denoted using either

XXXXX

or

XXXXX-XXXX

where X is a digit. An e-commerce website that ships within the United States would ensure that its customers' ZIP codes were entered in accordance to one of the preceding two formats.

Validating User Input in an ASP.NET Web Page

In ASP.NET input, validation is performed through the use of—you guessed it—Web controls. The Web controls that perform input validation are commonly called **validation Web controls**, or just **validation controls**.

We examine four kinds of validation controls in this hour, which are summarized in Table 12.1. Each of these Web controls is geared for providing one or more of the input validation classes discussed in the preceding sections.

TABLE 12.1 The ASP.NET Validation Web Controls

Validation Control	Type of Validation	Description
RequiredFieldValidator	Required Field validation	Ensures that data has been entered into a specific input.
CompareValidator	Data type validation and comparison validation	Ensures that a value in one input is less than, less than or equal, equal, greater than, greater than or equal, or not equal to some constant value or some user-inputted value. Can also be used to perform data-type validation.
RangeValidator	Range validation	Ensures that a numeric value in an input is between two constant numeric values.

TABLE 12.1 Continued

Validation Control	Type of Validation	Description
RegularExpressionValidator	Pattern validation	Ensures that a string value matches some specified pattern.

The following sections examine each of these validation Web controls in detail, focusing on how to add the validation control to an ASP.NET page, how to specify what user input they validate, and how to determine whether the user's input meets the required validation.

An ASP.NET Web Page for Examining the Validation Controls

Before we begin our examination of these four validation controls, let's first create an ASP.NET page that we can use throughout all these exercises. Specifically, we will create a page that collects the following information from users:

- **Name**, which is a required field
- **Age**, which is a numeric field that must be between 0 and 150
- **Social Security number (SSN)**, which is a string input with the format `NNN-NN-NNNN`, where `N` is a digit
- **Number of children**, which must be greater than or equal to 0
- **Number of male children**, which must be greater than or equal to 0 and less than or equal to the number of total children the person has

Start by creating a new ASP.NET page named `ValidationControlTestBed.aspx`. Next, add five TextBox Web controls for the five user inputs. Before each TextBox, enter a descriptive title, such as `Your name:`, `Your age:`, `Social Security number:`, and so on. Figure 12.1 shows Visual Web Developer after these five TextBox Web controls and their label text has been added.

Set the `ID` properties for these five TextBox Web controls. Set the first TextBox Web control's `ID` property to `Name`; the second's to `Age`; the third's to `SSN`; the fourth's to `TotalChildren`; and the fifth's to `MaleChildren`. For the `Age`, `TotalChildren`, and `MaleChildren` TextBox Web controls, also set the `Columns` property to 4.

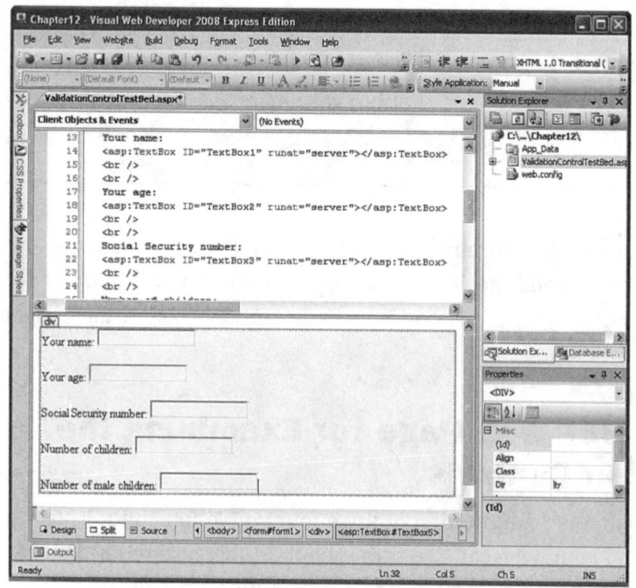

FIGURE 12.1 Five TextBox Web controls have been added, along with a title for each.

Next, add a Button Web control beneath the five TextBox Web controls. Set the Button's `ID` property to `SubmitButton` and its `Text` property to `Click Me`. Finally, add a Label Web control below the Button, clearing out its `Text` property and setting its `ID` to `Results`.

Your screen should now look similar to Figure 12.2.

At this point, you may want to test the `ValidationControlTestBed.aspx` ASP.NET page (you can see this page when viewed through a browser in Figure 12.7). Go ahead and enter some values into the various text boxes. Naturally, there is no input validation, meaning you can enter nonsensical text into any of these text boxes.

By the Way

> As we will see shortly, the ASP.NET validation controls will immediately display a warning message if a visitor enters invalid data.

We are ready to begin our examination of ASP.NET's validation controls, starting with the RequiredFieldValidator.

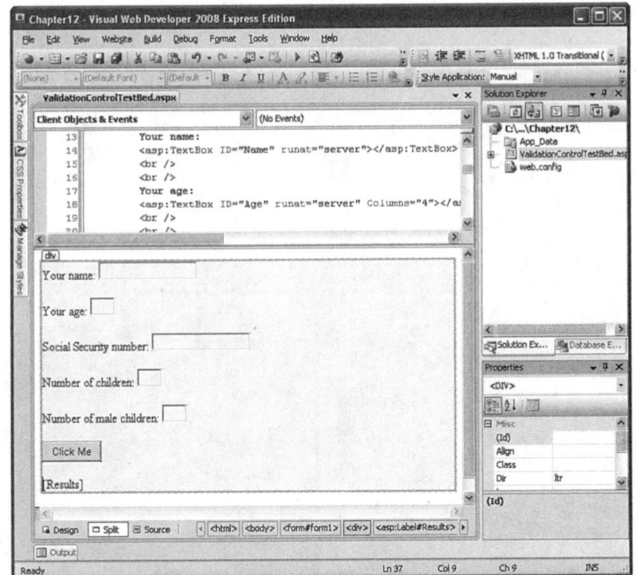

FIGURE 12.2
The TextBox Web controls have had their properties set, and a Button and Label Web control have been added.

Examining the RequiredFieldValidator Validation Control

User input can be divided into two categories: required input and optional input. Required input is the set of input that the user *must* provide, whereas optional input is the set of input that the user may choose to provide. To ensure that the user provides a response for a particular required input, use the RequiredFieldValidator Web control.

Add a RequiredFieldValidator validation Web control to the `ValidationControlTestBed.aspx` page by dragging it from the Toolbox onto the page; specifically, place the RequiredFieldValidator control immediately to the right of the `Name` TextBox.

By the Way

All the validation controls are grouped within the Validation section of the Toolbox.

When you drag and drop the RequiredFieldValidator validation control onto the designer, your screen should look similar to Figure 12.3. Although the image in this book doesn't show it, the text RequiredFieldValidator appears in a red font.

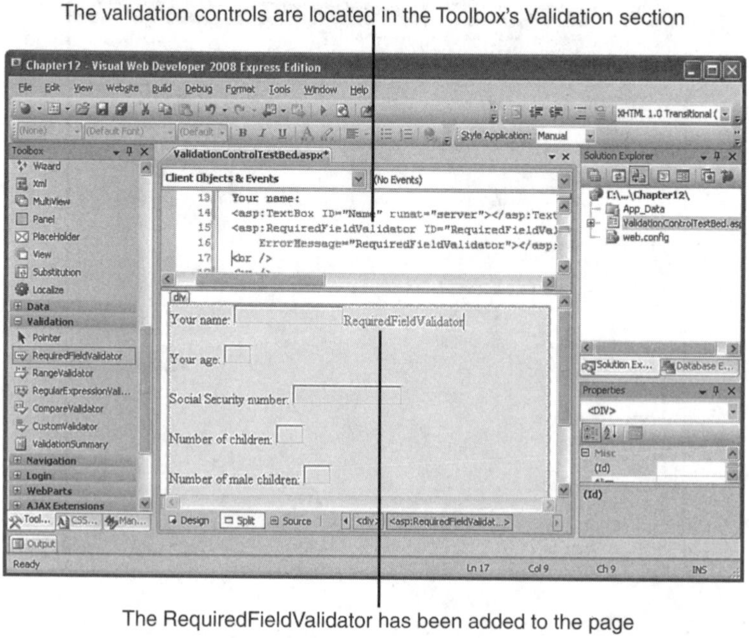

The validation controls are located in the Toolbox's Validation section

The RequiredFieldValidator has been added to the page

FIGURE 12.3
A RequiredFieldValidator has been added to the ASP.NET web page.

Specifying What Web Control the Validation Web Control Is Validating

The validation Web controls are designed to validate input for a particular **input Web control**. By input Web control, I mean a Web control that is used to collect user input, such as the TextBox Web control.

All validation Web controls contain a `ControlToValidate` property that specifies the `ID` of the input Web control to be validated. Because we want to require users to provide their name in the `Name` TextBox control, we need to add a RequiredFieldValidator to the page and set its `ControlToValidate` property to `Name`.

It is important to understand that each validation Web control added to an ASP.NET page can validate only *one* input Web control. Therefore, if the `ValidationControlTestBed.aspx` page had three required input fields (say `Name`, `Age`, and `SSN`), we would need to add three RequiredFieldValidator controls to the page. The first RequiredFieldValidator control would have its `ControlToValidate` property set to `Name`, the second's to `Age`, and the third's to `SSN`.

For our example, `Name` is the only required input Web control; therefore, we only need the one RequiredFieldValidator on the page. Set the `ControlToValidate` property of the RequiredFieldValidator that we just added to the page to `Name`. To do this, select the RequiredFieldValidator so that its properties are loaded in the Properties window. Next, click the `ControlToValidate` property, which will show a drop-down list of the various input Web controls on the page (see Figure 12.4). Select the `Name` option from the list.

FIGURE 12.4
Select the Web control you want the RequiredField Validator to validate.

If you forget to set the `ControlToValidate` property, when viewing the page through a browser you will get an error explaining that the `ControlToValidate` property cannot be blank (see Figure 12.5).

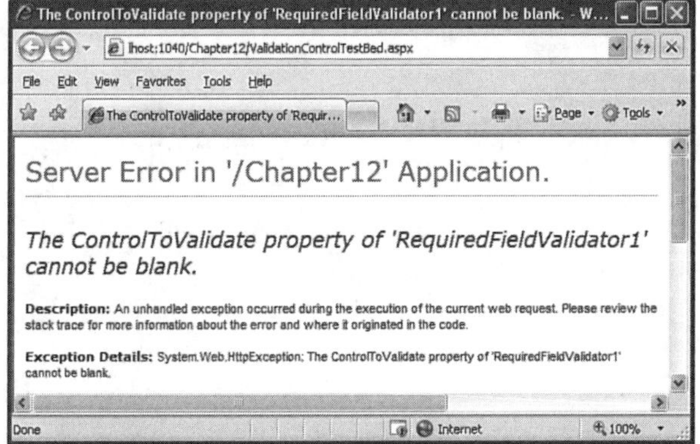

FIGURE 12.5
An error will occur if the validation Web control's `ControlTo Validate` property is incorrectly set.

If you set the `ControlToValidate` property to a specific Web control and then later change that Web control's `ID` property, you will get an error when visiting the ASP.NET page through a browser explaining that the validation control cannot find the control referenced by `ControlToValidate`. This error arises because the validation control's `ControlToValidate` property is not automatically updated when the Web control it validates has its `ID` property changed. Therefore, if you change a Web control's `ID` property after you have added validation controls to the page, double-check that the `ControlToValidate` properties are up to date.

Specifying What Error Message to Display for Invalid Input

Along with a `ControlToValidate` property, all validation controls contain an `ErrorMessage` property. This string property contains the text that is displayed when the user's input fails to meet the validation requirements. Typically, this text should provide a brief explanation as to the problem with the user's input and what she needs to do to fix it.

For example, for a RequiredFieldValidator, you might want to set the `ErrorMessage` to "You must provide a value for *input*," where *input* is the name of the information that the user is required to provide. Another common `ErrorMessage` value for RequiredFieldValidators is an asterisk. Many websites place asterisks next to required form fields that are missing values.

For the `ValidationControlTestBed.aspx` page, go ahead and set the RequiredFieldValidator's `ErrorMessage` to **`You must provide your name`**. After you enter this value, the text displayed for the RequiredFieldValidator control in the designer will update to reflect the new `ErrorMessage` value (see Figure 12.6).

FIGURE 12.6 The designer, after the RequiredField Validator's `ErrorMessage` property has been set.

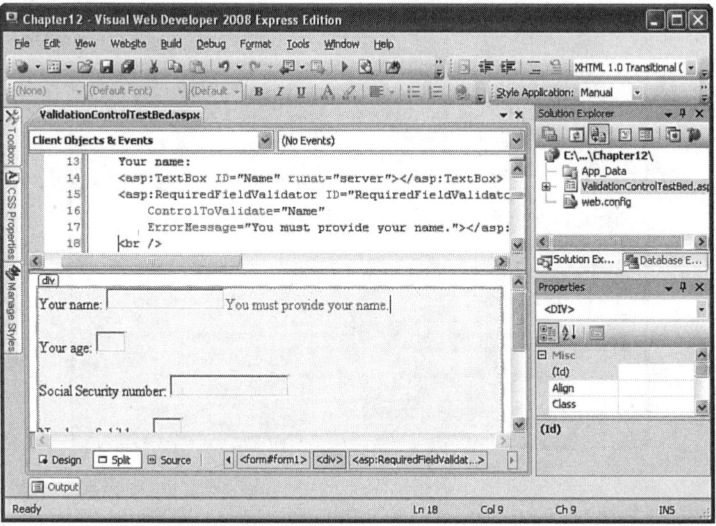

Testing the ASP.NET Page

With the `ControlToValidate` and `ErrorMessage` properties set, the RequiredFieldValidator will now display a warning to users if they do not provide a value for the `Name` text box. To test this, visit the `ValidationControlTestBed.aspx` page through a browser. Figure 12.7 shows this web page when first visited.

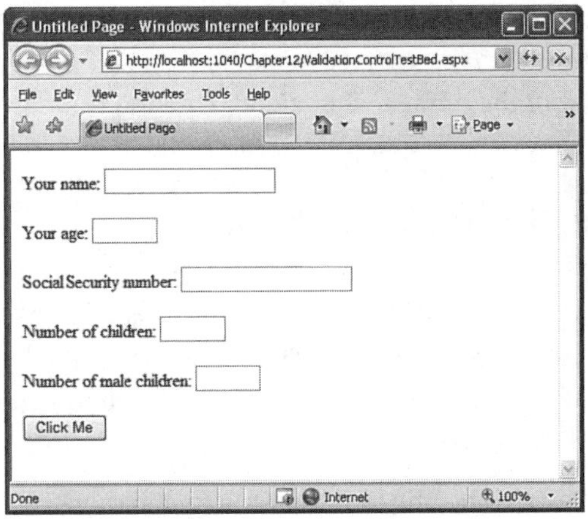

FIGURE 12.7
The ValidationControlTestBed.aspx web page, when first visited.

Note that there is a slight difference in the appearance of the web page when viewed through a browser (Figure 12.7) and when shown in the Design view (Figure 12.6). Specifically, in the browser the RequiredFieldValidator's `ErrorMessage` value is not displayed.

Now click the Click Me button without entering any text into the name text box. What happened? Clicking the button did not submit the form; instead, it displayed the message "You must provide your name" next to the name text box.

Figure 12.8 shows the `ValidationControlTestBed.aspx` page after the Click Me button has been clicked when there was no input entered into the name text box.

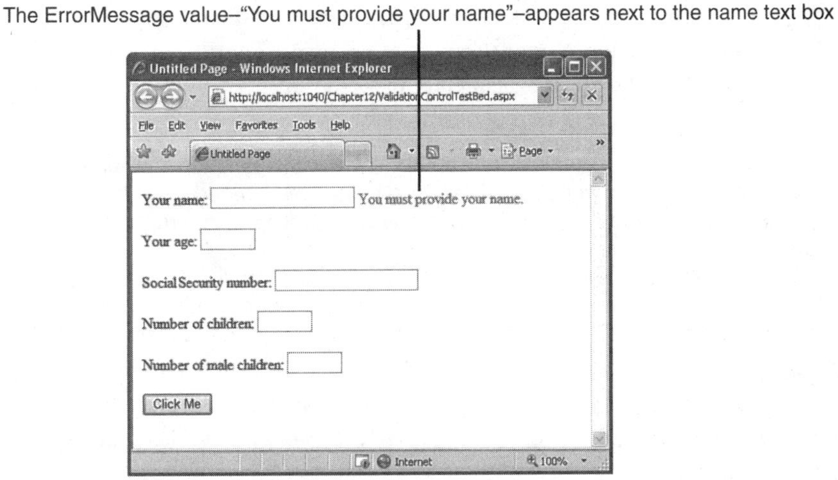

The ErrorMessage value–"You must provide your name"–appears next to the name text box

FIGURE 12.8
The message "You must provide your name" appears next to the name text box.

Now enter some text into the name text box. After you have done this, press the Tab key or click a different text box so that some other text box receives the focus. Moving the focus out of the name text box after entering text causes the "You must provide your name" message to magically disappear!

Client-Side and Server-Side Validation

What's going on here? How can the validation controls stop the button click from submitting the form if there's invalid data? And how does the "You must provide your name" error message automatically disappear after valid data is entered into the text box? This functionality is made possible by the **client-side script** emitted by the RequiredFieldValidator control.

Client-side script is JavaScript code that is sent to and executed by the visitor's browser. When the user tabs or clicks out of a text box, a piece of JavaScript code that determines whether the input provided is valid is run on the user's web browser; if the data is invalid, the client-side script automatically displays the validation Web control's `ErrorMessage` property value. Likewise, client-side script cancels the form submission in the face of invalid data.

Using client-side script to perform validation on the visitor's browser is referred to as **client-side validation**.

> Client-side validation can be used only if the visitor's browser supports client-side script. Although virtually all browsers today support client-side script, users can disable script through their browser's options.

Browsers that do not support client-side script or that have them disabled employ just **server-side validation**. Server-side validation, as the name implies, is validation that occurs in code that is executed on the web server.

> All validation controls, regardless of whether client-side validation is supported by the browser, perform server-side validation checks. This is good news because a user can easily sidestep client-side validation by disabling JavaScript in her browser.

Client-side validation's main advantage over server-side validation is that it provides immediate feedback to the user without requiring a postback to the web server. This has the advantage of saving the user time, especially if he is on a slow connection, because it does not require a round-trip to the web server to determine what inputs are invalid.

> **By the Way**
>
> To learn more about client-side validation, check out the article "Form Validation on the Client Side," at www.sitepoint.com/article/form-validation-client-side.

Programmatically Determining Whether the User's Input Is Valid

As we have seen, by simply setting the `ControlToValidate` and `ErrorMessage` properties of the RequiredFieldValidator control, users are automatically alerted if their input is invalid through client-side validation. But how can we determine whether all the user's input is valid from the page's source code portion?

Typically, we want to process the user's submitted input in some fashion, by performing some calculation on the input or, perhaps, by storing it in a database. Of course, we don't want to process the data unless it is valid.

To determine programmatically whether the user's input is valid, check the `Page.IsValid` property. The `Page.IsValid` property returns `True` only if all the validation Web controls on the ASP.NET page have indicated that the input entered into their respective input Web controls is in the proper format. Put another way, if any input is invalid, `Page.IsValid` will be `False`.

To demonstrate using this property, create an event handler for the Button Web control's `Click` event. Next, enter the following code into the generated `Click` event handler:

```
If Page.IsValid then
  'User input is valid
  Results.Text = "Input is valid..."
Else
  'There is at least one invalid input
  Results.Text = "Input is <b>not</b> valid..."
End If
```

A quick examination of the code reveals that if the `Page.IsValid` property is `True`, then the string "Input is valid..." is displayed; if there is any invalid input, however, the string "Input is **not** valid..." is displayed. This behavior can be seen in Figures 12.9 and 12.10, respectively.

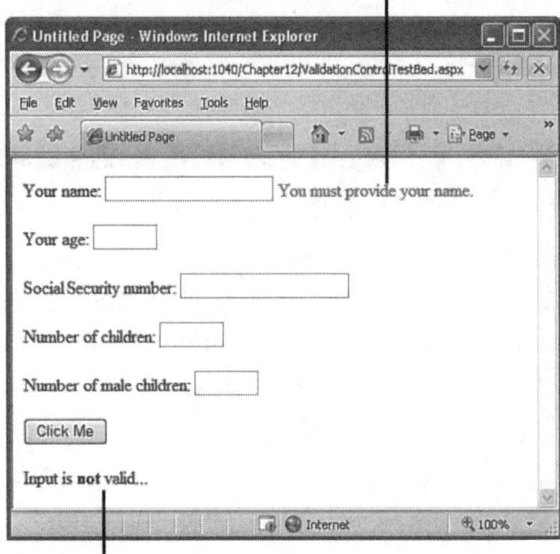

FIGURE 12.9 The form has been submitted with invalid user input.

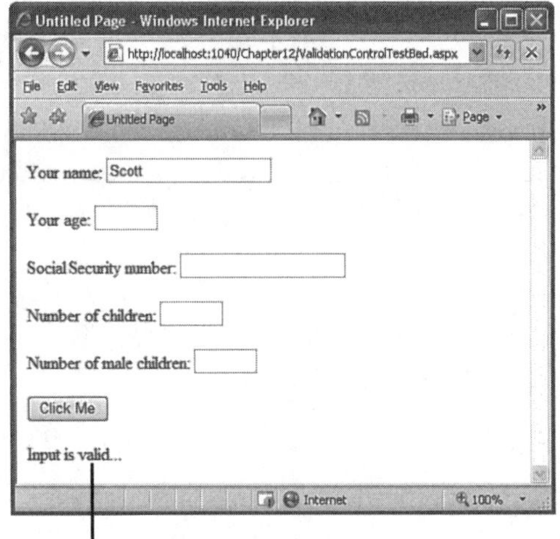

FIGURE 12.10 The form has been submitted, and all the user input is valid.

If you are visiting the page with a browser that supports client-side script, you will not be able get your screen to look like the screenshot in Figure 12.10 because the client-side validation script prohibits you from submitting the form without entering a value into the name text box. Because the form cannot be submitted with invalid data, the `Click` event handler is not executed, which is why you do not see the "Input is **not** valid..." message. The client-side validation ensures that the form is not posted back until the user has entered valid inputs.

Given that client-side validation suppresses the form from being submitted until the user's inputs are valid, you might reason that you need not bother checking the `Page.IsValid` property in the Button's `Click` event handler. However, you should *always* check to ensure that `Page.IsValid` is `True` before working with user-submitted data. A nefarious user can easily circumvent the client-side validation checks. Think of client-side validation as an added bonus, not as a foolproof way of ensuring valid input.

Summarizing the Basic Validation Control Features

Although a variety of validation Web controls are available, all of them share a number of similarities. First, all validation Web controls are designed to validate a single input Web control, and this control is specified via the validation control's `ControlToValidate` property. Furthermore, all validation controls contain an `ErrorMessage` property that specifies the text that is displayed if the input is invalid.

The validation controls emit client-side validation script that automatically shows or hides the validation control's `ErrorMessage` values, depending on whether the user inputs valid or invalid data. The client-side validation also prevents the form from being submitted if invalid inputs exist. Because client-side validation can be easily circumvented, the validation controls also perform server-side validation. To determine whether the input entered by a user is valid through code, check the `Page.IsValid` property.

Examining the CompareValidator

The CompareValidator validation control is useful for comparing the value of a user's input to a constant value or to the value of a different user input. For example, the last two inputs on the `ValidationControlTestBed.aspx` page ask users for the total number of children they have and the number of male children. These two inputs are prime candidates for the CompareValidator control.

The input that prompts users for their total number of children, for example, must be a value that is greater than or equal to 0. The input for the number of male children must be both greater than or equal to 0 and less than or equal to the value the user entered into the total number of children text box.

Let's first provide this validation check for the total number of children input. Start by adding a CompareValidator to the page, placing it to the right of the `TotalChildren` TextBox, as shown in Figure 12.11.

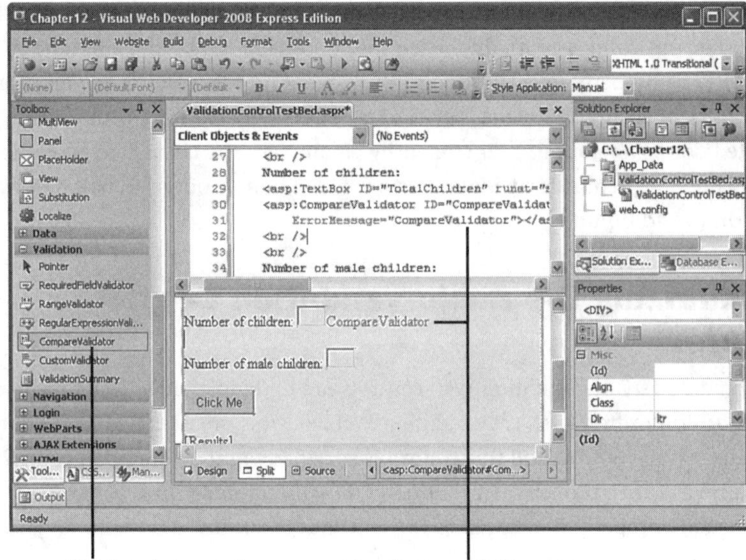
The CompareValidator is located in the Toolbox's Validation section
The CompareValidator has been added to the page

FIGURE 12.11
A Compare Validator Web control has been added.

The CompareValidator is capable of performing a number of comparisons. For example, the CompareValidator can compare an input to ensure that it's less than some value, greater than or equal to a value, or not equal to some value. The `Operator` property specifies what comparison the CompareValidator should perform.

Select the CompareValidator so that its properties are loaded in the Properties window and then scroll down to the `Operator` property. When you click this property, a drop-down list that contains the valid settings for this property appears. The `Operator` property can be set to one of the following comparisons:

- `Equal`
- `NotEqual`
- `GreaterThan`
- `GreaterThanEqual`
- `LessThan`
- `LessThanEqual`
- `DataTypeCheck`

Because we want to ensure that the number of total children entered by users is greater than or equal to 0, set the `Operator` property to `GreaterThanEqual`.

By the Way

> If you set `Operator` to `DataTypeCheck`, the CompareValidator will be considered valid only if the associated input Web control's contents are of the specified data type. The `DataTypeCheck` option is useful when you want to ensure that the user enters a value of the appropriate data type, but you don't care is less than or greater than some other value. For example, if a person was prompted to enter their favorite number, you could use a CompareValidator with its `Operator` property set to `DataTypeCheck` to ensure that the value entered was, indeed, a number.

In addition to the `Operator` property, we need to set the `Type` property. The `Type` property indicates what data type the users' input should be provided in. The `Type` property, which can be accessed via the Properties pane just like the `Operator` property, can be set to one of the following data types:

- `String`
- `Integer`
- `Double`
- `Date`
- `Currency`

Because we want the user to enter the total number of children as a numeric value without a decimal, set the `Type` property to `Integer`.

At this point we have specified what comparison should be performed and what data type the user's input should appear as. We must now specify the value we want to compare the user's input to. This value can be either a constant value or the value entered by the user in some other input Web control.

We want to ensure that the user's input is greater than or equal to a constant value, namely 0. Therefore, set the CompareValidator's `ValueToCompare` property to 0.

After this property has been set, all that remains is to set the `ControlToValidate` and `ErrorMessage` properties. Set the `ControlToValidate` property to `TotalChildren` and the `ErrorMessage` property to a descriptive message, such as `The total number of children must be a whole number greater than or equal to 0.`

After you have set all these properties, your screen should look similar to Figure 12.12.

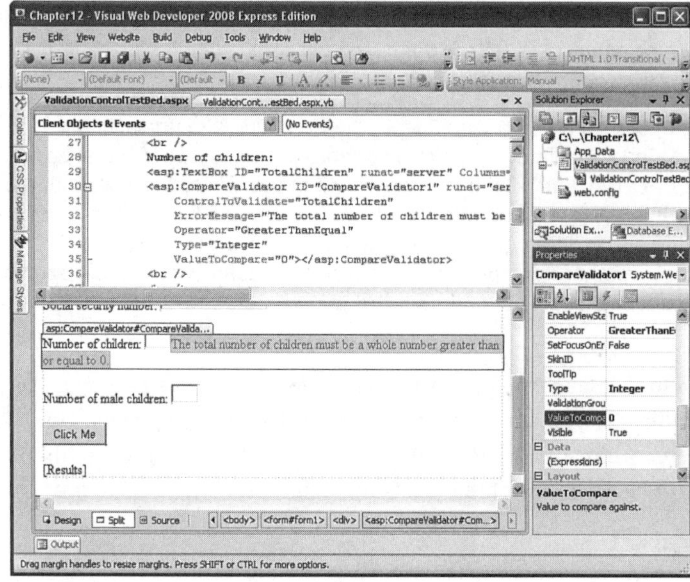

FIGURE 12.12 The Compare Validator will ensure that the input is greater than or equal to 0.

Test the functionality of the CompareValidator by visiting the `ValidationControlTestBed.aspx` page through a browser. Enter invalid input into the total number of children text box, such as **-33** or **Sam**. Doing so will display the validation control's error message as shown in Figure 12.13.

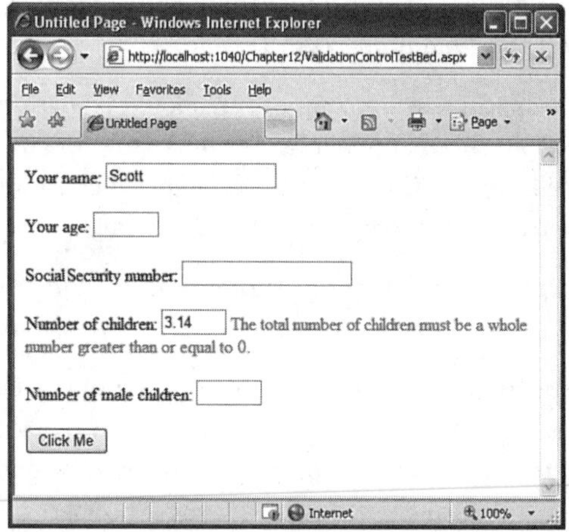

FIGURE 12.13 Invalid input produces an appropriate error message.

Invalid input is input that is not an integer and not greater than or equal to 0. Some examples of invalid input are

- Scott
- –4
- 3,456 (the presence of the comma makes this an illegal input)
- 3.14159

Some examples of legal input include

- 0
- 2
- 3456
- 45533

Did you Know?

Putting an upper bound on the total number of children input might make sense. For example, we can safely assume that no one will have more than 50 children. To place such an upper bound, we could add an additional CompareValidator and set its `Operator` property to `LessThanEqual` and its `ValueToCompare` property to 50.

Alternatively, instead of using two CompareValidators, we could use a single RangeValidator. We examine the RangeValidator Web control in the "Using the RangeValidator" section.

Keep in mind that if the user omits a value, the CompareValidator reports valid user input. In other words, if the user enters a value into the name text box but enters no value into the total number of children text box and clicks the Click Me button, the ASP.NET page will post back and display the "Input is valid..." message.

The RequiredFieldValidator is the only validation control that ensures that input is provided. All other validation controls perform their checks only if the user supplied an input. Consequently, if you want to require that the user enter a value into the total number of children input, you must add a RequiredFieldValidator for this input as well as a CompareValidator. (In the next section we look at having multiple validation controls validating a single input Web control.)

Using the CompareValidator to Compare One Input to Another

The preceding example used a CompareValidator to compare the total number of children input with a constant value—0. In addition to comparing the value of a user input with a constant value, CompareValidators can also be used to compare the value entered into one input Web control with the value entered into another. For example, the value entered into the number of male children input must be less than or equal to the value the user entered into the total number of children input.

The only difference between a CompareValidator that performs a comparison against a constant value and one that performs a comparison against the value in another input Web control is that in the former case, the CompareValidator's `ValueToCompare` property is set to the constant value to compare the user's input to. In the latter case, instead of setting the `ValueToCompare` property, set the `ControlToCompare` property to the `ID` of the input Web control whose value you want to compare.

To add a CompareValidator that ensures that the value entered into the number of male children input is less than or equal to the total number of children input, start by dragging a CompareValidator from the Toolbox onto the page, placing it to the right of the `MaleChildren` TextBox. Next, set the CompareValidator's `ControlToValidate` property to `MaleChildren`, its `Operator` property to `LessThanEqual`, its `Type` to `Integer`, its `ErrorMessage` to `The number of male children must be less than or equal to the number of total children`, and its `ControlToCompare` property to `TotalChildren`.

After you have set these five properties, your screen should look similar to Figure 12.14.

Now visit the ASP.NET page through a browser. If you enter a value of 4, for example, into the total number of children text box and a value of `8` into the number of male children text box, you will be shown the error message "The number of male children must be less than or equal to the number of total children." Similarly, if you enter a nonintegral value into the number of male children text box (such as `Scott` or `4.5`), you will get the same error message.

What, though, will happen if you enter a value of 5 into the total number of children text box and a value of –2 into the number of male children text box? No error message is displayed because –2 is less than 5, and –2 is an integer.

To prevent this, we must add another CompareValidator for the `MaleChildren` TextBox. This second CompareValidator will check to ensure that the value entered is greater than or equal to 0.

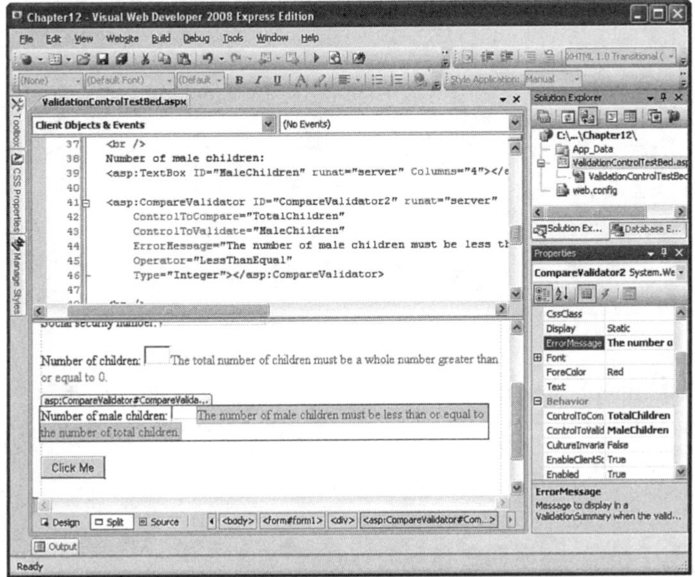

FIGURE 12.14 A Compare Validator has been added after the `MaleChildren` TextBox control.

Add another CompareValidator to the page, placing it to the right of the `MaleChildren` TextBox control's existing CompareValidator. Next, set this new CompareValidator's `ControlToValidate` property to `MaleChildren`, its `Type` property to `Integer`, its `Operator` property to `GreaterThanEqual`, its `ErrorMessage` property to `The number of male children must be greater than or equal to 0`, and its `ValueToCompare` property to 0.

Figure 12.15 shows the Visual Web Developer after this additional CompareValidator has been added and its properties have been set.

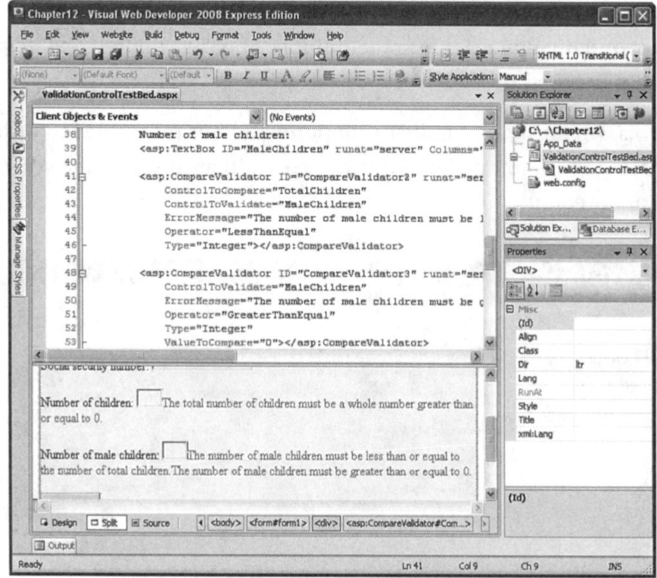

FIGURE 12.15 An additional CompareValidator has been added to help validate the number of male children input.

With this additional CompareValidator, an error message is displayed on the ASP.NET page if the user enters a negative value for the number of male children input.

Using the RangeValidator

As we saw in the preceding section, the CompareValidator can be used to ensure that an input maintains some relation with either a constant value or the value in another input Web control. But what if we need to ensure that a user's input is between a specified range of values? We could use two CompareValidator controls, one that did a `GreaterThanEqual` comparison on the lower bound of the range and one that did a `LessThanEqual` comparison on the upper bound of the range.

If the upper and lower bound of the range are constant values, we can use a single RangeValidator instead of using two CompareValidators. Let's use a RangeValidator in the `ValidationControlTestBed.aspx` ASP.NET page to ensure that the user's age falls within a sensible range (such as 0–150).

> **By the Way**
>
> The RangeValidator can be used only when *both* the upper and lower bounds of the range are constant values. The RangeValidator cannot be used to validate the number of male children input because the upper bound of the range is the value the user entered in the total number of children text box.

Add a RangeValidator to the right of the Age TextBox Web control. As with RequiredFieldValidator and CompareValidator, we need to set the RangeValidator control's `ControlToValidate` and `ErrorMessage` properties. Specifically, set the `ControlToValidate` property to `Age` and the `ErrorMessage` property to **`Age must be between 0 and 150`**.

The RangeValidator, like the CompareValidator, has a `Type` property that specifies the data type the input must be provided in. Because we want the user to enter his age as a number without decimals, set the `Type` property to `Integer`.

All that remains is to specify the upper and lower bounds of the acceptable range of values for the age input, which are configured through the RangeValidator's `MaximumValue` and `MinimumValue` properties. Set the `MaximumValue` property to 150 and the `MinimumValue` property to 0.

After you have set these properties, your screen should look similar to Figure 12.16.

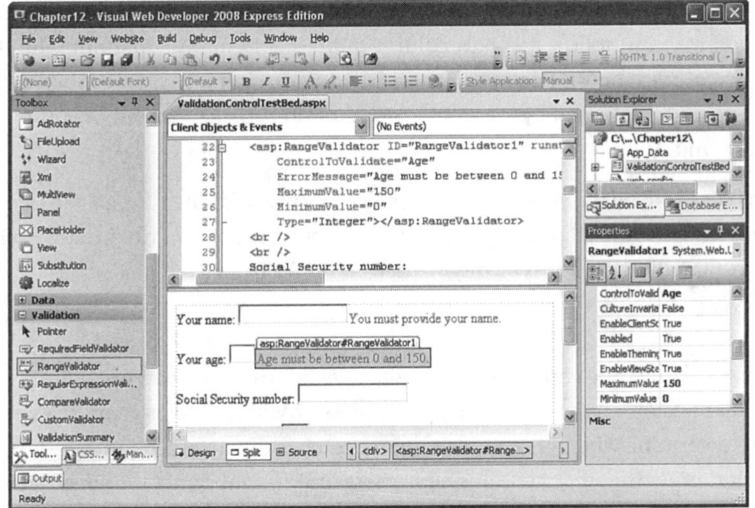

FIGURE 12.16
The properties of the RangeValidator have been set.

If you take a moment to view `ValidationControlTestBed.aspx` through a browser, you can see that an error message is displayed unless either no input is provided into the age text box or the input provided is an integer value between 0 and 150.

It is important that the RangeValidator's `Type` property be properly set because its value determines how the RangeValidator compares the user's input with the specified range. Consider what would happen if you forget to change the RangeValidator control's `Type` property to `Integer` and instead left it set to its default value, `String`. When its `Type` property is set to `String`, the RangeValidator performs a string comparison to determine whether the user's input is within the `MaximumValue` and `MinimumValue` bounds. The string **`1111`** is considered between the strings **`0`** and **`150`**, whereas the string **`29`** is not. Imagine the confusion your users would experience if they entered a value like **`45`** into the text box only to have a warning message appear saying, "Age must be between 0 and 150."

Validating Input with the RegularExpressionValidator

Many forms of user input must be entered in a certain format. For example, an email address must follow this particular format: one to many alphanumeric characters; the at symbol (`@`); one to many alphanumeric characters; and concluding with a period (`.`) followed by a top-level domain name, such as com, net, org, edu, us, uk, fr, and so on.

The `ValidationControlTestBed.aspx` page asks users for their Social Security number. In the United States, all citizens are given a Social Security number, which contains nine digits and is typically written in the form

```
XXX-XX-XXXX
```

To ensure that a string input meets some specified format, we can use a RegularExpressionValidator. The RegularExpressionValidator uses **regular expressions** to determine whether the user's input matches the accepted pattern. A regular expression is a string that contains characters and special symbols and specifies a general pattern. Fortunately, you do not need to be well versed in regular expression syntax to be able to use the RegularExpressionValidator.

Regular expressions are very useful when parsing or searching text and are definitely worth learning. However, an extensive examination of the topic is far beyond the scope of this book, especially because Visual Web Developer provides a number of built-in regular expression patterns that you can use in the RegularExpressionValidator without knowing a thing about regular expression syntax.

If you are interested in learning about regular expressions, I encourage you to read “An Introduction to Regular Expressions” at www.4guysfromrolla.com/webtech/090199-1.shtml and “Common Applications of Regular Expressions” at www.4guysfromrolla.com/webtech/120400-1.shtml. There’s also an extensive regular expression repository and community at www.regexlib.com.

To ensure that the Social Security number is inputted in a proper format, add a RegularExpressionValidator Web control to the ASP.NET page. Place it to the right of the `SSN` TextBox Web control.

Set the RegularExpressionValidator’s `ControlToValidate` property to `SSN` and its `ErrorMessage` property to `Your Social Security number must be in the format XXX-XX-XXXX`. After you set these two properties, the only other property you need to configure is the `ValidationExpression` property, which specifies the regular expression pattern that the user’s input must conform to.

To edit this property, click the `ValidationExpression` property; to the right you will see a pair of ellipses. Clicking these ellipses displays the Regular Expression Editor dialog box (see Figure 12.17).

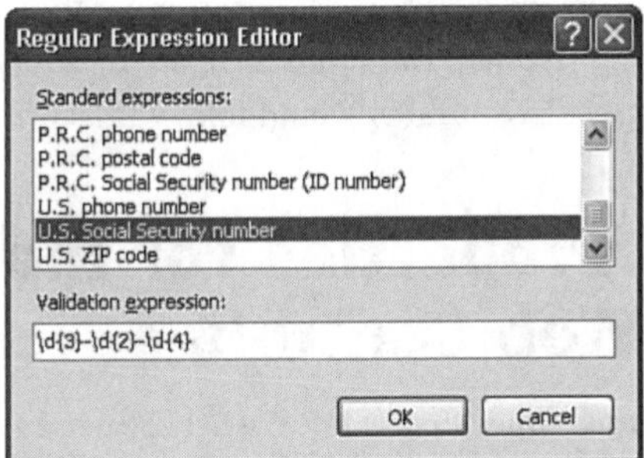

FIGURE 12.17
The Regular Expression Editor dialog box allows you to choose a predefined regular expression pattern.

The Regular Expression Editor dialog box contains a list of standard regular expression patterns that you can choose from. Alternatively, you can type a custom regular expression pattern into the Validation Expression text box. Scroll down and select the U.S. Social Security Number option.

After you select the U.S. Social Security Number option, its regular expression pattern is displayed in the Validation Expression text box. Click the OK button to set the RegularExpressionValidator’s `ValidationExpression`. At this point your screen should look similar to Figure 12.18.

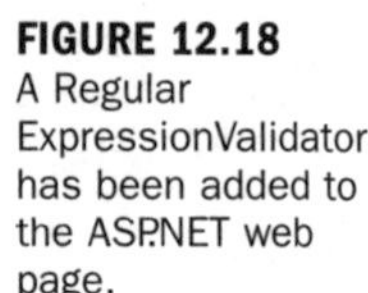

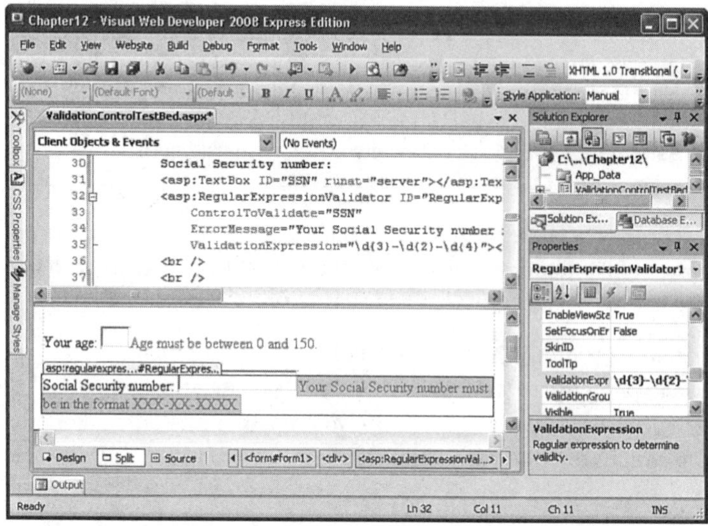

FIGURE 12.18
A RegularExpressionValidator has been added to the ASP.NET web page.

After you have set the key RegularExpressionValidator properties, take a moment to visit `ValidationControlTestBed.aspx` through a browser. Note that an error message is displayed if you provide a Social Security number that doesn't follow the correct format: three digits, a hyphen, two digits, a hyphen, and then four digits. For example, a legal social security number would follow this format: 123-45-6789.

Formatting Properties for the Validation Web Controls

As we have seen numerous times in this hour, when a user enters invalid input, the appropriate validation control's `ErrorMessage` is displayed. In all the examples, this error message has been displayed in a red font. However, the look and feel of the error message can be specified by setting the validation control's formatting properties.

As with all Web controls, the validation controls contain the typical formatting properties—`BackColor`, `BorderColor`, `BorderStyle`, `Font`, and so on. In addition to these standard formatting properties, the validation controls also contain a `Display` property.

The `Display` property specifies how the `ErrorMessage` is displayed when the user enters invalid input and can be assigned one of the following three values:

- `None`
- `Static` (the default)
- `Dynamic`

Setting Display to None hides the ErrorMessage, even if a user's input is invalid. When Display is set to Static, the validation control's ErrorMessage text consumes the same amount of space whether it's displayed or not. On the other hand, when Display is set to Dynamic, the validation control's error message takes up screen space only when it is displayed.

To illustrate the difference between the Static and Dynamic settings, create a new ASP.NET page named DynamicVsStatic.aspx. In the web page, add two TextBox Web controls, one right beneath the other. After each TextBox Web control, type in the text **This text appears right after a text box**. Figure 12.19 shows the Visual Web Developer designer at this point.

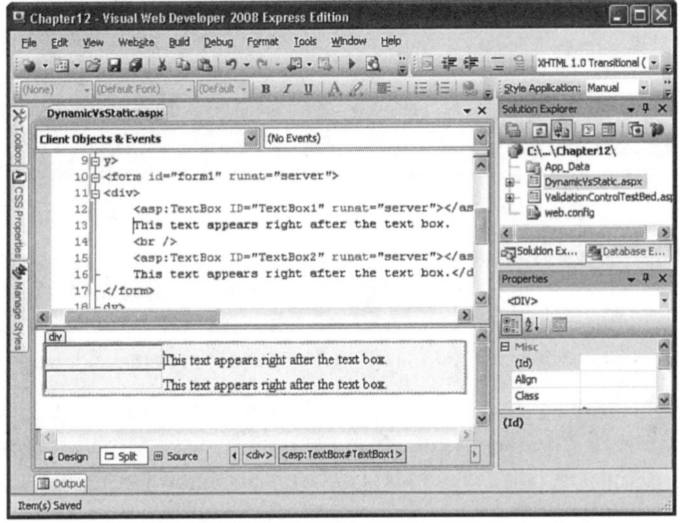

FIGURE 12.19 Two TextBox Web controls have been added to the designer.

Next, drop a RequiredFieldValidator control between the TextBox and the text to its right. Set the RequiredFieldValidator control's ControlToValidate properties to the ID values of the two TextBox Web controls. Set the ErrorMessage property to the value **This demonstrates the differences between Static and Dynamic Display**. Then set one of the two RequiredFieldValidator's Display properties to Dynamic, leaving the other's as Static.

Finally, add a Button Web control beneath both TextBox Web controls. Take a moment to make sure your screen looks similar to Figure 12.20.

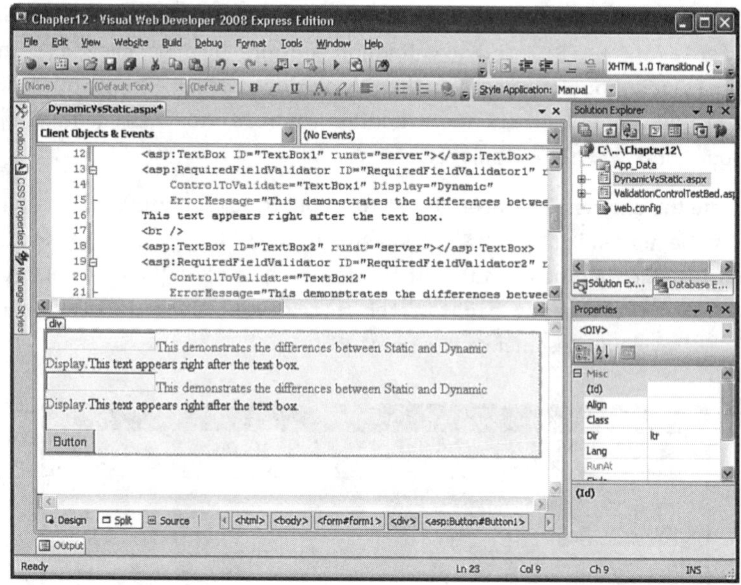

FIGURE 12.20 Two RequiredFieldValidators have been added to the page.

Now, view the `DynamicVsStatic.aspx` page through a browser. Notice that for the RequiredFieldValidator whose `Display` property was left as `Static`, the text "This appears right after a text box" is far from the right side of the text box. This gap represents the space where the RequiredFieldValidator's error message will be displayed.

For the RequiredFieldValidator whose `Display` property was set to `Dynamic`, however, the text "This appears right after a text box" appears immediately after the text box.

Figure 12.21 shows the `DynamicVsStatic.aspx` page when viewed through a browser. As you can see, I set the top RequiredFieldValidator's `Display` property to `Dynamic` and left the bottom's set to the default, `Static`.

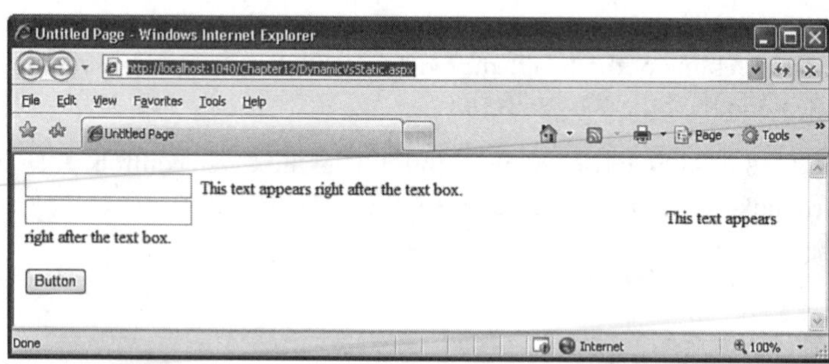

FIGURE 12.21 The gap you see occurs because the RequiredFieldValidator's `Display` property is set to `Static`.

Now, click the button on the web page without entering any input into either of the text boxes. This causes the error message to display for both of the RequiredFieldValidators. Figure 12.22 shows the page after both error messages are displayed. For the RequiredFieldValidator whose `Display` property was set to `Dynamic`, the text "This appears right after a text box" was automatically moved to the right to accommodate the error message.

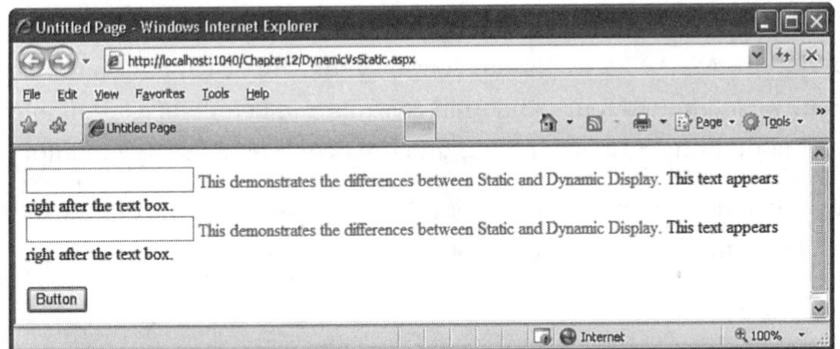

FIGURE 12.22
The page after the button has been clicked.

A Look at the Remaining Validation Controls

In addition to the four validation controls we examined in this hour, there are two more validation controls. The first is the CustomValidator, which is, as its name implies, a validation control that is customizable. The CustomValidator can be used to validate user input in a way that is not handled by the RequiredFieldValidator, CompareValidator, RangeValidator, or RegularExpressionValidator controls.

In my experience, I have found that I've rarely needed to use a CustomValidator. More often than not, one of the main four validation controls suffices. If, however, you find that you do need the power of a CustomValidator, I encourage you to read "Using the CustomValidator Control" at http://aspnet.4guysfromrolla.com/articles/073102-1.aspx.

The other validation control is the ValidationSummary control. The ValidationSummary control lists the `ErrorMessage` properties for all the validation controls on the page reporting invalid data.

By the Way

To learn more about the ValidationSummary control, see www.w3schools.com/aspnet/control_validationsummary.asp.

Summary

When collecting user input it is usually important that the input conform to some set of guidelines. Perhaps certain input is required or must be numeric. Maybe the input needs to be less than a certain value or between two constant values. Or perhaps the input needs to conform to some pattern, such as a telephone number or email address.

The process of ensuring that a user's input is in the correct format is referred to as input validation. ASP.NET's validation controls make input validation a breeze. In this hour we examined four validation controls: the RequiredFieldValidator, the CompareValidator, the RangeValidator, and the RegularExpressionValidator.

This hour concludes our examination of collecting user input. Starting with the next hour we'll be turning our attention to working with databases.

Q&A

Q. ***I noticed that the*** `Display` ***property can have one of three settings:*** `None`, `Static`, ***and*** `Dynamic`. ***I understand the*** `Static` ***and*** `Dynamic` ***settings, but why on earth would anyone want to ever use the*** `None` ***setting?***

A. When a validation Web control's `Display` property is set to `None`, the `ErrorMessage` property is never displayed, regardless of whether the data being validated is valid. It may seem confounding as to why anyone would ever want to do this.

One of the validation Web controls that we didn't discuss at length in this hour is the ValidationSummary control. This Web control lists all the validation errors on a web page. But if each validation control displays its error message and the ValidationSummary Web control displays each error message as well, then each error message is displayed twice on the page. For this reason, when using the ValidationSummary Web control, some developers prefer to set the various validation Web controls' `Display` properties to `None` so that the `ErrorMessage` property is displayed only once—in the ValidationSummary control.

Alternatively, you can specify what message should appear in the validation control's location and what message should appear in the ValidationSummary using the `ErrorMessage` and `Text` properties of the validation controls. If a validation control has values for both its `Text` and `ErrorMessage` properties, the `Text` value is displayed at the validation Web control's location, and the `ErrorMessage` property is displayed in the ValidationSummary control (if present). So another option is to have your validation controls include a detailed error explanation in the `ErrorMessage` property and an abbreviated message—perhaps just an asterisk (*)—for their `Text` property values.

Q. ***Whenever a user clicks a button, the validation controls perform their validation logic. What if I want a Cancel button on the page or some other button that, when clicked,* doesn't *invoke the validation logic?***

A. Button, LinkButton, and ImageButton Web controls all contain a `CausesValidation` property, which defaults to `True`. If you set this property to `False`, however, the button, when clicked, won't invoke the validation controls' validation logic.

For more information on some of the validation control features that we didn't examine in this hour, read "Dissecting the Validation Controls," available online at http://aspnet.4guysfromrolla.com/articles/112305-1.aspx.

Q. ***In Hour 10, "Using Text Boxes to Collect Input," you said that validation controls can be used to limit the amount of text that can be entered in*** `SingleLine` ***and*** `MultiLine` ***TextBox Web controls. What validation control would I use to do this?***

A. To limit the number of characters allowed in a TextBox Web control, use a RegularExpressionValidator control with its `ValidationExpression` property set to `[\S\s]{min, max}`, where min and max are the minimum and maximum number of characters needed in the TextBox for the input to be considered valid. For example, to permit no more than 100 characters in a TextBox, use a `ValidationExpression` of `[\S\s]{0, 100}`.

For more information on this technique, as well as other mechanisms for checking the quantity of text entered by a user, refer to http://aspnet.4guysfromrolla.com/articles/112404-1.aspx.

Workshop

Quiz

1. What property would you set to have a validation Web control display a particular error message when the data is invalid?
2. How does the `Display` property affect the display of the validation control's error message?

3. Many websites allow users to create accounts. When creating an account, the user often must choose a password. When choosing a password, she must enter her desired password twice, to ensure that there were no typos. Now, imagine that you are asked to create such a web page. What validation Web control would you use to ensure that the text entered into these two text boxes was identical?
4. True or False: A CompareValidator can be used to ensure that a user's input is a certain data type.
5. What are regular expressions, and what sorts of input validation are performed by the RegularExpressionValidator?
6. True or False: Each user input Web control can have at most one validation Web control associated with it.

Answers

1. The `ErrorMessage` property.
2. The `Display` property can be set to one of three values: `None`, `Static`, and `Dynamic`. If `Display` is set to `None`, the `ErrorMessage` property is never shown, regardless of whether the input data is valid. A value of `Static` allocates space on the web page for the validation Web control's error message, regardless of whether the error message is displayed. A value of `Dynamic` does *not* preallocate space for the error message. See Figures 12.21 and 12.22.
3. You would use a CompareValidator with its `ControlToValidate` and `ControlToCompare` properties being set to the two password TextBox Web controls. The CompareValidator's `Operator` property should be set to `Equal` and its `Type` property to `String`. (Exercise 3 asks you to implement this scenario.)
4. True.
5. A regular expression is a string that contains characters and special symbols and specifies a general pattern. A RegularExpressionValidator is a validation control that validates user input using a regular expression. Such a validation control is useful because it can be used to validate that a user's input conforms to a certain pattern. For example, you may want to ensure that the user provides his phone number as three digits, followed by a hyphen, followed by three digits, followed by a hyphen, followed by four digits. This can be easily accomplished with a RegularExpressionValidator, but could not be accomplished by any of the other validation Web controls.

6. False. Web controls may have an arbitrary number of associated validation Web controls. For example, if you had a TextBox Web control where the user needed to enter her Social Security number, you'd want to use both a RegularExpressionValidator, to ensure that the data was entered in the proper format, and a RequiredFieldValidator, to ensure that the user supplied a value and did not leave the text box blank.

Exercises

1. Build an ASP.NET page that uses a CompareValidator and two RequiredFieldValidators. Design the user interface so that it prompts the user for his two favorite ice cream flavors. There should be two TextBox Web controls, one for each of the user's two favorite flavors. Add the needed validation Web controls to ensure that the user provides input for both of these TextBoxes and that the values for the two TextBoxes are different from one another.

2. Create an ASP.NET page that prompts the user to provide her email address and the URL to her home page. Add the necessary validation Web controls to ensure that the user supplies an email address and that both the email address and home page URL are in the proper format. (Hint: The RegularExpressionValidator control's Regular Expression Editor contains predefined regular expressions for both Internet E-mail Addresses and Internet URLs.)

3. Many websites allow users to create an account. The account creation process usually prompts the user, at minimum, to provide a desired username, a password, and an email address. Create an ASP.NET page that has a TextBox Web control for the user's desired username, two TextBox Web controls for the user's password, and one TextBox Web control for the user's email address.

   For the user input to be valid, all TextBoxes must have a value entered. The user's email address must conform to the standard email address format, and the values entered into the two password TextBoxes must be equal. (Be sure to set the password TextBox Web control `TextMode` property to `Password`.)

   (As we will see in Hour 21, "Managing Your Site's Users," ASP.NET includes a number of Login controls that provide the user interface for many common user-related tasks, including creating a user account. Regardless, this exercise is still worthwhile because it gives you valuable practice working with input and validation Web controls.)

PART III

Working with Databases

HOUR 13

An Introduction to Databases

In this hour, we will cover

- What databases are
- How data is stored in a database
- What database tables, columns, and records are, and how they pertain to storing data
- The types of data that can be stored in a table column
- Some of the popular, commercially available database systems, as well as some of the free database systems
- How to create a new database and new database tables with Microsoft SQL Server 2005 Express Edition

One of the most powerful and useful features of ASP.NET is the capability for ASP.NET web pages to interact seamlessly with database systems. Databases, as we'll discuss in detail in this hour, are software applications designed to serve as efficient and powerful repositories of data.

In this hour, we look at what databases are and how data is stored in them. We'll also quickly examine a number of popular commercial and free database systems, focusing specifically on Microsoft SQL Server 2005 Express Edition, a free database system from Microsoft that you installed along with Visual Web Developer back in Hour 1, "Getting Started with ASP.NET 3.5."

By the end of this hour, you will have an understanding of database fundamentals, have created a database, and have populated this database with some data.

Examining Database Fundamentals

You may have heard the term **database** used before but might not be completely clear about what a database is or what it is used for. In the simplest terms, a database is a collection of structured information that can be efficiently accessed and modified.

Databases store data and permit four types of operations to be performed on that data: retrieval, insertion, modification, and deletion. Most commonly, databases are used as a means to retrieve already inserted data. Therefore, we will spend the bulk of our study of databases examining how to retrieve the database's data.

Before you can insert, update, delete, or query a database, you must first install the database software, create the database file, and define the structure of the data the database will hold.

By the Way

> Database systems usually provide some sort of application to assist database administrators with creating databases and inserting, deleting, updating, and querying the database's data.
>
> Databases can also be accessed through an ASP.NET web page. This means that we can create an ASP.NET page that reads data from a database and displays its contents to the visitor. This approach is common in a vast number of real-world websites. For example, when you search for a book at Amazon.com, the search results web page retrieves matching records from a database and then displays these records in a web page.
>
> Over the next several hours we examine how to insert, update, delete, and display database data from an ASP.NET page.

After we've examined the fundamental properties and aspects of a database, we'll turn our attention to the syntax databases used for inserting, updating, deleting, and retrieving data. This language, referred to as **Structured Query Language**, or **SQL**, is the topic for Hour 14, "Accessing Data with the Data Source Web Controls." We'll also see how to use the various ASP.NET Web controls that are designed to access and display database data.

In Hour 15, "Displaying Data with the Data Web Controls," and Hour 16, "Deleting, Inserting, and Editing Data," we'll see how easy it is to display and modify data using the GridView and DetailsView Web controls. In Hour 17, "Working with Data-Bound DropDownLists, RadioButtons, and CheckBoxes," we'll populate the contents of DropDownList, RadioButtonList, and CheckBoxList Web controls from data residing in a database.

A Look at Current Database Systems

Microsoft SQL Server 2005 is but one of many available database systems. Some of the more popular commercial database systems include

- **Microsoft SQL Server**—http://www.microsoft.com/sql/
- **Oracle**—http://www.oracle.com/

- **IBM's DB2**—http://www.ibm.com/software/data/db2/
- **Microsoft Access**—http://office.microsoft.com/access/
- **IBM's Informix**—http://www.ibm.com/software/data/informix/

These commercial database products are industrial strength, suited for large companies with demanding data needs. Because these are such high-grade database systems, the cost can be quite high, in the tens of thousands of dollars.

Fortunately for us amateur developers, a number of free database systems exist. These database systems are still impressive software accomplishments, but they lack the features and high performance that the commercial-grade database systems have. However, because we are just using these databases to test our ASP.NET pages, they more than meet our needs. Some of the more popular free databases include

- **PostgreSQL**—http://www.postgresql.com/
- **MySQL**—http://www.mysql.com/
- **SQLite**—http://www.sqlite.org/
- **Microsoft SQL Server 2005 Express Edition**—http://www.microsoft.com/sql/express/

Microsoft SQL Server 2005 Express Edition ships with Visual Web Developer; at this point you have already installed SQL Server 2005 Express Edition.

Although we'll be using Microsoft SQL Server 2005 Express Edition for the database examples through the remainder of this book, don't think that ASP.NET pages can communicate only with Microsoft's own database software products. On the contrary, virtually any database system can be accessed through an ASP.NET page. So, if you or your company is already using a database system other than SQL Server 2005 Express Edition, don't worry—you can still work with that particular database system. For the book's examples, though, I encourage you to follow along using SQL Server 2005 Express Edition.

By the Way

> When this book was written, Microsoft was close to releasing its latest database system, Microsoft SQL Server 2008, meaning that it will likely be released by the time you are reading this. Microsoft SQL Server 2008 includes a free Express Edition, just like Microsoft SQL Server 2005, and the examples in this book should work the same regardless of what version of Microsoft SQL Server you end up using.

Storing Structured Data

Databases structure their data by storing it into **tables**. A table is a combination of **columns** and **records** in the form of a two-dimensional grid. (Sometimes a table's columns are referred to as **fields** and its records referred to as **rows**; in this book, we'll use the words columns and records exclusively.) Each column corresponds to an attribute of the data, whereas each record corresponds to an actual data item. Furthermore, each table is assigned a unique name to differentiate it from other tables in the database.

To clarify these concepts, imagine that we wanted to use a database to store information about customers. Because we plan to store customer information in this database table, let's name the table `Customers`. Our first task is to decide what information, specifically, describes a customer. For this example, assume that we need to store the customer's name, phone number, and ZIP code, as well as the date the customer made his first purchase from our fictitious company.

These customer attributes make up the columns of the `Customers` table. Figure 13.1 shows a graphical representation of a table designed to store information about customers.

FIGURE 13.1
The `Customers` table's columns represent attributes of the customer.

Name	Phone	ZIPCode	DateBecameCustomer

Now, imagine that our company has five customers (it's amazing that it stays in business!). These five customers and their associated data might be

- Jisun Lee, 858-321-1234, 92109, January 27, 2001.
- Dave Yates, 619-123-4321, 92101, October 10, 2000.
- Todd Callister, 630-555-9898, 60126, August 27, 1989.
- Chris Mitchell, 212-555-1111, 10001, January 27, 1982.
- Sam, 858-555-4343, 92109, September 28, 2001.

Each of these five customers would be represented by one record in the `Customers` table. Figure 13.2 graphically represents the `Customers` table after these five records have been added to the table.

Name	Phone	ZIPCode	DateBecameCustomer
Jisun Lee	858-321-1234	92109	January 27, 2001
Dave Yates	619-123-4321	92101	October 10, 2000
Todd Callister	630-555-9898	60126	August 27, 1989
Chris Mitchell	212-555-1111	10001	January 27, 1982
Sam	858-555-4343	92109	September 28, 2001

FIGURE 13.2
The `Customers` table contains five records, one record for each customer.

Examining a Table's Columns

The columns of a database table, like variables in Visual Basic, have a name and a type. In our `Customers` table, the names of the four database columns might be `Name`, `Phone`, `ZIPCode`, and `DateBecameCustomer`. In addition to their names, these columns each have a type, which specifies the type of data that can be stored in the column.

For example, the `Name` column would likely have a type of `nvarchar(50)`; the `Phone` column, a type of `nvarchar(12)`; the `ZIPCode` column, a type of `nvarchar(5)`; and the `DateBecameCustomer` column, a type of `datetime`. Despite the type name differences, table columns can have types quite similar to the types that Visual Basic variables can have. The type `nvarchar(50)` is akin to a `String` type in Visual Basic, where the string can have, at most, 50 characters. The `datetime` table column type is synonymous with Visual Basic's `DateTime` type.

In addition to the `nvarchar(n)` and `datetime` types, there are a number of other types. Table 13.1 summarizes some of the more common table column types and their Visual Basic parallels.

TABLE 13.1 Commonly Used Table Column Types

Table Column Type	Description	Visual Basic Parallel
`nvarchar(n)`	A string of up to *n* characters in length	`String`
`int`	An integer	`Integer`
`bit`	Can be 0 or 1—a Boolean	`Boolean`
`datetime`	A date and time	`DateTime`
`money`	A monetary value	`Decimal`
`float`	A floating-point number	`Single`

When we create a database table later in this hour, you will see that many more column types exist than those listed in Table 13.1. However, the types presented in Table 13.1 are the ones you'll find yourself using most of the time. You can find a complete list of SQL Server 2005's data types at http://msdn2.microsoft.com/en-us/library/aa258271.aspx.

By the Way

The Different String Data Types

When you are creating a database table, you may notice that in addition to the `nvarchar` data type, there are similarly named data types `nchar`, `varchar`, and `char`.

The difference between `nvarchar` and `nchar` and `varchar` and `char` is that the types with `var` in the name are *variable length* character columns. That is, an `nvarchar(50)` column can have up to 50 characters but will take up only as many as are needed. An `nchar(50)` or `char(50)` typed column, on the other hand, will always take up 50 characters, regardless of whether the value stored there is one character long or 50. If the data stored is fewer than 50 characters, the database system automatically adds spaces to the end of the data to reach 50 characters.

The difference between the data types beginning with `n` (`nvarchar` and `nchar`) and those that don't (`varchar` and `char`) is that those prefixed with `n` store **Unicode** characters. Unicode is a character set that allows for a greater range of characters to be stored, enabling columns of this flavor to store characters in any alphabet. `varchar` and `char` data types, however, have a much smaller character set and are limited to the standard English alphabet.

Although each of the string data types has a time and place, the `nvarchar` data type is the one most universally used and is what we'll be using throughout this book to store string data in a table.

Regardless of the data type being used, database columns can store a special value referred to as **Null**. The Null value indicates an "unknown" value. Returning to the `Customers` database table in Figure 13.2, imagine that customer Jisun Lee never provided her ZIP code. We could store a value of Null in her `ZIPCode` column to represent this lack of information.

When defining a column, you can specify whether the column can be assigned the Null value. In some circumstances you might not want to allow an "unknown" value to be entered, in which case you can mark the column to not allow Nulls.

Primary Key Columns

Database tables often contain a **primary key column** in addition to their other columns. The primary key column uniquely identifies each record in a database table. It is typically a column of type `int` that has some special flags set. (We'll see how, specifically, to add a primary key column to a database table in the "Creating Database Tables" section.) Because the column that is marked as the primary key requires a unique value for each record in the table, primary key columns are often given the name `*TableName*ID`.

Furthermore, a numeric database column can be marked as an **Auto-increment column**. When a new record is added to a table, an Auto-increment column's value is automatically assigned an increasing numeric value. In other words, when you add a new record to the table, you cannot specify the value for an Auto-incrementing column; it is automatically given the next sequentially increasing number.

Many database tables uniquely identify each record by creating a primary key column of type `int` and marking it as an Auto-increment column. This combination provides a unique, sequentially increasing ID column whose value is automatically calculated when adding a new record.

By the Way

Primary keys and Auto-increment columns are two separate concepts: you can have a primary key column that is not an Auto-increment column, and you can have an Auto-increment column that is not a primary key. However, these two concepts are often used in tandem.

To make sense of this information, let's return to our `Customers` table example and add an Auto-increment primary key. Because primary key columns are usually named `*TableName*ID`, let's call the `Customers` primary key `CustomerID`. With the addition of this new column, the `Customers` table would have the structure shown in Figure 13.3.

CustomerID	Name	Phone	ZIPCode	DateBecameCustomer

FIGURE 13.3 A primary key column has been added to the `Customers` table.

Now, if we were to insert the five records examined earlier, the table's records would have the data shown in Figure 13.4. Note that the value in the Auto-increment primary key column is unique and increasing for each record added to the `Customers` table. Furthermore, realize that when inserting data, we would not specify the value for the `CustomerID` column; rather, the database system would automatically do this for us.

CustomerID	Name	Phone	ZIPCode	DateBecameCustomer
1	Jisun Lee	858-321-1234	92109	January 27, 2001
2	Dave Yates	619-123-4321	92101	October 10, 2000
3	Todd Callister	630-555-9898	60126	August 27, 1989
4	Chris Mitchell	212-555-1111	10001	January 27, 1982
5	Sam	858-555-4343	92109	September 28, 2001

FIGURE 13.4 Each record contains a unique `CustomerID` value.

Creating a New Database

The first step in using a database system like SQL Server 2005 Express Edition is to create a new database. Each database contains a group of one or more database tables.

Each SQL Server 2005 Express Edition database is implemented as a separate file. ASP.NET provides a special directory, `App_Data`, where you can place these database files for use in your web application. Creating a new database, then, is as simple as adding the appropriate database file to the `App_Data` folder.

To create a new database with Visual Web Developer, start by creating a new website using the ASP.NET website template. Recall that the ASP.NET website template, among other things, adds an `App_Data` folder to your website.

> If you do not have an `App_Data` folder in your website, right-click the Project name in Solution Explorer like you do to add a new ASP.NET page. From the context menu, select the Add ASP.NET Folder menu option, and then pick the `App_Data` option.

To add a database to your website, right-click the `App_Data` folder in the Solution Explorer and choose Add a New Item. This will bring up the Add New Item dialog box, which contains four choices, one of which is to add a new SQL Server Database (see Figure 13.5).

Select the SQL Database option and change the name of your database file in the Name text box from `Database.mdf` to `MyFirstDatabase.mdf`. After you click the OK button, Visual Web Developer starts to create your new SQL Server database file. When it has completed, the Solution Explorer shows the new database file in the `App_Data` folder (see Figure 13.6).

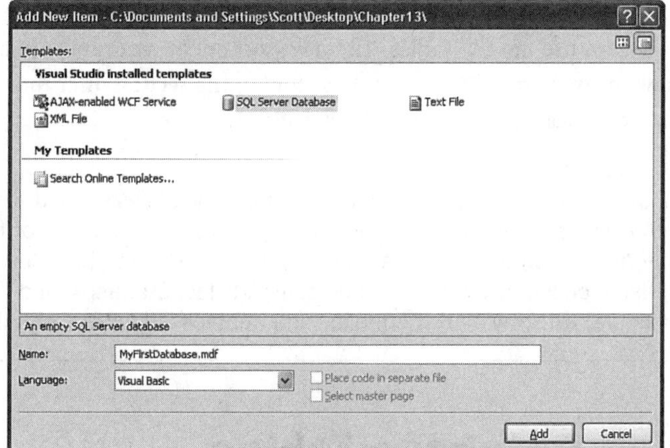

FIGURE 13.5
To add a database to your website, add a new SQL Server Database item.

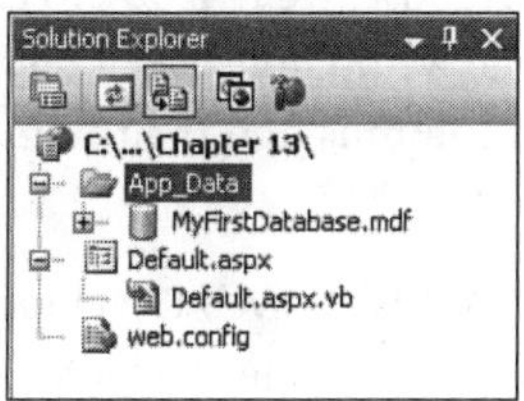

FIGURE 13.6
The new database is listed in the `App_Data` folder.

In addition to adding the database file to the `App_Data` folder, you should now see the newly added database within the Data Connections section of the Database Explorer window. By default, the Database Explorer window shares a pane with the Solution Explorer. If you don't see the Database Explorer on your screen, go to the View menu and select the Database Explorer option.

The Database Explorer provides a more detailed listing of a database's elements than the Solution Explorer. As Figure 13.7 shows, many database elements can be manipulated through Visual Web Developer, such as database diagrams, tables, views, stored procedures, and so on.

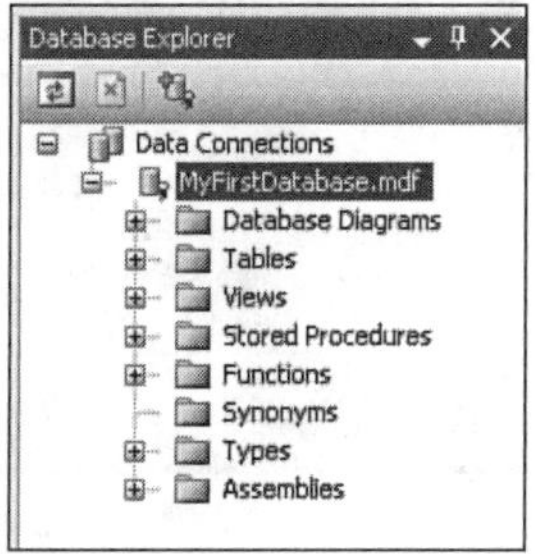

FIGURE 13.7
The Database Explorer lists the elements of the database.

For the data-driven examples we'll be exploring in this book, the only database elements we'll need to use are the tables. The next section, "Creating Database Tables," examines how to create and define database tables; the section after that looks at how to populate tables with data from Visual Web Developer.

By the Way

> More advanced data-driven web applications commonly use views and stored procedures; however, an exploration of these topics is beyond the scope of this book. For more information on these topics, I invite you to check out "SQL Server Views," available online at www.odetocode.com/Articles/299.aspx, and "Writing a Stored Procedure," at www.4guysfromrolla.com/webtech/111499-1.shtml.

Creating Database Tables

Now that we have created a database, we're ready to create our first database table. When creating a database table, we do not specify any of the data; rather, we just define the table's structure—its columns and their names, types, whether they allow Nulls, and other information.

Creating database tables through Visual Web Developer is quite easy. The Database Explorer (shown in Figure 13.7) has a Tables folder for each database. Simply right-click on the Tables folder and choose the Add a New Table option. This brings up the database table editor shown in Figure 13.8, where you can specify the column names and types for the new table.

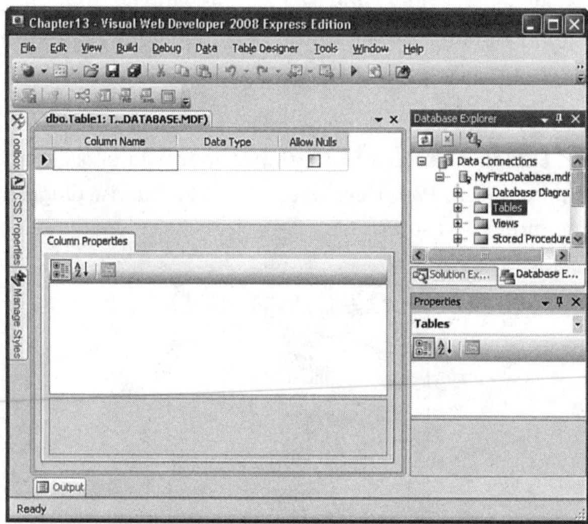

FIGURE 13.8
When creating a new database table, you need to specify the column names and data types.

Let's build a simple database table that could be used to store information about a book collection. When you're crafting a database table, it's important to first spend adequate time defining the attributes you want expressed in the table; these typically translate to the columns. For our book collection example, imagine that we want to capture the following information:

- The book's title
- The book's author
- The year the book was published
- The cost of the book
- The last date we read the book
- The number of pages in the book

Now that we have defined the information to capture, the next step is to translate this into columns in a database table. We'll use a single table, called `Books`, that has an appropriately typed column for each of the six bits of information required.

Start by adding a new column named `Title` that's of type `nvarchar(150)` and does not allow Nulls. To accomplish this, enter **`Title`** into the Column Name text box. Then, in the Data Type drop-down list, type in **`nvarchar(150)`**. Uncheck the Allow Nulls check box. After you perform these steps, your screen should look similar to Figure 13.9.

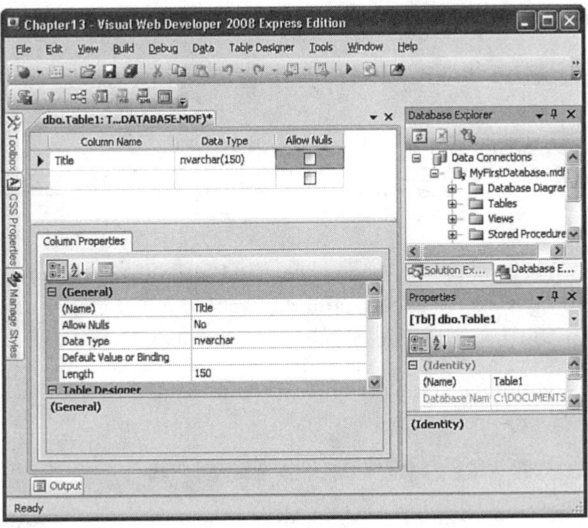

FIGURE 13.9
The `Title` column has been added to the table's definition.

Using the same technique, create the following columns:

- `Author`, of type `nvarchar(150)`, do not allow Nulls
- `YearPublished`, of type `int`, do not allow Nulls
- `Price`, of type `money`, do not allow Nulls
- `LastReadOn`, of type `datetime`, allow Nulls
- `PageCount`, of type `int`, do not allow Nulls

After adding these five additional columns, take a moment to ensure that your screen matches Figure 13.10.

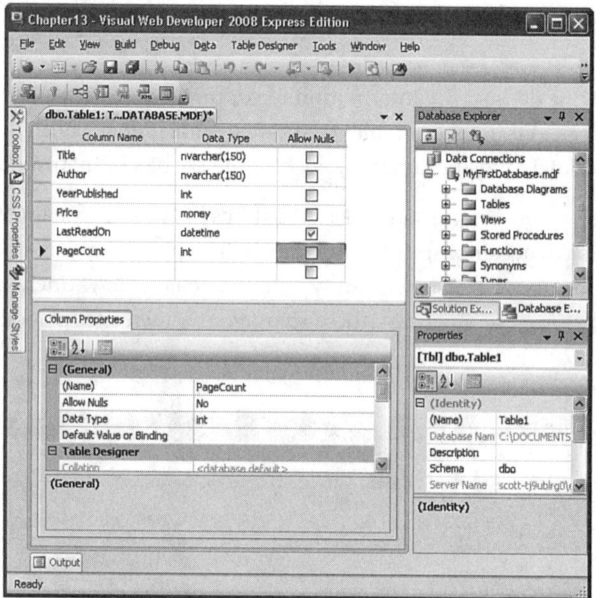

FIGURE 13.10
The table now contains six columns.

Save your new table by clicking the Save icon in the Toolbar or by going to the File menu and choosing the Save Table1 option. Visual Web Developer prompts you to specify the name for the new table. Name the table `Books`.

Congratulations, you have created your first database table!

A Discussion on Database Design

When you're building a data-driven application, the application's **database design** is of paramount importance. The database's design is the set of decisions made in structuring the database; it's the process of deciding what tables you need, what columns make up these tables, and what relationships, if any, exist among the tables. If you start building your application using a poorly designed database, you'll likely run into unseen shortfalls or limitations further in the development process. The later you find a shortcoming, the more energy, time, and effort it will take to correct. Therefore, it behooves you to invest the time to properly model the data.

Unfortunately, we do not have the time nor space to embark on a lengthy discussion of database design techniques, methodologies, and theories; entire books have been written on this subject. However, I'd like to take a moment to highlight a few quick concepts.

Uniquely Identifying Each Record

Because we'll often be interested in accessing, updating, or deleting a particular record in a database table, each record should be uniquely identifiable. This can be accomplished in a number of ways, but most often is done through an Auto-increment primary key column. When you make a column a primary key, the database automatically enforces that each value is unique. A primary key column alone, though, still requires that you provide the unique values. When you also make the column Auto-increment, the database system automatically provides a unique value for that column for each added record.

In our `Books` database table, we do not currently have a column that is guaranteed to be unique. The `Title` column might be a unique identifier if you are certain no two books in your collection will ever have the same title. To indicate that a book's title uniquely identifies each record, you need to make the `Title` column the table's primary key. To accomplish this, select the `Title` column in the table editor in Visual Web Developer and then click the primary key icon in the Toolbar (see Figure 13.11).

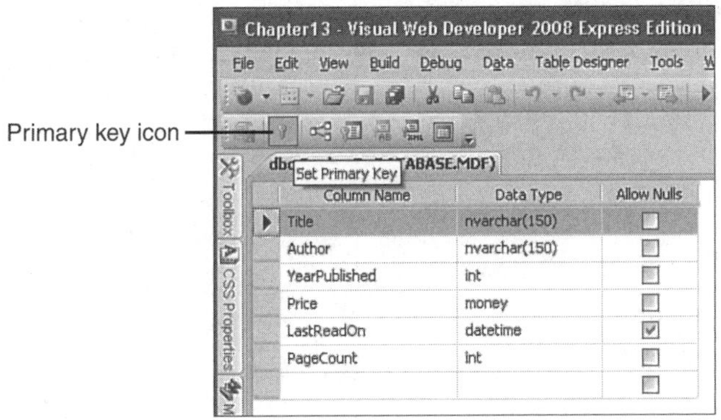

FIGURE 13.11
Select a column and click the primary key icon to mark it as the table's primary key.

What if a book's title, however, is not guaranteed to be unique? What if we might have two books in our collection with the same title? In that case we need to create a new column in our table whose explicit purpose is to uniquely identify each record. Typically, these types of columns are named *`TableName`*`ID`, where *`TableName`* is the name of the table the column is being added to.

Let's add an Auto-increment, primary key column to the `Books` table. Call this new column `BookID`, set its data type to `int`, configure it to not allow Nulls, and mark the column as a primary key by selecting the column and clicking the primary key icon in the toolbar.

Did you Know?

> You can add a new table column anywhere in the list of columns in the table editor: Just right-click the column in the editor and select the Insert Column option. For example, if you want to add `BookID` as the first column in the table, right-click the `Title` column (which is the first one listed) and choose Insert Column. This adds a blank row at the top of the column list into which you can enter the information for the new `BookID` column.

Next, we need to mark the column as an Auto-increment column. Select the `BookID` column; this loads the column's information in the Column Properties pane at the bottom of the screen. Scroll down through the various properties until you reach the Identify Specification property, which will have a value of `No`. Change this value to `Yes` (see Figure 13.12).

At this point `BookID` is now an Auto-increment, primary key column. Click the Save icon in the toolbar to save the table's changes.

Modeling a System's Logical Entities as Related Tables

When deciding what tables your database should contain, typically you'll want each table to represent a **logical entity** in your proposed system. For example, if you were creating an application to record the books in your collection, the logical entities in your system might include

- Books
- Authors
- Genres
- Publishers

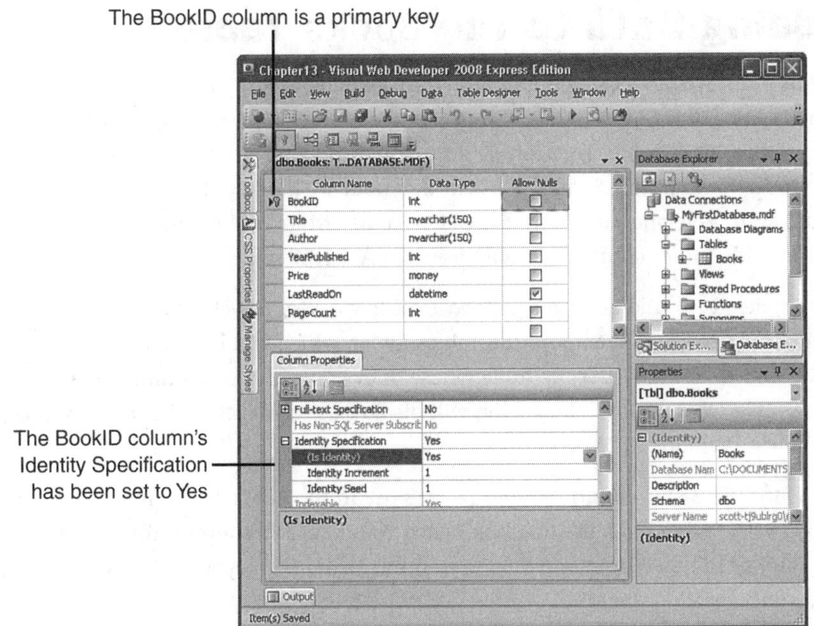
The BookID column is a primary key
The BookID column's Identity Specification has been set to Yes

FIGURE 13.12
The `BookID` column is an Auto-increment, primary key column.

For a system that tracked information about the books' authors, genres, and publishers, we'd most likely want four tables in our database, one to represent each logical entity. Moreover, we'd also want to model the relationships among these tables. For example, we would want to indicate that each record in the `Books` table could have one to many related records in the `Authors` table. This relationship would indicate who wrote the book. Similarly, we might indicate that each record in the `Books` table must be related to precisely one record in the `Publishers` table, indicating the book's publisher. Database systems include various techniques to indicate that a given table is related to another.

Although database models should ideally have a table for each logical entity and explicit relationships among the tables, most of the examples in this book will use a single-table design. This approach is not a recommended design approach; however, it makes creating, accessing, inserting, updating, and deleting the data much simpler.

By the Way

If you are interested in learning about good database design in greater detail, pick up a copy of Michael Hernandez's book *Database Design for Mere Mortals* (ISBN: 9780201752840) or Lynn Beighley's book *Head First SQL* (ISBN: 9780596526849).

Adding Data to the `Books` Table

At this point we have created a database and added to it a `Books` table. However, there is currently no information stored in our table! The next step, then, is to add data to the `Books` table. This can be accomplished either through Visual Web Developer or from an ASP.NET page. In this hour we'll add database records using Visual Web Developer; in Hour 16, "Deleting, Inserting, and Editing Data," we'll see how to add data to a database table from an ASP.NET page.

To edit, delete, or add data to a database table via Visual Web Developer, go to the Database Explorer and expand the Tables folder, which will list the tables of the database. Next, right-click the table whose data you want to edit and select the Show Table Data option. This action will display the contents of the selected table, as shown in Figure 13.13.

As Figure 13.13 shows, currently no records are in the `Books` table. To add a new record to the table, click the text box beneath the `BookID` column. You can now use the Tab key to move from one field to another, using the keyboard to enter the text you want to add to the table.

When entering data into these cells, keep in mind that the values you enter must correspond to the particular column's properties. That is, the `PageCount` column must be a legal value for the `int` type. If you try to enter a value such as **`Sam`** or **`one hundred pages`**, you will get an error message. Similarly, some columns can allow Null values, whereas others do not. Those columns that do not accept Null values must have a value explicitly entered, whereas the ones that can accept Nulls may optionally be left blank, which will add a value of Null.

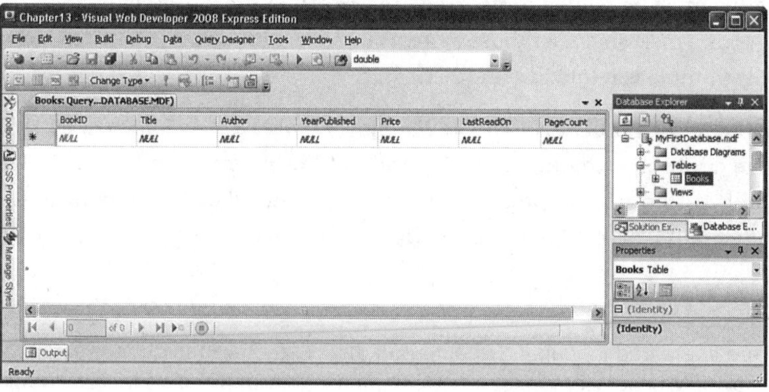

FIGURE 13.13
The contents of the `Books` table are shown in Visual Web Developer.

Similarly, for certain data types, the format you enter the data is important. For example, the `Price` column, which is of type `money`, accepts only numeric values, like 14.95. If you try entering a currency sign, you will get an error. Furthermore, when you enter dates, the date format depends on your computer's date/time settings. In the United States, you can enter the date as month/day/year, such as 11/19/2008 for November 19, 2008. In many European countries, the format is day/month/year, such as 19/11/2008. To circumvent any cultural date/time intricacies, you can always enter a date using the universal format, which is year-month-day, such as 2008-11-19 for November 19, 2008.

By the Way

> Don't worry if you happen to enter invalid data when trying to create a new record. You won't lose your database's data. Rather, you'll be presented with a helpful error message explaining the problem.

Add a new record to the table by entering **`Visual Studio Hacks`** in the `Title` cell, **`James Avery`** in the `Author` cell, **`2005`** for `YearPublished`, **`24.95`** for `Price`, and **`478`** for `PageCount`. Leave the `BookID` and `LastReadOn` cells with their default values, Null. At this point your screen should look similar to Figure 13.14.

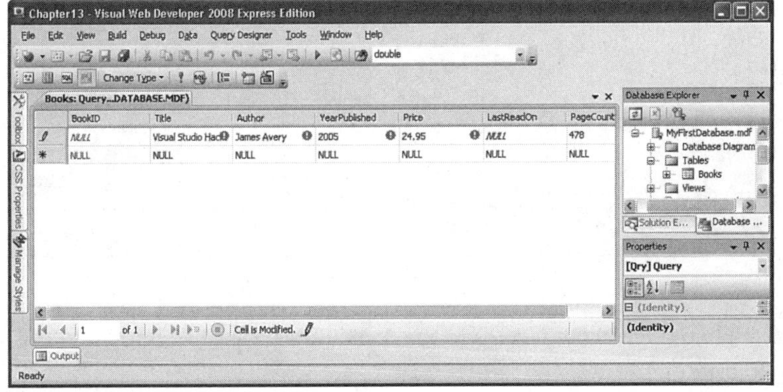

FIGURE 13.14 Our first book in the `Books` table is James Avery's Visual Studio Hacks.

Note that when you first start entering data in the record's cells, a new, blank record appears below the record you're typing in. Also, whenever you change a cell value and move to the next cell, a little red exclamation point icon appears. This indicates that the value of the cell has changed. If your cursor is still sitting in the `PageCount` cell and you still see the red exclamation point icons (as is the case in Figure 13.13), the new record has yet to be created. To commit the new record to the database, click in the next record (or press the Tab key to move the cursor down to the next record).

Watch Out!

The BookID column is an Auto-increment column, meaning that you cannot specify its value. Rather, you need to let the database system decide what value to use. Therefore, when adding a new record to the Books table, you must leave BookID as Null. If you attempt to enter a value, you will receive an error.

If you left BookID as Null and, when trying to save the record, were told that you needed to provide a value for BookID, you did not correctly mark the column as Auto-increment. Return to the "Uniquely Identifying Each Record" section and make sure to mark BookID as Auto-increment.

After you have tabbed to the next record, the red exclamation point icons disappear, and a value is automatically inserted into the BookID cell (see Figure 13.15). Remember that BookID is an Auto-increment column, meaning its value is automatically inserted by the database. For example, if you add another record to this table, the next record will have a BookID value of 2.

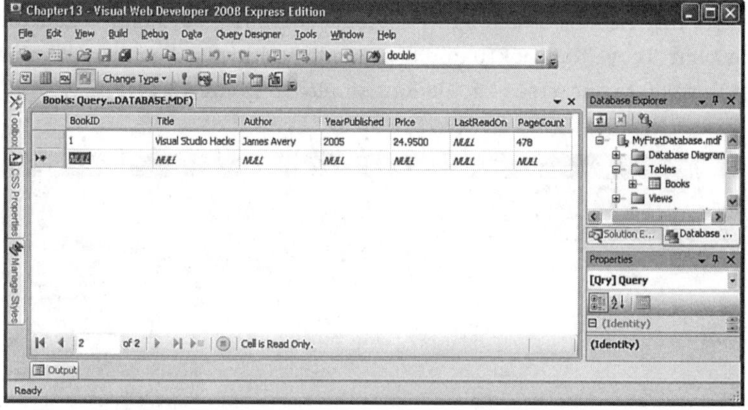

FIGURE 13.15
A new record has been added to the Books table.

Practice adding a few more records to the Books table. Go ahead and add the following four records:

- The book *Create Your Own Website* written by Scott Mitchell in 2006. The cost of this book is $19.99 and it is 224 pages long. Assume that you last read this book on February 1, 2008.
- The book *The Number*, by Alex Berenson. This book was published in 2003 at a cost of $24.95, and it is 274 pages in length. Assume that you last read this book on November 14, 2005.

- The book *The Catcher in the Rye* by J.D. Salinger. Your copy of this book was published in 1991 and costs $6.95. There are 224 pages. Assume you last read this book on June 12, 2004.
- The book *Fight Club*, by Chuck Palahniuk. This book was published in 1999 and costs $16.95. There are 187 pages. Assume that you have yet to read this book (that means to leave `LastReadOn` as Null).

After you have entered these four additional records into the `Books` table, your screen should look similar to Figure 13.16. Notice that the `BookID` value, which we never entered, has automatically increased with each new record added.

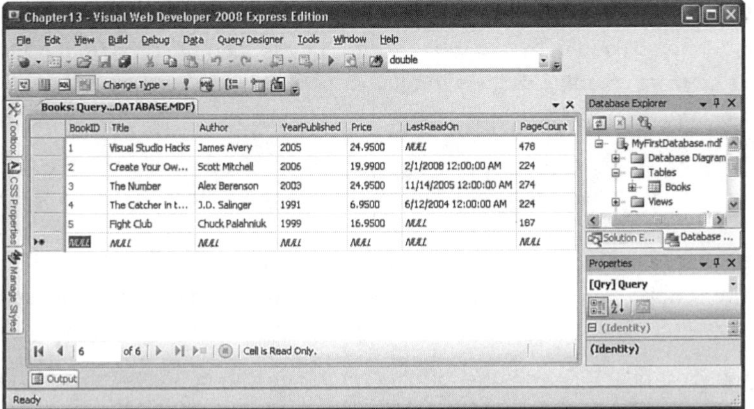

FIGURE 13.16
The `Books` table now contains five records.

Did you Know?

In addition to adding new records to the `Books` table, Visual Web Developer also makes it easy to edit and delete a table's existing data through the same interface. To change an existing record's contents, click in the appropriate record's area and make any changes needed. To delete a record, select it by clicking the box in its left margin and then press the Delete key.

Recall from the beginning of this hour that a database is a collection of structured information that can be efficiently accessed and modified. We've seen how to create the structures to hold information (database tables) and we've looked at how to add data to a table, but we've yet to examine the most useful aspect of databases: efficiently accessing the data stored within. This topic, though, will have to wait until the next hour.

Summary

In this hour we learned that databases are software systems designed for storing structured data that can be efficiently accessed and modified. Data in a database is structured by means of tables. A table is defined by its columns, which have a name and type.

In addition to columns, database tables contain records. The records in a table make up the table's data. For example, in Figure 13.16, the `Books` table has five records, which indicates that information about five books exists. To view, add, and edit the content of a database table in Visual Web Developer, right-click the Table name and choose the Show Table Data option.

Now that we've examined the structure of databases, how to create databases and tables, and how to add data to a table, we're ready to read the data from a table. In the next hour we examine a query language specifically designed for accessing database data.

Q&A

Q. ***Can I add new columns or remove existing columns from a database table after I have already created and saved the table? What if the table contains records?***

A. You most definitely can alter a table's structure after it has been saved—even if it has existing records. There are no rules when it comes to removing columns from an existing database table. Simply edit the table and remove the column. (Of course, you will lose the data expressed in the removed columns for all existing records.)

Adding new columns to an existing database table without any records is just as simple: Go into the table editor, add the new column(s), and save the results. This process is a little trickier if the table has existing records because the database table must decide what values to place into the new column(s) for the existing records. Here you have two options: You can either have the new column(s) allow Nulls, or you can specify a default value for the column. (You can set the default value through the Column Properties pane.) If you specify a default value for the new column(s), all existing records will have the default value inserted for the new column(s). If you do not specify a default value, but instead elect to allow Nulls, the new column(s) for the existing records will have a value of Null.

Workshop

Quiz

1. How are columns, tables, and databases related to one another?
2. A particular column for a particular record in a database table is a lot like a variable in a programming language in that it can be completely described by what three attributes?
3. What does a Null value represent?
4. How does an Auto-increment primary key column guarantee that it will uniquely identify each record?
5. True or False: When you create a database table, the table must have a primary key column.

Answers

1. A table contains one or more columns. A database contains one or more tables.
2. The column name, the column data type, and the value of the column for the specific record.
3. A Null value represents *unknown* or *no value*. For example, in the `Books` table, the `LastReadOn` column accepts Null values because we might not have read the book yet, in which case no value exists for this column.
4. When you insert a new record into a column with an Auto-increment primary key column, the database server decides the value of the Auto-increment primary key column. Because the database server gets to determine this value, it can ensure that the value is unique from all other records. This is accomplished by incrementing the Auto-increment primary key column value from the last-inserted record.
5. False. The vast majority of the time you will want your tables to include a primary key, Auto-increment column, but you can create tables without a primary key.

Exercises

1. To familiarize yourself with Visual Web Developer and SQL Server 2005 Express Edition, create a new database named `TestDB.mdf`. After creating the database, add a new database table named `Albums`. Imagine that you want to use this database table to hold information about the albums you own. Add columns with appropriate types and names. Some suggested columns include the following: an Auto-increment primary key column named `AlbumID`; an `nvarchar(50)` column titled `Name`; an `nvarchar(75)` column titled `Artist`; and a `datetime` column titled `DatePurchased`. (Take the time to add additional pertinent columns.) After creating the `Albums` table, add a number of records to the table.

   You lust and do not have. You murder and covet and cannot obtain. You fight and war. Yet[a] you do not have because you do not ask. 3 You ask and do not receive, because you ask amiss, that you may spend it on your pleasures.

2. In the "Storing Structured Data" section, we talked about a `Customers` table that captured information about potential customers, such as their names, phone numbers, ZIP codes, and so on (refer to Figure 13.3). Take a moment to create this database table with the appropriate schema; don't forget to add the `CustomerID` primary key column. Next, add the five records listed in Figure 13.4.

HOUR 14

Accessing Data with the Data Source Web Controls

In this hour, we will cover

- Working with data source controls
- Understanding SQL, the language of databases
- Retrieving specific columns from a database table
- Returning database data that meets certain criteria
- Ordering the results of a database query

In the preceding hour we examined, from a high-level perspective, what databases are, their internal structure, and their purpose. We looked at creating a database with SQL Server 2005 Express Edition through Visual Web Developer. We also saw how to create database tables and populate them with data.

Often we will want to retrieve information from a database and display it on an ASP.NET web page. To be able to do this, we need to learn how to retrieve data from a database. ASP.NET provides a set of Web controls—called **data source controls**—that are designed specifically to access data from an underlying database. With the data source controls, retrieving database data is as simple as dropping a control onto your ASP.NET page and stepping through a wizard, indicating the database data you want to grab.

Underneath the covers, the data source controls are simply sending commands to the database using a language called **Structured Query Language**, or **SQL** (pronounced either *S-Q-L* or *Seequell*). SQL is the language used by all modern database systems for retrieving and modifying data. In addition to examining the ASP.NET data source controls, we'll also spend a bit of time in this hour learning the general syntax of SQL.

Examining the Data Source Controls

ASP.NET contains a myriad of Web controls, which we grouped into various categories in earlier hours. For example, in Hour 8, "ASP.NET Web Controls for Displaying Text," we looked at those Web controls designed for displaying text content on an ASP.NET page. In this hour we'll examine a new class of Web controls—ones designed for accessing database data. This class of Web controls, referred to as **data source controls**, can be found in the Toolbox in the Data section (see Figure 14.1).

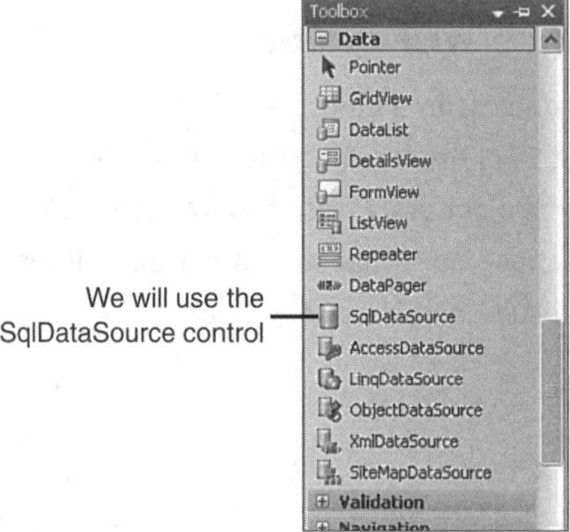

FIGURE 14.1 The Visual Web Developer Toolbox contains a number of data source controls.

ASP.NET includes six data source controls. Each data source control shown in Figure 14.1 has a name that ends in DataSource, such as SqlDataSource, AccessDataSource, and so on. Each data source Web control is designed for working with data from a different type of source. For example, the SqlDataSource and AccessDataSource controls are designed to retrieve data from databases; the XmlDataSource can be used to access data from an XML file; the SiteMapDataSource control is used to query a site map and return the website's navigational structure so that it can be displayed in a TreeView or Menu Web control.

By the Way

An **XML file** is a text file that contains data encoded in a special syntax. A thorough discussion of XML is beyond the scope of this book; for more information, refer to www.XMLFiles.com or www.w3schools.com/xml.

A **site map** is an XML file that is formatted in a particular way and contains information about a website's navigational structure. This information can then be displayed in the form of navigational breadcrumbs, menus, or trees. We'll examine ASP.NET's site map features and SiteMapDataSource in detail in Hour 20, "Defining a Site Map and Providing Site Navigation."

This hour focuses on accessing data from a database. There are two data source controls for working with database data: SqlDataSource and AccessDataSource. The AccessDataSource control is designed to work specifically with Microsoft Access databases, whereas the SqlDataSource control is a more general control and can work with Microsoft Access, Microsoft SQL Server, and other popular database systems. In Hour 13, "An Introduction to Databases," we created a Microsoft SQL Server 2005 Express Edition database; therefore, we will be using the SqlDataSource control.

By the Way

Data source controls serve as a bridge between the ASP.NET page and the database. That is, a data source control only retrieves database data and does *not* have any capabilities for displaying the retrieved data on the page. To display the data, we need to use an additional Web control, such as the DropDownList, GridView, DetailsList, CheckBoxList, and so on. This hour focuses on retrieving data using the data source controls. In the next hour, "Displaying Data with the Data Web Controls," we'll see how to display the data retrieved by a data source control in an ASP.NET page.

Working with the SqlDataSource Control

To practice using the SqlDataSource control, we'll need an ASP.NET website with a database. To save time in creating a new website and database, let's use the website and database from Hour 13.

Start by creating a new ASP.NET page named `AccessingData.aspx`. Next, drag a SqlDataSource control from the Toolbox onto the page. Each data source control is rendered in the Design view as a gray box with the data source control type followed by its `ID` value. As Figure 14.2 shows, after we add a SqlDataSource control to the page, the gray box reads `SqlDataSource - SqlDataSource1`. Here, `SqlDataSource1` is the `ID` of the control.

In addition to this gray box, there's also a **smart tag**. A smart tag is a list of common tasks that can be performed from the Web control. For the data source controls, the smart tag contains a single option, at first: Configure Data Source. Clicking this link starts the Configure Data Source Wizard, from which we'll specify what data we want to retrieve from the database.

To be able to work with a database's data, the SqlDataSource control needs to know two bits of information:

- How to connect to the database
- What query to issue to the database

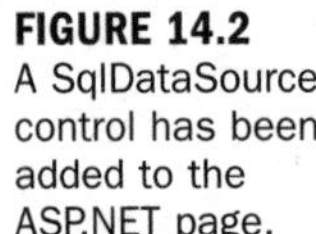

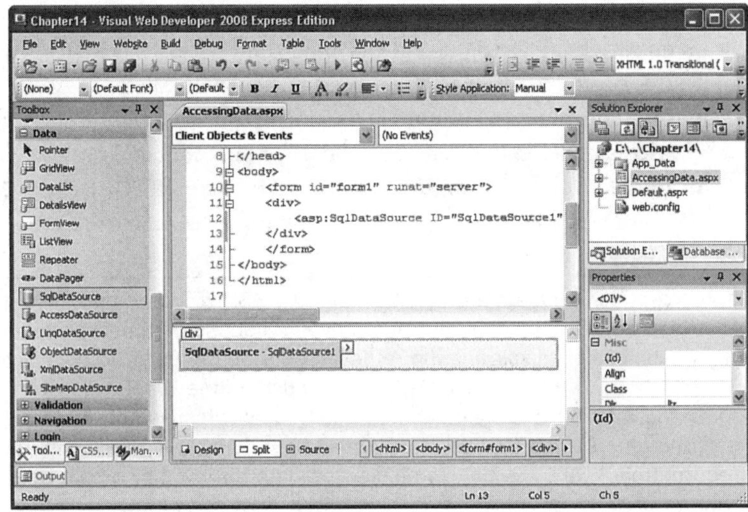

FIGURE 14.2
A SqlDataSource control has been added to the ASP.NET page.

The SqlDataSource control's wizard prompts you to provide these two vital pieces of information and does so in a very intuitive and developer-friendly manner.

Let's start examining the SqlDataSource control's wizard. Go ahead and click the Configure Data Source link.

Step 1: Choose Your Data Connection

The first step of the Configure Data Source Wizard prompts you to select the database to work with. A drop-down list contains those databases listed in your Database Explorer and should include the `MyFirstDatabase.mdf` database we created in the preceding hour. Go ahead and select this database from the drop-down list (see Figure 14.3).

Beneath the drop-down list of available databases is a Connection string label with a plus next to it. If you click this plus, it displays the **connection string** used to access the database data. A connection string is low-level information required by ASP.NET that provides the specific details for connecting to the database.

By the Way

> If you need to connect to a database that's not located in the `App_Data` folder, click the New Connection button to bring up a dialog box that prompts you for the connection information.

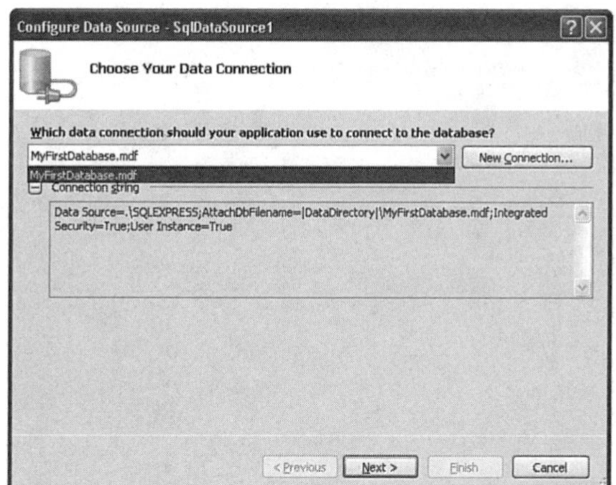

FIGURE 14.3
Select the `MyFirstDatabase.mdf` database from the drop-down list.

If this is the first time you've used a data source control to connect to this database, you'll be prompted to save the connection information in the web application's configuration file (see Figure 14.4). If you choose to save the connection string information in the web application's configuration file, which I heartily recommend, a new setting will automatically be inserted into the `web.config` file that associates the name provided in Figure 14.4 with the connection string.

The benefit of saving the connection string information in the web application's configuration file is that it adds a level of indirection in your application, which makes responding to changes easier. For example, imagine that you are using the `MyFirstDatabase.mdf` file and have created a dozen ASP.NET pages that work with this database's data. If you do not save the connection string in `web.config`, the database connection string will appear in each of these 12 ASP.NET pages. Now the gotcha: Imagine that your database's connection string changes. Perhaps you've renamed the database file, or you have deployed your website to a web hosting company that has moved your database from the `App_Data` folder to their database server. With the connection string hard-coded into each of the dozen ASP.NET pages, you'll have to go into each of those 12 pages and update the connection information. Had you stored the connection string information in `web.config`, however, you would have had to modify the connection string in only one place—the `web.config` file.

Because the data source control's wizard will handle adding the connection string setting in `web.config` automatically, there's no reason not to store the connection string there. Therefore, leave the check box in Figure 14.4 checked and click Next to proceed to the next step.

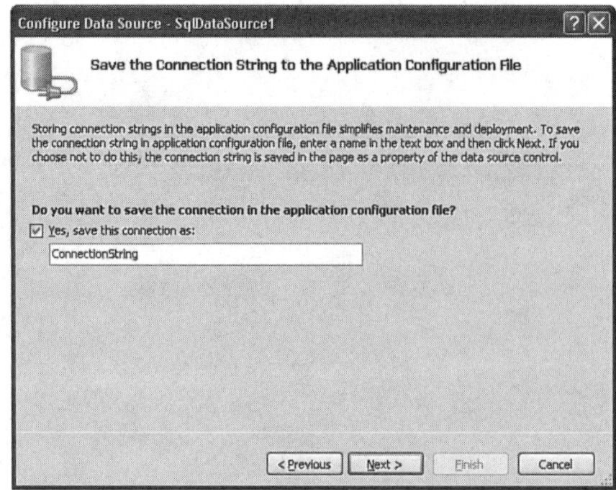

FIGURE 14.4 You can save the connection string in your website's configuration file.

Step 2: Configure the Select Statement

After choosing the database to use, the next step is to specify what data you want to retrieve from the database. With the SqlDataSource Wizard, you can select data in one of two ways:

- By specifying a database table, along with the columns to return
- By providing a **SQL SELECT query**

With the first option, you can pick the table and specify the columns to retrieve through the wizard. With the second option, you'll need to spell out the precise SQL query to use. Regardless of what approach you use, the result is the same: The SqlDataSource control concocts some SQL statement that is sent to the database to retrieve the data. We'll examine the basics of SQL later in this hour in the "A Look at SQL, the Language of Databases" section. For now, let's practice with using the first option.

In the Configure the Select Statement step of the wizard, you choose whether to select a database table or specify your own SQL query by selecting the appropriate radio button at the top of the dialog box. To pick a table, select the Specify Columns from a Table or View radio button (see Figure 14.5).

The tables in the database are listed in the drop-down list, with the selected table's columns listed underneath. Because only one database table is in our database—`Books`—it's the only option in the drop-down list. The area beneath lists the columns—`BookID`, `Title`, `Author`, `YearPublished`, `Price`, `LastReadOn`, and `PageCount`. There's also a `*` option list. This represents *all* columns.

We need to check those columns that we want returned from the Books table. If you want to retrieve all column values, select the * option, or check each of the individual columns. For this example, return all columns by checking the * check box. After you check this, a SELECT statement appears at the bottom of this dialog box. Specifically, you'll see the query syntax:

```
SELECT * FROM [Books]
```

SELECT queries are used to retrieve information from a database. There are many parts to the SELECT statement, some of which we'll examine further in this hour. For now, don't worry about the intricacies of the SQL syntax. Instead, focus on how the table data is selected through the SqlDataSource control's wizard.

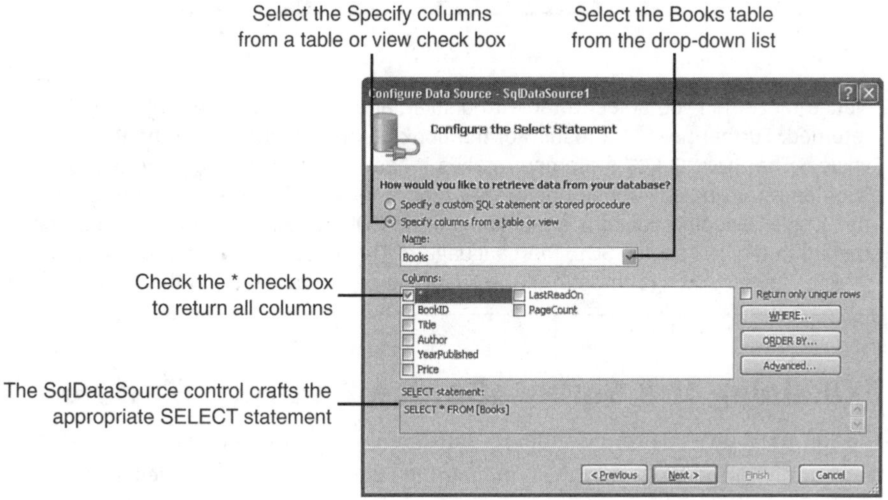

FIGURE 14.5
Pick the table whose data you want to retrieve.

Now that we've specified the data to return from the Books table, click the Next button to proceed to the final wizard step.

Step 3: Test the Query

The final step in the SqlDataSource control's wizard is the Test Query screen. The Test Query screen allows you to run the query to see what data, exactly, is returned. As Figure 14.6 shows, the SELECT * FROM [Books] SQL query returns all records from the Books table, with each record containing all the table's columns.

If you received the database results you expected, click the Finish button to complete the wizard. If something is awry, you can click the Previous button and adjust the query as needed.

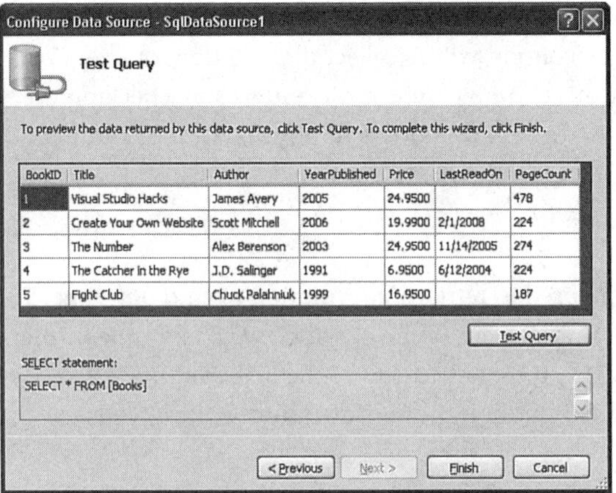

FIGURE 14.6 The query returns all columns and all rows in the `Books` table.

By the Way

Notice that when you select a table to display, all records from the table are returned. Furthermore, the results of the `Books` table are ordered by the `BookID` values. The SQL `SELECT` statement makes it easy to limit the records returned—such as retrieving only those books with a price less than $20.00—and to order the results by some column. We'll examine the SQL syntax for filtering and sorting results in the "A Look at SQL, the Language of Databases" section and see how to apply these settings through the SqlDataSource's wizard later in this hour.

Examining the SqlDataSource Control's Markup

The SqlDataSource control's Configure Data Source wizard simply sets a number of the control's properties. Let's take a moment to examine the markup generated in the Source view by the SqlDataSource control's wizard. After clicking the Finish button in the wizard you should find a SqlDataSource control declaration in the Source view like so:

```
<asp:SqlDataSource ID="SqlDataSource1" runat="server"
   ConnectionString="<%$ ConnectionStrings:ConnectionString %>"
   SelectCommand="SELECT * FROM [Books]">
</asp:SqlDataSource>
```

As you can see, the SqlDataSource control has three property values at this point:

- **`ID`**—This property uniquely identifies the data source control from all other Web controls on the page. Feel free to rename this to something more descriptive, like `BooksDataSource`, rather than the nondescript `SqlDataSource1`.

- **`ConnectionString`**—This property indicates the connection string used to connect to the database. If you opted to place the connection string information in the web application's configuration file, the value will be the name of the connection string setting in `web.config`. The syntax `<%$ connectionStringName %>` tells the data source control to look in the application's configuration to retrieve the appropriate information. If you decided against putting the connection string in `web.config`, the full connection string will be here in place of `<%$ connectionStringName %>`.
- **`SelectCommand`**—This property specifies the `SELECT` query issued to the database. Note that this property's value is identical to the `SELECT` statement displayed in the wizard.

At this point, the SqlDataSource's declarative markup is pretty simple. As we get into more involved examples that include interactive user filtering and updating, inserting, and deleting database data, the declarative markup generated by the SqlDataSource will quickly balloon. The lesson to take away from this discussion is that the SqlDataSource control's wizard is helpful in two ways: First, it helps us construct the appropriate SQL statements, rather than having to enter them ourselves by hand; and second, it saves a lot of tedious and cryptic typing of markup in the Source view.

A Look at SQL, the Language of Databases

For the SqlDataSource control to be able to retrieve database data, two pieces of information were required: the database's connection string and the query to issue to the database. As we discussed in the preceding section, the query issued to the database must be in a dialect that the database understands. The common dialect among all modern database systems is SQL.

To retrieve data from a database, we use a SQL `SELECT` statement. The `SELECT` statement, in its simplest form, specifies what database table to retrieve data from, along with what columns of data to return. For example, to return the title of each book in the `Books` table, we use the following SQL statement:

```
SELECT Title
FROM Books
```

We examine the SQL `SELECT` clause in great detail in the next section.

Although SQL is used primarily for retrieving database data, it can also be used to insert new data and update or delete existing data. These data modification capabilities are expressed using `INSERT`, `UPDATE`, and `DELETE` statements. In this hour we focus strictly on using SQL to retrieve data. However, starting in Hour 16, "Deleting, Inserting, and Editing Data," we examine how to delete and edit database data.

Delving into the SQL SELECT Statement

A `SELECT` statement must specify what database table and columns to return. It does so via the following syntax:

```
SELECT Column1, Column2, ..., ColumnN
FROM TableName
```

`Column1` ... *`ColumnN`* are columns from the database table *`TableName`*. For example, to retrieve the values from the `Title` and `Author` columns of the `Books` table, use the following SQL statement:

```
SELECT Title, Author
FROM Books
```

Note that this `SELECT` statement contains two clauses: the `SELECT` clause and the `FROM` clause. Clauses are keywords in the SQL `SELECT` statement that precede the data they operate on. The `SELECT` clause specifies the columns whose values are to be returned, and the `FROM` clause specifies the database table to retrieve the data from.

A `SELECT` statement may contain a number of optional clauses, many of which we examine in this section. For example, you can use the `WHERE` clause to return only those rows that meet certain criteria. The `ORDER BY` clause sorts the results by the values of a specified column.

The `SELECT` clause is a comma-delimited list of the columns whose values you are interested in. If you want to retrieve the values of *all* columns for a specific table, you may use the asterisk (`*`) instead of entering each column name.

Viewing SQL Queries Results in Visual Web Developer

When you're learning SQL, it helps to run queries against a database so that you can see the specific results returned by the SQL query. Fortunately, Visual Web Developer makes this task quite simple.

As we saw in the preceding hour, the Database Explorer window lists the databases used in the current ASP.NET website. Go to the Database Explorer, right-click the database name (`MyFirstDatabase.mdf`), and choose the New Query option from the context menu. This displays the query window, which first prompts you to select what tables to query. Because our database has only one table—`Books`—this is the only table listed (see Figure 14.7).

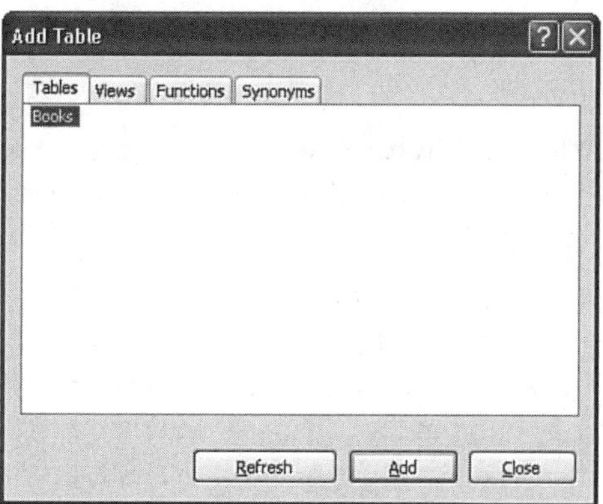

FIGURE 14.7
Select what table(s) you want to query.

Select the `Books` table and click the Add button; this adds the table to the query window. After adding the table, click the Close button in the dialog box. At this point your screen should look similar to Figure 14.8.

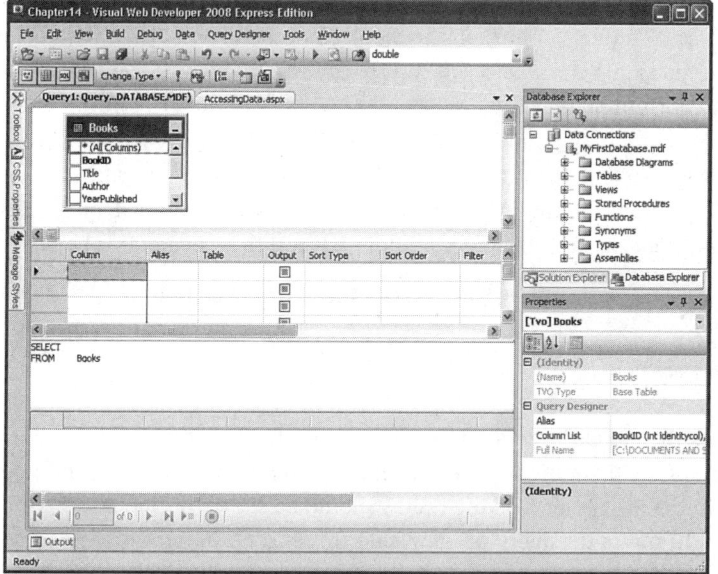

FIGURE 14.8
Create and run a query from the query window.

By default, the query window contains four regions:

- **Diagram Pane**—This pane lists the tables added, along with their columns at the top of the query window.
- **Criteria Pane**—This grid comes beneath the diagram pane and lists the columns that are returned by the query, along with any conditions (whether they're sorted, whether a filter applies, and so on).
- **SQL Pane**—This pane is beneath the criteria pane and lists the SQL query that will be executed.
- **Results Pane**—This final, bottommost pane lists the results after the query has been executed.

The first three panes work together, in a sense. For example, if you check a subset of columns in the `Books` table representation in the diagram pane and then execute the query, the criteria pane and SQL pane will be updated accordingly. Likewise, if you write a SQL query by hand in the SQL pane and then execute the query, the diagram pane and criteria pane will be updated. In short, the diagram, criteria, and SQL panes provide alternative ways to specify a SQL query. The results pane shows the results of the executed query, regardless of what pane was used to express the query.

Along the top of the query window are a series of icons that are especially useful (see Figure 14.9). Starting from the left, the first four icons toggle what panes are displayed. You can show or hide the panes you don't use. (Personally, I like to enter my SQL queries by hand, so I turn off the diagram and criteria panes.) Next is the Change Type icon, from where you can specify what type of SQL query you are interested in running (`SELECT`, `INSERT`, `UPDATE`, `DELETE`, and so forth). Next to that is the red exclamation point icon. This icon, when clicked, executes the query and displays the results in the results pane. The next icon, when clicked, validates the SQL query syntax, informing you of any syntax errors in your SQL query. The remaining icons are for functionality that's beyond the scope of this book.

Let's practice using the query window. Go ahead and type into the SQL pane the following query:

```
SELECT * FROM Books
```

Next, click the red exclamation point icon in the Toolbar to execute the query. At this point the diagram and criteria panes should update to reflect the SQL query entered in the SQL pane, and the results should be shown in the results pane. Figure 14.10 shows the query window after this `SELECT` statement is executed.

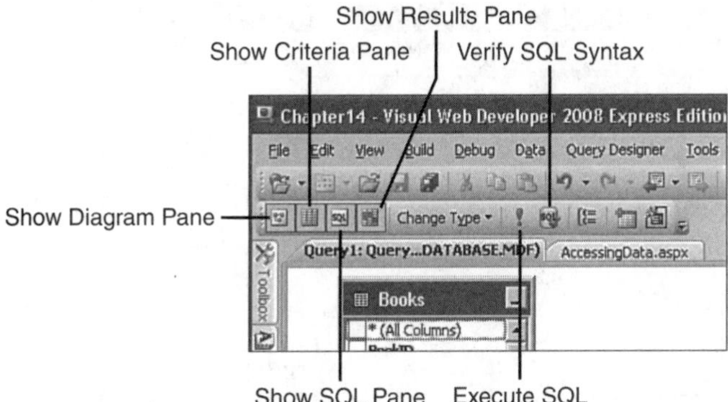

FIGURE 14.9
The Toolbar icons can be used to customize the query window.

Did you Know?

In addition to clicking the red exclamation point icon, you can also execute the query by going to the Query Designer menu and choosing the Execute SQL menu options. If you prefer executing the query using keyboard shortcuts, either Ctrl+R or Alt+X will work.

One thing to note is that at times the query engine will rewrite your SQL queries. I typed in `SELECT * FROM Books` as my query, but the query was rewritten to

```
SELECT     BookID, Title, Author, YearPublished, Price, LastReadOn, PageCount
FROM         Books
```

Of course, this query and my query are identical in their results. Also, note that the results in the results pane are identical to the results we saw in the Test Query step of the SqlDataSource control's wizard in Figure 14.6.

Let's try executing another `SELECT` statement. Change the SQL query in the SQL pane from `SELECT * FROM Books` to

```
SELECT Title, Author
FROM Books
```

This SQL query returns all of the rows from the `Books` table, displaying the values for just the `Title` and `Author` columns. After you have entered this query into the text box, execute the query; the results are shown in Figure 14.11. Notice how the diagram and criteria panes have been updated to reflect the new SQL query and how the results pane has only two columns returned instead of seven.

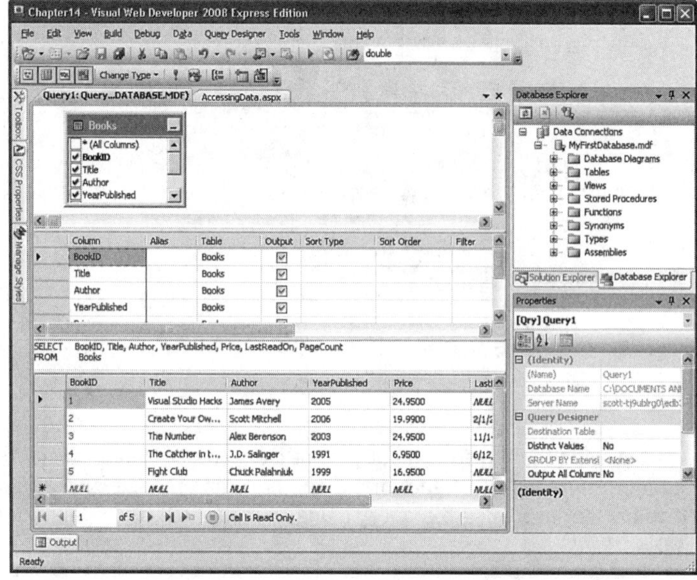

FIGURE 14.10
The results of the SQL query are displayed in the results pane.

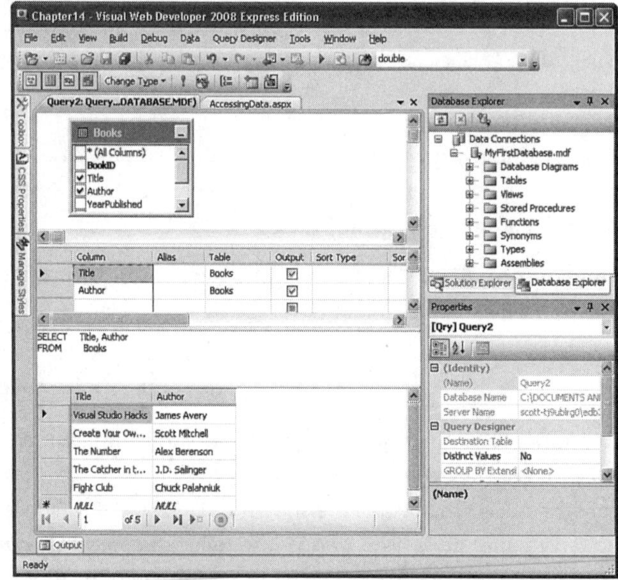

FIGURE 14.11
The SQL query returns the values for two columns.

Restricting Returned Rows Using the WHERE Clause

The SELECT statement, when composed of just the SELECT and FROM clauses, returns *all* rows of the specified database table. For example, the SQL query results shown in Figures 14.10 and 14.11 display all the rows in the Books table; the only difference between the two results is the columns whose values are returned.

Often, when querying database data, we are not interested in all the data in a table, but only a subset. For example, when you are searching Amazon.com for books on ASP.NET, the search results page lists only those books that match your search criteria rather than all the books in Amazon.com's database.

To limit the rows returned by the SELECT statement, we use the WHERE clause. The WHERE clause specifies conditions that a row must match to be returned by the SELECT statement. For example, the following SQL SELECT statement returns only those rows in which the Title column's value equals The Number:

```
SELECT *
FROM Books
WHERE Title = 'The Number'
```

Go ahead and enter this query into the SQL pane and click the Execute SQL Toolbar icon. The results should show all the columns of the Books table, but only one row—the book *The Number*.

Watch Out!

> Note that there are apostrophes around the string The Number in the WHERE clause. If you accidentally enter quotation marks instead of apostrophes, you will get a SQL Execution Error with the following error message: Invalid column name 'The Number'.

As you can see, the WHERE clause has a Boolean condition preceding it: Title = 'The Number'. The = operator here is synonymous with the = operator in Visual Basic, which we examined in Hour 5, "Understanding Visual Basic's Variables and Operators." In addition to the = operator, other comparison operators, such as <, <=, >, >=, and <>, can be used as well. Table 14.1 summarizes these other comparison operators.

TABLE 14.1 Comparison Operators That Can Be Used in the `WHERE` Clause

Operator	Example	Description
`=`	`Title = 'The Number'`	Compares two values, returning `True` if they are equal.
`<>`	`Title <> 'The Number'`	Compares two values, returning `True` if they are *not* equal.
`<`	`Price < 14.95`	Compares two values, returning `True` if the left value is less than the right value.
`<=`	`Price <= 14.95`	Compares two values, returning `True` if the left value is less than or equal to the right value.
`>`	`Price > 14.95`	Compares two values, returning `True` if the left value is greater than the right value.
`>=`	`Price >= 14.95`	Compares two values, returning `True` if the left value is greater than or equal to the right value.

In addition to the comparison operators, the logical operators `AND` and `OR` may be used to string together multiple Boolean expressions. The `AND` and `OR` keywords in a `WHERE` clause and are synonymous with the Visual Basic `And` and `Or` keywords. For example, the following SQL `SELECT` statement returns the `Title`, `Author`, and `Price` columns of books whose `YearPublished` equals `2006` or whose `Price` is less than or equal to `18.00`:

```
SELECT Title, Author, Price
FROM Books
WHERE YearPublished = 2006 OR Price <= 18.00
```

This query returns the Title, Author, and Price columns for three books: *Create Your Own Website, The Catcher in the Rye,* and *Fight Club.*

When comparing a column's value to a string or date/time constant, such as `WHERE Title = 'Fight Club'` or `WHERE LastReadOn < '2008-02-01'`, you must enclose the string or date/time constants (`Fight Club` and `2008-02-01`, in this example) in apostrophes. If, however, you are comparing a numeric column to a numeric constant, the numeric constant does not need to be surrounded by single quotation marks.

> Fortunately, we need to worry about this esoteric rule only when crafting SQL statements by hand in the query window. When we build SELECT statements through the SqlDataSource control's wizard, this minutia is handled for us automatically by the data source control.

Understanding What Happens When a WHERE Clause Is Present

When a WHERE clause is used, the following sequence of steps happens behind the scenes. Each record in the queried table is enumerated. The condition in the WHERE clause is checked for each record. If the condition returns the value True, the record is included in the output; otherwise, it is discarded.

For example, consider the following query:

```
SELECT Title, Author
FROM Books
WHERE Title <> 'The Number' AND BookID <= 3
```

The WHERE clause condition is analyzed for each row in the Books table. Starting with the first book, *Visual Studio Hacks*, we see that this book's title doesn't equal The Number and its BookID is indeed less than or equal to 3; therefore, the book *Visual Studio Hacks* is returned by this SELECT statement. The next book is *Create Your Own Website*. Again, this book's title does not equal The Number and its BookID is less than or equal to 3, so it's returned in the results as well.

The third book, however, is *The Number*. This book isn't returned because the Title <> 'The Number' condition returns False. The next book evaluated is *The Catcher in the Rye*; this book is also excluded from the resultset because its BookID is equal to 4, which is not less than or equal to 3. Similarly, *Fight Club* is omitted from the results because its BookID value is also greater than 3.

Therefore, the aforementioned SQL statement will return the values in the Title and Author columns for only two books: *Visual Studio Hacks* and *Create Your Own Website*.

Ordering the Results Using the ORDER BY Clause

You may have noticed that the results returned by the SQL queries we have examined so far have all been ordered by the BookID value. To see this point illustrated, refer to Figure 14.10, which shows the results of the query SELECT * FROM Books. What if we want the results ordered by some other column value, though?

The SELECT statement can include an optional ORDER BY clause, which specifies the column to sort the results by. For example, to retrieve books sorted alphabetically by title, use the following SELECT query:

```
SELECT *
FROM Books
ORDER BY Title
```

Figure 14.12 shows the query window when this SQL query is used. Note that the books are ordered by the values in the `Title` column, instead of by the values in the `BookID` column.

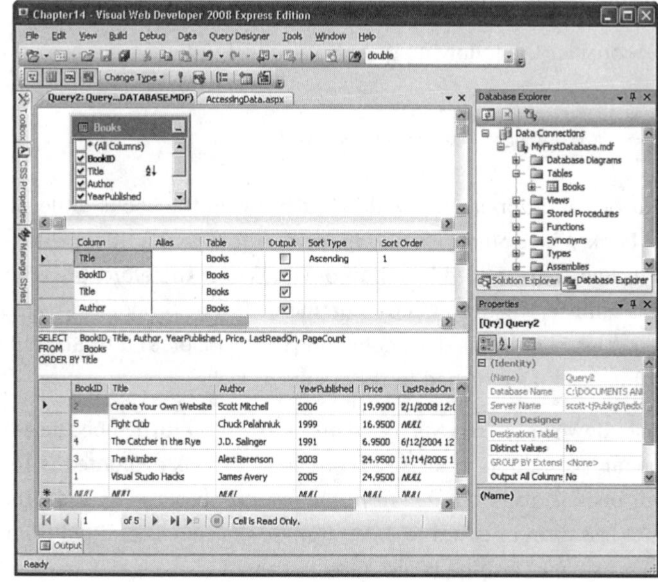

FIGURE 14.12 The books are ordered alphabetically by their `Title` column value.

Did you Know?

> If you want to construct a query that has both a WHERE clause and an ORDER BY clause, it is vital that the ORDER BY clause appear *after* the WHERE clause. The following is a legal SQL query:
>
> ```
> SELECT *
> FROM Books
> WHERE Title <> 'Fight Club'
> ORDER BY Author
> ```
>
> The following is not:
>
> ```
> SELECT *
> FROM Books
> ORDER BY Author
> WHERE Name <> 'Fight Club'
> ```

Sorting in Ascending and Descending Order

By default, the ORDER BY clause sorts the results of a query by a specified column in ascending order. You can specify that the sort ordering should be in descending order by adding the DESC modifier in the following fashion:

```
ORDER BY ColumnName DESC
```

As illustrated in Figure 14.12, sorting the results by a column that contains alphabetic characters in ascending order sorts the results in alphabetical order. If you want to sort the results in reverse alphabetical order, use the DESC keyword.

Filtering and Sorting Data from the SqlDataSource Control's Wizard

In the "Working with the SqlDataSource Control" section, we looked at how to use the SqlDataSource control's wizard to return all records from a specific table. However, we didn't examine how to filter or sort the results. Now that we have a bit more experience with the SQL SELECT statement, let's return to examining the SqlDataSource control's wizard and see how to filter and sort the results.

Start by returning to the AccessingData.aspx page we created earlier in this hour. Add another SqlDataSource control to the page and then click the Configure Data Source link from its smart tag. Because we've already created and stored a connection string for the MyFirstDatabase.mdf database in our web application's web.config file, the drop-down list in step 1 of the wizard lists this connection string name. Pick this connection string value and click the Next button.

From the Configure the Select Statement screen, choose the Books table from the drop-down list and click the * option to return all columns (refer to Figure 14.5). As we saw earlier in this hour, this issues a SELECT * FROM [Books] query to the database, which returns all records from the Books table ordered by the BookID values.

At this point we are ready to filter and sort the data as needed. Note the WHERE and ORDER BY buttons on the right of the Configure the Select Statement screen. These buttons bring up dialog boxes that we'll use to configure the WHERE and ORDER BY clauses of our SELECT statement.

Filtering the SqlDataSource Control's Data

As things stand now, all records from the Books table will be returned. Imagine, however, that we want to return only those records that have a BookID value of 3 or less and cost more than $20.00. We can add these WHERE clause filters via the

SqlDataSource's wizard by clicking the WHERE button. This will display the Add WHERE Clause dialog box, shown in Figure 14.13.

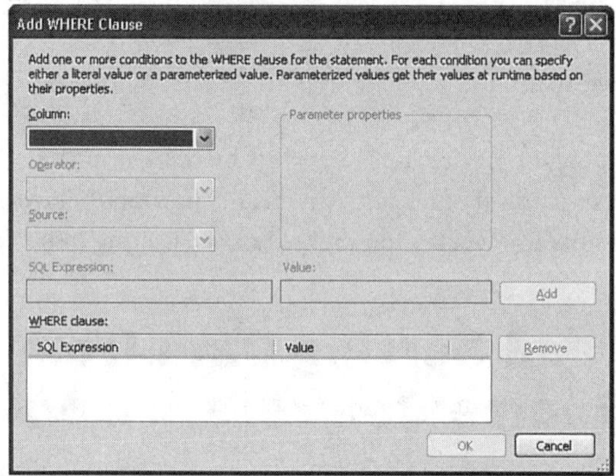

FIGURE 14.13 Filter the results using the Add WHERE Clause dialog box.

Adding a filter through the Add WHERE Clause dialog box involves a number of steps, such as choosing what column to filter on, the operator to filter with, and what value to use in filtering. To add the filter expression on the `BookID` column, perform the following steps:

1. Choose a column to filter. Because we want to filter on `BookID`, select the `BookID` value from the Column drop-down list.
2. Select the filtering operator from the Operator drop-down list. Because we want books with a `BookID` value less than or equal to 3, choose the <= operator from the list.
3. Specify the source of the filter value. The Source drop-down list contains the potential places where the filter value can be read from. For example, you might present a TextBox control to the user visiting the web page through which he could specify the `BookID` value to filter on. In that case you'd set the Source to the Control option. However, we want to enter a hard-coded value as our filter value (3, for this example). Therefore, choose None for the Source.
4. After you choose None, the Parameter Properties section displays a Value text box. Here, you can enter the hard-coded filter value. Enter **3**. (Figure 14.14 shows the Add WHERE Clause dialog box at the end of this step.)
5. Click the Add button to include the filter expression in the `WHERE` clause.

Congratulations, you have added your first `WHERE` clause expression using the SqlDataSource wizard!

Because we want our query to have two WHERE clause expressions, our work is only halfway done. Repeat the preceding steps, this time adding an expression that filters on the Price column for results with values strictly greater than $20.00. After adding both filter expressions, click the OK button to return to the Configure the Select Statement screen. At the bottom of this screen, you see the SQL query the wizard has constructed thus far:

```
SELECT * FROM [Books] WHERE (([BookID] <= @BookID) AND ([Price] > @Price))
```

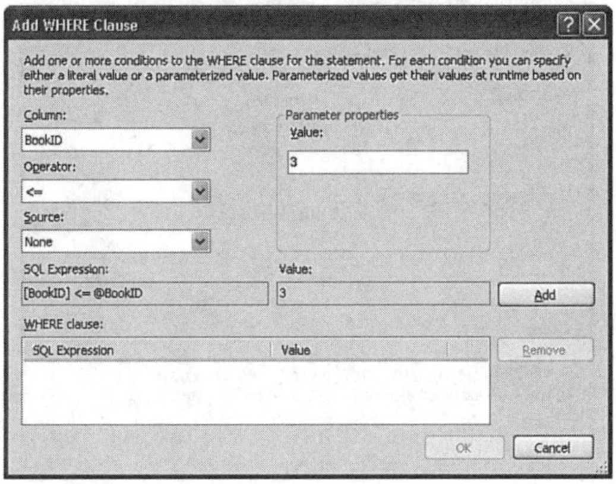

FIGURE 14.14
A less than or equal filter on BookID has been defined for the hard-coded value 3.

The Add WHERE Clause dialog box works great if you want to add only one filter expression or if all the filter expressions are joined by AND logical operators. However, if you want to have multiple filter expressions joined by OR operators, such as filtering on books with a BookID less than or equal to 3 *or* Price greater than $20.00, you'll need to craft the SQL statement yourself. From the Configure Select Statement screen, you'll need to select the Specify a Custom SQL Statement or Stored Procedure radio button and then provide the precise SQL query.

Sorting the SqlDataSource Control's Data

At this point we have added two filter expressions to the WHERE clause. However, the results returned will still be ordered by BookID. Let's instead have the books ordered by Price in descending order (from most expensive to least). If any ties occur in Price, let's break them by alphabetically sorting on the Title.

To accomplish this, click the ORDER BY button, which is beneath the WHERE button in the Configure Select Statement screen. This brings up the Add ORDER BY Clause dialog box, from which you can specify up to three columns to order the results.

The results are sorted by the column specified in the first drop-down list. If any ties occur in the results, the second column is consulted; finally, if any ties occur there, the third column specified is used to break those ties.

Figure 14.15 shows the Add ORDER BY Clause dialog box after it has been configured to sort first by `Price` in descending order, with ties being broken based on the alphabetical ordering of the `Title` column.

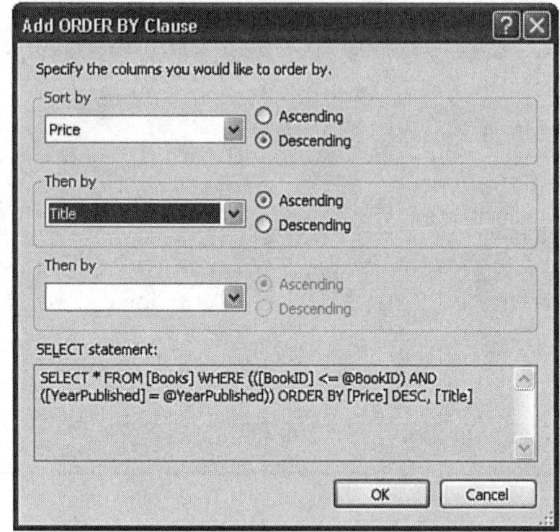

FIGURE 14.15 The results will be ordered by `Price` in descending order, with ties being broken by `Title`.

As Figure 14.15 shows, after we add the `ORDER BY` clause, the final SQL statement for our SqlDataSource control is

```
SELECT * FROM [Books] WHERE (([BookID] <= @BookID) AND ([Price] > @Price))
➥ ORDER BY [Price] DESC, [Title]
```

Testing Queries with `WHERE` Clauses

After you've entered the `ORDER BY` clause, click the OK button to return to the Configure Select Statement screen. At this point, our SQL query is complete; it returns all columns of the `Books` table records that have a `BookID` less than or equal to 3 and a price exceeding $20.00. These results are sorted by `Price` in descending order, breaking ties by sorting on `Title` alphabetically. Click the Next button to advance to the Test Query screen.

When you have a query that involves a `WHERE` clause, clicking the Test Query button prompts you to supply values for the `WHERE` clause filter expressions. For this example, we are prompted to enter values for `BookID` and `Price` (see Figure 14.16).

You can either leave in the default values—3 and 20.00, respectively—or enter different numbers.

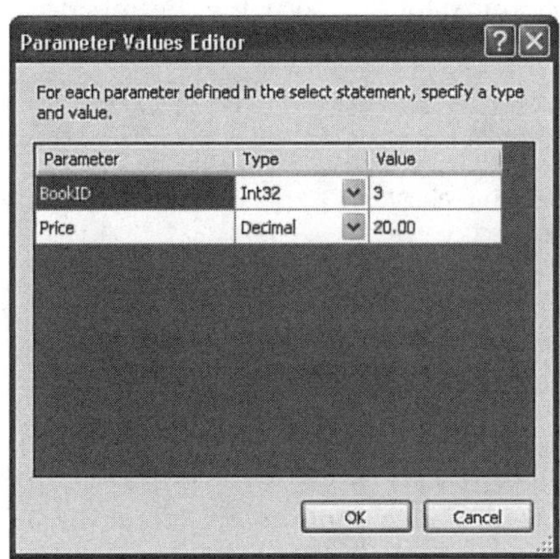

FIGURE 14.16
Specify the values for the `WHERE` clause filter expressions.

If you leave in the values of 3 and 20.00 for the `BookID` and `Price` filter expressions, you should see two books in the results—*The Number* and *Visual Studio Hacks* (see Figure 14.17). These are the only books that have `BookID` values less than or equal to 3 and prices greater than $20.00. *The Number* and *Visual Studio Hacks* have the same price—$24.95. *The Number* is listed first because its title comes before *Visual Studio Hacks* when sorted alphabetically.

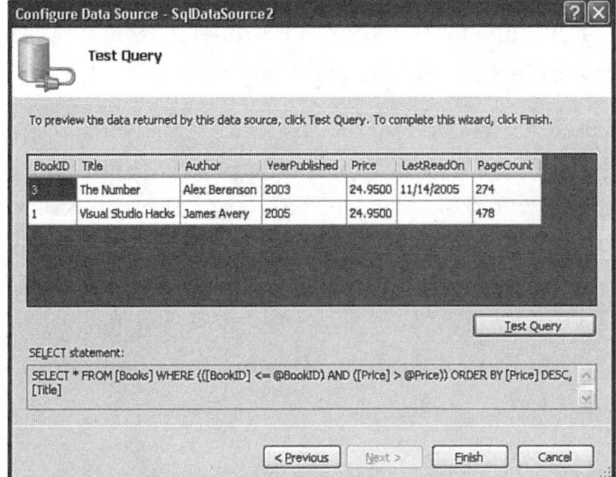

FIGURE 14.17
The query returns two records from the `Books` table.

To complete the SqlDataSource control's wizard, click the Finish button. For more practice with the Add WHERE Clause and Add ORDER BY Clause dialog boxes, click the Previous button to return to the Configure Select Statement screen.

A Look at the SqlDataSource Control's Markup

After you have configured the SqlDataSource control to include both WHERE and ORDER BY clauses, take a moment to inspect the control's declarative markup in the Source view:

```
<asp:SqlDataSource ID="SqlDataSource2" runat="server"
    ConnectionString="<%$ ConnectionStrings:ConnectionString %>"
    SelectCommand="SELECT * FROM [Books] WHERE (([BookID] &lt;= @BookID)
➥AND ([Price] &gt; @Price)) ORDER BY [Price] DESC, [Title]">
    <SelectParameters>
        <asp:Parameter DefaultValue="3" Name="BookID" Type="Int32" />
        <asp:Parameter DefaultValue="20.00" Name="Price"
➥Type="Decimal" />
    </SelectParameters>
</asp:SqlDataSource>
```

The ID and ConnectionString properties are nothing new; we examined them back in the "Examining the Data Source Controls" section at the start of this hour. The SelectCommand is more intricate, though, now including both a WHERE clause and an ORDER BY clause. Notice that no values are supplied for the filter expression values, even though we provided hard-coded values in the Add WHERE Clause dialog box. Instead, a **parameterized query** is used.

A parameter is a placeholder in a SQL statement that has the form *@ParameterName*. It serves as a location where a value will be inserted right before the actual SQL statement is sent off to the database. The SqlDataSource control lists the parameters for the SelectCommand in the <SelectParameters> element. There are two <asp:Parameter> elements within <SelectParameters>: one for the @BookID parameter and one for the @Price parameter. Here, their hard-coded values are specified in the DefaultValue properties.

When a user visits the ASP.NET page, the SqlDataSource control takes those parameter values and injects them into the appropriate places within the SELECT query before sending the query to the database. Although parameterized queries seem like overkill when filtering on hard-coded values, their utility will become more apparent when we start filtering based on values specified by the user visiting the page or from other external sources. We'll see how to base parameter values on user input in Hour 17, "Working with Data-Bound DropDownLists, RadioButtons, and CheckBoxes."

Summary

In this hour we discussed the ASP.NET data source controls, focusing specifically on the SqlDataSource control, which is designed to retrieve data from a database. The SqlDataSource control needs two bits of information to be able to grab data from a database: information on how to connect to the database and the SQL query to execute. As we saw in the "Working with the SqlDataSource Control" section, the SqlDataSource control contains a wizard that makes specifying this information a breeze.

The SqlDataSource control's wizard generates a SQL `SELECT` statement that specifies the data to retrieve from the underlying database. This query is written using the Structured Query Language, or SQL, which is the language used by all modern databases for retrieving, inserting, updating, and deleting data.

To retrieve rows from a database table, a `SELECT` statement is used, which has the syntax

```
SELECT Column1, Column2, ..., ColumnN
FROM TableName
WHERE whereConditions
ORDER BY ColumnName
```

The `SELECT` and `FROM` clauses are mandatory; `WHERE` and `ORDER BY` are optional.

Fortunately, we do not have to be SQL aficionados to retrieve database data from an ASP.NET web page. The SqlDataSource control's wizard allows us to construct our queries through an easy-to-use graphical interface.

Now that we have examined how to retrieve data from a database using the SqlDataSource control, the next step is to display that data in an ASP.NET page. This is accomplished through the use of data Web controls, which are examined in depth in the next hour.

Q&A

Q. ***Can SQL be used to retrieve data from multiple database tables?***

A. Yes. Although in this book we will be studying only examples that involve a single database table, database tables commonly share relationships. For example, imagine that we were working on a website for an e-commerce site, like Amazon.com. There might be a database table called `Orders`, which would contain a row for each order. Because each order could have one or more items, we might also have a table called `OrderItems`, which would contain a row for each item placed in each order.

These two tables obviously share a relationship with one another. That is, each row in the `OrderItems` table "belongs" to a particular row in the `Orders` table. This relationship can be expressed using **foreign keys**, which are special column types that relate a row in one table to a row in another.

After a relationship has been established between two tables, often you will want to retrieve results from both tables. For example, using the `Orders` and `OrderItems` example, we might want to issue a query that returns the list of orders and their associated items for a particular customer. Although such multitable SQL queries are quite common in the practice, they are beyond the scope of this book.

For more information on multitable relationships and more advanced SQL topics, consider picking up a copy of *Sams Teach Yourself SQL in 10 Minutes* (ISBN: 0672325675).

Workshop

Quiz

1. Imagine that you had a database table named `Albums` that contained the following columns: `AlbumID`, `Name`, `Artist`, and `DatePurchased`. Write a SQL query to retrieve the name of the albums, ordered alphabetically.

2. Write a SQL query to retrieve, in this order, the artist, name, and date the album was purchased, ordered alphabetically by the artist.

3. Write a SQL query that retrieves the names of all of the albums by the artist Nirvana, ordered by the date the album was purchased, starting with the most recently purchased.

4. True or False: The following two SQL queries would return the exact same data:

```
SELECT AlbumID, Name, Artist, DatePurchased
FROM Albums
```

and

```
SELECT *
FROM Albums
```

5. Describe the steps you would take to add a data source control that returned the name and purchase date of albums whose `AlbumID` is greater than 5 that were recorded by the artist Pavement.

Answers

1. The following SQL query would suffice:

```
SELECT Name
FROM Albums
ORDER BY Name
```

2. The following SQL query would suffice:

```
SELECT Artist, Name, DatePurchased
FROM Albums
ORDER BY Artist
```

3. The following SQL query would suffice:

```
SELECT Name
FROM Albums
WHERE Artist = 'Nirvana'
ORDER BY DatePurchased DESC
```

4. True.

5. Start by dragging a SqlDataSource control onto the Design view of an ASP.NET page and click the Configure Data Source link. Next, specify the database's connection information. From the Configure Select Statement screen, choose the `Albums` table from the drop-down list and select the `Name` and `DatePurchased` columns. Next, click the WHERE button to bring up the Add `WHERE` Clause dialog box.

   In that dialog box, add two filter expressions. For the first, on `AlbumID` use the > operator with a Source of None and a Value of 5. The second filter expression would be on the `Artist` column, using the = operator, with a Source of None and a Value of `Pavement`.

Exercises

1. This exercise is intended to improve your proficiency with SQL. Open the query window by right-clicking the database in the Database Explorer and choosing New Query.

   In the query window craft the SQL query to retrieve those books whose `BookID` is less than or equal to 3. (You can enter the SQL directly into the SQL pane or use the diagram or criteria panes if you prefer.) Note the list of books you see when testing the query. Now, run another query, this time retrieving those books that have a price greater than $10.00. (You are encouraged to experiment with the query window further.)

HOUR 15

Displaying Data with the Data Web Controls

In this hour, we will cover

- ▶ Associating data Web controls with data source controls
- ▶ Using the GridView and DetailsView controls
- ▶ Customizing the appearance of the GridView and DetailsView controls
- ▶ Displaying only a subset of data source columns in a data Web control

Displaying data in an ASP.NET page requires using two classes of Web controls. First, a data source control is used to access the data; next, a data Web control is employed to display the data retrieved by the data source control. In the preceding hour we discussed what data source controls are, focusing on the SqlDataSource control. In this hour we'll turn our attention to the data Web controls, which are a suite of controls that display the data from a data source control.

The data Web controls have a single function—to display data. The data Web controls do not provide any functionality to actually retrieve data. Instead, they take data from a data source and render it in an ASP.NET page. A number of data Web controls are available. Their differences lie in how they render the underlying data. For example, the GridView control displays data in a grid, with one row for each record in the data source control. The DetailsView, on the other hand, displays one record from the data source control at a time.

An Overview of Data Web Controls

ASP.NET contains a number of Web controls whose sole purpose is to display data from a data source control. These controls, which I call **data Web controls**, can be found in the Data region of the Toolbox above the data source controls. As Figure 15.1 shows, there are six data Web controls: GridView, DataList, DetailsView, FormView, ListView, and Repeater. In this hour we examine only two of these data Web controls—the GridView and the DetailsView.

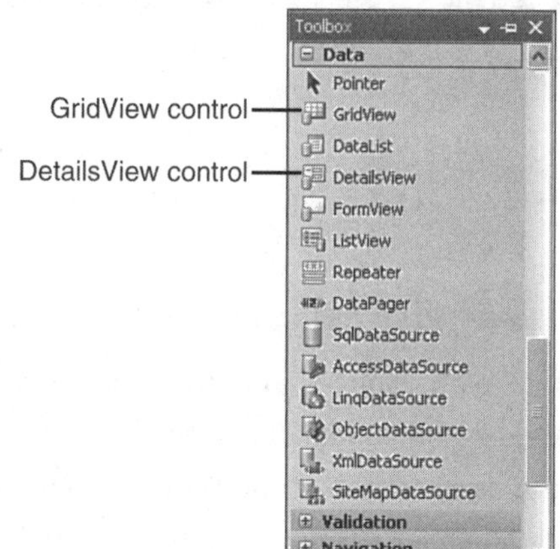

FIGURE 15.1 The Visual Web Developer Toolbox contains a number of data Web controls.

By the Way

The DropDownList, CheckBoxList, and RadioButtonList, which we examined in Hour 11, "Collecting Input Using Drop-Down Lists, Radio Buttons, and Check Boxes," can also be bound to data source controls. We'll look at binding data source controls to the DropDownList, CheckBoxList, and RadioButtonList controls in Hour 17, "Working with Data-Bound DropDownLists, RadioButtons, and CheckBoxes."

To display data with a data Web control, we need a populated data source control, such as the SqlDataSource control. After this data source control is added to the page and configured, displaying its data through a data Web control is a cinch: Simply drag the appropriate data Web control onto the ASP.NET page and, through its smart tag, specify what data source control to use. That's it!

To illustrate the simplicity in displaying data in an ASP.NET page, let's take the `AccessingData.aspx` page from the preceding hour and enhance it by adding a GridView control. (Recall that the `AccessingData.aspx` page has two SqlDataSource controls: one that returns all records and columns in the `Books` table and one that returns only those books whose `BookID` is less than or equal to 3 and whose price exceeds $20.00.)

Start by bringing up this page and going to the Design view. Next, drag a GridView control from the Toolbox's Data section onto the page. The GridView, which we'll be examining in much greater detail later in this hour as well as next hour, displays the data in the data source control in a grid. After you add the GridView to your page's Design view, your screen should look similar to Figure 15.2.

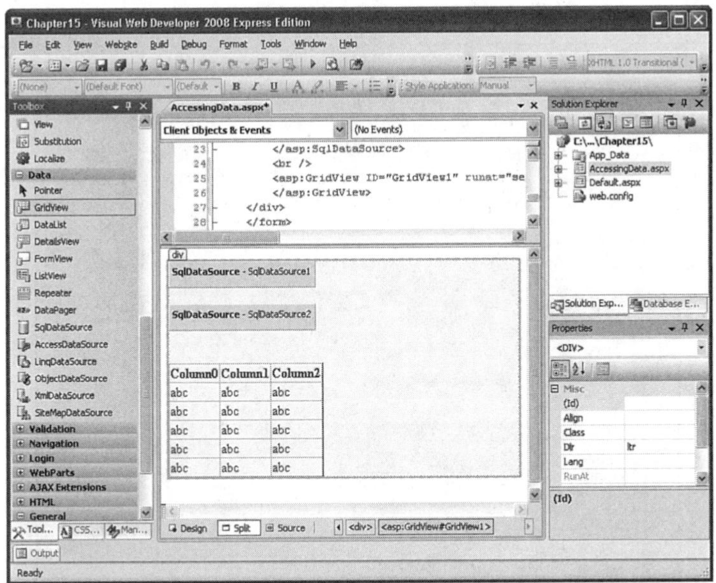

FIGURE 15.2
A GridView has been added to the page.

By default, the GridView shows up as a five-row grid in the Design view with generic field names Column0, Column1, and Column2. This is how the GridView appears in Visual Web Developer when no data source is associated with it.

There can be some confusion when using the word *column* when talking about database tables and GridViews. Both have columns, after all, thereby making it easy to confuse the context. To help remedy this, I will use the word *field* to refer to a GridView's columns and *column* to refer to the columns of a database table.

Assigning a data source control to the GridView is easy. In the smart tag there's a Choose Data Source task with a drop-down list that contains the data source controls on the page. Select the data source control whose contents you want to display in the GridView. After you make a selection, the GridView's field structure is updated to mirror the columns returned by the data source control.

Go ahead and select `SqlDataSource1` as the GridView's data source. When you make this selection, the GridView's appearance in the Design view is updated to include fields for the `BookID`, `Title`, `Author`, `YearPublished`, `Price`, `LastReadOn`, and `Price` columns returned by `SqlDataSource1`, as Figure 15.3 shows.

Did you Know?

> If selecting a data source merely changes the GridView's field headers from Column0, Column1, and Column2 to Databound Col0, Databound Col1, and Databound Col2, click the Refresh Schema link in the smart tag. This updates the GridView's display with the columns returned by the data source control.

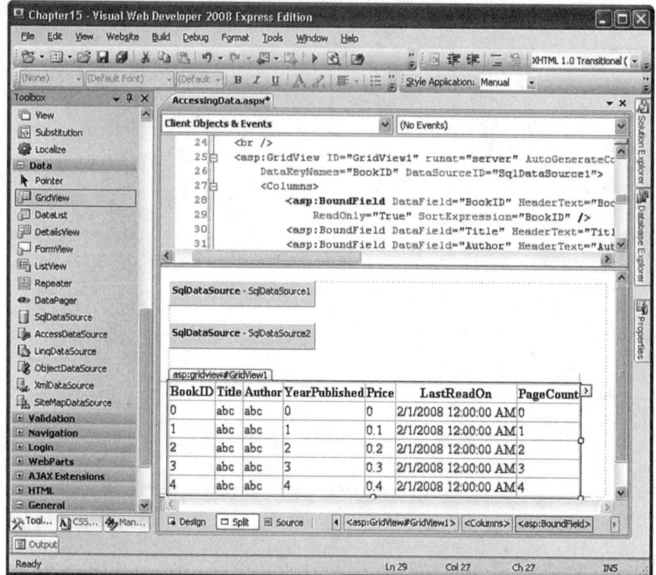

FIGURE 15.3 `SqlDataSource1` has been assigned as the GridView's data source control.

Congratulations, you now have an ASP.NET page that displays the contents of the query executed by `SqlDataSource1`. Take a moment to view the page in a browser (go to the Debug menu and choose Start Without Debugging). You should see a grid in your browser with a row for each of the five books in the Books table (see Figure 15.4).

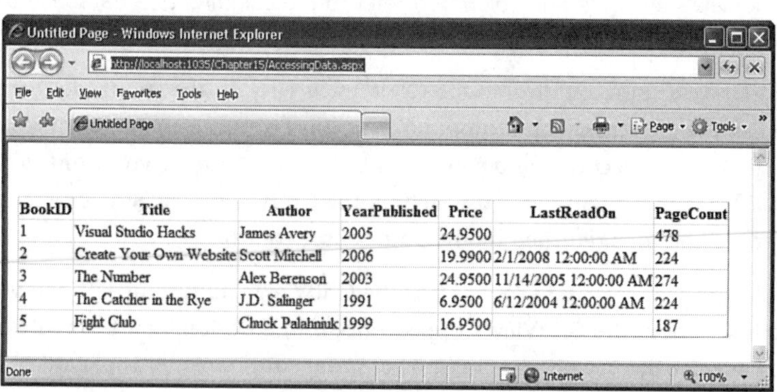

BookID	Title	Author	YearPublished	Price	LastReadOn	PageCount
1	Visual Studio Hacks	James Avery	2005	24.9500		478
2	Create Your Own Website	Scott Mitchell	2006	19.9900	2/1/2008 12:00:00 AM	224
3	The Number	Alex Berenson	2003	24.9500	11/14/2005 12:00:00 AM	274
4	The Catcher in the Rye	J.D. Salinger	1991	6.9500	6/12/2004 12:00:00 AM	224
5	Fight Club	Chuck Palahniuk	1999	16.9500		187

FIGURE 15.4 The contents of the `Books` table are displayed through an ASP.NET page.

By the Way

If you visit the page *before* specifying the GridView's data source, you'll see only a blank page. Similarly, if the GridView is assigned a data source control, but the data source control does not return any records (perhaps the underlying database table has no records, or the `WHERE` condition suppresses all records), you'll also see a blank page.

The GridView renders a grid only if it is assigned a data source control and if the data source control returns one or more records.

The output in Figure 15.4 is hardly ideal; it lacks any attractive fonts or colors, displays the columns in the order in which they were returned from the data source control, and applies no cell-level formatting. (For example, the `LastReadOn` value unnecessarily includes the time; the `Price` value does not include a currency symbol and has four decimal places rather than the typical two.) Don't worry, though, we'll look at how to customize the GridView later in this hour.

For now, take note of the process for displaying data in an ASP.NET page. The first step is to add the data source control that retrieves the appropriate subset of data. Following that, add a data Web control and, through its smart tag, specify what data source to use. Although our example in this section used the GridView, the process for associating a data source control with other data Web controls is identical.

Displaying Data with the GridView Control

When we're displaying data on a web page, more often than not we want to display all records from a particular query. The query might be a static query, such as `SELECT * FROM [Books]`, or it may be a more dynamic one whose filter expressions are based on the visitor's input. Regardless of the type of query, if you want to display all the results at once, consider using the GridView.

In addition to showing each of the records retrieved by the data source control, the GridView, by default, shows an additional header row, which lists the names of the displayed fields. By default, the GridView contains a field for each of the data source control's columns, although this can be customized as we'll see shortly.

In this hour we already examined adding a GridView to an ASP.NET page and associating it with a data source control. There are but two steps:

1. Add a data source control to the page and configure it to retrieve the data you are interested in displaying.

2. Add a GridView to the page and configure it to use the data source control added in step 1.

The result of these two simple steps is an ASP.NET page that displays the retrieved data in a grid.

A Look at the GridView's Declarative Markup

When adding the GridView control to our ASP.NET page, we did everything through the Design view. Like any other Web control, the GridView can also be configured declaratively, through the Source view. However, the tools available through the Design view can save you a great deal of typing. Figure 15.2 showed the Design view immediately after adding a GridView to the page. The declarative markup added to the Source view is very concise:

```
<asp:GridView ID="GridView1" runat="server">
</asp:GridView>
```

However, after you set the GridView's data source through the smart tag, the declarative markup explodes. Listing 15.1 contains the declarative markup after the GridView has been bound to `SqlDataSource1`. Figure 15.3 shows what the GridView looks like in the Design view after making this setting.

LISTING 15.1 The GridView's Markup, After It's Bound to a Data Source Control

```
<asp:GridView ID="GridView1" runat="server" AutoGenerateColumns="False" DataKeyNames="BookID"
    DataSourceID="SqlDataSource1">
    <Columns>
        <asp:BoundField DataField="BookID" HeaderText="BookID" InsertVisible="False" ReadOnly="True"
            SortExpression="BookID" />
        <asp:BoundField DataField="Title" HeaderText="Title" SortExpression="Title" />
        <asp:BoundField DataField="Author" HeaderText="Author" SortExpression="Author" />
        <asp:BoundField DataField="YearPublished" HeaderText="YearPublished" SortExpression="YearPublished" />
        <asp:BoundField DataField="Price" HeaderText="Price" SortExpression="Price" />
        <asp:BoundField DataField="LastReadOn" HeaderText="LastReadOn" SortExpression="LastReadOn" />
        <asp:BoundField DataField="PageCount" HeaderText="PageCount" SortExpression="PageCount" />
    </Columns>
</asp:GridView>
```

The <asp:GridView> tag (lines 1 and 2) has three new properties:

- **`AutoGenerateColumns`**—This property indicates whether the GridView bases its fields on the data source's columns or on the fields explicitly defined in the `<Columns>` tag. With `AutoGenerateColumns="False"`, the fields rendered are those specified in the `<Columns>` tag.
- **`DataKeyNames`**—This property specifies the column name(s) that uniquely identify each record being bound to the GridView. This is, by default, the primary key column(s). The smart tag was able to determine the primary key of the data source control and assign this property accordingly.
- **`DataSourceID`**—This property specifies the `ID` of the GridView's data source control.

Starting on line 3 is the `<Columns>` element, which defines the GridView's fields (lines 4 through 11). Each `<asp:BoundField>` element represents a field rendered by the GridView. As you can see from Listing 15.1, there are seven fields in the GridView, one for each of the columns returned by the data source control. Each `<asp:BoundField>` element contains an assortment of properties, specifying the name of the database column whose data is to be displayed (`DataField`) and the text shown in the column's header (`HeaderText`), among others. This tag can also contain column-specific formatting information, as we'll see shortly.

The purpose of Listing 15.1 is to highlight the benefit of the Design view in Visual Web Developer. Without the Design view, we would have to enter this declarative markup by hand.

Customizing the Appearance of the GridView

The GridView shown in Figure 15.4 is rather unattractive. It lacks any color; uses the default system font; displays, perhaps, fields that don't concern the user (such as `BookID`); and lacks any sort of formatting for currency and date values. Also, all values are left-aligned and look alike. Perhaps you'd like the `PageCount` right-aligned and the title of the book emphasized by displaying it in italics. Finally, the field names displayed in the grid's header are the precise names of the database columns—`BookID`, `YearPublished`, `LastReadOn`, and so on. Ideally, we would want these to be more readable names, such as ID, Published, and Last Read.

All these customizations can be easily accomplished with the GridView. The GridView allows customization of its appearance on a number of levels:

- **The GridView-level**—Changes specified at this level affect *all* the data in the GridView.

- **The Field-level**—Use this level to format a particular field in the GridView, such as the `Price` field.
- **The Row-level**—You can specify customized formatting for various classes of rows. For example, you can configure alternating rows to have a different background color, or you can have the header row displayed in a larger font size.

These various levels of settings can be set through the Auto Format dialog box, the Fields dialog box, or the Properties window. Let's examine how to tailor the GridView's appearance at each of the levels using the tools available.

Formatting from the Properties Window

GridView-level and row-level formatting can be accomplished directly through the Properties window. Select the GridView so that its properties are loaded in the Properties window. In the Appearances section (see Figure 15.5), you can set a number of GridView-level properties.

Table 15.1 lists these Appearance properties along with a brief description. Realize that these properties affect the *entire* GridView's formatting. That is, if you set the `BackColor` property to Green, for instance, all the rows and all the fields in the GridView will have a Green background color.

TABLE 15.1 The Appearance Properties Affect the Entire GridView's Formatting

Property	Description
`BackColor`	Specifies the GridView's background color.
`BackImageUrl`	Specifies an image to display in the GridView's background.
`BorderColor`	Specifies the color of the GridView's border.
`BorderStyle`	Specifies the GridView's border's style. Can be `NotSet`, `None`, `Dotted`, `Dashed`, and `Solid`, among others.
`BorderWidth`	Specifies the width of the border.
`CssClass`	Specifies the class name if you want to apply an external cascading style sheet (CSS) class to the GridView.
`EmptyDataText`	Specifies whether you want a message to be displayed in the event that there are no records. Recall that a GridView is rendered only if there are records returned by its data source control.
`Font`	Specifies the font settings for the GridView. Refer to Table 8.1 for a listing of the `Font` property's subproperties.

TABLE 15.1 Continued

Property	Description
`ForeColor`	Specifies the GridView's foreground color.
`GridLines`	Specifies how lines are drawn between the cells of the grid. Can be `None`, `Vertical`, `Horizontal`, or `Both` (the default).
`ShowFooter`	Specifies a Boolean value that indicates whether the footer row is shown; `False` by default.
`ShowHeader`	Specifies a Boolean value indicating whether the header row is shown; `True` by default.

Take a moment to try out some of these Appearance properties. Figure 15.5 shows Visual Web Developer after I set a number of properties. While making changes to these properties, notice how the GridView's appearance in the Design view is automatically updated to reflect the new formatting choices. Furthermore, note how the Appearance property settings affect the entire GridView.

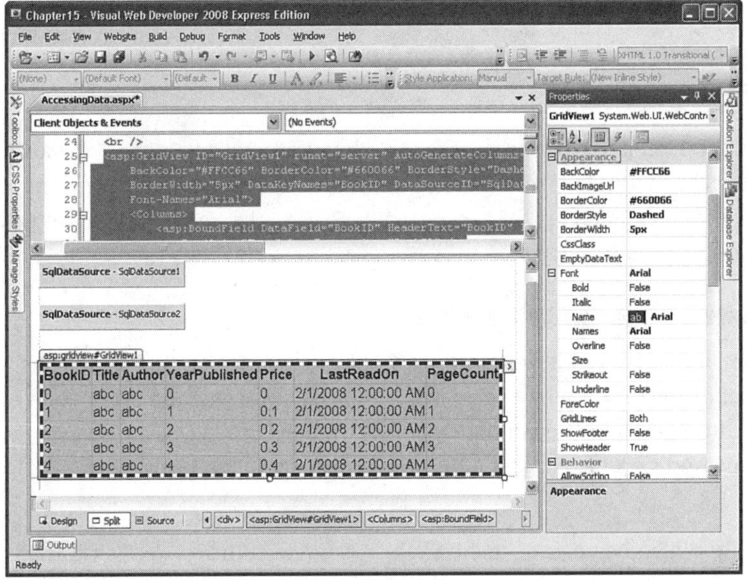

FIGURE 15.5 Customize the formatting of the entire GridView using the Appearance properties.

The Properties window also includes properties that you can set to specify the formatting at the row level. In the Styles section of the Properties window, you'll find a suite of properties that apply to various classes of rows. Table 15.2 lists these row-level style properties.

TABLE 15.2 The Style Properties Affect Various Classes of Rows

Property	Description
`AlternatingRowStyle`	Specifies style information for alternating rows.
`EditRowStyle`	Specifies the formatting for an editable row. When you're working with an editable GridView—a topic for Hour 16, "Deleting, Inserting, and Editing Data"—you will have a particular row being edited.
`EmptyDataRowStyle`	Specifies the style for a row if no records are in the GridView's data source and you have set the `EmptyDataText` property in the Appearance settings.
`FooterStyle`	Specifies the style of the footer row.
`HeaderStyle`	Specifies the header row style.
`PagerStyle`	Specifies the style for the GridView's paging controls. When you're creating pageable GridViews—again, a topic for Hour 16—a pager row is included.
`RowStyle`	Specifies the style for a GridView row.
`SelectedRowStyle`	Specifies the style for a selected row. Unfortunately, we won't have time to examine how to make a GridView row "selected."

Each of these properties has a number of subproperties: `BackColor`, `ForeColor`, `Font`, `CssClass`, `HorizontalAlign`, and the like. Take a moment to set some of the subproperties for `RowStyle`, `AlternatingRowStyle`, and `HeaderStyle`. Figure 15.6 shows Visual Web Developer after I customized my GridView's formatting a bit.

Formatting the GridView's Fields

At this point we've seen how to perform GridView-level formatting as well as row-level formatting. The only level we've yet to examine is field-level. You cannot edit the fields of the GridView through the Properties window; instead, go to the GridView's smart tag and click the Edit Columns link. This displays the Fields dialog box (see Figure 15.7).

The Fields dialog box lists the fields in the GridView in the bottom-left corner. Selecting a field from this list loads that field's properties in the list on the right. At the upper-left portion of the Fields dialog box is the list of types of fields that can be added to a GridView. Currently, all the fields used by the GridView are BoundFields. A BoundField simply displays the value from a particular column in the corresponding data source control. Other types of fields enable other functionality. For example, the HyperLinkField displays a hyperlink in each row; the ButtonField displays a button in each row. We'll examine some of these additional field types in more detail in Hour 16.

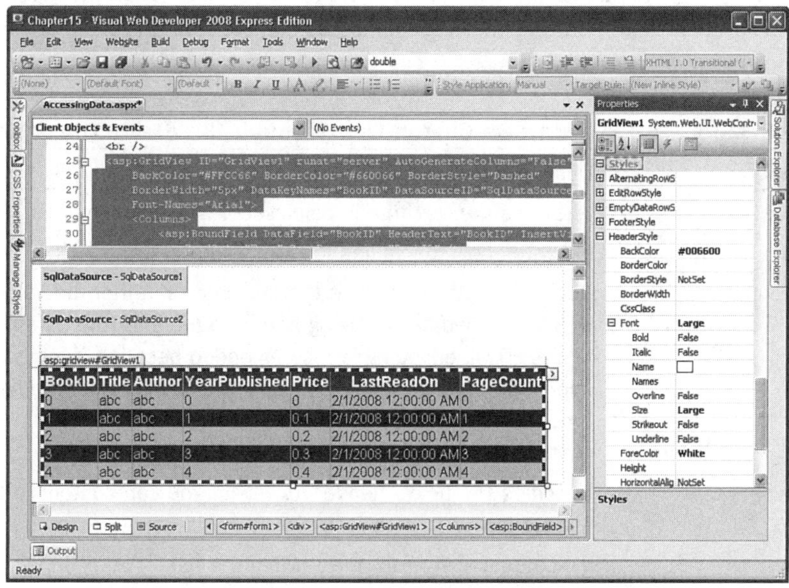

FIGURE 15.6
The Styles properties enable you to customize various classes of rows.

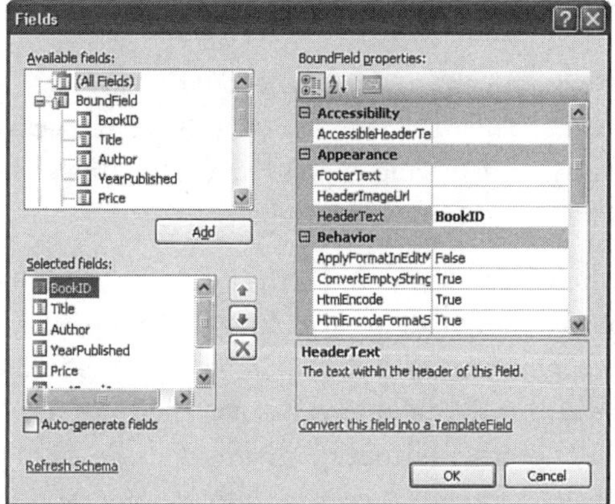

FIGURE 15.7
Customize the columns of the GridView through the Fields dialog box.

In addition to listing the GridView's fields, the Selected Fields list allows you to remove fields and reorder the fields in the GridView. Let's remove the `BookID` field from the GridView because end users don't need this information. To remove this field from the GridView, click the `BookID` field from the list in the bottom-left corner and then click the delete icon (the red X). Next, let's have the `PageCount` field displayed after the Author field. To accomplish this, click the PageCount field and then click the up-arrow icon until PageCount is the third field in the list.

To customize a particular field, first click the field in the Selected Fields list. This loads its properties in the right side of the dialog box. Table 15.3 lists some of the more germane field-level properties.

TABLE 15.3 A Field Can Be Customized Through the Fields Dialog Box

Property	Description
HeaderText	Specifies the text that is displayed in the field's header row.
DataFormatString	Indicates how the values for this field are formatted.
HtmlEncode	Specifies a Boolean value that indicates whether the value is HTML encoded before being bound to the grid (the default is True). HTML encoding is recommended because it removes <script> elements and other HTML that might not render properly in the grid. However, to have the DataFormatString property work, you must set HtmlEncode to False.
HeaderStyle	Specifies the field's header row style. You can customize the header row style on a field-by-field basis using this property.
ItemStyle	Indicates the style for the rows of the field. For example, you could have all the book titles displayed in italics by setting this property for the Title field.

Change the HeaderText properties of the PageCount, YearPublished, and LastReadOn fields to Pages, Published, and Last Read, respectively. Next, go to the Title field's ItemStyle property and expand it, locating the Font property. Expand the Font property and set the Italic subproperty to True.

Let's also configure the values displayed for the Price and LastReadOn fields. To format the values displayed in a field, we need to set two properties: HtmlEncode must be set to False, and DataFormatString should be set to the format string using the form {0:*format specifier*}. The format specifier indicates how the data is to be formatted. A number of built-in format specifiers are designed to format specific data types. For example, c formats a number into a currency; d formats a date and time so that it displays just the date portion. You can find a complete list of format specifiers by searching the Visual Web Developer help for "formatting."

To format the Price field as a currency and the LastReadOn field as just a date, set the HtmlEncode property to False for both fields and then set the DataFormatString properties to {0:c} and {0:d} for the Price and LastReadOn fields, respectively.

Click OK to close the Fields dialog box. When you return to the Design view, the GridView should be updated to show the new changes: The `BookID` field has been removed, the `Pages` field now comes after the `Author` field, the `Title` field is displayed in italics, and so on. Figure 15.8 shows the GridView when visited through a browser after making these field-level formatting settings.

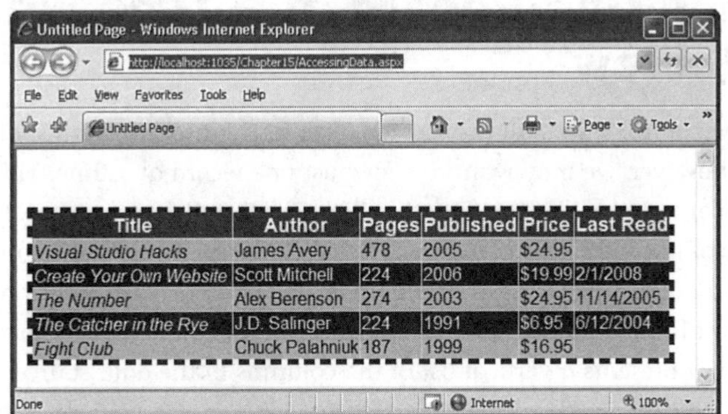

FIGURE 15.8 The fields of the GridView have been customized.

Formatting with the AutoFormat Dialog Box

As you may have gathered from the formatting I've applied to the GridView, its rows, and its fields, I am hardly one to be trusted with configuring the GridView's appearance. I have about as much artistic skill as a vegetable. We can be thankful that the GridView includes an AutoFormat option. From the smart tag, click the AutoFormat link, which shows the AutoFormat dialog box (see Figure 15.9). From this dialog box, you can pick one of a number of predefined styles.

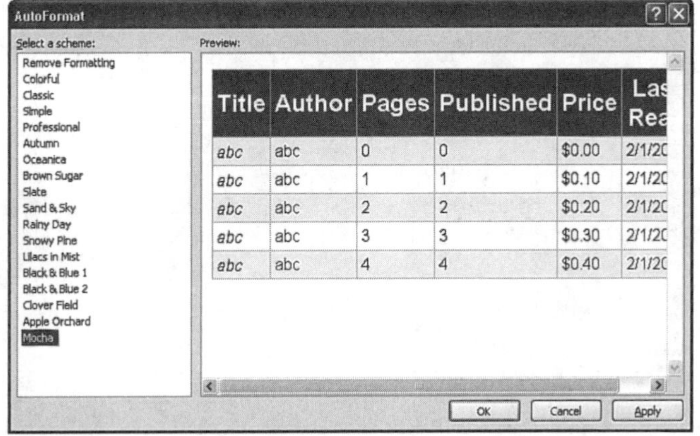

FIGURE 15.9 The Mocha style looks so much nicer than anything I could craft.

Selecting one of the AutoFormat styles will cause a number of Appearance and Styles properties to be automatically set to display the chosen format. If you are an artistic individual, you might prefer to define these formatting settings yourself. However, if you're like me, the AutoFormat feature will quickly become your best friend!

Showing One Record at a Time with the DetailsView

The GridView control shows all the records from its data source control at once. Sometimes, however, we may want to show just one record at a time. The DetailsView control provides this functionality. The DetailsView control is bound to a data source control in the same manner as the GridView. Drag the DetailsView onto a page with a data source control and then, from the smart tag, associate the DetailsView with the data source control. After you assign the data source control, the DetailsView presents a vertical list of the columns in the data source control.

To familiarize ourselves with the DetailsView control, let's create a new ASP.NET page called `DetailsView.aspx`. As in the preceding hour, add a SqlDataSource control to the page, configuring it to select all records and columns from the `Books` table. Next, add a DetailsView to the page and associate it with the SqlDataSource control. After you have completed these steps, your screen should look similar to Figure 15.10.

FIGURE 15.10
A DetailsView control has been added to the page and assigned a data source control.

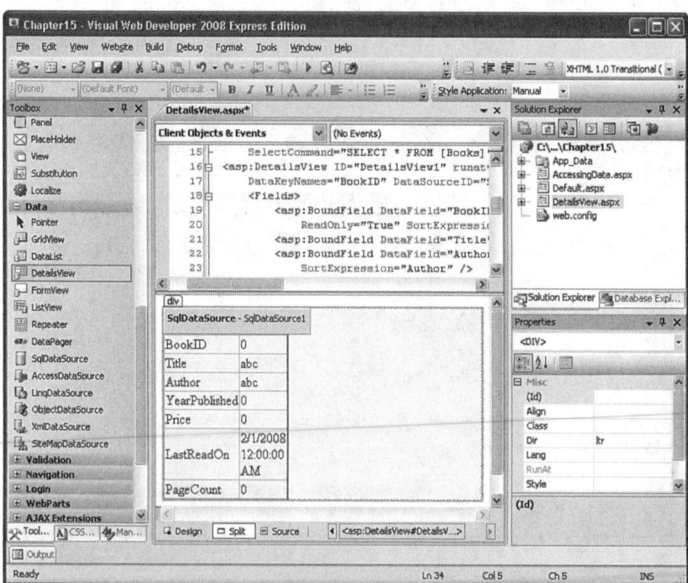

Take a moment to view the DetailsView in a browser. As Figure 15.11 shows, the DetailsView displays the first record returned by its SqlDataSource control.

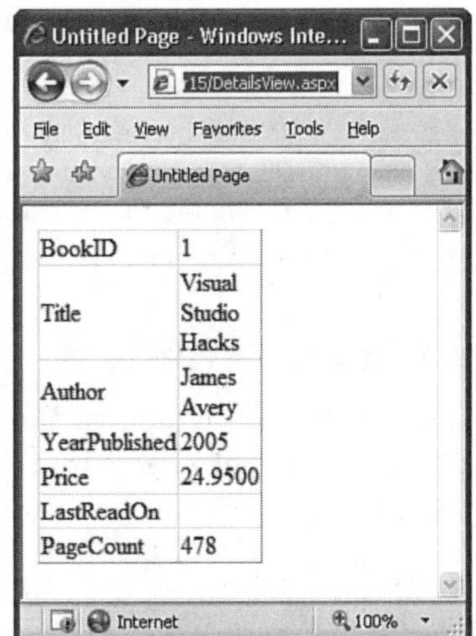

FIGURE 15.11
A single record from the data source control is displayed.

You may have noticed that the DetailsView, by default, doesn't provide any mechanism by which to view the next record in the data source. That is, with the DetailsView we see one record at a time, but there's no way to move to the next record. To provide a means to step through the records, check the Enable Paging check box in the DetailsView's smart tag. This adds a **pager row** to the bottom of the DetailsView that contains a user interface for stepping through the records. By default, the paging interface uses **page numbers** to allow the user to jump to a particular record.

After checking the Enable Paging check box, take a moment to view the page in a browser. Note that now there are five links at the bottom of the DetailsView, allowing you to navigate to any of the five records in the `Books` table by clicking the appropriately numbered link.

You can also configure the GridView control to support paging. Additionally, the user viewing the page can sort the GridView's data. We'll look at how to implement paging and sorting with the GridView later in this hour, in the "Paging and Sorting with the GridView" section.

The DetailsView shown in Figure 15.11 is narrow, causing the text in the `Title` and `Author` fields to wrap. This behavior occurs because Visual Studio automatically sets the DetailsView control's `Width` and `Height` properties to `125px` and `50px`, respectively, after it is bound to a data source control. The benefit of having a fixed width and height is that as the user pages through the records in the DetailsView, its size remains constant regardless of the length of each record's fields. However, I don't mind the DetailsView dynamically resizing based on the length of the data displayed, so I usually clear out these two property values. I encourage you to remove these property values to see the effect.

Customizing the Paging Interface

The DetailsView control's pager row can be customized through the Properties window. First, click the DetailsView in the Design view to load the properties. Next, scroll down to the Paging section of the Properties window. There, you'll see two properties:

- **`AllowPaging`**—This property indicates whether paging is supported (it defaults to `False`). When you checked the Enable Paging check box in the smart tag, this property was set to `True`.
- **`PagerSettings`**—This property contains a number of subproperties that customize the appearance of the pager row. For example, instead of having page number links, you can use Next/Previous links.

Let's change the `PagerSettings` property so that instead of the page number links, we use next, previous, first, and last links. Expand the `PagerSettings` property and go to the `Mode` subproperty. Here, you'll find a drop-down list with the various choices. By default, the `Numeric` option is selected; change this to the `NextPreviousFirstLast` option. Note how the DetailsView changes in the Design view in Visual Web Developer to include the next, previous, first, and last links. Figure 15.12 shows this pageable DetailsView when viewed through a browser.

By default, the next, previous, first, and last links are displayed as >, <, <<, and >>, respectively. You can change these, if you like, via the `PagerStyle`'s `NextPageText`, `PreviousPageText`, `FirstPageText`, and `LastPageText` properties. One important note—if you want to display < or >, you need to use the escaped HTML equivalent: `<` or `>`.

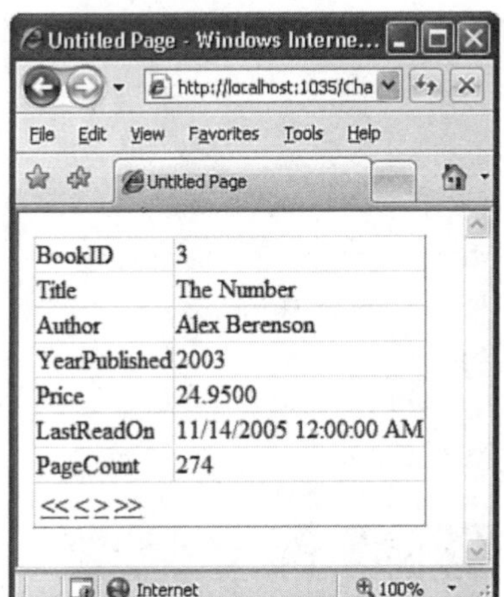

FIGURE 15.12
The DetailsView now supports paging and is showing information for the book `The Number`.

Customizing the Appearance of the DetailsView

The DetailsView's appearance can be customized just like the GridView's. There are DetailsView-level, row-level, and field-level formatting properties. The DetailsView-level and row-level properties can be configured through the Properties window in the Appearance and Styles sections, and the field-level properties are accessible through the smart tag's Edit Fields link, which displays the—you guessed it—Fields dialog box. The DetailsView also has an AutoFormat option in its smart tag, just like the GridView.

Although the process of customizing the formatting of the GridView and DetailsView is identical, some differences exist between the two controls' formatting properties. For example, the DetailsView does not have the notion of a "selected" row, so there's no `SelectedRowStyle`. As we'll see in the next hour, the DetailsView can be used to insert data into a database, and therefore it has an `InsertRowStyle` property.

For practice, take a moment to customize the appearance of the DetailsView. Go ahead and customize its fields like we did with the GridView. Add some color and font settings to liven up its display. Figure 15.13 shows the DetailsView in a browser after gussying up the appearance. Note that I applied the same field-level customizations that we did with the GridView (renaming the header rows, moving the `Price` field to come after the `Authors` field, formatting the `Price` as a currency, and so on.)

When setting the `DataFormatString` for the `Price` and `LastReadOn` fields, don't forget that you also need to set the `HtmlEncode` property to `False`. If you forget to do this, the formatting won't be applied to the field.

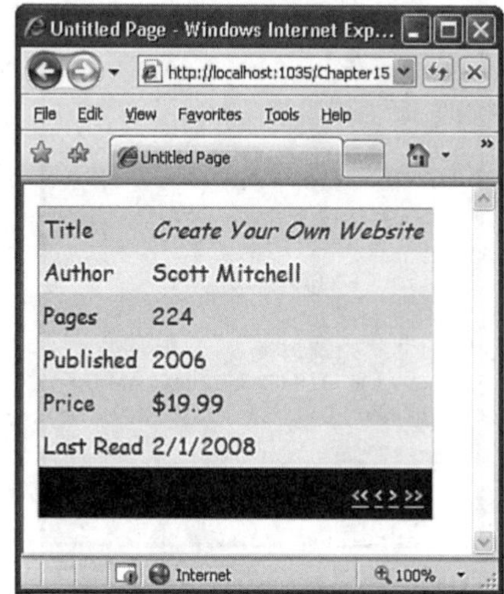

FIGURE 15.13
With some formatting, the DetailsView is much easier on the eyes.

Paging and Sorting with the GridView

By default, the DetailsView shows a *single* record from its data source control. To allow the user to view *all* records, stepping through them one at a time, we needed to configure the DetailsView to allow paging. This, of course, was as simple as checking the Enable Paging check box in the DetailsView's smart tag and then customizing the paging interface through the Properties window. (Refer to the "Customizing the Paging Interface" section for more information on this process.)

The GridView, by default, shows all the records in its data source control. Showing all the records, however, can lead to information overload if hundreds or thousands of records are being retrieved by the data source control. For example, in Figure 15.8 all the records of the `Books` table are displayed, but there's only five of them. Imagine that instead of five records in this table there were five hundred. Such a page would be unwieldy and would likely intimidate any users who were interested in what books we were reading. (Although they'd likely be impressed with the breadth of our library!) To help make the information more digestible, we can implement paging with a GridView, showing only a small subset of the records at a time.

In addition to paging, another helpful feature users are familiar with is sorting. When you go to a travel planning website to book a flight, the results are usually sorted by price, from the least expensive tickets to the most expensive. However, you may be interested in some other criteria, such as departure time or airline. Many sites offer users the ability to sort the results by these other criteria. ASP.NET makes it easy to add similar functionality to your site. The GridView provides a means for the user to sort the results by a particular field.

In the next two sections we'll see how to implement and customize the GridView's paging and sorting capabilities.

A Look at Paging

Enabling paging in the GridView is similar to enabling paging in the DetailsView: Go to the GridView's smart tag and check the Enable Paging check box. To customize the paging interface, go to the Properties window and locate the Paging section. The GridView's Paging section contains four properties:

- **`AllowPaging`**—This property indicates whether paging is supported (it defaults to `False`). When you checked the Enable Paging check box in the smart tag, this property was set to `True`.
- **`PageIndex`**—This property indicates the index of the page of data displayed. (The value is indexed starting at 0; to display the first page of data by default, leave this set at 0.)
- **`PagerSettings`**—This property contains a number of subproperties that customize the appearance of the pager row. For example, instead of having page number links, you can use Next/Previous links.
- **`PageSize`**—This property indicates the number of records to show per page.

The `AllowPaging` and `PagerSettings` properties should look familiar because they were the two properties in the Paging section of the DetailsView's properties. You probably won't ever need to set `PageIndex` through the Properties window; its default value of 0 ensures that the first page of data is displayed when the web page is first loaded in the user's browser. The final property, `PageSize`, specifies how many records to show per page. By default, 10 records will be shown per page. If you want to display more or fewer records per page, change this property value appropriately.

Testing the Paging Functionality

Because our `Books` table has only five records in total, leaving the PageSize at 10 would be uninteresting because there is only one page of data. Instead, let's set this property value to 2. After you have done that, take a moment to view the ASP.NET page through a browser. Figure 15.14 shows my browser when first visiting this page. Note that I'm using the Numeric mode for the paging interface (the default).

There are three pages in total, of which I am viewing page 1. Click the 3 hyperlink in the paging interface. This reloads the page, showing the third page of data (see Figure 15.15).

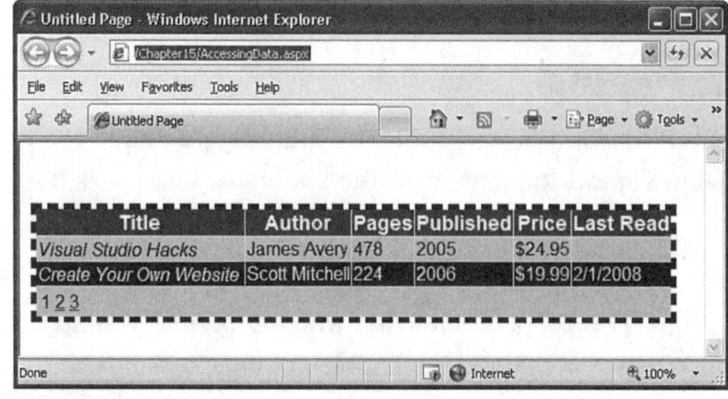

FIGURE 15.14 The first page of data is shown, displaying the first two books from the `Books` table.

FIGURE 15.15 The third page of data is shown, displaying the fifth and final book.

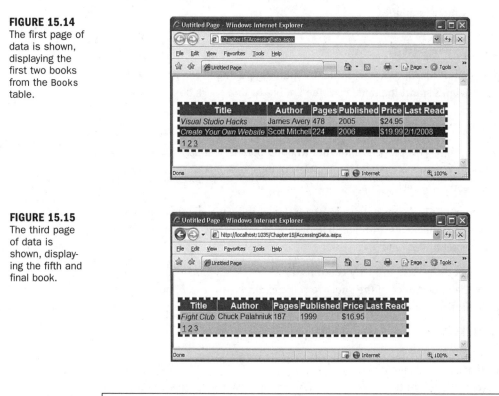

Watch Out!

> To page through the results of a SqlDataSource, the SqlDataSource control's `DataSourceMode` property must be set to `DataSet`. This is the default value, so paging should "just work."
>
> However, if you have changed this property to `DataReader` and attempt to page through its records with a GridView (or DetailsView), you will get an exception. Simply change this property back to `DataSet` to get things working.
>
> This caution also applies to sorting a GridView's data, which we'll be examining shortly.

Providing Sortable Data

In addition to allowing for its data to be paged, the GridView also makes it easy for the end user to sort its data. To indicate that a GridView's data should be sortable, click the Enable Sorting check box in the smart tag. That's all there is to it!

Enabling sorting will make the text in the header of each of the GridView's fields a link that, when clicked, will cause the ASP.NET page to be posted back. Upon postback, the GridView requeries the data from its data source control and applies the appropriate sort command.

Take a moment to check the Enable Sorting check box on your GridView and then view the page through a browser. As Figure 15.16 shows, with sorting enabled, the header of each field is rendered as a link. When one of these links is clicked, the data is sorted in ascending order by the field whose header link was clicked. If the user clicks the same field header again, the sort order is reversed, displaying the results in descending order.

Figure 15.17 shows the web page after the `Price` field's header link has been clicked.

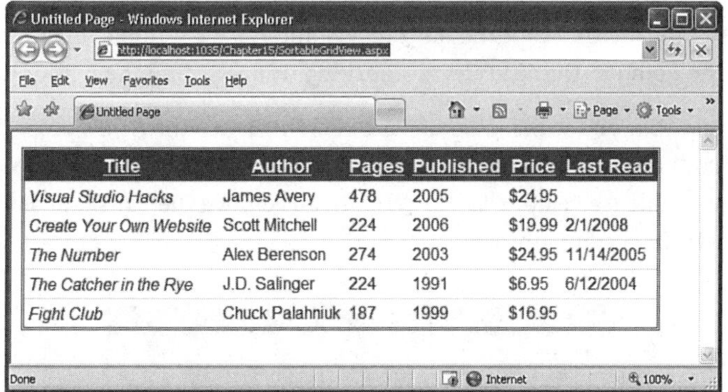

FIGURE 15.16 The data is initially sorted by `BookID`; each field's header is rendered as a link.

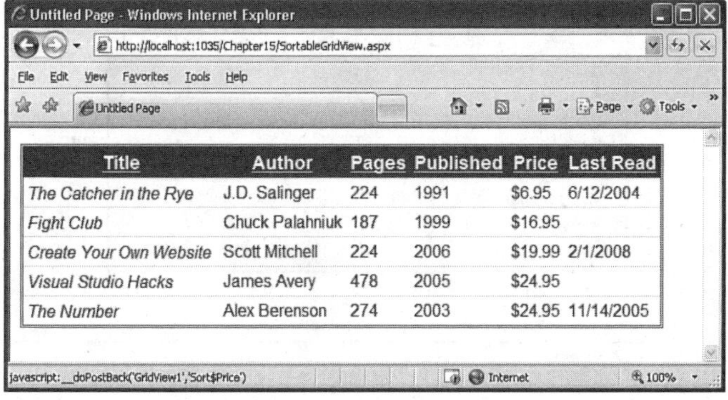

FIGURE 15.17 The `Price` field's header link has been clicked, sorting the books by price.

Did you Know?

When the GridView is sorted, any default ordering of the retrieved data specified by an `ORDER BY` clause is overridden. That is, if your SqlDataSource retrieves the contents of the `Books` table ordered by the `Price` column, and the user opts to sort by `Author`, the GridView's sorting preferences will trump the data source control's.

That doesn't mean that the data source control's `ORDER BY` clause isn't useful. You can use the `ORDER BY` clause to specify the default sort order; this is how the records will be sorted when the user first visits the page. The user, then, can override the sort order by clicking a particular column's header link.

Customizing the Sorting Interface

The GridView's sorting interface can be customized to the extent that you can indicate what fields should be sortable. (By default, all fields of a GridView are made sortable.) To indicate that a particular field should not be sortable, open the Fields dialog box by going to the GridView's smart tag and selecting the Edit Columns link.

Select the field that you want to be unsortable. This loads the field's properties on the right. Scroll down until you find the property named `SortExpression` and then clear out this value (see Figure 15.18). When you remove the `SortExpression` property, the field will become unsortable.

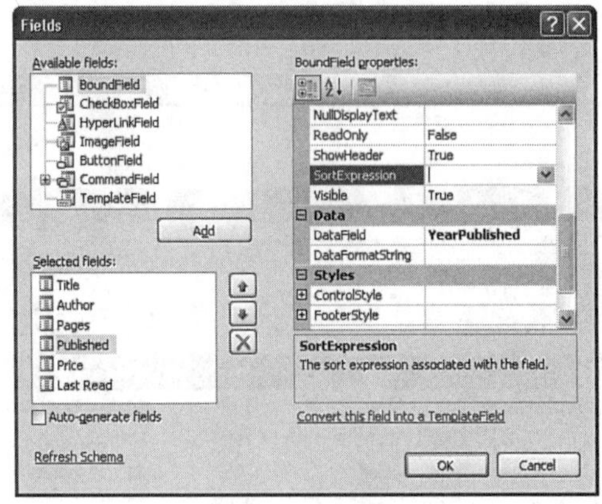

FIGURE 15.18 The `YearPublished` field's `SortExpression` property has been cleared out.

Did you Know?

At this point we've examined both paging and sorting in the GridView, but what about creating a pageable, sortable GridView? Although we've not looked at an example of such a GridView, providing such functionality involves simply checking Enable Paging *and* Enable Sorting.

Summary

In the preceding hour we saw how to retrieve data from a database in an ASP.NET page through the SqlDataSource control. In this hour, we saw how to take that data and display it in the page using a data Web control. All data Web controls essentially work the same: They are added to the page and assigned a data source control. When a user visits the page, the data source control grabs the data from the database, and the data Web control renders its content based on the data in its data source. There are five data Web controls, with the two most commonly used ones being the GridView and DetailsView.

The GridView displays all the records in its corresponding data source control in a grid. The DetailsView, on the other hand, displays only one record at a time. Both the GridView and DetailsView make it very easy to customize the appearance at a number of levels. The numerous control-level and row-level properties can be accessed through the Properties window, and field-level changes can be made through the Fields dialog box. Best of all, both controls sport an AutoFormat dialog box for artistically challenged individuals like myself.

This hour focused on displaying data. In the next hour we'll see how to use the data source controls and the data Web controls in tandem to edit, update, insert, and delete data.

Q&A

Q. ***The GridView and DetailsView look neat, but how can I customize the appearance further? I want to be able to have, for instance, three records displayed per table row rather than having one record per row as with the GridView.***

A. The GridView and DetailsView both include a number of formatting properties, but have a fairly rigid structure. The GridView is always going to display exactly one record per table row, and the DetailsView is going to use a two-column grid to display the columns of a particular database table record.

If you need to customize the output more radically, you'll need to use one of the other data Web controls. The other four controls—the ListView, DataList, Repeater, and FormView—use **templates**. A template allows you to specify a mix of HTML and Web controls, thereby allowing a greater degree of customizability. As we'll see in the next hour, both the GridView and DetailsView do have some support for templates, but the support is only at the field-level.

With the ListView, DataList, Repeater, or FormView, you can have row-level templates.

We'll look at the templated data Web controls in Hour 19, "Using Templated Data Web Controls."

Q. ***The GridView seems to have a lot of functionality. Where can I learn more about the GridView control?***

A. You're right, the GridView is a rather complex and feature-rich control. In the next hour we'll examine many useful features of the GridView, including editing, deleting, paging, and sorting of the data. However, in this book we are able to only scratch the surface of the GridView. For more in-depth information on the GridView, check out "GridView Examples for ASP.NET" at http://msdn2.microsoft.com/en-us/library/aa479339.aspx. It's an online article I authored with downloadable source code that includes more than 120 pages of GridView examples and lessons.

Another helpful resource is the 75 tutorials that make up my "Data Access Tutorials" series, available online at www.asp.net/learn/data-access.

Workshop

Quiz

1. How do you associate a data source control with a data Web control?
2. True or False: A data source control can be used to display data.
3. True or False: A data Web control can be used to retrieve data from a database.
4. How can a DetailsView control be configured to allow the user to step through the records of its data source control?
5. What are the formatting specifiers for formatting a numeric field as a currency? What about for formatting a date/time field as just a date?

Answers

1. Add the data Web control to the page. In the data Web control's smart tag, a Choose Data Source drop-down list will list the data source controls on the page. Select the data source control that you want to bind to the data Web control.

2. False. A data source control only retrieves data from a database. It's up to a data Web control to display it.

3. False. A data Web control merely displays data. It's the data source control that must get the data from the underlying data source. In this way, data source controls and data Web controls work in tandem.

4. By default, the DetailsView control does *not* support paging. That means when visiting the page through a browser, the user will see just the first record in the data source control. To allow the user to step through all the records in the associated data source control, you need to enable paging. You can do this by checking the Enable Paging check box in the DetailsView's smart tab or by setting the `AllowPaging` property to `True` in the Properties window.

5. The format specifier for a currency is `c`. To display just the date portion of a date/time field, use `d`. To use these format specifiers in a GridView or DetailsView field, you need to set the `HtmlEncode` property to `False` and set the `DataFormatString` to `{0:`*`format specifier`*`}`.

Exercises

1. Create a new ASP.NET page named `MyBookTitles.aspx`. Add a SqlDataSource control to the page and configure it to return only the `Title` column from the `Books` table, ordering the results alphabetically by `Title`. Next, add a GridView to the page and bind it to the SqlDataSource. Take a moment to format the GridView using the Auto Format dialog box.

   Test this page by visiting it through a web browser.

2. Create another ASP.NET page, this one named `MostRecentlyReadBook.aspx`. Add a SqlDataSource that returns all columns from the `Books` table but orders them by `LastReadDate` in descending order. Next, add a DetailsView to the page and bind it to the data source control. Do not enable paging in the DetailsView.

   Customize the field-level properties so that only the `Title`, `Author`, and `LastReadOn` fields are displayed, where the `Title` field is displayed in *italics* and the `LastReadOn` field is displayed in **bold**. Change the `LastReadOn` field's `HeaderText` property to `Finished Reading On` and have it formatted so only the date is displayed.

   Test this page by visiting it through a web browser.

HOUR 16

Deleting, Inserting, and Editing Data

In this hour, we will cover

- Configuring the SqlDataSource for updating, inserting, and deleting
- Learning the basics of the `UPDATE`, `INSERT`, and `DELETE` statements, which are SQL statements for modifying database data
- Editing and deleting data with the GridView
- Inserting data with the DetailsView

ASP.NET's data Web controls make displaying data a breeze—simply drag a GridView or DetailsView onto a page and bind it to a configured data source control. In addition to displaying database data, we may need to let a user *modify* the database's contents. For example, in the preceding hour we saw how to show the list of books in the `Books` table. It might be nice to allow visitors to add their own books to the table or leave comments about a particular book.

In addition to displaying data, the GridView and DetailsView controls can also be used to insert new records and delete and edit the data being displayed. Best of all, this can all be accomplished without having to write a single line of code! These code-free insert, update, and delete capabilities are possible thanks to the power of the data source controls.

We have a lot to cover in this hour. But after you've worked through this hour, you'll be able to display, edit, update, and delete data from a database through an ASP.NET page.

Updating, Deleting, and Inserting Data with the SqlDataSource

In addition to being able to retrieve data, data source controls can also be used to modify data. The SqlDataSource control can be configured to insert new records into the database and delete or modify existing records. After the SqlDataSource has been configured to support inserting, updating, and deleting, this functionality can be utilized by the GridView and DetailsView controls, allowing users not only to view, but also update, insert, and delete data from a database via a web page.

Adding support for inserts, updates, and deletions with the SqlDataSource control is as easy as checking a check box. To illustrate this process, take a moment to create a new ASP.NET page called `RichDataSourceEx.aspx`. Next, drag on a SqlDataSource control and configure the data source. As before, select the appropriate database or the connection string in the first step and then proceed to the Configure the Select Statement screen.

Make sure the `Books` table is selected in the drop-down list and then check the `*` option to retrieve all columns from the table. At this point you have configured the SqlDataSource control to retrieve all records and columns from the `Books` table using the query `SELECT * FROM [Books]`, just like we did in Hour 14, "Accessing Data with the Data Source Web Controls." To set up the SqlDataSource to support updating, deleting, and inserting, click the Advanced button, which brings up the Advanced SQL Generation Options dialog box (see Figure 16.1).

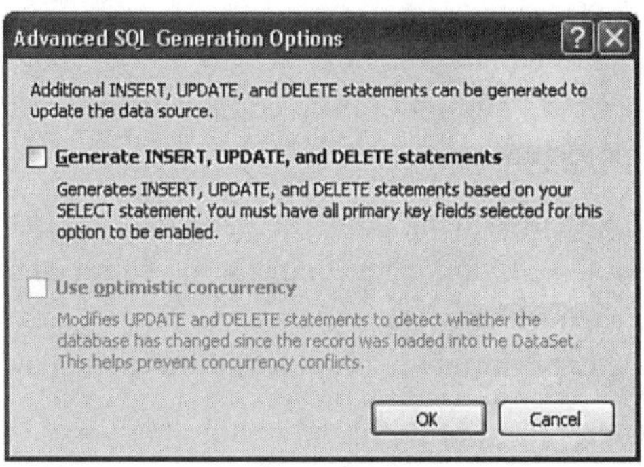

FIGURE 16.1 Add inserting, updating, and deleting support from the Advanced SQL Generation Options dialog box.

This dialog box has two check boxes: Generate INSERT, UPDATE, and DELETE Statements and Use Optimistic Concurrency. To enable the SqlDataSource's capabilities for inserting, updating, and deleting data, check the first check box. As we'll see in the section "Looking at the Data Modification SQL Statements," in addition to the

SELECT statement, SQL includes INSERT, UPDATE, and DELETE statements for inserting, updating, and deleting data. When we check the Generate INSERT, UPDATE, and DELETE Statements check box, the SqlDataSource automatically creates these data modification SQL statements in addition to the SELECT statement.

By the Way

Because the SqlDataSource wizard can generate INSERT, UPDATE, and DELETE statements only when the SELECT statement provides a means to uniquely identify each row, the Generate INSERT, UPDATE, and DELETE Statements check box is selectable only if the columns you selected in the Configure the Select Statement screen include the table's primary key. For our example, you must include BookID in the column list, either by selecting * (which will return all columns) or checking the BookID column name.

If you forgot to make the BookID column in the Books table a primary key column, the Generate INSERT, UPDATE, and DELETE Statements check box will never be selectable regardless of what columns are selected. In this case, take a moment to review the discussion on the creation of the Books table and the role of primary key columns in Hour 13, "An Introduction to Databases," and then update the table, making BookID a primary key.

The second check box, Use Optimistic Concurrency, is selectable only if the first check box is checked. Use Optimistic Concurrency allows updates and deletions to occur only if the data being updated or deleted has not changed since the data was last accessed from the database. It is useful if you expect to have multiple, concurrent users potentially updating or deleting the same data. Optimistic concurrency is an advanced topic that we don't have time to explore in this book. For more information, see "Implementing Optimistic Concurrency with the SqlDataSource Control," available online at www.asp.net/learn/data-access/tutorial-50-vb.aspx.

Check the first check box, Generate INSERT, UPDATE, and DELETE Statements, leaving the Use Optimistic Concurrency check box unchecked. Click the OK button to return to the Configure the Select Statement screen. Click Next to go to the Test Query screen and click Finish to complete the SqlDataSource wizard.

Looking at the SqlDataSource Control's Declarative Markup

After you've completed the SqlDataSource control's wizard, take a minute to view the declarative markup generated by the wizard. Go to the Source view; you should see markup identical to that shown in Listing 16.1.

LISTING 16.1 **The SqlDataSource Control's Markup Contains Commands for Deleting, Inserting, and Updating**

```
 1: <asp:SqlDataSource ID="SqlDataSource1" runat="server"
➥ConnectionString="<%$ ConnectionStrings:ConnectionString %>"
 2:      DeleteCommand="DELETE FROM [Books] WHERE [BookID] = @BookID"
➥InsertCommand="INSERT INTO [Books] ([Title], [Author], [YearPublished],
➥ [Price], [LastReadOn], [PageCount]) VALUES (@Title, @Author,
➥@YearPublished, @Price, @LastReadOn, @PageCount)"
 3:      SelectCommand="SELECT * FROM [Books]" UpdateCommand="UPDATE [Books]
➥SET [Title] = @Title, [Author] = @Author, [YearPublished] = @YearPublished,
➥ [Price] = @Price, [LastReadOn] = @LastReadOn, [PageCount] = @PageCount
➥WHERE [BookID] = @BookID">
 4:      <DeleteParameters>
 5:          <asp:Parameter Name="BookID" Type="Int32" />
 6:      </DeleteParameters>
 7:      <UpdateParameters>
 8:          <asp:Parameter Name="Title" Type="String" />
 9:          <asp:Parameter Name="Author" Type="String" />
10:          <asp:Parameter Name="YearPublished" Type="Int32" />
11:          <asp:Parameter Name="Price" Type="Decimal" />
12:          <asp:Parameter Name="LastReadOn" Type="DateTime" />
13:          <asp:Parameter Name="PageCount" Type="Int32" />
14:          <asp:Parameter Name="BookID" Type="Int32" />
15:      </UpdateParameters>
16:      <InsertParameters>
17:          <asp:Parameter Name="Title" Type="String" />
18:          <asp:Parameter Name="Author" Type="String" />
19:          <asp:Parameter Name="YearPublished" Type="Int32" />
20:          <asp:Parameter Name="Price" Type="Decimal" />
21:          <asp:Parameter Name="LastReadOn" Type="DateTime" />
22:          <asp:Parameter Name="PageCount" Type="Int32" />
23:      </InsertParameters>
24: </asp:SqlDataSource>
```

In Hour 14 we saw the declarative markup of the SqlDataSource when it was configured to issue just a `SELECT` statement, and it was much simpler than the 24 lines of markup shown in Listing 16.1. However, the simplicity from Hour 14 was possible because we were only retrieving data from a database; here, we need to include markup that specifies how to also insert, update, and delete that data.

In addition to the `SelectCommand` on line 3, three additional command statements are on lines 2 and 3: `DeleteCommand`, `InsertCommand` (both on line 2), and `UpdateCommand` (line 3). These command statements specify the SQL statements that will be passed to the underlying database when inserting, updating, or deleting data. In addition to these command statements, a number of related parameters exist, spanning from line 4 down to line 23. Recall that the SQL statements in a SqlDataSource control can use **parameters**, which are placeholders for values to be inserted at a later point in time. The parameters are denoted in the command statements using `@`*`ParameterName`*.

The parameters' names and types are defined in the `<DeleteParameters>`, `<UpdateParameters>`, and `<InsertParameters>` sections. For example, in the `DeleteCommand` statement, a single parameter, `@BookID`, is used to uniquely identify the row that's to be deleted. Then, in the `<DeleteParameters>` section (lines 4—6), a single `<asp:Parameter>` element identifies that the `BookID` parameter is an integer. Notice, however, that no value is specified for this parameter. Recall that in Hour 14, when we used the SqlDataSource wizard's capabilities to add filter expressions, we provided a hard-coded value for the `WHERE` clause. This hard-coded value then appeared in the associated `<asp:Parameter>` element.

The `<asp:Parameter>`s in the `<DeleteParameters>`, `<UpdateParameters>`, and `<InsertParameters>` sections, however, lack any hard-coded values. The reason is that their values will be determined at runtime. That is, the value of the `@BookID` parameter for the `DeleteCommand` depends on what row the user has decided to delete; that particular row's `BookID` will be used as the value for the `@BookID` parameter.

Later in this hour we'll be looking at how to work with the GridView and DetailsView controls to insert, update, and delete data. At that point it will become clearer how visitors will indicate what record they want to delete or update and how the data Web control plugs that information into the data source control. For now, though, just understand that checking the Generate INSERT, UPDATE, and DELETE Statements check box in the Advanced SQL Generation Options dialog box causes the data source control to provide commands and parameters for inserting, updating, and deleting the data specified in the Configure the Select Statement screen of the wizard.

Looking at the Data Modification SQL Statements

As we discussed in Hour 14, SQL is the language used by all modern databases to retrieve and modify data. We've already examined the `SELECT` statement, which is used to retrieve data. Let's now turn our attention to three other SQL statements: `INSERT`, `UPDATE`, and `DELETE`. These three statements are automatically generated by the SqlDataSource control when appropriately configured and are instrumental in modifying a database's content.

A thorough understanding of the `INSERT`, `UPDATE`, and `DELETE` statements is not required. After all, the SqlDataSource will create the necessary statements for you; all you need to do is check the appropriate check box! However, I do think it is worthwhile to have at least a cursory understanding of the syntax and semantics of these statements.

If you are already familiar with the basics of these three SQL statements, feel free to skip this section because it is intended for readers who are new to SQL. The "Editing and Deleting Data with the GridView" section begins our examination of modifying data through an ASP.NET page.

Examining the `INSERT` Statement

The `INSERT` statement, as its name implies, inserts a new record into a database table. The general syntax is as follows:

```
INSERT INTO TableName(Column1, Column2, ..., ColumnN)
VALUES(Column1Value, Column2Value, ..., ColumnNValue)
```

Here *`Column1`*, *`Column2`*, ..., *`ColumnN`* is a comma-delimited list of the column names of the table whose values you are providing in the `VALUES` portion. You do not want to include column names for any Auto-increment columns; furthermore, you may optionally omit a column if it either has a default value specified or accepts Nulls, in which case the default value will be used if it exists; otherwise, a Null value will be inserted. The *`Column1Value`*, *`Column2Value`*, ..., *`ColumnNValue`* is the place where you specify the values for the columns listed.

These rules for when to supply a column value for the `INSERT` statement should sound familiar. In Hour 13 we looked at adding records to an existing database table through Visual Web Developer. In that example, we did not specify values for the Auto-increment column (`BookID`) or those records where we wanted to insert a Null value. Similarly, we had to provide a value for those columns that did not allow Nulls.

Now that we've discussed the general form of the `INSERT` statement, let's look at a more concrete example. The following `INSERT` statement was generated by the SqlDataSource control's wizard (refer to Listing 16.1, line 2):

```
INSERT INTO [Books] ([Title], [Author], [YearPublished], [Price],
➥LastReadOn], [PageCount])
VALUES (@Title, @Author, @YearPublished, @Price, @LastReadOn, @PageCount)
```

Note that the `INSERT` statement adds a new record to the `Books` table and provides values for all fields except for `BookID`. `BookID` is omitted from the column list because it is an Auto-increment column, which means that the database system supplies the value. (Providing a value for `BookID` will result in an error when the code is executed.)

Rather than providing specific values in the VALUES clause, the InsertCommand uses parameters—@Title, @Author, @YearPublished, and so on. As we will see later in this hour, the DetailsView can be used to collect the visitor's input and use that input to insert a new record into the underlying database table. Specifically, when the visitor provides the data, the DetailsView control assigns it to the appropriate parameters of its data source control and then invokes the data source control's InsertCommand.

Deleting Data with the DELETE Statement

The general form of the DELETE statement is as follows:

```
DELETE FROM TableName
WHERE whereCondition
```

The WHERE condition is optional, but you'll almost always want to include it because the DELETE statement deletes all records from the table *TableName* that match the WHERE condition. Consequently, if you omit the WHERE clause (or forget to add it), *all* records from the table *TableName* will vanish into thin air!

Most commonly, the DELETE statement is used to delete one record at a time. For example, the DeleteCommand used by the SqlDataSource has a WHERE clause that's based on the Books table's primary key column, BookID. (Remember that the primary key column is what uniquely identifies each row in the table.)

```
DELETE FROM [Books]
WHERE [BookID] = @BookID
```

In some circumstances you might want to relax the WHERE condition to delete multiple records. For example, if you wanted to delete all books that were published in 2005, you could use this statement:

```
DELETE FROM [Books]
WHERE YearPublished = 2005
```

This might delete zero books, one, three, ... maybe all of them. The result would depend on the values of the YearPublished column.

Editing Data with UPDATE

The UPDATE statement is used to change the values of existing rows. With UPDATE you can specify what columns to change to what values; like the DELETE statement, the UPDATE statement contains a WHERE clause that specifies the scope of the update. That is, the UPDATE statement can be used to update a single row (which is how it is most commonly used), or it can be used to update a batch of records.

The general form of the UPDATE statement is as follows:

```
UPDATE TableName SET
  Column1 = Column1Value,
  Column2 = Column2Value,
  ...
  ColumnN = ColumnNValue,
WHERE whereCondition
```

The column/value list after the UPDATE *TableName* SET portion indicates what columns' values are being changed and to what values. The *whereCondition* indicates what rows this update applies to; if you omit the WHERE clause, the update applies to *all* records in the table.

The UpdateCommand in Listing 16.1 (line 3) updates a single record in the Books table and updates the values of all columns except for the Auto-increment column:

```
UPDATE [Books] SET
  [Title] = @Title,
  [Author] = @Author,
  [YearPublished] = @YearPublished,
  [Price] = @Price,
  [LastReadOn] = @LastReadOn,
  [PageCount] = @PageCount
WHERE [BookID] = @BookID
```

The WHERE clause is based on the primary key column, so only one record from the database table will be updated with this statement.

At this point we have examined how to configure a SqlDataSource to generate the INSERT, UPDATE, and DELETE commands through its wizard and have taken a cursory look at the related SQL statements. We're now ready to turn our attention to configuring the data Web controls to insert, update, and delete data. In the next section, "Editing and Deleting Data with the GridView," we'll see how to use the GridView to edit and delete data. Further on, in the "Inserting Data with the DetailsView" section, we'll see how to insert data using the DetailsView.

Editing and Deleting Data with the GridView

In addition to displaying data, the GridView can be used to edit and delete data. To edit or delete data, the GridView must be bound to a data source control that has an UpdateCommand and a DeleteCommand. Fortunately, these command statements can be automatically generated for us by the SqlDataSource control's wizard when retrieving data from a database table with a primary key.

Like adding sorting and paging support to a GridView, enabling editing and deleting support is as simple as checking a check box in the GridView's smart tag.

In this section we are going to examine editing and deleting as two separate tasks. However, there's no reason why you can't create a GridView whose data can both be edited and deleted. Just follow the steps from the editing and deleting sections on a single GridView.

Allowing Users to Delete Data

The GridView can be configured to provide the user with the ability to delete the GridView's underlying data, one record at a time. A deletable GridView adds a field of Delete buttons or links; to delete a particular row, the user visiting the page clicks the applicable row's Delete button. After the Delete button is clicked, the ASP.NET page is posted back. The GridView then populates the appropriate data source control parameters with the appropriate values and invokes its data source control's `DeleteCommand`. After it issues this command, the GridView reretrieves and redisplays its data from its data source control. From the user's perspective, she clicks a particular row's Delete button and that row disappears.

This interaction that occurs automatically is not trivial and deserves a bit of exploration. Before we worry about the intricacies, however, let's first create a working, deletable GridView. Start by creating a new ASP.NET page called `DeleteBook.aspx`. As you may have guessed, this page will list all the books in the `Books` table, providing a Delete button for each. The visitor to this page can then delete a book from the table by clicking the book's corresponding Delete button.

After the page is created, go to the Design view and drag on a SqlDataSource control. Configure the data source so that the query returns all records and all columns from the Books table, and have the wizard generate the `INSERT`, `UPDATE`, and `DELETE` statements (but don't check the Use Optimistic Concurrency check box).

After the data source has been configured, add a GridView to the page and specify its data source as the SqlDataSource you just added. If you configured the data source control correctly, in the GridView's smart tag there will be an Enable Deleting check box. Check this.

Checking the Enable Deleting check box will update the Design view to show a field of Delete links (see Figure 16.2). Congratulations, you've created a deletable GridView! Take a moment to test your page by going to the Debug menu and choosing Start Without Debugging. In the browser, if you click a particular row's Delete link—poof!—that record disappears because it has been deleted.

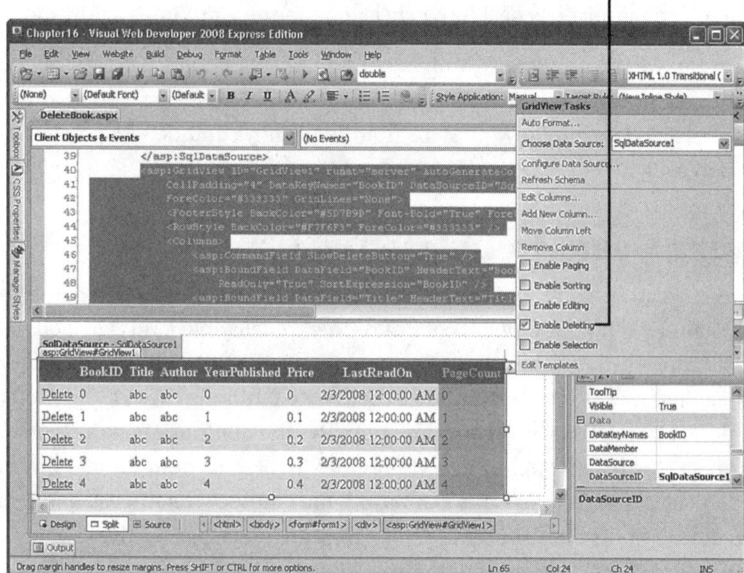

FIGURE 16.2 The GridView has been configured to support deleting.

Customizing the Delete Field

By default, the Delete field displays as a column of links with the word "Delete" as the text for each link. You can customize this field if needed, changing the link text or having the link displayed as a button or image. To accomplish this, go to the GridView's smart tag and click the Edit Columns link, which displays the Fields dialog box (see Figure 16.3).

In the bottom-left corner are the fields displayed in the GridView. In addition to the BoundFields for displaying the `BookID`, `Title`, `Author`, and other columns, there's also a CommandField called Delete. This CommandField was automatically added when the Enable Deleting check box was checked in the GridView's smart tag.

Selecting the Delete CommandField in the lower-left corner displays its properties on the right. The first property in the Appearance section is `ButtonType`, which dictates how the Delete field is displayed. Currently, it is set to its default value, `Link`, which causes the Delete field to render as a series of links. You can change the field's appearance by setting this property to `Button` or `Image`.

If you have `ButtonType` set to `Link` or `Button`, you can customize the text displayed in the button or link using the `DeleteText` property. If you are using a `ButtonType` value of `Image`, set the `DeleteImageUrl` property to the URL of the image to display.

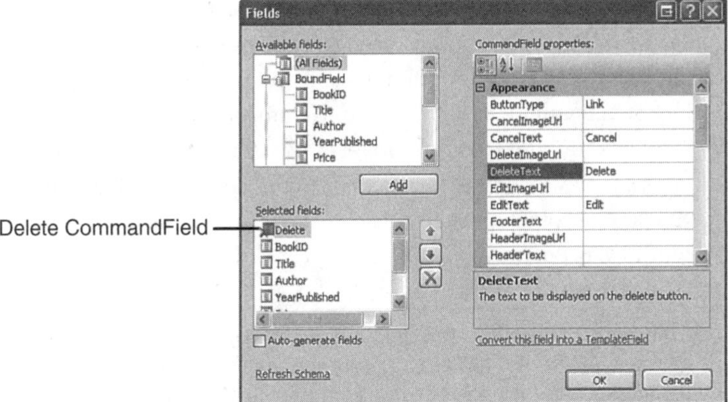

FIGURE 16.3
A CommandField named Delete was added when the Enable Deleting check box was checked.

Figure 16.4 shows the GridView in the Visual Web Developer Design tab after the Delete field has been customized to render as a button with the `DeleteText` "Delete Book."

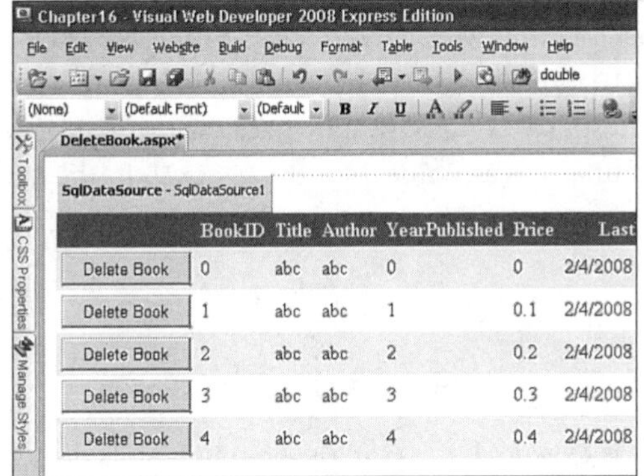

FIGURE 16.4
Each row in the GridView includes a Delete Book button.

The Delete field's aesthetic appearance—its background color, font, alignment, and so on—can be customized through the various properties in the Style section of the Fields dialog box. Refer to Hour 15, "Displaying Data with the Data Web Controls," for a more in-depth look at customizing the GridView's fields.

Looking at the Inner Workings of Deleting

What, exactly, happens when the end user clicks a Delete button? From the end user's perspective, the page flashes and the record whose Delete button he clicked vanishes. But what happens behind the scenes?

When a user clicks the Delete button, a postback ensues. On postback, the GridView notes that a particular row's Delete button has been clicked and in response raises its RowDeleting event. The GridView then takes the value that uniquely identifies the row (the BookID value), assigns that to its data source control's <DeleteParameters> @BookID parameter, and invokes the DeleteCommand. The data source control, then, issues the DELETE statement to the database, substituting in the value of the @BookID parameter. After it deletes the record via its data source control, the GridView raises its RowDeleted event.

Did you Know?

> If you need to programmatically tap into the deleting life cycle, you can do so by creating an event handler for the RowDeleting or RowDeleted events. The RowDeleting event handler can be used to programmatically abort the delete. For example, if the user attempts to delete a book authored by Scott Mitchell, you might want to cancel the delete. Check out the exercises at the end of this hour for some practice with programmatically canceling a deletion.

For example, imagine that the user visits DeleteBook.aspx and clicks the Delete button for the book *The Number*. This causes a postback, and the GridView control is notified that the Delete button was clicked for its third row. The GridView then determines that the BookID value for the third row is 3, assigns this to the @BookID parameter of its data source control, and invokes the DeleteCommand. The data source control substitutes in the value 3 for the @BookID in the DELETE statement, sending the following statement to the underlying database:

```
DELETE FROM [Books]
WHERE [BookID] = 3
```

This would delete *The Number* from the Books table.

After this statement is executed, the GridView reretrieves its data from its data source control. Because there are now only four books, the GridView is rendered with only four rows. The result is that the user visiting the page now sees the four remaining books in the Books table.

At this point you may be wondering how the GridView knows that the third row is uniquely identified by a BookID value of 3. The GridView control has a property called DataKeyNames that can be set to the name(s) of the primary key columns(s) of the data being bound to the GridView. If this property is set, the GridView automatically keeps track of each of the primary key column value(s) of each of its rows. When you bind a data source control to a GridView, this property is automatically set to the primary key column(s) returned by the data source control. (Take a moment to check out the Properties window for the GridView; you'll see that the DataKeyNames property is set to BookID.)

It is imperative that the underlying database table's primary key column or columns are specified in the GridView's `DataKeyNames` property. If this property value is missing, clicking the Delete button will cause the page to postback but won't delete the record because the GridView cannot determine the value that uniquely identifies the row. If clicking the Delete button leaves the page unchanged, take a moment to make sure that the `DataKeyNames` property is set.

Creating an Editable GridView

In addition to providing deleting support, the GridView also offers functionality that allows the end user to edit the GridView's underlying data. Specifically, when the GridView is configured to support editing, an Edit button is added to each row. When the end user clicks the Edit button, the row becomes **editable**, which means, by default, that its various editable fields turn into text boxes. Also, the Edit button is replaced by two new buttons: Update and Cancel. The user can then enter the new values for the record into these text boxes and click the Update button to save her changes, or she can click the Cancel button to return to the pre-editing GridView without saving any changes. Figure 16.6 shows a browser displaying an editable GridView where the user has clicked on the second row's Edit button.

The steps for creating an editable GridView are similar to those for creating a GridView that supports deleting:

1. Add a SqlDataSource to the ASP.NET page that is configured to include the `INSERT`, `UPDATE`, and `DELETE` commands.
2. Add a GridView to the page, binding it to the data source control added in step 1.
3. From the GridView's smart tag, check the Enable Editing check box.

In other words, the only difference is that instead of checking the Enable Deleting check box, you check the Enable Editing check box. (You can check *both* check boxes to create an editable GridView that supports deleting.)

Although enabling editing support is fairly straightforward, often we'll want to tailor the GridView's default editing interface. Fortunately, this is relatively easy and, like many of the other GridView's features, can typically be accomplished without having to write any code.

Before we delve into customizing the GridView's editing interface, let's first practice creating an editable GridView. Start by creating a new page named `EditBooks.aspx` and follow the three steps outlined at the beginning of this section. After you check the Enable Editing check box in the GridView's smart tag, the Visual Web Developer Design view should display an Edit field, as shown in Figure 16.5.

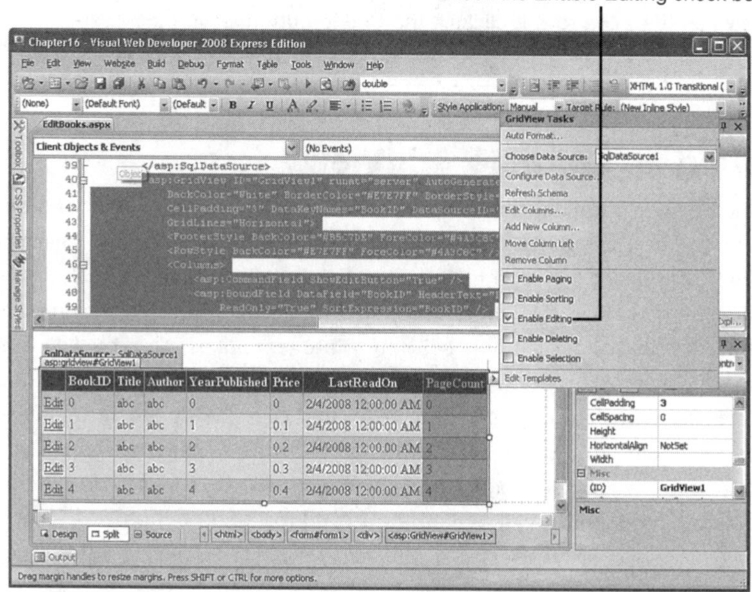

FIGURE 16.5
A CommandField named Edit was added when the Enable Editing check box was checked.

At this point you have created an editable GridView. Take a moment to try out this GridView in a browser. Each GridView row has an Edit link that, when clicked, makes the row editable. The end user can enter new values for the editable fields and click the Update link to save his changes (see Figure 16.6).

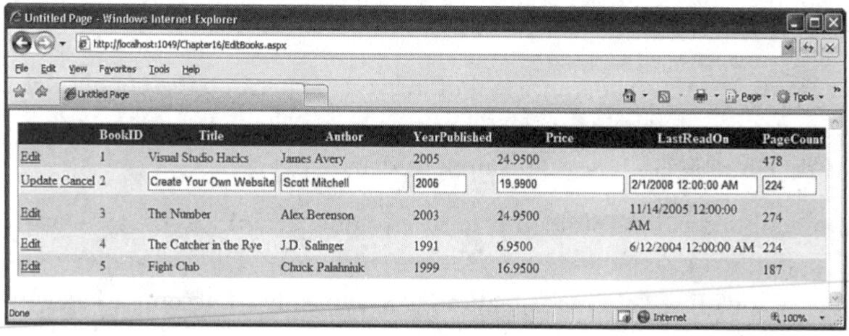

FIGURE 16.6
The user has opted to edit the second row of this editable GridView.

Watch Out!

As with deleting, editing data through a GridView requires that the underlying database table's primary key column or columns be specified in the GridView's `DataKeyNames` property. If this property value is reset, any changes specified to the editable record in a GridView won't be saved back to the underlying data. If you experience this when testing the GridView through a browser, ensure that the `DataKeyNames` property is set accordingly.

The format of the values entered into the editable row's text boxes is sensitive to the underlying database table's data type. For example, the `LastReadOn` field's underlying database table column's data type is `datetime`. Therefore, if you attempt to edit a row and enter an invalid `datetime` value—like **`Yesterday`**—you'll get an exception when you click the Update button.

Similarly, if a field does not accept Null values or doesn't have a default value defined, you must provide a value. In our example, if you clear out the `Title` field value and try to save the changes, you'll get an exception.

In the "Customizing the Editing Interface and Updating Rules" section, we'll see how to change the interface for each field in the editable row, including how to add validation controls to ensure that a value was entered or conforms to a particular data type.

Did you Know?

The GridView's Edit field's appearance can be customized just like the Delete field. That is, you can turn the Edit link into a button or image and change the text displayed in the Edit link or button. As with the Delete field, the Edit field's settings can be modified through the Fields dialog box.

Customizing the Editing Interface and Updating Rules

Take a moment to try out the editable GridView. Try entering different values for different fields or omitting values and see what happens. As you likely will discover, it is fairly easy to end up with an exception when saving an editable GridView. Simply omit the value for a required field (such as `Title` or `Author`) or put in a improperly formatted value (such as **`Long`** for the `PageCount` field). Figure 16.7 shows the resulting page in Internet Explorer when attempting to update the book *Visual Studio Hacks* with the `LastReadOn` value of **`Yesterday`**.

These exceptions arise because the GridView blindly passes back to its data source control whatever values the end user provides. When the data source control attempts to issue an `UPDATE` statement to the database with improperly formatted or missing values, the database raises an exception, which is what you see in Figure 16.7.

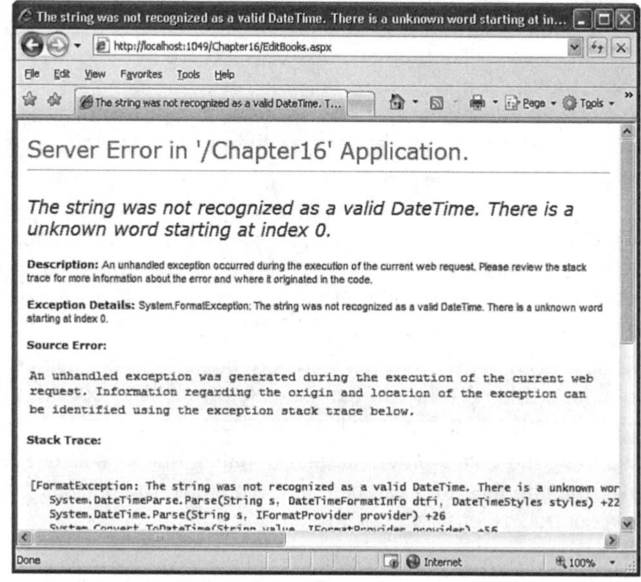

FIGURE 16.7 Attempting to input an improperly formatted string into the `LastReadOn` field results in an exception.

To prevent these types of errors, we need to customize the editing interface generated by the GridView. The GridView allows you to customize the markup used for each field. For example, for the `Title`, `Author`, `YearPublished`, `Price`, and `PageCount` fields, we need to include a RequiredFieldValidator control to ensure that the user has entered a value. A CompareValidator should be added to the `Price`, `LastReadOn`, `YearPublished`, and `PageCount` fields to ensure that the values entered by the user are of the proper data type and, perhaps, bounded by some value or values. (We might want to ensure that the value entered for `Price` is always greater than or equal to 0, for example.)

In addition to customizing the interface for an editable field, we might want to indicate that a particular field should not be editable. When the GridView row in Figure 16.6 is edited, notice that the `BookID` field remains as text, disallowing the end user from modifying the value of a row's `BookID`. The GridView automatically makes Auto-increment columns read-only because their values cannot be explicitly specified. We can easily indicate that other fields should be read-only as well. For example, we might not want to let a user change the title of a book.

Finally, the GridView provides options that can be set to indicate how the user-entered data should be sent to the database. If the user omits entering a value for a string data type (like `Title`, `Author`, and so on), should the database record be updated using Null or a blank string? These settings can be managed through the Fields dialog box.

Over the next few sections we'll examine each of these methods of customizing the editing interface and specifying database-related update rules.

Marking Fields as Read-Only

Making a field read-only is a two-step process:

1. Set the BoundField's `ReadOnly` property to `True`.
2. Remove the read-only field from the SqlDataSource's `UpdateCommand` and `UpdateParameters` properties.

For practice, let's make the `Title` field read-only. The first step is to set the `Title` field's `ReadOnly` property to `True`. Go to the Fields dialog box and select the `Title` field from the field list in the lower-left corner, loading its properties on the right. One of the properties in the Behavior section is named `ReadOnly`. Set this property to `True` (see Figure 16.8).

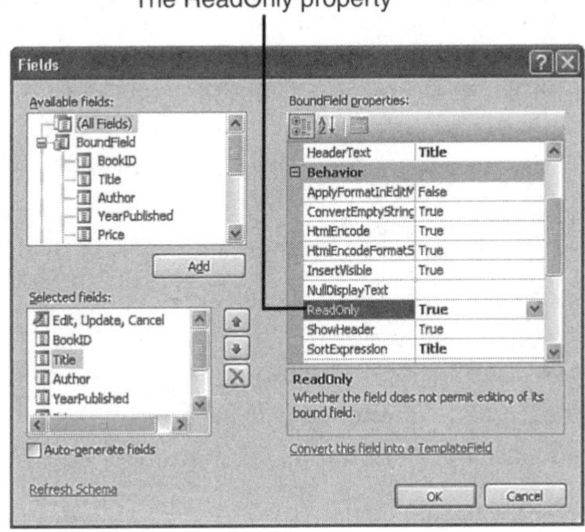

FIGURE 16.8
Set the `ReadOnly` property to `True` to make a field uneditable.

Visit the `EditBooks.aspx` page through a browser and click the Edit button for a row. Because the `Title` field's `ReadOnly` property was set to `True`, it is displayed as text, thereby disallowing the user to modify the value.

At this point we are only halfway done with making the `Title` field read-only. We still need to update the SqlDataSource control's `UpdateCommand` and `UpdateParameters` properties, removing references to `Title`. The easiest way to accomplish this is to select the SqlDataSource control from the Design view, loading its properties in the Properties window. Next, locate the `UpdateQuery` property and click the ellipses to bring up the Command and Parameter Editor dialog box (see

Figure 16.9). This dialog box displays the UpdateCommand and UpdateParameters properties.

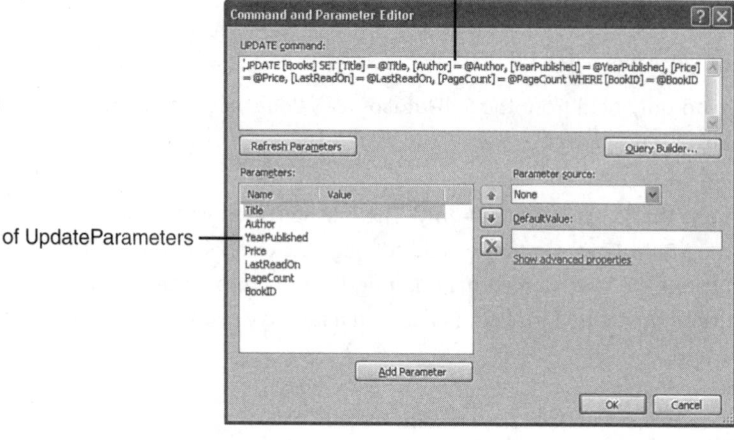

FIGURE 16.9 Update the SqlDataSource control's `UpdateCommand` and `Update Parameters` properties.

The `UpdateCommand` shown in Figure 16.9 contains a reference to the `Title` column and parameter:

```
UPDATE [Books] SET [Title] = @Title, ...
```

Remove this reference so that the `UPDATE` statement starts with

```
UPDATE [Books] SET [Author] = @Author, ...
```

Also remove the `Title` parameter by selecting it from the list of parameters in the lower-left corner and then clicking the red X icon. After making these modifications, click the OK button to close the Command and Parameter Editor dialog box.

Watch Out!

Don't forget that making a GridView field read-only is a two-step process. Consider what will happen if you perform only the first step—setting the field's `ReadOnly` property to `True`—but forget the second—removing the field from the SqlDataSource control's `UpdateCommand` and `UpdateParameter` properties. When the user editing a GridView row clicks the Update button, the GridView populates the values entered into the TextBoxes into the SqlDataSource's `UpdateParameters` collection.

Read-only fields lack a TextBox, so the GridView does not specify their values. Without a specified value, the SqlDataSource will use a Null value for the read-only field. This will have one of two effects: either the read-only field's value will be overwritten with a Null value, if the column allows Nulls; or, if the column disallows Nulls, an exception will be thrown indicating that Nulls are not allowed.

Editing and Formatted Fields

In the preceding hour we looked at how to format the values of the GridView fields, such as formatting the `Price` field as a currency and the `LastReadOn` field to display just the date and omit the time. By default, the formatting applied to a GridView field is not carried over to the default editing interface. To highlight this, take a moment to format the `Price` and `LastReadOn` fields using the currency and date-only format strings. To accomplish this, perform the following steps:

1. Open the Fields dialog box by clicking the Edit Columns link in the GridView's smart tag.
2. Click the appropriate field in the list of fields in the lower-left corner.
3. Set the `HtmlEncode` property to `False` for both the `Price` and `LastReadOn` fields, and set the `DataFormatString` property to `{0:c}` and `{0:d}`, respectively.

After you make these settings, the Design view in Visual Web Developer should show the fields formatted as specified. Next, view the page in a browser and click the Edit button for a row (see Figure 16.10). As you can see, the values for the `Price` and `LastReadOn` fields are properly formatted for the noneditable rows. For the row being edited, however, the text box shows the values in their unformatted state.

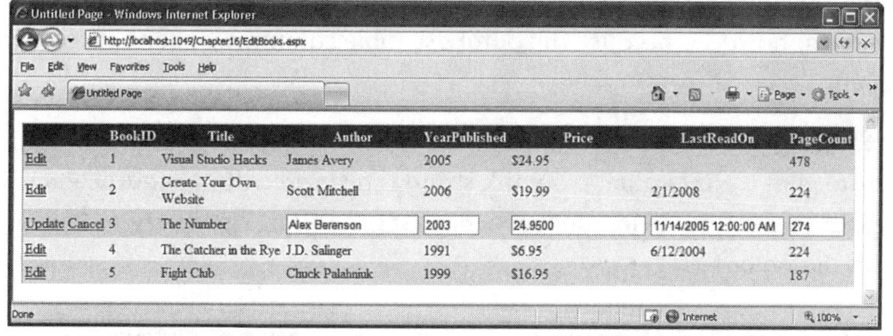

FIGURE 16.10 The formatting for the `Price` and `LastReadOn` columns isn't applied to the editable row.

You can indicate that the formatted values should apply for the editable view through the field's `ApplyFormatInEditMode` property, which is accessible through the Fields dialog box. By default, this value is `False`; if you set it to `True`, however, the formatting will apply to the row being edited. Because we are interested only in the date of the `LastReadOn` date field and not the time, it makes sense to set the `ApplyFormatInEditMode` property of the `LastReadOn` field to `True`.

Before you set the `ApplyFormatInEditMode` property of the `Price` field to `True`, realize that doing so will cause problems because the currency formatting introduces illegal characters. The `Price` field is tied to a database table column of type `money`, which expects a numeric value. If you apply the currency formatting, however, the formatted expression includes a currency symbol (such as a dollar sign). If the user edits a row and doesn't remove the currency symbol from the `Price` TextBox, when she saves the changes, the ASP.NET page will raise an exception. (There's no problem with formatting the `LastReadOn` field because if a date value lacks a time portion the database automatically assigns a time value of midnight.)

Using Nulls or Blank Strings

Some fields in the GridView map to database table columns that allow Nulls. For example, the `LastReadOn` column does not require a value; if we've yet to read the book, we can put a Null in this column. By default, if the user omits a value for a field, the GridView attempts to place a Null value in the corresponding database table column. To illustrate this concept, edit a row that has a `LastReadOn` date value and clear out this value from the text box. After saving this change, check out the database table's data; you'll see that a Null value has been placed in the book's `LastReadOn` column.

Sometimes, however, you may want to have the GridView use a blank string as opposed to a Null value. For example, imagine that you had a GridView field that mapped to a database table column that was of type `nvarchar` that did not allow Nulls. (Recall that `nvarchar` fields hold strings.) Now, if a user editing a GridView leaves off the value for this field, the GridView will use a Null value; this will cause an exception, however, because the database table column was configured to not allow Nulls.

To remedy this, you would need to have the GridView's field opt to use a blank string instead of a Null value. (A blank string is a string with no characters.) To accomplish this, set the field's `ConvertEmptyStringToNull` property to `False` via the Fields dialog box.

Replacing the Autogenerated TextBox with a Custom Editing Interface

When you click the Edit button in a GridView, by default all the editable fields are converted into text boxes. Sometimes, though, you might not want to use a text box as the editing interface, or you might want to augment the editing interface by tweaking the text box's appearance or by including validation controls. For example, it would be prudent to include RequiredFieldValidators for those GridView fields that map to database columns that do not allow Nulls and for which we do not want to allow a blank string to be present. Furthermore, we should add

CompareValidators to the numeric and date/time fields to ensure that the data format entered by the user conforms to the corresponding data type.

To customize the editing interface for a field, convert it from a BoundField into a TemplateField. The BoundField—which is added by default after associating a GridView with a data source control—displays the associated data source control column values as text for the noneditable rows and as a text box for the editable row. A TemplateField, on the other hand, allows us, the page developers, to specify precisely the Web controls that will be used in displaying the column values for both the editable and noneditable rows.

A TemplateField is defined as a collection of **templates**, where a template is a mix of Web controls and static HTML markup. The TemplateField offers five templates, all of which are optional:

- ItemTemplate
- AlternatingItemTemplate
- EditItemTemplate
- HeaderTemplate
- FooterTemplate

As the GridView is rendered row by row, a TemplateField is rendered depending on the row's type and the templates available. For example, if the TemplateField has a HeaderTemplate specified, when the field's header row is rendered, the HeaderTemplates markup is used. For noneditable items, the Item Templates or AlternatingItemTemplates are used, depending on whether the AlternatingItemTemplate is defined and, if so, whether the row is a normal row or an alternating row. For the editable row, the EditItemTemplate is used, if provided.

This may, understandably, sound a bit confusing at this point. I hope things will become clearer after you see an example. To illustrate using a TemplateField, we first need to create one. You can add a brand new TemplateField to the GridView if you like, but because we want to customize the editing interface of an existing BoundField template, we can turn those BoundFields into TemplateFields. To accomplish this, open the Fields dialog box, select the BoundField to turn into a TemplateField, and click the `Convert this field into a TemplateField` link at the bottom of the properties on the right (see Figure 16.11).

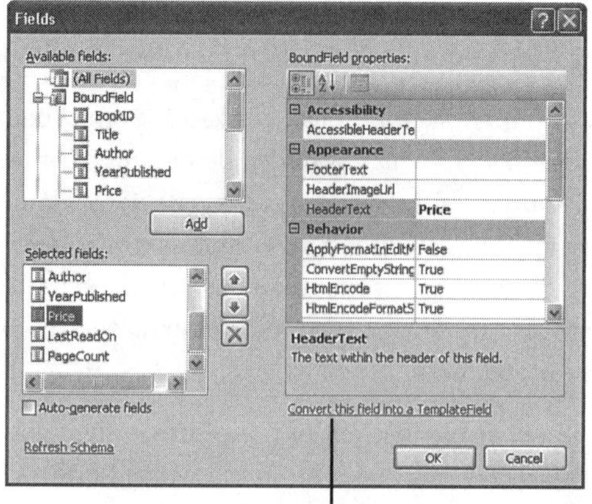

Click the Convert this field into a TemplateField link

FIGURE 16.11 To customize the editing interface, turn the BoundField into a TemplateField.

Take a moment to convert the `Price` field into a TemplateField and then close the Fields dialog box by clicking the OK button. You won't notice anything different in the Design view. In fact, if you test the page through a browser, it will behave just as it did before converting the field to a TemplateField. The reason is that converting the BoundField into a TemplateField creates a TemplateField with two templates: an ItemTemplate that contains a Label Web control and an EditItemTemplate that contains a TextBox Web control.

Listing 16.2 shows the GridView's declarative markup after converting the `Price` field into a TemplateField (pay particular attention to lines 10 through 17).

LISTING 16.2 The TemplateField Has an ItemTemplate and EditItemTemplate

```
 1: <asp:GridView ID="GridView1" runat="server" AutoGenerateColumns="False"
➥DataKeyNames="BookID"
 2:     DataSourceID="SqlDataSource1" BackColor="White" BorderColor="#DEDFDE"
➥ BorderStyle="None" BorderWidth="1px" CellPadding="4" ForeColor="Black"
➥GridLines="Vertical">
 3:     <Columns>
 4:         <asp:CommandField ShowEditButton="True" />
 5:         <asp:BoundField DataField="BookID" HeaderText="Book ID"
➥InsertVisible="False" ReadOnly="True"
 6:             SortExpression="BookID" />
 7:         <asp:BoundField DataField="Title" HeaderText="Title"
➥ReadOnly="True" SortExpression="Title" />
 8:         <asp:BoundField DataField="Author" HeaderText="Author"
➥SortExpression="Author" />
 9:         <asp:BoundField DataField="YearPublished" HeaderText="Published"
➥ SortExpression="YearPublished" />
10:         <asp:TemplateField HeaderText="Price" SortExpression="Price">
11:             <EditItemTemplate>
```

LISTING 16.2 Continued

```
12:                 <asp:TextBox ID="TextBox1" runat="server"
➥Text='<%# Bind("Price") %>'></asp:TextBox>
13:             </EditItemTemplate>
14:             <ItemTemplate>
15:                 <asp:Label ID="Label1" runat="server"
➥Text='<%# Bind("Price", "{0:c}") %>'></asp:Label>
16:             </ItemTemplate>
17:         </asp:TemplateField>
18:         <asp:BoundField DataField="LastReadOn" HeaderText="LastReadOn"
➥SortExpression="Last Read" ApplyFormatInEditMode="True"
➥DataFormatString="{0:d}" HtmlEncode="False" />
19:         <asp:BoundField DataField="PageCount" HeaderText="PageCount"
➥SortExpression="Pages" />
20:     </Columns>
21:     <FooterStyle BackColor="#CCCC99" />
22:     <RowStyle BackColor="#F7F7DE" />
23:     <SelectedRowStyle BackColor="#CE5D5A" Font-Bold="True"
➥ForeColor="White" />
24:     <PagerStyle BackColor="#F7F7DE" ForeColor="Black"
➥HorizontalAlign="Right" />
25:     <HeaderStyle BackColor="#6B696B" Font-Bold="True" ForeColor="White" />
26:     <AlternatingRowStyle BackColor="White" />
27: </asp:GridView>
```

Note that the `<EditItemTemplate>` (lines 11–13) and `<ItemTemplate>` (lines 14–16) sections contain a single Web control. Furthermore, the Web controls' Text properties are assigned a value using data binding syntax. Data binding syntax has the form `<%# Bind(`*`columnName`*`, `*`optionalFormatSpecifier`*`) %>` and grabs a particular column value from the data source control. In the `<ItemTemplate>` a Label Web control is configured to display the value of the `Price` column formatted as a currency (`{0:c}`); in the `<EditItemTemplate>`, a TextBox Web control's `Text` property is assigned the value of the `Price` column.

A TemplateField's templates can also be edited through the Design view. From the GridView's smart tag, click the Edit Templates link. This shows the ItemTemplate for the `Price` field. You can edit other templates by selecting them from the drop-down list. Figure 16.12 shows the Design view when editing the ItemTemplate of the `Price` field.

Did you Know?

To exit the template-editing interface and return to the GridView in the Design view, click the End Template Editing link in the smart tag (see Figure 16.12).

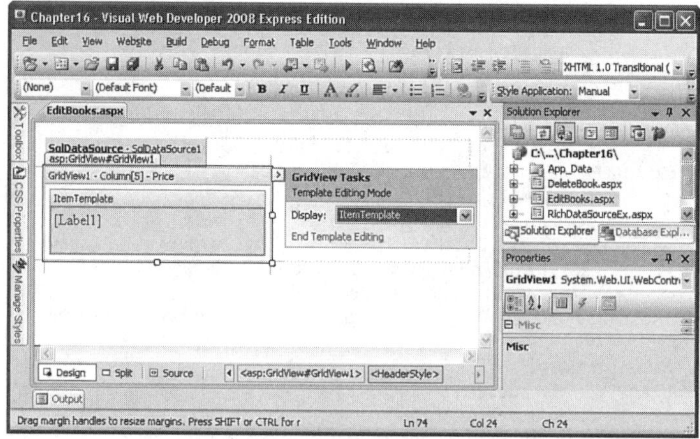

FIGURE 16.12
A TemplateField's templates can also be edited through the Design view.

Note that the ItemTemplate contains a Label Web control with ID `Label1`. This is the Label control whose declarative markup appeared on line 15 of Listing 16.2. Click the Label Web control and examine the Properties window. Note that the `Text` property has a little disc icon next to it; this indicates that the `Text` property is assigned using a data binding expression.

Did you Know?

You can edit the data binding expression for a Web control through the DataBindings dialog box, which is accessible by clicking the Edit DataBindings link in the Web control's smart tag.

By the Way

We'll be examining data binding syntax in much greater detail in Hour 18, "Exploring Data Binding and Other Data-Related Topics," and Hour 19, "Using Templated Data Web Controls."

Next, change the template being viewed from the ItemTemplate to the EditItemTemplate. You should now see a TextBox Web control whose `Text` property in the Properties window also has a disc icon. To customize the `Price` field's editing interface, make any necessary modifications to the EditItemTemplate. For our page, let's do the following:

1. Put a currency symbol in front of the TextBox Web control to indicate to the user that she doesn't need to enter a currency symbol. To accomplish this, click in the EditItemTemplate before the TextBox Web control and then type in the appropriate currency symbol.
2. Set the TextBox Web control's `Columns` property to 10, shortening the length of the TextBox.

3. Add a RequiredFieldValidator control to the EditItemTemplate by dragging it from the Toolbox into the EditItemTemplate. Set its `ControlToValidate` property to the `ID` of the TextBox in the EditItemTemplate, its `Display` property to `Dynamic`, and its `ErrorMessage` property to `You must enter a price.`
4. Add a CompareValidator control to the EditItemTemplate and configure it to require that the user enter a currency value greater than or equal to 0. (That is, set the `Type` property to `Double`, the `Operator` property to `GreaterThanEqual`, and the `ValueToCompare` property to `0`. Don't forget to set the `ControlToValidate`, `Display`, and `ErrorMessage` properties, as well.)

By the Way

If you need to refresh your memory on using the ASP.NET validation controls, consult Hour 12, "Validating User Input with Validation Controls."

After you have completed these four steps, view the page through a browser and attempt to edit the `Price` field. Note that if you omit the price or attempt to enter a noncurrency value or a currency value less than zero, you will receive a descriptive error message, and the value will not be saved to the database (see Figures 16.13 and 16.14).

In addition to adding validation controls and tweaking the TextBox Web control's aesthetic properties, when customizing the editing interface, you can replace the TextBox Web control with a more appropriate Web control, if needed. For example, if a GridView field displayed the gender of the book's author, we might want to have a drop-down list of genders rather than requiring the user to type in Male or Female. The exercises in this hour include a task that involves customizing the editing interface by replacing the TextBox with an alternative input Web control.

By the Way

We set the CompareToValidator's `Type` property to `Double` instead of `Currency` because the default format of the data returned by the database leaves the price with four decimal places (such as `6.9500`). However, the `Currency` data type used by the CompareValidator requires the value to have at most two decimal places. Therefore, if we used a `Type` of `Currency`, the validator would complain whenever we edited a row and did not manually pare down the value from four decimal places to two (or fewer).

A better workaround would be to adjust the data binding expression used in the `Text` property of the `Price` field's TextBox Web control. Ideally, we would have the result formatted to two decimal places, which could be accomplished using the following format specifier: `{0:0.00}`. Interested readers are encouraged to try to tweak the data binding expression to format the data like so; if you succeed, feel free to change the CompareValidator's `Type` to `Currency`.

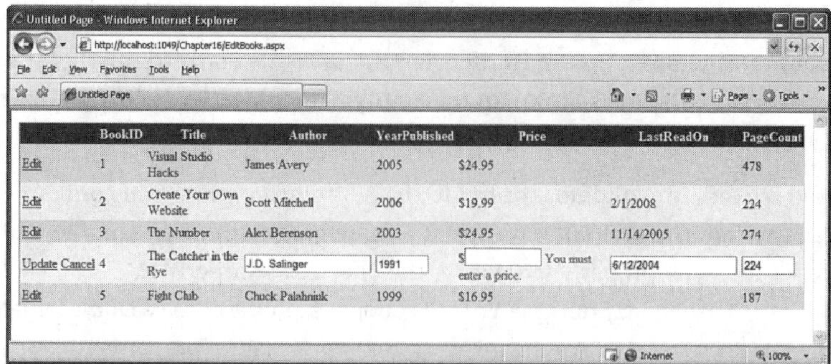

FIGURE 16.13
A message is displayed if the `Price` field value is omitted.

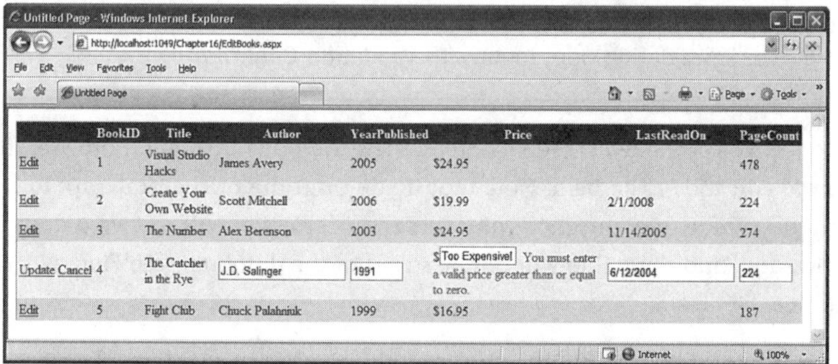

FIGURE 16.14
The GridView won't post back until a valid currency value is provided for the `Price` field.

Inserting Data with the DetailsView

Although the GridView makes editing and deleting data a breeze, it doesn't provide a way to insert a new record into the database. The DetailsView, however, does, and configuring the DetailsView to provide inserting support is quite similar to adding editing and deleting support to a GridView.

> In addition to providing inserting support, the DetailsView also offers editing and deleting capabilities. We won't be examining the DetailsViews' editing and deleting support; I leave that as an exercise for you. You'll find, though, that enabling and configuring editing and deleting support in the DetailsView is nearly identical to providing such functionality with the GridView.

As with the GridView, the first step in creating a DetailsView that supports inserting is to add a SqlDataSource control to the page that has been configured to include the `INSERT`, `UPDATE`, and `DELETE` statements. Take a moment to create a new ASP.NET page named `AddBook.aspx` and add and configure the SqlDataSource control as we've done throughout this hour.

Next, add a DetailsView to the Design view and bind it to the SqlDataSource control. In the DetailsView control's smart tag, you'll find an Enable Inserting check box. Check this. Doing so adds a New button beneath the other DetailsView fields, as shown in Figure 16.15. (Also take a moment to check the Enable Paging check box so that we can scroll through the records rather than just sitting at the first record.)

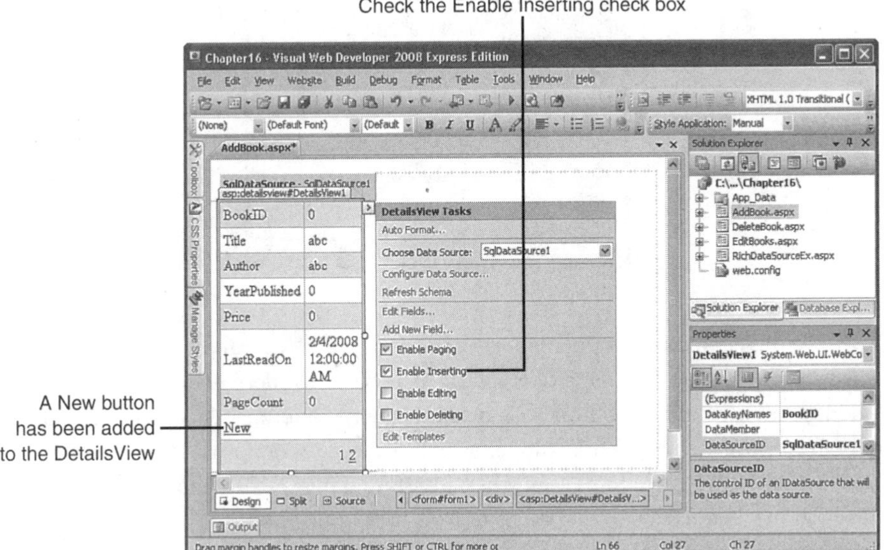
Check the Enable Inserting check box
A New button has been added to the DetailsView

FIGURE 16.15 The DetailsView has been configured to support inserting.

When you view the ASP.NET page through a browser, you'll see that the first book, *Visual Studio Hacks*, is displayed, with links to page through the results. Additionally, there's a New link that, when clicked, displays the DetailsView in an insertable mode (see Figure 16.16). When the DetailsView is in insertable mode, the user can enter values for the various editable fields, creating the new record by clicking the Insert button.

Customizing the Insertable DetailsView

Like the GridView, the insertable DetailsView is highly customizable. Enabling inserting in a DetailsView adds an Insert field to the DetailsView, which can be examined through the Fields dialog box. Like the Edit or Delete fields in an editable or deletable GridView, the Insert field's appearance can be customized. By default, it displays the text "Insert" as a link, but these appearance settings can be changed via the field's `ButtonType` and `InsertText` properties.

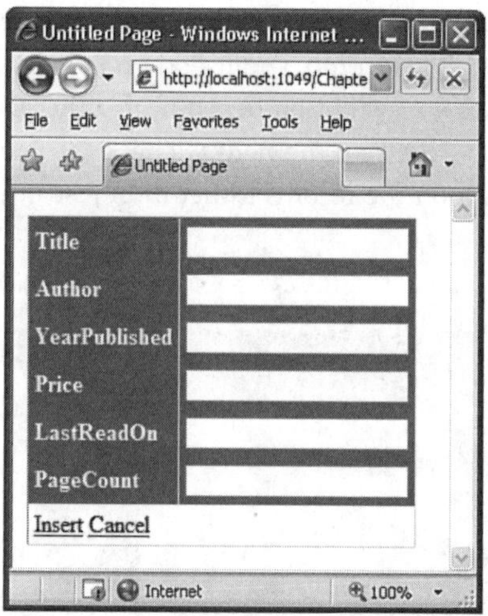

FIGURE 16.16 Clicking the New button displays the DetailsView in insertable mode.

Each DetailsView field has an `InsertVisible` property that can be set through the Fields dialog box. If this property is set to `False`, the field does not appear when adding a new record. By default, all Auto-increment columns—`BookID` in our example—have this `InsertVisible` property set to `False`. As Figure 16.16 shows, the `BookID` field is nowhere to be seen when inserting a new record into the `Books` table through the DetailsView's inserting interface.

By the Way

> The DetailsView fields also have a `ReadOnly` property; however, the `ReadOnly` property value is ignored when the DetailsView is in inserting mode. It is used, however, when we're working with an editable DetailsView control.

Like an editable GridView, an insertable DetailsView emits a default inserting interface, which results in a TextBox Web control for each field whose `InsertVisible` property is set to `True`. If you need to customize this inserting interface, convert the BoundFields into TemplateFields and edit their InsertItemTemplates accordingly.

As you can see, working with an insertable DetailsView is very similar to working with an editable GridView. The same issues and customization options exist with both data Web controls.

Summary

In this hour we looked at how to edit, delete, and insert data into a database through an ASP.NET page. As with displaying data, modifying database data through a web page involves both a data source control and a data Web control. To insert, update, or delete data, we need to configure the SqlDataSource control to generate the appropriate `INSERT`, `UPDATE`, and `DELETE` statements, which can be accomplished for us by the SqlDataSource control's Configure Data Source wizard.

When the SqlDataSource has been configured correctly, implementing editing and deleting support with the GridView is as simple as binding the GridView to the data source control and checking the Enable Deleting and Enable Editing check boxes from its smart tag. At a bare minimum, this is all that is needed to implement deleting and editing of the GridView's underlying data. However, often we'll want to customize the Edit or Delete field or tweak the editing interface. These tasks are not difficult—they require zero source code and can be accomplished through Visual Web Developer's Design view. If more advanced logic is required when updating or deleting a GridView's data, a number of related events are fired during the updating and deleting processes. (See the exercises section for practice on one of these GridView events.)

This hour concluded with a look at using the DetailsView to insert new records into the underlying database table. Creating an insertable DetailsView involved the same steps as creating an editable or deletable GridView. Additionally, the DetailsView provides similar mechanisms for customizing the inserting interface as the GridView does for customizing the editing interface.

In this hour and the preceding one, we examined how to display and modify database data using the GridView and DetailsView controls. In the next hour we'll look at binding database data to DropDownList, RadioButtonList, and CheckBoxList controls, and we'll also illustrate how to use the DropDownList and GridView Web controls in conjunction to filter the displayed data.

Q&A

Q. ***When I'm working with a GridView that supports deleting, is there any way to include a confirmation message when a user clicks the Delete button?***

A. You can configure the GridView to display a client-side confirmation message box when the user clicks a Delete button, asking her if she's certain she wants to delete the record (see Figure 16.17). This prompt is displayed before the page is posted back. If the user clicks OK, the page is posted back, and the Delete proceeds exactly as it would have had you omitted the client-side confirmation message box. If, however, the user clicks the Cancel button, the postback is canceled, and therefore the record is not deleted.

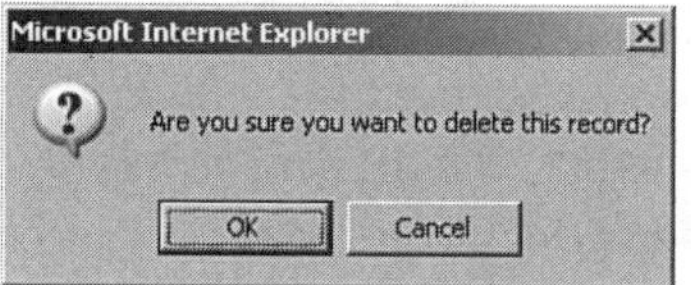

FIGURE 16.17 A client-side confirmation message box prompts the user as to whether she wants to delete the record.

To learn how to add a client-side confirmation message box to each Delete button in a GridView, refer to the "Utilizing Client-Side Script to Confirm Deletions" section of the article online at http://msdn2.microsoft.com/en-us/library/ms972940.aspx.

Workshop

Quiz

1. True or False: You can use the GridView to add new records to a database table.
2. What conditions must be true for the SqlDataSource control's wizard to be able to automatically generate `INSERT`, `UPDATE`, and `DELETE` commands?
3. How do we customize the editing interface of an editable GridView?
4. When a visitor clicks the Delete, Edit, or Insert buttons for the GridView or DetailsView, what sequence of events takes place?
5. What two GridView events fire during the deletion process?

Answers

1. False. The GridView supports only editing and deleting capabilities.
2. The table being queried must have a primary key, and the `SELECT` statement specified must, at minimum, return this primary key.
3. By default, a GridView renders each BoundField as a TextBox Web control. To customize the editing interface, convert the BoundField into a TemplateField and then edit the field's EditItemTemplate, making whatever changes are necessary.
4. When the user clicks one of these buttons, the ASP.NET page is posted back. Upon postback, the GridView or DetailsView notes that the Edit, Delete, or

Insert button was clicked and raises the first of two events: for the GridView, `RowDeleting` for deleting, and `RowUpdating` for updating; for the DetailsView, `ItemDeleting` for deleting, `ItemUpdating` for updating, and `ItemInserting` for inserting.

Next, the data Web control populates the parameters in its data source control's `InsertParameters`, `UpdateParameters`, or `DeleteParameters` collection. The `InsertCommand`, `UpdateCommand`, or `DeleteCommand` command is then invoked, which sends a SQL statement to the database, inserting, updating, or deleting the record. Finally, the data Web control signals that the data modification has completed, raising the `RowDeleted` or `RowUpdated` event for the GridView and `ItemDeleted`, `ItemUpdated`, or `ItemInserted` for the DetailsView.

5. `RowDeleting` and `RowDeleted`.

Exercises

1. In the "Allowing Users to Delete Data" section, we examined how to use the GridView to allow users to delete a record from the GridView. In that section I mentioned that when the user clicks the Delete button, a postback ensues and the GridView, before instructing its data source control to delete the data, raises the `RowDeleting` event. If we want the delete to be canceled if some condition is met, we can create an event handler for this event and determine whether to cancel the delete.

   Your task for this exercise is to create an ASP.NET page that lists the books from the `Books` database table in a GridView that supports deleting. In addition to this GridView control, add a Label Web control on the page. Set its `ID` property to `DeleteFailed`, `Visible` to `False`, and its `Text` property to **`Why oh why would you want to delete this book?`**. (When we set the `Visible` property to `False`, this control won't be rendered, so it won't appear in the user's browser until, on a postback, we set this property to `True`.)

   Next, create an event handler for the GridView's `RowDeleting` event. This event handler will be passed as its second parameter an object of type `GridViewDeleteEventArgs`, which has a property named `Cancel`. We can stop the user-initiated delete by setting this `Cancel` property to `True`. Additionally, this class has a property of type `Values`, which we can use as follows to grab a value from the row that the user is attempting to delete:

   ```
   e.Values(columnName)
   ```

Your task is to cancel the delete and have the `DeleteFailed` Label displayed if the user attempts to delete a book authored by yours truly (Scott Mitchell). If the user is deleting some other author's book, hide the `DeleteFailed` Label and let the delete continue unabated.

Here's a snippet of code to get you started; this will go inside the `RowDeleting` event handler:

```
If e.Values("Author") = "Scott Mitchell" Then
  ...
Else
  ...
End If
```

2. In the "Customizing the Editing Interface and Updating Rules" section, we saw how to use TemplateFields to customize a particular field's editing interface. In this hour we looked at customizing the `Price` field to include both a RequiredFieldValidator and a CompareValidator. These two validation controls ensured that the user provided a currency value for the `Price` that was greater than or equal to zero.

   Complete what we started here, adding RequiredFieldValidators to the `Author`, `YearPublished`, and `PageCount` fields in the `EditBooks.aspx` page. Also add CompareValidator controls to the `YearPublished` and `PageCount` fields to ensure that both fields' values are integers greater than zero.

3. In addition to adding validation controls to a TemplateField's EditItemTemplate, we can also replace the TextBox Web control with a different Web control. For this exercise, customize the editable interface for the `LastReadOn` field, replacing the TextBox with the Calendar Web control.

   To accomplish this, convert the `LastReadOn` field to a TemplateField. Next, delete the TextBox control from the EditItemTemplate and drag a Calendar control from the Toolbox into the EditItemTemplate. At this point test the functionality in the browser. You'll see that when the user tries to edit a row, a calendar is displayed in the editable row's `LastReadOn` field. However, no date is selected in the calendar (even if there's a `LastReadOn` value), and if you select a date from the calendar and click Update, the value is not saved.

   To have the current value displayed in the Calendar Web control and to have the user's selected value persisted back to the database, we need to use a data binding expression that assigns the `LastReadOn` field to the Calendar control's `SelectedDate` property. We can accomplish this through the Design tab by going to the Calendar control's smart tag and clicking the Edit DataBindings link. This will bring up the DataBindings dialog box. Select the appropriate

Web control property from the list on the left (`SelectedDate`) and then select the data source control field to bind to this value from the drop-down list on the right (`LastReadOn`). Make sure the Two-way Databinding check box is checked (see Figure 16.18).

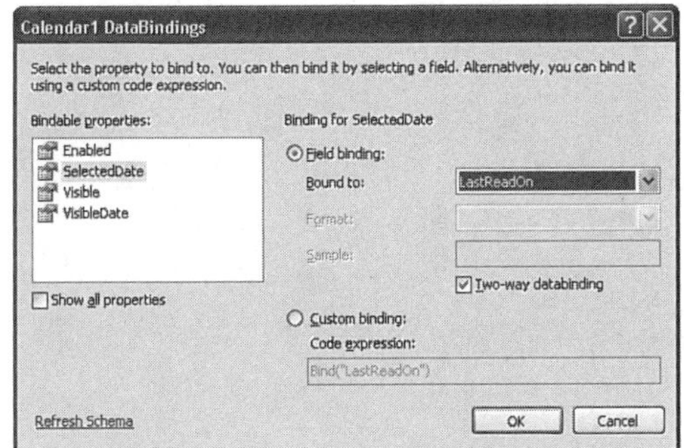

FIGURE 16.18 Bind the `LastReadOn` field to the Calendar's `SelectedDate` property using two-way data-binding.

After making this change, take a moment to test the page in a browser. If you edit a book that has a `LastReadOn` value, the Calendar control's `SelectedDate` property will be assigned to the Calendar. Furthermore, whatever date is selected in the Calendar control is what is saved as the `LastReadOn` value when the Update button is clicked. However, as you may have noticed, when the row is made editable, the Calendar control shows the month and year of the value of its `VisibleDate` property (which defaults to the current date). So if the `LastReadOn` value of the editable row is November 11, 2005, but the current date is March 13, 2006, you'll have to click back through the months to November to be able to see the selected date. Obviously, we want the month and year of the `LastReadOn` date to be shown when a row is first made editable. To accomplish this, go back to the Calendar's DataBindings dialog box and bind the `VisibleDate` property to the `LastReadOn` field value, but this time make sure Two-way Databinding is unchecked.

At this point the editable GridView should work as desired with rows that have a `LastReadOn` value; however, for those rows where this value is Null, you will get an exception when trying to edit. Why this happens, as well as why we had the Calendar's `SelectedDate` property use two-way databinding versus the one-way databinding used by the `VisibleDate` property, are topics we'll discuss in Hour 18, "Exploring Data Binding and Other Data-Related Topics."

HOUR 17

Working with Data-Bound DropDownLists, RadioButtons, and CheckBoxes

In this hour, we will cover

- Populating the items of a drop-down list with the results from a database query
- Creating check boxes and radio buttons based on the results of a database query
- Using the DropDownList control to filter the contents displayed in a GridView
- The benefits of using database information versus hard-coding drop-down list, check box, and radio button values

As we've seen over the past three hours, the data source controls enable us to easily work with database data. We simply specify what table and columns we want to work with and whether we need corresponding `INSERT`, `UPDATE`, and `DELETE` statements. When a data source control has been properly configured, one of a number of data Web controls can be used to interact with that data through an ASP.NET page. In addition to the GridView and DetailsView controls, ASP.NET includes a number of list controls that can also be bound to data source controls: the DropDownList, CheckBoxList, and RadioButtonList controls.

In Hour 11, "Collecting Input Using Drop-Down Lists, Radio Buttons, and Check Boxes," we looked at using the DropDownList, RadioButton, and CheckBox controls in an ASP.NET page, but we had to explicitly provide the values for the drop-down list items, radio buttons, and check boxes. Now that we know how to work with databases, we can reexamine these controls from Hour 11 and see how to populate them with data from a database.

An Overview of the List Web Controls

ASP.NET includes a bevy of Web controls designed for collecting user input, many of which we examined in Hours 10 and 11. The **list Web controls**, a special class of input collection Web controls, present the user with a list of options. The DropDownList, which we examined in Hour 11, falls into this category of list Web controls because it presents users with a series of options from which they must pick one. Although the CheckBox and RadioButton controls represent a single check box or radio button and, therefore, aren't list controls, often multiple radio buttons or check boxes are used in tandem to provide users with a list of check boxes or radio buttons to select among. ASP.NET does provide two Web controls designed to present a list of check boxes or radio buttons. These two Web controls—the CheckBoxList and RadioButtonList—are list Web controls.

The list Web controls share a number of features. Conceptually, they are all a collection of items of one sort or another. The DropDownList is a collection of drop-down list items; the CheckBoxList, a collection of check boxes; and the RadioButtonList, a collection of radio buttons. More concretely, they share a number of programmatic traits, such as

- Each list Web control provides programmatic access to its items through the `Items` property.
- Each item in a list Web control is an instance of the `ListItem` class.
- Each list Web control can optionally be configured to induce a postback when an end user makes a change in the selected state of the control. (This is discussed in the "Automatically Posting Back When a List Web Control Changes" section later in this hour.)
- If a list Web control's selected item or items are changed across postbacks, the `SelectedIndexChanged` event is raised.
- The list Web controls' `Items` collection can be propagated statically, programmatically, or through a data source control.

In Hour 11 we saw how to assign the items of a DropDownList control statically. Recall that the DropDownList's smart tag has an Edit Items link that, when clicked, displays the ListItem Collection Editor dialog box. This dialog box permits us to statically specify the items of a list control. The CheckBoxList and RadioButtonList also have a smart tag with an Edit Items option that likewise brings up the ListItem Collection Editor dialog box.

In addition to specifying a list Web control's items statically, we can assign the values through a data source control. That is, we can add a SqlDataSource control to our page, configure it to grab a set of records from a database table, and then bind that data to the list Web control. For each record returned by the SqlDataSource, the list Web control adds an item to its list.

Binding Data to a List Web Control

Binding data to a list Web control is very similar to binding data to a GridView or DetailsView. The only difference is that whereas a GridView or DetailsView can be bound to a variable number of database table columns, list Web controls can be bound to, at most, two columns. The reason is that each item in a list control has two properties, `Text` and `Value`. The `Text` property is the value displayed onscreen—the text shown in the drop-down list item or the text of the radio button or check box—whereas the `Value` property is not displayed, but provides an additional bit of information about each item.

Let's not get bogged down with the differences between the `Text` and `Value` properties at this point; if the distinction is not clear now, it will be as we work through some examples. For now, let's practice binding database results to the various list Web controls.

Start by creating a new ASP.NET page named `ListControls.aspx`. Next, add a SqlDataSource control to the page and configure it to return all columns and all rows of the `Books` table. You don't need to configure the SqlDataSource control to include the `INSERT`, `UPDATE`, and `DELETE` statements. After you have finished this, drag a DropDownList, CheckBoxList, and RadioButtonList onto the page, preceding each with text that shows the name of the control. After you have added the SqlDataSource control and the three list Web controls, your screen should look similar to Figure 17.1.

Each of these list Web controls has a smart tag with a Choose Data Source link. Clicking this link displays the Data Source Configuration Wizard, which prompts for the data source control to use and the column(s) to bind to the `Text` and `Value` properties of each list Web control. Take a moment to configure the data source for each of the three list Web controls, having each one display the `Title` column and use the `BookID` column as the value. Figure 17.2 shows this dialog box when configuring the DropDownList control's data source.

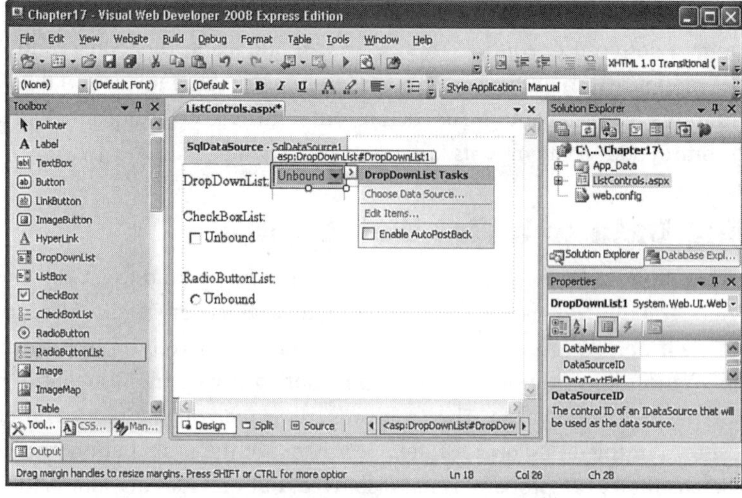

FIGURE 17.1
A SqlDataSource and the three list Web controls have been added to the page.

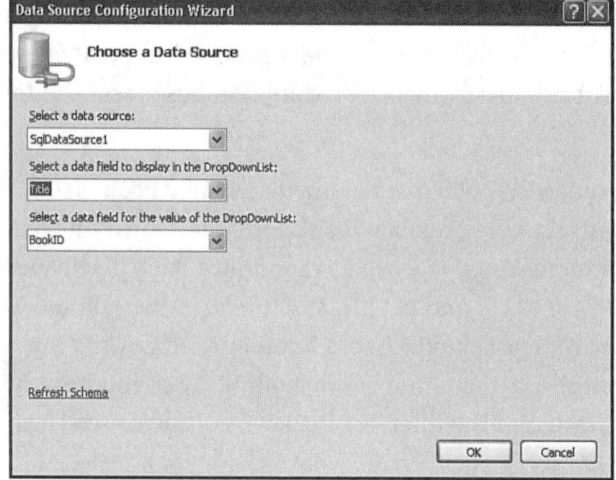

FIGURE 17.2
Choose the data source control and the columns to bind to the list Web control.

After you specify a data source for the list Web control, the Design view in Visual Web Developer will change slightly; instead of using the word `Unbound` for the DropDownList, RadioButtonList, or CheckBoxList (see Figure 17.1), the word `Databound` is used instead. To see the actual values displayed in the drop-down list, check boxes, or radio buttons, you'll need to view the ASP.NET page through a browser. Take a moment to do this and ensure that your screen looks similar to Figure 17.3.

Note that each list Web control has five items, one for each record returned by its SqlDataSource. The difference among the three list Web controls is the way they render their items.

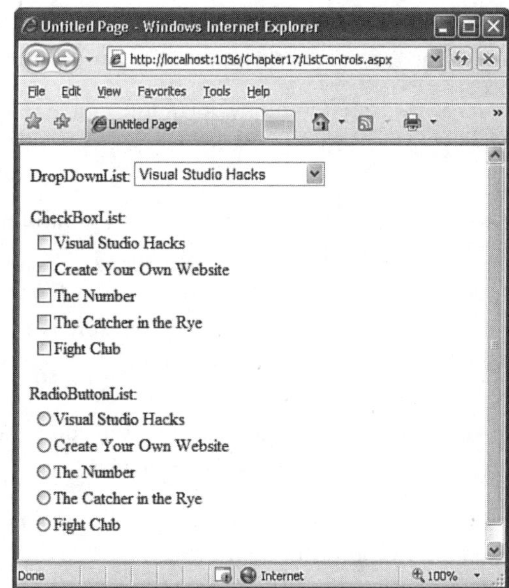

FIGURE 17.3
The list Web controls have five items, one for each book in the `Books` table.

The Benefits of Dynamically Populating a List Control

In Hour 11 we looked at how to populate the items in a DropDownList control statically, using the ListItem Collection Editor dialog box. Both the CheckBoxList and RadioButtonList can have their list items specified statically in this manner. Simply click the Edit Items link in their smart tags.

Although the list Web controls do support having their items set statically, it's often advantageous to do so dynamically, through binding the control to a data source. The problem with statically assigning the items to a list control is that if there are changes to the items to be displayed in the future, you must visit each and every page that uses this data and update the list control appropriately. If you dynamically bind your items, though, and if any changes occur, you can just update the database table from which the items are retrieved and you're done!

For example, in Hour 11 we looked at using a DropDownList that was statically populated with a list of ice cream flavors, from which we asked visitors to choose their favorite. These values were entered statically but could have been entered dynamically. That is, we could have created a table in our database called `IceCreamFlavors` that had two columns:

- **`IceCreamFlavorID`**—A primary key, Auto-increment field of type `int` that uniquely identifies each ice cream flavor
- **`Flavor`**— An `nvarchar(100)` column that contains the name of the flavor (Chocolate, Vanilla, and so on)

Then, in our ASP.NET page, we could use a SqlDataSource control to grab the contents of this table and bind it to the DropDownList. This may sound like a lot of work just to display some ice cream flavors, and this approach obviously isn't as quick as just typing in a handful of flavors in the DropDownList's ListItem Collection Editor dialog box. However, it will save you time if you need to replicate this functionality on other pages, if you expect the list of ice cream flavors to change in the future, or if you need to provide some association, for instance, in the database between users and their favorite ice cream flavors.

I encourage you to use dynamic list Web controls for all but the most trivial scenarios that are guaranteed not to change in the future, such as a drop-down list with gender options, Yes/No options, hours of the day, and so on.

By the Way

In Hour 13, "An Introduction to Databases," we briefly discussed how many real-world databases are composed of multiple, related tables. With such relational database models, scenarios often occur in which you need to populate related data using a list Web control. For such scenarios it is of the utmost importance to grab the data dynamically from the database, rather than hard-coding in the related options statically.

Programmatically Responding to a Changed Selection

When using list Web controls on a web page, we are often interested in knowing when a list control's selected item has changed. Each of the list controls contains a `SelectedIndexChanged` event that fires upon postback if the list control's selection has changed. Returning to our earlier example, `ListControls.aspx`, add a Button Web control and a Label Web control to the page. Set the Button's `ID` and `Text` properties to `SubmitButton` and `Click Me`, respectively. Set the Label's `ID` property to `Status`, and clear out its `Text` property.

Next, create a `SelectedIndexChanged` event handler for the DropDownList. You can accomplish this by double-clicking the DropDownList in the Design view, or by going to the code view and choosing the DropDownList's `ID` and the `SelectedIndexChanged` event from the drop-down lists at the top of the screen.

After you have added this event handler, your ASP.NET page's source code portion should look like this:

```
Partial Class ListControls
    Inherits System.Web.UI.Page

    Protected Sub DropDownList1_SelectedIndexChanged(ByVal sender As Object,
➥ ByVal e As System.EventArgs) Handles DropDownList1.SelectedIndexChanged

    End Sub
End Class
```

This event handler—`DropDownList1_SelectedIndexChanged`— executes whenever the page is posted back and a change has occurred in the selected item of the DropDownList. To test this, add the following line of code in the event handler:

```
Status.Text = "The drop-down list value is now " & DropDownList1.SelectedValue
```

Set a breakpoint at this line by positioning your cursor on the line and pressing F9, or by clicking in the margin; next, start the debugger by going to the Debug menu and choosing Start. This loads the ASP.NET page in a browser. Notice that on the initial page load, the `SelectedIndexChanged` event does not fire because there's been no change to the selected state of the DropDownList. At this point your screen should look similar to Figure 17.3, except with the addition of a button.

By the Way

> The basics of debugging an ASP.NET web page were discussed in Hour 4, "Designing, Creating, and Testing ASP.NET Pages." Feel free to return to Hour 4 to refresh your memory, if needed.

Without changing the value of the DropDownList, click the button, posting back the ASP.NET page. Again, the `SelectedIndexChanged` event does not fire because the selected DropDownList item—Visual Studio Hacks—has yet to change. This time, however, select a different book from the DropDownList and click the button. Upon postback, the `SelectedIndexChanged` event will fire, and the debugger will break on the breakpoint we set. Continue debugging by pressing F5. The browser window should now refresh, displaying a message in the `Status` Label indicating the `BookID` value of the selected book (see Figure 17.4).

Note that if you click the button again without changing the book selection, the `SelectedIndexChanged` event does not fire. As we've seen, it fires only on the postback immediately following a change in the list Web control's selection state.

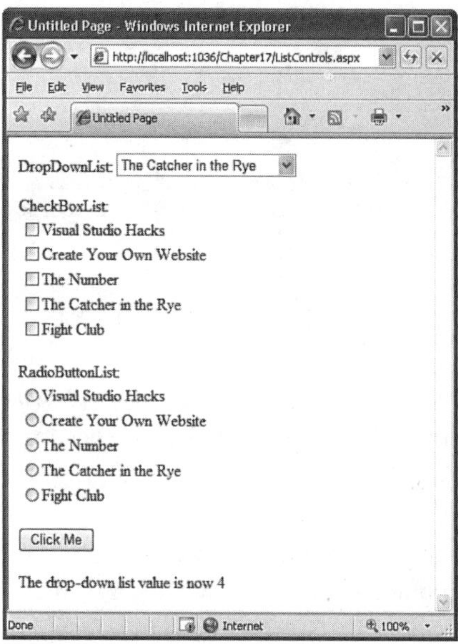

FIGURE 17.4
The Label displays the `BookID` of the currently selected book.

As we discussed in Hour 9, "Web Form Basics," server-side events and code, such as a list control's `SelectedIndexChanged` event and its associated event handler, can fire and execute on the web server only when the browser explicitly rerequests the page (a postback). By default, changing the selection of a list control does not cause a postback. Therefore, the control's `SelectedIndexChanged` event does not fire immediately after the user changes the selection state of a list control, but only when a postback ensues. For instance, in our previous example, you can change the drop-down list from *The Number* to *Visual Studio Hacks*, but the DropDownList Web control's `SelectedIndexChanged` event doesn't fire until the Click Me button is clicked, thereby causing a postback.

If the drop-down list's selection was changed from *The Number* to *Visual Studio Hacks* to *Fight Club*, and then the Click Me button was clicked, the `SelectedIndexChanged` event would fire only once, because from the web server's perspective, the drop-down list's selection has changed only once, from *The Number* to *Fight Club*. Similarly, if the drop-down list is changed from *The Number* to *Visual Studio Hacks*, and then back to *The Number*, and then the Click Me button is clicked, the `SelectedIndexChanged` event won't fire because from the web server's perspective, no selection change has been made—when the web server initially rendered the page, the DropDownList Web control's initial selection was *The Number* and on postback the selection was still *The Number*.

By the Way

In some scenarios, you might be interested to immediately know when a list Web control's selection state has changed. For example, a page might have a "Quick Links" DropDownList that contains some of the popular pages on your website. In this case you might want to have a `SelectedIndexChanged` event handler that redirects the user to the appropriate page whenever the DropDownList value is changed. In such scenarios the page needs to post back as soon as the user changes her selection; the next section discusses how to add such behavior to the list controls.

At other times, you may not really care when a list control's selection changes, but you are interested in what values are selected on postback. In this case, you can put your programmatic login in the Button Web control's `Click` event handler, which will run when the page is posted back.

Automatically Posting Back When a List Web Control Changes

In the smart tags for the list Web controls, you may have noticed a check box labeled Enable AutoPostBack. This check box indicates the value of the control's `AutoPostBack` property, which indicates whether the list Web control induces a postback upon having its selected state changed. As we've seen, by default the list controls don't cause postbacks on their own; rather, a postback is typically caused by the user clicking a Button Web control. Therefore, with list Web controls, the end user can make any sort of change to the list control—checking or unchecking the check boxes of a CheckBoxList, selecting different radio buttons from the RadioButtonList, or choosing different options in the DropDownList—and our server-side code won't know of these changes until the form is posted back.

However, we might want to be immediately alerted whenever a user changes the selection state of a list Web control. That is, if the user chooses a different DropDownList item, checks or unchecks a check box in a CheckBoxList, or picks a different radio button in a RadioButtonList, we might want to be notified right away, rather than having to wait for the user to click a button. We can implement this behavior by checking the Enable AutoPostBack check box in the list Web control's smart tag. With this option selected, the list control is rendered with additional client-side JavaScript that causes a postback as soon as the user alters the selection state. On postback, the list control's `SelectedIndexChanged` event fires.

The remainder of this hour focuses on using these three list Web controls in real-world situations. In the next section we'll see an example of using a DropDownList to filter the results displayed in a GridView. In this example, the DropDownList's `AutoPostBack` property will be set to `True` so that the data is automatically refreshed as soon as the DropDownList is changed. We'll also examine using the RadioButtonList and CheckBoxList to collect and process user input.

Filtering Results Using the DropDownList

In the past three hours we've been working with the Books database table and have seen how to use a GridView to display all the books in this table. In Hour 14, "Accessing Data with the Data Source Web Controls," we saw how to add hard-coded filtering expressions on the SqlDataSource control's SelectCommand to limit the books returned.

Specifying hard-coded filtering expressions is one way to limit the data returned by a data source control, but we might rather allow the user visiting the web page to be able to specify how, exactly, the data is filtered. When specifying the values for a filter expression through the SqlDataSource control's wizard, we can specify that the value be based on another Web control on the page, rather than a hard-coded value. For instance, we can craft a SqlDataSouce control so that its WHERE clause is based on the selected value of a DropDownList control.

To illustrate this, let's first add an additional column to the Books table by which we can easily filter the records. Take a moment to add a Genre column of type nvarchar(50) to the Books table. Because there are existing records in the Books table, you'll either need to give this column a default value or configure it to allow Nulls. For now, let the Genre column allow Nulls.

By the Way

If you need to review how to specify the definition of a SQL Server 2005 database table in Visual Web Developer, consult Hour 13.

Those with a database background know that rather than adding an nvarchar(50) Genre column, we should ideally create a new Genre lookup table, adding a foreign key GenreID to the Books table. Feel free to go this route, if this makes sense to you; if what I just said is Greek to you, don't worry; just create the Genre column as discussed.

After you've added this new table column, view the table data in Visual Web Developer and enter values for the genres for each of the books. I used the genre Technology for *Visual Studio Hacks* and *Create Your Own Website*, the genre Business for *The Number* and the genre Fiction for *The Catcher in the Rye* and *Fight Club*.

Next, create a new ASP.NET page named DropDownList.aspx. When we're done, this page will contain a DropDownList control that lists all the available genres and a GridView control that displays those books that match the genre selected in the DropDownList. This requires two SqlDataSource controls: one to retrieve the list of genres for the DropDownList and the other to grab those books that are of the selected genre for the GridView.

Listing the Genres in a DropDownList

Let's first concentrate on adding the DropDownList of genres. The DropDownList of genres will list each of the genres defined in the `Books` table. The user visiting the page can then filter the GridView results depending on the selected genre from the DropDownList. To create a DropDownList control listing the available genre choices, perform the following steps:

1. Add a SqlDataSource control that is configured to return just the `Genre` column from the `Books` table. Have the results ordered by the value of the `Genre` column in ascending order.
2. After completing the wizard, change this control's `ID` property from `SqlDataSource1` to a more descriptive `GenresDataSource`.
3. Enter the text `Choose a genre:` and then add a DropDownList control to the page. Bind the DropDownList control to the `GenresDataSource` SqlDataSource, using the `Genre` column as both the text and values of the DropDownList's items.
4. Change the DropDownList control's `ID` from `DropDownList1` to a more descriptive `Genres`.

At this point, test your ASP.NET page through a browser (see Figure 17.5). Notice that the drop-down list contains *five* items—one for each record in the `Books` table—even though the table contains only three unique genre values.

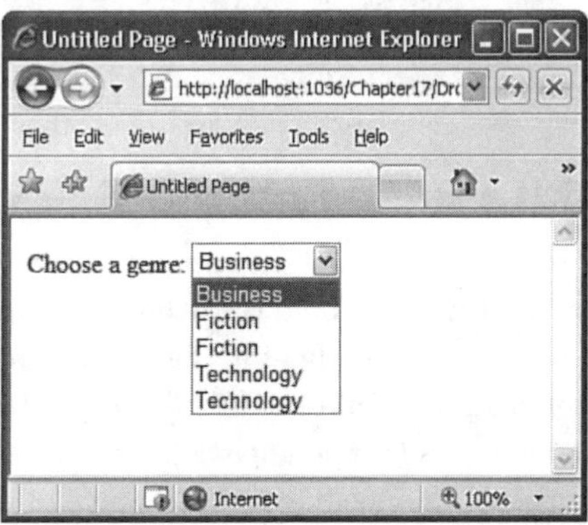

FIGURE 17.5
A drop-down list item is available for each record in the `Books` table, rather than one for each unique genre.

To remedy this, we need to configure the SqlDataSource to return only the *unique* genres in the `Books` table. To accomplish this, reopen the SqlDataSource control's wizard, and in the Configure the Select Statement screen, check the Return Only Unique Rows check box, as shown in Figure 17.6.

Watch Out!

> For this solution to work as needed, it is important that the `SELECT` statement return only a single column, `Genre`.
>
> The Return Only Unique Rows check box looks at *all* columns in the `SELECT` clause and considers a row a duplicate only if *every* value in the column list is equal to some other row's. That is, if you have the `SELECT` statement return, for instance, `Title` and `Genre`, currently all five records will be returned. If there were two books in the database with the same title and genre, then, and only then, would only one of these records be returned.

After making this change, view the page through a browser again. This time the drop-down list will have only three items: Business, Fiction, and Technology.

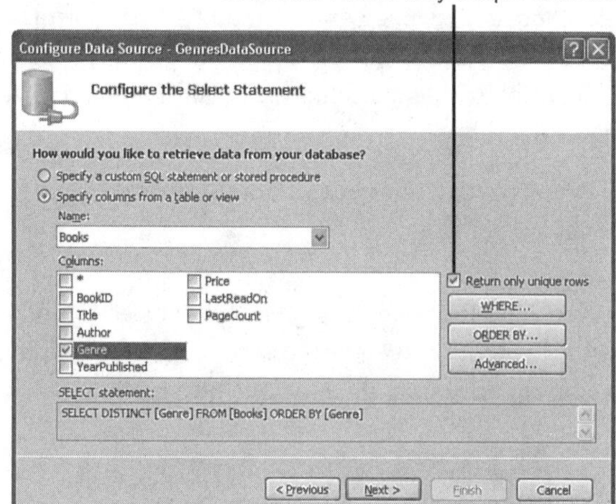

FIGURE 17.6
Only the unique genres will be returned.

Filtering the Data Based on the Selected Genre

Our next step is to add a GridView control that displays only those books that belong to the selected genre. Let's first add a GridView that displays all books from the `Books` table. We've done this many times in the past two hours, so this should be an easy task. Just drag a SqlDataSource onto the page and configure it to return all columns and all records from the `Books` table. As we did with the genre-returning SqlDataSource, change this SqlDataSource control's `ID` from `SqlDataSource1` to a more descriptive `BooksDataSource`. Next, add a GridView to the ASP.NET page, binding it to the `BooksDataSource` data source control. Rename the GridView's `ID` property to `Books`.

Take a moment to test the page in a browser. Because the `BooksDataSource` SqlDataSource isn't filtering the books based on the genre yet, the GridView shows all the books, regardless of what genre is selected from the drop-down list. Our next step, then, is to implement filtering within the `BooksDataSource` SqlDataSource. To accomplish this, return to the data source control's wizard and from the Configure Select Statement screen, click the WHERE button to bring up the Add WHERE Clause dialog box.

We want to add a `WHERE` clause to the `SELECT` statement that looks like this:

```
SELECT *
FROM [Books]
WHERE [Genre] = Genre selected in the DropDownList
```

Because we want this `WHERE` clause to operate on the `Genre` column, choose `Genre` from the Column drop-down list. Select the = operator from the Operator drop-down list and then, from the Source drop-down list, choose Control because we want the filter expression to be based on the value of a Web control on the page. Choosing the Control option updates the Parameter Properties box in the upper-right corner to provide a drop-down list titled Control ID and a text box titled Default Value. From the Control ID drop-down list, select the `Genres` control (the `ID` of our DropDownList); you don't need to pick a default value, so you can leave this text box blank.

Make sure your screen looks similar to Figure 17.7 and then click the Add button to add the parameter to the SqlDataSource. Click OK to return to the Configure the Select Statement screen and then complete the wizard.

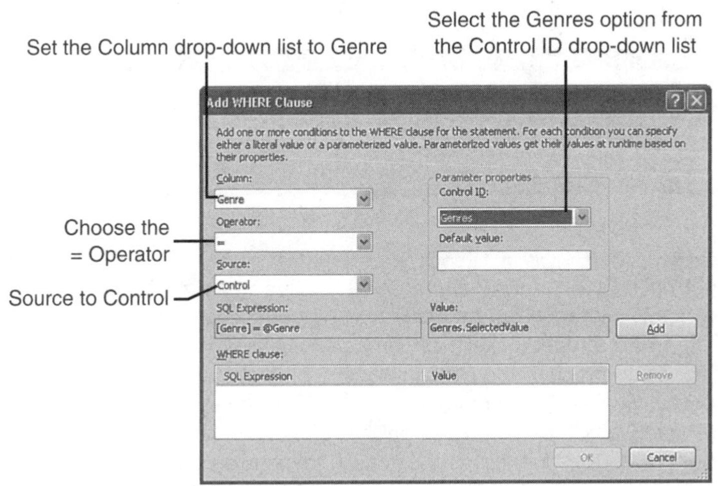

FIGURE 17.7
Add a `WHERE` clause parameter whose value is the selected value of the genres DropDownList.

View the ASP.NET page through a browser again. This time, when the page first loads, the GridView should display only one book, *The Number*, because that's the only book that falls within the Business genre (see Figure 17.8). Go ahead and try changing the drop-down list to another genre. Nothing happens! We still see the GridView with one record, listing *The Number*. The reason is that we've yet to enable `AutoPostBack` in the DropDownList control. Simply changing the DropDownList doesn't cause a postback unless the DropDownList's `AutoPostBack` property is set to `True`. Take a moment to fix this and then revisit the page. Now selecting a different genre from the drop-down list invokes a postback and causes the GridView to be updated (see Figure 17.9).

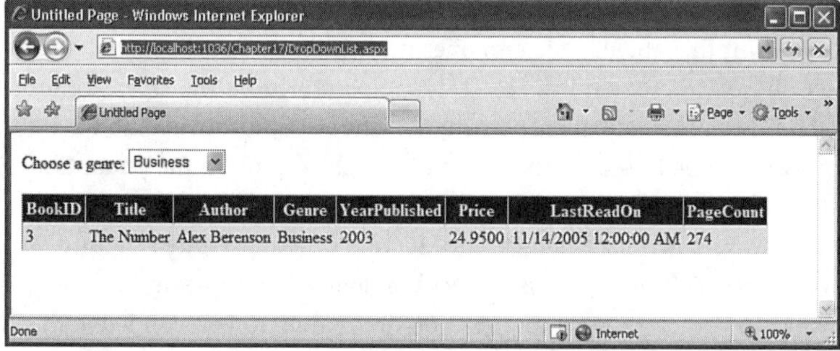

BookID	Title	Author	Genre	YearPublished	Price	LastReadOn	PageCount
3	The Number	Alex Berenson	Business	2003	24.9500	11/14/2005 12:00:00 AM	274

FIGURE 17.8 The `DropDownList.aspx` page, when first visited.

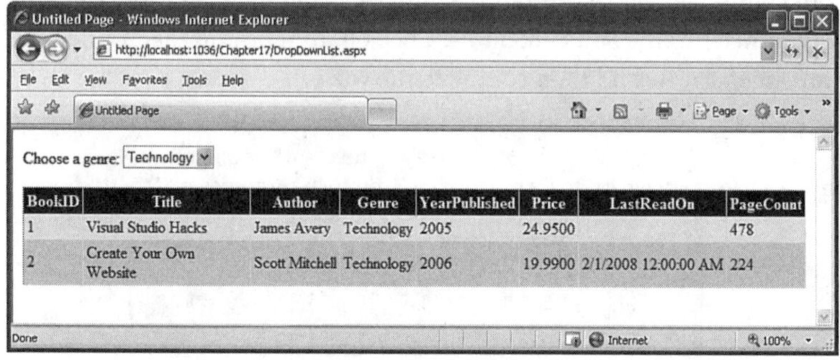

BookID	Title	Author	Genre	YearPublished	Price	LastReadOn	PageCount
1	Visual Studio Hacks	James Avery	Technology	2005	24.9500		478
2	Create Your Own Website	Scott Mitchell	Technology	2006	19.9900	2/1/2008 12:00:00 AM	224

FIGURE 17.9 The page after the user has changed the drop-down list's selection from Business to Technology.

By the Way

Setting the DropDownList's `AutoPostBack` property to `True` was not necessary. We could have optionally added a Button Web control to the page after the DropDownList with a `Text` property like "Refresh." Clicking this would have induced a postback and refreshed the GridView based on the user's drop-down list selection. In essence, we need a postback to refresh the GridView's display, which can be accomplished by either setting the DropDownList's `AutoPostBack` property to `True` or by adding a Button that the user can click to instigate the postback.

Collecting User Input with CheckBoxLists and RadioButtonLists

In Hour 11 we saw how to use the CheckBox and RadioButton controls to collect user input. When using these individual controls, we had to manually add one CheckBox or one RadioButton control for each check box or radio button needed. Rather than using a series of single CheckBox or RadioButton controls, we can use, instead, the CheckBoxList or RadioButtonList.

By the Way

> Recall that a series of check boxes allows the user to select zero to many items from the list of choices. With radio buttons, however, the user is restricted to selecting *one* of the available choices.

The CheckBoxList and RadioButtonList's items can be specified statically via the ListItem Collection Editor dialog box, which you can reach by clicking the Edit Items link in the control's smart tag. The process for adding items to a CheckBoxList or RadioButtonList using the ListItem Collection Editor dialog box is identical to adding items this way for a DropDownList. These steps were covered in detail in Hour 11.

The CheckBoxList and RadioButtonList can also be bound to a data source control as we saw in the "Binding Data to a List Web Control" section earlier in this hour. What we didn't look at earlier, though, was how to determine what item or items, in the case of a CheckBoxList, were selected by the user. There are a couple ways to accomplish this:

- Enumerate the list control's items, checking each item to see if it has been selected.
- Use the `SelectedItem` property to get a reference to the item that was selected.

Let's examine both of these techniques. First, let's create a new ASP.NET page named `CheckAndRadio.aspx` and add a SqlDataSource control, a CheckBoxList, and a RadioButtonList. Configure the SqlDataSource to return all columns and all records from the `Books` table. Bind this SqlDataSource to both the CheckBoxList and RadioButtonList, having the list controls display the `Title` column with their values set to the `BookID` column.

Finally, add a Button Web control and a Label Web control, setting their `ID` properties to `SubmitButton` and `Results`, respectively. Set the Button's Text property to `Click Me` and then create an event handler for its `Click` event. Clear out the `Text` property of the Label control.

Take a moment to view the page through a browser. You should see a series of check boxes listing each of the five books in the table, followed by a series of radio buttons listing the same books.

Enumerating the List Web Control's List Items

As discussed earlier in this hour, all three list Web controls have an `Items` property that is a collection of list items. This collection can be programmatically enumerated using the following code:

```
'Enumerate the list of items in the CheckBoxList
For Each li As ListItem In listWebControlID.Items
  ' Work with the list item, li
Next
```

Within the `For Each` loop, you can access the properties of the current list item (`li`); the germane ones are

- **`Selected`**—A Boolean value indicating whether the list item has been selected by the user
- **`Text`**—The displayed text of the list item
- **`Value`**—The value assigned to the list item

If we wanted to display a list of the selected items in the `Results` Label Web control, we could use the following code:

```
Results.Text = String.Empty

'Enumerate the list of items in the CheckBoxList
For Each li As ListItem In CheckBoxList1.Items
    If li.Selected Then
        Results.Text &= li.Text & " was selected!<br />"
    End If
Next
```

This code starts by clearing out the `Text` property of the Label control and then enumerates the list items of the CheckBoxList `CheckBoxList1`. If an item is selected—that is, if `li.Selected` is `True`— the Label's `Text` property has appended a string indicating that the particular list item was selected. (The `<br />` in the string is an HTML element that adds a breaking line; it's used to help improve the readability of the output in the page.)

Figure 17.10 shows this ASP.NET page. Note that for each selected check box a corresponding message is displayed in the Label. (This approach works equally well for RadioButtonLists.)

FIGURE 17.10
The Label's output is dictated by what check boxes were selected.

Using `SelectedItem` and `SelectedValue`

In Hour 11 we saw how to programmatically determine the selected item or value of the DropDownList using the `SelectedItem` and `SelectedValue` properties. The `SelectedItem` property returns the `ListItem` instance of the selected item; `SelectedValue` returns the value of the selected item. Both the RadioButtonList and CheckBoxList have these two properties as well; however, more care must be taken when using these properties with either of these two controls.

When you're using a RadioButtonList or CheckBoxList, understand that the user may not choose any item. With either of these controls, the user can avoid selecting a check box or radio button. (This concern doesn't exist with the DropDownList control.) Before using these properties, then, you must first ensure that a value was selected. The simplest way to ensure that a value has been selected is to test to see whether the `SelectedItem` property is equivalent to `Nothing`; if it is, that means an item was not selected.

We can use the following code to proceed within the conditional only if an item has been selected. That is, we test to see whether `SelectedItem` is not `Nothing` and, if so, we can then work with the `SelectedItem` or `SelectedValue` properties (see Figure 17.11):

```
'See what item was selected in the RadioButtonList
If RadioButtonList1.SelectedItem IsNot Nothing Then
    results.Text &= "From the RadioButtonList you selected " &
➥RadioButtonList1.SelectedItem.Text
End If
```

Watch Out!

> If you do not use a conditional statement to ensure that `SelectedItem` is not `Nothing`, you will get an exception if the user has not selected any item and you try to access the `SelectedValue` property or one of the properties of `SelectedItem` (such as `SelectedItem.Text`).

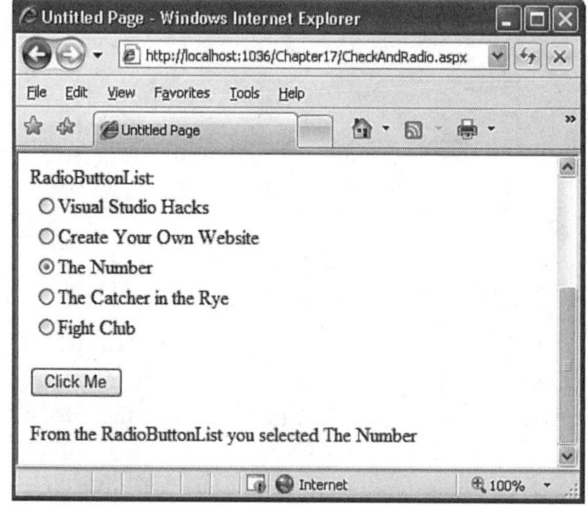

FIGURE 17.11 The selected radio button's text is displayed in the `Results` Label.

Another concern with `SelectedItem` and `SelectedValue` is that they return a single `ListItem` instance or value. How does this work with the CheckBoxList, which might have multiple selected items? `SelectedItem` and `SelectedValue` return the *first* selected item from the list. Therefore, we typically use `SelectedItem` or `SelectedValue` only with DropDownLists or RadioButtonLists. For determining the selected items in a CheckBoxList, stick with enumerating the CheckBoxList's `Items` collection, as we saw in the previous section.

Customizing the Appearance of the RadioButtonList and CheckBoxList Controls

Like the other ASP.NET Web controls we've examined throughout this book, the RadioButtonList and CheckBoxList controls have `Font`, `ForeColor`, `BackColor`, and other common formatting properties we've seen before. As with other Web controls, these properties can be found in the Appearance section within the Properties window.

The RadioButtonList and CheckBoxList also have some properties in the Layout section worth noting. By default, both the RadioButtonList and CheckBoxList are rendered in a single column. Although a one-column layout will likely suffice for CheckBoxLists or RadioButtonLists with a small number of items, displaying dozens of check boxes or radio buttons in this vertical, single-column manner can easily chew up a lot of screen real estate. Rather than confining the items to a single column, we might want to have the check boxes or radio buttons span multiple columns.

To accomplish this, use the `RepeatColumns` property, which specifies how many columns to display and can be assigned any non-negative integer value. The `RepeatDirection` property indicates the direction the items are laid out and can be either `Horizontal` or `Vertical` (the default).

Figure 17.12 shows a CheckBoxList and RadioButtonList with three columns. The figure also illustrates the effects of the `RepeatDirection` property: The CheckBoxList has its `RepeatDirection` property set to `Vertical`, whereas the RadioButtonList's is set to `Horizontal`. The results here are ordered by `BookID`, so *Visual Studio Hacks* is the first book, then *Create Your Own Website*, followed by *The Number*, and so on. As you can see, with the CheckBoxList, the first two books are in the first column, the second two in the second column, and so on. In essence, the output is grouped by row. With the RadioButtonList's `Horizontal` `RepeatDirection` value, the output is grouped by column, with the first three books in the first column and last two books in the second column.

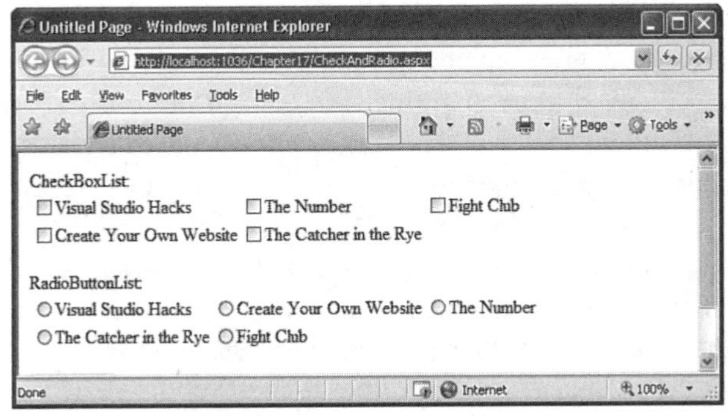

FIGURE 17.12
A RadioButtonList and CheckBoxList, with `RepeatColumns` set to 3.

Summary

In this hour we examined the ASP.NET list Web controls: the DropDownList, CheckBoxList, and RadioButtonList. These three controls are composed of a series of list items that can be specified statically, programmatically, or through data binding. The manner by which these three controls differ is in how they render their list items. A DropDownList control renders as a drop-down list, with each item an option in the list. A CheckBoxList renders each of its items as a check box, and the RadioButtonList renders its items as radio buttons.

A common use of these controls is to list a particular column from a database table, enabling a visitor to easily filter displayed results. We saw an example of this in the "Filtering Results Using the DropDownList" section. In our example, a DropDownList contained the various genres, and a GridView displayed only those books of the selected genre.

Q&A

Q. ***Earlier in this hour we worked on an example of filtering a GridView's data using a DropDownList. Would it have been possible to use a RadioButtonList in place of the DropDownList?***

A. Sure, a RadioButtonList would have worked equally as well; in fact, exercise 1 asks you to build an ASP.NET page that filters the data displayed using a RadioButtonList.

When using a RadioButtonList to filter results, however, there is one point to keep in mind: by default, a RadioButtonList doesn't have a selected item. Therefore, when the page first loads the parameter used to filter, the SqlDataSource will be missing and an exception will be raised. To circumvent this problem, you'll need to add a default value to the parameter when constructing your `WHERE` clause parameter in the SqlDataSource control's wizard. Use as a default value one of the values of the `Genre` column, such as Business, or a blank string if you don't want any results returned initially.

Q. ***When filtering the GridView's data using a DropDownList, the DropDownList defaulted to the first option, Business. Consequently, when the page is first visited the GridView lists those books in the Business genre. How would I go about adding a "Choose a Genre" item to the DropDownList that would be selected by default and, when selected, would not display any books in the GridView?***

A. To add a "Show All Genres" option to the DropDownList you need to add the "Show All Genres" option through the ListItem Collection Editor dialog box. As discussed in Hour 11, this dialog box is accessible through the Properties window. Set the new list item's Text property to `Choose a Genre` and its `Value` property to `-1` (or some other value that does not map to a valid `Genre` value).

By default, when database data is bound to a DropDownList it overwrites any statically added list items (such as the "Show All Genres" option). To override this behavior and append the data bound items those list items added statically, set the DropDownList's `AppendDataBoundItems` property to True. That's all there is to it!

Workshop

Quiz

1. Name some of the ways in which the three list Web controls examined in this hour are similar to one another.
2. Name some ways in which the list Web controls differ from one another.
3. What is the name of the event that is raised when a list Web control's selected state is changed across postbacks?
4. What properties must you set to have the RadioButtonList or CheckBoxList controls render their items laid out horizontally using multiple columns?
5. The DropDownList, RadioButtonList, and CheckBoxList controls all have an `AutoPostBack` property. What happens when this property is set to `True`?

Answers

1. All are composed of list items and contain a similar set of base properties—`Items`, `SelectedItem`, `SelectedValue`, and so on. They all have a `SelectedIndexChanged` event that fires on postback if the selected state of the control has changed. Additionally, they all can have their list items specified in one of three ways: statically, through the ListItem Collection Editor dialog box; programmatically; and through a data source control.

2. Each list Web control renders its list items differently. The DropDownList will always have one selected item, whereas the RadioButtonList can have zero or one, and the CheckBoxList can have zero to many selected items.

3. `SelectedIndexChanged`.

4. The `RepeatColumns` property specifies how many columns the RadioButtonList or CheckBoxList's items will use; the `RepeatDirection` property indicates whether the items are laid out vertically or horizontally.

5. When `AutoPostBack` is set to `True`, any client-side change in the control's selection state causes a postback. For example, with a DropDownList whose `AutoPostBack` property is set to `True`, when the user chooses a new option from the list, the page automatically posts back and the DropDownList's `SelectedIndexChanged` event is fired.

Exercises

1. Using the same techniques discussed in the "Filtering Results Using the DropDownList" section, create an ASP.NET page that uses a GridView to display the books from the `Books` table and a RadioButtonList of all the authors to allow the user to filter the books displayed. (Be sure to set the RadioButtonList's `AutoPostBack` property to `True`.)

   As in our earlier example, make sure that the RadioButtonList displays only *unique* author names. Also, because on the initial page load, the RadioButtonList will not have any item selected, you'll need to set a default value for the parameter you create in the GridView's SqlDataSource Wizard. Set the default parameter value to a blank string. With this setting, when the page first loads, before a user selects an author from the list of radio buttons, the GridView should not be shown because there should be no authors with a blank string. Upon selecting a new author, the page will post back and the books that the selected author has written will be displayed.

   When testing this, be sure to edit the `Books` table so that there are at least two books written by the same author. Also, take a moment to set the GridView's `EmptyDataText` property to an applicable message. Recall that the value of this property is displayed when binding a GridView to a data source control that returns no records, as is the case with this exercise when the user first visits the page, before selecting an author.

HOUR 18

Exploring Data Binding and Other Data-Related Topics

In this hour, we will cover

- The different fields available for the GridView and DetailsView controls
- Displaying hyperlinks, check boxes, and images in the GridView and DetailsView controls
- Using wildcards in the SQL `WHERE` clause
- Understanding data binding and the data-binding syntax

Over the past five hours we've covered a number of data-related topics. In Hour 13, "An Introduction to Databases," we talked about the structure and purpose of databases and looked at how to create a SQL Server 2005 Express Edition database using Visual Web Developer. Next, in Hour 14, "Accessing Data with the Data Source Web Controls," we saw how to get data from the database to an ASP.NET web page through ASP.NET's data source controls. In particular, we focused on the SqlDataSource control, which is designed for accessing data from a database. And in the preceding three hours we examined a variety of ASP.NET controls designed to display and modify the data retrieved from a data source control.

However, a number of data-related topics didn't fit naturally into any of the previous hours. This hour examines some miscellaneous data-related topics. Hour 19, "Using Templated Data Web Controls," examines the ListView and FormView controls and concludes our examination of ASP.NET's data capabilities.

Looking at the GridView's and DetailsView's Fields

As we saw in Hour 15, "Displaying Data with the Data Web Controls," when a SqlDataSource control is bound to a GridView, a BoundField is added to the GridView for each database column specified in the SqlDataSource control's `SelectCommand`. We can edit the GridViews fields by going to the smart tag and clicking the Edit Columns link. As we have seen in past hours, this brings up the Fields dialog box (see Figure 18.1). The bottom-left corner of the Fields dialog box lists the current fields of the control; from here we can reorder, remove, or configure the assorted BoundFields.

The BoundField is not the only type of field. A total of seven field types exist. Each field type renders a different interface. As you already know, the BoundField displays the values of a specified database column either as plain text or in a TextBox Web control, depending on whether the data is in read-only, edit, or insert mode.

Another field type that we've used in past hours is the CommandField, which provides an interface for the end user for inserting, editing, selecting, and deleting data. The CommandField can show any combination of insert, edit, select, and delete buttons; you can indicate which of these you want present through the `ShowInsertButton`, `ShowEditButton`, `ShowSelectButton`, and `ShowDeleteButton` properties. When you use the GridView's smart tag to turn on support for inserting, editing, selecting, or deleting, a CommandField is automatically added with the appropriate properties' values set accordingly.

The seven field types are displayed in the upper-left corner of the Fields dialog box (see Figure 18.1). Table 18.1 lists the seven field types along with a brief description of each.

TABLE 18.1 The GridView and DetailsView Can Be Composed of a Number of Fields of Differing Types

Field	Description
BoundField	Displays a corresponding data source control column's value as text or in a text box when being edited or when inserting a new value. When binding a GridView or DetailsView control to a data source control through the smart tag, a BoundField is automatically created for each column in the associated data source control.
CheckBoxField	Renders a check box whose checked state depends on the value in a specified data source control column. Useful for displaying the value of a `bit` database column. (Recall that a `bit` database column is a Yes/No type of column, one that can have a value of either 0 or 1.)

TABLE 18.1 Continued

HyperLinkField	Creates a HyperLink control whose `Text` and `NavigateUrl` property values can be either hard-coded or based on values from columns in the data source control.
ImageField	Renders as an Image Web control whose `ImageUrl` property is based on some database column value.
ButtonField	Renders as a Button Web control. Useful if you have some action you want the user to be able to initiate on a record-by-record basis other than editing, deleting, or selecting. (Those functions are already provided by the CommandField.)
CommandField	Renders the interface for inserting, updating, deleting, or selecting records. Automatically added when enabling any of those functionalities through the control's smart tag.
TemplateField	Allows for a mix of static HTML markup, Web controls, and data binding syntax. In Hour 16, we used TemplateFields to customize the editing interface for the GridView.

We've already looked at using the BoundField, CommandField, and TemplateField. Over the next few sections we'll examine the CheckBoxField, HyperLinkField, and ImageField.

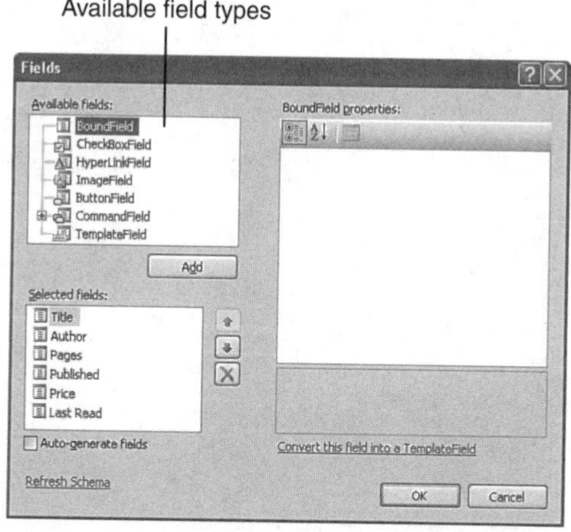

FIGURE 18.1 The Fields dialog box lists the fields in the data Web control, along with the field types that can be added.

Looking at How `Bit` Columns Are Displayed

As we discussed in Hour 13, a database table is composed of a number of columns, each of which has a data type that indicates what types of values can be stored in the column. The `Title` column in the `Books` table, for example, has an `nvarchar(150)` data type, meaning that it can store strings with up to 150 characters; the `LastReadOn` column has a `datetime` data type, meaning it can store date and time values. One database column data type that we've yet to use in the `Books` table is the `bit` data type. A column that has a data type of `bit` can store one of two values: 0 or 1. Typically, a bit column is used to store a Yes/No or True/False type value.

Let's take a minute to add a `bit` column to our `Books` table. Go to the Database Explorer in Visual Web Developer, drill down to the `Books` table, right-click its name, and choose the Open Table Definition option. This brings up the list of columns that make up the table. Next, add a new column named `Recommended` and choose a Data Type value of `bit`. Because the table contains existing data, this column either must allow `Nulls` or we must provide a default value. Let's use the latter approach.

First, uncheck the Allow Nulls check box. We need to specify a default value for this column. In the Column Properties pane, search for the property titled Default Value or Binding in the General section. Then put in the default value there. Let's use a default of 0. Take a minute to ensure that your screen looks similar to Figure 18.2 and then save the table changes.

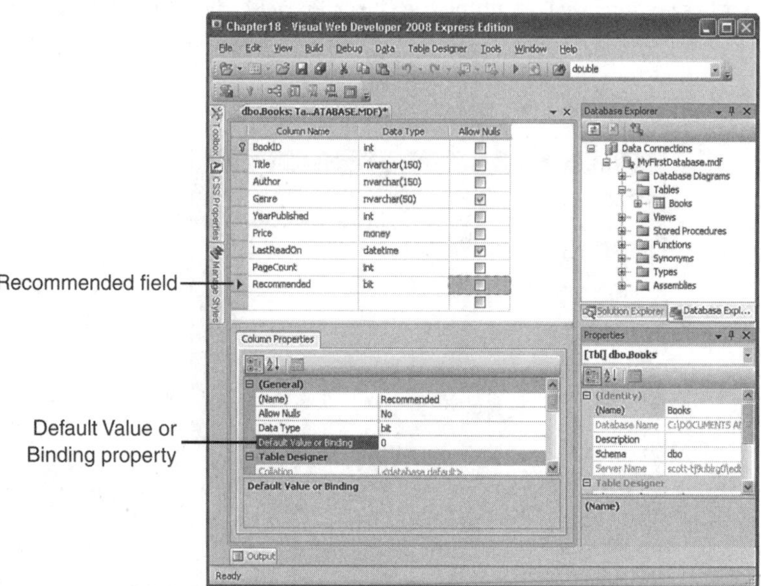

FIGURE 18.2 The `Recommended` column has been added; it's a `bit` column with a default value of 0.

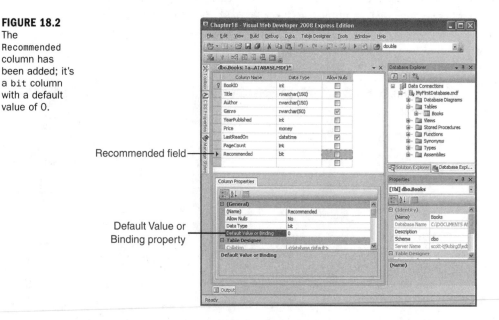

Now that we've added this new column, create an ASP.NET page that displays all rows and all columns in an editable GridView. As soon as you bind the GridView to the SqlDataSource control through the GridView's smart tag, the `Recommended` field in the GridView is shown as a series of check boxes. Visual Web Developer is smart enough to note that a particular column being bound to the GridView is a `bit` column. For such columns, it automatically uses a CheckBoxField instead of the standard BoundField (see Figure 18.3).

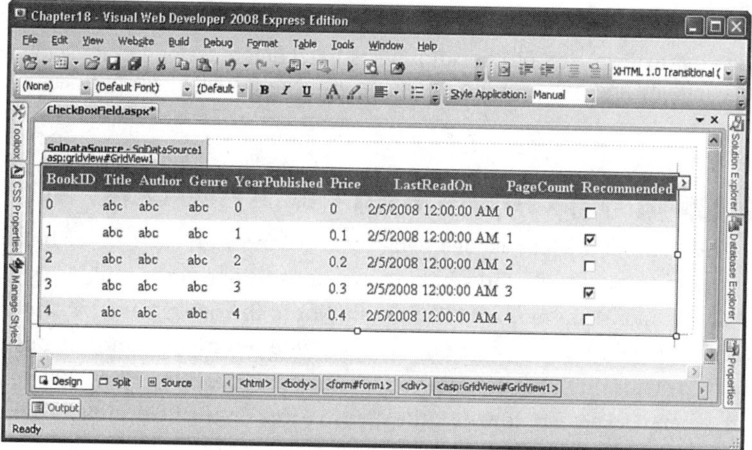

FIGURE 18.3 The `Recommended` field is displayed as a series of check boxes.

To see that the `Recommended` field is indeed a CheckBoxField, go to the GridView's smart tag and click the Edit Columns link, bringing up the Fields dialog box. As Figure 18.4 shows, from the bottom-left corner listing of the fields in the GridView, the `Recommended` field is a CheckBoxField. Selecting the `Recommended` field loads its properties on the right. As with the BoundField, you can customize the CheckBoxField's appearance through the properties in the Styles section.

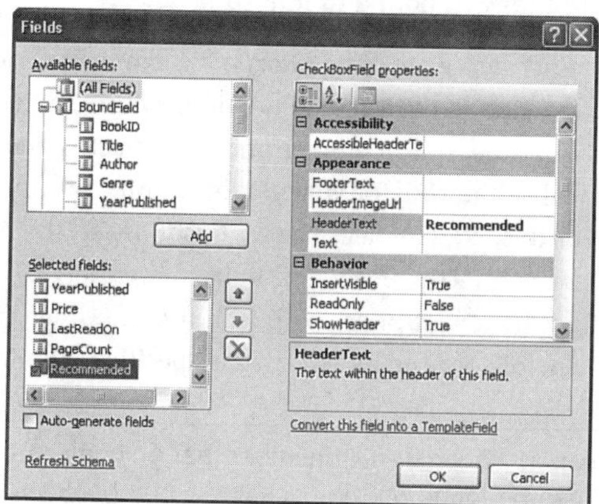

FIGURE 18.4 The GridView automatically uses a CheckBoxField for `Recommended`.

Take a moment to test this ASP.NET page through a browser. When you visit the page, each row in the Recommended field is displayed as a disabled check box. When a particular row is edited, the editable row's check box is enabled, allowing the end user to change the check box's value. This functionality is made possible thanks to the CheckBoxField.

By the Way

> Although our examination of CheckBoxFields has centered around the GridView, the functionality and behavior are the same with the DetailsView control.

Displaying Hyperlinks with the HyperLinkField

With the addition of a Recommended field, users visiting your site can see both what books are in your bookshelf and what books you heartily recommend. A visitor who notes that the books you read and like are similar to the books he reads and likes might be interested in buying some of the books you recommend that he has yet to read. To help streamline this process, you could add a link titled "Buy" in each book row that, when clicked, would whisk the user to some online bookstore, displaying the details of that particular book.

Adding such functionality through the GridView (or DetailsView) is possible and quite simple thanks to the HyperLinkField. As its name implies, the HyperLinkField displays a field of HyperLink Web controls. When visited through a browser, the HyperLink control renders as a link that, when clicked, takes the visitor to a specified URL. With the HyperLinkField field, we can set the `Text` and `NavigateUrl` properties of the HyperLink control based on database values so that the text and URL of the rendered link for each row in the GridView is based on the values of the columns of the database record that was bound to that row.

If this doesn't make much sense yet, don't worry; an example should help. Because we want to add a "Buy" link to each row in a GridView that, when clicked, sends the visitor to an online bookstore, our first order of business is to determine what online bookstore to use and what the URL for viewing the details for a particular book on that site looks like. For this exercise, let's use www.isbn.nu as the online bookstore. isbn.nu doesn't sell books directly; instead, it links to a variety of online bookstores, helping the visitor find the lowest price. With isbn.nu, the URL `http://www.isbn.nu/`*`ISBN`* displays the details for the book with the specified ISBN value.

By the Way

> The **ISBN** of a book is a 10- or 13-digit number that uniquely identifies the book. Typically, the ISBN can be found on the back cover of a book.

To provide such a link, we need to store the ISBN for each of the books; therefore, we need to add an `ISBN` column to the `Books` table. Because a book's ISBN can be up to 13 characters, create the ISBN column using the `nvarchar(13)` data type. We don't want to allow Nulls, but because there's already data in the Books table, we'll initially need to allow Nulls for this new column until we have a chance to provide values for the ISBN column for the existing rows. Take a moment to add this new column.

After adding the `ISBN` column, edit the table's data (right-click the `Books` table in the Database Explorer and choose Show Table Data). Enter an `ISBN` for each of the books, omitting any hyphens (see Figure 18.5). The `ISBN` for the five books in the `Books` table are as follows:

- *Visual Studio Hacks*—9780596008475
- *Create Your Own Website*—9780672329265
- *The Number*—0375508805
- *The Catcher In The Rye*—0316769487
- *Fight Club*—9780805076479

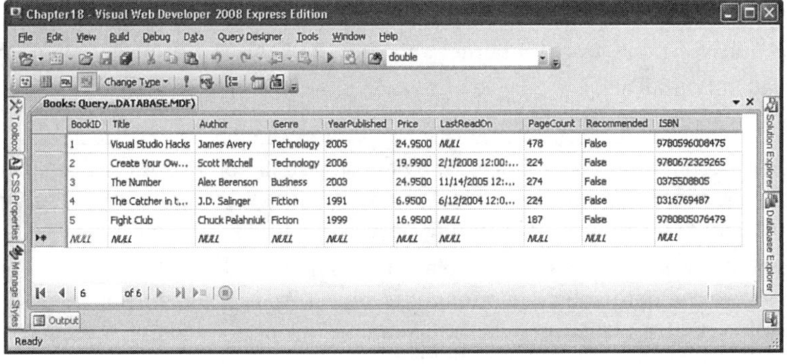

FIGURE 18.5
The ISBN values for the five books have been added.

After you've supplied the ISBN values for all the records in the `Books` table, return to editing the table's definition and uncheck the Allow Nulls check box for the `ISBN` column.

Next, create an ASP.NET page with a SqlDataSource that retrieves all the columns and rows from the `Books` table. Add a GridView control and bind it to the SqlDataSource. At this point the GridView displays the value of the `ISBN` column using a BoundField. We need to replace this BoundField with a HyperLinkField. To accomplish this, go to the Fields dialog box.

The lower-left corner of the Fields dialog box lists the fields currently being used by the GridView, one of which is an `ISBN` BoundField. Remove this field from the GridView by selecting it and clicking the Delete icon to the immediate right of this list, as shown in Figure 18.6.

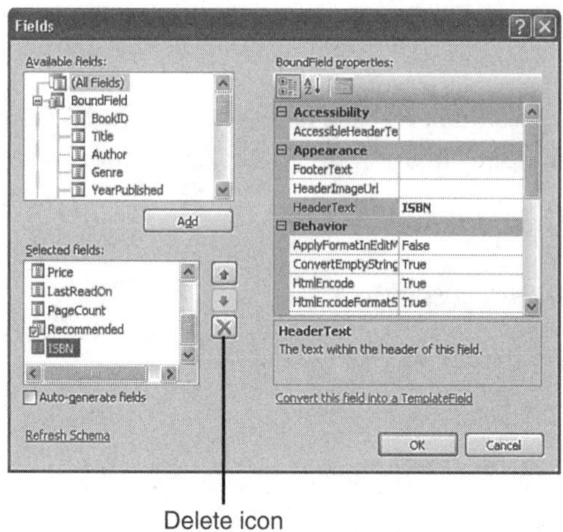

FIGURE 18.6
Select the `ISBN` BoundField and delete it.

You can also delete any other BoundFields that you aren't interested in displaying. For this ASP.NET page, let's not bother showing the `BookID`, `YearPublished`, or `LastReadOn` BoundFields.

Watch Out!

> If you are working with an editable GridView or editable or insertable DetailsView, you cannot blindly remove BoundFields from the data Web control because the SqlDataSource control is configured to save these values as well.
>
> If you do not want certain fields displayed when editing or inserting data, be sure to configure the data source control not to return those column values. For more discussion on this issue, refer to the "Marking Fields as Read-Only" section in Hour 16, "Deleting, Inserting, and Editing Data."

We're now ready to add the `Buy` HyperLinkField. From the Available Fields list in the upper-left corner, scroll down and select the HyperLinkField option and then click the Add button. This will add a HyperLinkField to bottom of the list of fields in the lower-left corner. Take a moment to move this HyperLinkField to the top of the list so that it is displayed in the far left of the GridView. We now need to set the HyperLinkField's properties, indicating what the rendered link's text and URL values should be.

The HyperLinkField's text and URL values can be static or dynamic. A dynamic value differs for each row in the GridView based on the data bound to that particular row; a static value is the same among all rows. For our task we want a static text value—`Buy`—and a dynamic URL value, varying on each book's ISBN.

If you want to set the text or URL values to static values, use the `Text` or `NavigateUrl` properties. The `Text` property can be found in the Appearance section of the properties list; `NavigateUrl` is located in the Behavior section. Because we want the link's text to be `Buy` for all rows, set the `Text` property of the HyperLinkColumn to `Buy`.

To specify a dynamic value for the text or URL values, we need to use two properties. For the text, we can use the `DataTextField` and `DataTextFormatString` properties; for the URL, we can use the `DataNavigateUrlFields` and `DataNavigateUrlFormatString` properties. These four properties are found in the Data section of the HyperLinkField's properties. The properties work in tandem in the following manner: the `DataTextField` or `DataNavigateUrlFields` properties specify what database column values are used in the text or URL of the rendered link; the `DataTextFormatString` or `DataNavigateUrlFormatString` properties can be used to surround the database value with static text. With the `DataTextFormatString` and `DataNavigateUrlFormatString` properties, the string `{0}` is used to inject the dynamic value.

For our example, we want the URL to be dynamic based on the book's ISBN; therefore, set the `DataNavigateUrlFields` property to `ISBN`. Because we want the URL to be `http://www.isbn.nu/`*`ISBN`*, use `http://www.isbn.nu/{0}` as the value for the `DataNavigateUrlFormatString` property. This instructs the HyperLinkColumn to inject the current row's `ISBN` value at the `{0}` position, resulting in a properly formatted hyperlink.

After you set these properties and click the OK button in the Fields dialog box, your screen should look similar to Figure 18.7. Note that the GridView now has a `Buy` HyperLinkField at its far left and that the `BookID`, `YearPublished`, and `LastReadOn` BoundFields have been removed.

View the ASP.NET page in a browser. Each row in the rendered GridView contains a `Buy` link that, when clicked, will whisk you to isbn.nu. For example, clicking the `Buy` link for *Create Your Own Website* will take you to http://www.isbn.nu/9780672329265. Notice how the ISBN value for this book—9780672329265—is injected into the URL of the link precisely where the `{0}` string was placed in the HyperLinkField's `DataNavigateUrlFormatString` property.

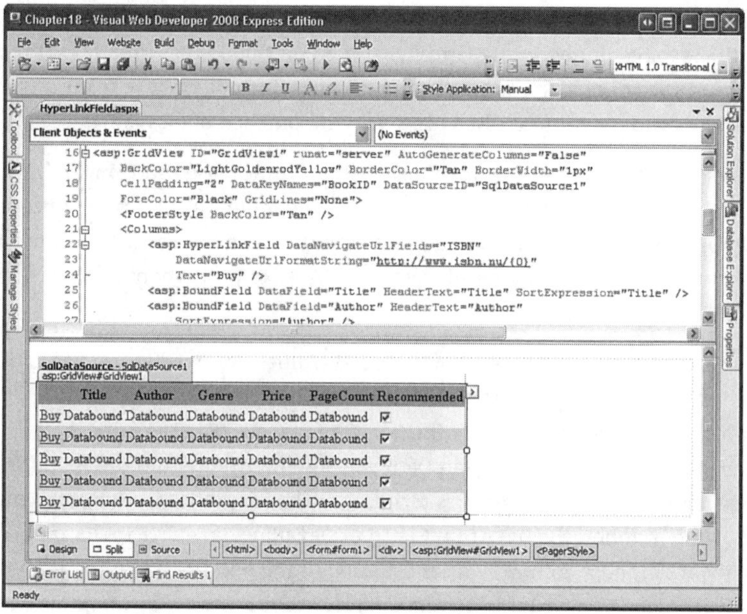

FIGURE 18.7
A HyperLinkField has been added to the GridView.

Did you Know?

> You can have the URL value of the HyperLinkField include multiple values from database columns. To do so, specify each database column name you need in the `DataNavigateUrlFields`, separated by commas. Then, in the `DataNavigateUrlFormatString`, use `{0}` to inject the value of the first column in the column list, `{1}` to inject the second column's value, `{2}` to inject the third's, and so on. The `DataTextField`, however, can only include one database column name.

Displaying Images with the ImageField

The ImageField is designed to display an image whose URL is based on a database value. The ImageField injects an Image Web control, which renders as an HTML `<img>` element. Like the HyperLinkField, the ImageField has a pair of properties that can be used to specify a database column and a format string: `DataImageUrlField` and `DataImageUrlFieldString`.

Let's augment the GridView we created in the "Displaying Hyperlinks with the HyperLinkField" section to include an ImageField that displays each book's cover.

The first step is to find the cover images and save them to your computer. The isbn.nu website lists a small cover image at www.isbn.nu/*ISBN*. Visit the isbn.nu site for each of the books in the database. Right-click the cover image and save it to your website's root folder, naming the file `BookID.jpg`. For example, save the cover image for *Visual Studio Hacks* using the filename `1.jpg`; for *Create Your Own Website*, use `2.jpg`, and so on.

After you have saved the cover images to your computer, add an ImageField to the GridView using the following steps:

1. From the GridView's smart tag, click the Edit Columns link to open the Fields dialog box.
2. Add a new ImageField to the GridView.
3. Click on the ImageField to load its properties. Set the `DataImageUrlField` property to `BookID` and the `DataImageUrlFieldString` property to `{0}.jpg`.

After step 3, your Fields dialog box should look similar to the one in Figure 18.8. After verifying this, click the OK button and then view the ASP.NET page through a browser. You should see the thumbnail images for each of the book's covers, as shown in Figure 18.9.

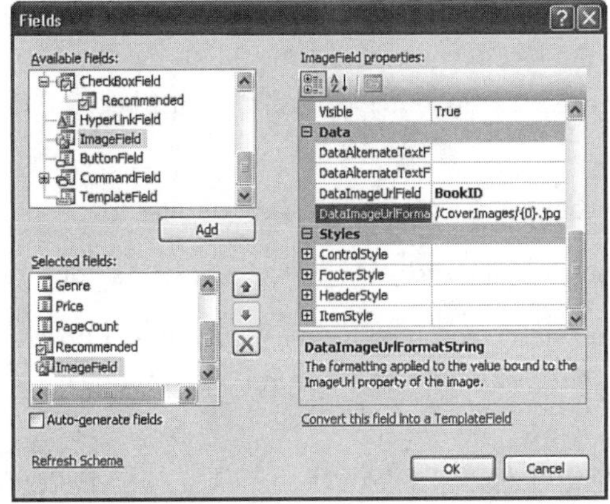

FIGURE 18.8 Set the properties of the ImageField through the Fields dialog box.

FIGURE 18.9
A thumbnail image of the cover is shown for each book.

Using Wildcards in a WHERE Filter Expression

In previous hours we saw how to use the SqlDataSource's wizard to add `WHERE` filter expressions to limit the results returned by the database. When creating a filter expression through the SqlDataSource control's wizard, recall that we must specify three things:

- The database column the filter expression applies to
- The filter expression operator—=, <>, <, <=, >, and so on
- The filter value, which can be a hard-coded value or based on some external value, such as the value of a Web control on the page

One of the operators that we've yet to look at is the `LIKE` operator. The `LIKE` operator uses wildcards around the parameter value and works only with string or date/time database columns. We can use the `LIKE` operator to build an interface for the user to search the `Books` table, returning all rows where the `Title` column value contains some user-entered search term.

Let's create a page to demonstrate this filter expression operator. Before adding a SqlDataSource control to this page, first enter the text **`Search for books by title:`**, followed by TextBox and Button Web controls. Set the TextBox Web control's

ID property to TitleSearch and the Button control's ID and Text properties to SearchButton and "Search," respectively. The user interface we've just added will allow the user visiting our page to enter a search term into the text box. Upon clicking the Search button, the page will post back and the GridView will display those books with matching titles.

Now that we have the user interface implemented, the next step is to add the SqlDataSource and GridView controls. Configure the SqlDataSource control to return all columns from the Books table. Add a WHERE clause filter expression on the Title column using the LIKE operator based on the TitleSearch control (see Figure 18.10).

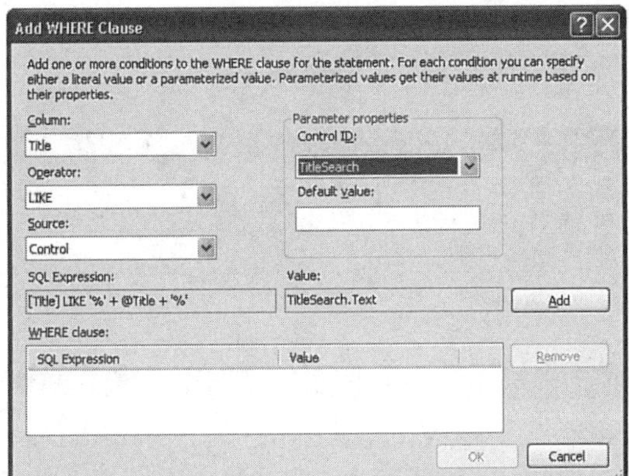

FIGURE 18.10
Add a LIKE filter expression on the Title column.

The LIKE operator can be applied only to string (nvarchar, nchar, char, or varchar) or date/time columns.

After you add this filter expression and return to the wizard's Configure the Select Statement screen, the wizard's proposed SELECT statement should look like

```
SELECT * FROM [Books] WHERE ([Title] LIKE '%' + @Title + '%')
```

Note that the WHERE clause uses the LIKE operator in conjunction with wildcard characters (%) to return all records whose Title column value contains the value of the @Title parameter. This @Title parameter value will be set to the value of the Text property of the TitleSearch TextBox control.

Complete this page by adding the GridView control and binding it to the SqlDataSource. When the page is first visited through a browser, no records will be shown because the user has yet to enter a value into the text box. Similarly, if the user enters a search term that does not appear in any of the books' titles, no books will be returned by the SqlDataSource. These two scenarios may confuse the end user. To help alleviate any confusion, enter a helpful message into the GridView's `EmptyDataText` property. As we've discussed before, this value of the `EmptyDataText` property is displayed when no records are returned by the GridView's associated data source control. Also feel free to tailor the GridView's columns as you see fit; I used the column configuration from our ImageField discussion earlier in this hour.

After setting the `EmptyDataText` property, take a moment to test this page in a browser. Figure 18.11 shows the page the user searches on the term "the". This produces two results: *The Number* and *The Catcher in the Rye*. When a user enters a search term that is not in any title, such as "Rolla", no results will be returned by the SqlDataSource control, and the GridView will display the value of its `EmptyDataText` property (see Figure 18.12).

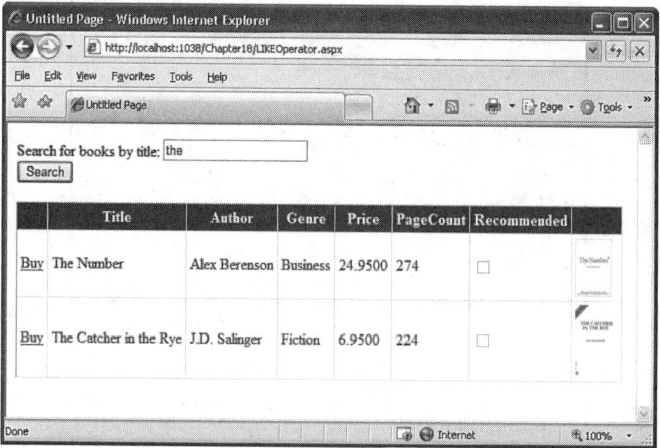

FIGURE 18.11 Two books match when searching on "the".

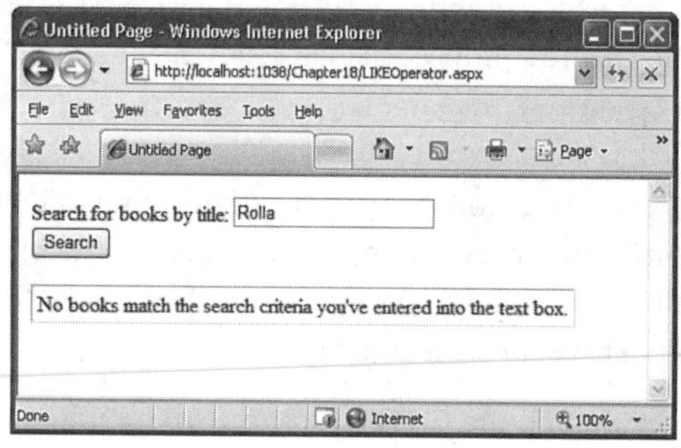

FIGURE 18.12 The GridView's `EmptyDataText` property value is displayed when no matching book titles are found.

An Examination of Data Binding

Data binding is the process of tying a property of a Web control to the value of a database column; this process happens automatically all the time with the data Web controls. When we're using BoundFields, CheckBoxFields, or ImageFields, the GridView or DetailsView control handles all the data binding for us behind the scenes. For example, the BoundField uses a Label Web control and automatically binds the Label's `Text` property to the corresponding database column; with a CheckBoxField, a CheckBox Web control is used, and its `Checked` property is data bound to the corresponding database column.

In Hour 16 we saw how, when creating an editable GridView or DetailsView, the BoundFields rendered a TextBox Web control whose `Text` property was set to the value of the field's corresponding database column. Sometimes we may need to customize the editing interface, adding validation controls, changing the properties of the TextBox Web control, or replacing the TextBox control with other Web controls altogether.

As we saw in Hour 16, this customization can be accomplished using a TemplateField. There are two ways to add a TemplateField: by adding a new TemplateField to the GridView or DetailsView, just like we added a HyperLinkField and an ImageField earlier in this hour; or by converting an existing BoundField into a TemplateField. In situations where you need to customize the editing interface for a BoundField, I encourage you to convert an existing BoundField into a TemplateField rather than deleting the BoundField and then adding a new TemplateField. Converting a BoundField to a TemplateField automatically performs a number of steps for you. Specifically, it creates the ItemTemplate and EditItemTemplates for the TemplateField, with a data-bound Label control in the ItemTemplate and a data-bound TextBox control in the EditItemTemplate. If you add a TemplateField manually, you'll need to add the Label and TextBox controls and configure the data binding yourself.

The Difference Between One-Way and Two-Way Data Binding

ASP.NET supports two flavors of data binding: one-way and two-way. One-way data binding takes a specified database column's value and binds it to a specified Web control property. Two-way data binding can not only assign a database column's value to a Web control property, but can also do the inverse: It can take the value of a Web control's property and assign it to the value of a data source control parameter.

One-way data binding is used when working with a nonmodifiable data Web control. When we're using a data Web control that supports editing, inserting, or deleting, two-way data binding is used instead.

When working with BoundFields, CheckBoxFields, HyperLinkFields, or ImageFields, you do not need to concern yourself with the differences between one-way and two-way data binding; all the intricacies are automatically handled by the various fields. However, when adding data-bound Web controls to a TemplateField, you need to specify whether the data binding should be one-way or two-way. If the Web control is used only to display the information, use one-way data binding; if the Web control is also used to collect user input and save those values back to the database, use two-way data binding.

Specifying the Data Bindings for a Web Control

If you add a TemplateField manually or want to replace a converted TemplateField's Label or TextBox Web control with a different control, you'll need to specify the data bindings for the new controls you add to the TemplateField (including whether the data bindings are one-way or two-way). The data binding simply ties a particular property of the Web control to the field's corresponding database column.

To practice working with data bindings and custom TemplateFields, let's create an editable GridView with a customized editing interface. Specifically, we'll create a GridView that lists the `BookID`, `Title`, and `Genre` columns from the database. By default, the `BookID` field will be read-only, and the `Title` and `Genre` fields will have a TextBox Web control for their editing interface. However, when editing a GridView row, we might want to instead have the `Genre` field displayed as a DropDownList with all the existing genres. To accomplish this, we'll need to convert the `Genre` BoundField into a TemplateField and replace the TextBox Web control in the EditItemTemplate with SqlDataSource and DropDownList controls. In doing so, we'll need to use data binding to tie the DropDownList control's `SelectedValue` property to the value of the edited book's `Genre` column.

Let's not get too far ahead of ourselves here. Before we worry about creating a customized, data-bound editing interface for the `Genre` field, let's first create an editable GridView that uses the default editing interface. Recall from Hour 16 that this involves first adding a SqlDataSource control configured to support updating. Because we want to allow the user to edit only the `Title` and `Genre` fields, in the SqlDataSource's wizard, be sure to bring back only the `BookID`, `Title`, and `Genre` columns, as shown in Figure 18.13. Also, don't forget to click the Advanced button and check the Generate INSERT, UPDATE, and DELETE Statements check box.

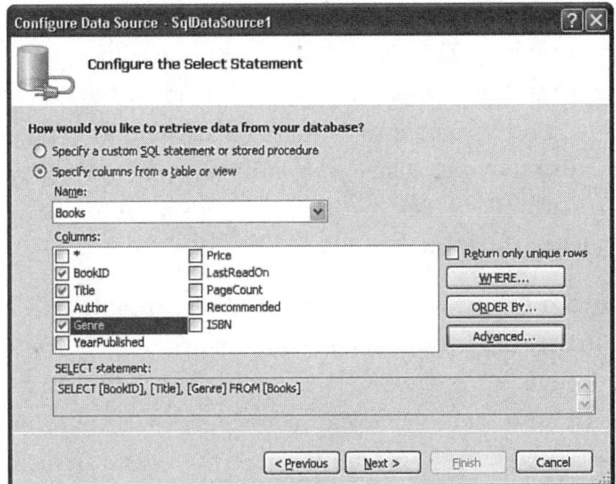

FIGURE 18.13 From the Configure the Select Statement screen, check the `BookID`, `Title`, and `Genre` columns.

Next, add a GridView to the page and bind it to the SqlDataSource control. Check the Enable Editing check box in the GridView's smart tag. Take a moment to view the page through a browser, editing the value for a particular book. Note that when you click the Edit button, the editing interface shows a text box for both the `Title` and `Genre` fields (see Figure 18.14).

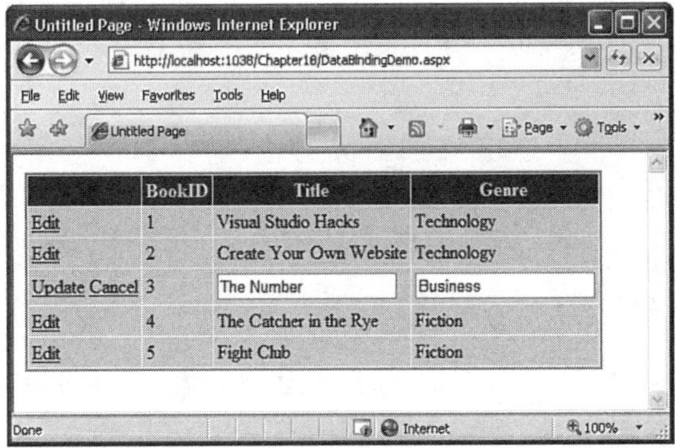

FIGURE 18.14 Both the `Title` and `Genre` fields use the default editing interface.

Let's now look at how to customize the `Genre` field so that it displays a DropDownList of the current genre values in the table, rather than using a TextBox control. To start, go to the Fields dialog box and convert the `Genre` BoundField into a TemplateField. This automatically creates an ItemTemplate with a data-bound Label Web control and an EditItemTemplate with a data-bound TextBox. In fact, if at this point you retest your page through a browser, there will be no discernable difference from the editable interface in Figure 18.14.

To change the `Genre` field's EditItemTemplate, go to the GridView's smart tag and click the Edit Templates link. This displays the template editing view of the GridView, with the smart tag listing the available templates. Choose the EditItemTemplate. You should see a TextBox Web control in the EditItemTemplate; this is the data-bound TextBox control that was added automatically when we converted the `Genre` BoundField to a TemplateField. Because we no longer want to use a TextBox in the editing interface, delete this Web control.

We now need to add a DropDownList to the EditItemTemplate that lists the genres in the `Books` table. To accomplish this, we need to first create a SqlDataSource control that retrieves the unique list of genres. This can be added directly to the `Genre` field's EditItemTemplate. After adding the SqlDataSource to the EditItemTemplate, set its `ID` property to `GenreDataSource`. Next, run through the wizard, returning just the `Genre` column and checking the Return Only Unique Rows check box, like we did in the preceding hour when using a DropDownList to filter the GridView results by genre.

After configuring the `GenreDataSource` SqlDataSource control, add a DropDownList to the EditItemTemplate. Click the Choose Data Source link in the DropDownList's smart tag and bind it to the `GenreDataSource` control, with the `Genre` column serving as both the field to display and the value field. After you've added both the SqlDataSource control and the DropDownList to the EditItemTemplate, and configured both, your screen should look similar to Figure 18.15.

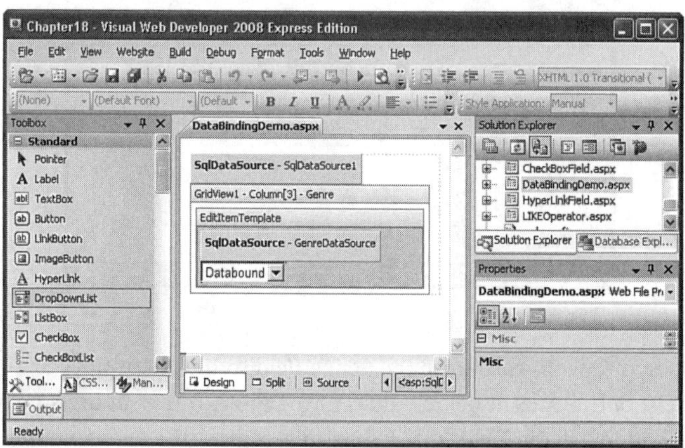

FIGURE 18.15
A SqlDataSource and DropDownList have been added to the `Genre` TemplateField's EditItemTemplate.

Test the ASP.NET page through a browser. When you edit a particular row, the `Genre` field is displayed as a drop-down list with the various genre values in the `Books` table (Business, Fiction, and Technology), as shown in Figure 18.17. However, notice that the first item of the DropDownList is selected, regardless of the edited book's actual Genre value. That is, if you edit *Visual Studio Hacks*, which has the genre Technology, the drop-down list has the Business genre selected. Furthermore, if you save the edits, by clicking the Update button, a value of Null is saved for the book's genre, regardless of what option you've selected from the drop-down list.

What's going on here? What we've yet to do is implement data binding on the DropDownList control in the EditItemTemplate. Right now the DropDownList doesn't know the value of the row's `Genre` column, nor does it provide its selected value to the GridView's SqlDataSource control when the data is updated. We need to have the DropDownList properly data bound to have this interaction occur correctly.

Return to Visual Web Developer and go back to the `Genre` field's EditItemTemplate. Open the DropDownList's smart tag and click the Edit DataBindings link. This displays the DataBindings dialog box, from which you can tie together the DropDownList's properties and the column values returned by the GridView's SqlDataSource control. Because we want the DropDownList's selection to be based on the Genre column value, select the `SelectedValue` property from the list on the left and pick the Genre field from the drop-down list on the right, as shown in Figure 18.16. Because the `SelectedValue` value also dictates the value of the edited book's Genre value, make sure that the Two-way Databinding check box is checked.

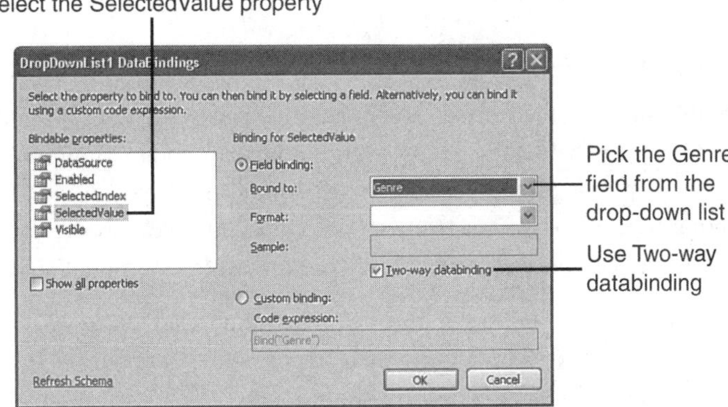

FIGURE 18.16
Bind the `SelectedValue` property to the `Genre` column value using two-way data binding.

After binding the `SelectedValue` property to the `Genre` column, revisit the page in the browser. This time the item in the DropDownList is properly set to the book's `Genre` value, and when you save the edits, the selected DropDownList value is saved. Figure 18.17 shows the ASP.NET page in action.

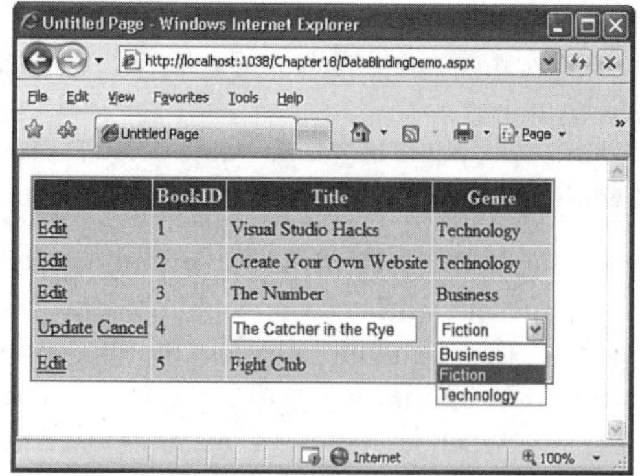

FIGURE 18.17
The `Genre` field provides a customized, data-bound editing interface.

Watch Out!

> Because the DropDownList in the `Genre` EditItemTemplate lists the unique genres that already exist in the `Books` table, you can lose options from the DropDownList. For example, *The Number* is the only book that is in the Business genre. If we edit this book and change its genre to Fiction, the next time we edit a row, the genre drop-down list will have only two options: Fiction and Technology.
>
> As discussed in previous hours, ideally we would implement the concept of genres as a separate table in the database, giving the `Books` table a foreign key to this genre table. With that approach, we'd have a well-defined set of available genres and not lose existing genre choices based on a user's actions.

A Look at the Declarative Markup

Visual Web Developer makes it very easy to specify the data bindings for a Web control. As Figure 18.16 showed, the DataBindings dialog box allows us to pick one of the Web control's properties, specify the database column to bind it to, and indicate whether to use one-way or two-way data binding. These steps, although done through the Design view, can also be performed through the Source view.

It's always worthwhile to see how actions in the Design view affect the page's declarative markup, so let's take a moment to peruse the Source view. Listing 18.1 shows the `Genre` TemplateField's declarative markup.

LISTING 18.1 The Genre TemplateField's Declarative Markup

```
<asp:TemplateField HeaderText="Genre" SortExpression="Genre">
    <EditItemTemplate>
        <asp:SqlDataSource ID="GenreDataSource" runat="server"
            ConnectionString="<%$ ConnectionStrings:ConnectionString %>"
            SelectCommand="SELECT DISTINCT [Genre] FROM
➥ [Books]"></asp:SqlDataSource>
        <asp:DropDownList ID="DropDownList1" runat="server"
```

LISTING 18.1 Continued

```
 7:                DataSourceID="GenreDataSource" DataTextField="Genre"
➥DataValueField="Genre"
 8:                SelectedValue='<%# Bind("Genre") %>'>
 9:            </asp:DropDownList>
10:        </EditItemTemplate>
11:        <ItemTemplate>
12:            <asp:Label ID="Label1" runat="server" Text='<%# Bind("Genre")
➥%>'></asp:Label>
13:        </ItemTemplate>
14: </asp:TemplateField>
```

The TemplateField contains an ItemTemplate and an EditItemTemplate. The ItemTemplate is defined on lines 11 through 13; the EditItemTemplate, on lines 2 through 10. The EditItemTemplate contains two Web controls: a SqlDataSource named `GenreDataSource` on lines 3–5 and a DropDownList control on lines 6–9. The effects of the data binding performed in Figure 18.16 are shown on line 8: The DropDownList control's `SelectedValue` property has been bound to the `Genre` column using `SelectedValue='<%# Bind("Genre") %>'`.

I find it a lot quicker and easier to use the Design view to specify the data bindings for controls in TemplateFields, but do realize that a one-to-one correspondence exists between what we do through the Design view and the page's declarative markup.

The two-way data binding uses the `Bind(`*`columnName`*`)` syntax; one-way data binding uses `Eval(`*`columnName`*`)`.

Summary

In this hour we looked at a hodgepodge of data-related topics, starting with an examination of the fields available for use with the data Web controls. The three fields we looked at were the CheckBoxField, HyperLinkField, and ImageField. The CheckBoxField is automatically used when binding a bit column to a GridView or DetailsView. The HyperLinkField renders a link, and the ImageField renders an image. Both the HyperLinkField and ImageField have pairs of properties that allow us to associate a database field value with the properties of the fields' corresponding HyperLink or Image controls.

We also looked at how to use `WHERE` clause filter expressions with wildcards. This technique is useful if you want to allow the user to search for a particular substring within a database field. This hour concluded with an examination of data binding. Although the data Web controls natively handle data binding for us most of the time, if we add a TemplateField or want to use a Web control other than the TextBox in the editing or inserting interface, we need to bind the appropriate database column values to the appropriate Web control properties. We can accomplish this by clicking the Edit DataBindings link in the smart tag of a Web control in a TemplateField.

Q&A

Q. ***In the "Displaying Hyperlinks with the HyperLinkField" section, we learned that the HyperLinkField's URL value can be constructed using multiple database values by setting the*** `DataNavigateUrlFields` ***property to a comma-delimited list of database column names. Does this also apply to the text value (***`DataTextUrlField`***)?***

A. No, the HyperLinkField supports multiple column names only in its URL portion. The `DataTextUrlField` property can accept only one column name. Similarly, the ImageField's `DataAlternateTextField` and `DataImageUrlField` properties can be assigned only to a single column name.

Q. ***In the "Using Wildcards in a*** `WHERE` ***Filter Expression" section, we saw how to display all books where the title contained a search term entered by the user. Would it be possible to make a more general search engine, one that would return a book whose title, author, or genre matched the search term entered by the user?***

A. Yes, this would be possible. You would need to add multiple `WHERE` clause conditions, using the same pattern for each. However, when you specify the `SELECT` clause through the Specify a Selected Statement screen of the SqlDataSource wizard, the `WHERE` clause filter expressions specified are joined by `AND`s. That is, if you followed the steps outlined earlier in this hour and added three filter expressions to the `Title`, `Author`, and `Genre` columns using the `LIKE` operator with a parameter value based on the `TitleSearch` TextBox, the resulting `SELECT` query would be

```
SELECT *
FROM [Books]
WHERE ([Title] LIKE '%' + @Title + '%') AND
      ([Author] LIKE '%' + @Author + '%') AND
      ([Genre] LIKE '%' + @Genre + '%')
```

Note that the three conditions in the `WHERE` clause are joined by an `AND`. That means the only rows that will be returned will be those whose `Title` column value contains the user's search term and whose `Author` column value contains the user's search term and whose `Genre` column value contains the user's search term. What you probably want, though, is to have all books returned where any of those columns contain the search term.

To accomplish this, you'll have to craft the `SELECT` statement yourself through the SqlDataSource wizard's Define Custom Statements or Stored Procedures screen. (This screen was first discussed in Hour 14.)

Q. ***What if I want to display an image (or hyperlink), but I need more control over the way the image or hyperlink is rendered than the ImageField or HyperLinkField grants? For example, what if I want to have two images in the field, or I want some nonlinked text to appear after the hyperlink?***

A. For simple links and images, the HyperLinkField and ImageField work wonderfully. However, if you need greater flexibility in the appearance of these fields, you'll need to use a TemplateField instead. You can convert the HyperLinkField or ImageField into a TemplateField and then customize the ItemTemplate as needed.

Workshop

Quiz

1. What HyperLinkField properties would you set to what values if you wanted to display a hyperlink with the text `Buy` ***`Title`*** that whisked the user to the URL `http://www.buybooks.com/Buy.aspx?ISBN=`*`ISBN`*, where *`Title`* was the title of the book and *`ISBN`* is the ISBN?
2. If you set the `DataNavigateUrlFields` property to multiple column names—like `BookID,ISBN`—what would you set the `DataNavigateUrlFormatString` property to in order to have a URL generated with the form `http://www.books.com/Details.aspx?BookID=`*`BookID`*`&ISBN=`*`ISBN`*?
3. True or False: The `LIKE` operator in the `WHERE` clause can be used with columns of any data type.
4. What are the seven types of fields that can be added to GridView or DetailsView controls?
5. How do one-way and two-way data binding differ?

Answers

1. To configure the URL portion of the hyperlink, you would set the `DataNavigateUrlFields` property to `ISBN` and the `DataNavigateUrlFormatString` property to `http://www.buybooks.com/Buy.aspx?ISBN={0}`. To configure the text portion, you would set the `DataTextField` property to `Title` and the `DataTextFormatString` property to `Buy {0}`.
2. You would use `{0}` to inject the value of the first database column (`BookID`) and `{1}` to inject the value of the second (`ISBN`). Therefore, you would use `http://www.books.com/Details.aspx?BookID={0}&ISBN={1}`.
3. False. The `LIKE` operator must be used with string or date/time column types.
4. The seven fields are: BoundField, CheckBoxField, HyperLinkField, ImageField, ButtonField, CommandField, and TemplateField.
5. One-way data binding takes a specified database column's value and binds it to a specified Web control property. Two-way data binding can not only assign a database column's value to a Web control property, but can also do the inverse: It can take the value of a property and assign it to the value of a data source control parameter.

Exercises

1. In this hour we looked at one example that used a HyperLinkField and an ImageField to display a `Buy` link and the book's cover image. Create a new page that includes a HyperLinkField and ImageField, but change the HyperLinkField's text to `Buy` *`Title`*, where *`Title`* is the title of the book. Have the book's cover image centered in the table cell. (Hint: To center the book's cover image, use the `ItemStyle` property of the ImageField.)
2. In this hour we added a `Recommended` field to the `Books` table. Because users might be interested in seeing only books that are recommended, create a page that has a DropDownList with two options—Recommended and Not Recommended—with values of 1 and 0, respectively. Next, add a SqlDataSource control that has a `WHERE` clause filter expression on the `Recommended` field based on the value of the DropDownList. Finally, add a GridView to the page, bind it to the SqlDataSource, and test the page in a browser.
3. In the "Specifying the Data Bindings for a Web Control" section this hour, we created an editable GridView that used a DropDownList for the `Genre` field's editing interface. Re-create this page, but this time use a RadioButtonList in place of the DropDownList.

HOUR 19

Using Templated Data Web Controls

In this hour, we will cover

- Using the ListView and FormView controls to display data
- Creating the ListView's templates by hand and through the Configure ListView dialog box
- Sorting data with the ListView
- Paging through data with the DataPager control
- Paging through the FormView's records

As we have seen through the past several hours, the GridView and DetailsView controls make displaying, inserting, editing, and deleting database data as easy as point and click. However, these two controls render a rather boxy and unimaginative interface. By default, the GridView and DetailsView use BoundFields to display the database columns returned by their data source controls, which simply display the value as text when in read-only mode and as a text box when in edit or insert mode.

In the preceding hour, "Exploring Data Binding and Other Data-Related Topics," we saw how to customize the GridView and DetailsView using alternative field types. The TemplateField offers the most flexibility because its templates can contain a mix of HTML, Web controls, and data binding syntax. TemplateFields are often used to customize the editing or inserting interfaces by adding validation controls or replacing the text box with a more suitable input Web control. But even with TemplateFields, the GridView and DetailsView controls still produce a boxy interface.

The ListView and FormView controls are two data Web controls that offer the same rich features found in the GridView and DetailsView—sorting, paging, inserting, editing, and deleting—but with a much more flexible layout. Rather than using fields, the ListView and

FormView controls define their layout via templates. Because templates allow for a mix of HTML, Web controls, and data binding syntax, the ListView and FormView controls can be configured to render any values from their data source controls using any Web control and in any order.

Displaying Data Using the ListView Control

Like the GridView, the ListView control displays all the records returned by its data source control. Instead of displaying its underlying data as a grid, the ListView renders its contents based on its templates. Templates provide a finer degree of control over the rendered markup and therefore enable the ListView to display data in more interesting and customizable ways than is possible with the GridView.

By the Way

> The ListView control is new to ASP.NET version 3.5. Prior to version 3.5, developers used the DataList or Repeater controls to display multiple records using a template. The DataList and Repeater controls are still available in ASP.NET version 3.5 and can be found in the Toolbox along with the ListView. This book focuses on the ListView because it includes additional features not found in the DataList or Repeater.

Let's practice using the ListView control to display data. Create a new ASP.NET page and add a SqlDataSource to the page, naming it `BooksDataSource`. Configure the `BooksDataSource` control to return all the columns from the `Books` table. Next, add a ListView control to the page. The ListView control is located in the Data section of the Toolbox alongside the other data Web controls and data source controls.

The ListView control is displayed in the Design view as a gray box until its ItemTemplate and LayoutTemplate are defined. The ItemTemplate and LayoutTemplate are two of the ListView's templates and are both required. These templates can be created manually or automatically through the Configure ListView dialog box. Regardless of how these templates are created, we first need to specify the control's data source. To accomplish this, go to the ListView control's smart tag and choose the `BooksDataSource` from the drop-down list. Upon selecting the data source, the smart tag is refreshed and includes a new option, Configure ListView (see Figure 19.1).

By the Way

> If you do not see the Configure ListView option in your ListView's smart tag after binding it to a data source, click the Refresh Schema link in the smart tag.

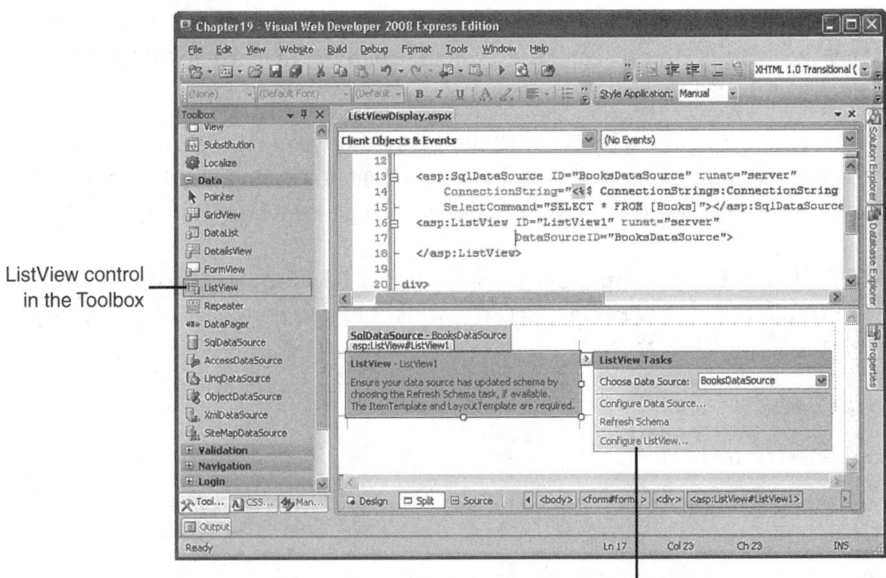

FIGURE 19.1 You can configure the ListView control after it has been bound to a data source control.

At this point we're ready to create the LayoutTemplate and ItemTemplate. Before we examine how to create these templates, let's first discuss how these two templates are used by the ListView when rendering its output.

Examining How the ListView Renders Its LayoutTemplate and ItemTemplate

The GridView displays the contents of its underlying data source control in a grid. Each record returned by the data source control is rendered as a row; the grid's columns are defined by the GridView's fields.

The ListView, on the other hand, displays the contents of its underlying data source control using templates. The LayoutTemplate is rendered exactly once and includes any HTML or text that you want to appear around the data. For example, if you want to display a message above the data, you can do so by typing in the text in the LayoutTemplate.

The ItemTemplate is rendered once for each record returned by the data source control and typically contains HTML, Web controls, and data binding syntax. Recall from Hour 18 that data binding syntax is markup in the form `<%# Eval("columnName") %>` or `<%# Bind("columnName") %>`. These expressions return the value of the database column *columnName* for the current data source record.

Finally, the LayoutTemplate must contain a server-side control that has its `ID` set to `itemPlaceholder`. This specifies the location within the LayoutTemplate that the contents of the ItemTemplate are added.

If all this information is a bit overwhelming, don't worry, an example should clear things up. Listing 19.1 shows the declarative markup of a sample ListView control. The LayoutTemplate is defined in lines 2–5, the ItemTemplate in lines 6 through 12.

LISTING 19.1 A Simple ListView Control's Declarative Markup

```
 1: <asp:ListView ID="ListView1" runat="server" DataSourceID="BooksDataSource">
 2:     <LayoutTemplate>
 3:         <h2>My Bookshelf</h2>
 4:         <asp:PlaceHolder runat="server" ID="itemPlaceholder">
➥</asp:PlaceHolder>
 5:     </LayoutTemplate>
 6:     <ItemTemplate>
 7:         <p>
 8:             <asp:Label ID="TitleLabel" runat="server" Text='<%#
➥Eval("Title") %>'></asp:Label>
 9:             <br />
10:             (Written by: <%# Eval("Author") %>)
11:         </p>
12:    </ItemTemplate>
13: </asp:ListView>
```

The LayoutTemplate displays the text `My Bookshelf` in an `<h2>` HTML element on line 3. `<h2>` is an HTML element that displays its inner content in a large, bold font. The `<asp:PlaceHolder>` markup on line 4 specifies the location where the rendered ItemTemplate contents will be placed. As its name implies, the PlaceHolder control's purpose is to serve as a marker. Because the PlaceHolder's `ID` is set to `itemPlaceholder`, the ListView will place the rendered contents of its ItemTemplate here.

The ItemTemplate displays the `Title` and `Author` columns using data binding syntax. A Label Web control is used on line 8, with the `Title` column assigned to the Label's `Text` property. Data binding expressions can be used outside of Web controls, as the syntax on line 10 shows.

In addition to the data binding syntax, the ItemTemplate contains text and HTML elements. The `Author` value displayed on line 10 is prefaced with the text `Written by:`. There's also a paragraph element (lines 7 and 11) and a line break element (line 9) to add some whitespace when displayed in the browser.

Watch Out!

When assigning a database column value to a Web control property using data binding syntax, it is imperative that you use apostrophes to delimit the property value and quotation marks to delimit the column name in the `Eval` or `Bind` method. For example, the markup used on line 8 to assign the `Title` column value to the `TitleLabel`'s `Text` property is:

```
Text='<%# Eval("Title") %>'
```

Note that apostrophes delimit the value assigned to the `Text` property, and quotation marks delimit the column name (`Title`). The following examples are invalid and will result in an error:

```
Text="<%# Eval("Title") %>"
Text="<%# Eval('Title') %>"
```

Figure 19.2 shows this ListView control when viewed through a browser.

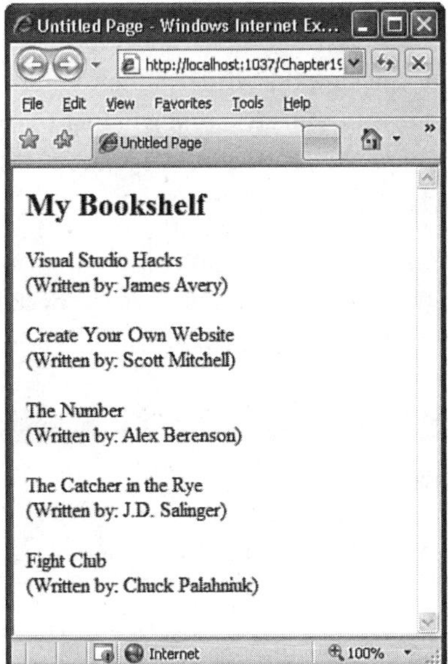

FIGURE 19.2
The `Title` and `Author` columns are displayed for the five books in the `Books` table.

When the ASP.NET engine rendered the ListView control shown in Figure 19.2, it started by emitting the contents in the LayoutTemplate, namely the title `My Bookshelf`. It then enumerated the records in the data source control and, for each record, rendered the ItemTemplate. This resulted in HTML that displayed the book's title and author within a paragraph element. For example, the following markup was rendered for the ItemTemplate rendered for the book *Visual Studio Hacks*:

```
<p>
   <span id="ListView1_ctrl0_TitleLabel">Visual Studio Hacks</span>
   <br />
   (Written by: James Avery)
</p>
```

By going to your browser's View menu and choosing Source, you can see the complete HTML that was generated.

The important concept to take away from this discussion is that the ListView generates it markup by first rendering the LayoutTemplate and then rendering the ItemTemplate for each record, placing the rendered markup at the location in the LayoutTemplate designated by the server control whose `ID` is `itemPlaceholder`.

Adding Templates Using the Configure ListView Option

After specifying the ListView's data source, its smart tag is refreshed to include a Configure ListView option. Clicking this displays the Configure ListView dialog box, from which we can pick a layout and style and whether to include paging support. After specifying these options and clicking the OK button, Visual Web Developer automatically generates the ListView's templates.

Let's practice using the Configure ListView option. For this example, use the Grid layout and Professional style; leave the Enable Paging check box unchecked. Figure 19.3 shows the Configure ListView dialog box after these selections have been made.

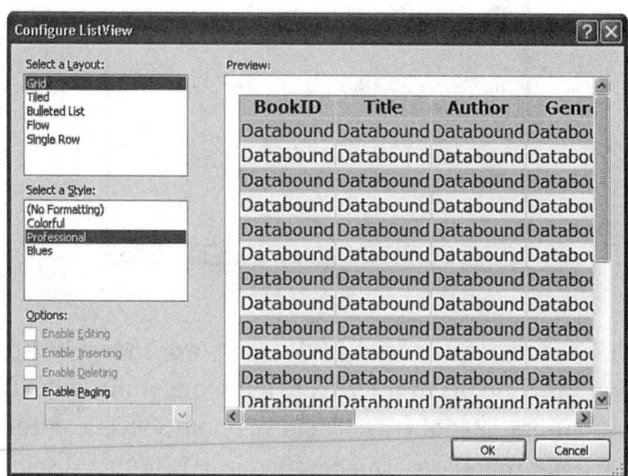

FIGURE 19.3 Specify the ListView's Layout and Style settings.

Based on your choices made in the Configure ListView dialog box, Visual Studio creates a series of templates for the ListView. The Grid layout uses an HTML <table> element in the LayoutTemplate to create a gridlike configuration. The Professional style adds assorted style-related markup to the templates to apply various formatting rules, such as the grid's background colors and border settings.

Take a second to peer through the Source view. Along with the LayoutTemplate and ItemTemplate, the Configure ListView dialog box created the following additional templates:

- AlternatingItemTemplate
- InsertItemTemplate
- SelectedItemTemplate
- EmptyDataTemplate
- EditItemTemplate

Table 19.1 summarizes the ListView's most commonly used templates.

TABLE 19.1 The Most Commonly Used ListView Templates

Template	Description
AlternatingItemTemplate	If present, this template is rendered in place of the ItemTemplate for alternating rows.
EditItemTemplate	If the ListView is configured to support editing, this template is used to render the editing interface.
EmptyDataTemplate	Rendered if no records are returned by the data source control.
GroupTemplate	A ListView can be configured to render several ItemTemplates as a "group." The markup for each group is defined by this template.
InsertItemTemplate	If the ListView is configured to support inserting, this template is used to render the inserting interface.
ItemSeparatorTemplate	If specified, this template's markup is injected between each rendered ItemTemplate.
ItemTemplate	This template is rendered once for each record returned from the data source control. This template is required.
LayoutTemplate	This template is rendered once for the entire control and specifies where the contents of the ItemTemplate are located. This template is required.

Figure 19.4 shows the ListView when viewed through a browser.

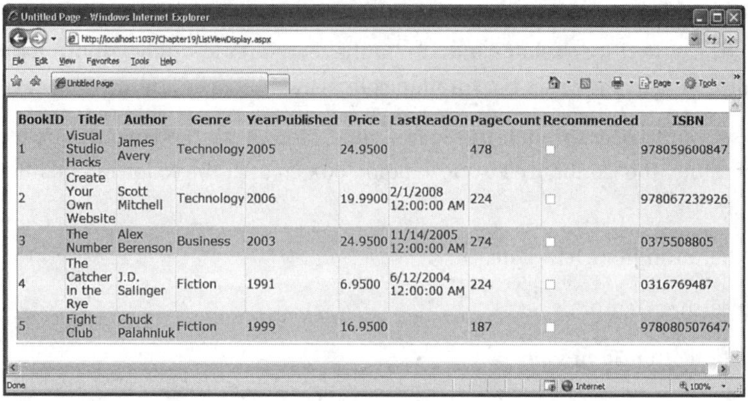

FIGURE 19.4
The ListView, when configured with the Grid layout and Professional style.

BookID	Title	Author	Genre	YearPublished	Price	LastReadOn	PageCount	Recommended	ISBN
1	Visual Studio Hacks	James Avery	Technology	2005	24.9500		478		978059600847
2	Create Your Own Website	Scott Mitchell	Technology	2006	19.9900	2/1/2008 12:00:00 AM	224		978067232926
3	The Number	Alex Berenson	Business	2003	24.9500	11/14/2005 12:00:00 AM	274		0375508805
4	The Catcher In the Rye	J.D. Salinger	Fiction	1991	6.9500	6/12/2004 12:00:00 AM	224		0316769487
5	Fight Club	Chuck Palahniuk	Fiction	1999	16.9500		187		978080507647

Adding Templates Manually

As we've seen in previous hours, the GridView and DetailsView controls include an Edit Templates option in their smart tags that, when clicked, displays a template editing interface in the Design view. Unfortunately, the ListView does not include a template editing interface. All template content must be added directly to the Source view.

To practice specifying the markup for these templates manually, create a new page named `SimpleListView.aspx`. Add a SqlDataSource control and configure it to return all records from the `Books` table. Next, add a ListView control to the page and bind it to the SqlDataSource control. Finally, type in the LayoutTemplate and ItemTemplate content from Listing 19.1 (lines 2–12) into the ListView control's declarative markup. After entering these templates, the ListView no longer displays as a gray box in the Design view, but instead offers a WYSIWYG interface (see Figure 19.5).

Let's try another example. Create a new page named `SimpleListView2.aspx` and add a SqlDataSource and ListView control like before. This time, define the LayoutTemplate so that it includes an `<h2>` element displaying the text `Welcome to My Bookstore` and indents the contents of the ItemTemplates using the `<blockquote>` element.

In the ItemTemplate, use an `<h3>` element to display the `Title`. Beneath that, display the `Genre` and `Price` values, formatting the price as a currency. Include a CheckBox Web control and set its `Checked` property to the value returned from the `Recommended` database column. Also set the CheckBox's `Text` property to `Recommended` and the `Enabled` property to `False`.

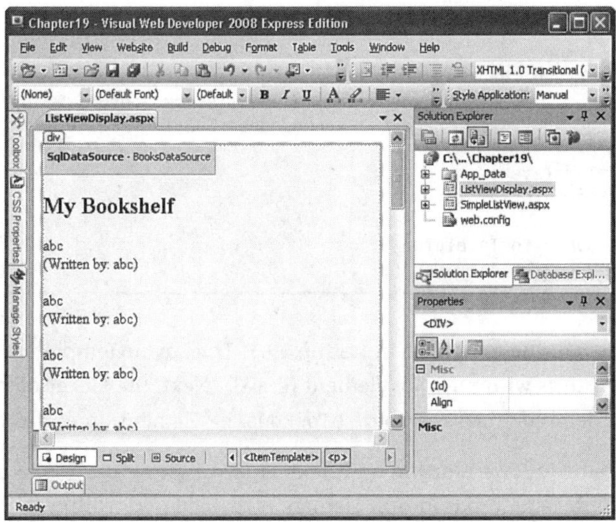

FIGURE 19.5
With the LayoutTemplate and ItemTemplate specified, the Design view offers a WYSIWYG view of the ListView.

Finally, use the `<hr />` HTML element to display a horizontal rule between each rendered item. As noted in Table 19.1, the ListView's ItemSeparatorTemplate's content is rendered between each ItemTemplate, so put this HTML there.

The markup for these three templates is provided in Listing 19.2. However, I encourage you to first try to create the markup for these three templates on your own. Don't worry about making a mistake or doing things wrong; just try your best, knocking off one little piece at a time. Frequently check your progress by viewing the WYSIWYG display in the Design view and by visiting the page through a browser.

LISTING 19.2 This ListView Uses Three Templates: LayoutTemplate, ItemTemplate, and ItemSeparatorTemplate

```
<asp:ListView ID="ListView1" runat="server" DataSourceID="BooksDataSource">
    <LayoutTemplate>
        <h2>Welcome to My Bookstore</h2>
        <blockquote>
            <asp:PlaceHolder runat="server" ID="itemPlaceholder">
➥</asp:PlaceHolder>
        </blockquote>
    </LayoutTemplate>
    <ItemTemplate>
        <h3><%#Eval("Title")%></h3>
        <p>
            <b>Genre: </b>
            <asp:Label runat="server" id="GenreLabel"
➥Text='<%# Eval("Genre") %>'></asp:Label>
            <br />
            <b>Price: </b>
            <%#Eval("Price", "{0:c}")%>
```

LISTING 19.2 Continued

```
16:             <br />
17:             <asp:CheckBox ID="RecommendedCheckBox" runat="server"
18:                           Checked='<%# Eval("Recommended") %>'
19:                           Text="Recommended" Enabled="false" />
20:         </p>
21:     </ItemTemplate>
22:     <ItemSeparatorTemplate>
23:         <hr />
24:     </ItemSeparatorTemplate>
25: </asp:ListView>
```

Let's review each of the templates in Listing 19.2. The LayoutTemplate spans lines 2 through 7. It starts with an <h2> element (line 3). Next, the PlaceHolder with ID itemPlaceholder is defined within a <blockquote> element (lines 4–6).

The ItemTemplate follows, starting on line 8. Line 9 displays the Title column in an <h3> element. Next, a paragraph element is defined and, within that, the Genre, Price, and Recommended columns are displayed. The Genre column value is bound to the Text property of the GenreLabel Label Web control (line 12). Recall that the Eval and Bind methods can display the specified column using a format specified. The Eval method on line 15 is passed two input parameters: Price and {0:c}. This displays the value of the Price column using the currency format. A CheckBox is used to indicate whether a book is recommended. Because the value of the Recommended column is bound to the CheckBox's Checked property, the resulting check box will be checked only if Recommended is True.

ItemSeparatorTemplate is the third and final template (lines 22–24). It indicates that a horizontal rule should separate each ItemTemplate.

Figure 19.6 shows the SimpleListView2.aspx page when viewed through a browser.

By the Way

Although the Configure ListView dialog box automatically generates the templates for you, it's likely that you'll need to further customize the templates' contents. Because no Edit Templates interface exists, these customizations must be made through the Source view. Therefore, I suggest that you become comfortable with creating and editing the ListView's templates through the Source view.

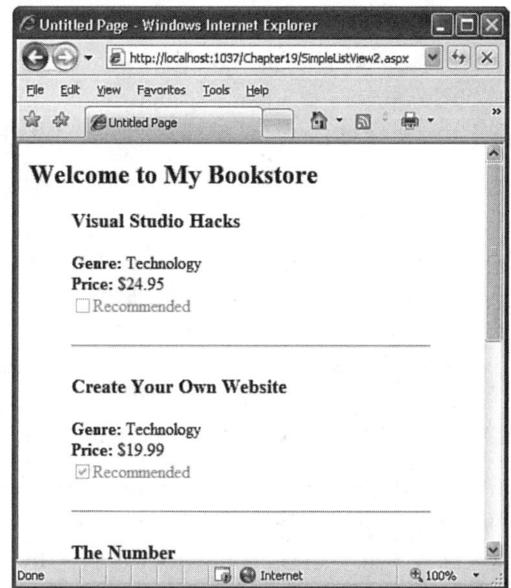

FIGURE 19.6 Each book's `Title`, `Genre`, `Price`, and `Recommended` values are displayed.

Paging and Sorting the ListView's Data

Like the GridView, the ListView can be configured to include options for the user to sort and page through the data. Recall that with the GridView, configuring the sorting and paging features is as simple as checking the Enable Sorting and Enable Paging check boxes in the GridView's smart tag. Enabling sorting converts each of the GridView's column headers from plain text to a LinkButtons that, when clicked, causes a postback and redisplays the GridView data sorted by the selected column. With paging enabled, the GridView includes a paging interface with page numbers or next and previous links.

Implementing sorting and paging in the ListView control requires a little more work on our end. Because of the ListView's highly customizable layout, it cannot automatically insert sort LinkButtons or render a paging interface. Instead, we must define the sorting and paging interfaces. The good news is that this can be accomplished by adding various Web controls to the ListView's templates, and it does not require us to write any code.

The next two sections look at implementing sorting and paging in a ListView. In "Creating a Sorting Interface" we will look at how to add sorting LinkButtons to the ListView. The "Adding Paging Support" section builds on the sortable ListView and adds a paging interface.

Creating a Sorting Interface

Defining a sorting interface for the ListView entails adding specially configured LinkButton controls to the ListView's templates. Usually these LinkButtons are placed in the LayoutTemplate so that they appear just once; defining them in the ItemTemplate would have them appear once for each record returned by the data source control.

Create a new page named SortAndPageListView.aspx. Add a SqlDataSource control and configure it to return all the records from the Books table; set its ID to BooksDataSource. Next, add a ListView control, binding it to the BooksDataSource SqlDataSource; set the ListView's ID property to BookList. Re-create the templates from SimpleListView2.aspx and Listing 19.2 in the BookList ListView. You can reenter the templates' syntax or copy and paste the declarative markup.

Let's add two sorting options to the ListView—one to sort by title and one to sort by price. Add two LinkButton controls to the LayoutTemplate beneath the <h2> element, but above <blockquote>. Set the LinkButtons' ID properties to SortByTitle and SortByPrice. Similarly, set the Text properties to Sort By Title and Sort By Price.

View the SortListView.aspx page through a browser. You should now see the two sort LinkButtons below the Welcome to My Bookstore title. Clicking these links causes a postback, but the data is not sorted. For these LinkButtons to sort the data, we need to configure two of their properties:

- **CommandName**—This property must be set to Sort.
- **CommandArgument**—Set this property to the column name by which to sort the results.

Set the SortByTitle LinkButton's CommandName property to Sort and its CommandArgument property to Title; likewise, set the SortByPrice LinkButton's CommandName property to Sort and its CommandArgument property to Price. With these changes in place, your ListView's LayoutTemplate should look similar to the following

```
<LayoutTemplate>
    <h2>Welcome to My Bookstore</h2>
    <asp:LinkButton ID="SortByTitle" runat="server"
                    Text="Sort By Title"
                    CommandName="Sort"
                    CommandArgument="Title"></asp:LinkButton> |
    <asp:LinkButton ID="SortByPrice" runat="server"
                    Text="Sort By Price"
                    CommandName="Sort"
                    CommandArgument="Price"></asp:LinkButton>
```

```
    <blockquote>
        <asp:PlaceHolder runat="server" ID="itemPlaceholder"></asp:PlaceHolder>
    </blockquote>
</LayoutTemplate>
```

Visit the page through a browser again. This time, clicking the LinkButtons not only causes a postback, but sorts the data by the specified column. Moreover, clicking a particular LinkButton multiple times toggles between sorting the data in ascending and descending order.

Did you Know?

> The `SortListView.aspx` page uses LinkButtons for the sorting interface. Alternatively, you can use Buttons or ImageButtons. The same configuration steps apply—namely, set the `CommandName` and `CommandArgument` properties.

Figure 19.7 shows the results of clicking the Sort By Title LinkButton. Refer to Figure 19.6 to see what the page looks like when first visited, before a sort LinkButton has been clicked.

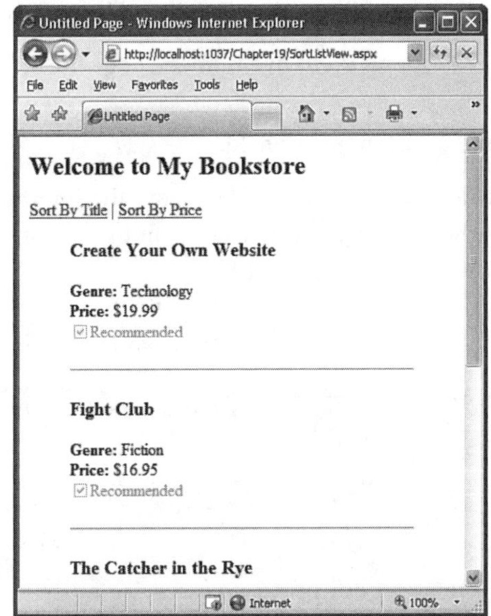

FIGURE 19.7 The books are sorted by their titles.

Adding Paging Support

The ListView does not offer built-in paging support itself. Instead, paging is provided through a separate Web control, the DataPager. The DataPager control renders a paging interface for a specified data Web control. To allow the user to page through the ListView's records, then, add a DataPager to the page wherever you want the paging interface to appear and configure its properties.

By the Way

> Like the ListView, the DataPager control is new to ASP.NET version 3.5. The DataPager works only with the ListView control, but I wouldn't be surprised if in future versions of ASP.NET the DataPager also works with the GridView, DetailsView, and FormView controls.

Let's update the `SortAndPageListView.aspx` page so that visitors can page through the books using a First, Previous, Next, Last paging interface. Add a DataPager to the page, placing it beneath the ListView control. The DataPager control is located in the Data section of the Toolbox.

The Design view displays the DataPager control as a gray box until its **pager fields** are defined. The pager fields are what make up the paging interface. The DataPager's smart tag contains a Choose Pager Style drop-down list with two common pager field options:

- **Next/Previous Pager**—Displays First, Previous, Next, and Last buttons
- **Numeric Pager**—Displays up to five numeric page links

You may optionally use a custom pager field.

For now, choose the Next/Previous Pager option from the smart tag's drop-down list. As Figure 19.8 shows, the DataPager now appears in the Design view as four Button controls labeled First, Previous, Next, and Last.

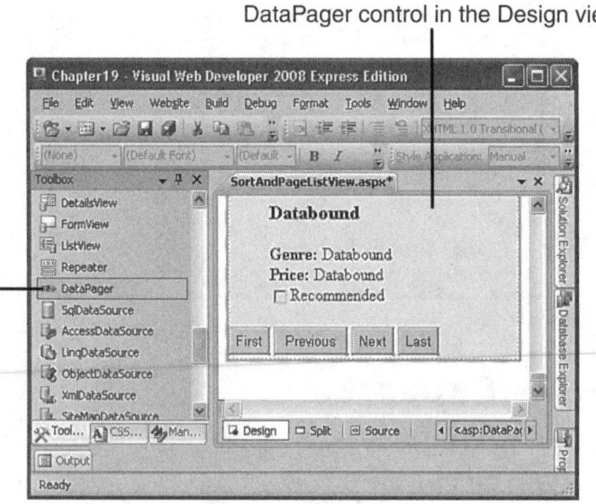

FIGURE 19.8
The DataPager appears in the Designer as First, Previous, Next, and Last buttons.

To customize the DataPager's appearance, select the Edit Pager Fields option from its smart tag. This launches a dialog box from which you can customize the pager field's properties (see Figure 19.9). For example, you can specify whether to display the First and Last options by configuring the Next/Previous Pager Field's `ShowFirstPageButton` and `ShowLastPageButton` properties. To alter the text displayed in these buttons, use the `FirstPageText`, `PreviousPageText`, `NextPageText`, and `LastPageText` properties.

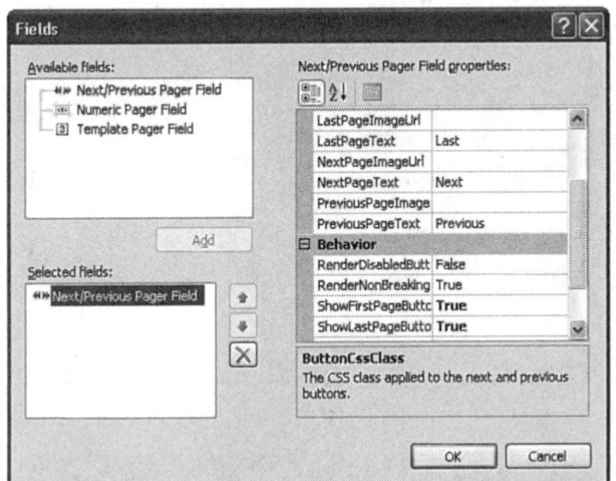

FIGURE 19.9
It is easy to customize the pager field's appearance.

After you have the pager field looking the way you want, the last step is to wire up the DataPager to the ListView control. This is accomplished by setting the DataPager's `PagedControlID` property to the `ID` of the ListView. Select the DataPager to load its properties in the Properties window. The `PagedControlID` property lists the available ListView controls on the page in a drop-down list—select `BookList`.

The DataPager's `PageSize` property indicates how many records to display per page and defaults to 10. Because only five books are in the `Books` table, if we leave property set at its default, all the records will be displayed on the first page, and the paging interface will be disabled. Therefore, set the `PageSize` to 2 so that the list of books is spread across three pages.

After making these changes, visit the page through a browser. As Figure 19.10 shows, when the page is first visited, only the first two books are displayed—*Visual Studio Hacks* and *Create Your Own Website*. The Next and Last buttons are enabled.

Figure 19.11 shows the page after the Next button is clicked. The books *The Number* and *The Catcher in the Rye* are listed, and all four pager buttons are enabled.

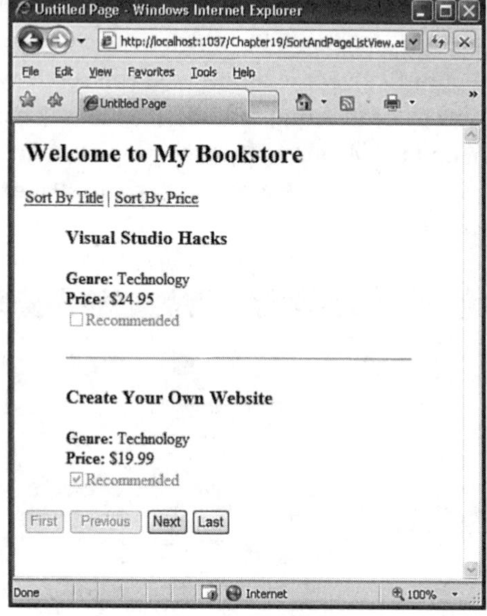

FIGURE 19.10 The first page of data is displayed.

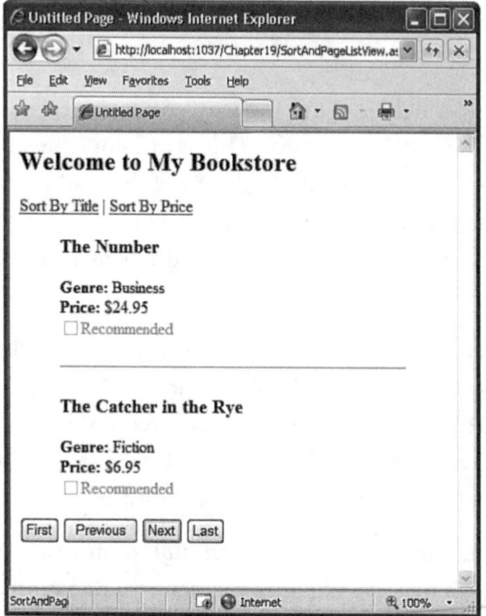

FIGURE 19.11 Clicking Next displays the second page of data.

Did you Know?

If you want to include a paging interface at the top and bottom of the ListView controls, place one DataPager control above the ListView and another beneath it. Just put a DataPager control in every location you want a paging interface to be rendered.

Displaying One Record at a Time with the FormView Control

The ListView control displays all the records from its data source control using, at minimum, a LayoutTemplate and ItemTemplate. The FormView is similar to the ListView in that it uses templates to render its output, but instead of displaying all the records from its data source, it displays only one at a time, much like the DetailsView control.

Let's practice using the FormView control. Create a new page named `FormView.aspx`. Start by adding a SqlDataSource to the page; configure it to return all columns from the `Books` table and set its `ID` property to `BooksDataSource`. Next, add a FormView control to the page. The FormView can be found in the Data section of the Toolbox.

Like the ListView, the FormView initially appears in the Design view as a gray box. It cannot be rendered in the Design view until its ItemTemplate is defined. The FormView's smart tag includes three options:

- **Auto Format**—This option works like the DetailsView's Auto Format option. Selecting it displays a number of predefined styles in the Auto Format dialog box, and choosing one of the styles sets a number of the FormView's formatting properties.
- **Choose Data Source**—Select the data source to bind to the FormView from the drop-down list.
- **Edit Templates**—This option displays the same WYSIWYG template editor available from the GridView and DetailsView's smart tags.

Bind the FormView to the `BooksDataSource` SqlDataSource control by selecting it from the Choose Data Source drop-down list. This automatically creates an ItemTemplate, EditItemTemplate, and InsertItemTemplate for the FormView control. Moreover, the smart tag is updated to include an Enable Paging check box.

The ItemTemplate that was automatically generated by Visual Web Developer when selecting the FormView's data source displays the name and value of each column returned by the data source control. Figure 19.12 shows the FormView when viewed through the Design view. The Designer lists each column name and then `0` or `abc` to represent where the value of the column will be displayed.

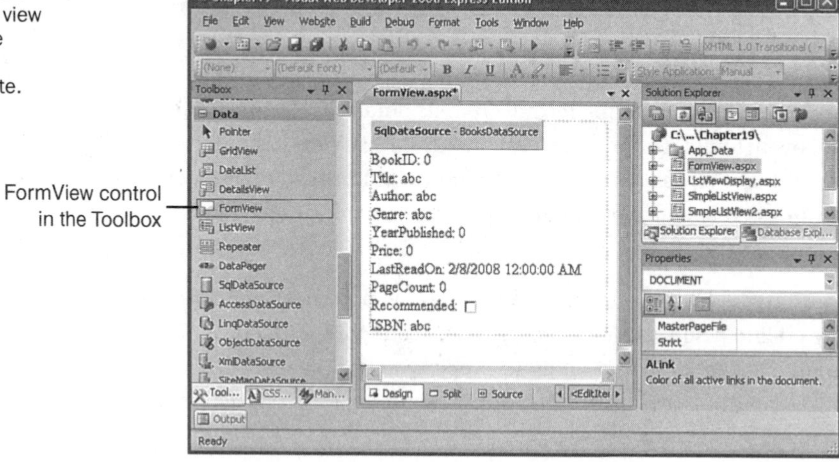

FIGURE 19.12 The Design view displays the FormView's ItemTemplate.

View the FormView through a browser. As Figure 19.13 shows, the FormView displays only the *first* record returned by its data source control (*Visual Studio Hacks*).

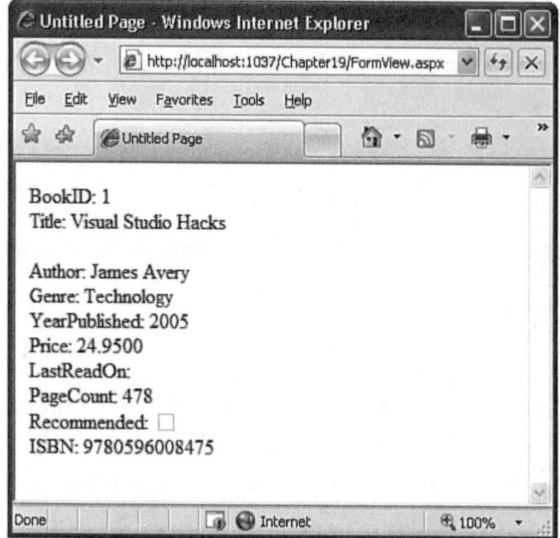

FIGURE 19.13 The FormView renders the first record returned by its data source control.

Paging Through the Records One at a Time

You may have noticed that the FormView, by default, doesn't provide any mechanism by which to view the next record in the data source. Like the DetailsView, we see just one record at a time, but there's no way to move to the next record. To provide a means to step through the records, check the Enable Paging check box in the

FormView's smart tag. This adds a paging interface to the bottom of the FormView's rendered markup. By default, the paging interface uses page numbers to allow the user to jump to a particular record, but the paging interface is configurable through the `PagerSettings` property.

After checking the Enable Paging check box, take a moment to view the page in a browser. Note that now there are five links at the bottom of the DetailsView, allowing you to navigate to any of the five records in the `Books` table by clicking the appropriately numbered link. Figure 19.14 shows this default paging interface.

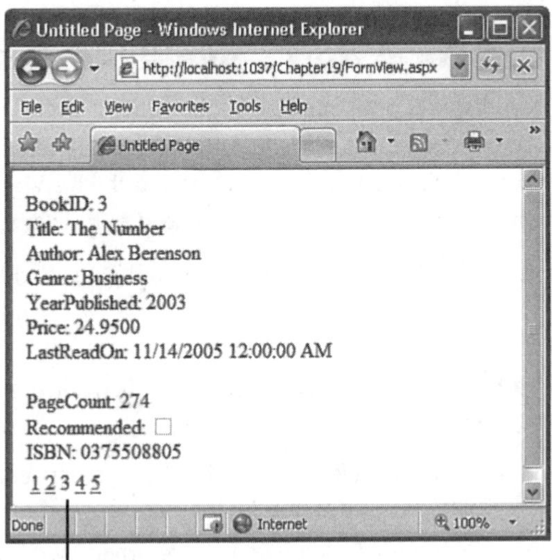

FIGURE 19.14
The FormView's default paging interface uses a series of page numbers.

The paging interface can be customized through the Properties window. From the Properties window, scroll down to the Paging section. There, you'll find two properties:

- **`AllowPaging`**—This property indicates whether paging is supported (it defaults to `False`). When you checked the Enable Paging check box in the smart tag, this property was set to `True`.
- **`PagerSettings`**—This property contains a number of subproperties that customize the appearance of the pager row. For example, instead of having page number links, you can use Next/Previous links.

These paging options should be familiar because the DetailsView control offers the same paging-related properties.

You may have noticed that the FormView is more similar to the DetailsView than the ListView is to the GridView. For example, the FormView's smart tag includes an EditTemplates option. Paging is enabled through the FormView's `AllowPaging` property rather than the DataPager control. The reason is that the FormView control was introduced in ASP.NET version 2.0, at the same time as the GridView and DetailsView controls. Not surprisingly, they all have roughly the same set of features and configuration options. The ListView and DataPager controls, however, were added to the ASP.NET Toolbox in version 3.5, which explains why they may seem like the oddballs of the data Web controls.

Examining the FormView's Available Templates

Because the FormView displays only one record at a time, it does not need as many templates as the ListView. For example, the ListView has an ItemSeparatorTemplate that, if present, is rendered between each item bound to the ListView. With the FormView, only one item is rendered, so there's no need to have a separator template.

Table 19.2 lists the FormView's seven templates. The only required template is the ItemTemplate.

TABLE 19.2 The FormView's Seven Available Templates

Template	Description
EditItemTemplate	If the FormView is configured to support editing, this template is used to render the editing interface.
EmptyDataTemplate	Rendered if no records are returned by the data source control.
FooterTemplate	If present, this template's rendered markup appears after all other templates.
HeaderTemplate	If present, this template's rendered markup appears before all other templates.
InsertItemTemplate	If the FormView is configured to support inserting, this template is used to render the inserting interface.
ItemTemplate	This template is rendered for the current data source record. This template is required.
PagerTemplate	The FormViewUse automatically renders a paging interface. Use this template to render a custom paging interface.

Customizing the Templates

The ItemTemplate generated by Visual Studio is rather bland and uninspiring. Let's update this default ItemTemplate so that it displays only a subset of the database column values. Furthermore, let's format the values we do display so that they stand out more.

Working with the FormView's templates is much easier than working with the ListView's because the FormView offers the WYSIWYG Edit Templates interface. Go to the FormView's smart tag and click the Edit Templates link. This displays the template editing view, with the smart tag listing the available templates.

The ItemTemplate displays each column name as text. This text is followed by a Label Web control or a CheckBox Web control, depending on the column's data type. Let's remove the text and Label controls that display the `BookID`, `YearPublished`, `LastReadOn`, and `ISBN` columns. To remove this content, click within the ItemTemplate editing interface and use your keyboard's Delete or Backspace keys.

Let's format the Title column so that it displays in a large, bold font. First, remove the `Title:` text preceding the `TitleLabel` Label control. Then select the `TitleLabel` so that its properties are loaded in the Properties window. From there, expand the `Font` property and set its Bold and Size subproperties to `True` and `X-Large`, respectively.

At this point your screen should look similar to Figure 19.15.

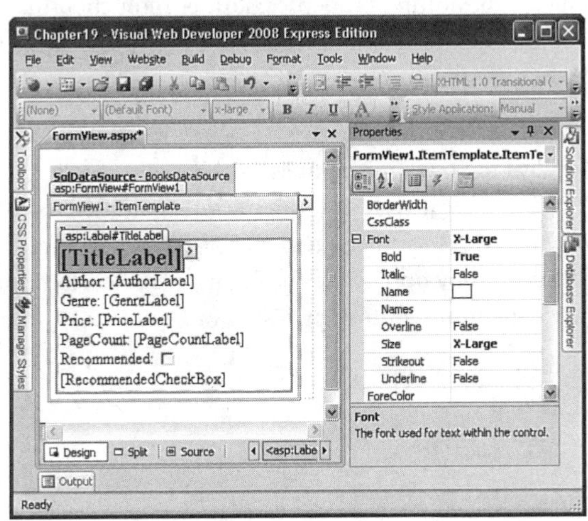

FIGURE 19.15 Customize the FormView's ItemTemplate through the Edit Templates interface.

Next, change the `Author:` and `PageCount:` text to **`Written By:`** and **`Pages:`**. Last, format the value of the `Price` column as a currency. To accomplish this, bring up the `PriceLabel`'s smart tag and choose the Edit DataBindings option. This brings up the `PriceLabel` DataBindings dialog box, indicating that the Label's `Text` property is bound to the `Price` column value. This dialog box includes a Format drop-down list that's currently set to None—change this to Currency (see Figure 19.16).

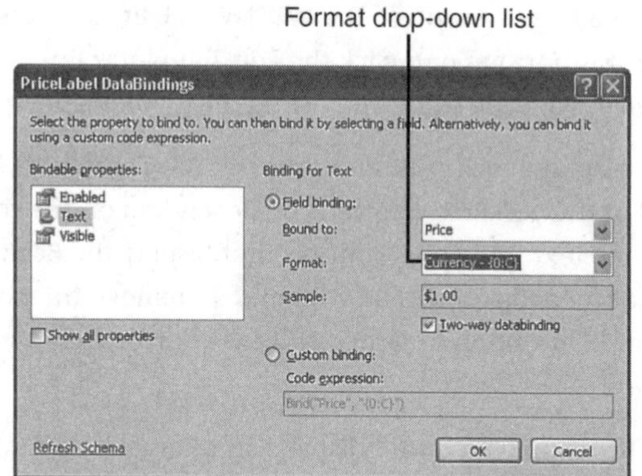

FIGURE 19.16
Format the `Price` database column value as a currency.

Finally, let's add some color to our FormView. Exit the Edit Template interface by selecting the End Template Editing link from the smart tag. Next, choose the Auto Format option from the smart tag and pick a scheme. Like with the GridView and DetailsView controls, picking a scheme from the Auto Format dialog box sets a number of the control's formatting properties. Rather than choosing a predefined format scheme, you can alternatively select custom colors and styles from the Properties window in the Appearance, Layout, and Style sections.

After completing these customizations, view the page through a browser. The FormView now displays the book information in a more appealing format: the title is bold and displayed in a large font size; the price is formatted as a currency; superfluous columns, like `BookID`, have been removed from the display; and a dash of color has been added. To fully appreciate the changes and customizations we just made, compare the appearance of the FormView in Figure 19.17 with the one in Figure 19.13.

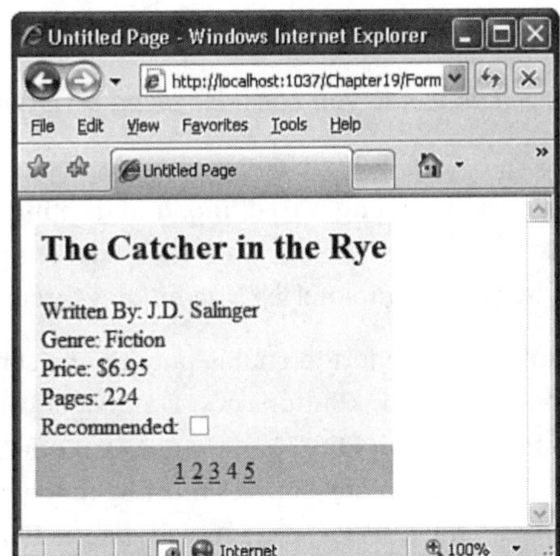

FIGURE 19.17
The FormView's appearance has been vastly improved.

Summary

ASP.NET offers a number of data Web controls that are ideal for different situations. The past several hours focused on two of the most commonly used controls, the GridView and DetailsView. In some scenarios, however, a more flexible layout is needed, which is where the ListView and FormView controls come in.

Like the GridView, the ListView control displays a set of records from its data source control, but instead of using fields, the ListView's makeup is defined via templates. In particular, a ListView must use two templates—LayoutTemplate and ItemTemplate—and these templates may be defined manually through the Source view or automatically via the Configure ListView dialog box. As we saw in the "Adding Paging Support" section, the DataPager control is used to implement paging within the ListView control.

The FormView control is similar to the DetailsView in that both display one record at a time. Moreover, both controls offer paging support, which can be enabled and customized through the `AllowPaging` and `PagerSettings` properties. Like the ListView, the FormView renders its contents using templates.

This hour wraps up our look at accessing and modifying database data through an ASP.NET web page. Working with data through a web page is a very common task, so it's important that you're comfortable with the processes examined in the past several hours. Before you continue, it behooves you to spend adequate time practicing creating data-driven ASP.NET pages. I strongly encourage that you work through all the exercises from Hour 13 through Hour 19 before moving onward in your studies.

Q&A

Q. ***In what circumstances would you consider using a ListView over a GridView?***

A. Both the ListView and GridView are designed to display a set of records. It is easier to implement sorting, paging, editing, and deleting with the GridView than with the ListView. Moreover, the GridView's Edit Templates interface allows you to manage its TemplateFields' templates through the Design view.

The ListView requires more effort to enable paging and sorting, because you have to add and configure LinkButtons or a DataPager control rather than just checking a check box. And the ListView does not offer an Edit Templates interface, meaning any template changes must be made directly through the Source view. However, the ListView offers much greater flexibility in its rendered output.

Personally, I strive to use the GridView more often than the ListView because of its ease of configuration. However, certain pages require a more fluid layout than the GridView can offer, and in those cases I'll use a ListView.

Q. ***I noticed that the Configure ListView dialog box offers a Tiled layout option, which appears to display data source records in a multicolumn table. Where can I learn more about this?***

A. The ListView examples we examined in this hour focused on the LayoutTemplate and ItemTemplate. However, the ListView includes a GroupTemplate that, if present, groups together the rendered output of multiple ItemTemplates. The ListView's `GroupItemCount` property indicates how many ItemTemplates to render per group. This behavior can be utilized to generate HTML that will display data records in a multicolumn table.

To generate a multicolumn table layout, you can either select the Tiled layout from the Configure ListView dialog box or you can build the necessary LayoutTemplate, GroupTemplate, and ItemTemplate by hand. In either case, the value of the `GroupItemCount` property specifies how many columns appear in the table.

For more information on using the GroupTemplate, as well as a simple example of using the LayoutTemplate, GroupTemplate, and ItemTemplate in tandem to display data in a multicolumn table, refer to http://aspnet.4guysfromrolla.com/articles/010208-1.aspx.

Q. ***The GridView and DetailsView controls offer inserting, updating, and deleting support. Are these features found in the ListView and FormView controls?***

A. The ListView and FormView can be configured to support inserting, editing, and deleting. Unfortunately, we did not have time in this hour to cover these topics, but I invite you to try out these features on your own. To start, add a SqlDataSource to the page and have it generate the `INSERT`, `UPDATE`, and `DELETE` statements. Then add a ListView or FormView control and bind it to this SqlDataSource.

To enable inserting, editing, or deleting in the ListView, click the Configure ListView option from the smart tag. The Configure ListView dialog box will include check boxes labeled Enable Editing, Enable Inserting, and Enable Deleting.

When binding a SqlDataSource to a FormView, Visual Web Developer automatically generates an InsertItemTemplate and EditItemTemplate. If the SqlDataSource control has `INSERT`, `UPDATE`, and `DELETE` statements, the ItemTemplate includes a New and Edit LinkButtons that, when clicked, render the inserting or editing interface.

Workshop

Quiz

1. True or False: The ListView, DataPager, and FormView controls are new to ASP.NET version 3.5.
2. How can you have the ListView's templates automatically generated?
3. What steps do you need to perform to add sorting support to a ListView?
4. In what ways are the ListView and FormView controls alike? In what ways do they differ?
5. What is the purpose of the DataPager control?

Answers

1. False. Although the ListView and DataPager controls are new to ASP.NET version 3.5, the FormView was first added to ASP.NET in version 2.0.
2. After the ListView has been bound to a data source control, its smart tag includes a Configure ListView option. Clicking this displays the Configure ListView dialog box, from which you can specify the ListView's layout and style settings. The corresponding ListView templates are then created for you.
3. To add sorting support to a ListView, you need to manually create and configure the sorting interface. This entails adding a LinkButton, Button, or ImageButton control for each sorting option and then setting its `CommandName` property to `Sort` and its `CommandArgument` property to the value of the column to sort by.
4. The ListView and FormView are alike in that they both define their content through templates, and both offer inserting, editing, and deleting capabilities. They differ in that the ListView control is designed to display multiple records, whereas the FormView displays one record at a time, like the DetailsView.
5. The DataPager control renders a paging interface for a ListView control.

Exercises

1. The HTML elements `<ul>` and `<li>` work in tandem to render a bulleted list using the following pattern:

```
<ul>
    <li>List Item 1</li>
    <li>List Item 2</li>
    ...
    <li>List Item N</li>
</ul>
```

Use a ListView to display the `Title`, `Author`, and `Price` columns in a bulleted list. The rendered output should look something like this:

```
<ul>
    <li>Visual Studio Hacks: James Avery - $24.95</li>
    <li>Create Your Own Website: Scott Mitchell - $19.99</li>
    ...
    <li>Fight Club: Chuck Palahniuk - $16.95</li>
</ul>
```

Here's a hint: the `<ul>` and `</ul>` tags will appear in the LayoutTemplate, whereas the `<li>` element will appear in the ItemTemplate along with three databinding expressions.

2. Create two ASP.NET pages named `BookSummary.aspx` and `BookDetail.aspx`. In `BookSummary.aspx`, use a GridView to display each book's `Title` column value. Also include a HyperLinkField that displays a link titled `View Details` that, when clicked, takes the user to `BookDetail.aspx?BookID=`*`BookID`*.

   In `BookDetail.aspx`, use a FormView control to display all the column values of the book whose `BookID` value was passed through the querystring. Customize the FormView's ItemTemplate so that the `Title` is displayed in a large, bold font. Format the `Price` column value as a currency; format the `LastReadOn` column value so that just the date is displayed. Finally, add a HyperLink control to the page that, when clicked, takes the user back to `BookSummary.aspx`.

PART IV

Site Navigation, User Management, Page Layout, AJAX, and Deployment

HOUR 20

Defining a Site Map and Providing Site Navigation

In this hour, we will cover

- The basics of site navigation with ASP.NET
- Creating and defining your website's structure
- Showing the user's current location in the site's structure using a breadcrumb
- Displaying the site's structure using the TreeView Web control
- Using the Menu Web control

At its most granular level, a website is nothing more than a collection of discrete web pages. Typically these pages are logically related and categorized in some manner. For example, Amazon.com has its site broken into product categories, such as books, music, DVDs, and so forth. Each of these sections is further categorized by genre. The classification of a website's pages into logical categories is defined by a **site map**.

After a site map has been defined, most web developers create the **site navigation**. The site navigation is the collection of user interface elements that assist users in browsing the site. Common navigation elements include menus, treeviews, and breadcrumbs. These user interface elements serve two tasks: They let the users know where in the site they are currently visiting, and they make it easy for the users to quickly jump to another part of the site.

An Overview of ASP.NET's Site Navigation Features

ASP.NET provides a means to specify a hierarchical site map and includes Web controls for displaying site navigation controls based on a structure specified by the site map. The site map is implemented as an **XML file** that defines the logical sections of the site and optionally ties each section to a particular URL.

By the Way

> **XML**, which stands for **eXtensible Markup Language**, is a technology for expressing data in a text-based format using elements that can contain attributes and text content, much like the static HTML and Web controls are expressed through the HTML portion of an ASP.NET page. XML documents, however, are more flexible than HTML's syntax, allowing the creator of the XML document to define the elements that may appear in the markup. ASP.NET uses a special set of elements in the site map file.

ASP.NET provides three navigation Web controls:

- **SiteMapPath**—This Web control provides a **breadcrumb**, which is a single line of text showing the user her location in the website's structure. For example, at an online bookstore, if a user had drilled down to *Visual Studio Hacks*, the breadcrumb might look like Home, Computers, Programming, Visual Studio Hacks, with each section—Home, Computers, and so forth—rendered as links back to the previous section. A breadcrumb allows the user to quickly see where she is in the site and to navigate back through the logical hierarchy. (Figure 20.7 shows the SiteMapPath control when viewed through a browser.)
- **TreeView**—This Web control provides a hierarchical view of the site's structure. For an online bookstore, the top level would contain the main categories—Computers, Fiction, History, and so on—and each of those main categories could be expanded to show subcategories. (Figure 20.8 shows the TreeView control when viewed through a browser.)
- **Menu**—A menu offers the same data as in the treeview; the only difference is in how the data is displayed. The treeview renders as an expandable/collapsible tree, whereas the menu is composed of menu items and submenus. (Consult Figure 20.11 to see the Menu control in action.)

Because the navigation Web controls' contents are rendered based on the page being visited and the contents of the site map, updating the site map immediately updates the navigation controls used throughout the site. If you want to add a new section to your website, create the appropriate ASP.NET pages and then tie those new pages into the site map. As soon as these changes are made and saved, the navigation Web controls used throughout the site will automatically be updated to include this new section!

Before we can start using the navigation Web controls, we need to define our website's structure in a site map. In the next section we create the site map file. In the sections after that, we examine each of ASP.NET's three navigation Web controls.

Defining the Website's Structure Using a Site Map

Although a very small and trivial website composed of only a handful of pages might not have an easily identifiable site structure, all sufficiently large websites possess a logical structure that is usually easy to identify. The contents of the site, whether items for sale, discussions in online forums, or informational articles, can be classified in some manner. These classifications define the structure of a site.

Because we've yet to create any multipage websites, let's take a minute to build a website with a number of related web pages. These pages won't do anything interesting; rather, we'll use them simply to create a mock website structure. For this example, imagine that we are building an online bookstore.

Start by creating a new ASP.NET website project in Visual Web Developer. This new project should already include one ASP.NET page, `Default.aspx`. (If you used a project type that does not include `Default.aspx`, add it now.) Next, add four new ASP.NET web pages: `OnSale.aspx`, `Legal.aspx`, `Privacy.aspx`, and `About.aspx`. Add three folders to the website: `Business`, `Fiction`, and `Technology`. In each of these folders, add a single ASP.NET page, `Default.aspx`. Finally, in the Technology folder, add two subfolders, `Computers` and `Electronics`, adding a `Default.aspx` page to each of these subfolders.

> **Did you Know?**
> To add a new folder, right-click the project name in the Solution Explorer and choose the New Folder menu option. To add a web page to a particular folder, right-click that folder in the Solution Explorer and choose Add Item.

After you have added these web pages and folders, your Solution Explorer should look similar to Figure 20.1.

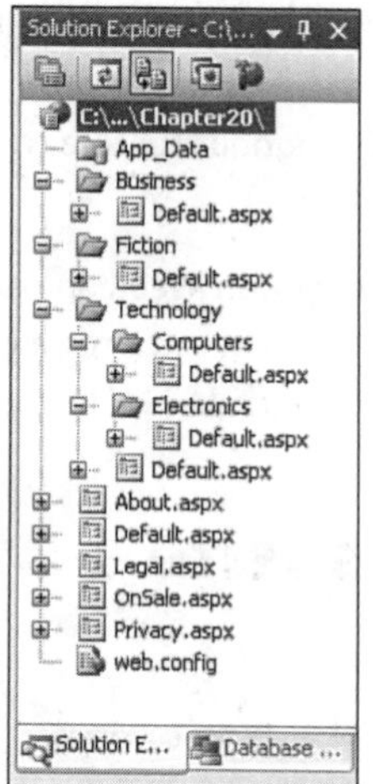

FIGURE 20.1
A number of new folders and web pages have been added to the project.

In each of these pages, add a short bit of text in the page, providing a summary of the page's functionality. For example, in the root directory's `Default.aspx` page, I put `Welcome to my online book store!`; in `OnSale.aspx`, I used `This lists the books currently on sale.`; in the `Business` folder's `Default.aspx` page, I added `This lists the books in the Business genre`. Add a similar brief summary for each page in the site.

Adding the Site Map

Now that we have created the pages for our mock website, we're ready to add the site map. To create the site map, follow the same steps as you normally would to add an ASP.NET web page to the project—right-click the project name in the Solution Explorer and choose the Add Item menu option. From the Add Item dialog box, choose the Site Map option (see Figure 20.2) and click the Add button. This adds a site map named `Web.sitemap` to your project.

When adding a site map to your project, put the site map in the root directory and leave the name of the file as `Web.sitemap`. If you place this file in another folder or choose a different name, the navigation Web controls won't be able to find the site map because, by default, they look for a file named `Web.sitemap` in the root directory.

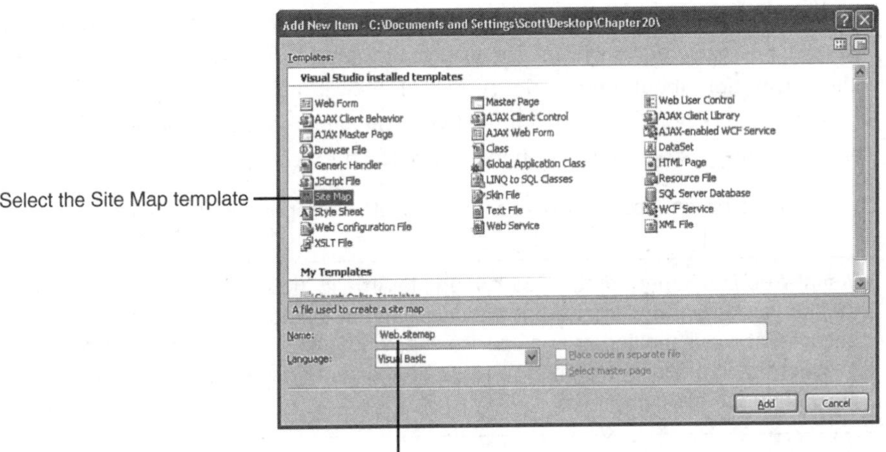

FIGURE 20.2 Add a new site map to the website.

After you have added the site map, open it by double-clicking the `Web.sitemap` file in the Solution Explorer. Listing 20.1 shows the default site map markup.

LISTING 20.1 The Default Content of the Site Map

```
1: <?xml version="1.0" encoding="utf-8" ?>
2: <siteMap xmlns="http://schemas.microsoft.com/AspNet/SiteMap-File-1.0" >
3:     <siteMapNode url="" title=""  description="">
4:         <siteMapNode url="" title=""  description="" />
5:         <siteMapNode url="" title=""  description="" />
6:     </siteMapNode>
7: </siteMap>
```

The site map file is an XML file that expresses the logical structure of the website. To define the site map, you need to edit this file manually. Don't forget that XML documents impose strict formatting rules. One rule is that XML is case sensitive. If you try to add a `<siteMapNode>` element using improper casing, such as `<SITEMapNode>`, you'll get an exception when attempting to use the navigation Web controls. Another rule of note is that all elements must have opening and closing tags. Notice how the `<siteMap>` element has an opening tag on line 2 and a closing tag on line 7. The `<siteMapNode>` element on line 3 has its opening tag there and its closing tag on line 6. The two `<siteMapNode>` elements on lines 4 and 5 don't have an explicit closing tag because they use the shorthand notation, `/>`.

By the Way

An XML element with no inner content can have its closing tag expressed in one of two ways: verbosely, such as *`<myTag attribute1="value1" ...></myTag>`*, or more tersely, using `/>` like so: *`<myTag attribute1="value1" ... />`*.

The site map begins with a <siteMap> element (line 2), which contains a number of <siteMapNode> elements within. The `url`, `title`, and `description` attributes provide information about a particular section of the website's structure, and the location of the <siteMapNode> element relative to the other <siteMapNode> elements determines the position of the section relative to other sections.

If this isn't clear yet, don't worry; a more concrete example ought to help.

Visual Web Developer notifies you if you enter invalid XML when creating the site map. If you enter an element that the site map does not know about, either because of a misspelling or improper casing, Visual Web Developer underlines the suspect tag in blue. If you forget to close an element, Visual Web Developer underlines the element in red.

Building the Site Map

Given the mock website we've created, let's define a site map that exhibits the logical hierarchy shown in Figure 20.3. Each node in the hierarchy shows the title and URL for the section along with the section's place in the hierarchy.

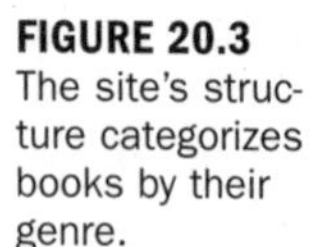

FIGURE 20.3
The site's structure categorizes books by their genre.

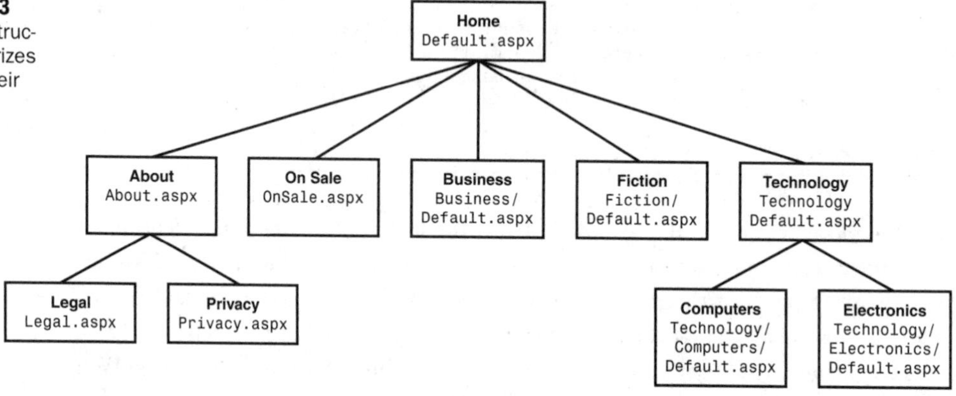

To implement this site structure in an ASP.NET site map, start by clearing out the <siteMapNode> elements from the default site map (remove lines 3 through 6 in Listing 20.1). Next, begin at the top section and work your way down the hierarchy, adding a <siteMapNode> for each section. Those sections that appear beneath a given section in the hierarchy will be nested within a <siteMapNode> element.

To put these concepts into practice, add a `<siteMapNode>` element for the Home section, like so:

```
<siteMapNode url="Default.aspx" title="Home"  description="" />
```

Notice that I used the section URL in Figure 20.3 as the value for the `url` attribute and the section title as the `title` attribute value. I am going to leave the `description` attribute blank, but feel free to enter a meaningful value here if you like. Also, note that for the Home `<siteMapNode>` element, I used the terse closing tag syntax, `/>`. After you add this element, your site map should look like this:

```
<?xml version="1.0" encoding="utf-8" ?>
<siteMap xmlns="http://schemas.microsoft.com/AspNet/SiteMap-File-1.0" >
   <siteMapNode url="Default.aspx" title="Home"  description="" />
</siteMap>
```

Because the next sections in the hierarchy exist as descendents of the Home section, the corresponding `<siteMapNode>` elements will be nested within the Home `<siteMapNode>` element. There are five such sections, requiring five `<siteMapNode>` elements:

```
<siteMapNode url="About.aspx" title="About" description="" />
<siteMapNode url="OnSale.aspx" title="On Sale" description="" />
<siteMapNode url="Business/Default.aspx" title="Business" description="" />
<siteMapNode url="Fiction/Default.aspx" title="Fiction" description="" />
<siteMapNode url="Technology/Default.aspx" title="Technology" description="" />
```

Watch Out!

XML's formatting rules prohibit the characters <, >, &, and " from appearing within an element's text content or as the value for an attribute. If you want to include any of these characters in the `title` or `description` attributes, you instead need to use `<`, `>`, `&`, or `"`, respectively. For example, if you wanted to have the `title` attribute for a site map node be `Business & Investing`, you need to use the text `Business & Investing`.

These five `<siteMapNode>` elements should be nested within the Home `<siteMapNode>` element, resulting in the following site map:

```
<?xml version="1.0" encoding="utf-8" ?>
<siteMap xmlns="http://schemas.microsoft.com/AspNet/SiteMap-File-1.0" >
   <siteMapNode url="Default.aspx" title="Home"  description="">
      <siteMapNode url="About.aspx" title="About"  description="" />
      <siteMapNode url="OnSale.aspx" title="On Sale"  description="" />
      <siteMapNode url="Business/Default.aspx" title="Business"
➥description="" />
      <siteMapNode url="Fiction/Default.aspx" title="Fiction"
➥description="" />
      <siteMapNode url="Technology/Default.aspx" title="Technology"
➥description="" />
   </siteMapNode>
</siteMap>
```

Notice how the Home <siteMapNode>'s closing tag was changed from the terse dialect (/>) to the more verbose form (</siteMapNode>). The reason is that the verbose form is needed when an element contains inner content; because the Home <siteMapNode> element now contains children elements, we have no choice but to use the verbose syntax.

Watch Out!

> Each `<siteMapNode>` element *must* contain a `title` attribute; the `url` and `description` attributes are optional. Furthermore, each provided `url` attribute *must* be unique. You cannot have two `<siteMapNode>` elements with the same value.

If you continue this process through the remainder of the sections in Figure 20.3, you'll eventually wind up with the site map shown in Listing 20.2.

LISTING 20.2 The Completed Site Map Contents

```
<?xml version="1.0" encoding="utf-8" ?>
<siteMap xmlns="http://schemas.microsoft.com/AspNet/SiteMap-File-1.0" >
    <siteMapNode url="Default.aspx" title="Home" description="">
      <siteMapNode url="About.aspx" title="About" description="">
        <siteMapNode url="Legal.aspx" title="Legal" description="" />
        <siteMapNode url="Privacy.aspx" title="Privacy" description="" />
      </siteMapNode>
      <siteMapNode url="OnSale.aspx" title="On Sale" description="" />
      <siteMapNode url="Business/Default.aspx" title="Business"
➥description="" />
      <siteMapNode url="Fiction/Default.aspx" title="Fiction"
➥description="" />
      <siteMapNode url="Technology/Default.aspx" title="Technology"
➥description="">
        <siteMapNode url="Technology/Computers/Default.aspx"
➥title="Computers" description="" />
        <siteMapNode url="Technology/Electronics/Default.aspx"
➥title="Electronics" description="" />
      </siteMapNode>
    </siteMapNode>
</siteMap>
```

By the Way

> Although a page developer can use folders to help organize the files in his website, the site's structure as defined in the site map need not model this folder hierarchy. For example, in the site map hierarchy shown in Figure 20.3, the Privacy and Legal sections are subsections of the About section, even though `About.aspx`, `Privacy.aspx`, and `Legal.aspx` all exist in the same folder.
>
> Often, though, there is a correlation between the site's folder structure and the site map. The book genre sections illustrate this: Technology is one section with subsections for Computers and Electronics, and there's a `Technology` folder in the website with `Computers` and `Electronics` subfolders.

Displaying a Breadcrumb with the SiteMapPath Control

ASP.NET provides three navigation Web controls for displaying a navigation user interface based on the site map: the SiteMapPath, the TreeView, and the Menu. The SiteMapPath control, which is the focus of discussion in this section, displays a breadcrumb, showing the user where in the site he is currently visiting. All three of these controls are available from the Navigation section of the Toolbox (see Figure 20.4).

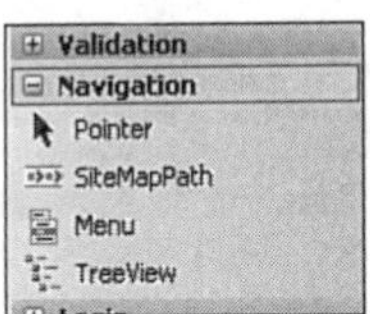

FIGURE 20.4
The navigation Web controls can be found in the Toolbox under the Navigation label.

Watch Out!

If you want to work with the SiteMapPath—or any of the other navigation Web controls, for that matter—it's imperative that a legally formatted site map exist in the root directory and be named `Web.sitemap`. If you followed along with the steps in the previous section, you should have, at this point, a valid `Web.sitemap` file in your root directory containing the contents in Listing 20.2.

Did you Know?

Breadcrumbs are especially useful for sites that have a particularly deep structural hierarchy. As users drill down through the levels of hierarchy in a site, they can easily become disoriented. A breadcrumb control shows them where in the hierarchy they are currently visiting and provides a means to quickly move back to a higher level, if necessary.

To add the SiteMapPath control to an ASP.NET page, drag it from the Toolbox onto the page. Take a moment to add the SiteMapPath control to the `Default.aspx` pages in the root directory, in the `Technology` folder, and the `Computers` subfolder. When we view the SiteMapPath in the pages' Design views, the SiteMapPath control shows the layout based on the values in the site map. Figure 20.5 shows the Visual Web Developer Design view for the `Default.aspx` page in the `Computers` subfolder.

By the Way

If you do not see the SiteMapPath rendered in the Visual Web Developer Design view, as shown in Figure 20.5, one of several things could be awry. If you see a gray box with a warning message, the `Web.sitemap` file contains invalid XML, returning to the site map and fixing the specified problems should remedy this situation.

If you see Root Node > Current Node > Parent Node in the Design view, you likely have not created a site map (or you have not named it `Web.sitemap` and placed it in the root directory). If you have a properly named and placed site map file, go to the View menu and choose Refresh.

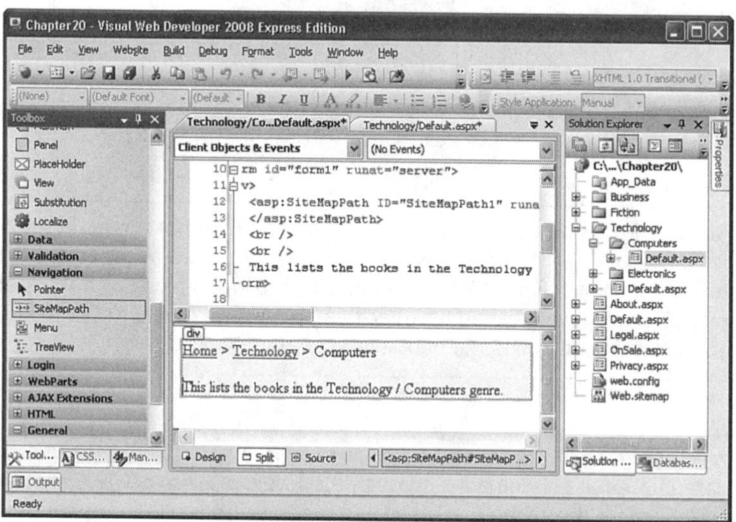

FIGURE 20.5 The SiteMapPath shows the breadcrumb relative to the current page.

At this point we've successfully added three SiteMapPath controls to our ASP.NET website! That was easy. Take a minute to try out these three pages in a browser. The SiteMapPath renders the same as in the Design view; clicking the links in the breadcrumb whisks you back to the appropriate section. (Refer to Figure 20.7 to see the SiteMapPath control on `Technology/Computers/Default.aspx` when viewed through a browser.)

Customizing the SiteMapPath's Appearance

Like most of the Web controls we've examined throughout this book, the SiteMapPath control has a number of properties that can be used to customize its appearance. These properties can be set manually through the SiteMapPath's properties listed in the Appearances and Styles sections of the Properties window.

To understand how these properties affect the rendered appearance of the SiteMapPath, we first need to discuss the components of the SiteMapPath. The SiteMapPath builds up a list of **nodes** and **path separators**. A node is a section in the site map hierarchy (a `<siteMapNode>` element); the path separator is what separates each node. For example, the SiteMapPath in the `Technology/Computers/Default.aspx` page has three nodes: Home, Technology, and Computers. Each node is separated by a path separator: >, by default. There are three possible types of nodes:

- **Root Node**—A SiteMapPath contains a single Root Node; it's the node that contains the section at the top of the site map hierarchy. In all pages that use the site map in Listing 20.2, the Root Node is Home.
- **Current Node**—A SiteMapPath contains a single Current Node. The Current Node is the section that corresponds to the page the user is visiting. In the SiteMapPath in the `Technology/Computers/Default.aspx` page, the Current Node is Computers.
- **General Nodes**—A SiteMapPath contains zero to many General Nodes, depending on the depth of the Current Node in the site map hierarchy. In the `Technology/Computers/Default.aspx` page, there's a single General Node, Technology.

Table 20.1 lists the SiteMapPath's appearance-related properties, along with a brief description. Some of these properties affect the look and feel of the entire SiteMapPath, whereas others affect particular components of the SiteMapPath, such as only the Current Node or only the path separators.

TABLE 20.1 The SiteMapPath's Appearance Properties

Property Name	Description
`BackColor` `ForeColor`	Specify the background and foreground colors for the entire SiteMapPath.

`BorderColor`
`BorderStyle`
`BorderWidth`
	Indicate the border settings for the SiteMapPath.

`CssClass`	Specifies the name of the cascading style sheet (CSS) class to be applied to the SiteMapPath's rendered HTML element.
`Font`	Specifies the font-related settings for the entire SiteMapPath.
`PathDirection`	Can be one of two values: `RootToCurrent` (the default) or `CurrentToRoot`. With `RootToCurrent`, the breadcrumb is rendered as `Root > ... > Current`; with `CurrentToRoot`, it's rendered as `Current > ... > Root`.

TABLE 20.1 Continued

Property Name	Description
PathSeparator	Specifies the string that separates each node. Defaults to >.
RenderCurrentNodeAsLink	Specifies a Boolean value that indicates whether the Current Node is rendered as a link. Defaults to False.
NodeStyle	Specifies the default style for *all* the nodes in the breadcrumb. Applies to the Root Node, Current Node, and General Nodes. This and the other style properties have subproperties such as BackColor, ForeColor, Font, and so on.
CurrentNodeStyle	Indicates the appearance settings applied to the Current Node. Any settings here override the NodeStyle settings for the Current Node.
RootNodeStyle	Specifies the appearance settings applied to the Root Node. Any settings here override the NodeStyle settings for the Root Node.
PathSeparatorStyle	Indicates the appearance settings applied to the path separator.

Take a moment to tinker with these properties and note the results in the Design view.

If you don't trust your artistic skills, the SiteMapPath contains an Auto Format option, just like the GridView and DetailsView controls we examined back in Hour 15, "Displaying Data with the Data Web Controls." For some assistance in formatting the SiteMapPath, click the Auto Format link in the control's smart tag. Figure 20.6 shows the SiteMapPath's AutoFormat dialog box, and Figure 20.7 shows the SiteMapPath control in `Technology/Computers/Default.aspx` when viewed through a browser after the AutoFormat dialog box's Colorful setting has been applied.

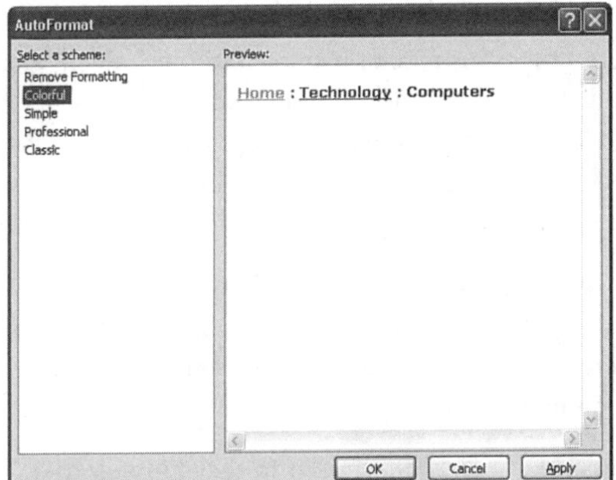

FIGURE 20.6
Let the AutoFormat dialog box aid you in specifying the SiteMapPath's appearance.

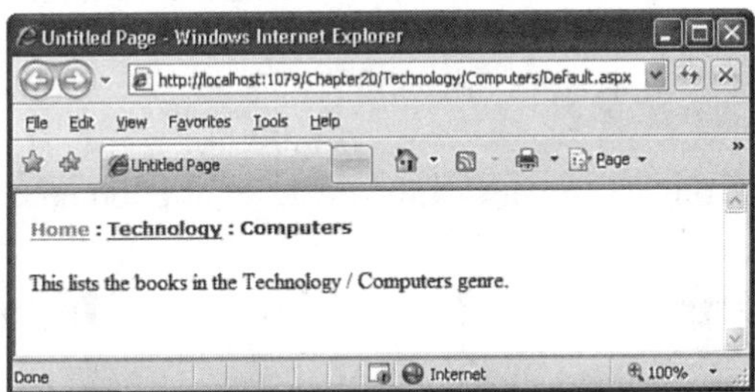

FIGURE 20.7
The SiteMapPath control when visiting `Technology/Computers/Default.aspx` through a browser.

Showing the Entire Site Structure

As Figure 20.7 shows, the SiteMapPath control displays only the current section based on the page where the user is visiting and those immediate ancestor sections. Although the breadcrumb interface provided by the SiteMapPath makes it easy for a visitor to pinpoint his location in the site's navigational hierarchy and navigate further up the hierarchy quickly, it does not enable him to easily jump to any section of the site.

For example, imagine that a visitor comes to our online bookstore's home page. Although only text exists right now, imagine that the page has links to the various genre pages titled `Business Books`, `Fiction Books`, and `Technology Books`. Our imaginary visitor might click `Technology Books`, which would take her to the `Technology/Default.aspx` page, where there might be some technology books listed as well as links to drill down into the subcategories `Computer Books` and `Electronics Books`. Suppose that our user clicks the `Computer Books` link. On this page the SiteMapPath shows `Home > Technology > Computers` and would list the computer books for sale. However, at this point if the user decides that she wants to look at books on electronics instead, or if she realizes technology books aren't her thing and she'd rather browse the fiction titles, she has to click her browser's Back button or go back via the breadcrumb to the appropriate parent level, and then drill down into whatever category she's interested in. The point is, the user can't jump directly from the computer books page to the electronics books or fiction books pages.

To allow a visitor to quickly hop to any section from any page, we need to use a navigation user interface element that lists the entire site structure. The final two ASP.NET navigation Web controls—the TreeView control and the Menu control—provide this functionality.

The Menu and TreeView controls are similar to the GridView and DetailsView controls examined in Hour 15 in that they require a data source control that contains the data to display. ASP.NET provides a SiteMapDataSource control that automatically retrieves the data from the site map and provides it in a manner that the TreeView and Menu controls can work with. Unlike the SqlDataSource control we used when working with the GridView and DetailsView, the SiteMapDataSource control doesn't have any wizard or require any configuration on our part.

Displaying the Site's Structure in a TreeView

The TreeView control lists the sections of the website as defined in the site map in a collapsible tree. A visitor can quickly see all the sections of the site and his position in the site structure hierarchy. Each node in the tree is rendered as a hyperlink that whisks the user to the appropriate section when clicked.

Let's add a TreeView to the Home section (`Default.aspx` in the root folder). To do so, we must first add a SiteMapDataSource control to the page; this control can be found in the Data section of the Toolbox. Next, add the TreeView control to the page and, from its smart tag, specify the data source as the SiteMapDataSource we just added to the page. After the TreeView's data source has been specified, its appearance in the Design is updated, mirroring the hierarchy expressed in site map.

Take a moment to visit this page through a browser (see Figure 20.8). When trying out this control, notice that you can jump to any section in the site by clicking the appropriate section title in the TreeView. Furthermore, you can expand or collapse the TreeView's nodes by clicking the + or - icons on the left of those nodes that have child nodes. Also, note that the SiteMapDataSource control does not result in any visual effect in the browser. Like the SqlDataSourceControl examined in previous hours, the SiteMapDataSource simply retrieves data from a source—in particular, the site map—and does not render any HTML.

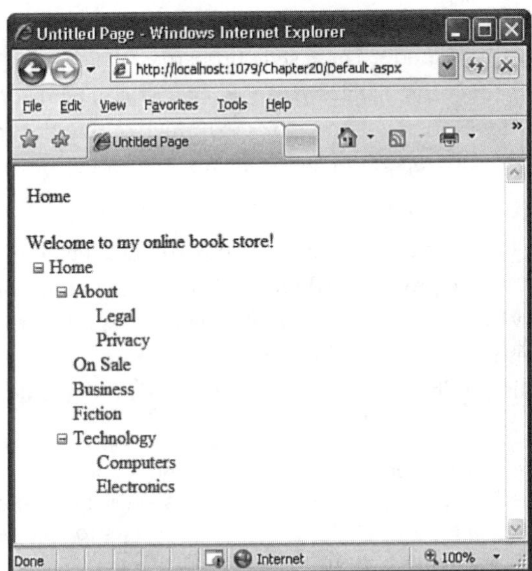

FIGURE 20.8
The TreeView's structure mirrors the site map.

Customizing the TreeView's Appearance

Like the SiteMapPath control, the TreeView contains a number of appearance-related properties, as well as an Auto Format option, that we can use to highly customize the look and feel of the TreeView. The TreeView is made up of a number of **nodes**, with each node representing a section defined in the site map. Each node has zero or one parent nodes and zero to many children nodes. For example, in the TreeView shown in Figure 20.8, the Home node has no parent and five children—About, On Sale, Business, Fiction, and Technology. The About node has one parent—Home—and two children—Legal and Privacy. The Business node has one parent—Home—and no children.

The four types of nodes in a TreeView are

- **Root Nodes**—These nodes have no parent (Home).
- **Parent Nodes**—These are nodes other than the Root Nodes that have children nodes (About and Technology).
- **Leaf Nodes**—These nodes have a parent but no children nodes (Legal, Privacy, Business, Fiction, Computers, and Technology).
- **Selected Node**—The selected node is the one that corresponds to the current page being visited. So when we're visiting the Home section, the Home node is the Selected Node; when we're visiting the business books section, Business is the Selected Node.

Each of these types of nodes has style properties, which can be found in the Styles section of the Properties window. These style properties, which have subproperties like `BackColor`, `BorderColor`, `BorderWidth`, `BorderStyle`, `Font`, and so on, affect the appearance of these classes of nodes. For example, setting the `LeafNodeStyle` property's `BackColor` subproperty to `Red` will cause all Leaf Nodes to have a red background color.

In addition to the `RootNodeStyle`, `ParentNodeStyle`, `LeafNodeStyle`, and `SelectedNodeStyle` style properties, there are two additional node-related style properties: `NodeStyle` and `HoverNodeStyle`. `NodeStyle` specifies the default style applied to all nodes in the TreeView. `HoverNodeStyle` indicates the style settings to be applied when the user hovers his mouse pointer over a particular node.

Did you Know?

> Using the `HoverNodeStyle` property helps to provide feedback to the visitor, showing him what node he's currently hovered over. Personally, I like to set the `HoverNodeStyle`'s `ForeColor` and `BackColor` properties to complementary values, both of which stand out from the default node style.

The Styles section in the Properties window also includes a `LevelStyles` property. This property allows you to specify style information for particular levels of the TreeView, with the first level being the set of Root Nodes, the second level being those nodes that are children of the first-level nodes, the third level being the children of the second-level nodes, and so on. To specify a unique style for each level, go to the `LevelStyles` property in the Properties window and click the ellipses icon to the right of the property name. This brings up the TreeNodeStyle Collection Editor dialog box, from which you can define the style for each level.

Click the Add button to add a new level to the list of levels on the left. For each level, you can specify its appearance-related properties from the list on the right. Note that the topmost level in the list on the left corresponds to the first level (the set of Root Nodes), the second level from the top corresponds to the second level (the children of the Root Nodes), and so on. Figure 20.9 shows the TreeNodeStyle Collection Editor dialog box for a TreeView control that has the style settings made for the first two levels.

In addition to the properties in the Styles section of the Properties window, the TreeView contains a number of styles in the Appearances section worth noting. Of course, the usual properties exist—`BackColor`, `CssClass`, `Font`, and so on—but there are also a number of TreeView-specific properties. These appearance-related TreeView-specific properties are listed in Table 20.2.

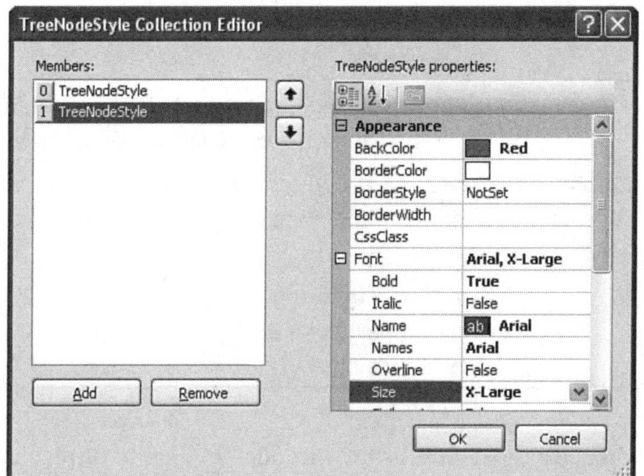

FIGURE 20.9 The styles for the TreeView's first two levels have been specified.

TABLE 20.2 The TreeView-Specific Appearance Properties

Property Name	Description
`CollapseImageTooltip` `ExpandImageTooltip`	Indicate the tooltip shown to the end user when she hovers the mouse pointer over the collapse or expand icons for a node. Any instances of `{0}` in the property value are replaced with the node's text. For example, an `ExpandImageTooltip` value of `Expand {0}` would display `"Expand Home"` when the user hovers her mouse pointer over the Home node's expand icon. (A **tooltip** is a small yellow box with a brief explanation or help message that appears when the user's mouse pointer hovers over a particular region on the web page.)

`CollapseImageUrl`
`ExpandImageUrl`
`NoExpandImageUrl`
	Specify the image URLs to use for the collapse and expand icons for non-Leaf Nodes (those that can be expanded or collapsed), as well as the image to use for Leaf nodes (those nodes that cannot be expanded or collapsed because they have no children). You can also use the `ImageSet` property to indicate the collapse and expand icons.

`ImageSet`	Allows the TreeView's images to be custom defined or based on a packaged set of predefined images. Set this property to `Custom` to choose your own images or pick one of the numerous options to use predefined images. Defaults to `Custom`.
`NodeIndent`	Specifies the number of pixels to indent each level of the TreeView. Defaults to 20.

TABLE 20.2 Continued

Property Name	Description
NodeWrap	Specifies a Boolean property that indicates whether a node's text should be wrapped. Defaults to False.
ShowExpandCollapse	Specifies a Boolean property that indicates whether the expand and collapse icons are shown. Defaults to True.
ShowLines	Specifies a Boolean property that indicates whether lines are drawn between each node and level in the TreeView. This property can also be turned on or off from the TreeView's smart tag.

The `ImageSet` property provides a list of packaged images to display next to each icon. This list includes choices such as `WindowsHelp`, `BulletedList`, `Events`, and `Contacts`, each providing a different set of images for expand and collapse icons for non-Leaf Nodes, as well as images for the nonexpandable, noncollapsible Leaf Nodes. (Figure 20.10 shows the icons used when the `ImageSet` property is set to `Contacts`.) If you want to provide your own images, set `ImageSet` to `Custom` and then provide the URLs to your custom images in the `CollapseImageUrl`, `ExpandImageUrl`, and `NoExpandImageUrl` properties.

If you would rather let Visual Web Developer choose the appearance-related property settings, you can always use the Auto Format option, which is available through the TreeView's smart tag. Figure 20.10 shows the TreeView's AutoFormat dialog box when choosing the Contacts Auto Format option.

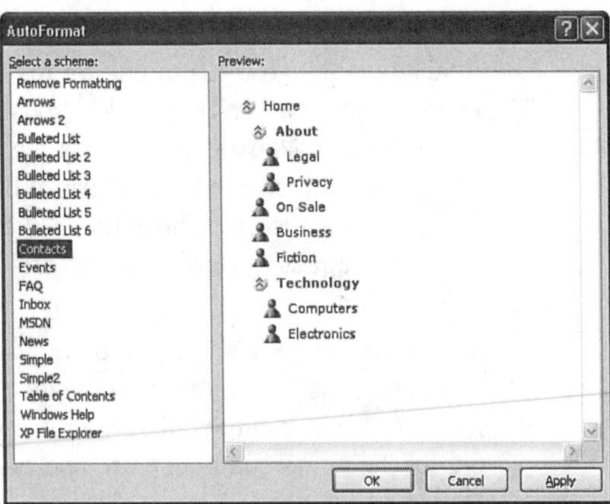

FIGURE 20.10
Let the AutoFormat dialog box help you improve the appearance of the TreeView.

Using Menus to Show the Site's Structure

Like the TreeView control, the Menu control displays the entire contents of the site map. Rather than displaying the contents of the site map as a tree, however, the Menu control displays the items using a menu interface. By default, each section defined in the site map is rendered as an item in the menu with submenus used to reflect the hierarchy. To display navigation using a Menu control, we must first add a SiteMapDataSource control to the page.

Let's add a Menu control to the `Default.aspx` page in the `Fiction` folder. Open this page in Visual Web Developer and start by adding a SiteMapDataSource control; next, add the Menu control and bind it to the SiteMapDataSource control just added. After you specify the Menu control's data source, the Menu will be updated in the Design view to reflect the structure of the site map. By default, the menu shows just the top-level element in the site map hierarchy—Home, for our site map.

After setting the data source, take a minute to view this page in a browser. The menu displays a single, visible menu item, Home. If you move your mouse pointer over the Home item, though, a submenu appears, listing Home's children nodes: About, On Sale, Business, Fiction, and Technology. If you move your mouse pointer over About or Technology, another submenu appears, listing the appropriate items (see Figure 20.11). Clicking a menu item whisks you to the corresponding section in the site.

Configuring the Menu's Static and Dynamic Portions

A Menu control is composed of both a static and a dynamic portion. The static portion of the menu is always shown when viewing the page, whereas the dynamic portion is shown only when the user interacts with the menu. By default, only the top-level node in the site map is static; all other site map sections are placed in the dynamic portion. In Figure 20.11, only the Home menu item is shown when the page loads; the other sections are displayed only when the user hovers her mouse pointer over the Home menu item.

The number of levels in the site map hierarchy that make up the static portion of the menu can be specified by the Menu control's `StaticDisplayLevels` property. The default value for this property is 1. If we change this to 2, however, all the sections in the first and second levels of the site map hierarchy—Home, About, On Sale, Business, Fiction, and Technology—are shown as static menu items. Figure 20.12 shows the Menu control in the Visual Web Developer Design view after the `StaticDisplayLevels` property has been set to 2.

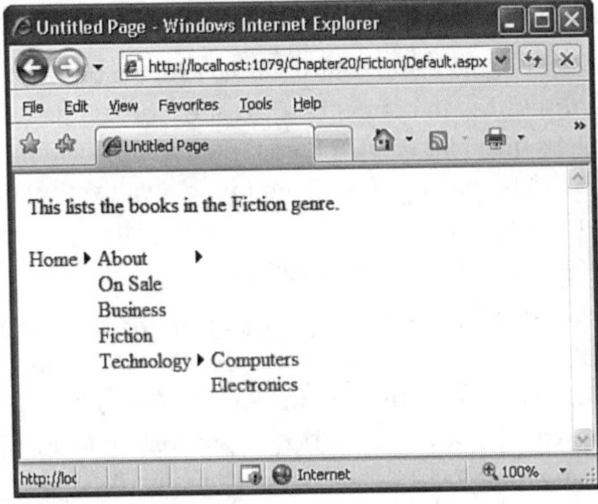

FIGURE 20.11 The menu's Home and Technology options have been selected.

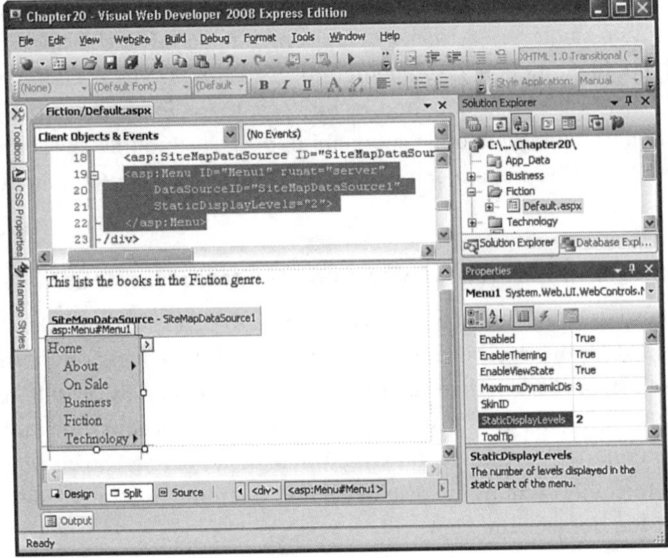

FIGURE 20.12 The menu shows the first two levels of the site map hierarchy statically.

Now instead of just the Home menu item showing when the page loads, Home, About, On Sale, Business, Fiction, and Technology will be displayed. The third level, which includes Legal, Privacy, Computers, and Electronics, will still be displayed in the dynamic portion. That is, the user will have to hover her mouse pointer over the About menu item to be able to see the Privacy or Legal menu items.

Did you Know?

When the user's mouse pointer leaves a dynamically displayed submenu, the submenu remains visible for a period specified by the Menu control's `DisappearAfter` property. This value defaults to 500 milliseconds, which leaves a dynamic menu displayed for 0.5 seconds after the user's mouse pointer leaves the submenu. You can increase or decrease this time as needed.

Customizing the Menu's Appearance

The Menu control contains a wide array of appearance-related properties—far too many to cover in this hour. Rather than enumerate all these properties, let's instead look at the more germane ones and focus on the concepts rather than the specifics.

By the Way

As always, I encourage you to tinker around with all the Menu control's properties, not just those that we cover here. Try changing them and observe the effects when viewing and interacting with the menu through a browser. Review the description of the properties using the MSDN Library. (We discussed using the MSDN Library in Hour 3, "Using Visual Web Developer.")

You should not be surprised that the Menu control has the base set of appearance-related properties: `BackColor`, `ForeColor`, `Font`, and the like. In addition to these properties, it has appearance-related properties for the dynamic and static portions of the Menu. The names of these properties start with either `Static` or `Dynamic`, such as `StaticItemFormatString` and `DynamicItemFormatString`. The prefix indicates whether the property value applies to the dynamic or static portion of the Menu control.

Table 20.3 lists a number of the Menu control's appearance-related properties. Figure 20.13 shows a Menu control after a number of these properties have been set.

TABLE 20.3 The Menu Control Contains Properties That Apply to Its Dynamic and Static Portions

Property Name	Description
`DynamicEnableDefaultPopOutImage` `StaticEnableDefaultPopOutImage`	Specify a Boolean property that indicates whether an image is displayed to show that an item has a submenu. Defaults to `True`. In Figure 20.11, the arrow icon next to Home was present because `StaticEnableDefaultPopOutImage` was set to `True`, and the arrow image next to About and Technology was present because `DynamicEnableDefaultPopOutImage` was set to `True`.

TABLE 20.3 Continued

Property Name	Description
`DynamicItemFormatString` `StaticItemFormatString`	Specify the text displayed in the menu item. Use `{0}` to inject the title of the menu item's corresponding site map section. That is, using `Visit {0}` would display `"Visit Business"` (instead of `"Business"`) for the Business menu item.
`DynamicPopOutImageTextFormatString` `StaticPopOutImageTextFormatString`	Specify the tooltip text displayed for the pop-out image. Include a `{0}` to inject the current site map section's title.
`DynamicPopOutImageUrl` `StaticPopOutImageUrl`	Specify the URL to your own image if you want to use a pop-out image other than the default arrow.
`StaticSubMenuIndent`	Specifies the indentation between a static menu item and its static submenu. As Figure 20.12 shows, when displaying multiple levels in the static portion, there's an indentation between levels. Use this property to tailor the amount of indentation. (Defaults to 16 pixels.)
`Orientation`	Specifies whether the menu is laid out horizontally or vertically. Can be either `Vertical` or `Horizontal`; defaults to `Vertical`.
`DynamicHorizontalOffset` `DynamicVerticalOffset`	Specify the offset in pixels between the right border of a menu item and the left border of its submenu item (or of the bottom border of a menu item and the top border of its submenu item). Both properties default to 0.
`ItemWrap`	Specifies a Boolean property that indicates whether the text in a menu item should be wrapped. Defaults to `False`.

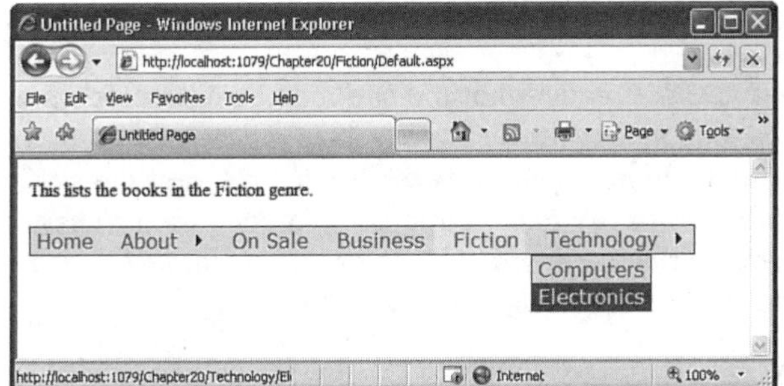

FIGURE 20.13 This menu has a `Horizontal Orientation` and was further customized using the AutoFormat dialog box.

By the Way

Like the SiteMapPath and TreeView controls examined earlier in this hour, the Menu control also offers an Auto Format option, which is available through its smart tag.

Furthermore, the Menu control has a number of properties in the Styles section of its Properties window that you can use to customize the appearance of the static and dynamic submenus and menu items.

Summary

In this hour we saw how to create a site map and navigation user interface. The site map is an XML-formatted file that expresses the structural hierarchy of a website. Often it helps to first sketch out the proposed site structure (as we did in Figure 20.3) and then convert the items in the sketch into the appropriate XML elements in the site map file.

After the site map file has been created, the three ASP.NET navigation Web controls can be used to render the site map information into a user interface. The SiteMapPath displays a breadcrumb, showing the user the current page he is visiting and its location in the site map hierarchy. The TreeView and Menu controls display the entire site map, either as a tree or a menu. To use either of these controls, you need to first add a SiteMapDataSource control to the page.

All three of these controls offer a high degree of customization, making it easy to tailor the appearance of the navigation controls to fit your site's look and feel. Furthermore, there is a clean separation between the navigation controls and the site map, making updating the site's structure a breeze. To add a new section to your site or remove some existing sections, simply update the site map file. The navigation controls used throughout the site automatically reflect these changes.

Q&A

Q. ***Why does ASP.NET require that the site map be expressed as a particularly formatted XML file? What if I already have a database or my own custom XML file with site map information? Or what if I want the site map to be based on my website's folder structure and don't want to have to bother with mirroring the folder structure in the site map file? Does that mean I can't use the ASP.NET navigation controls?***

A. Actually, ASP.NET allows for developers to specify their own site map formats. You can create your own **site map provider** that would allow for a different mechanism for storing the site map information. A site map provider is a class that you would write to instruct ASP.NET on how to retrieve site map information. The default site map provider uses an XML file with the format we examined in this hour; however, there's no reason why you couldn't create your own provider.

A discussion on creating and working with custom providers is beyond the scope of this book. If you are interested in learning more, though, be sure to check out "Examining ASP.NET's Site Navigation" at http://aspnet.4guysfromrolla.com/articles/111605-1.aspx.

Q. ***In this hour we added various navigation controls to various pages. If I want the Menu or the SiteMapPath control to exist on all pages in my site, must I manually go to each page and add the appropriate controls, or is there a better way?***

A. When creating a website, typically we want all pages to have a similar look and feel, such as all pages having a menu across the top. A simple way to accomplish this is to repeat the desired look and feel on each page. This approach, though, is asking for trouble, because if we decide to update our site's look, we then need to make changes to each and every page in the site!

A better approach is to use **master pages**. Master pages allow us to create a single page that specifies a standard look and feel. For example, the master page may contain a menu along the top and a list of common links at the bottom of the page. Then, when creating a new page, we can specify that it use the master page. The result is that all pages that use the master page have a consistent look and feel. Furthermore, any changes to the master page are immediately reflected on those pages that use that master page, thereby making updating the site's appearance as easy as editing the master page.

We'll examine master pages in depth in Hour 22, "Using Master Pages to Provide Sitewide Page Templates."

Workshop

Quiz

1. What name must you give the site map file?
2. True or False: The site map file can appear in any folder in the web project.
3. What attributes can be found in the <siteMapNode> element? What attributes, if any, are required?
4. What control must be added to the page to have the TreeView or Menu controls display the site's structure?
5. What is the difference between the static and dynamic portions of the Menu control?

Answers

1. `Web.sitemap`.
2. False. The site map file must appear in the web project's root directory.
3. The `<siteMapNode>` can contain the `url`, `title`, and `description` attributes. The `title` attribute is required.
4. The SiteMapDataSource control.
5. The static portion of a Menu control is always shown in the user's browser. The dynamic portion is shown only when the user interacts with the menu in some manner.

Exercises

1. Alter the site map created during this hour so that a new section titled Books is created. When specifying the Books section in the site map file, do *not* provide a value for the `url` attribute.

   Move the Business, Fiction, and Technology sections (and their subsections) to reside underneath this new Books section. Additionally, move the On Sale section here as well. Figure 20.14 shows the new site structure hierarchy.

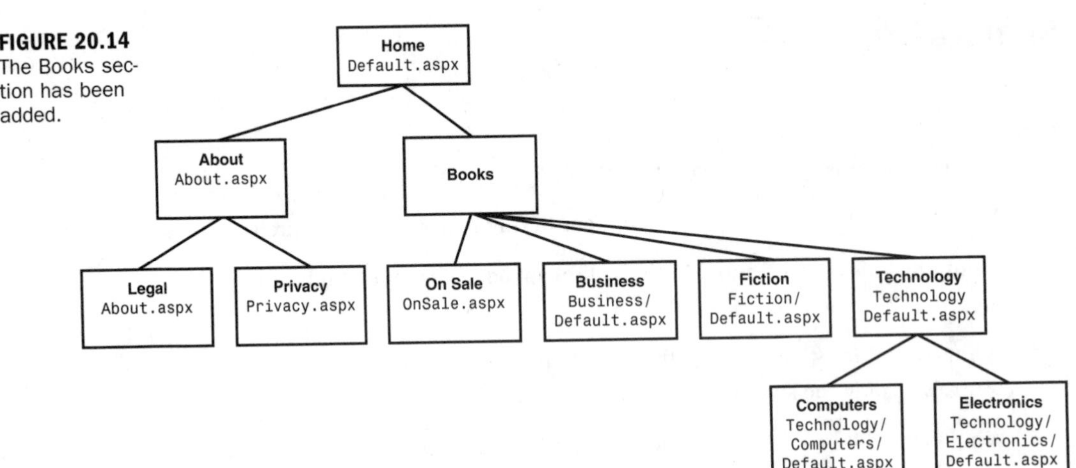

FIGURE 20.14
The Books section has been added.

2. In this hour we looked at only a handful of the Menu control's appearance-related properties. In particular, we didn't examine any of the properties in the Styles section of the Properties window.

   Add a Menu control (and, of course, a SiteMapDataSource control) to the `Legal.aspx` page and practice with these Styles properties, noting the effects in the Design view and when visiting the page through a browser. Finally, be sure to try out the level-related style properties—`LevelMenuItemStyles`, `LevelSelectedStyles`, and `LevelSubMenuStyles`. These level-related style properties are similar to the `LevelStyles` property of the TreeView control.

HOUR 21

Managing Your Site's Users

In this hour, we will cover

- How to configure a website to support user accounts
- How and where user account information is stored
- Creating and managing user accounts and roles through the ASP.NET Website Administration Tool
- Granting and denying access to folders based on users, user type, or role
- Logging users on to the site using the Login control

Many websites allow visitors to create user accounts and log on to the site. If you bank online or have ever purchased an item from an online retailer, you're already familiar with the process of creating an account and logging on to a website from the end user's perspective. But what steps are required from the web developer's perspective to add support for user accounts? How and where is user account information stored? What steps need to be taken to create a new user? How does a user log on to the site or log off?

ASP.NET includes a plethora of features designed to make supporting user accounts as easy as possible. As we'll see in this hour, we can configure our website to support user accounts with just a few clicks of the mouse. When the website has been configured properly, the login Web controls provide the user interface necessary for performing user account-related tasks, including logging in and out of the site, creating a new user account, sending a user his forgotten password, and so on.

An Overview of User Accounts in ASP.NET

When you make a purchase from an online retailer for the first time, you are prompted to create a **user account**. When creating a user account, you are asked to enter information that uniquely identifies you, along with some bit of information known only to you. This identification information is referred to as **credentials**. Typically, the credentials are a username and password, although some websites use an email address and password, or require not only a password, but also a personal identification number (PIN).

In addition to credentials, a user account can also store additional user-specific information. An online retailer would likely collect billing information and a shipping address, and an online banking site might require that you provide your account numbers, Social Security number, and so on.

A site that supports user accounts must store the user account information somewhere; most often, this information is stored in a database. Commonly, websites that need to provide such support will add a database table called `Users` (or something similar) that has one record for each user account in the system. The columns for this table usually have names like `Username`, `Password`, `Email`, and so on. After this database table has been defined, the process of creating a user account becomes trivial because it involves creating an ASP.NET page that prompts the user for the required inputs—username, password, and so on—and stores this information in a database. (We saw how to insert records into a database table in Hour 16, "Deleting, Inserting, and Editing Data.")

With ASP.NET you do not need to create your own user account database tables because ASP.NET provides built-in support for user accounts through a feature called **membership**. To take advantage of this feature, we first must configure our website to support membership.

Configuring an ASP.NET Website to Support Membership

To configure our website to support membership, we must launch the **ASP.NET Website Administration Tool**. To accomplish this, either click the ASP.NET Configuration icon at the top of the Solution Explorer or click the Website menu's ASP.NET Configuration option. Either way opens a web browser pointed to a page through which the ASP.NET site can be configured. Figure 21.1 shows the ASP.NET Website Administration Tool.

For help on using the ASP.NET Website Administration Tool, click the `How do I use this tool?` link in the upper-right corner of the web page.

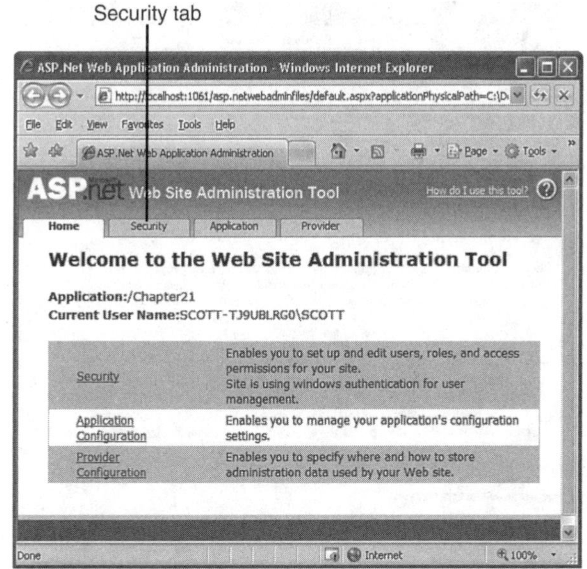

FIGURE 21.1
Configure your website through the ASP.NET Website Administration Tool.

To add user account support, click the Security link. This takes you to the Security screen shown in Figure 21.2. From this screen, you can specify the user accounts in your system, what roles exist, and the access rules for users.

By default, an ASP.NET website is set up to use **Windows authentication**. **Authentication** is the process of identifying a user. For Internet sites that support user accounts, typically authentication is achieved by prompting users for their credentials in a logon page. This style of authentication is commonly referred to as **forms-based authentication** because users are prompted for their credentials through a form. Windows authentication, on the other hand, is useful if you are building a website that is used on an **intranet**. An intranet is a local, private network within a company or organization. In such a setting, users typically log on to the network from their desktop computers. They can then visit the intranet and, because they've already logged on to their workstations, this logon information can be detected automatically by the intranet web server.

By the Way

In this book we examine only **forms-based authentication**. If you are developing an application on an intranet, you'll likely want to explore Windows authentication.

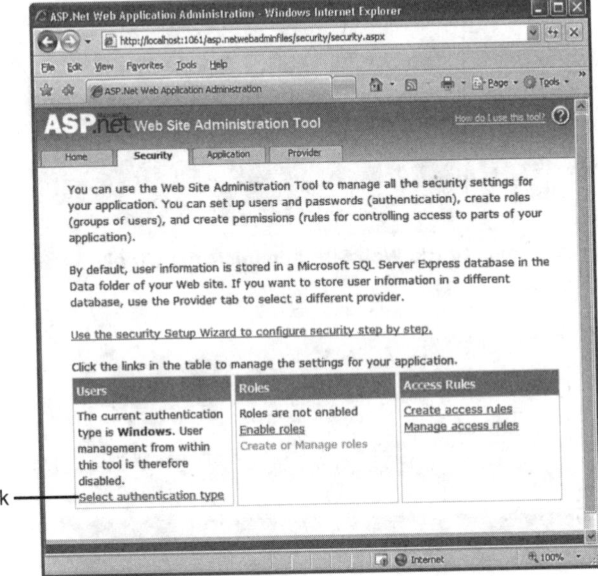

FIGURE 21.2 Configure your website's security-related settings from the Security screen.

To change the current authentication model from Windows authentication to forms-based authentication, click the link titled `Select authentication type` at the bottom of the Users box. This loads the screen shown in Figure 21.3, where you can select how users will access your site:

- **From the Internet**—This option configures the website to use forms-based authentication and creates the necessary database tables to support membership.
- **From a local network**—This option configures the website to use Windows authentication.

Select the `From the internet` option button and then click the Done button. Doing so not only configures your application to use forms-based authentication, but also automatically creates a SQL Server 2005 Express Edition database named `ASPNETDB` with predesigned tables to support user accounts.

When you return to the Security screen, the Users box should now list the number of existing users—0—along with links titled `Create user` and `Manage users`.

Let's examine the `ASPNETDB` database that was created for us. Close the ASP.NET Website Administration Tool, returning to Visual Web Developer. From the Solution Explorer, right-click the `App_Data` folder and choose Refresh Folder. You should now see the ASPNETDB.MDF file listed in this folder. Go to the Database Explorer and drill down into the tables of the ASPNETDB database. There are 11 tables in total, providing functionality that extends beyond simple user accounts.

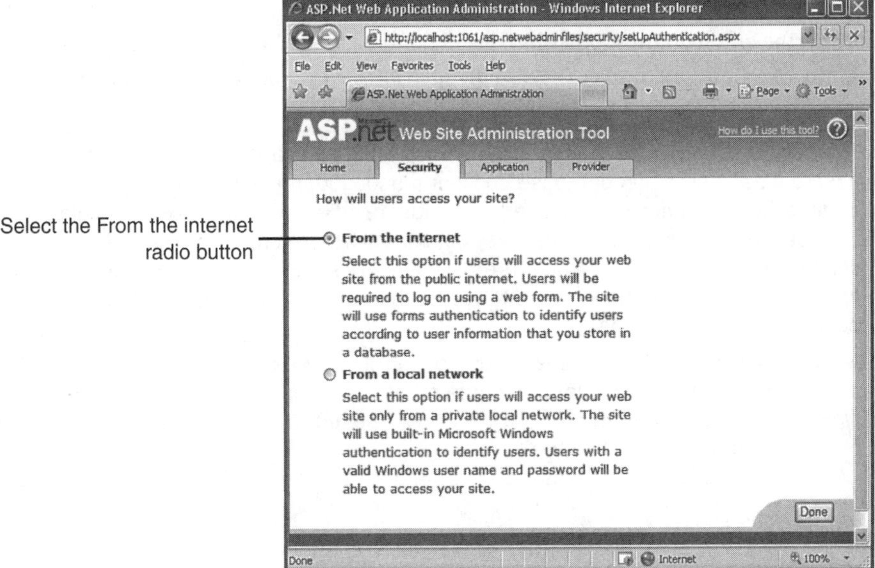

FIGURE 21.3 Indicate that users will connect to your site from the Internet.

By the Way

Using the Same Database

The Membership system stores information about users and roles in the ASPNETDB.MDF database, which is automatically created from the ASP.NET Web Site Administration Tool (see Figure 21.3). But you may have already created another database to store your application's data. For example, in Hour 13, "An Introduction to Databases," you created a database named MyFirstDatabase.mdf.

Although it is possible to have your application's data and user accounts stored in two separate databases, most applications aren't designed this way. If you plan to deploy your website to a web-hosting company—a topic discussed in Hour 24, "Deploying Your Website"—chances are the web hosting company will require that you use just one database for your site.

There are two ways to remedy this two-database solution. The simplest approach is to add your application's database tables to the ASPNETDB.MDF database. Alternatively, you can configure the membership system to store the user accounts in your database. This topic is a bit more difficult to implement, however. For step-by-step instructions on this task, refer to http://aspnet.4guysfromrolla.com/articles/040506-1.aspx.

For now, concentrate on just the aspnet_Users and aspnet_Membership tables. These database tables store user account information. Each user account in the website will have a corresponding record in these two tables. The aspnet_Users table contains the base set of columns to identify a user, essentially the username. The aspnet_Membership table has columns that provide information required for a user account, such as the email address, password, last login date, date the account was created, security question and answer (in case the user forgets his password), and so on.

By the Way

The aspnet_Users and aspnet_Membership tables illustrate two related database tables, a common database concept mentioned in previous hours. A record in either table is uniquely identified by the UserId field (in database vernacular, the UserId column in the primary key column). Furthermore, a **foreign-key constraint** ensures that for each UserId value in aspnet_Membership there is a matching UserId value in aspnet_Users, thereby cementing the relationship between these two tables.

A foreign-key constraint is a special database rule that ensures that one column in one table contains a value from some other column in another table. These constraints help ensure the integrity of the data used to establish relationships between tables.

Creating and Managing Users

As the site administrator, you can add new user accounts through the ASP.NET Website Administration Tool. In addition to creating new users, you can also manage existing users.

To create a new user account through the ASP.NET Website Administration Tool, go to the Security screen and click the Create user link in the Users box. This brings up the screen shown in Figure 21.4.

To create a new user account, provide the username, password, email, and security question for the new user and then click the Create User button. The security question is asked if the user forgets her password. The security answer is the answer the user must provide to be able to recover her password.

When we're creating a new user account a number of validation checks are automatically performed. You must provide values for the username, password, confirm password, and security question and answer text boxes. Furthermore, the username must be unique, the password must meet a certain password "strength" (by default, be seven characters long with at least one nonalphanumeric character), and the email address must in the proper format.

If you enter invalid data when creating a new user, a validation error message will be displayed, prohibiting the new user account from being created until the errors are corrected.

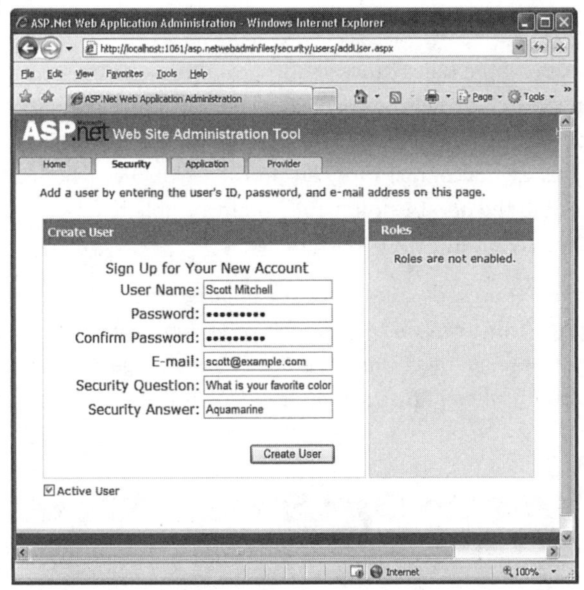

FIGURE 21.4
Create a new user account.

To manage the set of existing users, click the `Manage users` link in the Security screen. This takes you to the screen shown in Figure 21.5, which lists all user accounts in the system. From here you can edit or delete users, or mark them as active or inactive.

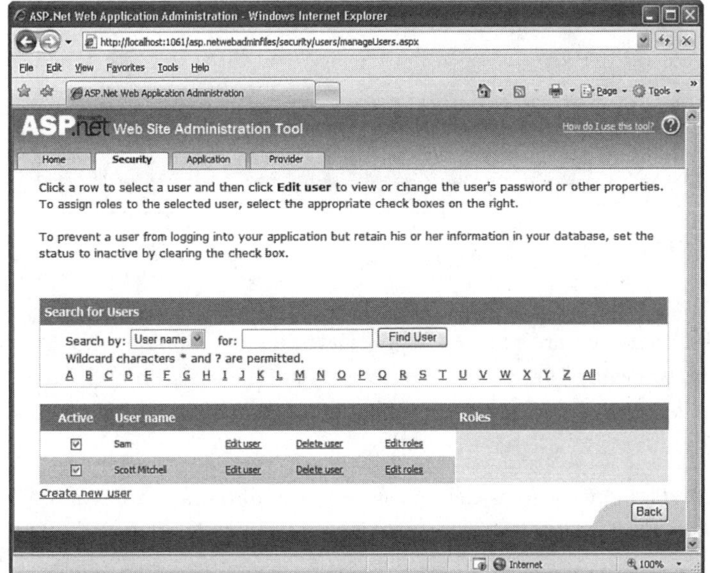

FIGURE 21.5
Edit and delete users from the Manage Users screen.

Classifying Users by Role

You may have noticed the Roles functionality from the Security screen and the screens for managing and creating users. You can categorize users into roles and then allow or deny functionality based on users' roles. For example, you may have a site that requires user accounts, with certain users classified as administrators. Those users added to the administrator role might be able to access web pages in a certain folder that are off-limits to other users.

If you need to classify users by roles, click the `Enable roles` link in the Roles box of the Security screen. This turns on role support, after which you can create and manage the roles in the system by clicking the `Create` or `Manage` roles link. Figure 21.6 shows the Create or Manage Roles screen, into which I've added a role named Administrators.

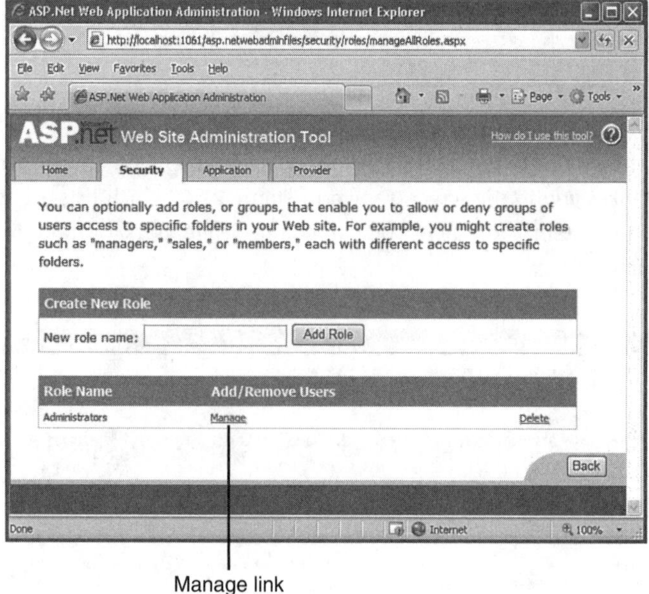

FIGURE 21.6
The Administrators role has been added to the system.

After the roles have been created, assign users to the appropriate roles. Click the `Manage` link shown in Figure 21.6 to see a listing of the users who belong to the selected role. You can add new users to the role by searching for them and then checking the `User Is in Role` check box (see Figure 21.7).

Along with adding users to a selected role, you can also assign roles to a selected user through the Manage Users screen (refer to Figure 21.5). Click the `Edit roles` link for a particular user. A check box list of available roles displays, and you can select which roles, if any, the user belongs to.

Role information is stored in the ASPNETDB database's `aspnet_Roles` table. The association between users and roles is captured by the `aspnet_UsersInRoles` table.

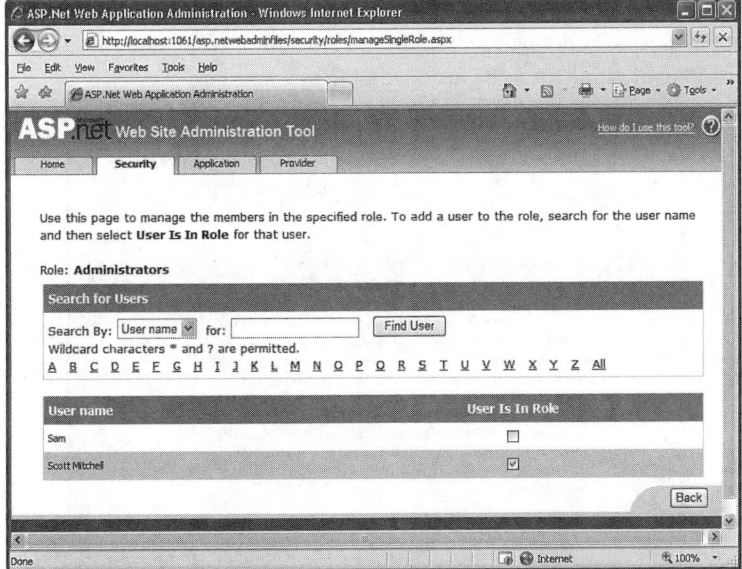

FIGURE 21.7
User Scott Mitchell has been added to the Administrators role.

Creating and Managing Access Rules

After you have users or roles defined in the system, you can, optionally, specify access rules. Access rules dictate whether particular users or roles are granted or denied access to the ASP.NET pages in particular folders in the website. As discussed earlier, you might want to allow only users in the Administrators role to access web pages in a particular folder. Or you might want to require that only logged-in users can visit a certain folder in the website.

To create an access rule, go to the Security screen and click the `Create access rules` link in the Access Rules box. This takes you to the screen shown in Figure 21.8. From here, you can select what folder the access rule applies to; whether the access rule applies to a role, a particular user, all users, or anonymous users; and whether the rule is to allow or deny access.

By the Way

An **anonymous user** is one who has yet to log in to the site—that is, a user who has yet to be authenticated.

Because our website currently lacks any folders other than the default `App_Data` folder, we really can't define meaningful access rules unless we want them to apply to the entire site. Take a minute to add two folders to the project: `Admin` and `Users`. Don't bother adding any ASP.NET pages to either of these folders yet, we'll do that later in this hour. For now, understand that those web pages in the `Admin` folder are meant to be accessed only by users in the Administrators role, and those pages in the `Users` folder are meant to be accessed only by logged-on users.

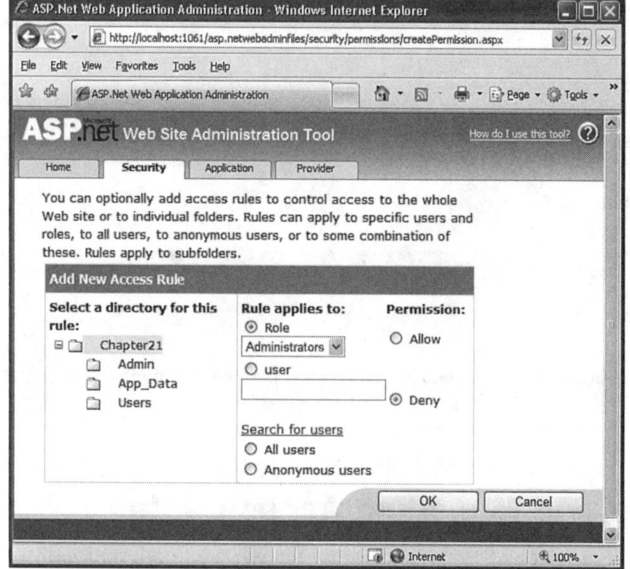

FIGURE 21.8
Define the access rules for the folders of your website.

To achieve these access rights, add the following access rules:

- For the `Admin` folder, allow access for the Administrators role.
- For the `Admin` folder, deny access to all users.
- For the `Users` folder, deny access to anonymous users.

Notice that for the `Admin` folder, we first allowed access for Administrators and then denied access to all users. This might seem a bit confusing at first. Why not just allow access for Administrators and be done at that?

If you do not explicitly deny access to a particular role or user type, those particular users can access that resource. So simply allowing Administrators to access the `Admin` folder would also permit others to view this folder because we did not explicitly deny access to those users outside of the Administrators role. Therefore, we needed to both allow Administrators to access this folder and deny all users.

By the Way

> Keen logicians may still see a bit of a paradox here because users in the Administrators role are still in the set of all users. Because there's a rule to deny access to all users, won't Administrators be denied access to the `Admin` folder, too?
>
> When a user attempts to access a resource, ASP.NET processes the access rules from the top down. So in our case it starts by saying, "Is this user in the Administrators role? If so, she can access this folder." If the user is indeed in the Administrators role, she is granted access. If she is not, ASP.NET proceeds to the next rule and asks, "Is this user in the set of all users? If so, deny access."

To delete existing access rules or reorder the rules for a particular folder, click the `Manage access` rules link from the Security screen. This takes you to a screen that lists the access rules for a selected folder. From here, you can remove any access rules or reorder the existing access rules.

By the Way

> Whereas the user accounts and roles are stored in the `ASPNETDB` database, the access rights are stored in the configuration file, `web.config`. Specifically, a `web.config` file is added to each folder that has access rights specified, along with an `<authorization>` element that spells out the access rights for that folder.

At this point we have seen how to configure an ASP.NET website to support user accounts. Doing so automatically creates the needed database (`ASPNETDB`) and database tables (`aspnet_Users`, `aspnet_Membership`, `aspnet_Roles`, and `aspnet_UsersInRoles`, among others). With the user account system set up, we can use ASP.NET's login Web controls in our website to allow visitors to create a new account and log in and out of the site. We examine these login controls throughout the remainder of this hour.

Configuring a Website's SMTP Settings

A number of the login Web controls provide built-in email features. For example, the CreateUserWizard control can be configured so that when a user creates a new account, he is automatically sent an email that includes his username, password, and other information. For the login Web controls to be able to send emails, the website must be configured to support sending email, which can be accomplished through the ASP.NET Website Administration Tool.

The ASP.NET Website Administration Tool lists four tabs:

- Home
- Application
- Security
- Provider

In the preceding sections we examined the Security option. To configure the website to send email, click the Application tab. From the Application screen, click the `Configure SMTP e-mail settings` link; this displays the screen shown in Figure 21.9. From here, you can provide the email server name, port, and authentication information (if required), along with the address that the email messages will be sent from.

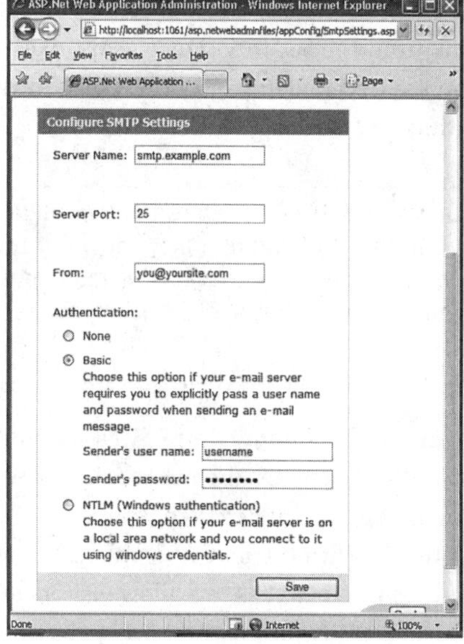

FIGURE 21.9
Configure your website's email settings.

By the Way

Email messages are sent by sending the message to an **SMTP server**. The Configure SMTP E-Mail Settings screen prompts you for the information needed to connect to an SMTP server. If you are hosting your website with a web-hosting company, the company will provide you with the SMTP server, port, and authentication information needed. If you are not using a web-hosting company, you can configure these settings to use the same SMTP server settings you use in your desktop email program.

After you have provided the appropriate values for the SMTP server, click the Save button. The settings specified in this screen are saved in the website's `web.config` file, in the `<mailSettings>` element; you can edit these values either directly through `web.config` or from the ASP.NET Website Administration Tool.

Allowing Visitors to Create New User Accounts

Although you can create user accounts through the ASP.NET Website Administration Tool, chances are you'll want to also allow users to create accounts on their own. This process can be handled by ASP.NET's CreateUserWizard Web control, which provides a user interface very similar to that shown in the ASP.NET Website Administration Tool's Create User screen (refer to Figure 21.4).

Create a new ASP.NET page in your website named `CreateAccount.aspx`. Add a CreateUserWizard control to the page. (The CreateUserWizard control, along with the entire suite of login Web controls, can be found in the Login section of the Toolbox.) Figure 21.10 shows Visual Web Developer after this control has been added to the ASP.NET page.

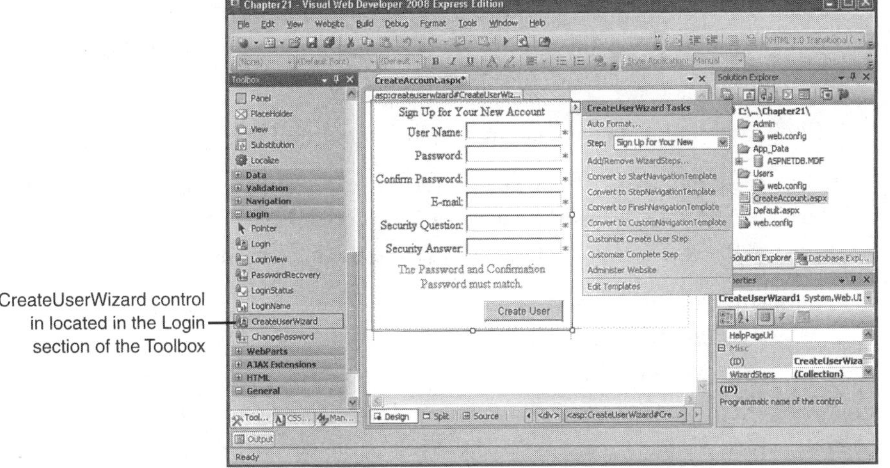

FIGURE 21.10
The CreateUserWizard login control allows the user to create an account.

The CreateUserWizard control is a **wizard Web control**. Wizard Web controls consist of a number of steps that the user progresses through. By default, the CreateUserWizard has two steps: Sign Up for Your New Account and Complete.

The first step prompts the user to choose a username, password, email, and security question and answer, just as we did when creating the user through the ASP.NET Website Administration Tool. The user is taken to the Complete step after successfully creating an account; this step displays a `Your account has been created` message. You can toggle between the two steps through the CreateUserWizard control's smart tag.

Take a moment to try out the CreateUserWizard control in your browser. When you first visit the page, you'll see the Sign Up for Your New Account step. After entering your user account and clicking the Create User button, you'll be taken to the Complete step, informing you that your new account has been created. In addition to creating a new account, the user is also logged in as this newly created account.

Along with a message, the Complete step includes a Continue button. If you try to click it, you'll see that nothing happens. If you want the user to be whisked to a particular page after clicking this button, set the control's `ContinueDestinationPage` property to the appropriate URL. For our site, when the user clicks the Continue button, let's have him automatically sent back to `Default.aspx`; therefore, set the `ContinueDestinationPage` property to `Default.aspx`.

Customizing the CreateUserWizard Control

The CreateUserWizard control contains a cornucopia of properties that can be tweaked to customize the appearance. These appearance-related properties can be broken into the following three classifications:

- Properties that dictate the control's colors, fonts, and borders.
- Properties that specify the text used for the user interface elements in the control. This includes elements like the labels preceding each text box, the default text in the text boxes, the text displayed in the buttons, and so on.
- Properties that indicate what bits of information are collected by the Create User Account Wizard.

In previous hours we've examined the formatting properties common to all Web controls, which include `Font`, `ForeColor`, `BackColor`, `BorderStyle`, and so on. Rather than rehash these properties, let's focus on the properties that specify the text used for the user interface elements and dictate what bits of information are collected by the control.

Specifying the Text for the Labels, Text Boxes, and Buttons

By default, the CreateUserWizard control labels each text box with text such as User Name, Password, Confirm Password, E-mail, and so forth. Furthermore, it specifies default text for the error messages that are displayed if the user enters an invalid email address or does not correctly duplicate her password in the Confirm Password text box. These defaults are all customizable through the control's properties, along with the text displayed in the Create User and Continue buttons. You can even provide default values for the text boxes in the create user step, if you so desire.

Table 21.1 lists a number of the properties that can be set to customize the labels, text boxes, and buttons in the control. For brevity, not all properties that fall into this classification are listed.

TABLE 21.1 The Text in the Labels, Text Boxes, and Buttons Can Be Customized

Property Name	Description
`UserNameLabelText`	Specifies the text displayed for the username text box label. (Defaults to `User Name:`.)
`UserName`	Provides the default value displayed in the username text box. (Empty, by default.)
`PasswordLabelText`	Specifies the text displayed for the password text box label. (Defaults to `Password:`.)
`ConfirmPasswordLabelText`	Specifies the text displayed for the confirm password text box label. (Defaults to `Confirm Password:`.)
`EmailLabelText`	Specifies the text displayed for the email text box label. (Defaults to `E-mail:`.)
`Email`	Provides the default value displayed in the email text box. (Empty, by default.)
`QuestionLabelText`	Specifies the text displayed for the security question text box label. (Defaults to `Security Question:`.)
`Question`	Provides the default value displayed in the security question text box. (Empty, by default.)
`AnswerLabelText`	Specifies the text displayed for the security answer text box label. (Defaults to `Security Answer:`.)
`Answer`	Provides the default value displayed in the security answer text box. (Empty, by default.)

TABLE 21.1 Continued

Property Name	Description
`CreateUserButtonText`	Specifies the text displayed in the Create User button.
`ContinueButtonText`	Specifies the text displayed in the Continue button.
`UserNameRequiredErrorMessage`	Specifies the error message that is displayed if the user does not provide a username. (Defaults to `User Name is required.`)
`PasswordRequiredErrorMessage`	Specifies the error message that is displayed if the user does not provide a password. (Defaults to `Password is required.`)
`EmailRequiredErrorMessage`	Specifies the error message that is displayed if the user does not provide an email address. (Defaults to `E-mail is required.`)

In addition to `UserNameRequiredErrorMessage`, `PasswordRequiredErrorMessage`, and `EmailRequiredErrorMessage`, a number of other error message properties exist. You can find all of them in the Validation section of the Properties window. In the next section we'll explore some properties that can prohibit certain questions from being asked, such as the user's email address. If the user is not prompted for his email address, the `EmailRequiredErrorMessage` property becomes moot.

Dictating What Information Users Must Provide

By default, the CreateUserWizard control requires that the user provide a username, password, email address, and security question and answer to be able to create a new account. You can, however, decide whether to prompt the user for an email address or password. In the Behavior section of the Properties window, you'll find the `AutoGeneratePassword` and `RequireEmail` Boolean properties.

When `RequireEmail` is `True` (the default), the user is prompted to enter an email address when signing up. If you do not need to know the user's email address, you can set `RequireEmail` to `False`. I recommend leaving this property as `True` because it provides a communication channel between you and the user. Furthermore, various login Web controls, including the CreateUserWizard, provide the capability to email an informational message to the user. Of course, for this functionality to be utilized, the user's email address must be known.

The `AutoGeneratePassword` property, if `True`, does not prompt the user to enter and confirm a password; rather, the system automatically creates a random password.

When AutoGeneratePassword is False (the default), the user chooses her own password.

A usability concern with assigning a random password is how to inform the user of his autogenerated password. Imagine that you set the AutoGeneratePassword property to True, thereby removing the Password and Confirm Password text boxes from the user interface. After the user enters his username, email address, and security question and answer, and clicks the Create User button, an account is created with a random password and the user is logged in. The problem is, the user doesn't know his password! How will he log back in to the site at some later point in time?

The common solution is to email the user his autogenerated password after he has created his account, along with instructions on how to change his password.

Emailing Users a Message After Creating Their Accounts

The CreateUserWizard control can optionally send an email message to the user who just created the account. This email message can provide the user with her username and password, along with any instructions and information necessary. To provide this functionality, the website must be configured to support sending email; we examined how to accomplish this earlier in this hour in the "Configuring a Website's SMTP Settings" section.

To send an email to new users, we must first define the content of the email message in a file. This file must exist within the website project and can be a text file or an HTML file, depending on whether you want the email message to be plain text or HTML-formatted. In this file we can optionally use the placeholders <%UserName%> and <%Password%> to indicate where the user's username and password should appear.

Imagine that we wanted to send a user a plain-text email message that invited him to our site and contained only his username. We could accomplish this by creating a new text file in our website project with the contents shown in Listing 21.1. If, instead, we wanted to provide an HTML-formatted email that listed, for instance, both the user's username and password in a bulleted list, we could create an HTML file in our website project that contained the markup shown in Listing 21.2.

Did you Know?

> To add a text file or HTML page to your website, right-click the project name in the Solution Explorer and choose the Add New Item menu option. In the Add New Item dialog box, you'll find Text file and HTML page file types.

LISTING 21.1 This Plain-Text Email Includes the User's Username

```
Hello <%UserName%>!

You have just created a new account on MySite.com. Thanks!
You can login at any time by visiting http://MySite.com/Login.aspx

If you have any problems logging in, please contact help@mysite.com.
```

LISTING 21.2 This HTML-Formatted Email Includes Both the Username and Password

```
<!DOCTYPE html PUBLIC "-//W3C//DTD XHTML 1.0 Transitional//EN" "http://www.w3.org/TR/xhtml1/DTD/xhtml1-transitional.dtd">
<html xmlns="http://www.w3.org/1999/xhtml" >
  <head>
    <title>Welcome to My Website!</title>
    <style type="text/css">
      body { font-family: Verdana; font-size: medium; }
    </style>
  </head>
  <body>
    <h1>
      <span style="color: #990000; ">Welcome to My Website!</span>
    </h1>
    <p>
        According to our records you have created a new account on our website. Your login
        information is:
    </p>
    <ul>
        <li>Username: <%UserName%></li>
        <li>Password: <%Password%></li>
    </ul>
    <p style="text-align: center">
        If you have any questions, please email me at </span>
        <a href="mailto:my@email.com"><em>my@email.com</em></a>
    </p>
  </body>
</html>
```

After the contents of the email message have been defined in a separate file, having the CreateUserWizard send the email message is as simple as setting a few subproperties in the control's `MailDefinition` property. `MailDefinition` has four germane subproperties:

- **`BodyFileName`**—This is the name of the file that contains the email body of the message.
- **`From`**—The From address of the email sent to the user. Recall that when the website was configured to support email, we specified a default From address. If you want this default From address used, leave this subproperty blank.

- **`IsBodyHtml`**—A Boolean property that indicates whether the email is sent as HTML-formatted or as plain text. It defaults to `False`, meaning emails are sent as plain text.
- **`Subject`**—The subject of the email message.

After these properties have been set, any newly created user will automatically receive an email. Figure 21.11 shows the email message received when the HTML-formatted email template from Listing 21.2 is used.

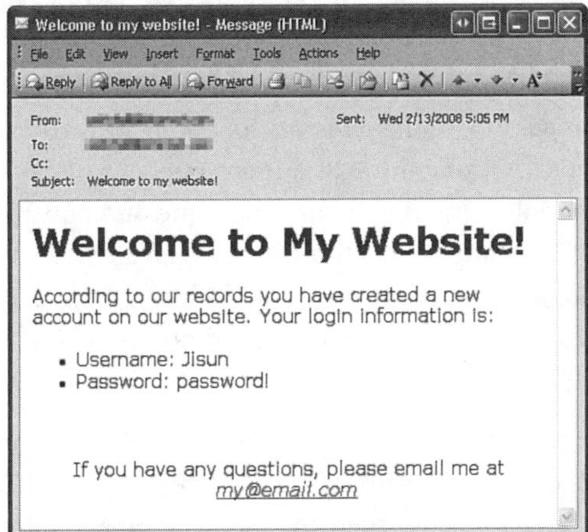

FIGURE 21.11 The email message sent to new user accounts.

Creating Inactive User Accounts

Whereas most sites allow users to create a new account by providing a username, password, and email address, some sites are more selective about their membership and want to make members **inactive** by default. An inactive member cannot log in to the site until an administrator marks her account as active. Recall that in the ASP.NET Website Administration Tool's Manage Users screen, shown in Figure 21.5, we could mark users active or inactive.

By default, newly created user accounts are active, but this is configurable through the CreateUserWizard control's `DisableCreatedUser` property. By default, this is set to `False`, which means the created user is active and can log into the site. To make new users inactive, set this property to `True`. As you may have guessed, when this property is set to `True`, the user is not automatically logged in after creating her account.

If you make newly created users inactive, rather than redirecting them to the site's home page after creating a new account, you may want to send them to a page that explains that their account is currently inactive. This page should also include the policies used by your site to determine whether a user is marked as active.

Furthermore, if you send an instructional email, as discussed in the "Emailing Users a Message After Creating Their Accounts" section, be sure to inform the users that their account is currently inactive.

Logging In to the Website with the Login Control

Any site that supports user accounts must include some means for the users to log in to the site. This is typically done through a **login page**. In the login page, the user is queried for his credentials—in our case, his username and password. Creating a login page in ASP.NET is quite simple thanks to the Login Web control, which renders the typical login user interface. To see this Web control in action, start by creating a new ASP.NET page named `Login.aspx`, adding the Login control to the page (see Figure 21.12).

As Figure 21.12 shows, the Login control contains two TextBox controls to capture the user's credentials. Additionally, there's a Remember Me Next Time check box. If the user logs on to the site without checking the Remember Me Next Time check box, she remains logged on to the site for the duration of her browser session; after she closes her browser and revisits the site, she'll need to log on again. If, however, the user checks this check box when signing on, she'll remain logged on across browser and computer restarts.

By the Way

Online banking websites and other security-conscious sites often don't provide a Remember Me Next Time option to help prevent another person using the same computer from logging on to the first user's account. You can dictate whether this Remember Me Next Time check box appears through the Login control's `DisplayRememberMe` property.

When visiting this page, if a user enters invalid credentials or the credentials for an inactive account, he will be shown an appropriate message—`Your login attempt was not successful. Please try again.` by default. If he enters valid credentials, he will be logged on to the site and redirected to the URL specified by the Login control's `DestinationPageUrl` property. (If no value is specified for this property, the user will be sent to `Default.aspx`.) Try out this page on your own in a browser.

Go to `Login.aspx` and observe what happens when you enter invalid credentials, or when you omit the username or password. Also, make sure to see what happens when you provide valid credentials.

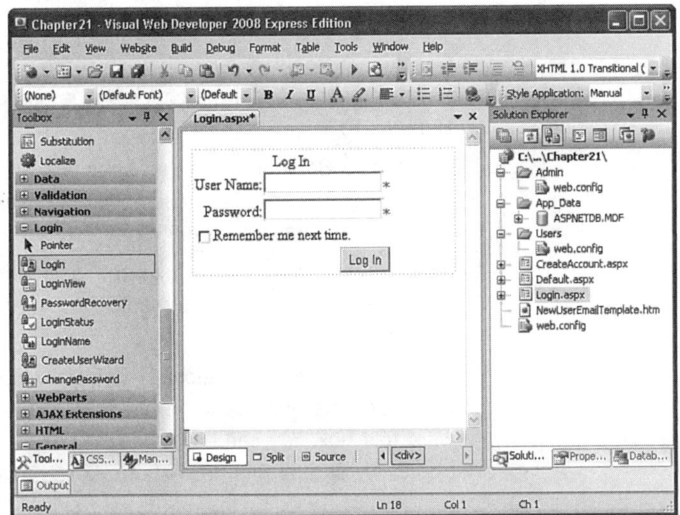

FIGURE 21.12
The Login control provides the standard login user interface.

By the Way

If the user attempts to visit a page that he does not have access to, he will automatically be redirected back to the login page. For example, earlier in this hour we created a `Users` folder and configured its access rights to disallow anonymous users. Take a moment to add a `Default.aspx` page to the `Users` folder and then, when logged out, try visiting this page. You'll find that you are automatically sent back to the login page, at which point you can enter your credentials. Upon being authenticated, you will be automatically sent back to the `Users/Default.aspx` page.

Customizing the Login Control

Like the Web controls examined in the preceding hour, the Login control has the usual suite of appearance-related properties. Furthermore, like the CreateUserWizard control, the Login control has properties that can be used to customize the labels, text box content, and error messages. Rather than go over these common properties, let's focus on the Login control-specific properties.

The Login control properties worth noting include those in the Link and Behavior sections of the Properties window. Table 21.2 contains a listing of the control's more interesting properties, along with a brief description for each.

TABLE 21.2 Customize the Login Control Using These Properties

Property Name	Description
`DestinationPageUrl`	Indicates the URL the user is sent to after successfully logging in. Defaults to an empty value, which ends up sending the user to `Default.aspx`.
`DisplayRememberMe`	Specifies a Boolean value that indicates whether the Remember Me Next Time check box is present. Defaults to `True`.
`RememberMeSet`	Indicates a Boolean value that specifies whether the Remember Me Next Time check box is checked by default. Defaults to `False`.
`VisibleWhenLoggedIn`	Indicates whether the Login control is rendered when the page is visited by an authenticated user. Defaults to `True`.
`Orientation`	Has a `Vertical` orientation, by default, which causes the username text box to be placed above the password text box. You can have the text boxes laid side-by-side by setting this property to `Horizontal`.
`TextLayout`	Can be one of two values—`TextOnLeft` or `TextOnTop`. Specifies the position of the labels relative to the text boxes.

`CreateUserText`
`CreateUserIconUrl`
`CreateUserUrl`
	Include a link from the Login control to the create account page by setting the `CreateUserUrl` and one or both of the `CreateUserText` and `CreateUserIconUrl` properties.

`HelpPageText`
`HelpPageIconUrl`
`HelpPageUrl`
	Allow you to add a link to this page if you have created a help page, explaining the login process and policies.

`PasswordRecoveryText`
`PasswordRecoveryIconUrl`
`PasswordRecoveryUserUrl`
	Provide a link to a web page from which the user can reset her password.

If you add a Login control to your site's home page, you likely want the control to appear only for unauthenticated users. That is, if a user is already logged in, there's no reason to show the Login control on the home page. To accomplish this, you can set the control's `VisibleWhenLoggedIn` property to False. Another option, though, is to use the LoginView Web control, which lets you define precisely what content is shown for logged-in users versus that shown for unauthenticated users. We'll discuss this control in more detail later in this hour in the "Displaying Content Based on Authentication Status" section.

Logging Out

Although being able to log on to a site is important, it's also equally important to allow users to log off. This is usually accomplished through a Logoff link that, when clicked, signs the user out of the site. The LoginStatus Web control provides this functionality. When an authenticated user visits the site, the LoginStatus control displays a Logoff link; it renders a Login link for anonymous visitors.

Add the LoginStatus control to `Default.aspx`. In the control's smart tag, you'll see that there are two views: Logged In and Logged Out. Toggling between these views shows what visitors to the site will see depending on whether they're authenticated. The `LoginText` and `LogoutText` properties specify the text that's displayed for the Login and Logout links. If you would rather have these links displayed as clickable images, you can set the `LoginImageUrl` and `LogoutImageUrl` properties to the corresponding login and logout images.

Did you Know?

> You'll likely want to have the LoginStatus control appear on all the pages in your website, thereby enabling users to log on or log off from anywhere on the site. Although this can be accomplished by manually adding a LoginStatus control to each and every page of the site, a better, more maintainable approach is to use **master pages**, which are the topic of our next hour.

By default, when the user clicks the logout link, he will be logged out but remain on the same page. If you want the person redirected to a specific URL after being logged out, use the `LogoutAction` and `LogoutPageUrl` properties. The `LogoutAction` property specifies what action is taken when the user clicks the Logout link; it can have one of three values:

- **`Refresh`**—The user is logged out and stays on the same page.
- **`Redirect`**—The user is logged out and redirected to the URL specified by the `LogoutPageUrl` property.
- **`RedirectToLoginPage`**—The user is logged out and redirected to the login page.

When an unauthenticated user visits a page with a LoginStatus control and clicks the Login link, he is taken to the login page with the URL of the page he was on passed along in the querystring. After the user successfully provides his credentials, not only is he logged on, but he is automatically redirected back to the page he came from.

Specifying the Login Page URL

If you scan the list of the LoginStatus control's properties, you'll notice that although a `LogoutPageUrl` property exists, there's no corresponding `LoginPageUrl` property. There's no explicit way to tell the LoginStatus control where to send the user when she clicks the Login link. By default, the website uses the URL `Login.aspx` as its login page. If, however, you need to customize this, you can do so through the site's `web.config` file. Specifically, you need to find the `<authentication>` element and add a `<forms>` child element. In the `<forms>` element, use the `loginUrl` attribute to specify the URL of the site's login page.

For example, to create a site whose login page was at `SignOn.aspx` instead of `Login.aspx`, we'd go to the `web.config` file and locate the `<authentication>` element, which should look like this:

```
<authentication mode="Forms" />
```

We need to add the `<forms>` element as an inner element of the `<authentication>` element. Therefore, replace the preceding line with the following:

```
<authentication mode="Forms">
   <forms loginUrl="SignOn.aspx" />
</authentication>
```

> To avoid having to muck around in the `web.config` file, I make sure to name my login page `Login.aspx`. If you decide to use a login page other than the default `Login.aspx`, don't forget that the `web.config` file is case sensitive. Make sure to enter the `<forms>` element and `loginUrl` attribute with the correct casing.

Displaying Content Based on Authentication Status

Often we need to display different content based on whether the user visiting the page is authenticated or anonymous. If the visitor is not logged on to the site, we might want to display the Login control; however, if the user has already been authenticated, in place of the Login control, we might want to display a short message like `Welcome back` *`username`*, where *`username`* is the name of the logged-on user.

As we saw in the preceding section, the Login control can be conditionally displayed based on the user's authentication status via the `VisibleWhenLoggedIn` property. Although setting this property to False will indeed hide the Login control from authenticated users, it doesn't provide a mechanism to replace the login control with a customized message. To accomplish that, we'll need to use the LoginView Web control.

Go to `Default.aspx` and add a LoginView control to the page. As the control's smart tag shows, the LoginView control provides two views: Anonymous Template, which is shown for unauthenticated users; and Logged In Template, which is shown for authenticated users. To add content that should appear only when the visitor is authenticated or not, add the content to the appropriate view.

To have `Default.aspx` show a Login control for unauthenticated users, switch to the Anonymous Template view and then drag and drop a Login control from the Toolbox into the LoginView control. Next, switch to the LoginView control's Logged In Template. Whatever static HTML or Web controls we add here will appear for authenticated users. Begin by putting your mouse cursor inside the Logged In Template and click to give focus. Then type in the text **`Welcome back`**. Finally, drag the LoginName control from the Toolbox into the Logged In Template, placing it after the text you just added (see Figure 21.13).

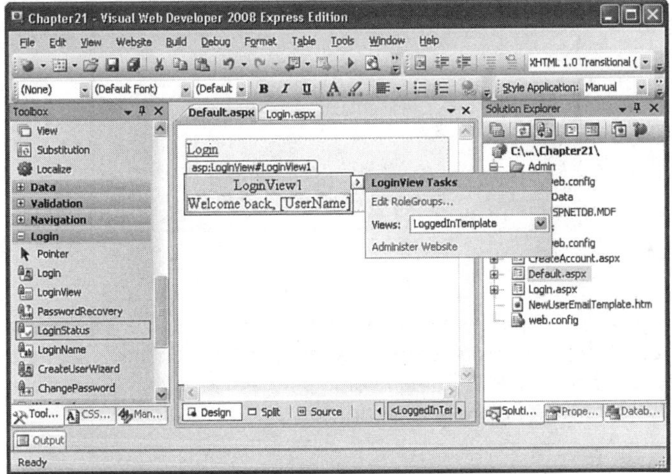

FIGURE 21.13
The LoginName control has been added to the LoginStatus control's Logged In Template.

As you may have guessed, the LoginName control displays the username of the logged-on user. If an anonymous user visits a page, the LoginName control displays nothing.

Figure 21.14 shows `Default.aspx` when viewed by an anonymous user, whereas Figure 21.15 shows the page when visited by a logged-on user.

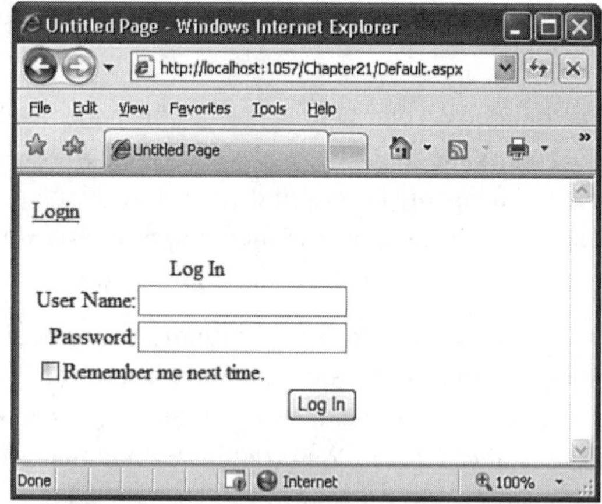

FIGURE 21.14 For anonymous users, the Login control is shown.

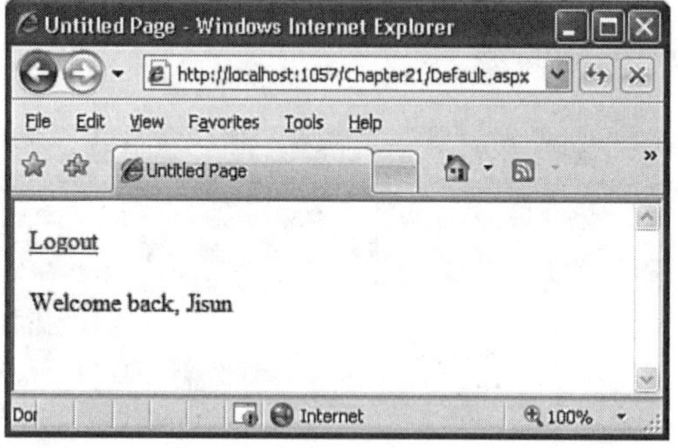

FIGURE 21.15 After Jisun has logged on, she sees `Welcome back, Jisun`.

Did you Know?

The LoginView control can also be configured to display content based on the logged-in user's role. For more information on this feature, check out Part 2 of my article "Examining ASP.NET's Membership, Roles, and Profile," available online at http://aspnet.4guysfromrolla.com/articles/121405-1.aspx.

Summary

Building a website that supports user accounts is trivial with ASP.NET, thanks to ASP.NET's built-in user account support and login Web controls. When we configure the ASP.NET website to use forms-based authentication, the ASP.NET Website Administration Tool automatically adds a database to our project, `ASPNETDB`. This database contains the tables needed to store user accounts and roles. Additionally, the ASP.NET Website Administration Tool simplifies adding and managing users, roles, and access rights.

After this database has been created, a host of login Web controls aid in performing common user account-related tasks. The CreateUserWizard control allows users to register new accounts, whereas the Login control logs a user on to the site. The LoginStatus control displays a Login or Logout link, depending on whether the user is logged in, while the more flexible LoginView control allows us to specify a user interface for authenticated and anonymous visitors.

For a more in-depth look at forms-based authentication, authorization, and ASP.NET's membership and role-based features, check out my ASP.NET security tutorials, online at www.asp.net/learn/security.

Q&A

Q. ***I like how ASP.NET provides inherent user account support, but it seems to make a lot of assumptions for me. For example, users' passwords must be seven characters long and include nonalphanumeric characters. I want to change some of these defaults. Is this possible?***

A. Yes. The membership feature of ASP.NET is highly customizable through the website's `web.config` file. For more information, consult the "How To: Use Membership in ASP.NET" documentation at http://msdn2.microsoft.com/en-us/library/ms998347.aspx. Also check out "Examining ASP.NET's Membership, Roles, and Profile" at http://aspnet.4guysfromrolla.com/articles/120705-1.aspx.

Q. ***In this hour you showed us how to configure the CreateUserWizard control to automatically send an email message to the new user. Are there other controls that offer this feature? Can I send an email message from an ASP.NET page on my own, without having to use one of these controls?***

A. Along with the CreateUserWizard control, the PasswordRecovery and ChangePassword controls may be configured to send an email message to a user. Although we did not examine the PasswordRecovery and ChangePassword controls in this hour, to use them simply add them to a page and configure their properties. As you may have guessed, the PasswordRecovery control emails a user his password in the event that he has forgotten it; the ChangePassword control enables a user to change his password.

It is also possible to send an email message from an ASP.NET page by writing a few lines of code. For details and step-by-step instructions on how to accomplish this, read "Sending Email in ASP.NET," at http://aspnet.4guysfromrolla.com/articles/072606-1.aspx.

Workshop

Quiz

1. What is authentication? How is authentication performed with forms-based authentication?
2. What three pieces of information do you need to provide when specifying an access right?
3. Imagine that on a web page you wanted to show anonymous users the user interface for logging in to the site as well as for creating a new user account, whereas for logged-on users you simply wanted to display a Logout link. What Web controls would you use to accomplish this?
4. What does the LoginName Web control do?
5. True or False: It is possible to configure the CreateUserWizard control to automatically send an email to the new user.

Answers

1. Authentication is the process of identifying a user. Forms-based authentication requires that the user provide her credentials through a Web Form.
2. To create an access right, you need to specify the following: the folder, the user or role, and whether to allow or deny access.
3. Use the LoginView control. In the Anonymous Template view, add the Login and CreateUserWizard Web controls; in the Logged In Template view, add the LoginStatus control. Recall that the LoginStatus control displays a Login link for anonymous users and a Logoff link for authenticated users. Because the LoginView control's Logged In Template view is displayed only for authenticated users, the LoginStatus control will always show the Logoff link.
4. The LoginName Web control displays the logged-in user's name. If the visitor is anonymous, it displays nothing.
5. True. To accomplish this, configure the `MailDefinition` property as described in the "Emailing Users a Message After Creating Their Accounts" section.

Exercises

1. In Hour 16, "Deleting, Inserting, and Editing Data," we looked at displaying and editing the contents of the `Books` table through a GridView. If we were building a website to showcase our favorite books, we'd want to make sure that only we could update the contents of the `Books` table, whereas other visitors could only view the results. For this exercise, create a website that supports user accounts and has an Administrator role defined. Next, add a folder to the website named `Admin` and then create two web pages: `BookList.aspx`, in the root folder; and `Default.aspx`, in the `Admin` folder. Have `BookList.aspx` list the contents of the `Books` table in a read-only GridView, with `Admin/Default.aspx` providing an editable GridView. Finally, configure the `Admin` folder to only allow access by those users who belong to the `Administrator` role.

2. Repeat Exercise 1, but instead of having a separate `Admin` folder, have only one page, `BookList.aspx`, in the root folder. Add a LoginView control and add a GridView to both the Anonymous and Logged In Templates. Finally, configure the GridView in the Logged In Template to allow editing, while keeping the GridView in the Anonymous Template read-only. With this setup, any authenticated user can edit the contents of the `Books` table, but anonymous users will be presented with a read-only interface.

3. Repeat Exercise 2, but this time instead of using two GridViews in a LoginView control, add just one GridView to the page. Configure the GridView to support editing. Next, turn the GridView's Edit, Update, Cancel column into a TemplateField through the Fields dialog box. This new TemplateField will have an ItemTemplate that contains a LinkButton with the text Edit and an EditItemTemplate with two LinkButtons: Update and Cancel.

   Add a LoginView control to this new TemplateField's ItemTemplate, leaving the Anonymous Template empty and placing the Edit LinkButton in the Logged In Template. When an anonymous user visits the website, the field that normally contains the Edit button will be blank; when an authenticated user visits, however, he'll see the Edit button, which he can click to edit the contents of the corresponding record in the `Books` table.

   (Both Exercises 2 and 3 allow any authenticated user to edit the `Books` table. You could restrict this functionality to users in the Administrator role by utilizing the LoginView's role-based features.)

HOUR 22

Using Master Pages to Provide Sitewide Page Templates

In this hour, we will cover

- ▶ Creating a master page
- ▶ Defining editable regions within a master page
- ▶ Associating a newly created page with an existing master page
- ▶ Making an existing page use a master page
- ▶ Adding source code to a master page

Virtually all professionally done websites have a very consistent look and feel across their pages. The common look and feel usually includes both the layout of the page—where various user interface elements appear and how they are oriented with respect to one another—and the fonts, colors, and graphics used within the page. For example, if you visit sports channel ESPN's website at ESPN.com, you'll find that regardless of where you go on the site, the top of the page includes the ESPN logo, a search box, and a menu listing the sports covered by ESPN. At the bottom of each page is another search box, along with the links to the most recently published stories.

When you create the web pages for a website, you do not want to manually add the common sitewide features to each and every page. The web designers at ESPN.com would be remiss to repetitively add the search box, logo, and common links to each and every page. Not only would this add significantly to the time required to build each page, but it would make updating the website's layout a nightmare. If the designers at ESPN.com wanted to remove the search box from the top or add to their menu of sports covered, they would have to visit and update each and every page in the site.

The approach used by professional web developers is to design a single site template that contains the HTML content that should be present on each and every page. This is accomplished in ASP.NET through the use of a **master page**. A master page is like a regular ASP.NET page in that it contains both a code portion and an HTML portion, but rather than defining the HTML for a specific page the master page contains the website's common layout content. New ASP.NET pages can optionally inherit the master page's look and feel. With the master page model, updating the master page automatically updates the common content in all the ASP.NET pages that are associated with the master page.

With master pages, creating a unified site layout that can be easily updated is a snap!

An Overview of Master Pages

Programs for designing websites and creating web pages, like Microsoft FrontPage and Adobe Dreamweaver, have long offered template features. With these tools, a designer can create a single template page that contains both common, sitewide content as well as regions that can be customized by each page that uses the template.

With ASP.NET and Visual Web Developer, a page developer provides a sitewide template by creating a **master page**. Just like the template files in FrontPage and Dreamweaver, a master page consists of two pieces: content that appears on each and every page that inherits the master page and regions that can be customized by the **content page**. A content page is the ASP.NET page that is bound to the master page. The master page model in ASP.NET outshines simple HTML-based templates because master pages, like any ASP.NET page, can contain not only HTML, but Web controls and server-side source code as well.

Before we jump into creating our own master pages, let's first look at how the entire master page model works. Imagine that we wanted a website where each page on the site had the following four common user interface elements:

- The website's name on the top of the page
- A navigation breadcrumb at the top of the page
- A navigation treeview on the left of the page, showing the site's structure
- A copyright statement and a series of links—Legal, Privacy Policy, About Us, and so on—at the bottom of the page

The navigation treeview and breadcrumb on the pages in our site would ideally be implemented using the site navigation features and the SiteMapPath and TreeView Web controls examined in Hour 20, "Defining a Site Map and Providing Site Navigation."

Figure 22.1 shows the About page on this site.

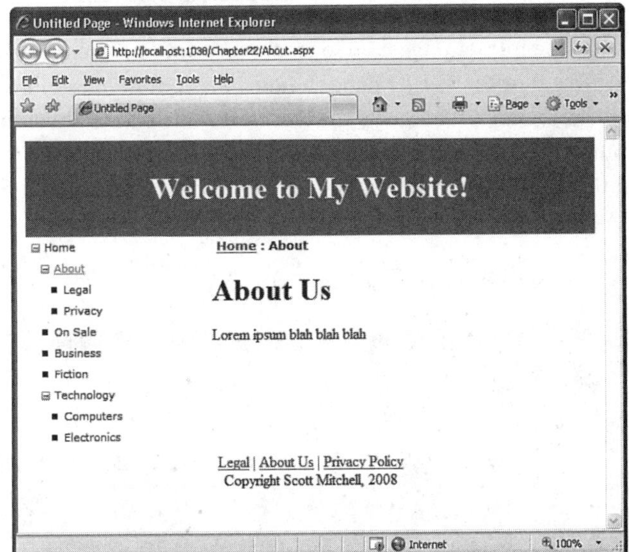

FIGURE 22.1
Each page in the site will have the same look and feel.

The title at the top of the page (`Welcome to My Website!`), the treeview on the left, the breadcrumb, and the list of links at the bottom will exist on each page in our site precisely as they appear in the About page in Figure 22.1. The remaining portion of the page, the part that says `About Us` and `Lorem ipsum blah blah blah`, can be unique to each of the web pages on the site.

To accomplish this in an ASP.NET website, we first create a master page. A master page needs to specify *both* the regions of the page that are common to all content pages as well as the regions that are customizable on a page-by-page basis. The content that is common to all content pages can be added to the master page the same as you add content to a regular ASP.NET page. You can enter the HTML and Web controls by hand, in the Source view, or by using the WYSIWYG designer.

To indicate a region in the master page that is customizable on a page-by-page basis, use the ContentPlaceHolder Web control. As Figure 22.2 shows, this Web control renders as a box in the Design view of the master page. Later, when creating an ASP.NET page that inherits from this master page, we will be able to add content only inside this box.

Did you Know?

> A master page may have multiple ContentPlaceHolder Web controls. Each ContentPlaceHolder control represents a location on the master page that can be customized by its content pages.

Figure 22.2 shows the master page used to create the common user interface shown in Figure 22.1. Note that the master page contains the common user interface elements—the title at the top of the page, the TreeView control (and SiteMapDataSource control), the SiteMapPath control, and the links at the bottom of the page—along with a ContentPlaceHolder control. (We'll look at the steps in creating a master page in greater detail later in this hour.)

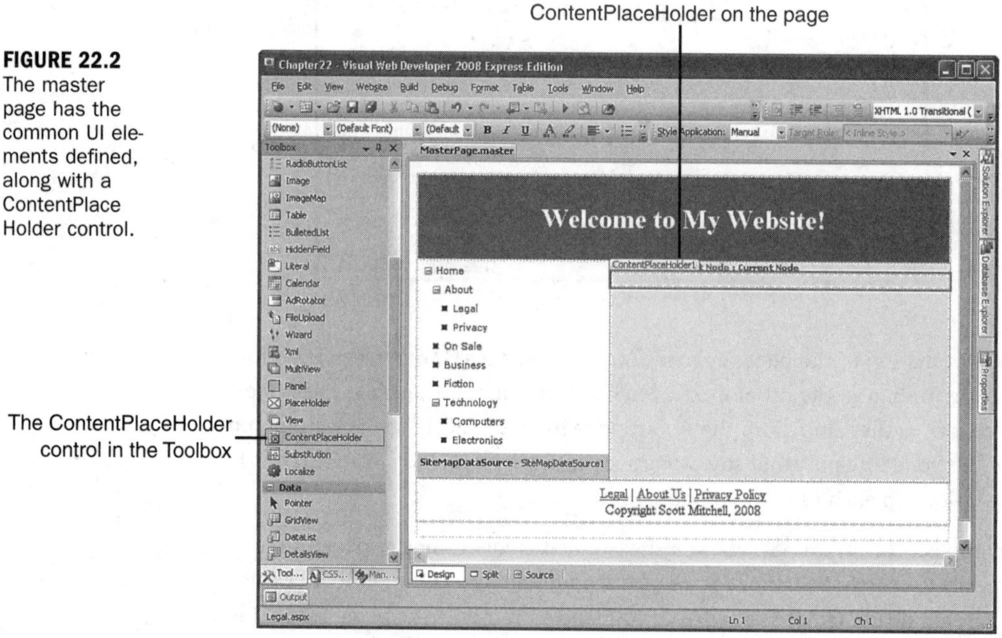

FIGURE 22.2 The master page has the common UI elements defined, along with a ContentPlace Holder control.

With this master page created, the next step is to create an ASP.NET page that inherits from the master page, a topic that we'll delve into later this hour. After such a page has been created, the Design view for the ASP.NET page shows both the noneditable master page content as well as the editable content regions. Figure 22.3 shows the Design view of the About page.

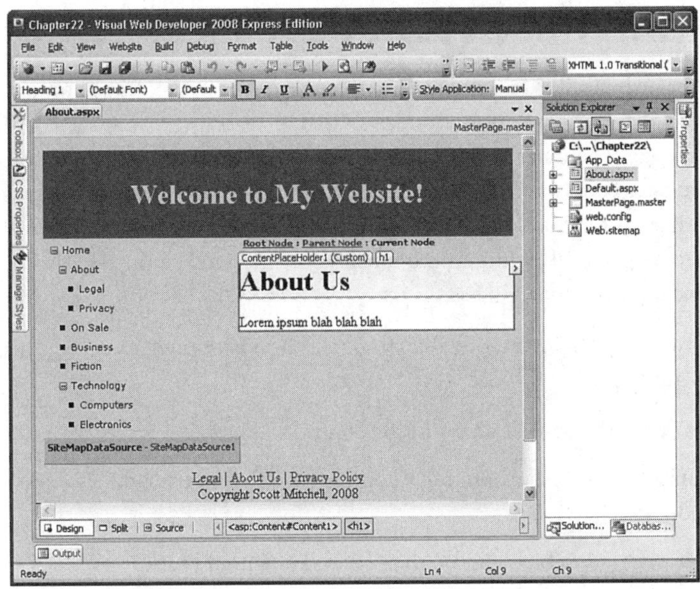

FIGURE 22.3 The About page's only editable region is the Content region.

We don't need to re-create the common page elements—the title, TreeView control, and so on. They are automatically shown in the page's Design view, inherited from the master page. Although it may not be particularly clear from the figures in this book, these common master page elements are grayed out and cannot be modified by the ASP.NET page. Rather, the only modifiable region on the page is the Content region, which shows up precisely where the ContentPlaceHolder control was added to the master page.

With this master page setup, we can easily adjust the overall look and feel of the site by updating the master page. For example, if we wanted to change the text displayed at the top of the page or wanted to add new links to the bottom of this page, we could edit the master page. After the master page was modified and saved, those content pages that inherited from this master page would immediately show the updated look and feel.

To summarize, defining a sitewide template with master pages involves two steps, which should be done in the following order:

1. Create a master page that specifies the common, sitewide user interface elements and the regions that are customizable on a page-by-page basis.
2. Create the site's ASP.NET pages, with the pages configured to use the master page created in step 1.

The remainder of this hour examines these two steps in greater detail.

Creating a Master Page

A master page is similar to the ASP.NET pages we've been creating throughout this book. Like ASP.NET pages, master pages consist of Web controls, static HTML, and server-side code. The main difference between a master page and an ASP.NET page is that a master page's purpose is to define a template for the website. As we discussed earlier in this hour, the master page defines both the user interface elements common to all pages that inherit the master page, as well as the regions that are editable on a page-by-page basis.

To get started defining a sitewide template, add a master page to your project using the following steps:

1. Right-click the project name in the Solution Explorer.
2. Choose the Add New Item menu option, displaying the Add New Item dialog box.
3. From this dialog box, choose the Master Page item type.
4. Choose a name for the master page. By default, the name is `MasterPage.master`. Feel free to leave it as this or change it to something else. Just be sure to keep the file extension as `.master`.
5. Check the Place Code in Separate File check box, if it's not already checked. As we discussed in previous hours, checking this check box places the master page's source code portion in a separate file.
6. Click the Add button to add the master page to your project.

After you add the new master page, the Design view shows a page with a single ContentPlaceHolder Web control (see Figure 22.4). This ContentPlaceHolder indicates the region that can be edited by the ASP.NET pages that inherit this master page. You can have multiple ContentPlaceHolders in your master page. In fact, the page already contains two ContentPlaceHolders: one within the `<head>` HTML element and one within the Web Form. (The one you see in the Design view in Figure 22.4 is the ContentPlaceHolder in the Web Form; the one in the `<head>` is not displayed.)

To add a new ContentPlaceHolder, drag the ContentPlaceHolder control from the Toolbox onto the master page.

By the Way

> The ContentPlaceHolder Web control can be added only to master pages, not to ASP.NET pages. Therefore, when viewing a master page in Visual Web Developer, you will find the ContentPlaceHolder control in the Toolbox; however, it is not displayed in the Toolbox when working with an ASP.NET page.

Take a moment to view the declarative markup of the master page (see Listing 22.1). If you compare the default declarative markup for a master page to that of a regular ASP.NET page, you'll see two differences. The first is that the master page starts with a `<%@ Master %>` directive (line 1), whereas ASP.NET pages start with the `<%@ Page %>` directive. Furthermore, the master page contains, by default, two ContentPlaceHolder controls: one on lines 8 and 9 and the other spanning lines 14 to 16.

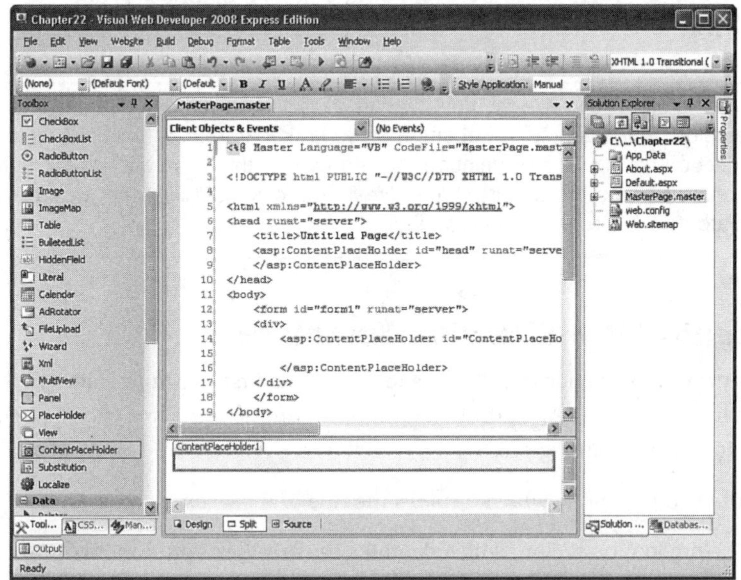

FIGURE 22.4 New master pages contain a single ContentPlace Holder control.

LISTING 22.1 The Default Declarative Markup for a Master Page

```
 1: <%@ Master Language="VB" CodeFile="MasterPage2.master.vb"
➥ Inherits="MasterPage2" %>
 2:
 3: <!DOCTYPE html PUBLIC "-//W3C//DTD XHTML 1.0 Transitional//EN"
➥ "http://www.w3.org/TR/xhtml1/DTD/xhtml1-transitional.dtd">
 4:
 5: <html xmlns="http://www.w3.org/1999/xhtml">
 6: <head runat="server">
 7:     <title>Untitled Page</title>
 8:     <asp:ContentPlaceHolder id="head" runat="server">
 9:     </asp:ContentPlaceHolder>
10: </head>
11: <body>
12:     <form id="form1" runat="server">
13:     <div>
14:         <asp:ContentPlaceHolder id="ContentPlaceHolder1" runat="server">
15:
```

LISTING 22.1 Continued

```
            </asp:ContentPlaceHolder>
        </div>
        </form>
</html>
```

To create the sitewide look and feel, add the appropriate HTML and Web controls to the master page. Again, you can do this by manually entering the HTML and control syntax through the Source view, or in a more graphical way through the Design view.

A website project can have multiple master page files, each one defining a different template. For example, a website may be broken into three sections, with each section having its own unique look and feel. In this case we would create three master pages for the site. When creating a new ASP.NET page, we would associate it with the appropriate master page.

Designing the Sitewide Template

Let's create a master page that has the look and feel first shown in Figure 22.1—a title at the top, a TreeView control along the left, and so on. This design has each page laid out into four regions:

- The header region, which displays the title of the website.
- The navigation region, which contains the TreeView control and appears on the left of the page beneath the header region.
- The main region, which contains the SiteMapPath control and the ContentPlaceHolder control. This region is located beneath the header region and to the right of the navigation region.
- The footer region, which contains the common links—Legal, About Us, and so on—along with the copyright statement.

To provide this page layout, let's use **tables**. A table is an HTML element that can be used to arrange a page into various columns and rows. For this site design, we want a table that takes up the entire page with two columns and three rows, with the top and bottom rows spanning two columns. Figure 22.5 illustrates this design concept graphically.

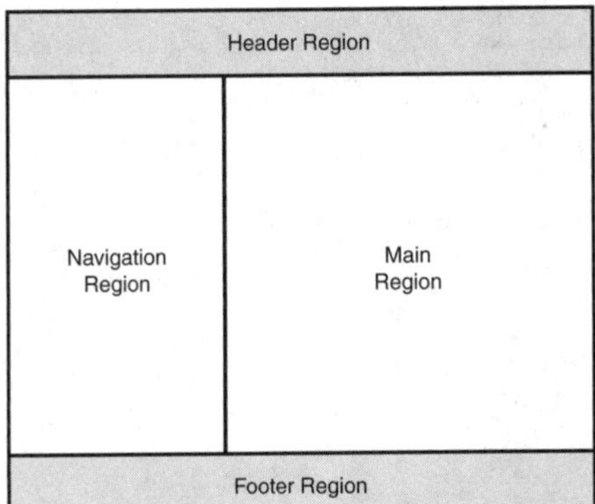

FIGURE 22.5 The site's design lays out pages using a two-column, three-row table.

To create such a layout in HTML, you can manually enter the appropriate HTML table markup, or you can use Visual Web Developer. If you prefer entering the HTML by hand, feel free to do so.

If you are not an HTML aficionado and would rather have Visual Web Developer assist with creating the page's layout, follow these steps. First, go to the master page's Design view and make sure that the focus is on the `<div>` element in the Web Form and not on the ContentPlaceHolder control.

Next, go to the Table menu and choose Insert Table. This displays the Insert Table dialog box, from which you can specify the precise table settings, indicating the number of rows and columns, the alignment, the width and height, and so on (see Figure 22.6). Create a table with two columns and three rows. We want the table to fill the width of the page, so check the Specify Width check box, enter 100 into the text box, and select the In Percent option button. Finally, set the Cell spacing to 0 and the Cell padding to 5.

The Insert Table dialog box adds the new table to the page before the ContentPlaceHolder Web control. Because we want the ContentPlaceHolder control in the main region, take a moment to drag the ContentPlaceHolder from beneath the table into the second column in the second row of the table.

Creating the Header Region

The header region is currently divided into two cells. We want to merge these two cells into one so that we can enter the website title here. To accomplish this, select both cells from the Design view. Then right-click the cells and, from the Modify menu option, choose to Merge the cells.

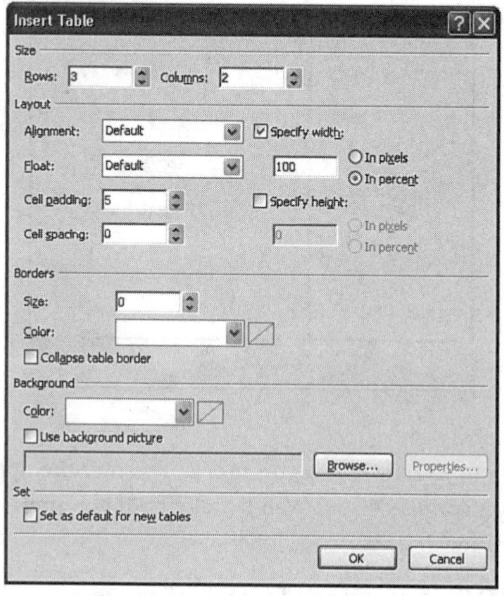

FIGURE 22.6
Add a table to the master page using the Insert Table dialog box.

Now enter the site's title here, such as `Welcome to My Website!`. I've opted to have this title centered, bolded, and displayed using the `X-Large` font size. These settings can be specified when typing in the website name, through the myriad of formatting options along the toolbar or through the Format menu. Alternatively, you can add a Label Web control for the title and configure its formatting properties to achieve the desired effect.

These settings can also be made to apply to the entire table cell, rather than just the particular piece of text being entered. To tailor the entire header region, perform the following steps:

1. Click inside the table cell and then go to the Properties window.
2. Click the `Style` property, which displays a set of ellipses.
3. Click these ellipses. This displays the Modify Style dialog box where you can set the font, background, layout, and other options that apply to the entire table row (see Figure 22.7).

For example, to have the header region display white text on an olive background, from the Font tab, select the white color from the color drop-down list, and from the Background tab, choose olive from the background-color drop-down list. To specify the height of the header region, use the height drop-down list in the Position tab. You can also specify font sizes, alignment, and a host of other settings through the Style Builder dialog box.

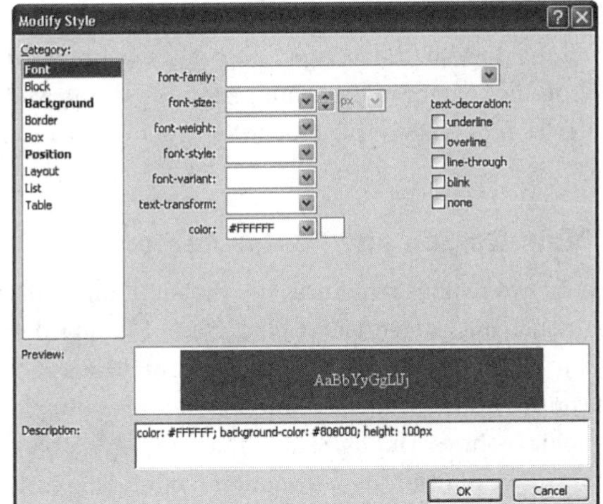

FIGURE 22.7
Customize the appearance of the header region through the Style Builder dialog box.

Crafting the Navigation Region

The purpose of the navigation region is to provide the visitor with a complete listing of the site's structure, making it easy to quickly move to another page on the site. As we discussed in Hour 20, "Defining a Site Map and Providing Site Navigation," the ASP.NET TreeView Web control can be used in tandem with a SiteMapDataSource control to display the site's structure, assuming that there is a properly defined site map. For this hour, I am using the same site map used in Hour 20.

After you have created your site map, add the SiteMapDataSource and TreeView controls to the first column in the second row of the table, configuring the TreeView control to use the SiteMapDataSource.

By default, the content in a table cell is vertically placed in the middle of the cell. If the navigation region's row is particularly tall, which can happen in pages that include lengthy content in the main region, whitespace will appear between the header region and the TreeView control. In fact, if the main region holds several pages' worth of content, the visitor may have to scroll down to see the TreeView.

Often the common sitewide elements are formatted so that their position is not affected by the page-specific content. To accomplish this, we need to have the navigation region's content appear at the top of the cell, rather than in the middle. This is configurable through the table cell's `valign` property. To set this property, click inside the cell that makes up the navigation region, go to the Properties window, and set the `valign` property to `top`. This causes the navigation region's content to be vertically aligned with the top of the table cell, regardless of how much or how little content is in the main region.

In addition to the vertical alignment, we should fix the navigation region's width. If we don't specify a fixed width, the navigation region's width will depend on the width of the page-specific content in the main region. To set the width, load the navigation region cell's properties in the Properties window and set the `Width` property to `200px`.

Creating the Main Region and Footer Region

At this point the only two regions remaining are the main and footer regions. The main region already has the ContentPlaceHolder control (dragged into it after adding the table) but still needs the SiteMapPath control, which shows a breadcrumb. Drag this control from the Toolbox into the main region, placing it above the ContentPlaceHolder control. Finally, set the main region's table cell's `valign` property to `top`, just as we did with the navigation region. This ensures that regardless of how little content is in the main region, it will appear at the top of the cell.

Finally, add the content for the footer region in the bottommost row. But first merge the bottom row's two cells, just like we did with the header region. My footer region contains three links: Legal, About Us, and Privacy Policy. I manually typed in these links, although you could opt to use three HyperLink Web controls, if you prefer.

Refer to Figure 22.2 to see the completed master page when viewed through the Visual Web Developer's Design view.

Did you Know?

Creating an aesthetically pleasing sitewide design can be difficult if you are new to HTML or if you are not artistically inclined. Fortunately, there are many websites that offer pre-designed sitewide templates. One such site is www.OpenDesigns.org, which includes hundreds of free website designs that you can use in personal and commercial web applications.

Creating a Content Page

With our master page created, the next step is to create a content page. A content page is an ASP.NET page that inherits from a master page. When creating a content page, we must define the content that belongs in the master page's ContentPlaceHolder controls. We *cannot* add any additional content outside these regions. To create a content page, when adding a new ASP.NET page to the project, check the Select Master Page check box (see Figure 22.8).

After you check Select Master Page and click the Add button, the Select a Master Page dialog box appears, as shown in Figure 22.9. This dialog box lists the master pages in the website project.

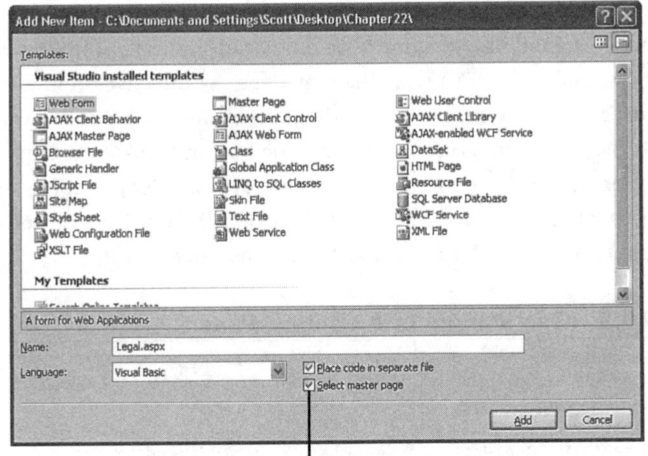

FIGURE 22.8 Associate the new ASP.NET page with a master page by checking Select Master Page.

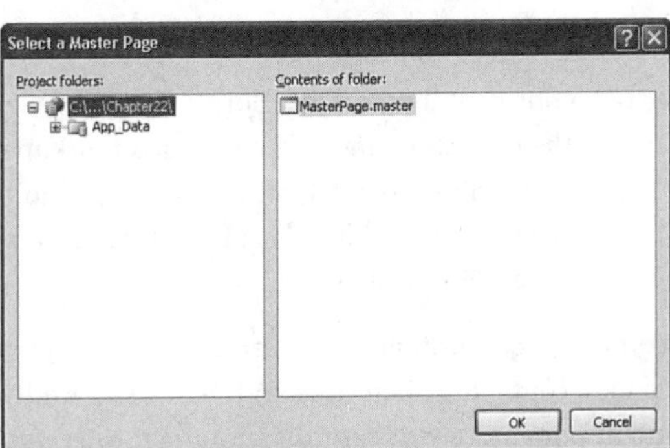

FIGURE 22.9 Select the new ASP.NET page's master page.

After you choose a master page, the new ASP.NET page's Design view shows the master page's sitewide markup as grayed-out, uneditable content (refer to Figure 22.3). The master page's ContentPlaceHolder controls are replaced with Content controls, which are editable regions whose content is unique to the particular ASP.NET page. You can type directly into the Content region or drag controls from the Toolbox.

If you create the content page before saving the master page, the content page's Design view displays an error message explaining that the content page has one or more Content controls that do not correspond with ContentPlaceHolders. To remedy this, save the master page file; the content page's Design view will then refresh and the error message will go away.

Listing 22.2 shows the declarative markup of the new content page. As you can see, the declarative markup for a content page differs substantially from the default markup for a regular ASP.NET page. The `<%@ Page %>` directive on line 1 includes a `MasterPageFile` attribute that indicates the path to the master page. And rather than having the typical markup, a content page has, in its place, a Content control for each ContentPlaceHolder control in the associated master page. The Content control's `ContentPlaceHolderID` property associates the Content control with a particular ContentPlaceHolder control in the master page.

LISTING 22.2 The Markup of a Content Page

```
1: <%@ Page Language="VB" MasterPageFile="~/MasterPage.master"
➥AutoEventWireup="false" CodeFile="Legal.aspx.vb" Inherits="Legal"
➥title="Untitled Page" %>
2:
3: <asp:Content ID="Content1" ContentPlaceHolderID="head" Runat="Server">
4: </asp:Content>
5: <asp:Content ID="Content2" ContentPlaceHolderID="ContentPlaceHolder1"
➥ Runat="Server">
6: </asp:Content>
```

Because our master page has two ContentPlaceHolder controls (`head` and `ContentPlaceHolder1`), the corresponding content page's markup contains two Content controls: `Content1`, on lines 3 and 4, which is mapped to the `head` ContentPlaceHolder; and `Content2`, on lines 5 and 6, which is mapped to the `ContentPlaceHolder1` ContentPlaceHolder.

When you visit a content page through a browser, the ASP.NET engine grabs the associated master page's content. It then fuses in the markup and Web controls specified in the content page's Content controls into the master page's corresponding ContentPlaceHolder controls. Because this infusion of master page and ASP.NET page occurs when the page is visited through a browser, any changes to the underlying master page are immediately reflected in its content pages.

An ASP.NET page does not lose any functionality when it inherits from a master page. All the examples we have examined throughout this book would have worked the same had we associated a master page with the ASP.NET page.

Having an Existing Page Inherit from a Master Page

Creating a *new* ASP.NET page that inherits from a master page is easy enough: Just check a check box and choose the master page. However, taking an existing, master page-less ASP.NET page and having it inherit from a master page is, unfortunately, not as simple. To take an existing page and have it inherit an existing master page, we must do two things:

- Add a `MasterPageFile` attribute to the page's `<%@ Page %>` directive.
- Create a Content control for each ContentPlaceHolder control in the master page, with the page's existing HTML and Web control markup moved into the appropriate Content controls.

The first step is simple enough to accomplish. Start by opening the ASP.NET page that you want to have inherit a master page and go to the Source view. Next, place your cursor in the `<%@ Page %>` directive and type in **`MasterPageFile=`**. At this point, a drop-down list should appear containing the various master pages in your project. Choose which master page file you want to use and press the Tab key. In the end, the `<%@ Page %>` directive should include an attribute that looks like `MasterPageFile="~/`*`masterPageFileName`*`"`.

With the `MasterPageFile` attribute specified, the final step is creating a Content control for each of the master page's ContentPlaceHolders and moving over the appropriate markup. Assuming the existing page already has content, what I do is typically cut all the content inside the Web Form and paste it into Notepad. After I have removed the content from inside the Web Form, I delete all the content in the web page except for the `<%@ Page %>` directive. (Recall that the Web Form is denoted by `<form runat="server">`.)

Finally, I go to the Design view of the ASP.NET page. Because the ASP.NET page now inherits the master page, it shows the master page's sitewide content as non-editable along with the content regions. To create the Content controls, right-click the content regions in the Design view and choose the Create Custom Content menu option. After you have created the Content control for each of the ContentPlaceHolder controls in the master page, go back to the Source view and paste the code saved in Notepad back into the appropriate content regions.

Did you Know?

> Because having a new ASP.NET web page inherit a master page is much easier than having an existing page inherit a master page, I recommend that you create a master page when starting on a new site. Keep the master page simple; I usually just have it contain the default ContentPlaceHolder controls.
>
> When creating new web pages for the site, have them all inherit from the master page. At some later point, you can go back to the master page and actually implement the sitewide design. Because all pages inherit the master page, they'll all immediately reflect the update to the master page.

Providing Default Content in a Master Page

The ContentPlaceHolder controls in a master page represent the portions of the template that are editable on a page-by-page basis. Typically, these regions are customized in the content page. However, in some circumstances a content page may not want to customize a particular ContentPlaceHolder region, instead falling back on some default value specified by the master page.

For example, imagine that instead of having the title `Welcome to My Website!` displayed on each page in the header region, you wanted to allow each page to customize this title. However, you suspect that the majority of the pages will probably use the value `Welcome to My Website!` To accomplish this, you could add a ContentPlaceHolder control in the master page's header region and specify the default value of the ContentPlaceHolder as the title `Welcome to My Website!` Then, in the content pages, you could indicate whether the page should use the master page's default content or specify its own customized content.

To illustrate creating a default value in a master page's ContentPlaceHolder control, let's create a new master page called `DefaultExample.master` that has the same layout as the `MasterPage.master` master page we created earlier.

By the Way

When adding a master page, make sure that the Select Master Page check box is unchecked; otherwise, you will be creating a master page that is configured to inherit from *another* master page. Although it is possible to have master pages that inherit from other master pages, this is an advanced topic that we won't be covering in this book.

Did you Know?

To quickly copy the layout from `MasterPage.master` to `DefaultExample.master`, go to the Design view of `MasterPage.master`. Select all content by going to the Edit menu and choosing Select All. Next, go to the Edit menu and choose Copy. Return to `DefaultExample.master`'s Design view and select all content in this page and then go to the Edit menu and choose Paste.

Voila! You've just copied the content from one master page to another.

In the `DefaultExample.master` page, replace the text `Welcome to My Website!` with a second ContentPlaceHolder control. Set this ContentPlaceHolder control's `ID` property to `HeaderRegion`. To specify a default value for the `HeaderRegion` ContentPlaceHolder, add the default content to the ContentPlaceHolder, much like you would on an ASP.NET page to customize a particular content region. Because we want the default title to still be `Welcome to My Website!`, type this text into the ContentPlaceHolder in the header region. That's all there is to it!

Choosing to Use Default or Custom Content in an ASP.NET Page

A content page can opt to provide custom content for a master page region or, instead, rely on the master page's default content for that region. To illustrate this, take a moment to add a new content page that inherits from the `DefaultExample.master` page we just created.

The `DefaultExample.master` master page has three ContentPlaceHolder controls:

- **`head`**—The ContentPlaceHolder in the <head> element
- **`HeaderRegion`**—The ContentPlaceHolder we just added in the header region.
- **`ContentPlaceHolder1`**—The ContentPlaceHolder in the main region.

Because only two of these ContentPlaceHolder controls are in Web Form, you'll see only two Content controls in the content page's Design view. The content page's declarative syntax, however, has Content controls for all three ContentPlaceHolders:

```
<%@ Page Language="VB" MasterPageFile="~/DefaultExample.master"
➥AutoEventWireup="false" CodeFile="DefaultExample.aspx.vb"
➥Inherits="DefaultExample" title="Untitled Page" %>

<asp:Content ID="Content1" ContentPlaceHolderID="head" Runat="Server">
</asp:Content>
<asp:Content ID="Content2" ContentPlaceHolderID="HeaderRegion" Runat="Server">
</asp:Content>
<asp:Content ID="Content3" ContentPlaceHolderID="ContentPlaceHolder1"
➥Runat="Server">
</asp:Content>
```

To use the master page's default content for a region, rather than custom content, you need to remove the associated Content Web control from the ASP.NET page. To use the default content for the header region, delete the Content control whose `ContentPlaceHolderID` equals `HeaderRegion`. You can accomplish this by manually removing the Content control syntax from the Source view or by going to the Design view, right-clicking the editable region, and choosing the Default to Master's Content option. After this Content Web control has been removed from the ASP.NET page, the page will use the default content from the master page (Welcome to My Website!).

To stop using the master page's default content and to create custom content for the page, you need to add back the Content Web control. You can do this manually, through the Source view, or by going to the Design view, right-clicking the content region, and selecting Create Custom Content.

Working with a Master Page's Source Code Portion

A master page has all the functionality found in an ASP.NET page. That means that it can have Web controls in addition to static HTML. The Web controls in the master page can collect user input or retrieve data from a data source. For instance, the master page created in the "Creating a Master Page" section had SiteMapDataSource and TreeView controls, which queried and displayed the site's structure based on the site map. Websites that support user accounts often allow visitors to log in from any page on the site. We could accomplish this by adding a Login control to the master page.

In addition to Web controls and static HTML, a master page can also have a server-side source code portion. This source code portion can contain event handlers for the Web controls added to a master page or code that is to run each time a content page is visited. To illustrate the server-side source code portion capabilities of master pages, create a new master page named `CodeDemo.master`.

Let's add a Label Web control that displays the current date and time along with a mechanism to search the Internet from our site. Start by adding the Label Web control above the ContentPlaceHolder. Clear out its `Text` property and set its `ID` to `CurrentDateTime`. Next, type in the word **`Search`** and, after that, add a TextBox Web control, setting its `ID` to `SearchTerm`. Finally, add a Button Web control after the TextBox, setting its `ID` and `Text` properties to `SearchButton` and "Search," respectively. After you have completed these steps, your screen should look similar to Figure 22.10.

With these Web controls in place, we're ready to add the server-side source code for the master page. Start by creating the `Page_Load` event handler. This event fires each time an associated content page is visited. Add the following code to the `Page_Load` event handler:

```
CurrentDateTime.Text = "It is now " & DateTime.Now
```

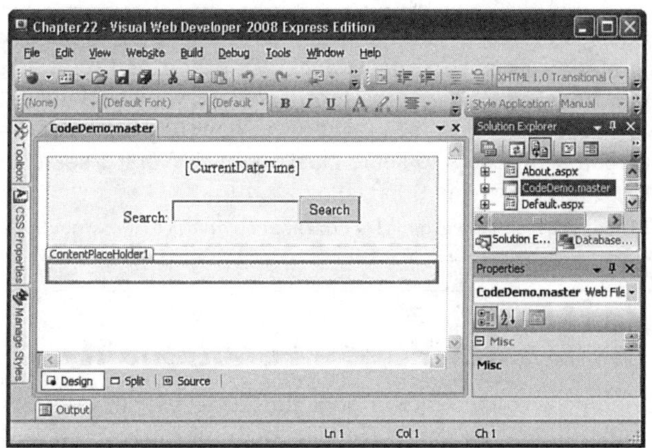

FIGURE 22.10 The master page includes three Web controls: a Label, a TextBox, and a Button.

For the search interface, when the user enters a search term and clicks the Search button, a postback will ensue, and the Button Web control's `Click` event will fire. For this example, let's have the user search the Internet using Google. This can be accomplished by sending the user to `http://www.google.com/search?q=`*`searchTerm`*. To accomplish this, create an event handler for the Button's `Click` event and then use `Response.Redirect(`*`url`*`)` to send them to Google's site, passing in the search term through the querystring:

```
Response.Redirect("http://www.google.com/search?q=" & SearchTerm.Text)
```

Listing 22.3 contains the complete source code portion for the master page.

LISTING 22.3 The Master Page Has Two Event Handlers

```
Partial Class CodeDemo
    Inherits System.Web.UI.MasterPage

    Protected Sub Page_Load(ByVal sender As Object, ByVal e As
➥System.EventArgs) Handles Me.Load
        CurrentDateTime.Text = "It is now " & DateTime.Now
    End Sub

    Protected Sub SearchButton_Click(ByVal sender As Object, ByVal e
➥ As System.EventArgs) Handles SearchButton.Click
        Response.Redirect("http://www.google.com/search?q=" &
➥SearchTerm.Text)
    End Sub
End Class
```

Did you Know?

You can use Google to search just the pages on your site by prepending the user-entered search term with `site:yourDomain+`. For example, if you wanted to search just `www.YourSite.com` for the term `Terrier`, you could use the URL `http://www.google.com/search?q=site:www.YourSite.com+Terrier`. Therefore, you can allow users to search just your site (versus searching the entire Internet) by changing line 9 in Listing 22.4 to

```
Response.Redirect("http://www.google.com/search?q=site:www.YourSite.com+" &
➥SearchTerm.Text)
```

Testing the Master Page's Functionality

At this point we have created a master page that displays the current date and time along with an interface for searching the Web through Google. Unfortunately, we've yet to test this master page's functionality in a browser. To do so, we must create an ASP.NET page that is bound to this new master page.

Take a moment to create a new ASP.NET page, using `CodeDemo.master` as its master page. Add a short blurb to the Content control in the ASP.NET page and then view it in a browser. As Figure 22.11 shows, when visiting the page, you'll see the current date and time displayed at the top of the page. Furthermore, when you enter a search term into the text box and click the button, you are whisked to Google's search results for the entered search term. Figure 22.12 shows a user's browser after he has entered the term **`Scott Mitchell`** into the search text box and clicked the button.

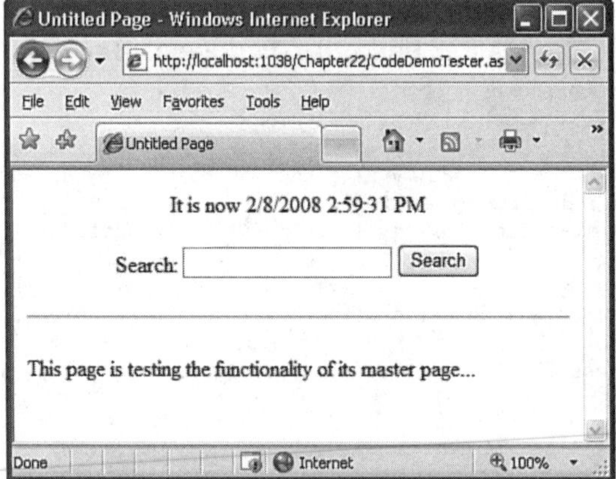

FIGURE 22.11 The current date and time is displayed at the top of the page.

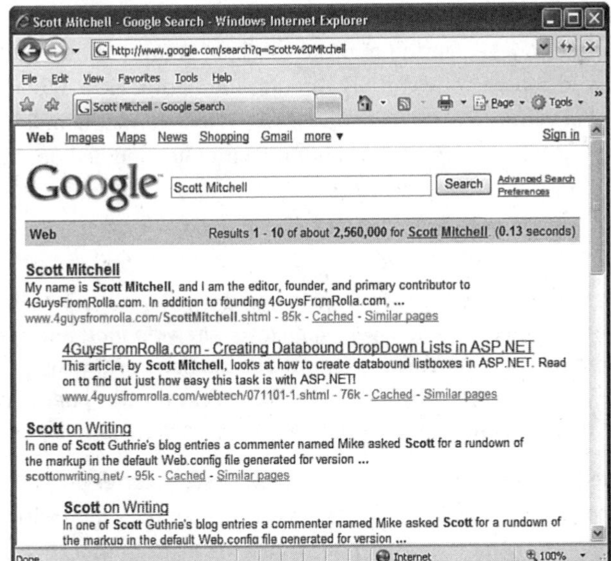

FIGURE 22.12 Users can enter a search term and be taken to Google's results page.

Summary

When creating a website, designers strive to have all pages share a common look and feel. This includes a consistent color and font scheme along with consistent user interface elements. For example, most designers strive to have navigation controls and login-related controls available on all pages throughout the site. Implementing a consistent, sitewide design with ASP.NET is easy and hassle-free, thanks to master pages. A master page contains both sitewide user interface elements along with regions that can be customized on a page-by-page basis. These editable regions are indicated in the master page by ContentPlaceHolder controls.

After a master page is created, an ASP.NET page can inherit from this master page. This is accomplished by selecting the master page when adding the ASP.NET page to the project. When an ASP.NET page is associated with a master page, it contains a Content Web control for each of the ContentPlaceHolder controls in the master page. The content placed in these editable regions is fused with the master page's content when the page is viewed through a browser. Because the melding of the master page and the ASP.NET page is performed when the page is requested, any changes to a master page are automatically and instantly reflected in its content pages.

As we saw throughout this hour, Visual Web Developer provides rich design-time support for master pages. Creating a master page is tantamount to creating an ASP.NET page and can be done entirely through the Design view. When an ASP.NET page is associated with a master page, the Design view shows the master page's sitewide content grayed out, indicating that it cannot be modified on this page.

Q&A

Q. ***Can master pages be nested? That is, can a master page inherit a master page? For example, I want a very high-level sitewide look and feel defined by a parent master page. Then, for various sections of the site, I want a sectionwide template that borrows from the parent master page's look and feel, but defines some settings unique to the section. Is this possible?***

A. Yes, nested master pages are allowed. With nested master pages, the "root" master page can have HTML and Web control syntax, along with ContentPlaceHolders. A master page that inherits from that root master page can have only Content Web controls, just like a normal ASP.NET page that inherits from a master page. However, inside these Content Web controls can be additional ContentPlaceHolders.

For more information on nested master pages and master pages in general, check out "Master Pages in ASP.NET" at www.odetocode.com/Articles/419.aspx, as well as Microsoft's official master page-related documentation, available at http://msdn2.microsoft.com/en-us/library/18sc7456.aspx.

Q. ***Is it possible to have the master page's content updated in response to some action in a content page?***

A. Yes, it is possible for the master page and its content page to interact with one another in a variety of ways. This is a rather advanced topic, however, and beyond the scope of this book. For more information on this concept, refer to "Passing Information Between Content and Master Pages," online at http://aspnet.4guysfromrolla.com/articles/013107-1.aspx.

Workshop

Quiz

1. What is the purpose of a ContentPlaceHolder control in a master page?
2. True or False: A master page can have no more than one ContentPlaceHolder Web control.
3. What content is an ASP.NET page composed of when it is set up to inherit a master page?
4. What steps must be taken to create a new ASP.NET page that inherits a master page?
5. What steps must be taken to have an existing ASP.NET page inherit a master page?
6. How do you have an ASP.NET page use the master page's default content for a given region?
7. True or False: Master pages can contain a server-side source code portion.

Answers

1. The ContentPlaceHolder control indicates a region in the master page where content pages can optionally define the content. All other content in a master page is *not* editable by the content page.
2. False. A master page can have an arbitrary number of ContentPlaceHolder controls.
3. Content pages contain a reference to the master page in their `<%@ Page %>` directive (specifically, `MasterPageFile="`*`pathToMasterPage`*`"`) as well as a Content Web control for each ContentPlaceHolder control in the master page.
4. To have a newly created ASP.NET page inherit from a master page, check the Select Master Page check box in the Add New Item dialog box. Doing so will bring up a list of the master pages in the project, from which you can select the one to inherit from.
5. If you have an existing ASP.NET page that you want to inherit from an existing master page, start by adding the appropriate `MasterPageFile` attribute to the page's `<%@ Page %>` directive. Next, replace the page's declarative markup portion with a Content Web control for each of the master page's

ContentPlaceHolder controls. Some tips for accomplishing this step are discussed in the "Having an Existing Page Inherit from a Master Page" section.

6. An ASP.NET page that inherits a master page can opt to use the master page's default content for a given ContentPlaceHolder. To accomplish this, remove the ASP.NET page's Content control(s) that corresponds to the ContentPlaceHolder control(s) for which you want to use the default content. You can do this by manually removing the Content control from the Source view or by going to the Design view, right-clicking the Content region, and selecting the Default to Master's Content option.

7. True.

Exercises

1. In the preceding hour we looked at how to provide user account support in an ASP.NET website. Commonly, such sites have various user account-related Web controls on every page.

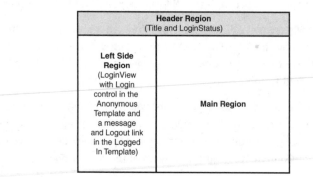

   Return to the examples from the preceding hour and create a master page that has a header region, left-side region, and main region. In the header region, put the website's title and the LoginStatus control. (Recall that the LoginStatus control displays a Login link for anonymous users and a Logout link for those who are logged in.) In the left-side region, use a LoginView control. In the control's Anonymous Template, put a Login Web control; in the Logged In Template, display the message `"Welcome back, username"` and include a Logout link. Figure 22.13 shows a diagram of the site template that your master page should implement.

   After you have created this master page, take a moment to convert the existing pages in the site to inherit this master page. Furthermore, create at least one new page that inherits from this master page.

FIGURE 22.13
The site design contains three regions.

HOUR 23

Building More Responsive Web Pages with ASP.NET AJAX

In this hour, we will cover

- ▶ The benefits of AJAX-enabled websites
- ▶ How AJAX improves the responsiveness of web pages
- ▶ Implementing AJAX with the UpdatePanel control
- ▶ Using Multiple UpdatePanels on an ASP.NET page
- ▶ Displaying a `Loading` message with the UpdateProgress control

Throughout this book we have created many ASP.NET pages that execute server-side code based on some user action. Clicking a button causes the Button Web control's server-side `Click` event handler to execute. Selecting an item from a DropDownList control whose `AutoPostBack` property is set to `True` causes the DropDownList's `SelectedIndexChanged` event to fire. Clicking the header column of a GridView that is configured to enable sorting sorts the grid by that column.

For server-side code to execute in response to a client-side action, the client must communicate with the web server. As we saw in Hour 9, "Web Form Basics," this is commonly performed through the HTML `<form>` element. When a postback form is submitted—be it through the user clicking a submit button or client-side JavaScript initiating the submission—the browser rerequests the same page from the web server, sending along the names and values of the form's `<input>` elements. The web server processes the request and then retransmits the entire page's HTML back to the browser, which redisplays it.

Submitting a form and redisplaying the resulting HTML is costly in terms of performance. Even with a high-speed Internet connection, this interaction may take several seconds to complete, depending on how many `<input>` elements are in the form, the length of the `<input>` elements' values, and the size of the retransmitted HTML. This workflow can be greatly enhanced by using **AJAX**, a set of technologies offering a more streamlined approach to transferring data between the browser and web server. In this hour we discuss the benefits of AJAX and see how to create AJAX-enabled ASP.NET pages.

An Overview of AJAX

A traditional Web Form postback involves the web browser sending *all* the form's `<input>` elements' names and values to the web server and the web server returning the entire HTML for the page. For example, imagine that you were designing a page that had two sortable GridView controls on the page showing data from two different database tables. Using the techniques we've examined throughout this book, if the user clicked one of the first GridView's sort links the page would be posted back. On postback, the ASP.NET page would reretrieve the data for the first GridView, sort it by the specified column, and rebind it to the grid. Then the page's *entire* HTML would be returned to the browser and redisplayed. The net effect, from the end user's perspective, is that she clicked on a sort link and, after a delay of a second or two, the page was redisplayed with the grid's data sorted by the specified column.

This approach is inefficient because much of the data exchanged between the browser and the web server is superfluous. Most notably, the web server returns the entire page's rendered HTML to the browser, even though the only modified HTML is for the GridView that was just sorted. The rest of the page's HTML—including the HTML for the second GridView—was needlessly rerendered by the ASP.NET engine and returned to the browser.

AJAX is a set of interrelated technologies that improves this data exchange by transmitting only the necessary `<input>` element names and values and returning only the HTML portions of the page that need to be updated.

By the Way

> Because AJAX submits a subset of `<input>` elements and receives only a portion of the page's rendered HTML, an AJAX-enabled postback is referred to as a **partial page postback**, or simply a **partial postback**.

The workflow of a partial page postback is depicted in Figure 23.1.

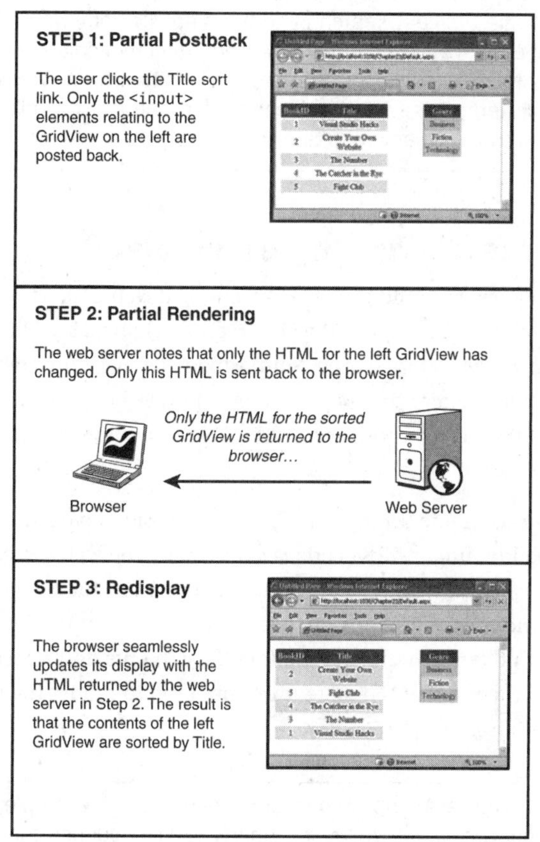

STEP 1: Partial Postback
The user clicks the Title sort link. Only the <input> elements relating to the GridView on the left are posted back.
STEP 2: Partial Rendering
The web server notes that only the HTML for the left GridView has changed. Only this HTML is sent back to the browser.
Only the HTML for the sorted GridView is returned to the browser...
Browser
Web Server
STEP 3: Redisplay
The browser seamlessly updates its display with the HTML returned by the web server in Step 2. The result is that the contents of the left GridView are sorted by Title.

FIGURE 23.1 A partial page postback transmits only a subset of the <input> elements and rendered HTML.

Because less information is shuttled between the browser and web server, and because the browser dynamically updates only those portions of the page that have changed, the user's browser display is updated more quickly when using an AJAX-enabled page. Furthermore, the browser is able to seamlessly update the modified regions and avoid the page flash that is sometimes present when redisplaying the HTML from a full postback. The net result of AJAX's reduced transmission payload is a page that is much more responsive than one using traditional full postbacks.

More and more websites are using AJAX to improve the user experience. Two great examples of AJAX-enabled user interfaces are Google's Gmail service (www.gmail.com) and the Google Suggest search page (www.google.com/webhp?complete=1&hl=en). Gmail employs AJAX to load selected email messages in the window without a full postback. Google Suggest prompts visitors for a search term. As you type in the search term, suggested searches are dynamically displayed in a drop-down list, along with how many results exist in Google's database.

A Look at the Technologies Involved

As you may have guessed, building an AJAX-enabled web page requires added functionality to both the web browser and web server. As Figure 23.1 illustrates, the web browser must know how to make a partial postback (Step 1), the web server must know how to partially render the page and return only the necessary HTML back to the browser (Step 2), and the browser must be able to update its display to integrate the returned HTML (Step 3).

The browser works its magic through the use of client-side JavaScript. JavaScript is a powerful scripting language whose code is supplied by the web server, but is executed on the user's computer. JavaScript includes functions for sending information to a web server, and these functions are used to initiate the partial page postback. Moreover, JavaScript can dynamically update the contents and structure of the web page displayed in the browser. These features are used to render the partial HTML returned by the web server.

We've already utilized JavaScript in previous examples. For example, setting the DropDownList control's `AutoPostBack` property to `True` causes the ASP.NET engine to inject a JavaScript that automatically submits the Web Form when the user changes her drop-down list selection.

On the web server side, ASP.NET includes the capability to selectively render and return the markup for a portion of the page.

At this point it's only natural to feel a bit overwhelmed. We've talked sparingly about JavaScript, and this is the first mention of ASP.NET's ability to partially render a page. The good news is that we won't be responsible for writing JavaScript code or handling the partial rendering logic. That task falls to **ASP.NET AJAX framework**, which is a rich AJAX library created by Microsoft and built into ASP.NET version 3.5.

With the ASP.NET AJAX framework, utilizing AJAX techniques is as easy as dragging and dropping.

Using the ASP.NET AJAX Framework

The ASP.NET AJAX framework includes a handful of Web controls. The most important ones are

- **ScriptManager**—Provides the necessary JavaScript functionality for performing partial postbacks and updating the browser's display.
- **UpdatePanel**—Defines a region on the page that can participate in a partial postback.
- **UpdateProgress**—Displays content during the partial postback; this control is useful in providing users feedback that their request is being processed.

The ScriptManager control handles the complex communications between the visitor's browser and the web server, and *must* appear on every ASP.NET page that uses the ASP.NET AJAX framework. To use the UpdatePanel on a page, for example, you must also include a ScriptManager control.

Did you Know?

> If you are building a website using master pages where the majority of the ASP.NET pages are AJAX enabled, it makes sense to place the ScriptManager in the master page so that it is automatically included in each content page. In fact, when adding a new item to a website through Visual Web Developer, one of the options is to add an AJAX Master Page. If you select this option, Visual Web Developer creates a master page that includes a ScriptManager control.

The UpdatePanel control defines a region on the page that can participate in a partial postback. As we will see shortly, after an UpdatePanel has been added to the page, additional Web controls may be added within the UpdatePanel. When the user visiting the page interacts with one of these controls in a manner that would normally cause a full page postback—such as clicking a submit button—a partial page postback occurs instead. The UpdatePanel, along with JavaScript routines added by the ScriptManager control, automatically handles all the AJAX-related tasks: initiating the partial page postback from the browser, performing the partial page rendering on the web server, and updating the browser's display with the returned markup.

When a user clicks a submit button in a web page using full page postbacks, the browser indicates that a postback is occurring by displaying a progress bar and providing other visual feedback. But during a partial page postback, the browser itself does not provide any visual feedback. The UpdateProgress control is useful for informing the user that a partial page postback is in progress. For example, you could configure the UpdateProgress control to display a message titled `Loading... please wait`. We examine the UpdateProgress control in the "Displaying a Progress Message for Long-Running Partial Postbacks" section.

Working with the UpdatePanel Control

To demonstrate the principals behind AJAX, as well as how to use the UpdatePanel control to add AJAX functionality to an ASP.NET web page, create an ASP.NET page named `AJAXSimple.aspx`. Add a Label Web control to the page named `CurrentTime` and clear out its `Text` property. Beneath the Label, add a Button Web control and set its `ID` and `Text` properties to `FullPostBackButton` and `Full Postback`, respectively.

Next, create an event handler for the page's `Load` event and write code that sets the `CurrentTime` Label's Text property to the current date and time.

```
Protected Sub Page_Load(ByVal sender As Object, ByVal e As System.EventArgs)
➥Handles Me.Load
    CurrentTime.Text = DateTime.Now
End Sub
```

With this code in place, visit the page through a browser. When the page is first loaded, you should see the current date and time displayed. Each time the button is clicked, the page performs a full postback, the `Page_Load` event executes, and the displayed date and time are updated.

Return to Visual Web Developer and add an UpdatePanel control to the page below the existing Label and Button controls. The UpdatePanel is located in the AJAX Extensions portion of the Toolbox. We also need to add a ScriptManager control to the page. A page can have at most one ScriptManager control and the ScriptManager must appear before any UpdatePanel controls.

At this point your screen should look similar to Figure 23.2.

> If you forget to add the ScriptManager control, or locate it below any UpdatePanel controls on the page, an error message is displayed when the page is viewed through the browser. The error message is pretty self-explanatory: `The control with ID` *`UpdatePanelID`* `requires a ScriptManager on the page. The ScriptManager must appear before any controls that need it.`

Next, add another Label Web control and another Button Web control to the page, but this time, add them *within* the UpdatePanel. To accomplish this, switch to the Design view and then drag the Label and Button from the Toolbox and drop them within the UpdatePanel. Set the Label's `ID` property to `CurrentTimeAJAX` and clear out its `Text` property; set the Button's `ID` and `Text` properties to `PartialPostBackButton` and `Partial Postback`, respectively.

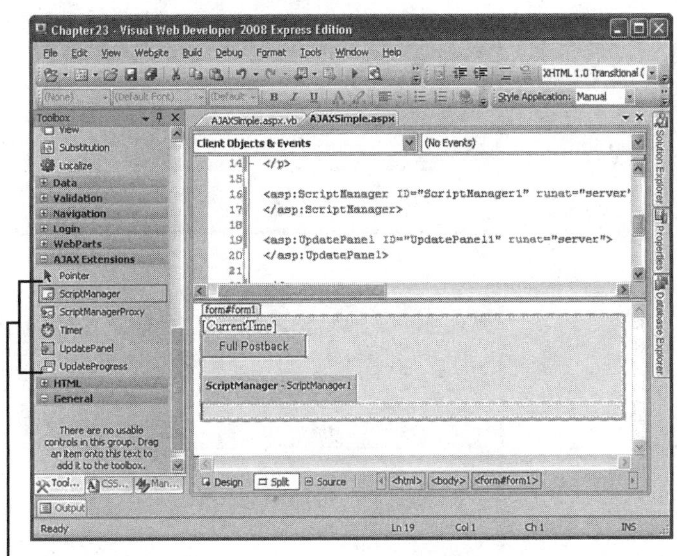

ScriptManager and UpdatePanel controls are located in the AJAX Extensions section of the Toolbox

FIGURE 23.2
A partial page postback transmits only a subset of the `<input>` elements and rendered HTML.

We now need to update the page's code so that the `CurrentTimeAJAX` Label's `Text` property is also assigned the current date and time on page load. To accomplish this, update the `Page_Load` event handler as follows:

```
Protected Sub Page_Load(ByVal sender As Object, ByVal e As System.EventArgs)
➥ Handles Me.Load
    CurrentTime.Text = DateTime.Now
    CurrentTimeAJAX.Text = DateTime.Now
End Sub
```

With this code in place, visit the page through a browser. Both Label controls should display the same date and time value (see Figure 23.3). However, clicking the `Partial Postback` button only updates the date and time value displayed by the `CurrentTimeAJAX` Label (see Figure 23.4). Now click the `Full Postback` button. The Label controls are back in synchrony, displaying the same value. What's going on here?

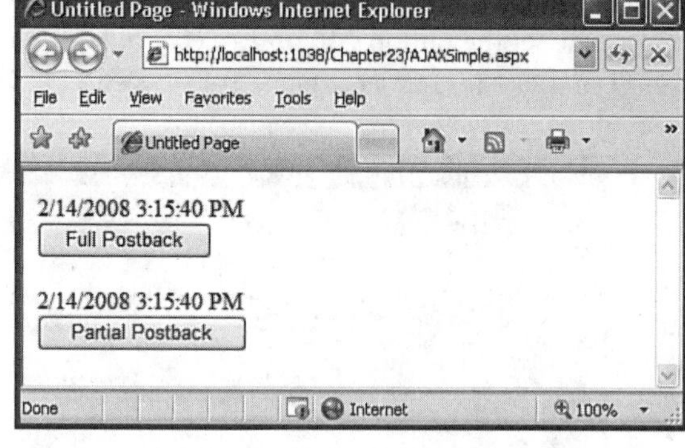

FIGURE 23.3 The two Label controls display the same date and time value.

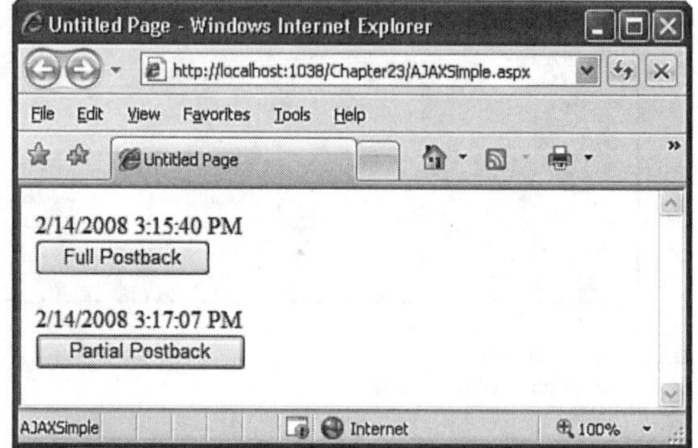

FIGURE 23.4 The two Labels values differ.

When the page is first visited or whenever the `Full Postback` button is clicked, the entire page is rerendered and redisplayed in the browser. However, when the `Partial Postback` button is clicked, a partial postback ensues. The web server only renders the markup for the controls within the UpdatePanel, and only this markup is returned to the browser. Consequently, only the content within the UpdatePanel—the `CurrentTimeAJAX` Label—is refreshed.

The UpdatePanel control defines a region within which user actions that would normally cause a full page postback instead trigger a partial page postback. When a partial postback occurs, the web server refreshes only the contents of the UpdatePanel; areas outside the UpdatePanel are not updated. A full page postback, however, refreshes the entire contents of the page, including the content within UpdatePanel controls.

By the Way

> As noted earlier, the key benefit of AJAX is that it produces a more responsive user experience because the interaction between the client and the server is much quicker with AJAX than when using full page postback. However, you may not have noticed any difference in speed between the full postback and partial postback in the current date and time example.
>
> One of the main bottlenecks in a web application is the time it takes to transfer data between your computer and the web server. AJAX improves the responsiveness of a page by reducing the amount of data exchanged. But when testing an ASP.NET application locally, this bottleneck is a nonissue. In short, the speed benefits of AJAX are best seen when visiting a remote website. We'll look at how to move your web application to a web hosting company in the next hour, "Deploying Your Website."

Using Multiple UpdatePanel Controls

An ASP.NET page may contain multiple UpdatePanels. This is useful if you have multiple regions on the screen whose content is updated independently. Consider a web page with two sortable GridView controls on the page, showing different data. With full page postbacks, sorting one grid causes the entire page to reload, but this is a waste of bandwidth because only the contents of one grid have changed. Such a page is a prime candidate for using two UpdatePanel controls—one for each GridView control on the page.

Create a new page named `MultipleUpdatePanels.aspx`. Start by adding a ScriptManager control at the top of the Web Form. Next, add two UpdatePanel controls. Then add a SqlDataSource control to the first UpdatePanel. Name the SqlDataSource `BooksDataSource` and configure it to return the `BookID` and `Title` columns from the `Books` table. Next, add a GridView to the same UpdatePanel, set its `ID` to `BooksGrid`, and bind it to the `BooksDataSource` control. Repeat these steps in the second UpdatePanel, but this time name the SqlDataSource control `GenreDataSource` and have it return the distinct `Genre` values from the `Books` table. Name the GridView `GenreGrid` and bind it to the `GenreDataSource`. Enable sorting for both GridViews.

Next, add three Label controls to the page, clearing out the `Text` properties for all three. Place one Label outside the UpdatePanel controls and name it `CurrentTime`; put another one inside the first UpdatePanel and name it `CurrentTimeAJAX1`; put the third Label inside the other UpdatePanel, setting its `ID` to `CurrentTimeAJAX2`. Create the `Page_Load` event handler and set each Label's `Text` property to the current date and time.

```
Protected Sub Page_Load(ByVal sender As Object, ByVal e As System.EventArgs)
➥Handles Me.Load
    CurrentTime.Text = DateTime.Now
    CurrentTimeAJAX1.Text = DateTime.Now
    CurrentTimeAJAX2.Text = DateTime.Now
End Sub
```

Add a Button Web control outside of the UpdatePanels. Set its `ID` and `Text` properties to `FullPostbackButton` and `Full Postback`, respectively.

After adding these controls, your screen should look similar to Figure 23.5.

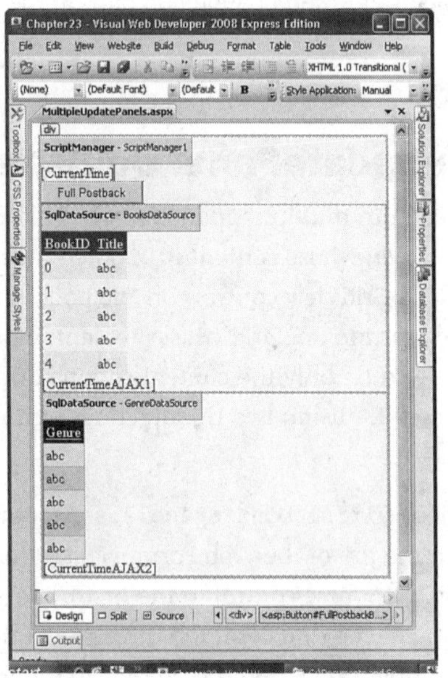

FIGURE 23.5
Two sortable GridViews have been added to two UpdatePanels.

Visit the page through a browser. Each Label control displays the date and time that the portion was last refreshed. When the page is first visited, or whenever the `Full Postback` button is clicked, all Labels should show the same value. Clicking one of the sort links in either GridView causes a partial postback. As you may have expected, sorting either of the grids leaves the `CurrentTime` Label outside of the UpdatePanels unaffected. What you might not have expected, though, is that *both* UpdatePanels are updated when either grid is sorted, as evidenced by the fact that both UpdatePanels' Label controls show the same date and time value (see Figure 23.6).

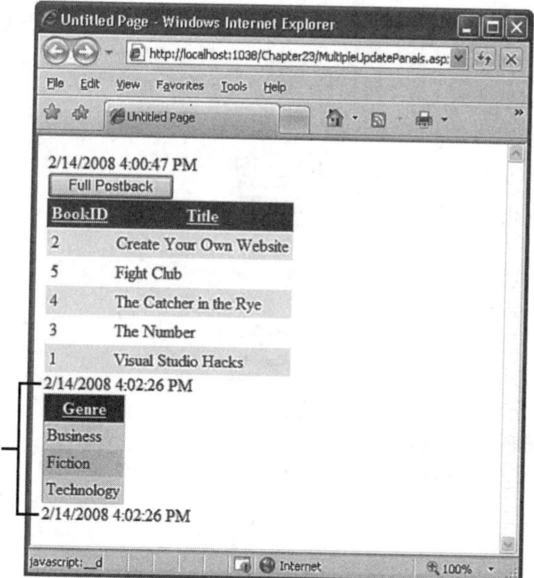

FIGURE 23.6 Sorting either GridView updates both UpdatePanels.

By default, when any UpdatePanel on the page instigates a partial postback, all the UpdatePanels' displays are updated. In this example, the contents in the two UpdatePanels are independent, so when a partial postback is instigated from one UpdatePanel there's no need to update the other's contents. To instruct an UpdatePanel to update its contents only when it triggers a partial postback, change its `UpdateMode` property from `Always` (the default) to `Conditional`.

After setting both UpdatePanels' `UpdateMode` properties to `Conditional`, revisit the page. This time, sorting a grid updates only the contents of the grid's UpdatePanel. Figure 23.7 shows the results of sorting the `BooksGrid` by `Title`. Note the discrepancy between the two UpdatePanels' Labels, indicating that the sort operation in the first UpdatePanel did not also refresh the content of the second UpdatePanel.

Did you Know?

> The UpdatePanel control can be configured to refresh based on a user action elsewhere in the page. For example, you can add a Button to the page that, when clicked, performs a partial postback and causes a specific UpdatePanel to refresh. For more information on additional means for triggering an UpdatePanel to refresh, read "Using the UpdatePanel" at http://aspnet.4guysfromrolla.com/articles/102407-1.aspx.

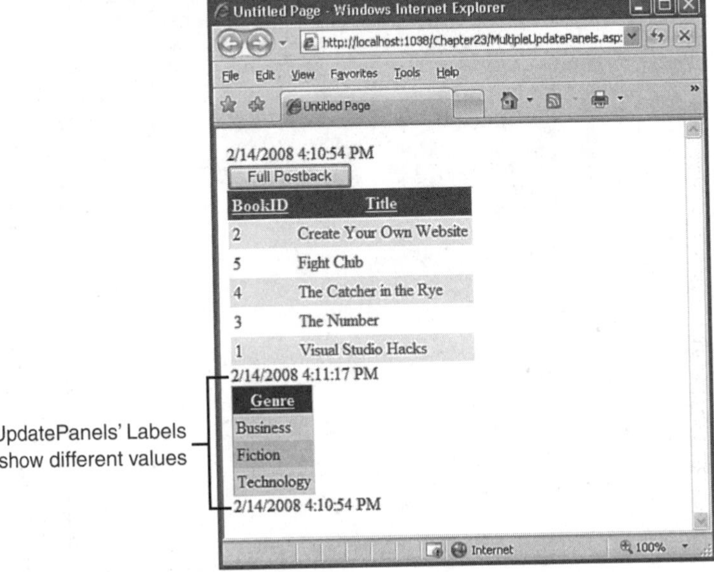

FIGURE 23.7 Now only the UpdatePanel that triggered the partial postback is refreshed.

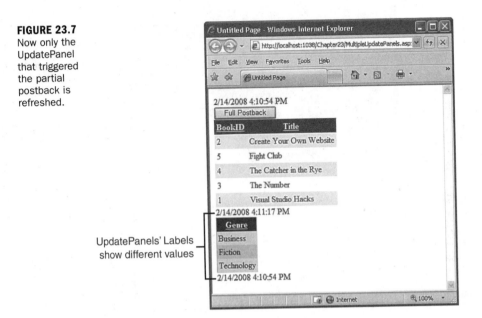

Displaying a Progress Message for Long-Running Partial Postbacks

Ideally, all requests to the web server will be quickly handled and the resulting markup speedily returned to the requesting browser. But sometimes it may take several seconds for the communication between the browser and the web server to complete, even when using AJAX techniques. There are many potential causes for such a slowdown. Real-world projects usually involve querying large databases or require complex database queries that may take several seconds to complete. The web server may be under an unusually high load if there is a sudden spike of traffic. And delays are commonplace for users who have a slow connection to the Internet.

Regardless of the reasons behind a slow serving page, it helps to provide users with visual feedback so that they know their request is being processed. Displaying such feedback during a partial page postback is easy, thanks to the UpdateProgress control. The UpdateProgress control displays its contents for a particular UpdatePanel after a specified number of milliseconds have elapsed.

To see the benefits of the UpdateProgress control, we need to first devise a long-running scenario. Right now, the partial page postbacks return so quickly that the UpdateProgress control does not have time to display feedback. However, we can write code that introduces an artificial delay.

Start by creating an ASP.NET page named `UpdateProgress.aspx`. Add a ScriptManager to the page followed by an UpdatePanel. In the UpdatePanel, add a Label and a Button control. Set the Label control's `ID` property to `StatusMessage` and clear out its `Text` property. Set the Button's `ID` and `Text` properties to `SlowOperationButton` and `Start Slow Operation`, respectively.

Create an event handler for this Button's `Click` event and add the following code:

```
Protected Sub SlowOperationButton_Click(ByVal sender As Object, ByVal e As
➥ System.EventArgs) Handles SlowOperationButton.Click
    'Pause for 5 seconds
    System.Threading.Thread.Sleep(5000)

    StatusMessage.Text = "Slow operation complete! The current time is: "
➥ & DateTime.Now
End Sub
```

The statement `System.Threading.Thread.Sleep(5000)` pauses the processing of this page for 5,000 milliseconds, or 5 seconds. It then sets the `StatusMessage` Label's `Text` property to the current date and time.

Visit this page through a browser and click the `Start Slow Operation` button. This causes a partial postback that will take 5 seconds to complete. During that time, there is no feedback as to what's happening. A confused user may click the button again, thinking that the first click did not register somehow. After 5 seconds, the `StatusMessage` Label indicates that the slow running operation has completed.

Let's update this page to include feedback that the partial page postback is in progress. Add an UpdateProgress control to the page. Add whatever markup you want to display during the partial postback within the UpdateProgress control. You can enter text, drag on a Label Web control, or add an Image Web control. For this example, add a Label control into the UpdateProgress control and set its `Text` property to `Loading...`. Feel free to also set any of the Label's formatting properties.

The UpdateProgress control has two properties of interest:

- **`AssociatedUpdatePanelID`**—Set this property to the `ID` of a UpdatePanel control. When this UpdatePanel instigates a partial postback, the UpdateProgress control's contents are displayed.
- **`DisplayAfter`**—Specifies a delay, in milliseconds, between when the partial postback begins and when the UpdateProgress's contents are displayed. This property defaults to 500, or 0.5 seconds. It is useful to prevent the UpdateProgress from displaying for partial postbacks that complete very quickly.

Set the UpdateProgress's `AssociatedUpdatePanelID` to the `ID` of the UpdatePanel on the page and then revisit the page through a browser. This time when the `Start Slow Operation` button is clicked, the `Loading...` message appears and remains until the partial postback completes (see Figure 23.8).

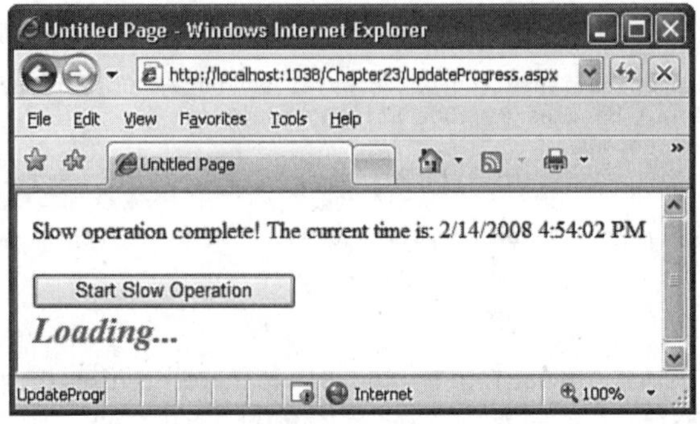

FIGURE 23.8 The `Loading...` message appears during the partial postback.

Did you Know?

Many websites use a small animated image file, such as a rotating circle, to inform users that their request is being processed. To create an AJAX loading image for your site, check out www.ajaxload.info. You can specify the style of animation and the foreground and background colors, and this neat website generates a free AJAX loading image based on your settings.

Summary

AJAX is a set of complementary web technologies that work together to provide a more responsive web interface. This goal is accomplished by reducing the amount of information typically exchanged in a full page postback by selectively posting back, rendering, and updating the display for the affected regions of the page.

Although communications and workflow between the client and server in an AJAX-enabled application is complex, the ASP.NET AJAX framework makes building such applications as easy as dragging and dropping. The key components of the framework are the ScriptManager and UpdatePanel controls. The ScriptManager provides the necessary client-side JavaScript, whereas the UpdatePanel defines a region on the screen that can participate in partial page postbacks. In addition to these controls, there's the UpdateProgress control, which is useful for displaying a progress message during a partial postback.

Many websites today use AJAX to offer a more responsive user interface. As AJAX has matured, it has become easier to build AJAX-enabled web pages. I encourage you to explore the ASP.NET AJAX framework in more depth. Two great resources are the suite of AJAX tutorials and training videos, available online at www.asp.net/learn/ajax and www.asp.net/learn/ajax-videos.

Q&A

Q. ***It sounds like AJAX uses a lot of advanced JavaScript techniques. Are there any browsers that Microsoft's ASP.NET AJAX framework will not work with?***

A. AJAX does rely heavily on JavaScript, so the UpdatePanel and other ASP.NET AJAX framework features may not work when visited by older browsers or browsers that have disabled JavaScript support. Microsoft's ASP.NET AJAX framework works with the following browsers:

- Microsoft Internet Explorer 6.0 and later
- Mozilla FireFox version 1.5 and later
- Opera version 9.0 and later
- Apple Safari version 2.0 and later

Q. ***I know that the UpdatePanel can be used in tandem with the standard ASP.NET Web controls to provide an AJAX-enabled web page. Do any ASP.NET controls designed specifically to use AJAX techniques exist?***

A. Microsoft offers a rich suite of AJAX controls in its ASP.NET AJAX Control Toolkit. This toolkit includes controls such as an AJAX-enabled Calendar, a content rating control, a slider, a filtered text box, and many others. Unfortunately, this toolkit is not yet built in to ASP.NET like the core ASP.NET AJAX framework and its Web controls—ScriptManager, UpdatePanel, and UpdateProgress. Perhaps future versions of ASP.NET will include the AJAX Control Toolkit controls by default.

To download the ASP.NET AJAX Control Toolkit, visit www.asp.net/ajax/ajaxcontroltoolkit. You'll find a plethora of live demos and examples online at www.asp.net/ajax/ajaxcontroltoolkit/samples.

Workshop

Quiz

1. Why do AJAX-enabled web applications offer a more responsive user interface than traditional web applications?
2. How does a partial page postback differ from a full page postback?
3. True or False: JavaScript is an essential part of any AJAX-enabled website.
4. What ASP.NET AJAX framework control must be added to all AJAX-enabled web pages? What happens if you forget to add this control?
5. True or False: You cannot have more than one UpdatePanel control on an ASP.NET page.
6. What is the purpose of the UpdateProgress control?

Answers

1. Because AJAX techniques streamline the data exchanged between the browser and web server, partial page postbacks are faster than full page postbacks.
2. In a full page postback, all the form's `<input>` elements' names and values are sent to the web server, and the entire page's markup is rendered and returned to the browser. In a partial page postback, the browser transmits only the necessary `<input>` fields to the web server. The web server then renders and returns the markup for just the application portion of the page. The browser then updates its display using the HTML returned from the browser. Refer to Figure 23.1 for a more detailed look at the steps that compose a partial postback.
3. True.
4. The ScriptManager control. If you omit this essential control, the ASP.NET engine displays an error message when the page is visited through a browser.
5. False. You can have any number of UpdatePanel controls on a page.
6. The UpdateProgress control displays its content during a specified UpdatePanel control's partial postback. It provides visual feedback that the user's requested action is being processed.

Exercises

1. Create an ASP.NET page and add ScriptManager and UpdatePanel controls. Next, add a SqlDataSource and DetailsView control within the UpdatePanel and configure them so that the visitor can add new records to the `Books` table. If you need to brush up on inserting data into a database using the DetailsView control, return to Hour 16, "Deleting, Inserting, and Editing Data."

   Like the examples in this hour, add two Label Web controls to this page—one outside the UpdatePanel and the other within the UpdatePanel. Have the Label `Text` properties assigned to the current date and time on each page load. When testing the page, note that when the page is first visited, the two Labels' values match, but when a new record is added through the DetailsView control, the Label within the UpdatePanel is updated, but one outside the UpdatePanel is not.

2. Extend the page created in the first exercise by adding a second UpdatePanel control. Drag a GridView control into this second UpdatePanel and bind it to the same SqlDataSource control used by the DetailsView. Also add a Label Web control to this second UpdatePanel and configure it to display the current date and time on each page visit. What happens when a new record is added through the DetailsView control? What happens if you set the two UpdatePanels' `UpdateMode` properties to `Conditional`? Try to figure out how to add a trigger to the second UpdatePanel so that it is updated only when a new record is added via the DetailsView control.

HOUR 24

Deploying Your Website

In this hour, we will cover

- Finding a web-hosting company
- The steps involved in deploying an ASP.NET application
- Techniques for uploading your website's files
- Replicating a database with the Database Publishing Wizard and SQL Server Management Studio
- Updating the connection string information in `web.config`

With the lessons learned through the past 23 hours, you are able to create useful data-driven ASP.NET web applications using Visual Web Developer and Microsoft SQL Server 2005 Express Edition. The only problem is that all the websites we have created in this book have been stored locally, on your own computer. Hosting your website locally has many advantages: you can test while offline; it's fast; advanced debugging features are available; and it's secure. The main disadvantage of hosting ASP.NET applications locally is that they can be viewed only from your computer. For someone to visit your site, the user must be sitting at your computer.

Most ASP.NET websites are developed and tested locally. After the website has been completed and thoroughly tested, it is then deployed to a web-hosting company. At this point you have the background to create and test ASP.NET websites locally. All that remains is to deploy the finished application to a web-hosting company so that anyone with a connection to the Internet can visit it.

In this hour we walk through the process of moving an ASP.NET application from your computer to a web-hosting company.

Choosing a Web-Hosting Company

A web-hosting company has a number of Internet-accessible computers for individuals or companies to place their websites. These computers contain web servers that are accessible from any other computer on the Internet. When setting up an account, you can ask the company to register a **domain name** for you if you don't already have one. A domain name is the text that a person would enter into their web browser to visit your website. (For example, the domain name of Microsoft's site is Microsoft.com. For my personal website, I might choose ScottMitchellInfo.com.)

Did you Know?

> You can choose only a domain name that has not already been registered by somebody else. To determine whether your desired domain name is still available, visit www.netsol.com, where you can enter a domain name to check on its availability, and register it if it is available.

The benefits of using a web-hosting company to host your site include

- **A publicly available website**—With a web-hosting company, any visitor who has an Internet connection can visit your website!
- **Use of a domain name**—You can register a domain name and have it point to your website so that visitors can reach your site through a name like www.mysite.com.
- **Ability to focus 100% on building your website**—Installing a web server, applying the latest security patches, properly configuring domain names, and so forth can be tricky tasks. By using a web-hosting company, you are paying for this service, which allows you to concentrate on building your website.

By the Way

> You can choose from literally thousands of web-hosting companies, ranging dramatically in price, performance, features, support, and other qualities. A great place to start shopping for a web-hosting company is at a website like www.tophosts.com or www.hostindex.com. These websites catalog thousands of web-hosting companies and allow you to search through their database looking for companies that match your price range, feature needs, and so forth.
>
> When you choose a web-hosting company that you'd like to do business with, be sure to contact the company and make certain it supports ASP.NET development.

After your web-hosting account is set up, you can move your site's web pages and databases from your computer to the web-hosting company's computers. Then you, or anyone else on the Internet, can visit these pages. For example, if you upload a web page named `Default.aspx` and your domain name was `SamsDogPound.org`, anyone could view the page by typing **`http://www.SamsDogPound.org/Default.aspx`** into their browser's Address bar.

Getting Started with a Web-Hosting Company

Before you can create an account with a web-hosting company, you need to find a company that supports the following:

- **ASP.NET version 3.5**—Some web-hosting companies focus on non-Microsoft web technologies, such as PHP and JSP, and do not offer web-hosting plans for ASP.NET websites.
- **Microsoft SQL Server**—If you plan to deploy a data-driven web application, ensure that the hosting plan you buy includes a Microsoft SQL Server database account. Most web-hosting companies do not allow Microsoft SQL Server 2005 Express Edition database files in the `App_Data` folder. Instead, they provide a **database server**, which is a computer whose sole task is to host databases. To work with databases through your ASP.NET application, you must have access to this server through a database account. Some web hosts charge extra for these accounts.
- **FTP access**—The easiest way to upload files from your computer to the web-hosting company's is through the **File Transfer Protocol**, or **FTP**. Virtually all web-hosting companies provide FTP access, but double-check to ensure that you can use this protocol to upload files to your account.

In my opinion, the easiest way to find a web-hosting company that supports ASP.NET 3.5 and offers database accounts, and allows FTP access, is to check sites such as TopHosts.com and HostIndex.com, which list thousands of web-hosting companies. You can search these sites' databases for web-hosting companies that meet certain criteria, such as cost per month, geographical location, web server platforms used, database availability, and so forth.

Costs for web-hosting companies can range from a few dollars per month to hundreds or thousands of dollars per month, based on the features provided. Additionally, most web-hosting companies have a setup fee in the $20 to $100 range. On top of the web-hosting costs, you will probably want to register a domain name, which typically costs between $10 and $35 per year, depending on the domain name registrar used.

After you have picked out a web-hosting company and have double-checked that it supports ASP.NET development and offers database accounts, contact the company's sales staff to create an account.

By the Way

Can I Host a Website from My Personal Computer?

Readers who have always-on broadband connections, such as through a cable modem or DSL, and a static IP address may be able to host a website from their personal computers. For more information on this option, contact your broadband provider.

If you want a public website, I personally recommend that you go with a web-hosting company. Setting up your computer to host a public website can be a difficult process and, if not done correctly, can leave your computer open to a number of security threats. For example, in July 2001 an Internet worm named Code Red spread quickly across the Internet, infecting Microsoft web servers. (A *worm* is a program that replicates and distributes itself over a computer network.) Specifically, the worm defaced web pages by adding the following text: `HELLO! Welcome to http://www.worm.com! Hacked By Chinese!` (For more information on the Code Red worm, see www.cert.org/advisories/CA-2001-19.html.) By setting up a public web server on your personal computer, you open yourself up to this sort of attack.

You can neutralize such threats by keeping abreast of the latest security patches from Microsoft, along with gaining the know-how on how to best secure systems. Chances are, the professionals at the web-hosting company have more experience setting up, administering, and securing web servers than you, and therefore it's likely they can provide a better line of defense.

Understanding the Deployment Process

Deploying an ASP.NET website to a web-hosting company involves the following steps:

- **Uploading the website files**—You need to copy the web pages, image files, and other web content from your computer to the web-hosting company's computer.
- **Replicating the database**—If your local web application uses a database, you need to replicate your local database's schema and table on the web-hosting company's database server.
- **Updating `web.config`**—As discussed in Hour 13, "An Introduction to Databases," the application's database connection strings are stored in the `web.config` file. These connection strings need to be updated to point to the web-hosting company's database servers. This includes updating connection string information used by the membership and roles systems.

Keep in mind that deployment is often cyclical; it is not a one-time event. After deploying your website for the first time, you will find bugs or have other features or changes to add. These enhancements should be made locally. After testing these changes, upload the added and modified ASP.NET pages. If any database changes occur, apply these changes to the database on the web-hosting company's database server.

Let's create a simple data-driven ASP.NET web application and then look at the precise steps for deploying the sample application to a web-hosting company's computers.

Building the Sample Web Application

Create a new ASP.NET application and place it on your computer's file system. Because some additional steps are needed when deploying an application that uses the membership or roles systems, let's configure this sample application to use membership. Launch the ASP.NET Web Site Administration Tool. From the Security tab, set the website's authentication to authenticate users from the Internet. This configures the application to use forms-based authentication and automatically creates the `ASPNETDB.MDF` database file in the `App_Data` folder.

By the Way

> For a refresher on ASP.NET's membership system, forms-based authentication, and the ASP.NET Web Site Administration Tool, refer to Hour 21, "Managing Your Site's Users."

After configuring the ASP.NET Web Site Administration Tool to authenticate users through the Internet, the Security screen should include a link titled `Create user`. Click this and add a user account named Admin (see Figure 24.1). Close the ASP.NET Web Site Administration Tool and return to Visual Web Developer.

In addition to supporting user accounts, let's have the `ASPNETDB.MDF` database also store application data. Imagine that this sample website was going to be used as an employee directory, enabling visitors to quickly find contact information for the employees at your company. Such an application would need a database table that included a row for each employee, with columns to capture each employee's name, phone number, email address, and other pertinent information.

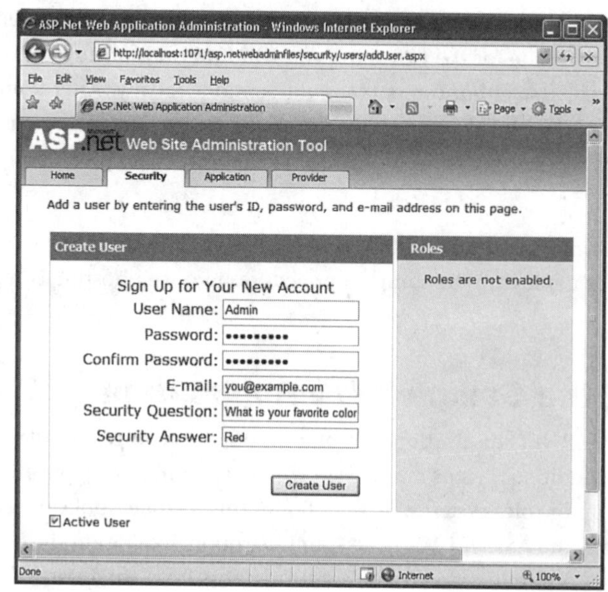

FIGURE 24.1 Create a user account named `Admin` using the ASP.NET Web Site Administration Tool.

From the Database Explorer, drill into the `ASPNETDB.MDF` database and add a new table with the following columns:

- **`EmployeeID`**—This column uniquely identifies each record, so set its data type to `int` and disallow Nulls. Also mark the column as an Auto-increment and make it the primary key.
- **`Name`**—Make this column of type `nvarchar(100)` and disallow Nulls.
- **`Email`**—Make this column of type `nvarchar(100)` and allow Nulls.
- **`PhoneNumber`**—Make this column of type `nvarchar(25)` and allow Nulls.

At this point your screen should look similar to Figure 24.2. Save the table, naming it `Employees`.

Add a handful of records to the `Employees` table through Visual Web Developer by right-clicking the `Employees` table in the Database Explorer and choosing the Show Table Data option.

Next, open the `Default.aspx` page. Let's build a user interface here to allow visitors to search the `Employees` table by name. Add the text **`Search by name:`** followed by a TextBox and Button control. Set the TextBox control's `ID` property to `NameSearch` and the Button's `ID` and `Text` properties to `SearchButton` and `Search`, respectively.

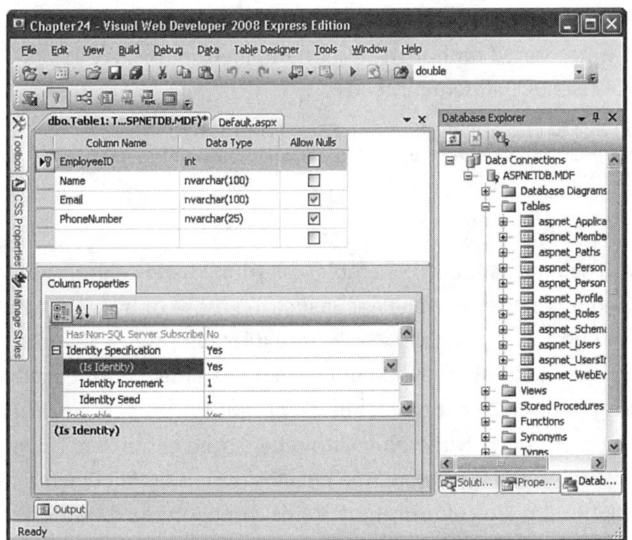

FIGURE 24.2 The table is composed of four columns: `EmployeeID`, `Name`, `Email`, and `PhoneNumber`.

Beneath the Button, add a SqlDataSource control and name it `EmployeesDataSource`. Configure the data source to return the `Name`, `Email`, and `PhoneNumber` columns from the `Employees` table.

Click the WHERE button and add a `WHERE` clause on the `Name` column. Specifically, set the Column drop-down to `Name`, the Operator to `LIKE`, and the Source to Control, choosing the `NameSearch` option from the Control ID drop-down list (see Figure 24.3). Click the Add button to add the `WHERE` clause to the SqlDataSource control's `SELECT` statement and then click OK to return to the wizard.

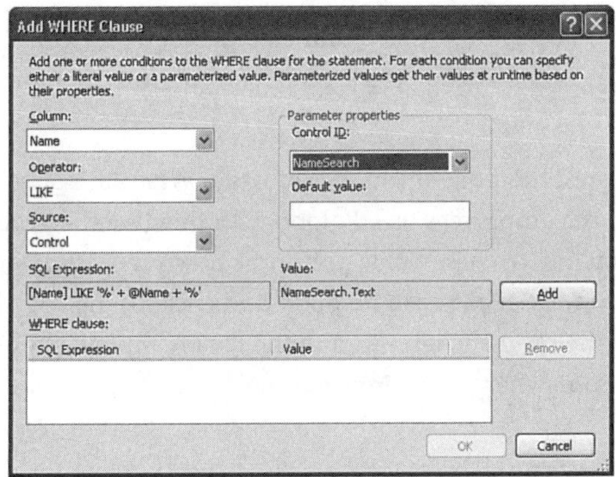

FIGURE 24.3 Add a `WHERE` clause to the `SELECT` statement to query on the `Name` column.

Click the ORDER BY button and select the Name column from the drop-down list so that the results are sorted alphabetically by employee name. At this point the SqlDataSource's SELECT statement reads:

```
SELECT [Name], [Email], [PhoneNumber] FROM [Employees]
➥WHERE ([Name] LIKE '%' + @Name + '%') ORDER BY [Name]
```

Click Finish to complete the wizard.

This WHERE clause returns the list of employees whose Name column value contains the text entered by the user in the NameSearch TextBox control. But what is displayed if the user leaves the NameSearch TextBox empty? By default, the SqlDataSource uses a database Null value when one of its parameters lacks any value, resulting in a WHERE clause of: `WHERE ([Name] LIKE '%' + Null + '%')`. Concatenating a database Null value with other string characters (such as %) results in a database Null value. Therefore, the WHERE clause is boiled down to: `WHERE ([Name] LIKE Null)`. No columns match this condition. As a result, if the user omits a value from the NameSearch TextBox, no records are returned from the SqlDataSource control.

To have the SqlDataSource return all the Employees records when no value is entered into the NameSearch TextBox, we need to configure the parameter so that it does not convert an empty value in the NameSearch TextBox to a database Null value. To accomplish this, select the SqlDataSource to load its properties in the Properties window. Go to the SelectQuery property and click the ellipses to bring up the Command and Parameter Editor. Select the Name parameter from the list of parameters on the left and then click the Show advanced properties link on the right. Set the ConvertEmptyStringToNull property to False, as shown in Figure 24.4, and then click OK to close this dialog box.

With the SqlDataSource control added and configured, add a GridView control to the page, binding it to the EmployeesDataSource control. Configure the GridView to enable paging and sorting.

Take a moment to test the page through a browser. When the page is first visited, you should see all the employees listed along with their contact information. You can sort the grid by any of these fields or narrow down the list of employees by typing a name into the NameSearch text box and clicking the Search button. Figure 24.5 shows the results when filtering the list of employees by those that contain the letter "s" somewhere in their name.

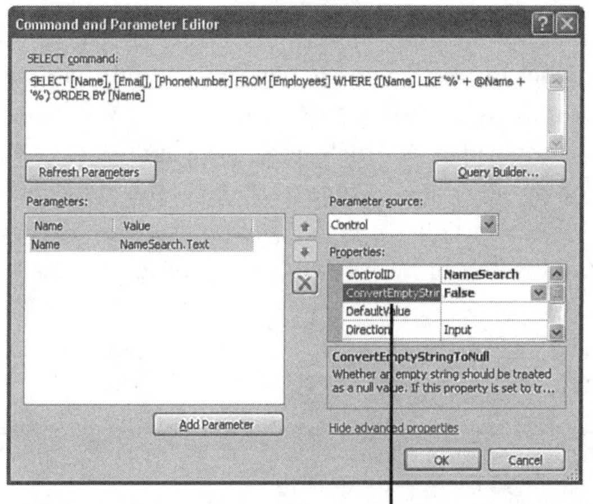

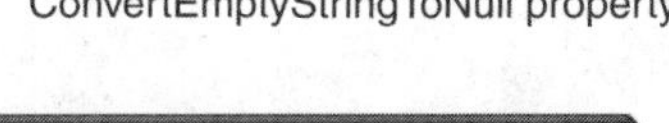

FIGURE 24.4 Configure the `Name` parameter so that it does not convert empty string values to Nulls.

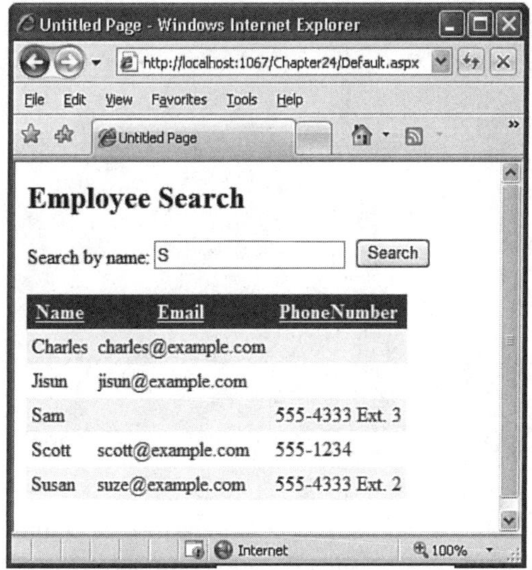

FIGURE 24.5 Employees whose name contains the letter "s" are displayed.

At this point, our application is complete, tested, and ready to be deployed! After a web-hosting account has been procured, deployment involves three steps: uploading the website's files; replicating the database; and updating the connection strings in `web.config`.

This sample application is pretty simple. I encourage you to extend it by adding a page for the `Admin` user to add, update, and delete records from the `Employees` table.

Uploading the Website's Files

To move files from your local computer to your web-hosting company, go to the Website menu in Visual Web Developer and choose Copy Web Site. This brings up the Copy Web interface, which lists the contents in your website and the contents of a remote site in side-by-side panes. Figure 24.6 shows this screen when a remote website has not yet been specified. The left column lists the contents of the local website—`Default.aspx`, `Default.aspx.vb`, `Web.config`, and the `App_Data` folder.

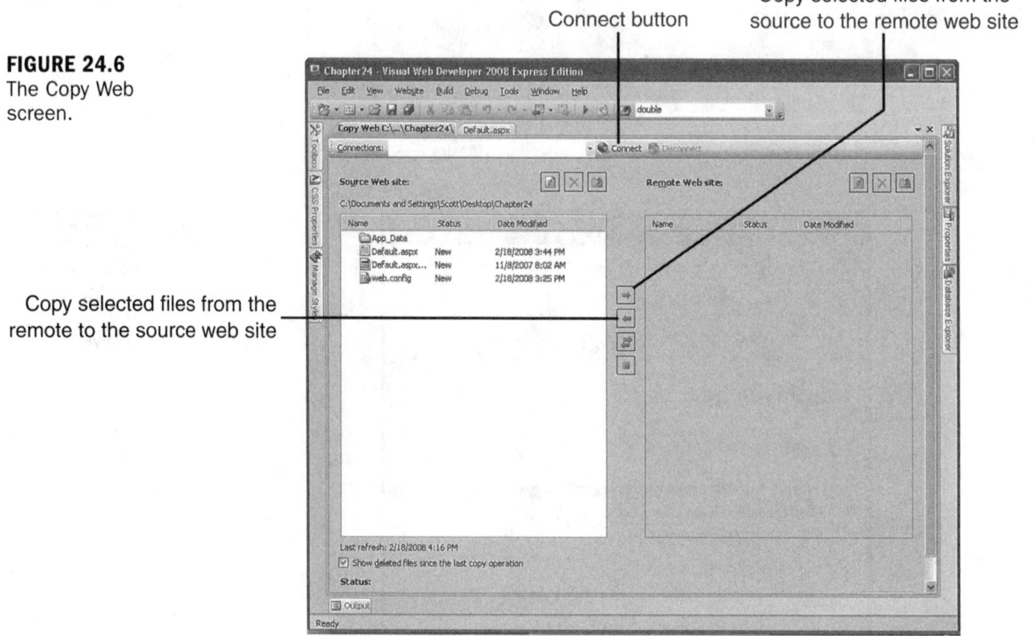

FIGURE 24.6
The Copy Web screen.

To connect to your web-hosting company, click the Connect button at the top of the screen. This brings up the Open Web Site dialog box. Select the FTP Site option and then enter the connection information. If you are unaware of the server, port, directory, and other FTP configuration information, contact your web-hosting company's support staff.

After supplying the FTP information and clicking Open, the Copy Web screen lists the contents of the remote website. You can copy files between your local computer and the remote website by selecting a file from one column and then clicking the appropriate arrow icon.

When deploying a website for the first time, copy over all files except for the Microsoft SQL Server 2005 Express Edition database files (the `.mdf` files in the `App_Data` database). If you are redeploying the site after making additions or changes, you need to upload only the new and modified files.

Because this is the first deployment for this sample web application, upload all the files in the root directory: `Default.aspx`, `Default.aspx.vb`, and `Web.config`. Figure 24.7 shows the Copy Web screen after these files have been copied over.

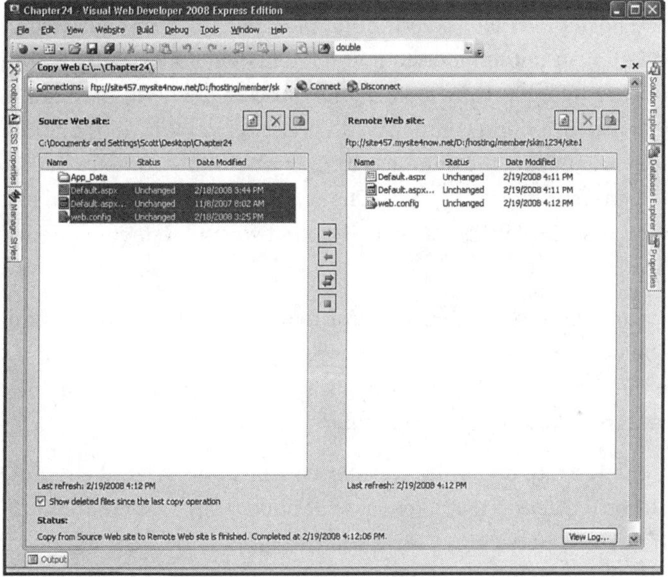

FIGURE 24.7 Upload `Default.aspx`, `Default.aspx.vb`, and `Web.config` to the remote site.

You don't have to use Visual Web Developer to copy files from your computer to the web-hosting company. Any FTP client will suffice. There are many free and commercial FTP clients available. One of my favorites is FileZilla, a free FTP client available at www.FileZilla-Project.org.

Replicating Your Database

As we have seen throughout the latter half of this book, Visual Web Developer and Microsoft SQL Server 2005 Express Edition make it easy to create and manage databases. Traditionally, working with databases required installing and configuring a database server. But with SQL Server 2005 Express Edition, new databases are simply added to the web application's `App_Data` folder.

Unfortunately, Microsoft SQL Server 2005 Express Edition introduces security and configuration issues for web-hosting companies. Consequently, few, if any, web-hosting companies support Express Edition. Instead, most require that you transfer your database to their database server.

Moving your database to your web-hosting company's database server involves replicating the database's tables and their data. There are a variety of ways to accomplish this:

- **Start developing on the web-hosting company's database server**—If you already have procured a web-hosting plan prior to starting development, you can do all your database design on the remote database server. With this setup, your web pages are created on your computer, but they communicate with your web-hosting company's database server. With this approach there's no need to replicate the database to the web-hosting company's database server because it's already there. The only downside to this approach is that you must be connected to the Internet when developing or testing your application locally.
- **Ask your web-hosting company for help**—Some web-hosting companies may be willing to replicate your Express Edition database for you if you send them the `.mdf` file. Others have tools in place to upload a `.mdf` file and automatically attach it to the database server.
- **Copy the website using the Database Publishing Wizard**—Visual Web Developer includes a tool to assist with publishing your database file. Using the Database Publishing Wizard you can select a local database to replicate and it will generate a script that contains the SQL commands to create the schema and data. You can then execute this script on the web-hosting company's database server.

The first two options are the simplest and don't require any further examination. The third option—using the Database Publishing Wizard—deserves more discussion.

Using the Database Publishing Wizard

The Database Publishing Wizard is a tool created by Microsoft that is included with Visual Web Developer 2008. To launch it, go to the Database Explorer, right-click on the database to publish, and choose the Publish to Provider menu option. This launches the Database Publishing Wizard.

The Database Publishing Wizard starts by displaying a welcome screen that explains its purpose. The subsequent screen, shown in Figure 24.8, prompts for the database to replicate.

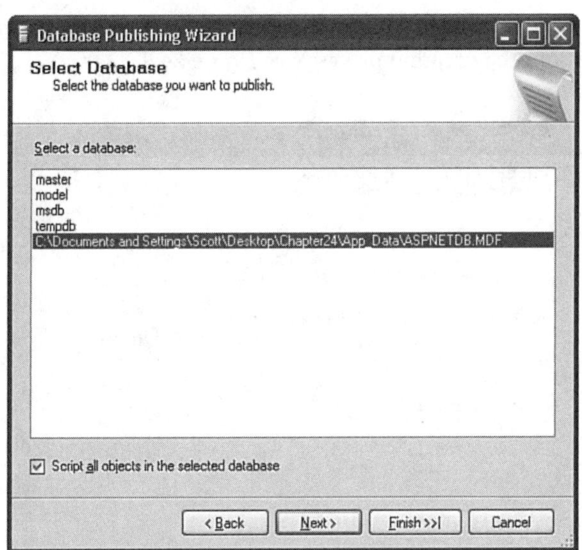

FIGURE 24.8
Specify the database to replicate.

By the Way

By default, the Database Publishing Wizard replicates *all* database objects to the destination server. If you want to replicate only a subset of database objects, uncheck the Script All Objects in the Selected Database check box shown at the bottom of Figure 24.8. If this option is unchecked, the subsequent screens have you select what database objects to copy over.

After specifying the source database, the wizard asks where to publish the database. There are two options:

- **Script to File**—This choice creates a script file with the necessary SQL commands to replicate the source database's structure and data.
- **Publish to a Shared Hosting Provider**—The Database Publishing Wizard can publish the database changes directly to the remote database server if the web-hosting company supports Microsoft's SQL Server Database Publishing Services protocol. Check with your web-hosting company to see if they offer this support.

The Script to File option works for any web-hosting company, regardless of whether they support Microsoft's SQL Server Database Publishing Services protocol. Therefore, let's look at using this option. Select the Script to File option and choose the location to place the file. Then click Next to review the settings.

After you have verified that the appropriate database objects are being copied over, click Finish to begin the scripting process (see Figure 24.9).

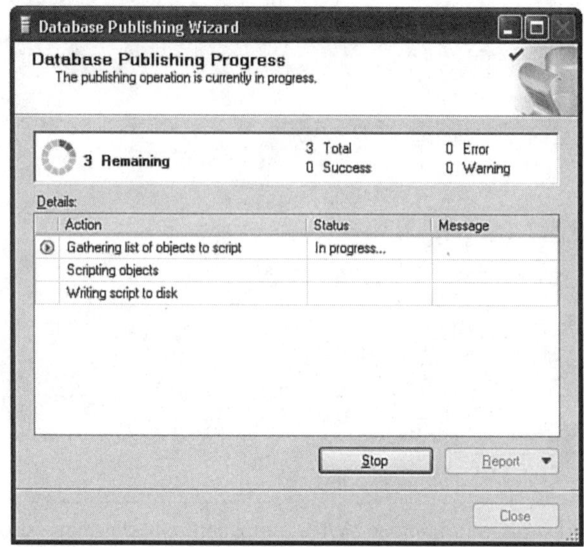

FIGURE 24.9 The wizard is generating the SQL scripts needed to copy the source database to the web-hosting company's database server.

Executing the Output Script on the Web-Hosting Company's Database Server

At this point the Database Publishing Wizard has created the scripts to replicate the source database's content and data. Our final step is to execute this script file on the web-hosting company's database servers. The easiest way to execute a script file on a database is to download Microsoft SQL Server Management Studio Express Edition, which is a free application for managing Microsoft SQL Server databases.

Did you Know?

If you have any of the non-Express Editions of Microsoft SQL Server 2005 installed on your computer, chances are you have SQL Server Management Studio installed on your computer. If this is the case, you can use the already installed version and do not need to download SQL Server Management Studio Express Edition.

To download Microsoft SQL Server Management Studio Express Edition, visit www.microsoft.com/downloads/details.aspx?FamilyID=c243a5ae-4bd1-4e3d-94b8-5a0f62bf7796&displaylang=en.

By the Way

> The Microsoft SQL Server Management Studio Express Edition download page includes two download options: `SQLServer2005_SSMSEE.msi` and `SQLServer2005_SSMSEE_x64.msi`. You'll likely want to download the first option, as the latter one is for 64-bit systems.

After you've downloaded and installed Management Studio, launch it. Management Studio starts by asking you what server to connect to. Go ahead and click Cancel for now—we'll provide this information later.

Go to the File menu and select the Open child menu. Next, select to open a file and browse to the file created by the Database Publishing Wizard. After selecting the file, Management Studio again prompts for the database server name and credentials. Fill in the server name and credentials needed to connect to the web-hosting company's database server (see Figure 24.10).

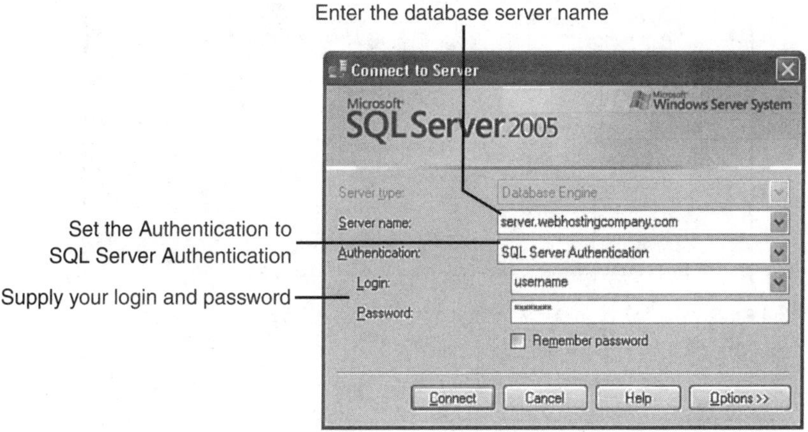

FIGURE 24.10 Connect to the web-hosting company's database server.

After entering the database server name and your credentials, Management Studio displays the contents of the selected file in a query window. Go to the Query menu and choose Execute to run this query on the database server.

By the Way

> It may take anywhere from several seconds to several minutes for the SQL script file to finish executing. The time required depends on how many database objects were created by the Database Publishing Wizard, how many records were in these tables, the processing power of the database server, and other related factors.

To verify that the database has been replicated on the web-hosting company's database server, go to the File menu and choose the Connect Object Explorer file option.

This redisplays the Connect to Server dialog box shown in Figure 24.11. Reenter your credentials and click Connect.

The Object Explorer lists those database objects on the server that you have permission to examine. Drill down into the Databases folder and into your database. Expand the Tables folder. You should see the same set of Tables on the web-hosting company's database server that is on your local database.

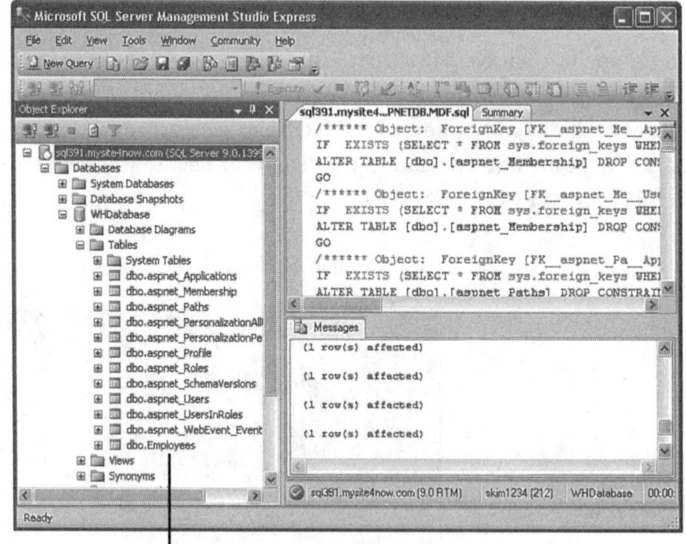

FIGURE 24.11 The local database's tables have been replicated to the web-hosting company's database server.

By the Way

Keep in mind that the Database Publishing Wizard replicates both the database schema *and* the database data. The `Admin` user account and the records you added to the `Employees` table through Visual Web Developer have been replicated to the remote database server.

Updating the Connection Strings in `Web.config`

After the database has been replicated, the final step is to update the connection string settings in `web.config` so that they point to the web-hosting company's production server. You need to make these changes on the `web.config` file on the web-hosting company's computer. To accomplish this, modify the `web.config` file on your computer and then upload it to the web-hosting company through the Copy Site screen. After uploading the `web.config` file to the web-hosting company, you may undo the changes so that the local web.config file's connect strings still point to the local SQL Server database in the App_Data folder.

The connection string value in web.config should look similar to the following:

```
Data Source=.\SQLEXPRESS;AttachDbFilename=|DataDirectory|\ASPNETDB.MDF
➥;Integrated Security=True;User Instance=True
```

Replace this string with the connection string information provided by your web-hosting company. The web-hosting company will provide you with a database server, a database name, and a username and password. If the database is a SQL Server 2005 server, use the following connection string value:

```
Data Source=databaseServer;Initial Catalog=databaseName;
➥User Id=username;Password=password;
```

For alternative databases, such as SQL Server 2000 or SQL Server 2008, consult www.ConnectionStrings.com for sample connection strings. If you have trouble formulating the correct connection string, contact the web-hosting company's support for assistance.

Did you Know?

> In addition to updating web.config on the web-hosting company's computer, you can also update your local web.config file to point to the remote database. Doing so means that when developing and testing your website locally, you will be interfacing with the web-hosting company's database server. This has its advantages—during development you get to see real data—and perils—because the data is the live data, users may be upset if you accidentally delete a record.

If your web application uses the membership or roles systems, you will need to update the web.config at the web-hosting company to include an additional connection string setting. By default, the membership and roles systems use a hard-coded connection string named LocalSqlServer to connect to the database where user account and role information is stored. This connection string points to the ASPNETDB.MDF database in the App_Data folder. The remote web application, however, does not have an App_Data folder; the user accounts and roles systems are instead stored on the database server.

We need to update the LocalSqlServer connection string to point to the database server. If you forget to do this, you will get an error message when visiting a page that attempts to work with user accounts or roles.

Currently, the <connectionStrings> section in web.config looks similar to the following:

```
<connectionStrings>
    <add name="ConnectionString" connectionString="connectionString"
        providerName="System.Data.SqlClient" />
</connectionStrings>
```

We need to add two additional XML elements within the `<connectionStrings>` element:

- **A `<clear />` element**—This clears out the hard-coded connection string names, including `LocalSqlServer`. This should appear as the first markup within the `<connectionStrings>` element.
- **An `<add />` element**—Use this to create a custom connection string value for `LocalSqlServer`.

After making these additions, your `web.config` file's `<connectionStrings>` section should look like the following:

```
<connectionStrings>
    <clear />

    <add name="ConnectionString" connectionString="connectionString"
        providerName="System.Data.SqlClient" />

    <add name="LocalSqlServer" connectionString="connectionString"
        providerName="System.Data.SqlClient" />
</connectionStrings>
```

The *`connectionString`* values in the two `<add />` elements should be the same, pointing to your database on the web-hosting company's database server.

Visiting the Remote Website

After uploading your ASP.NET files and replicating the database, visit the remote site. If you have already purchased a domain name and pointed it to your web-hosting company's computers, you should be able to visit the site by entering www.YourDomainName.com. If you do not yet have a domain name, your web-hosting company can provide you with a temporary server name, which might be something like www.WebHostingCompany.com/*AccountName*.

Figure 24.12 shows the uploaded website when viewed through a browser. Note the URL in the browser's Address bar—http://site457.mysite4now.net/skim1234/site1/Default.aspx. We're no longer visiting the website locally! It is now accessible to any user on the Internet.

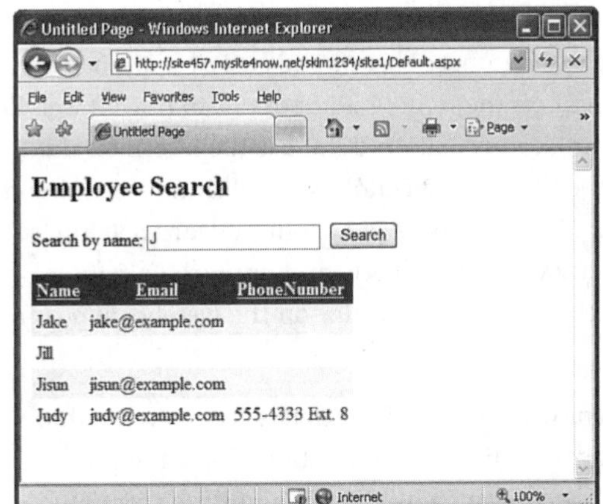

FIGURE 24.12 The local database's tables have been replicated to the web-hosting company's database server.

Did you Know?

If you get an error when visiting a page on the production server, ASP.NET shows a rather unhelpful error page that lacks any information as to the cause of the error. This uninformative error page is used because it is a security risk to divulge error details to a web visitor because it may highlight a potential vulnerability in your application. To override this default behavior, add the following markup within the `<system.web>` section of `web.config`:

```
<customErrors mode="Off" />
```

Alternatively, you can configure your ASP.NET application to automatically email you the details of an error whenever one occurs. For more information on this approach, check out http://msdn2.microsoft.com/en-us/library/aa479332.aspx.

Summary

ASP.NET applications are usually developed and tested locally and then deployed to a web-hosting company when completed. By deploying the site to a web-hosting company, any person with an Internet connection can visit the site. Deployment involves three steps: uploading the website's files, replicating the database, and updating `web.config`.

When uploading the website's files, all files except for the Microsoft SQL Server 2005 Express Edition database files need to be copied up. This includes `.aspx` pages, `.vb` pages, `web.config` files, image files, and so forth. Visual Web Developer's Copy Web Site option makes it easy to transfer files from your computer to the web-hosting company's.

The hardest step in the deployment process is replicating the local database to the web-hosting company's database server. The easiest approach is to simply start database development on the remote database or to have a web-hosting company that will import your Express Edition database file into their database server. Barring that, you need to use the Database Publishing Wizard and SQL Server Management Studio. The Database Publishing Wizard generates the SQL scripts to create the necessary database objects and data in the remote database. Use Management Studio to execute this script on the web-hosting company's database server.

Learning how to deploy an ASP.NET site is like learning anything else—it's hard and slow-going the first couple times through, but after some practice it becomes easier. If you get stuck, the best resource is your web-hosting company's support staff—you're paying them, in part, for their expertise and help. Another great resource is the Configuration and Deployment forum at http://forums.asp.net/26.aspx.

Q&A

Q. ***I have deployed my website and would now like to add new users accounts through the ASP.NET Web Site Administration Tool. How do I do this?***

A. Unfortunately the ASP.NET Web Site Administration Tool is designed to work only on local sites. You cannot use this tool to manage user accounts, roles, and authorization rights on a remote site. The good news is that many ASP.NET developers have created their own Web Site Administration Tool-like applications. One of my favorite ones is from Dan Clem. The complete source code along with instructions on how to set up and use it can be found at http://aspnet.4guysfromrolla.com/articles/052307-1.aspx.

Workshop

Quiz

1. What three features should you ensure that any prospective web-hosting company offers?
2. True or False: Deployment is usually a cyclical task, occurring multiple times over the lifetime of an application.
3. Deploying an ASP.NET application involves what three steps?

4. True or False: When deploying a website, you should not copy up the Microsoft SQL Server 2005 Express Edition database files.
5. What is the purpose of Microsoft's Database Publishing Wizard?
6. What portion of the `web.config` must you update when deploying a website for the first time?

Answers

1. You should ensure that a web-hosting company supports ASP.NET version 3.5; Microsoft SQL Server database accounts; and FTP access.
2. True.
3. Uploading the website's files, replicating the database, and updating `web.config`.
4. True.
5. The Database Publishing Wizard generates the SQL script that replicates the source database's schema and data to a destination database.
6. The connection strings in `web.config` need to be updated to point to the database on the web-hosting company's database server.

Exercises

There are no exercises for this hour.

Index

Symbols

A

B

C

E

F

I

J-K

L

N

O

P

Q

R

S

U

V

W-X-Y-Z

THIS BOOK IS SAFARI ENABLED

INCLUDES FREE 45-DAY ACCESS TO THE ONLINE EDITION

The Safari® Enabled icon on the cover of your favorite technology book means the book is available through Safari Bookshelf. When you buy this book, you get free access to the online edition for 45 days.

Safari Bookshelf is an electronic reference library that lets you easily search thousands of technical books, find code samples, download chapters, and access technical information whenever and wherever you need it.

TO GAIN 45-DAY SAFARI ENABLED ACCESS TO THIS BOOK:

- Go to **http://www.samspublishing.com/safarienabled**
- Complete the brief registration form
- Enter the coupon code found in the front of this book on the "Copyright" page

If you have difficulty registering on Safari Bookshelf or accessing the online edition, please e-mail customer-service@safaribooksonline.com.

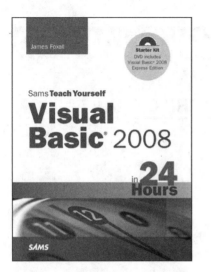